FOUNDATIONS OF GUIDANCE AND COUNSELING

Multidisciplinary Readings

Edited by

C. E. SMITH and O. G. MINK

Division of Clinical Studies
College of Human Resources and Education
West Virginia University

J. B. Lippincott Company
Philadelphia and New York

DEDICATION

To our parents, wives, and children

CONSULTING EDITOR: Dr. Richard E. Ripple, Cornell University

PREFACE

RECENTLY four significant events have stimulated an examination of the interdisciplinary foundations of guidance and its emergent professional specialty, counseling. The four events are the National Defense Education Act of 1958 and subsequent amendments; the "Wrenn Report,"[1] sponsored by the American Association for the Advancement of Science; the adoption of official role and preparation statements by the American Personnel and Guidance Association at its 1964 convention[2]; and the establishment and continuing contributions of the Interprofessional Research Commission on Pupil Personnel Services.[3] Each event includes a call for stronger training of the school counselor to include further emphasis on the foundations disciplines of the behavioral and social sciences.

Other events related to this examination include a project at Columbia University which was designed to contribute toward meeting "the need of professional guidance in education for a broader and deeper theoretical foundation." This project resulted in a brief but noteworthy publication of readings[4] by behavioral scientists representing various disciplines that potentially offer such a foundation. A symposium at Fordham University resulted in another collection of readings, entitled the *Interdisciplinary Roots of Guidance*.[5] Finally, a "critical-incidence" (essential concepts, terms, names, titles) procedure used with several hundred graduate students in numerous introductory courses in guidance resulted in a syllabus-workbook[6]

[1] Wrenn, C. Gilbert. *The counselor in a changing world*. Washington, D.C.: American Personnel and Guidance Association, 1962.

[2] Loughary, John W., Robert O. Stripling, and Paul W. Fitzgerald (Eds.). *Counseling: a growing profession*. Washington, D.C.: American Personnel and Guidance Association, 1964, pp. 77–106.

[3] For example, see IRCOPPS. *Pupil Services Department: Functions, Organization, Staffing*. Arlington, Va.: Educational Service Bureau, 1968.

[4] Lloyd-Jones, Esther & Esther Westervelt. *Behavioral science and guidance: proposals and perspectives*. New York: Teachers Press, Teachers College, Columbia University, 1963.

[5] Hennessey, Thomas, S. J. *The interdisciplinary roots of guidance*. New York: Fordham University Press, 1966.

[6] Mink, Oscar G. & Charles E. Smith. *Guidance: foundations and services*. Dubuque: William C. Brown, 1967.

containing units on both academic foundations areas and traditional services. Additionally, several articles from an Arden
House Conference on interdisciplinary foundations are included
in sections of this book.

The need is obvious for continuing attention to infusing
counselor education with a clarified multidisciplinary foundation consisting of both knowledge and methods of inquiry. The
present book is a contribution to this area.

The increased importance of the counselor's role is but one
factor contributing to the need for strengthening the academic
portion of counselor education. From the knowledge explosion
and concomitant changes in both job structure and general
social structure in recent years, extensive and profound altera-
tions are being wrought in the scope and depth of a counselor's
education. For example, the average Ph.D. finds the knowledge
gained in pursuing his degree at least half obsolete seven years
later. Likewise, primarily because of the changing job structure,
on the average a man changes his occupation about every eight
years. Such factors inevitably affect the definition and practice
of the guidance function and consequently that of counselor
education.

At present guidance as an applied scientific discipline is
an infant supported by a family of psychology, sociology, economics, anthropology, statistics, and measurement. Counselor
educators do students a disservice if they teach only techniques.
Techniques alone may become useless in the ensuing decade, if
they are not in fact already dysfunctional. It is therefore also
the responsibility of counselor educators to help students master
basic principles and absorb the rationale of the academic disciplines on which guidance rests, so that students are better able
to develop basic methods of inquiry from which techniques
may be derived and new skills acquired. Nonetheless, "methods
and techniques" constitute the principal focus of many textbooks currently published for use in the basic courses in guidance. Discontent with such an approach has been expressed
in a growing body of literature.

Recognizing the complexities of professional role development, many programs in counselor education have begun to
emphasize the importance of the multidisciplinary foundations
of their programs. The present book of readings follows such
an emphasis. It unfolds around three themes: conceptual elements basic to guidance, the purposes and major rationale of

several basic disciplinary areas undergirding guidance, and the definitions of the discipline or major function and consequent implications for guidance. The text is intended as a vehicle to provide the counselor in training with a sound cognitive schemata for continuing professional growth during and after further training.

In Piaget's terms, learning may take place generally either by assimilating experiences or by accommodating to them. Simply defined, Piaget presented assimilation as possession of skills that encompass an experience. Accommodation is the addition of new facets to a schema that is not yet adequate to subsume the experience. In accord with such ideas, this collection is based upon the belief that study of foundations disciplines and of major functions will yield a more viable schemata for the student's professional development than will a technique-oriented, "principles and practices," approach. Essentially, counselors in training must be not only *technically* equipped for the here and now but also prepared for continued growth. Such a reader—the counselor in training—is then the primary target of this volume. The volume will also be helpful to the educator or other professional who has use for a conceptual understanding of guidance and counseling.

Foundations of Guidance and Counseling is divided into two main parts. The first part, "Multidisciplinary Foundations," is subdivided into several disciplines which have theoretical and practical relevance for guidance. Articles in the "Foundations" section were chosen for their conceptual rather than their exhaustive-content qualities. Accordingly, while a great amount of substantive content may be present or alluded to, such content primarily serves as a vehicle to define—to conceptualize—the foundations discipline or the major function under consideration.

The second part is entitled "Major Functions" and is organized around elements and purposes which are appropriate to guidance, without regard to specific job setting. The collection is relevant, then, not only to the preparation and training of the school counselor, but also to that of the rehabilitation counselor, the employment service counselor, the counselor in a college counseling center, or any other professional counselor. Such a focus is a reflection of the editors' opinion that a productive step for the development of professional personnel workers[7] at the present time is to emphasize the similarities and to minimize the differences of the various counseling professions. Thus, competence speaks to competence, and the differences which do exist in technical skills, knowledge of research and theory, and in job performance, are minimized. Further, such differences are more likely to be a function of the quality and the amount of training rather than true differences between predominantly independent professions. This is not to deny that differences in emphasis on primary functions or knowledge do vary across job setting. It is, for example, more likely that a skilled rehabilitation counselor will know more about medically disabling aspects of human functioning than will the comparably skilled college counselor. Similarly, in terms of job definition, the counselor in a college will probably spend more time in long-term therapeutic counseling than will the typical secondary school counselor, yet the college counselor may have significantly fewer organizational and administrative tasks.

Differences such as these and others result in different emphases in counselor training programs. Nonetheless, competency at a professional level in each of the major functions in Part II is generally seen as necessary for the preparation of counselors regardless of their anticipated work setting. The editors would agree that viable differences in job performance and thus perhaps in training do exist. However, the intent of this collection is to emphasize commonalities.

For critical comments and help in manuscript preparation we owe a special note of thanks to Loretta Culiz, R. F. Forestandi, Linda Freed, Don Mastrogiuseppi, Fran Stillman, and Jewel Washington. The support and technical help of Sally W. Arbuthnot and Alex Fraser of J. B. Lippincott were invaluable. Finally, a customary but real extra note of appreciation is due our temporarily abandoned wives and children.

January, 1969   C. E. SMITH
Morgantown, W. Va.   O. G. MINK

---

[7] To clarify terminology which is used with variation in the literature, the editors concur that *personnel* workers implement the *guidance* function primarily through their professional skills in *counseling*. There are many guidance "services or activities," which is a loose way of speaking of activities which are designed to implement the guidance function. These activities are performed by personnel workers who may be counseling psychologists, school counselors, rehabilitation counselors, employment service counselors, industrial personnel psychologists, social workers. Personnel workers compose one set of many who perform in the general field of the "helping professions."

CONTENTS

Bibliography for Quick-Reference Chart

ARBUCKLE, DUGALD S. *Counseling: philosophy, theory and practice.* Boston: Allyn & Bacon, Inc., 1965.

ARBUCKLE, DUGALD S. *Pupil personnel services in American schools.* Boston: Allyn & Bacon, Inc., 1967.

BIGGE, MORRIS & MAURICE P. HUNT. *Psychological foundations of education.* New York: Harper & Row, Publishers, 1962.

BLANCHARD, HOWARD & LAURENCE FLAUM. *Guidance: a longitudinal approach.* Minneapolis: Burgess Publishing Co., 1962.

DOWNING, LESTER. *Guidance and counseling services: an introduction.* New York: McGraw-Hill Book Co., 1968.

GLANZ, EDWARD. *Foundation and principles of guidance.* Boston: Allyn & Bacon, Inc., 1964.

HUTSON, PERCIVAL. *The guidance function in education.* New York: Appleton-Century-Crofts, Inc. (2nd ed.), 1968.

ISAKSEN, H. L., O. G. MINK, & C. E. SMITH. *The guidance function.* Philadelphia: J. B. Lippincott Co., 1969.

KOWITZ, GERALD & NORMA KOWITZ. *Operating guidance services for the modern school.* New York: Holt, Rinehart and Winston, Inc., 1968.

MATHEWSON, ROBERT. *Guidance policy and practice.* New York: Harper & Row, Publishers, 1962.

MILLER, CARROLL H. *Guidance Services.* New York: Harper & Brothers, 1965.

MILLER, FRANK. *Guidance principles and services.* Columbus: Charles E. Merrill Books, Inc., 1961.

MINK, O. G. & C. E. SMITH. *Guidance: foundations & services.* Dubuque: William C. Brown, 1967.

McGOWAN, JOHN & LYLE SCHMIDT. *Counseling: readings in theory and practice.* New York: Holt, Rinehart & Winston, Inc., 1962.

OHLSEN, MERLE M. *Guidance services in the modern school.* New York: Harper & Row, Publishers, 1962.

PETERS, HERMAN J. & GAIL F. FARWELL. *Guidance: a developmental approach.* Chicago: Rand McNally & Co., 1967.

SCHERTZER, BRUCE & SHELLEY STONE. *Fundamentals of guidance.* Boston: Houghton Mifflin Co., 1966.

STEWART, LAURENCE H. & CHARLES F. WARNATH. *The counselor and society.* Boston: Houghton Mifflin Co., 1965.

TRAXLER, ARTHUR & ROBERT NORTH. *Techniques of guidance.* New York: Harper & Row, Publishers, 1966.

WRENN, C. GILBERT. *The counselor in a changing world.* Washington, D.C.: American Personnel and Guidance Association, 1962.

Correlation of FOUNDATIONS OF GUIDANCE AND COUNSELING: MULTIDISCIPLINARY READINGS with leading guidance and counseling texts. Note: See Bibliography on page xi for titles of texts; use index to locate short discussions of specific subjects.

CHAPTER	Arbuckle (1965)	Arbuckle (1967)	Bigge & Hunt (1962)	Blanchard & Flaum (1967)	Downing (1968)	Glanz (1964)
I Historical						25–69
II Philosophical	3–45		29–54			
III Empirical				56–97 306–332		
IV Psychological		51–94	Entire Text			193–213
V Anthropology & Sociology		3–40	55–109			
VI Economics						
VII Appraisal		292–334		98–131 306–333	103–128	
VIII Information		244–291		286–305	183–201	
IX Counseling	49–117 153–384	211–243		249–264	129–181	92–121
X Administration & Evaluation		372–396		132–151 265–285	247–278	340–357

Hutson (1968)	Isaksen, Mink, Smith (1969)	Kowitz & Kowitz (1968)	Mathewson (1962)	Miller, C. (1965)	Miller, F. (1961)	Mink & Smith (1968)
3–29	Chapters II		71–96	1–21	3–18 27–48	38–42
24–29 30–176	VIII		131–188			7–12
757–776 431–502	X	97–114		369–394	111–153 228–251	13–24 65–69
133–176	IX		9–41			30–37
30–92	VI, VII	12–32	42–70	22–46		25–29
93–132	VII		335–357			
377–584	XIV	95–113	262–272	156–195	193–227	43–47
177–184 185–202 243–376 697–720	XV			79–155	79–177	48–52
177–184 585–696	IV, XVI	127–132	308–321	196–233	170–192	53–57
177–184 203–242 721–776	I, III, V	74–94 153–177 200–218	191–260	316–368	153–169	58–64

McCowan & Schmidt (1962)	Ohlsen (1962)	Peters & Farwell (1967)	Schertzer & Stone (1906)	Steward & Warnath (1965)	Traxler & North (1966)	Wrenn (1962)
7–23	7–18	1–31	37–76	3–21	1–5	
100–127						1–4
538–554	473–506	544–569		235–254	156–170	111–126
276–319	25–60	32–55 351–384		93–120 203–234		4–8 53–65
		56–89	3–29	65–91		11–19 28–39
					8–10	19–28 39–47
495–522	217–303	158–185	184–267 395–423	145–174	74–155	
	304–334	186–221	268–290	123–143		96–106
241–537	61–181	222–287	137–183	255–302	303–330	69–74 126–134
	21–24 182–439 426–439	447–543	347–391	175–201 303–330	5–18 171–268	140–159

PART ONE

Multidisciplinary Foundations

SECTION ONE

An Emerging Profession:
Historical Foundations

A SECTION on historical foundations was chosen to begin this collection because in a sense such a section provides a broad conceptual theme for the entire book. Beginning with a brief portrayal of the social reformist climate of the early twentieth century, four significant trends—(1) vocational guidance, (2) mental health, (3) testing, and (4) progressive education —and numerous associated and interrelated events are delineated in terms of their impact on the development of guidance as a profession.

This section differs slightly in approach from the following foundations sections in that it provides descriptive content of the historical development of guidance. Other sections provide only brief samples of the relevant knowledge content of the discipline under study for its real or potential contribution to guidance. Content that is present in later sections is primarily a vehicle illustrative of second order abstractions such as definitions, viable issues, schools of thought and systematic positions, methods of inquiry, and basic assumptions of the particular discipline. The impact—potential or real—of these second order abstractions upon guidance constitutes the unifying rationale of the remaining foundations sections. Those articles were selected which seemed best to provide, either explicitly or implicitly, meaningful representations of supporting concepts drawn from the interdisciplinary base sampled.

The articles in this section differ, however, by *not* capitalizing on history as a social science with a distinct methodology and knowledge pool that has obvious and largely untapped relevance for both the theory and practice of guidance. Sociology and psychology—two major areas identified by the profession as providing disciplinary bases of counselor training—most often use a reductionistic methodology. The historian, however, attempts to synthesize from his sources a coherent statement of what the human past was like. Thus, the historian contributes immeasurably to man's knowledge, not as a chronicler of events, but as a creator of a *whole* view of past events through objective means and systematic analysis. As the institutionalization of the guidance function grows in both scope and depth, the personnel worker, be he industrial psychologist or school counselor, will have an increasing need to study the history of his professional origins as a means for coping with developing complex events in the increasingly diverse society he serves.

In the initial selection Rockwell and Rothney survey the social ideas of five pioneers in the guidance movement and relate the ideas to the broader social thought of the late nineteenth century. Beginning with Frank Parsons, the recognized "Father" of vocational guidance, and concluding with David Hill, who advocated and applied the scientific method to social programs, all five pioneers held a belief in the evolutionary quality of society. Undoubtedly influenced by the then recent force of Darwinism, these pioneers, whose legacy with respect to a society conceived of in evolutionary terms still remains, believed in human society as a progressive development in which human weakness could be changed by appropriate human effort. Rockwell and Rothney suggest that guidance itself may not have evolved so very far from the pioneers' view of fitting man to society's values of the moment. The issue posed indicates that guidance can still profit from a heightened awareness of its past.

In the second selection E. G. Williamson examines the vocational guidance movement in terms of seven dimensions or phases of development. While praising the genius of Frank

Parsons, Williamson finds that the original concept of vocational guidance as a one-step process is obsolete. Current thinking emphasizes that vocational development is a life-long process in which individuals have a continuing need for reconsideration and reassessment of capabilities and opportunities in a series of choice points.

Donald Super, in what is now a classic article, continues describing the conceptual development of the vocational guidance movement in an account of the transition from a relatively naive and excessively cognitive vocational guidance to a more sophisticated counseling psychology, a profession he helped "create" in the early 1950's. Professor Super has made life-long contributions to vocational development theory and research.

No selection has been chosen specifically to reflect the historical march of the testing movement. Such information is already contained in several of the previous selections, and Alexakos and Anastasia each contribute relevant articles in Section Seven, *The Appraisal Function*. Both articles could well be perused by the reader at this point for a more extended view of both the historical development and specific characteristics of major instruments of the testing movement. Similarly, the portion of Samler's article entitled "The Problems of Being in Charge" in Section Eight outlines major federal legislation of import to the guidance movement.

The noted educational historian, Lawrence Cremin, develops the case in "The Progressive Heritage of the Guidance Movement" that the personnel worker is the chief heir to the progressive movement in education. Bearing this burden the counselor continues to be influenced by several contradictory ideas that need reappraisal and revision. Not only does the counselor need to be wary of what goals and commitments he takes for granted, but he must examine also his concepts of education, vocation, and community. Too often, says Cremin, the counselor exaggerates his view of his function and potential accomplishment—a legacy from the now defunct progressive movement.

In a statement of particular relevance to the purpose of the present book, Cremin observes that the professional counselor should make the humanities an area of continuing study and should acquire competency in the humanities as foundation disciplines to his enterprise. The latter point has not been covered in the present volume, although the editors are of the opinion that the idea has much merit.

The selections described thus far reflect historical influences primarily from four major movements: (1) vocational guidance, (2) mental health, (3) testing, and (4) progressive education. The final article of the section is a postscript by C. Gilbert Wrenn to his widely distributed and significant book, *The Counselor in a Changing World.* The selection is reprinted from a definitive American Personnel and Guidance Association account of the professionalization of school counseling. Wrenn's postscript offers a particularly lucid view across many disciplines of some of the more current and likely future trends in the development of counseling as a profession.

1. Some Social Ideas of Pioneers in the Guidance Movement

Perry J. Rockwell, Jr., and John W. M. Rothney

The guidance movement was born in the welter and confusion of protest, reform, utopian idealism, and defenses of the status quo which were rampant in the late nineteenth and early twentieth centuries. Those who have written about the beginnings of the guidance movement have tended to touch very lightly on the many social factors which led to the development of guidance services. The social ideas which inspired pioneers to initiate organized guidance services have not been given enough consideration. In the study described below an attempt was made to do this by examining the writings of five of the pioneers in guidance during its organizational period (1900–1916). The criteria of selection of the individuals were their activity in organizing guidance services, the extent to which they published the results of their efforts, the availability of their publications for study, and the geographical area in which they did their work. Using the methodology of historical research and analysis, the published writings of Frank Parsons, Jessie B. Davis, Anna Y. Reed, Eli W. Weaver, and Davis S. Hill were examined for evidence about their

Perry J. Rockwell and John W. M. Rothney, "Some Social Ideas of Pioneers in the Guidance Movement," from *Personnel and Guidance Journal,* December, 1961, pp. 349–354. Copyright © 1961 by the American Personnel and Guidance Association, Inc., Washington, D.C. Reprinted by permission.

views of society. The ideas are noted below under the heading of social reform, the social gospel, social Darwinism, and the new science.

SOCIAL REFORM

The writings of Frank Parsons, a utopian social reformer, ranged from a lengthy tome about the history and political development of New Zealand to brief paragraphs of comment about incidents of the day which seemed to him to be of some social significance. He expressed his ideas about society often and at length. The culmination of his career of concern for the welfare of mankind was reached in the organization of the Vocational Bureau in Boston in 1908 (Parsons, 1908).

His study of history and economics had led him to formulate what he called his philosophy of mutualism, a kind of gradual socialism. This idea was the frame of reference for all his thinking and writing. He believed in the perfectability of mankind and in the movement of society toward that perfection on earth.

Parsons was against private ownership by monopolies and what he considered the evils of competition. He believed that government should play a major role in causing changes in society by legislating hours of work, prohibiting child labor, and controlling the growth of industry. Parsons studied and wrote about successful government ownership experiments in Switzerland, Northern Europe, and in New Zealand (Parsons, 1904, 1906). He wanted to develop in the American system the democratic methods which had brought about the success of these experiments.

Many of the reforms for which he fought have been realized. Our senators are chosen by the direct vote of the people, and the initiative, referendum, and direct primaries are part of our state political systems. Women have achieved the right to vote and the progressive income tax has become a large source of support of our government. Monopolies have grown to undreamed-of proportions but so have the regulations which encompass their movements, and government seems to have more control of business practices today than at any other time in our history. Guidance has become an accepted part of the school system in all states of the union and has been recognized by federal legislation.

A fundamental concept in Parson's counseling was the belief that counselee had the power to analyze himself and to make wise decisions on the basis of that analysis. The forms developed by Parsons for use with the Vocational Bureau were aimed at helping the individual make as complete an analysis of himself as was possible (Parsons, 1909). A person would be asked such questions as "Are you honest?" In the context of social reform it seemed logical that a counselor should ask such questions since one of the basic tenets of the reform group was faith in man's ability to control his evolution to higher stages through conscious purposeful actions.

Another characteristic of Parsons' counseling was his prescriptive advice to counselees. If he noted a peculiarity about a client which he felt would hinder him in achieving his goal, Parsons would inform the client and tell him that the characteristic should be modified or eliminated. Otherwise, he indicated, failure would surely result. Parsons also recommended certain books to be read to improve the client's mind or stimulate his interest in civic affairs.

The peculiarities noted by Parsons were those which might make life as a member of a closely knit cooperative society a bit difficult. The books recommended for reading included much of the reform and exposé literature published by the social reform group and critics of the power class. Henry D. Lloyd and Ida Tarbell's accounts of the Standard Oil Company's rise to power, the economics of John R. Commons and Richard T. Ely, the sociology of Lester F. Ward and E. A. Ross and many of his own works about needed social improvements were prominent on his recommended reading lists.

Activities such as those noted above indicated that Parsons wanted counselors to work toward social goals as well as the development of the individual client. It suggests that Parsons' guidance could have been used as a means toward the achievement of the mutualistic society which he sought.

THE SOCIAL GOSPEL

While attending Cornell University Jessie B. Davis worked through his uncertainty of career choice by self-analysis, occupational study, and an examination of self in relation to his chosen occupation. As soon as he could he introduced the study of self and occupations to his classes in Detroit and later in Grand Rapids. His description of counseling (Davis, 1914), suggests that he preached to students about the moral value of hard work, ambition, honesty, and the development of good character as assets to any person who planned to enter the business world.

As principal of a school in Grand Rapids he launched his program in English classes because they reached every pupil in the school and because composition work in English classes lent itself to his technique of occupational study. In order to help students to think about careers he had them write themes on such topics as "The Kind of Man (or Woman) I Should Like to Be," "What I Will Do When I Grow Up," "A Call to

Service," and "To What Extent Am I Indebted to the Social Interest of Others?" (Davis, 1914).

Examination of his published writings reveals that Davis was an advocate of what social historians have called the social gospel. This was essentially an attempt to bring the church closer to the mass of the people. The practice of the Golden Rule was looked upon as a panacea for the ills of society. It was most popular in urban centers where the evils of an industrialized society seemed to be most prominent. Adherents to the social gospel were concerned equally with the effects upon the individual of the excesses of corporate wealth and the formation of a socialistic state as advocated by the naturalists of the social reform movement. The social gospel was developed as a compromise between unrestrained competition on the one hand and socialism on the other.

Since the social gospel was concerned with social problems, its adherents often supported many of the same reforms as the social utopians. Theirs, too, was a campaign to alter current society until it recognized the goodness of each individual. There is no suggestion in Davis' writings of the achievement of a socialistic state but there is recognition and discussion of some of the evils existing in society. He referred frequently to the need for making morally sound decisions.

Davis' position within the social gospel philosophy was enhanced by his use of the "call" concept of the ministry in relation to the way one should choose a vocation. When an individual was "called" to a vocation he would approach it with the noblest and highest ideals which would serve society best by uplifting humanity.

The significance for guidance of the social gospel approach lies in the accent placed upon the development of the individual in accord with the particular moral code of the Christian concept of brotherly love. Individuals who made choices not consistent with this ideal needed to be guided toward the correct path. The social gospel of Jessie Davis brought to guidance a touch of a supernatural force. The moral code would be the standard by which the excellence of decisions by counselors and counselees alike could be judged.

SOCIAL DARWINISM

The ideas of Anna Y. Reed and Eli W. Weaver were both identified with the concept of social Darwinism although they did their work in areas geographically a continent apart. Eli Weaver worked with the High School Teachers' Association in New York City to establish a vocational guidance service while Anna Reed established her service in the schools of Seattle. Of the two, Anna Reed was the most fluent and prolific in the presentation of her ideas.

Working with Seattle school leaders and their employers, Reed accepted the prevailing concepts of business and business ethics in a free enterprise system. She seemed to equate morality and business ethics. She was much concerned that any course of action on a social question be taken on the basis of social research, economy, and how it would be accepted by the business world.

The system rather than persons seemed most important to Reed. She urged that schools use the example of business and keep the dollar sign before children since it was something every pupil understood (Reed, 1916). She advocated stiff competition for grades in school and suggested that only 100 per cent success was good enough in school as it was in industry. Whenever she advocated curriculum changes such as the addition of commercial courses, she justified them by reference to complaints she had received from business men about employees they hired directly from the schools. Business standards and moral principles seemed synonymous in her lexicon, and she urged educators to be thoroughly imbued with them so that they might better serve their pupils (Reed, 1917). She believed that by adding guidance services to a school system she would help prevent much of the "waste" of the educational product. Her guidance services were organized and operated with business methods (Reed, 1917). She believed that the social service attitude did not have a place in a guidance organization because quick decisions associated with successful business methods were required.

Her admiration of business philosophy and methods resulted in criticism of all programs of guidance which placed the welfare of the individual above the needs of industry. In the guidance services which she developed an individual's worth was judged by his acceptability to employers. Other guidance programs, she said, "savored too much of a philanthropic or social service proposition and too little of a practical commercial venture" (Reed, 1920).

Anna Reed looked upon life in American society as a competitive struggle. The success which an individual achieved in the struggle depended upon his adjustment to the demands of business which dominated society. She accepted the dominance of business philosophy and methods as positives and did not join in Davis' and Parsons' criticisms of the activities of business.

Eli Weaver, on the other hand, gained the respect of Davis, Reed, and other pioneers in guidance by his quiet, capable and persistent work with students in New York City. He did not write much about his work but reported to the First National Conference on Vocational Guidance in 1910 that every high school in the city of New York had a committee of teachers who were actively attempting to aid boys and girls to discover what they could do best and how to secure a job in which their abilities could be used to the fullest advantage of both employer and employee (Rockwell, 1958).

He did not comment about the organization of society as a whole in his writing. He did, however, advise young persons to develop character as the best means of securing and holding a job. He seemed content to work within the framework of society as it existed and to look upon guidance as a means of keeping the wheels of the social machinery well oiled. Employers, he felt, should set up standards which they wished workers to have and publicize them through the schools so that students would know what was expected of them and be able to prepare themselves more effectively.

The ideas of Reed and Weaver seem to be an integral part of the Social Darwinist doctrine so popular as a defense for some of the business practices of the day. The supporters of Social Darwinist doctrine maintained, as Darwin had in biology, that man and his social forms had evolved from lower to higher forms through a competitive process of natural selection which allowed only the strongest and best to survive.

The wealthy businessman of the day was identified as the strongest and best in the evolutionary concept and was believed to be highest on the social evolutionary scale. Competition was the means by which he had evolved and by which newer forms would be developed. The possession of money was the measure of his success.

Social Darwinists believed that education should mirror and prepare students for entry into the competitive world by teaching self-dependence, adjustment to the existing system, and for fighting for survival. The implication of this view is that guidance of an individual should be toward conformity with whatever social mores had come to be respected within the society. It suggests that the training which an individual needs is that training which will enable him to be most like the current power group. If an individual adjusted to whatever demands an employer made and maintained his loyalty to that employer he might advance to higher and higher positions within his employer's company and, if his competitive spirit and strength among his peers was of a high enough order, he might take over the company and become an employer.

Acceptance of the Social Darwinist evolutionary concept in guidance would lead a counselor to the position of guiding individuals toward conformity with the expectancies of superiors while urging them to fight their co-workers for advanced status. In a school, the authorities would determine what "outward" social mores should be. A system of rewards and punishments for those who succeeded or failed within its framework would be established. Simultaneously the peer culture would determine what "inward" school social mores would be and develop a system of rewards and punishments based largely upon the idea of social acceptance. Since these systems of the school and of the group might clash, the Social Darwinist counselor would call the attention of a counselee to the points of conflict and the possible results of choosing one course over another. When this had been done and the individual had made a decision he would be "on his own" to survive or fail according to his capacity to succeed in the course he had chosen.

THE NEW SCIENCE

Perhaps the most significant of all the approaches to the development of guidance services was the scientific approach used by David S. Hill, Director of the Educational Research Bureau in New Orleans. His concern for guidance did not grow out of a conscious desire to direct the reform of society toward a specific social or economic goal. It grew out of his belief that any decisions which would affect the educational system, and thus society, should be based upon sound scientific research.

Hill used more complete methods to study individuals than any of his contemporaries. He utilized the techniques of medical science to examine the physical fitness of boys and girls who were referred to his research bureau, used the newest psychological tests including the Binet individual intelligence test, and he sent a trained social investigator into homes to learn about the environments of children.

Society, according to Hill (1907), was constantly evolving, and it was necessary for an individual to adapt himself to the changing conditions within the society in order to survive. It was the obligation of all to study scientifically the changes that were occurring and to guide youth toward a more perfect society. He did not strike out at specific abuses of wealth nor formulate definite plans to alleviate poverty. His recognition of them as problems on the social scene was couched in general terms and usually as a prelude to the statistical study in which he was currently engaged (Hill, 1914, 6–8). He mentioned the need for a scientific approach to education to eliminate political influence and corruption in government, labor-capital strife, spread of poverty, and the waste of natural resources.

Most of the forces active in bringing about changes in society were beyond the control of man, but Hill believed that man had the ability to work toward a goal and to make choices of behavior which would help him to achieve the goal. The school was society's tool for changing boys and girls into men and women who, by their choices toward what was beautiful, good, and true, would improve society.

His research revealed the great diversity of aims and objectives of those for whom American education was designed. He concluded that vocational guidance and diversified curricula were necessary for the fullest development of the individual student and the transmission to the future of the convictions, aspirations, and faith of the American people in the democratic process.

Hill's scientific approach to social problems was based on the assumption that answers to social problems could be discovered through research on specific problems. If the immediate situation were resolved perhaps the solution to the problem could be applied to other problems and society would be improved. Through the methods of science man could learn about the forces which caused social evolution, and by controlling his environment man could control the direction of evolution.

Scientific methodology so permeated the thinking of early twentieth century society that none of the pioneers in guidance was unaffected by it. Anna Reed used many techniques of social science research in her studies of state institutions, children in Seattle, and newsboys. Jessie Davis used the technique of personal visitation, interview, and discussion in his attempts to get more accurate information about occupations. Parsons used research continuously in his approach to social problems and in his discussion of techniques for use with counselees.

An approach to guidance problems through scientific research implies that answers to a problem can be obtained through a study of the problem itself. A scientific frame of reference required that techniques for studying individuals and their environments be developed. It meant that guidance would be a continuous process of helping persons solve their problems until they became skillful in doing so.

Summary

Regardless of their approach to social problems each of the guidance pioneers discussed above indicated that there was a need for guidance services and each looked to education as the proper instrument for implementing such services. Each was affected by several streams of thought which flowed through society in the late nineteenth and early twentieth centuries. Their acceptance or rejection of these broad streams of thought affected the conception of guidance which each developed.

Despite the diversity of social ideas among the pioneers in guidance they had many ideas in common. Each of them viewed society as a progressive development. Each believed that man had the power to change his weaknesses to strength or to fortify his areas of strength if he were aware of them. If the desires of the masses of the people could be changed through the increase of political reforms, the application of Christian ethics to everyday living, the increased acceptance of business methods, or the application of scientific procedures, society could be changed.

All of the guidance activities organized by these early workers were designed to make the individual fit closer to a mold that would include all the values which these workers thought would result in successful living. To achieve this would require that guidance counselors know what was best for society and that they guide their counselees to fit the best mold. Current comments in the press and statements by guidance workers about the use of guidance services to "straighten out" individuals and to recruit certain kinds of workers for selected occupations indicate that the issue has not been completely resolved. Toward what kind of a society are guidance workers dedicated today? How much real change has occurred during the first 50 years of the guidance movement?

REFERENCES

DAVIS., J. B. *Moral and vocational guidance.* New York: Ginn and Co., 1914.

HILL, D. S. "The education and problems of the protestant ministry." *Amer. J. Rel. Psychol.,* 1907, 2, 204–256 & 1908, 3, 29–70.

HILL, D. S. *An experimental study of delinquent and destitute boys in New Orleans and notes concerning preventive and ameliorative measures in the United States.* New Orleans: Commission Council, 1914.

HILL, D. S. *Facts about the public schools of New Orleans in relation to vocation.* New Orleans: Commission Council, 1914.

HILL, D. S. "Problems of vocational guidance in the South." *Sch. & Soc.,* 1915, 1, 257–263.

HILL, D. S. "Significant problems of education in New Orleans." *Sch. & Soc.,* 1916, 4, 197–203.

HILL, D. S. *Educational research in public schools.* New Orleans: Div. of Educ. Res., 1915.

HILL, D. S. *A study of manufacturing establishments of New Orleans and mechanical occupations of boys and men with reference to education.* New Orleans: Commission Council, 1916.

PARSONS, F. The philosophy of mutualism. *The arena,* 1894, 10, 783–815.

PARSONS, F. *The story of New Zealand.* Philadelphia: C. F. Taylor, 1904.

PARSONS, F. "Nationalization of railways in Switzerland." *The arena,* 1906, 36, 557–658.

PARSONS, F. "The Vocation Bureau." *The arena,* 1908, 40, 3–19, 171–183.

PARSONS, F. *Choosing a vocation.* Boston: Houghton Mifflin Co., 1909.

REED, ANNA Y. *Vocational guidance report 1913–1916.* Seattle: Board of School Directors, 1916.

REED, ANNA Y. "Vocational guidance—problem of organization and administration." *N.E.A. Proc.,* 1917, 443–449.

REED, ANNA Y. *Newsboy service.* Yonkers-on-Hudson: World Book, 1917.

REED, ANNA Y. *Junior wage earners.* New York: Macmillan, 1920.

ROCKWELL, P. J. *Social concepts in the published writing of some pioneers in guidance, 1900–1916.* Unpublished Ph.D. dissertation. University of Wisconsin, 1958.

U. S. BUREAU OF EDUCATION. *Papers presented at the organization meeting of the Vocational Guidance Association, Grand Rapids, October, 1913.* Bull. 14, 5–94. Washington, D. C.: GPO, 1914.

2. An Historical Perspective of the Vocational Guidance Movement

E. G. Williamson

As practiced in American schools, organized vocational guidance was originated by Frank Parsons and described in his 1909 book, *Choosing A Vocation*. Parsons (1909, pp. 91–92) makes a casual comment that he had been practicing vocational guidance for "more than a dozen years." In the 1890 decade Parsons began counseling underprivileged youth in Boston. His methods, as described in his book, consisted of three categories of techniques:

1. A joint and cooperative analysis of the individual's capabilities, interests and temperament.

2. The student's study of occupational opportunities, requirements, and employment statistics.

3. A joint and cooperative comparison of these two sets of information.

PARSONS' PRECURSORS

While I do not reduce the respect that one experiences in contemplating the amazing invention of Parsons, yet his was not the first conception of systematic guidance of youth with regard to their choice of an adult job. Eliot (1892) of Harvard spoke of individualized diagnosis of pupils' temperament, constitution and mental aptitudes and defects in 1892. Gilman (1897) of Johns Hopkins made a similar proposal concerning vocational counselors in 1898. In 1899, Harper (1905, pp. 321–323) of Chicago delivered two speeches in which he outlined diagnosis of individuality, a considerable formulation of his own. Harper also predicted

E. G. Williamson, "An Historical Perspective of the Vocational Guidance Movement," from *Personnel and Guidance Journal*, April, 1963, pp. 854–859. Copyright © 1963 by American Personnel and Guidance Association, Inc., Washington, D.C. Reprinted by permission.

that 50 years hence there would be specialized counselors in the schools available for the diagnosis of individuality, prior to instruction. Also in 1899, Munsterberg (1899, p. 141) said: ". . . recently the proposition was made for the appointment of special school psychologists attached to the superintendent's office in large cities." Munsterberg was possibly referring to Parsons, whose "counseling" he had observed directly. Or perhaps he had in mind Witmer's innovation in 1896 of the clinical use of psychology.

To return to Parsons: In my opinion, the essential and the then most unique feature of his three-part formula is the first step, the diagnosis of the individual's capabilities, *prior to choice*. But even more amazing were the methods and techniques employed by Parsons. He was not trained as a psychologist, but he was a teacher and an administrator in colleges. The story of how he stumbled upon the then emerging psychologist's experimental tests of man's capabilities is unknown. He seems to have modified current psychological laboratory tests, according to Munsterberg (1913, p. 45), and adapted them for the diagnosis of the individual's capabilities prior to choosing a life career.

In the evaluation of the psychological tests available at the time Parsons was inventing his method, Boring (1929, pp. 545–549) says that there were three originations of psychological tests of capabilities.

1. One by Francis Galton of the character of psychomotor capacities such as strength of hand grip and visual acuity.

2. Those brought to America by the students of Wilhelm Wundt of Leipzig, particularly his student, Cattell. These were psychophysical functions such as number checking and memory for numbers heard.

3. And the third type of tests of man's capabilities were those constructed by Binet and Simon which finally developed into the modern intelligence tests. Binet's tests were tests of complex mental processes and Boring says that the third pattern proved to be the most useful in the diagnosis of human beings, particularly with regard to diagnosis of learning capability of the school curriculum.

No one has traced the fascinating story of the development of psychological techniques of diagnosis from Parsons' day to the contemporary Differential Aptitude Tests and the General Aptitude Test Battery. But the more I study this fascinating story the more I am impressed with the inventive genius of Parsons who borrowed psychological techniques for psychometric diagnosis of unique aptitudes prior to choice. To be sure, Parsons also advocated the tryout method of observation through visitations to jobs, a technique still in current use, although they are presently critically evaluated by Barry and Wolf (1962).

Unfortunately, after Parsons' death in 1908 his successor as director of the Vocations Bureau of Boston, Bloomfield (1911, pp. 26, 27), abandoned psychological tests on the grounds that they had not yet been perfected and also because various occupations had not yet been subjected to the type of psychological experimentation advocated by Munsterberg, the founder of American applied psychology. That is, there were then no available occupational ability profiles, as we now call them, and therefore Parsons' successor thought that psychological tests were not yet promising of utility in occupational diagnosis.

But Parsons' successors abandoned psychometric methods of diagnosis of aptitude and turned to self-analysis of capabilities and interests and to observational methods of collecting occupational information. Kitson (1929, 1931, 1938, 1947) later became a most vocal exponent of self-diagnosis, without giving indication that he sought experimental validity of self-diagnosis. Kitson's (1917) own doctoral thesis under Angel at the University of Chicago employed the Wundtian and Cattellian type of psychological tests correlated with grades in the School of Commerce.

SEVEN DIMENSIONS

In this paper I am not writing history but rather formulating my own appraisal of more than a half century of organized guidance. I will make this appraisal in terms of seven major dimensions of the vocational guidance movement.

1. The first significant dimension is the objectivity of the analysis of man's capabilities, employing an external criterion. No one has written the complete history of man's efforts at placing the young in work (freedom of choice was not a prevalent concept in the early centuries of Western civilization); nevertheless, probably before the 1890 decade there was little objectivity in the appraisal and estimation of man's capabilities. Perhaps an 18th century document was characteristic of early methods of vocational guidance. Campbell (1747) published in 1747 a description of the trades, professions and arts then practiced in the cities of London and Westminster, a manual "calculated for the information of parents and instruction of youth in their choice of business." This manual, which to the historians may prove to be characteristic of the prevailing methods, contained "Advice to parents how to study and improve the Natural Genius of their children, before they bind them apprentice."

But objective, rather than observation and estimation, means of identifying talents were not available until late in the 19th century to replace "crude" methods of estimation. Thus it was that methods of subjective appraisal and observation, as well as "tryout" under the master workman, had to suffice as means of identifying capabilities. But near the turn of the century, objective techniques of testing aptitudes were invented in the psychologists' laboratories for research studies of mental organization. Parsons "borrowed" some of these techniques and demonstrated their use.

2. A second revolution in vocational guidance originated apparently in France and Germany around the turn of the century when psychological tests were applied by Lahy (1913) and Clarapede (1922) to the identification of workers in various industries who were either accident prone, as we would say, or unsatisfactory in meeting the requirements of the employer. About this time Frederick Taylor (1911), in American industry, standardized work units by means of objective observation and studies of time and motion of workers. For the first time we had available an *objective external criterion* against which to check and to correlate the emerging psychometric tests of aptitudes. This use of an external criterion in validating aptitude tests proved to be not only significant for the emerging psychology of work and of human capabilities, but it also made possible the diagnosis of capabilities required for various tasks *before training or employment was undertaken*. This invention was as significant for western industrial civilization as was the invention of the wheel in earlier centuries.

In calling attention to the use of an external criterion of "satisfactoriness" of work tasks in school and occupation, I still am mindful of the reality of "subjective" criteria as employed in that part of industrial psychology which deals with "job satisfaction" and also in psychotherapy which seeks to aid individuals to "feel better" about their interpersonal relationships and other dimensions of personal experience. A careful reading of the industrial classics of Viteles and Scott and Clothier will establish the fact that early industrial psychologists for decades were concerned not only with externally observed work tasks, but as much also with how the worker *felt* about his work and thus with his feeling of satisfaction (Scott et al, 1958). Moreover I have not observed disregard of "feelings" in vocational counseling; rather have I concluded that counselors of all persuasion, to be sure in varying ways, are sensitive to feeling, or whatever one calls the "subjective" dimension of experience.

3. A third dimension of the vocational guidance movement has been referred to, the employment of *experimental* methods as a basic technique for determining job requirements of capabilities. These experimental methods replaced the ancient techniques of observation and estimation. Industrial psychology thus became applied research in its basic methods. And a new research design became well founded in industrial psychology: The differentiation of "successful" from "unsuccess-

ful" workers in an occupation and of one occupational group from a different one; these were basic experimental methods of describing the requirements of any occupation. The experimental design of objective differentiation of defined *criterion groups*, first employed in industrial psychology, has now provided counselors with techniques of analysis of the individual with respect to aptitudes, interests, and personality traits.

4. A fourth unique invention underlying modern counseling and vocational guidance is the contribution of Munsterburg and other industrial psychologists in their description of work or jobs in the same terms that workers are described (Alexander, 1934). This was a new kind of occupational information gradually emerging in the *occupational ability profile* and now used in the new type of *scholastic aptitude* profiles and differential predictions for school tasks.

There are two research designs employed in this type of job worker description. The first is exemplified in Munsterberg's (1913) experimental comparison of workers using objective tests of aptitudes and skills. The second design, pioneered by Paterson, Viteles, Munsterberg, Bingham, and others decades ago, is exemplified, currently, by the "estimates" of Worker Trait Requirements, employing trained occupational analysts who "estimated" the job-man requirements including specified aptitudes, temperaments, interests, physical capacities, and working conditions (Fine, Heinz, 1957).

5. A fifth characteristic of vocational guidance, viewed historically, is the revolutionary reconstruction of educational guidance, as it was earlier called. The Army psychologists, trained in manpower analysis and job descriptions in terms of manpower abilities, turned to the occupation of "studentship" as though it were a vocation, subject to psychometric description by means of experiment. And the very extensive literature on predicting the criterion of scholastic success is a tribute to these industrial psychologists. Even though we still bemoan the fact that our correlations with the criterion of grades are less than perfect, still they are far better than the "estimation" and teacher's ratings of a half century ago. I conclude that we must either accept the slow and limited methods of science in improving our predictive accuracy, or, as did Kitson, we turn to self-analysis or estimation or to some other technique of unknown validity and reliability.

6. A sixth major breakthrough in the establishment of vocational guidance was the pioneering work of E. K. Strong, Jr., preceded at Carnegie Institute of Technology by B. V. Moore, Jay Bean, and Max Freyd (Ferguson, 1952, p. 14). This was the objective measurement of that elusive phenomenon called "interest." Perhaps for the first (?) time in man's history the methods of psychological research and psychometric

measurement were applied to a motivational phenomenon. And E. K. Strong, Jr. and Frederick Kuder have now given us technical literature which makes possible much improved vocational guidance over that which is based upon self-diagnosis of interests.

7. A seventh significant contribution is the development of rational reasoning about self in communicable terms so that counselor and student can understand the student's capabilities relevant to the prediction of a given criterion as a fundamental preparation for *his* rational choice of adult career objectives. Viteles seems to be one of the early innovators to develop such an instrument, known as the individual psychograph, later adapted by Paterson in the Minnesota Employment Stabilization Research Institute to the guidance of the adult unemployed through objective, communicable reasoning about capabilities. Paterson's pioneering work in Minnesota laid the foundation for a new type of employment counseling and placement service in the U.S. Employment Service and also in the U.S. Office of Vocational Rehabilitation. Thus the new pattern of vocational guidance was adapted to adults and Parsons' step three, "true reasoning" about man and job, was given new meaning and new techniques.

These are, for me, seven of the most significant breakthroughs and stages of development viewed in historical perspective. But without undervaluing these magnificent innovations, I come away from a review of this historical evolution with the conviction that the method of research is the only known instrumentality for improving techniques and for determining the effectiveness of their use in counseling.

CHOICE WITHOUT KNOWLEDGE

I conclude that man's recently won freedom of choice of vocation is relatively meaningless, if not downright precarious, when he makes his choices without some *valid* knowledge of his own capabilities and potentialities. And I believe that the method of self-analysis, while it is simple and thus appealing in its simplicity, is of questionable validity and reliability.

But there are some deficiencies still current in our thinking about vocational guidance, after more than a half century of development, including some basic research. I mention one deficiency which is being corrected today by incorporating knowledge and techniques not available to Parsons. In his day there was very little understanding among American psychologists of the psychology of motivations. To be sure, G. Stanley Hall and William James were familiar with Freud and other European therapists, and Munsterberg himself earned a medical degree in psychotherapy and published a book on that topic in 1909. Moreover, G. Stanley Hall brought Freud to lecture at Clark University in 1910. And Clifford Beers wrote his book, *A Mind That Found Itself*, in 1908, and the child guidance (therapy) clinic was organized in Chicago in 1910. Unfortunately, Parsons and his immediate successors seem to have been uninformed about the development of psychodynamics and, therefore, evidenced no well-founded understanding of motivation, except a practical understanding that the choice of the wrong career meant frustration of motivation. But in Parsons' day the psychology and theory of emotions and feelings was not as well elaborated or developed in theory or research as were psychophysical and psychometric tests and the theory of states of consciousness and mental organization.

Thus the desirable *rapprochement* between the psychology of aptitudes and the psychology of motivations was long delayed. But at long last the 1951 Northwestern Conference (Super, 1956) of counseling psychologists revealed that we were beginning to integrate these two separate, but related fields of knowledge about man into a comprehensive theory and practice of the whole individual. We may confidently anticipate that the research of Tyler on interest development, related to capabilities, and Roe's work on motivational factors of vocational choice and satisfaction will eventually yield a much more sophisticated pattern of this dimension of vocational guidance. And Samler recalled us to a new critical examination of Walter Dill Scott's dictum, "the worker in his work unit," to a rewriting of occupational information in terms of the psychological dimensions of work, far beyond Parsons' and Munsterberg's centering on aptitudes for work tasks (Samler, 1961).

I mention one other deficiency that is now being corrected. Apparently because of Parsons' humanness of understanding of misery resulting from the wrong vocational choice during adolescence, and because of his own sampling of case materials, he specialized in the problems of the early adolescent because they were the ones most notably at hand calling for some kind of helping relationship.

Vocational guidance was thus originally a one-step operation. It was to occur prior to training and perhaps prior to employment. But it was a sort of emergency service and life planning operation. The concept of applying vocational guidance at successive stages in one's life does not seem to have occurred to Parsons, and, in fact, organized guidance, for the most part in this country, has been a problem of early adolescence or at least a problem that centered largely just prior to or in the early stages of school and college.

But Super's adaptation of Buehler's concept of life stages of human development now provides us with a new pattern of thinking that Parsons would have applauded, I am sure. This is so well known that I need not discuss it, but it promises to make vocational guidance a lifelong process for many individuals at various stages of emerging need for reconsideration and rediagnosis of capabilities and then rematching them with opportunities.

I turn now to some future stages of evolvement. To be sure, many, if not all, of the stages appraised are not yet completed in either our understanding of the basic problems or in our forging of valid techniques of counseling practice. I might, therefore, project into future years incomplete and persistent technical problems. But I rather choose to identify another incomplete problem which is basic to the counseling process itself. I refer to that complex of unknowns which Meehl (1954) identified in his book, *Clinical versus Statistical Prediction*. He asserted, and later established by research (1956), that certain kinds of personality descriptions and diagnoses are as accurately made by means of standard and generalized interpretations of personality test profiles as by interpretations of clinical psychologists. Sarbin (1960) reported a similar finding comparing predictions of grades using a battery of tests and high school grades with predictions made by counselors (psychologists) with knowledge of these tests and traditional case data, following *personal interviews with students*. These findings, needing replication, to be sure, are clear: the counselor's interview and knowledge of case data, including tests, added little if anything to the statistical accuracy of prediction using the test battery for prediction alone.

These findings recall Clark Hull's 1928 book *Aptitude Testing* (pp. 487–490), in which he describes a forecasting machine, first sketched in 1923, involving use of a standard battery of aptitudes. The 40 or 50 different equations, for as many occupations, would be applied by the machine to the test scores of each student to be counseled. His proposal was criticized by many as irrelevant to the task of the counseling interview. Despite these early criticisms, Horst (1955) at the University of Washington today mans a program of differential predictions for each freshmen in terms of regression equations with standard weightings for each course enrolling freshmen.

And the use of College Board test batteries, the DAT as well as other available probability tables for colleges and curricula, have revolutionized the diagnostic function of Parsons' step one, analysis of the individual in terms of some identified external criterion in school.

I now come to the crucial questions raised, for me, by these recent developments: What is the utility of the counselor? of the interview? of case data? That is, if the counselor's interview and case data yield no increase in forecasting efficiency of test batteries, then what is their utility? Let me make explicit my personal belief, or hypothesis, that the counseling relationship does add significantly to human development. But I also hypothesize that research, rather than tribal dogma, will be productive in establishing whatever that relationship does, in actuality, contribute to human development.

Instead of seeking to ignore, or to question Sarbin's findings, we need to research these questions with professional vigor. We thus must be ready to re-examine the *traditional wisdom* rather than clinging to tribal ritual. Such an open-minded examination of prevalent techniques and presuppositions constitutes a continuation of Parsons' pioneering search for new and more productive techniques of assistance to American youth. In such a spirit of research, Parsons would, I conclude, have welcomed the out-dating and up-dating of his repertoire of techniques as well as his theory of career counseling.

REFERENCES

ALEXANDER, WILLIAM P. "Research in guidance." In Donald G. Paterson, ed., "Analysis of the individual." *Occupations,* 1934, *12,* 76.

BARRY, RUTH, & WOLF, BEVERLY. *An epitaph for vocational guidance.* New York: Bureau of Publications, Teachers College, Columbia Univ., 1962.

BLOOMFIELD, MEYER. *The vocational guidance of youth.* Boston: Houghton Mifflin, 1911.

BORING, EDWIN G. *A history of experimental psychology.* New York: D. Appleton-Century Company, 1929.

CAMPBELL, R. *The London tradesman,* Table of Contents. London: T. Gardner, 1747.

CLARAPEDE, EDOUARD. "L'orientation professionnelle." In *Problems and methods of vocational guidance.* Geneva: International Labor Office, 1922.

ELIOT, CHARLES W. "Undesirable and desirable uniformity in schools." *National Education Association Journal,* 1892, p. 90.

FERGUSON, LEONARD W. "A look across the years, 1920 to 1950." Chapter 1 in *Applications of psychology, Essays to Honor Walter V. Bingham.* New York: Harper, 1952.

FINE, SIDNEY A., & HEINZ, CARL A. "The estimates of worker trait requirements." *Personnel guid. J.* 1957, *36,* 168–174.

See also: Estimates of worker trait requirements for 400 jobs, as defined in the *Dictionary of occupational titles,* U.S. Dept. of Labor, 1956.

GILMAN, DANIEL G. "Modern education: Does it educate in the broadest, most liberal sense of the term?" *Cosmopolitan,* 1897, *23.*

HARPER, WILLIAM RAINEY. *The trend in higher education.* Chicago: Univ. Chicago Press, 1905.

HORST, PAUL. "A technique for the development of a multiple absolute prediction battery." *Psychol. Monogr.* 1955, *69,* No. 5 (Whole No. 390).

HULL, CLARK L. *Aptitude testing.* New York: World Book Co., 1928.

KITSON, HARRY DEXTER. *How to find the right vocation.* New York: Harper, 1929, 1938, 1947.

KITSON, HARRY DEXTER. *I find my vocation* (3rd. ed.). New York: McGraw-Hill, 1931, 1947.

KITSON, HARRY DEXTER. "The scientific study of the college student." *Psychol. Monogr.,* 1917, *23,* 1–18.

LAHY, J. M. "Les conditions psycho-physiologiques de l'aptitude au travail dectylographique." *J. Physiol. Pathol. Gen.,* 1913, 826–834.

MEEHL, PAUL. *Clinical versus statistical prediction.* Minneapolis: Univ. Minnesota Press, 1954.

MEEHL, PAUL. "Wanted—a good cook book." *Amer. Psychologist*, 1956, 2, 263–272.

MUNSTERBERG, HUGO. "Scientific vocational guidance." Chapter V in *Psychology and industrial efficiency*. Boston: Houghton Mifflin, 1913.

MUNSTERBERG, HUGO. *Psychology and life:* Boston: Houghton Mifflin, 1899.

PARSONS, FRANK. *Choosing a vocation.* Boston: Houghton Mifflin, 1909.

SAMLER, JOSEPH. "Psycho-social aspects of work: a critique of occupational information." *Personnel guid. J.,* 1961, 39, 458–465.

SARBIN, T. R., *et al. Clinical inference and cognitive theory.* New York: Holt, Rinehart and Winston, 1960.

SCOTT, THOMAS B., DAVIS, RENE V., ENGLAND, GEORGE W., & LOFQUIST, LLOYD H., *et al. A definition of work adjustment.* Minneapolis: Univ. Minnesota Press, Minnesota Studies in Vocational Rehabilitation, 1958, 10; 1961, 12; 1962, 13.

SUPER, DONALD E. "Counseling psychology as a specialty." Report of the APA Committee on Definition of Counseling Psychology, *Amer. Psychologist*, 1956, 2, 282–285.

TAYLOR, FREDERICK W. *The principles of scientific management.* New York: Harper, 1911.

3. Transition: From Vocational Guidance to Counseling Psychology

Donald E. Super

In 1951, rather suddenly but not unexpectedly, a new psychological job title came into use in the United States, and a hitherto somewhat amorphous and debatable field of psychology emerged as clearly a field in its own right. The job was that of *counseling psychologist*, the field was that of *counseling psychology.*

These terms were adopted at a meeting which took place at Northwestern University immediately prior to the annual meeting of the American Psychological Association in September, 1951, at a special conference called by C. Gilbert Wrenn of the University of Minnesota, president of what was then called the Division of Counseling and Guidance of the American Psychological Association. The conference was attended by some sixty leading psychologists interested in vocational guidance and in counseling. The way had been paved for this conference by a Committee on Counselor Training headed by Francis P. Robinson of the Ohio State University, and two co-ordinate subcommittees, one on Doctoral Training

From: Donald E. Super, "Transition: from vocational guidance to counseling psychology," *Journal of Counseling Psychology*, 2, 1955, pp. 3–9. Copyright by the American Psychological Association, and reproduced by permission.

Programs headed by Edward S. Bordin of the University of Michigan and one on the Practicum Training of Counseling Psychologists chaired by the present writer.

The work of these committees and of the Northwestern Conference, published in the June, 1952, issue of the *American Psychologist* (APA, 1952a, 1952b), crystallized current thinking and standardized terminology, giving birth to the term *counseling psychology* and creating an awareness among psychologists of some of the important differences between this and the related fields of applied psychology. It may be of general interest to outline the origins of this new development.

Origins

Vocational guidance began, in the United States, as a movement by philanthropically-minded citizens to improve the post-school vocational adjustments of boys and girls (Brewer, 1942). They allied themselves with social agencies such as Civic Service House in Boston and the Young Men's Christian Association in some communities, and with the schools in many cities such as Providence and Grand Rapids, to provide occupational information and orientation for boys and girls leaving school or adrift in the chaotic world of work. This movement was soon joined by psychologists working in the field of psychometrics, for at the very time that Frank Parsons began his vocational guidance work in Boston, Alfred Binet published his intelligence scale in Paris, and World War I effected a partial merger of these two important streams in the U.S.A. That the merger was only partial was made clear by the different emphases, in the 1920's, of educators such as John Brewer (Brewer, 1932) with his stress on exploratory experiences in guidance, and of psychologists such as Clark Hull (1928), with his hopes for psychological tests as the basis of vocational counseling.

The economic depression of the 1930's added a new current to the stream of history. Large-scale unemployment highlighted vocational guidance as a job-placement activity as well as an educational function. The Minnesota Employment Stabilization Research Institute experimented with psychological tests, occupational information, and retraining as methods of getting adult workers back into the active labor force. Then many private and public vocational counseling centers, together with the United States Employment Service, quickly took over the research and counseling methods developed in this pioneer project. The union of education, of social work, and of psychometrics in the vocational guidance of youth and adults was now somewhat more complete, as shown by the strength of the National Vocational Guidance Association and the activities of the National Occupational Conference. NVGA's membership came from the fields of education, psychology, community service, business, and government. Psychology as an organized field at this time showed some interest in guidance only through a small group of applied psychologists who, in 1937, organized the American Association for Applied Psychology, but it is significant that while this organization included sections concerned with clinical, consulting, educational, and industrial psychology, none was concerned particularly with vocational guidance.

During the 1930's another movement gathered force, this one under the auspices of clinical psychology, namely, an interest in psychotherapy. One of the products of this new focus of psychological research and practice was Carl Rogers' book on *Counseling and Psychotherapy* (Rogers, 1942). The years following its publication in 1942 saw a growth of interest in psychotherapeutic procedures which soon became even greater than interest in psychometrics. This movement, and the numerous research and theoretical contributions which have accompanied it, has had its impact on vocational guidance (Super, 1951, pp. 88–92). It has made vocational counselors, whether psychologists or otherwise, more aware of the unity of personality, of the fact that one counsels *people* rather than *problems*, of the fact that problems of adjustment in one aspect of living have effects on other aspects of life, and of the complexity of the processes of counseling concerning any type of individual adjustment, whether in the field of occupation, of group living, or of personal values. It has, perhaps even more importantly, provided counselors of all types with a better understanding of counseling processes and techniques. It is significant, as pointed out elsewhere (Super, 1954, pp. 123–124), that the three North American textbooks which in the 1930's purported to deal with counseling methods actually dealt only with diagnostics, that of the three which were published in the 1940's only one actually dealt with counseling, while of the ten which had appeared during the 1950's, up to the time of writing, as many as seven actually dealt with counseling methods in some detail.

The merging of these several streams of development means that the movement which started as vocational guidance in the United States, first with an emphasis on vocational orientation activities and then with a parallel and eventually merging emphasis on aptitude testing, both leading to placement, recently also assimilated a psychotherapeutic approach and has emerged as the "new" field of counseling psychology. While it includes vocational guidance, it goes beyond it to deal with the person as a person, attempting to help him with all types of life adjustments. Its underlying principle is that it is the adjusting individual who needs help, rather than merely an occupational, marital, or personal problem which needs solution. However, counseling psychology recognizes, unlike some therapeutic approaches, that the adjusting individual lives in a real world in which situational as well as attitudinal problems are encountered, and hence it uses aptitude tests, occupational information, exploratory activities, and structured situations as well as therapeutic interviews (APA, 1952a).

PHILOSOPHY, SCOPE, AND METHOD

This leads us to questions of the philosophy, scope, and method of counseling psychology. Even with the clarification which has taken place so rapidly during the past few years many American psychologists ask what difference exists between counseling psychology, on the one hand, and clinical, educational, or personnel psychology on the other. In fact, there are presently quite a few clinical psychologists who believe that counseling psychology is logically a branch of clinical psychology, and that the two should officially merge. It is significant, however, that the same belief is encountered among a number of educational, school, and personnel psychologists, each field stressing its kinship to counseling psychology while denying equal kinship to the other special fields.

It is frequently stated by counseling psychologists that their field is concerned primarily with the normal person (Gustad, 1953). These psychologists state that the objective of this field is to help the normal individual, whether student, worker, parent, or other, to achieve a better integration and to find more adequate outlets than he otherwise might in our complex and confused world. While this is true so far as it goes, many other counseling psychologists, including this writer, maintain that this is not enough. Counseling psychology is also concerned with handicapped, abnormal, or maladjusted persons, but in a way which is different from that which has characterized clinical psychology.

Clinical psychology has typically been concerned with diagnosing the nature and extent of *psychopathology*, with the abnormalities even of normal persons, with uncovering adjustment difficulties and maladaptive tendencies, and with the acceptance and understanding of these tendencies so that they may be modified (Louttit, 1939).

Counseling psychology, on the contrary, concerns itself with *hygiology*, with the normalities even of abnormal persons, with locating and developing personal and social resources and adaptive tendencies so that the individual can be assisted in making more effective use of them (Gustad, 1953).

Some clinical psychologists are beginning to say, now that counseling psychology has made clear this surprisingly novel philosophy and these nonetheless time-honored methods, that clinical psychology made a serious error in defining itself as it did, that it should have been more independent of psychiatric traditions and interests and concerned itself with hygiology as well as with pathology. Perhaps in due course the two fields will merge, in a more broadly trained and oriented field.

SETTING

Another important distinction between counseling psychology and the other applied fields is that of setting. Clinical psychologists function, with rare exceptions, in medical settings (unless their functions are instructional). Educational psychologists are typically professors, and when employed in other capacities they generally work as researchers in educational settings. School psychologists, as their nomenclature indicates, work in schools, and their orientation is educational even though their work in many ways resembles that of clinical psychologists. Personnel psychologists typically work in government, industry, or business, and they are often appropriately more concerned with their administrative-productive-distributive setting than they are with individuals.

Counseling psychologists, on the other hand, work in a variety of settings. They are employed in university counseling centers, in secondary schools, in hospitals, in rehabilitation centers, in social welfare agencies, in industry, in business, in government. They work in educational, medical, social work, and administrative settings—wherever there are people who need help in mobilizing their personal resources and in using the environment in order to make better adjustments. Wherever they work, they share one common treatment philosophy, one common collection of methods, and they acquire varying situational orientations according to the nature of the setting in which they are to work with people. In this, perhaps, lies counseling psychology's unique strength and its rapidly developing future: the counseling psychologist sees beyond the setting, whether it be medical, educational, social, or other, and deals with the individual who lives and functions in a variety of settings.

STRUCTURE AND ORGANIZATION

The principal professional association for vocational guidance in the United States has been the National Vocational Guidance Association. It has been brought out, also, that leadership in organizing the field of counseling psychology was exercised by the American Psychological Association's Division of Counseling and Guidance, now officially renamed the Division of Counseling Psychology. There is, of course, some overlapping of membership in these two organizations, but there are important differences.

We have seen that NVGA is made up of persons from the fields of education, community service, psychology, and business, while the Division of Counseling Psychology consists solely of psychologists. This means that NVGA contains many members whose primary affiliation is elsewhere, whereas APA's Division 17 (Counseling Psychology) contains members who tend to think of it as their primary affiliation. It means that NVGA has a revolving membership, as high school counselors become principals and drop their guidance activities, as social workers move from agencies doing vocational counseling to other agencies without this function, as businessmen move from personnel work to some other branch of management. Division 17, on the other hand, has a stable membership of persons who tend to keep up their interest in the field regardless of transfers or promotions. NVGA members may have considerable or little professional training in guidance, while Division 17 members have at least two years of specialized graduate preparation plus experience in their field. All this gives the Division of Counseling Psychology, with 700 members, a homogeneity and strength which NVGA, with 4,000 members, does not and perhaps cannot have.

There is another important reason why leadership in this evolving area has been exercised by psychology rather than by the heterogeneous field of guidance. This is the general recognition of the unity of the individual, the widespread emphasis on the guidance of persons and on the guidance of development, the current interest in life adjustment which includes vocation rather than merely in vocational choice and adjustment. The major advances in understandings, methods, and techniques of life adjustment have been psychological: psychology developed the tests used in diagnosis, prediction, and assessment; psychology systematized the study of occupations (except for trend studies contributed by economists); psychology (building partly on psychoanalysis) analyzed interviewing and counseling methods and applied this new understanding to life adjustment problems.

While the National Vocational Guidance Association spent a score of years in the sporadic but animated debate of whether or not to drop the adjective *vocational* from its title and statement of purpose, psychologists interested in counseling concerning life adjustment problems found a focus for their interest in the developing divisions of the American Association for Applied Psychology and of the American Psychological Association with which it merged during World War II. Better prepared to study, understand, and assist individual development and adjustment than most educators; closer to their scientific foundations and hence more versatile than most social workers; more interested in people than most administrators in business, industry or government—counseling psychologists had a clearer idea of what needed to be done and how to do it than had most others interested in guidance.

In 1952 the National Vocational Guidance Association merged with several other similar associations to form the American Personnel and Guidance Association, thereby giving more adequate expression to the current interest in general adjustment while preserving the necessary special interest in occupational problems in its divisional structure. The APGA is today a strong and important association. But it is still more an *interest* than a *professional* association, and the contributions made by psychology to guidance were implicitly recognized in the new association by the election of two counseling psychologists both to its first and to its second slate of three officers, and by the inclusion of five counseling psychologists in its fifteen-member Executive Council of 1953–54. (This is in contrast with the one psychologist who was on the eleven-man Board of Trustees of NVGA twenty years earlier.) Four of APGA's five psychologist-council members have been officers of APA's Division of Counseling Psychology, including two past-presidents (C. Gilbert Wrenn and the writer) and two past-secretaries (Frank M. Fletcher and Clifford P. Froehlich).

We have seen that the American Psychological Association's Division of Counseling Psychology has set standards for the training of counseling psychologists, standards which are now used by the APA's Education and Training Board in accrediting doctoral training programs in the universities. In addition, the Division has been regularly represented not only on the committees of that Board but also on the American Board of Examiners in Professional Psychology (ABE pp. 1953) (currently by Austin B. Wood and C. Gilbert Wrenn) which has, since 1947, issued the Diploma in Counseling and Guidance to persons with the doctorate and five subsequent years of experience in counseling psychology who pass appropriate written, oral, and practical examinations. It has also been represented on the Committee on Ethical Standards which, in 1953, published the APA's Code of Ethics (APA, 1953) which deals, among other topics, with counseling.

Further recognition of the importance of this field of applied psychology in the United States exists in the program for financing the training of counseling psychologists established in 1952 by the Veterans Administration. In this program substantial numbers of university-selected men and women are currently pursuing doctoral studies which include a paid internship in a veterans hospital (Moore, 1952). The Veterans Administration initiated this and a related in-service education program in order to fill more adequately its own unmet needs for counseling psychologists in its hospitals and regional offices. It did this after rewriting job specifications and requirements for vocational counselors to replace the latter with counseling psychologists as turnover or upgrading of incumbents and the availability of trained personnel makes it possible (this has since World War II been a shortage field, with only a handful of clearly qualified practitioners in 1940).

The role of the counseling psychologist in rehabilitation work is being studied by Veterans Administration psychologists and by other counseling psychologists interested in the work of the federal and state civilian rehabilitation programs. They are concerned with making sure that the more extensive and intensive professional training which counseling psychologists are bringing to the work of the vocational counselor finds ways of making the greatest possible contribution to the rehabilitation process. Counseling psychologists in industry and in education have been doing this for some time, but now rehabilitation also has begun to make demands on vocational counseling which are appropriate to counseling psychology and which command its attention.

As implied in the above, the development of the field of counseling psychology has been reflected also in the programs of American universities. For example, in 1951–52 the Department of Guidance of Teachers College, Columbia University, made a thorough study of its programs and reorganized some of them while renaming others. It was recognized that in the Guidance Department the twenty-five-year-old area of specialization locally known as Vocational Guidance and Occupational Adjustment had, for some time in fact, been offering five different programs: a doctoral program for counseling psychologists, another doctoral program for personnel psychologists, and three master's programs for school counselors, vocational counselors in social agencies, and personnel technicians in business, industry, or government. This recognition led to a departmental reorganization. The doctoral programs in counseling and in personnel psychology were so named and associated more closely with those in clinical and in school psychology, all in an area called Psychological Services. The master's program for school counselors was merged with that in another, nonpsychological, area called Student Personnel Administration. In many other universities a similar but not identical reorganizing and renaming of existing programs has taken place during the past three years, with the result that a total of eighteen programs in counseling psychology are now accredited by the American Psychological Association (APA, 1954).

For a field to be of age it must have not only a professional organization, professional certification, professional training programs, a professional code of ethics, and professional employment outlets but also a professional journal. This the field now has, in the *Journal of Counseling Psychology*, founded by some twenty psychologists and first published early in 1954.

Conclusions

The field of counseling psychology is still evolving, and important developments will most certainly take place during the next few years, especially in connection with rehabilitation work. Counseling psychology, already closely affiliated with clinical psychology in some universities and agencies but closer to educational psychology or to personnel psychology in others, may move even closer to one or all of these in the years to come. Already there is some talk of a need for a second "Boulder Conference" (Raimy, 1950) and a second "Northwestern Conference" (APA; 1952a, 1952b), the Runnymedes respectively of clinical and of counseling psychology, this time as two co-ordinated conferences or one joint conference, at which progress in the two fields might be reviewed and the rapprochement desired by some might be effected.

Perhaps the end result will be the emergence of a field of applied individual psychology, or consulting psychology, in which psychologists will be prepared to function as consultants to people in varying situations and with varying types of adjustment problems. Perhaps, on the other hand, true differences in the several fields will emerge more clearly, and both applied psychologists and the general public will develop a new recognition of and respect for the various applied specialties. In either case, the current trends in counseling psychology in the United States impress those of us who are involved in them as full of challenge, demanding the best that scientific method, professional skill, and human understanding can bring to bear.

REFERENCES

American Board of Examiners in Professional Psychology. *The certification of advanced specialists in professional psychology.* Washington: American Psychological Association, 1953.
American Psychological Association, Committee on Ethical Standards for Psychology. *Ethical standards for psychologists.* Washington: American Psychological Association, 1953.
American Psychological Association, Division of Counseling and Guidance, Committee on Counselor Training. "Recommended standards for training counseling psychologists at the doctorate level." *Amer. Psychologist,* 1952, 7, 175–181.
American Psychological Association, Division of Counseling and Guidance, Committee on Counselor Training. "The practicum training of counseling psychologists." *Amer. Psychologist,* 1952, 7, 182–188.
American Psychological Association, Education and Training Board. "Doctoral training programs in clinical psychology and in counseling psychology." *Amer. Psychologist,* 1954, 9, 258.
BREWER, J. M. *History of vocational guidance.* New York: Harper and Brothers, 1942.
BREWER, J. M. *Education as guidance.* New York: Macmillan, 1932.
GUSTAD, J. W. "The definition of counseling." In R. F. Berdie, ed., "Roles and relationships in counseling." *Minnesota Studies in Student Personnel Work,* No. 3, 1953.

HULL, C. L. *Aptitude testing*. Yonkers: World Book Co., 1928.

LOUTTIT, C. M. "The nature of clinical psychology." *Psychol. Bull.*, 1939, *36*, 361–389.

MOORE, B. V., & BOUTHILLET, LORRAINE. "The VA program for counseling psychologists." *Amer. Psychologist*, 1952, *7*, 684–685.

PEPINSKY, H. B. "Selection and use of diagnostic categories in clinical counseling." *Psychol. Monogr.*, 1948, No. 15.

RAIMY, V. C. *Training in clinical psychology*. Englewood Cliffs, N.J.: Prentice-Hall, 1950.

ROGERS, C. *Counseling and psychotherapy*. Boston: Houghton Mifflin, 1942.

SUPER, D. E. "Vocational adjustment: implementing a self-concept." *Occupations*, 1951, *30*, 88–92.

SUPER, D. E. "Comments on current books." *J. counsel. Psychol.*, 1954, *1*, 123–124.

4. The Progressive Heritage of the Guidance Movement

Lawrence A. Cremin

It is now almost twenty years since the psychologist, Lawrence K. Frank, first published his intriguing little essay, "The Historian as Therapist." In it, Frank pleaded for historians who would serve society much in the fashion of psychoanalysts, clearing away distorted versions of the past so that men would be freed to contend more effectively with the problems of the present.

Frank's proposals, of course, raise all sorts of difficulties for any historian who would take them seriously, notably in their subtle invitation to read the problems of the present into the story of the past. And yet, I would suspect my students and I had something of Frank's "therapeutic" goal in mind as we set out in the early 1950's to write a history of the progressive education movement. We wanted to do away with the cartoons and caricatures that had long dominated pedagogical discussion, and to substitute a clear and accurate account of what progressive education had really meant in the American tradition. Our goal, to be sure, was to discover the facts; but we also wanted to report those facts in such a way as to enable contemporary educators to respond more intelligently to the situations in which they found themselves.

From *The Education Digest*, *30*, pp. 18–21, December, 1964. This article is condensed from *Guidance in American Education: Backgrounds and Prospects*, which was published by the Harvard Graduate School of Education. It is reprinted here by permission of Lawrence Cremin, *The Education Digest*, and the original publisher, Harvard Graduate School of Education.

I sketched some of our findings two years ago in a book called *The Transformation of the School,* and would like to use those findings as a basis for this paper. Perhaps I might summarize them in seven brief propositions:

First, what Americans refer to as *progressive education* began not in 1919 with the founding of the Progressive Education Association, but rather in the 1890's as the educational phase of the broader progressive movement in American life and thought.

Second, progressive education was not a single movement but rather a congeries of separate—frequently contradictory—movements, each seeking to contend in its own way with the central educational problem of the early twentieth century: how to adapt the popular school system to the needs of a democratic-industrial civilization.

Third, these movements enjoyed widespread support from businessmen, labor leaders, rural publicists, clergymen, academics, and social workers; they were not dreamed up and put across by a conspiracy of professional educators.

Fourth, these movements influenced all levels of education, public as well as private, rural as well as urban, southern as well as northern, western as well as eastern.

Fifth, John Dewey was the hero of the progressive education movement, not because he created it singlehandedly, but rather because he saw it whole; he was able to weave the *social reformism* of the urban settlement workers, the *individualism* of the Rousseauan pedagogues, and the *scientism* of the university psychologists into a reasonably consistent view of education. Seen in this light, the genius of *The School and Society,* the first great manifesto of the movement, and of *Democracy and Education,* its most comprehensive theoretical statement, resides less in their complete originality than in their synthetic character.

Sixth, the rise and fall of the movement was a political phenomenon comprehensible in political terms; progressive education collapsed as an organized movement in the 1950's partly because of internal dissension and party because the political coalition supporting it in the schools dissolved.

Seventh, although the organized movement is dead, the ideas and ideals of the progressive era retain a distinctive relevance for our own time; but they need searching reappraisal and substantial restatement to render them intellectually tenable and politically viable.

Needless to say, the effects of the progressive revolution I have described here are everywhere with us: in the architecture of schools, in the arrangement of classrooms, in the programs of students, and in the attitudes of teachers. Nowhere are the effects more apparent, however, than in the work of the guidance counselor. Beyond any other individual in today's education system, he incarnates the aims and ideals of progressivism. He is the most characteristic child of the progressive movement, and as such is heir to all of its vigor and optimism, and all of its diversity and contradiction.

Consider, for a moment, the legacy of diversity and contradiction. The fact is that each of the principal facets of progressive education is reflected in a particular way in the early development of the guidance movement. The social reformism of the urban settlement workers, for example, is patently involved in the beginnings of vocational counseling during the first years of the present century. One need only recall that the work of Frank Parsons and Meyer Bloomfield emerged as part of the program of the Civic Service House, a Boston settlement. It was Parsons' idea that a Vocation Bureau attached to the settlement could be of substantial assistance to young people, especially those of limited means, in helping them arrive at wise, well-founded occupational choices. And he saw wise, well-founded occupational choices as the foundation of useful and happy lives (Brewer, 1942; Parsons, 1909).

The key to Parsons' ultimate goal, of course, lay in his notion of the useful and happy life. Parsons, a significant figure in the history of American reform, believed not only that vocational counseling would lead to greater individual fulfillment, but that people suited to their jobs would tend to be active in the creation of a more efficient and humane industrial system. Intelligently practiced, the craft of vocational guidance would serve not only the youngsters who sought counsel, but the cause of social reform as well. Thus did the earliest, and to date the most stubbornly central, thread of the guidance movement connect with the broader progressive program.

In like manner, the effort to individualize education—which had always been the essence of the new pedagogy—was at the heart of what came to be known as "educational guidance." In 1908, the very year Parsons and Bloomfield opened the Vocation Bureau in Boston, a young teacher named Jessie B. Davis organized a program of vocational and moral guidance in the schools of Grand Rapids, Michigan. His effort included not only job counseling, but counseling with respect to courses and extra-curricular activities as well (Davis, 1914). Six years later, Truman Lee Kelley wrote a Ph.D. dissertation at Teachers College, Columbia University, entitled *Educational Guidance*, in which he urged the need for general counseling programs that would aid youngsters in their choice of studies. The concept broadened steadily during the 1920's, especially under the influence of the child guidance clinics pioneered by the National Committee for Mental Hygiene. By 1932, Professor John Brewer of Harvard was advancing a conception of guidance that came close to being synonymous with the whole of education. Pupils, Brewer argued, should be guided in *all* of their life activities; the ultimate goal of guidance was unified, integrated, harmonious personalities (Brewer, 1932).

Finally, the effort to develop a science of education, also at the heart

of the progressive movement, was reflected in the spirited interest in tests
and measurements that grew up in the United States shortly after the
turn of the century. By the time of World War I, a variety of intelligence
and aptitude tests was already in fairly general use in the schools; and
the wartime work of the Army Committee on Classification of Personnel
(mainly in developing and administering the Army Alpha and Beta tests)
really made testing a household notion throughout the country. Needless
to say, the possibility of precise instruments for measuring and predicting
achievement proved a boon to counselors, who were ever eager to make
their work more scientific; and the tests rapidly became a standard
counseling device. Thus the idea developed of the guidance worker as a
trained professional, wise in administering and interpreting scientific instruments for the prediction of vocational and educational success.

DIVERSITY AND CONTRADICTION

Now, my effort here has not been to sketch a history of the guidance
movement; that has been done elsewhere and well (Barry & Wolf, 1955).
Rather, I have attempted to document the close and inextricable tie
between the guidance movement and the broader progressive movement
of which it was part. Both movements have had a heritage of diversity,
and both have had a heritage of contradiction. Just as various schools of
progressives began to argue among themselves during the 1930's and
1940's over whether teachers ought to "build a new social order" or
"develop the whole child" or "apply scientific techniques in the classroom," so did various schools of counselors argue the merits of vocational
versus educational guidance, of systematic testing versus non-directive
interviewing. One need only follow the long and tedious discussion over
what kind of organization should represent guidance workers and what it
should be called, to grasp the significance of these differences.

More important for our purposes, perhaps—and here I'm reminded
of Lawrence Frank's plea—these differences and contradictions continue
to affect the practice of guidance today; they are inherent in the very
assumptions the counselor brings to his work. Permit me to illustrate with
a few questions that might well come up in the day-by-day activities of
any high-school counselor. How much social reformism, for example, of
the sort implicit in Parsons' notion of vocational guidance, is the counselor going to permit himself in advising minority-group youngsters with
respect to vocations from which they have traditionally been excluded?
How much does the counselor's commitment to individual fulfillment in
such cases ultimately conflict with his commitment to social reform? Or
again, to what extent does the commitment to individual fulfillment in

counseling lower-class children conflict with the knowledge that middle-class values are generally more appropriate to white-collar or professional occupations (Friedenberg, 1963)? Or again, to what extent does the commitment to a notion of individuality lead the counselor to skepticism concerning scientific test data (Hersey, 1960; Thorndike, 1963)? Universities, after all, are constantly taking chances on highly motivated youngsters who do poorly on every conceivable predictive measure. Or again, to what extent does a counselor support a personal sense of vocation where the market seems to call for different aptitudes (there's the old saw about Einstein doing poorly in school mathematics), or indeed, where there is little or no market for such a vocation? How much does "realism" about the job market sometimes fly in the face of the deepest meanings of vocation?

One could go on with such questions, but perhaps my point has been made. My concern is not with the dozens of decisions a counselor has to make every day in the very nature of his work. It is rather with the contradictory values and loyalties he brings to his work as heir to a contradictory heritage. Ultimately, it is only as he becomes aware of these contradictions that he can really enter upon the difficult task of resolving them; and it is only as he resolves them that he can eventually overcome the confusions they inevitably generate.

REAPPRAISAL NEEDED

One other problem derives from the progressive heritage of the guidance movement: it concerns the need for a searching reappraisal of progressive doctrine to separate those notions that are still tenable from those that are not. In the extent to which progressivism has become the "conventional wisdom" of our time, it is increasingly prone to obsolescence. As John Kenneth Galbraith pointed out some years ago, the ultimate enemy of the conventional wisdom is not so much ideas as the march of events. The conventional wisdom accommodates itself not to the world it is meant to interpret, but rather to the public's view of that world. And since the public tends to prefer the comfortable and familiar, while the world moves on, the conventional wisdom is ever in danger of obsolescence.

The implications for guidance are profound. It is no news that the movement has entered a period of vigorous expansion, aided in large measure by the federal government's financial assistance and Dr. Conant's moral assistance. Yet at this very time, some of the most fundamental assumptions of the movement, insofar as they derive from the progressive tradition, stand in need of drastic reformulation. Put another way, contemporary guidance theory is shot through with terms and concepts handed down from the progressive era that are now anachronistic in their meanings. Let me cite three by way of example.

First, the concept of *education*. As I read the contemporary guidance literature—and I admit to oversimplifying here to make my point—I come away with the notion that the counselor is dealing with a changing individual who is growing up in a changing world that has a changing occupational structure. Yet in all of this, the agencies of education somehow remain constant. The point, of course, is that this is simply not true. The structure of education is changing more rapidly in our time than at any other in history; witness the rapid rise of public, social and recreational facilities, of quasi-public social service organizations, of teaching programs in business and industry, and most important, perhaps, of the mass media of communication, notably television (Mead, 1958). All of these institutions educate, and as the counselor considers the range of educational possibilities open to his clients, he must bear them all in mind (Dienstfrey, 1963). Few of these institutions existed during the formative period of progressivism, and hence the progressives thought almost exclusively in terms of an expanding *school*. To do so today is plainly anachronistic. An exciting case in point, by the way, is New York's Higher Horizon's program, in which counselors have turned to all of the city's educational resources—museums, parks, concert halls, theatres, libraries, zoos, and aquaria—in their effort to raise the intellectual sights of slum children.

A second progressive holdover I find in the guidance literature is a concept of *community* that almost always implies locality. Now, the community in turn-of-the-century America *was* the locality, and the early progressives—except for the more far-sighted among them—had every right to assume that most people would spend their adult lives in the communities into which they were born. Indeed, many progressives, especially rural publicists concerned with the flight of farm youngsters to the city, took this goal as not only probable but eminently desirable. Much of what we know about contemporary America indicates that this is no longer so. Consider a passage from a recent report of the United States Census Bureau:

About 35.5 million, or 20.0 percent, of the 177.4 million persons 1 year old and over who were living in the United States in March 1961 had moved at least once since March 1960. Although this overall mobility rate has reflected to some slight extent some of the postwar changes in business conditions, it has remained relatively stable in the 14 successive surveys conducted since 1948. . . .

Of the 35.5 million persons 1 year old and over who were living in a different house in March 1961 from that in 1960, about 24.3 million, or 13.7 percent of the total population 1 year old and over, had moved within the same county; 5.5 million, or 3.1 percent had moved between counties in the same State; and 5.8 million, or 3.2 percent, had moved between States. In addition to these persons who moved within the United States, about 0.6 percent of the 1961 population had been living abroad in 1960. . . . (Current Population Reports, 1962)[1]

Given these statistics, it is simply erroneous to assume that most graduates of a local high school are going to remain in the local community for the rest of their lives, and hence ought to be trained with reference to the occupational structure of that community. Today, the counselor must think in terms of a national—indeed, international—community if young men and women are to be prepared realistically for the world in which they will undoubtedly live.

A third anachronism from the progressive era that suffuses the literature of guidance is a particular notion of *vocation*. Based on the situation that prevailed in the first years of the present century, too many counselors have continued to assume that choice of occupation plays *the* determinative role in the development of adult character. Yet, as I read the sociology of occupations today, we seem to be moving into a period in which, paradoxically, occupation will probably play an ever more central role in the lives of those who enter the professions, but a less and less central role for those who enter the trades—witness the recent victory of the New York electricians' union in winning a five-hour basic workday (Merton, et al., 1959). If this be the case, the counselor will have to develop a much broader concept of vocational choice, one concerned with total life-style rather than merely with occupation. Here, I find myself much in agreement with the arguments of my colleague Edward Joseph Shoben, Jr. in his essay in this volume. Dr. Shoben proposes that the counselor assist the youngster not merely in choosing a vocation, but in the whole process of choosing the personal models he takes for himself, or, if we use the Socratic terminology, in the process of learning to live the examined life. Incidentally, I might add that if the counselor is to play this role, he will have to prepare himself for it with a good deal more humanistic study than is currently present in most guidance curricula.

In connection with Dr. Shoben's proposal, I might also remark on one other educational change of extraordinary significance: the contemporary curriculum reform movement. The reader is no doubt aware of the excitement generated by recent curriculum revision in mathematics and the natural sciences; and no doubt there is equal awareness of the effort to extend this revision into the social sciences and humanities. This is not the place to debate the merits of the new reforms; suffice it to say they have produced some striking results that are patently here to stay.

[1] . . . There are no accurate statistics on the mobility of the American population at the turn of the century; the earliest Census Bureau statistics refer to the period between 1935 and 1940.

But they have also raised some thorny problems, one of which is a growing specialization, and consequent fragmentation, in the curriculum. Now, it may be that such specialization is unavoidable, given the nature and rapid expansion of knowledge in our time; I for one have not yet made up my mind on the matter. But I do know that as specialization moves down into the elementary and secondary schools, the role Dr. Shoben asks the counselor to play becomes all the more important. Ultimately, the counselor may end up as one of the few professionals primarily responsible for seeing the child's education whole.

THE PROBLEM OF OPTIMISM

My final comment is really in the nature of a postscript. Insofar as guidance is the child of the progressive movement, it is also heir to the characteristic vigor and optimism—some would say utopianism—of that movement. And this, too, has raised problems. After all, the counselor has dedicated his life to taking some of the waste, the accident, and the needless inefficiency out of the difficult business of becoming an adult. Yet however much he achieves his goal, he is ever doomed to a measure of failure. As Morris R. Cohen once remarked in a critique of John Dewey's perennial optimism: "So long as human beings lack omniscience they will lack omnipotence and will therefore have to face insuperable difficulties and evils" (Cohen, 1949). The failure to recognize this, I would suspect, is the original sin of pride.

Some years ago, Ruth Barry and Beverly Wolf observed the following about the literature they had read in connection with their history of the guidance movement:

The guidance and personnel literature indicates that personnel workers are also unrealistic about their own work. Personnel work has had its successes and presumably its failures, but the literature would lead a reader to believe that no program or no aspect of a program had ever failed. Mathematically, the odds against 100 percent success in personnel work are infinite; yet, apparently no one ever fails in personnel work. Writers admit that a guidance program could be better, but never was it unsuccessful. . . . By refusing to recognize failure, personnel work creates a myth, an impossible ideal, a stereotype, which does not fool the public, but may mislead individual workers in the field. By reinforcing stereotypes, personnel work tacitly promises that it can be all things to all people and that each personnel worker can be everything to each individual student (Barry and Wolf, 1955).

I'm afraid I, too, come away with much the same impression. Somehow the guidance literature seems to promise that with more money, more personnel, and more effort, counselors could usher in some sort of utopia.

I think counselors would do themselves and the public a great deal more good if they simply promised that they would try to make life a bit more planful, a bit more intelligent, and a bit more humane.

REFERENCES

BARRY, R. E. & WOLF, B. *A History of the Guidance Personnel Movement in Education.* New York: Columbia University Press, 1955.

BREWER, J. M. *Education as Guidance.* New York: Macmillan, 1932.

BREWER, J. M. *History of Vocational Guidance.* New York: Harper and Row, 1942, pp. 303–308.

COHEN, M. R. *Studies in Philosophy and Science.* New York: Holt, Rinehart and Winston, 1949, p. 169.

Current Population Reports: Population Characteristics. Series P-20, No. 118, August, 1962, p. 1.

DAVIS, J. B. *Vocational and Moral Guidance.* Boston: Ginn, 1914.

DIENSTFREY, H. "Doctors, Lawyers and Other TV Heros." *Commentary,* 1963, 519–524.

FRIEDENBERG, E. Z. "An Ideology of School Withdrawal." *Commentary,* 1963, 492–500.

HERSEY, J. *The Child Buyer.* New York: Knopf, 1960.

MEAD, M. "Thinking Aloud: Why Is Education Obsolete?" *Harvard Business Review,* Nov.–Dec., 1958, 23–30.

MERTON, R. K., BROOM, L. and COTTRELL, L. S., JR., eds. *Sociology Today.* New York: Basic Books, 1959, pp. 442–458.

PARSONS, F. *Choosing a Vocation.* Boston: Houghton Mifflin, 1909.

THORNDIKE, R. L. *The Concept of Over- and Under-achievement.* New York: Teachers College, Columbia University, 1963.

5.   A Second Look

C. Gilbert Wrenn

In being asked to take "a second look" at what was proposed in *The Counselor in a Changing World* (American Personnel and Guidance Association, 1962), I am reminded of what Dael Wolfle, Willis Dugan and others told me in 1960—"In your cultural projections be sure to state your assumptions—only if these conditions prevail is this and this likely to happen—a given innovation or invention is likely to change radically your extrapolation of a present curve—what you are recommending is a 1962 recommendation only—make it clear that different recommendations might be in order a few years hence—etc." To the extent that I was not appropriately cautious in either social projections or counseling recommendations, I am now grateful for this chance to take a second look.

CULTURAL PROJECTIONS REVISITED

It now seems apparent that I was not imaginative enough with regard to scientific and technological developments—and I was too optimistic about the speed of social innovation and change. This is my 1964 reaction to what I wrote in 1960. I am not aware of any scientific discovery that markedly changes our concept of man and the world and therefore changes the slope of our curves of extrapolation, but technological changes are "ahead of schedule." In spatial exploration, the development of effective oral contraceptives, and the development of computorized and automated systems, as examples, greater strides have been taken in four years than I had thought at all possible. I am not a professional student of many areas of science and technology, perhaps not even of any one, but I am pleasantly excited about our world-wide advancement in the physical and biological sciences and related technologies.

There is also a firm advance in the more or less structural elements of our society. Our 1964 Gross National Product of $600 + billion is a little ahead of where it should be if the projected $750 billion for 1970 is to become a reality. The latest statement of a 1965 GNP is a projection of $685 billion with 1970 seen as $825 billion. The same is true of metropolitan development. The explosion of suburbs and physical action to counteract economic and social decay within the Central City is more rapid than seemed possible in 1960.

Social innovation, however, is another story. I failed, in 1962, to allow sufficiently for the time element involved in the operation of the social principle which says that "things must get worse before they get any better." Nor did I anticipate the magnitude of physical and intellectual violence as a protest for change. Social innovation has not produced new jobs rapidly enough to care for those displaced by automation and other technological changes. We will have—I now predict—a constantly large and probably increasing segment of the population who are unemployed. Some will be temporarily unemployed because they are in the process of retraining and replacement, but some, for a variety of reasons, will increase the size of the chronically unemployed group. We need a new economic and social theory to fit the inescapable reality that *from now on there will be more people than jobs.*

The family is adjusting at a slow pace to the new demands made upon it in the light of greater freedom of action available to children and the impersonalized, mobile nature of urban life.

The clash is very real in a number of other social areas where bad conditions will probably get worse before constructive action outweighs destructive tendencies. Four areas are illustrative, (1) Young people, faced with what seems to them to be an unrealistic school program, vocational uncertainty, and adult unsureness in the declaration of firm values, become resentful and turn to violence, expressions of contempt for law, and disregard for the rights of others. This will probably continue for some time since the causes are basic in our society and not easily modified. (2) Attempts to hasten the slow change of attitudes toward racial and color-line differences is and will be accompanied by more violence than was anticipated. The solution is not yet apparent, nor by what avenues we will arrive at a solution. The violence of resistance to educational, political and economic integration indicates that status quo with all of its attendant injustices is more acceptable to some and more deeply resented by others than students of the subject appeared to realize. Here the violence dimension discussed in (1) becomes an augmenting factor and has, for both sides, retarded movement toward constructive behaviors.

(3) The movement toward what is generally regarded as more liberal economic and political assumptions (more Federal concern with education, employment, and physical and social health at state and community levels) is being resisted vigorously. Name calling is relied upon; the Bible is invoked for the meeting of conditions not dreamed of by the writers of that day; people are denying economic and political realities with an undreamed-of intensity. The organized fashion of this resistance, recently demonstrated in a national political campaign, was not anticipated. The "it must get worse" attribute of the situation is enhanced by the failure of those who are in favor of change to make allowance for the *normality* of the psychological resistance to be encountered. Name calling, labeling, and invalid inferences from facts are indulged by both proponents and opponents, and the social change movement is reduced to a crawl.

(4) The projected increase in GNP, and therefore in average family income, will probably result in an increase in the gap between those who have much and those who have little. The 35 million people whose annual income is less than $3,000 will not keep up with the projected increase in family income. They will fall further behind. Those who are fortunate in

family support and in amount and kind of education will be *rewarded* more and those without these advantages will be *penalized* more. There will be pressure on community and, in particular, educational leaders to develop educational programs and non-employment activity outlets appropriate to the disadvantaged and the nonemployed. There will be pressure also on the government to provide a living "wage" for all who are low in income and only partially employable. There will be resentment also of those who have by those who haven't.

SOME HOPEFUL SIGNS

Not all of the developments seen from 1965 are dark. In the United States the annual birth rate per 1,000 was reported in the spring of 1964 as 22.6, down from 25+ in 1960. This is in the face, however, of a world population annual increase of 2.1 per cent reported in the *Demographic Yearbook* as the highest ever recorded. (The increase is highest in Central America with annual increases averaging 2.9 per cent since 1958. By comparison, the annual increase reported in 1964 was 1.6 per cent in the United States and 0.9 in Europe.)

The Economic Opportunity Act (Anti-Poverty Bill) is a brave attempt to iron out some of the unevenness of opportunity in our country. It may well be too much of a crash program but if its objectives are reached to only a limited degree, however, hundreds of thousands will benefit, and the gap in family income mentioned earlier will be slightly less formidable.

The Manpower Development and Training Act of 1962 was strengthened by substantial amendments in 1964, several of which make it a more effective instrument for youth—lowering the age limit to 17, increasing mobility of training and placement, providing for basic literacy training where this was needed to make a person eligible for vocational training (up to a total of 72 weeks for a combination of basic and vocation-training), etc. Here again the intent was sound but the objective was a short-range one—as though basic and enduring economic and vocational dislocations could be settled by an "emergency" program. In my testimony August 12, 1964, before the House Select Sub-Committee on Labor, I said, "It is crucial for all Americans to realize that unemployment is and will be a constant factor in our society. Different administrations may affect it some, but the changing technology of our day and of the immediate future will affect it far more. It may be easier to get emergency legislation adopted, but the emergency or temporary concept of unemployment is not honest. People speak of full employment as though it were achievable. It is not and it will not be. I am concerned that the task of the United States Employment Service and its contributions to the local offices be seen as a permanent social and economic need which will not be placated by emergency and short-run legislation."

It has been encouraging too to see the response, mostly of young people, to the appeal of the Peace Corps. Most of them want to *serve* and they develop a healthy respect for the necessity of understanding other people before they can help them. The selection program for the Peace Corps has been appropriately vigorous. I hope we can develop an equally effective selection and educational program for those (again mostly young people) who will work in the Youth Opportunity Centers through the State Employment Offices. The start made was only a fair one, particularly on matters of selection for the CAUSE program and employment by the State Offices afterward. But again most of the young people responded in terms of a desire to serve, to be of some worth to disadvantaged youth. More of the same spirit was seen in the college students who wanted to help disadvantaged Negroes get to the polls. Their sacrifice was often real. Only time will tell how socially constructive was this 1964 program. It meant much to the young people and to many individual Negroes.

These responses of young people to needs at home and abroad balance in some measure the violence and hostility shown in other quarters. The year and the quadrennium saw the white flames of hope and charity as well as the red glare of hatred and the dead embers of despair.

COUNSELOR DEVELOPMENTS SINCE 1960

1. Secondary School Counselors have increased markedly in sheer numbers—from 7,000 full time in 1959 to 18,000 full time in 1963. Counseling in schools, in the public Employment Service, and in social agencies is getting quite a "play"—the acceptance of counseling as an essential social function is almost embarrassing. The 1963 President's Manpower Report to Congress contains an estimation of 32,000 additional full-time counselors to be needed in the schools and other public agencies by the end of Fiscal Year 1967. This number of counselors who could be called qualified cannot, of course, be supplied in so short a time—this is more than a 50 per cent increase of all full time people called counselors in 1964. Embarrassing also are the expectations accompanying this wave of popularity—many of them are grossly unrealistic. Counselors find it impossible to live up to what parents, in particular, now hopefully expect of them.

2. The publication of this present book and all of the cooperative endeavor that made it possible is one of the encouraging developments of

the past four years. The possibility of such a combined report by APGA and two of its Divisions seemed quite remote in 1960 although it was specifically proposed in *The Counselor in a Changing World* (pp. 178–179). I have developed some real inner excitement as I read the reports and the chapters of this book that analyze them.

Stoughton's chapter portrays statemanship upon the part of the APGA committee over these recent years in limiting the scope of its operations and in recognizing the more specific responsibilities that each Division has to its own membership. I believe too that the "implementation" concepts apparent in this chapter and that by Fitzgerald on the ASCA report is a wise feature. Steps to put ideas into use must be clearly formulated and change must be *phased in,* not administered in one dose. It is particularly significant that the ASCA study, analyzed by Fitzgerald, and the ACES study, reported by Stripling, "went to the people" for both the details of their proposals, and in the case of ASCA, for reactions on the final draft.

The ACES study was the "original" and had the larger range in time development. The involvement of 1,000 people in the ACES study and the seeking of the reactions of over 2,500 ASCA members to the final draft suggests a strong sense of responsibility to the membership of the Divisions. The fact that 80 per cent of the ASCA members approved the Policy Statement on Counselor Role and that 90 per cent endorsed the Guidelines for Implementation of Policy means that for the first time we have a strong national consensus of agreement on counselor function. In only two states did as much as one-fifth of the members voting disapprove the policy (31 per cent in Iowa and 24 per cent in Illinois) and in 12 states the agreement was unanimous. A marked step forward was taken in the ASCA involvement of the officers of the National Association of Secondary School Principals and the American Association of School Administrators in the development of the report. This was the first national move that had been taken to put into action another proposal of *The Counselor in a Changing World* (p. 178). A move in this same direction was taken by ACES in its conferences on accreditation with the National Commission on Accreditation and the National Commission on Accreditation in Teacher Education.

3. Another major step forward for counselors taken by APGA was the adoption of a code of ethics at Denver in 1961, published and distributed to the membership in that same year (*Personnel guid. J.,* 1961, *40,* 204–209). This adoption of a set of standards for the total and quite varied membership of APGA leads inevitably to the development of codes specifically designed for the membership of each Division. But *now* we have an essential foundation block in the further professionalization possibilities of counselors and of all members of APGA.

4. The development in 1961 of the Interprofessional Research Commission on Pupil Personnel Services with its consequent five-year grant of $1,300,000 from the National Institute for Mental Health is a marked step forward in interdisciplinary study. Twelve national professional associations concerned directly or tangentially with pupil personnel work and mental health in schools banded together and planned what is one of the most striking interprofessional efforts of the decade—all in the interests of pupil personnel work! Three additional associations asked for inclusion in the study after the grant had been made, making 15 in all—APGA and APA, NEA and ASCD, four medical associations, school administrators, elementary and secondary principals, speech and hearing, exceptional children, social workers, etc. In the summer of 1963 four centers of research were established at the University of Maryland (also the headquarters of the central staff, Dr. Walter B. Waetgen, General Director), University of Michigan, University of Texas, and University of California at Los Angeles. Each of these has a distinctive program of research—community cultures and vocational choice, professional role of different specialists, the function of child behavior consultants, the school learning environment, etc. The central staff anticipates making a national survey of pupil personnel specialists, establishing criteria for the evaluation of pupil personnel services, collecting and disseminating professional information, etc.

5. Counseling has received several vigorous nods of recognition in employment and welfare legislation passed by Congress during the quadrennium. Counseling is seen as essential in meeting retraining and employment needs—1962 Manpower Development and Training Act, 1964 Economic Opportunity Act, counseling of those rejected by Selective Service, etc. There is encouragement also in the provisions for counseling in the Vocational Education Act, in the extensions of school counselor education to the elementary school as well as to technical schools and higher education in the 1963 and 1964 amendments to NDEA, in the Social Security Administration's use of counselors as "expert witnesses" in their appeal cases.

These developments have both positive and negative implications. The very real danger is that too much is expected of too few. In particular, counseling functions are being loaded on the Employment Service by such legislation with no provision in the legislation for additional counselors or the professional upgrading of the 2,900 employment counselors (42 per cent of whom spend less than half-time in counseling, according to a May, 1964, report). The exception is the legislative provision for a bare minimum of "counselor aide" preparation for those who will work in Youth Opportunity Centers. Legislation was introduced in July, 1964, but not passed, by Representative Holland, Chairman of the

House Select Sub-Committee on Labor, which provided for fairly substantial subsidization of the professional education of presently employed employment counselors ($4,000 Fellowships).

To be remembered is that the United States Employment Service *proposes,* but the 1,900 local employment offices are *staffed* and *administered* by the 50 State Employment Services under widely varying state standards and personnel merit systems. Not all that goes into the national hopper comes out at the local office end. USES has developed some excellent standards, tools, and procedures, but local office pay schedules and general lack of concern for professional counselor standards keep legislative intent from being realized. Nevertheless, I count as gain all such recent national attention to counseling.

A SECOND LOOK AT COUNSELOR ROLE

Influenced by my experiences in meeting with state and city counselor organizations in 29 states during the last three years, by some excellent papers heard at national meetings, and by the work of the three committees reporting in this volume, I would build certain emphases into a 1965 statement. To a considerable extent these would *be built upon* the 1960 writing, not replace it.

1. The school counselor is a team worker always—with teacher, parent, and principal at least. This means understanding what the other team members think is important, in helping them to achieve some of *their* goals with the student as well as expecting them to work with the counselor. He remains a specialist in the understanding of human behavior, both youth and adult behavior, and in the counseling knowledges and skills that contribute to student living and planning for living, to student growth in the process of decision making, to student understanding and modifications of his own behavior. Because these ends can often be best reached through the "important others" in a student's life, the counselor may spend as much time with adults as with the students. He is a team worker with other pupil personnel specialists if they are in the school or system. If they are not, he is a "general practitioner" in his field, performing functions that would be performed by school psychologists, school social workers, or even remedial teachers if these were available. Hopefully he can be on both the general school team and a pupil personnel team.

2. The school counselor is a member of the educational staff of the school and system. As such he is not immune to the weary plague of housekeeping duties. Certainly he is not superior to them. Two considerations should guide both the counselor and his principal in the assignment

of housekeeping duties to a counselor: (a) Does the assignment of this task reduce the time the counselor can spend on activities that are uniquely his own, essential work that he can perform somewhat better than anyone else in the school? In other words, is this assignment "getting the most mileage" out of the counselor, a consideration which would have some significance for both school board and parents. (b) Is the nature of the school task to be performed by the counselor likely to support the image of the counselor that both principal and counselor want others to have of him? Or does it distort that image and make it harder for the counselor to be of help to students? These constitute the basis for decision, not whether the counselor likes the nature of the housekeeping duty. This suggests that the counselor must have a clear idea of the image he wishes to project and that his principal shares this perception.

3. It is important that the counselor assist the student in better self-understanding, in gaining some sense of self-identity, but I see this now more as *a means to an end* than as an end in itself. The outcomes should include observable behavior changes as well as changes in self-attitudes. There is still too little proof that one follows the other, although that is the assumption, and certainly we now know that behavior changes can be developed without attitude change. The evidence is not all in that, in spite of claims to that effect, attitude change always follows behavior change. It would appear that neither the phenomenologist nor the behaviorist has the full truth, but rather that each has *evidence bearing on a portion of the total complex of human behavior.* Counselors must be alert to specific disequilibriums and specific behavior syndromes *as well as* to the student's confusion about self and to his misperceptions of himself.

Counselor emphasis moves in cycles. From sentiment and persuasion early in the century we moved to a diagnostic emphasis in the 20's and 30's, with the rational process of the counselor looming largest. In the 40's and 50's we become very aware of student emotion, affect, and self-attitudes. One *felt* in counseling rather than thought. Now comes a healthy adjustment in the direction of saying cognition *and* emotion, feelings *and* behavior. At each state the new builds upon the old rather than replacing it so that we do not have to abandon affect if we bring cognition into focus.

4. Vocational counseling could have new meaning for counselors if they were to see occupation as *part* of one's vocation, of one's purpose in or commitment to life. The chapter on "Human Values and Work in American Society" (Wrenn, 1964) . . . has made me very thoughtful about the meaning of work for many young people today and many more in the future. A job, or even one's occupation, does not bring meaning into life for so many, perhaps a third of our high school and college graduates. Havighurst writes that two-thirds of those now in the Ameri-

can labor force are in "society-maintaining" as opposed to "ego-involving" occupations. Occupation for many is simply a way to make a living and no counseling can make it personally significant.

But *life* can be significant and a sense of purpose and contribution can be developed. This is vocational counseling, helping students plan for nonemployed as well as employed activity in life. The non-employed activity may give meaning to life even if the routine and trivial nature of one's occupation does not do so. Loughary's brilliant chapter has made this point most effectively and there is need here only to say "please read again."

"What Has Happened to Vocational Counseling in Our Schools?" was the title of an article written for the Tenth Anniversary Issue of *The School Counselor* (March, 1963) in which I analyzed what is now seen as the complex nature of vocational counseling. If vocational counseling is now being given inadequate attention because it requires increasing knowledge and skill, and this is certainly part of the explanation, the future will see the task grow more difficult, not less. It is one of the most vital and distinctive tasks of the secondary school counselor. No counselor should be allowed to substitute "counseling for college" or any other emphasis for vocational counseling. As the decade advances it will be more and more apparent that this country will not have enough jobs for all the workers. Counseling for life activity, with occupation in the picture for those who will have jobs, takes on new meaning.

In the comprehensive and detailed ASCA statement on counselor role and responsibility, I fear that the over-riding significance of psychologically meaningful vocational counseling is lost. For the sake of troubled young people in a rapidly shifting vocational and social world, it must not be lost.

CONCLUDING LOOK AT ROLE AND PROGRAM

In the preceding paragraphs two elements of program relationship and two of counselor relationship to students have been refocused. The other elements of these two kinds of relationships (Chapters 5 & 6 of *The Counselor in a Changing World*) are, however, not to be excluded. In considering these I would still have the counselor work with staff and parents more than I believe is suggested in the ASCA Implementation statement. I believe it would be more significant to propose that approximately two-thirds of the counselor's work week be spent in personal contact with some combination of students, staff and parents than to establish a standard of 50 per cent of his "assigned time in counseling" to be spent with the students. As stated earlier, a counselor may be *able to help students* more by providing assistance and understanding to the adults in the students' lives than by using the same amount of time with individuals or even groups of students.

It was probably not appropriate in the broad-gauged ASCA policy statement to call attention to particular groups or categories of students. I would again, however, express the conviction that (a) the anticipation of the changing role of women in our society and (b) the creative, divergent-thinking students' need for recognition deserve special attention by counselors. Both of these groups of students are likely to be the victims of prejudicial attitudes upon the part of the adults. Girls are not really as important as boys because "man is the breadwinner" while divergent thinkers have too little respect for adults and "must be kept in their place." The counselor must fight against these attitudes in his own relations with such students. He needs to give particular attention to the vocational counseling of girls and to the identification and encouragement of students who are "different" since the needs of these groups of students are likely to be neglected by everyone else.

Many of the developments of the past four years point to the extreme importance of women and of creative individuals of both sexes to the future of our society. The proportion of women in our labor force in 1964 is only one per cent less than the 38 per cent predicted by the Labor Department in 1960 that would be the proportion *in 1970*. It is estimated that 8 out of 10 girls now in high schools will have jobs outside the home as well as in the home for some major part of their adult lives. Are counselors taking seriously the task of assisting girls to plan for these two work-lives? The Women's Bureau writes, "about one half of today's young women are married by age 20 and have their last child by age 26; by the time the youngest is in school, the mother may have 40 or more years of her life before her." Are the counselors of girls acting within this framework of reality?

Social innovations will be needed in large measure in the near future if the strides of technological development are matched and serious social dislocation is prevented. Are counselors helping these "uncomfortable" creative students to respect themselves and their uniqueness of thinking, to dedicate their talents not only to the discovery of truth but to the development of societal health? I fear that *if* the counselor fails to see not only the loneliness but the preciousness of these individuals they will be lost to mediocrity.

My reading in existentialist philosophy and psychology over the past four years would make me stress more than before the importance of helping students to develop self-reliance and a sense of personal responsibility for themselves. Each person is responsible for choices involving himself, and he must not let the Establishment make them for him. People generally, youth in particular, do not want the anguish of making choices and being responsible for the outcomes. So a student (or an adult) makes loud noises about authority—and then leans upon authority for his decision when permitted. Are counselors themselves self-responsible and therefore able to help students become more so? Part of this means getting students to be self-involved in a cause, in a principle. Can students be helped to *care* about *something?*

A Second Look at Counselor Education

The most pressing modification needed for my 1960 proposals is more stress on the evolutionary nature of counselor education. The entire chapter by Loughary makes this point—as counselor functions and procedures change we must make sure that counselor education is flexible enough to change accordingly. His illustrations are apt—the changing function of work and, therefore, of vocational counseling, the systematic supplying of individualized information to students, the utilization of automation for certain counselor procedures, the changing nature of the teacher-pupil relationships which counselors must understand—all of these call for changed emphases in counselor education. Nor is it enough that counselor education keep apace of changes in the counseling function; it must anticipate such changes by some years.

In fact the counselor education curriculum should always represent a judicious blend of preparation for presently emphasized counselor competencies and of preparation for those anticipated in the immediate future. Such a curriculum should be close to the present in a major part of its emphasis but always on the growing edge of the future for the balance.

What is needed is a built-in provision for vigorous self-criticism and consequent modification at stated intervals. Although not written into the ACES standards, a three-year revision was stipulated by the assembly when they were endorsed. This should result in bringing the objectives "up to date" as well as in revision intended to make the policy more "workable"—the latter probably means patterning closer to the comfortable present! A policy statement such as this could well include provision for an arbitrary review each two years to work out the operational "bugs" located through experience, and each five years to bring the statement up to date. It is too easy for an organization or a faculty to admire its efforts, excellent for the time, and then to continue for far too long a time to bask in the glory of that achievement.

UNDERSTANDING OF COUNSELORS BY NON-COUNSELORS

I would now place more stress on efforts to make counselor education (and the counselor's role which determines much of the content of the curriculum) better understood by *employers of counselors*. Very little has been done in that regard during the last four years. The Commission on Guidance in American Schools chose to bend its first efforts toward securing action and a consensus by those in the counseling field. Its second step, never achieved, was to produce a much briefer statement on counseling for parents and members of legislatures. This was not done in part for lack of funds and in part because my attention was turned elsewhere after almost two solid years on *The Counselor in a Changing World*. We made one attempt for a second and smaller grant to do two things: (1) Prepare a *Reader's Digest* type condensation of *The Counselor in a Changing World* for quite general distribution and (2) develop research ideas for testing some of the basic assumptions made in the book. When our first try for a grant failed, we did not go further. *The Counselor in a Changing World* has been used more widely than we had hoped (some 35,000 to 40,000 copies in less than three years), but largely by professional people in our field and in counselor education and sociology classes. We still have not made enough of an impact upon principals, superintendents, teachers and school board members. Will APGA, ASCA, and ACES pursue this more vigorously? If the professional organizations most concerned have now reached reasonable consensus among themselves could not the next step be a vigorous attack on a condensed and simplified statement for the employers and supporters of counseling?

CERTIFICATION

The lag in accreditation procedures also deserves more thought than it has received to date. Always lagging behind the emphasis in the major graduate schools, and frequently behind good practice in the schools, counselor certification standards may lag still further behind as counseling practice and counselor education take decided steps forward. As counselor education programs lay more stress on concepts and less on techniques, the strong techniques emphasis in the state certification plans that were analyzed in 1960 has probably changed very little. With both counselors and counselor educators agreeing upon two years of graduate study as the desirable goal, less than half of the states require even a year's graduate work.

ASCA's proposal of more than one level of professional preparation and certification is realistic. So is its expectation of graduate school endorsement for certification. It is a reasonable goal to specify both "counselor" and "master counselor" with at least one of the latter in each school having 500 students or more. A single counselor in a school with no supervision should be a master counselor. Could not certification standards be thus appropriately devised, certification that provides for the *best* of practice in the state as well as for the average and the minimal?

Is it significant that only ASCA speaks at all on the point of state certification? Why not ACES? *The Counselor in a Changing World* recommended (pp. 176–179) that counselor educators work not only with school principals on what is needed in counseling and who might succeed in graduate school as well as on the job, but also with state departments of education in periodic reviews of school counselor certification standards. Granted that the present ACES statement on counselor education is broader than school counselors, but *now* perhaps it is possible for ACES to pick up the urgent problems of school counselor certification. It is a team job—counselor, counselor employer, counselor educator, and state department. The graduate school counselor educator is often in the least vulnerable position and should assume vigorous leadership in establishing periodic review.

SPECIFICS IN THE CONTENT OF COUNSELOR EDUCATION

There is really little point in gilding the lily. The ACES statement has been five years in the making and has involved hundreds of people and thousands of hours. It is a strong and comprehensive statement on content and the basis for determining content. It established guidelines that are based upon both scholarship standards and professional demands. Both the APGA and ASCA statements contain additional attention to professional preparation. A study of these documents will provide insight into the thinking of perhaps a thousand thoughtful people in the field. My personal comments would add but little for I am appreciative of the fact that what was said four years ago is in relatively good harmony with these 1964 documents. Two years of graduate work, a core of preparation in psychology and the social-behavioral sciences, less emphasis on technique courses, fundamental attention to supervised experience, service research and computer understanding, ethical relationships and legal responsibilities—all are here and more too.

It is good also to reflect that you have seen each of these emphases demonstrated in various developing programs over the last four years. The 1960 proposals can be seen in action in 1964—and in large measure, I believe, because of the impetus to innovation given by the NDEA Institutes. So I will only reflect very briefly upon things that I would "do better" were I writing in 1964.

1. More attention to learning theory and research as well as to personality theory. I am no longer bothered by labels—if anyone wishes to call me a behaviorist because I think there is much to be learned from learning research, let them. I remain basically a centralist in my theory

orientation but with great respect for the methodology of learning research and for what it can be worth in contributing to counseling. Nor are all behavioristically focused research workers committed to operant conditioning or any other one theoretical scheme. John Krumboltz of Stanford University and Lee Meyerson of Arizona State University are examples of methodological behaviorists who have much to contribute to counseling.

2. More attention to the purposes and objectives of counseling. We are far too vague about our objectives in counseling, our desired outcomes. These are of two sorts—broad philosophical purposes that provide a link between what Life means and what counseling can mean to Life, and specific operational objectives that are expressed in observable behavior changes. I would distinguish, as Richard Byrne did so admirably in *The School Counselor*, between immediate, intermediate, and ultimate goals in counseling with the first two being gauged to the specific individual at a specific time. They are researchable while the ultimate goal is only logically defensible. Here again I want "the best of two worlds" for I am convinced that life is meaningful in terms of both specifics and ultimates, not one or the other.

3. I would do no differently in 1964 on the teacher-experience issue. The ASCA statement on the point is an admirable further step.

4. I would ask again for more attention in counselor education to the psychology of the adult, not only for dealings with colleagues and with parents but because the burgeoning junior college field will demand real understanding of adult counselees.

5. If pressed, I would plead for careful attention to the education of employment counselors—no, I could not because my treatment was of school counselors! Well, employment counselors must work in an increasingly close relationship to schools as more adults return to school for re-education or retraining, so perhaps I could.

We are in a lively field, we counselors and counselor educators. We are vulnerable to the temptations of too much "press," of too much expected of us. We can feel important and develop a Jehovah complex rather easily, slide along on glib assumptions with no testing of anything. Other professions, psychiatry comes to mind, have been tempted this way. The search for tested truth is demanding, *yet it is our way* if we represent a vocation that professes to be based upon a science. To search yet never to find completely, this is our fate. And Emerson once said, "you may seek either Truth or repose; you must choose, for you cannot have both."

REFERENCES

"A Code of Ethics." *Personnel and Guid. J.* 1961, 40, 204–209.
WRENN, G.G. "Human Values and Work in American Society." In H. Borow, ed., *Man in a World at Work*. Boston: Houghton Mifflin, 1964.

SECTION TWO

Philosophical Aspects

Psychology has proved to be the discipline of major influence in the historical development of the guidance movement. Since psychology itself split from philosophy fewer than one hundred years ago, it is therefore no surprise that the rekindled interest in philosophical issues in psychology has direct relevance for counselors and personnel workers in general. Thus, most if not all the selections in Section Four, *Psychological Foundations*—where the major focus is the conceptualization of psychology as a discipline and consequent implications for guidance—are inseparable in many ways from the present section. This relationship is particularly apparent, for example, in Gordon Allport's classic "Psychological Models for Guidance," which deals primarily with philosophic assumptions undergirding differing conceptions of the discipline of psychology.

The necessity for the guidance profession to explore its philosophical foundations in the social and behavioral sciences is of paramount importance. Unlike the experimental psychologist who might rest comfortably within a simple mechanistic view of life and events, the counselor must grapple with fundamental problems philosophers have been considering for centuries. This point of view follows from the assumption that science provides at best a limited and truncated view of the human condition.

The readings in this section deal with essentially two

branches of philosophy: *axiology,* which explores the nature
and types of values; and *metaphysics,* which is concerned with
first principles and deals with the nature of being and reality
(*ontology*), the structure of the world and universe (*cosmology*), and the theory of knowledge (*epistemology*).

In the first article of the section Rudolf Dreikurs, a psychiatrist noted for his work with children and parent groups, explores
epistomological issues relevant to the helping professions. In a
view which draws from both the physical and social sciences
Dreikurs makes a strong case for the inadequacy of the philosophical and methodological bases of the behavioral sciences.
Since psychology and sociology have borrowed from the physical
sciences the deterministic presumptions of strict causality,[1] they
have been left behind while the modern physicist has moved on
to the more sophisticated concept of statistical causality. Simply
speaking, statistical causality means that predictions of the movements or changes in the aggregate are tenable, while it is admitted that the behavior of the single atom or quantum is unpredictable. A general unwillingness of psychologists to admit an
uncertainty principle applicable to individual behavior and the
attempt of sociologists to fit rigid predictive models to highly
complex social behavior leaves both disciplines at the level of
classical physics. In predicting a new form of science ready to be
born, Dreikurs makes suggestions for a new epistemology: what
can the behavioral scientist properly call knowledge and how
can his subjective bias as an observer be minimized?

Stroup, by contrast, attacks the epistemological problem in
counseling dialogue from the vantage point of current philosophical study. The nature of what can be communicated between counselor and client is examined in a series of "contraries": private *versus* public, present *versus* past, and content
versus structure.

A shift of emphasis is Martin Astor's brief consideration of
the ontological problem of "free will." Stressing the need for

---

[1] Mechanical causality has been a somewhat dead issue in philosophy since David
Hume. The legacy of a "billiard ball universe" kind of determinism is, strangely
enough, a function of the British empiricist-associationistic tradition in psychology.
The reader who has a serious interest in intellectual history (not always defined as
philosophy) will want to read the appropriate sections in E. G. Boring's monumental
A History of Experimental Psychology (New York: Appleton-Century-Crofts, 1950);
and Robert I. Watson's *The Great Psychologists* (Philadelphia: J. B. Lippincott Co.,
1968).

"tentativeness and commitment," Astor believes that counselors can participate in a self-understanding process and thereby optimize the possibility of free choice and self-determination by adopting a modified existential viewpoint.

Orville Walters presents a survey of the philosophical positions taken by writers dealing with an applied science of man. Ranging from Freud to the existentialist Victor Frankl, Walters concludes that a counselor's philosophical outlook matters very much in his dealings with the client. Whether recourse is taken to metaphysics, religion, or existentialism, the counselor must align himself with the view that man is "something more" than any one doctrine of human nature such as science can offer. The Judeo-Christian view of man is in many respects the most moderate and accurate one the counselor may choose, Walters concludes.

McCully expands the point of "something more" by defining the helping professions and advancing the arguments that because practitioners deal with existential affairs they must rely more on values than science. McCully identifies the age-old question, "What is man, and what is his destiny in terms of his potential?" as a most relevant question for the helping professions—a course which serves as an inadvertent rationale for the study of the humanities by counselors. The McCully statement may be compared with a similar position taken by Cremin in Section One.

6.   The Scientific Revolution

Rudolf Dreikurs

One of the cornerstones of humanism is reliance on science rather than on revelation, a simple proposition as long as the concept of science was clear and the nature of the scientific method unquestioned. But this is no longer true; and unless we recognize the inadequacy of present scientific methods we bring science into discredit at the very same time that we are trying so hard to kindle a scientific spirit in our midst.

Reprinted by permission of *The Humanist* ©, 125 El Camino del Mar, San Francisco, California.

The revolutionary changes in epistemology which have been occurring since Planck's discovery of the quantum around the turn of the century are not yet known to the majority of our contemporaries, lay people and scientists alike. Our universities do not yet teach the new concepts, except in the departments of physics and chemistry and perhaps at times in philosophy.

Quantum theory inevitably led science into a new era and to the Copenhagen agreement of 1927 in which Niels Bohr (1958) took a leading part. It marked the beginning of a new scientific era, ending the one which began with Kepler, Newton, and Galileo. It not only opened new perspectives in theoretical physics, but new visions for all the sciences, new ways of thinking and problem solving.

What are some of the elements of these revolutionary developments?

The crucial issue is the problem of causality. What appears as a casual connection can be observed only if a great number of particles are involved. Statistical probability gives the impression of rigid causality, but it does not pertain to the movement of any individual particle. Any organic whole—from the quantum to man—places limits on certainty and predictability.

Heisenberg's Uncertainty Principle indicates limitations of knowledge. We can determine accurately either the location of an electron at a given moment, or its speed. Knowing one permits only a vague impression of the other. This imposes limitations on the heretofore basic requirement of scientific research: accuracy of observation and measurement.

Certainty of diagnosis and certainty of prediction have vanished. If one cannot know simultaneously where a particle is and the speed with which it moves, then one cannot predict exactly where it will be at any time. Predictability has become merely a question of statistical probability. Radium offers a typical example of our inability to predict events. Its atoms explode, and we know that within 1600 years half of the atoms will disintegrate. But no one can predict whether any given atom will explode in the next one tenth of a second or in a thousand or two thousand years.

Classical Newtonian mechanics obviously has lost validity in the domain of subatomic and submolecular processes and must be replaced by quantum or wave mechanics. However, are quantum mechanics limited to electrons or do they have validity on higher levels of organization? Both theoretical physicists and students of human behavior are inclined to assume that the new concepts are limited to the subatomic level. But evidence seems to indicate the opposite. In our exploration of the Psychological Uncertainty Principle (Dreikurs, 1963) it appears that quantum mechanics is a general principle pervading all forms of existence, from the subatomic level through the physical, chemical, and biological, to the human-social level.[1] It seems to apply wherever organic wholes exist, and therefore, is part of the holistic system (Smuts, 1926).

BEYOND THE SUBATOMIC LEVEL

The first demonstration of quantum mechanics beyond the subatomic level was observed in the behavior of big molecules suspended in a fluid, the so-called Brownian movements. Einstein found that they obey the laws of quantum mechanics rather than those of classical physics. They do not follow the strict causal dependency on forces to which they are exposed. London (1950) described quantum mechanics on a microscopic scale in the strange behavior of a metal or of superfluid helium under exceedingly low temperatures. Thus, the assumption that quantum mechanics is micro-mechanics, relevant exclusively to the understanding of the mechanisms on a submolecular level, had to be discarded. In superconductivity and super-fluidity a whole piece of metal, a whole pot of liquid helium become and act as organic wholes.

Recently, in the field of biology, particularly in genetics, peculiar observations have been made. According to Mendelian laws, new species and races can only develop through a new mixture of already existing genes. Suddenly it was found that new organisms, independent from their genetic inheritance, could develop. Like the quantum jumps which puzzled the physicists, the mutations puzzled the geneticists. In their mechanistic, scientific tradition, they looked for the "cause" of these nature jumps. They first believed that cosmic rays were responsible for the mutations because radiation did bring about mutations. Now we know that changes in genes may occur "spontaneously," since genes are complex molecules, and highly unstable like radium atoms. Therefore, new species are constantly created by nature.

Thus we find limitations of causal determination on the biological as well as on the subatomic and atomic levels.[2]

"TRUTH," DOGMA, AND OTHER PITFALLS

The consequences of these new scientific concepts are far-reaching. They limit what can be known. Truth is merely a statistical phenomenon.

---

[1] It was my great privilege to present my ideas about the Psychological Uncertainty Principle first to the Danish Psychological Society in 1962 at the Psychology Department of the University of Copenhagen, probably the only department of psychology strongly affected by the ideas of Niels Bohr.

[2] A certain freedom has been recognized as a universal quality. Only on the human level can this freedom of movement, of choice, be called free will. Man is a

Absolute truth cannot be perceived since all our knowledge is only approximate. Attempts to find what is true or false is hopelessly snarled by what Bohr (1958) described as "complimentarities." Interpretations of facts can contradict each other and yet both be correct. The quantum can be regarded either as mass or as a spurt of energy. It is up to the observer to determine what he considers it to be; but after he makes this decision, he will come to different formulations. This spells the end of the Aristotelian logic (Korzybski, 1933). Ordinary logic such as we use in arithmetic is "two-value" (Hayakawa, 1939). An answer is either right or wrong. This logic is also called "the law of the excluded middle," meaning that something is either A or not A. The concept of complimentarities contradicts the principle of the excluded middle.

In order to apply these new perspectives we must first free ourselves from the shackles of contemporary scientific assumptions. There is an increasing body of literature indicating the pitfalls of the so-called Scientism which is characteristic of present research. Let us look at some of the statements dealing with this issue. "Western thought now idolizes 'science.' Since Newton, the 'exactness' of science was the magic that would bring order to the universe. Everything was to be neat and tidy, and in its place. That was the bright promise of science. Gone were the murky dogmas of theology and the 'thinkers' in philosophy. . . . In the generation of Newton, when all was light, the belief in science swiftly became the faith of Scientism—the magical conception of natural science as omniscient and omnipotent" (Matson, 1964).

It was a scientist (Andrade, 1957) who observed that modern man may have succeeded in emancipating himself from his belief in the magical powers of supernatural agencies only to plunge into an equally naive commitment to the magical powers of science—"a belief that precise measurement and prodigious calculation will lead not only to widespread human happiness . . . but to a knowledge of ultimate reality, which the philosophers have vainly sought through the ages."

Frazer (1951) compares primitive magic with modern science: "Underlying the whole system is a faith, implicit but real and firm. In the order and uniformity of nature. . . . The anology between the magical and scientific conceptions of the world is close. In both of them, the succession of events is assumed to be perfectly regular and certain, being determined by immutable laws, the operation of which can be foreseen and calculated precisely."

Let us look at what Whitehead (1933) has to say. "The restless modern search for increased accuracy of observation and for detailed explanation is based upon unquestioning faith in the reign of law. Apart

---

quantum, a whole, and like all wholes cannot be understood or explained on the basis of causal determinism.

from such faith, the enterprise of science is foolish, hopeless. . . . During the medieval epoch in Europe, the theologians were the chief sinners in respect to dogmatic finality. During the last three centuries, their bad preeminence in this habit passed to the men of science. . . . Systems, scientific and philosophic, come and go. In its prime, each system is a triumphant success; in its decay, it is an obstructive nuisance."

On another occasion, Whitehead (1929) makes the following statement. "Some of the major disasters of mankind have been produced by the narrowness of men with a good methodology. Evidence which lies outside the method simply does not count. . . . Scientists animated by the purpose of proving that they are purposeless constitute an interesting subject for study. . . . Obscurantism is the refusal to speculate freely on the limitations of traditional methods. A few generations ago, large sections of the clergy were the outstanding examples of obscurantism. Today their place has been taken by scientists. The obscurantists of any generation are in the main the practitioners of the dominant methodology. Today, scientific methods are dominant, and the scientists are the obscurantists. . . . In scientific investigations the question 'true or false?' is usually irrelevant. The important question is: in what circumstances is this formula true and in what circumstances is it false?"

This brings us to a central issue of science. The scientist believes that he is examining "facts." Little is he aware, as yet, that facts do not exist as such. As Dewey (1938) says, "Data are selected, they are discriminated for a purpose." Bentley and Dewey (1949) speak against the fallacy of dogmatism in the behavioral sciences, against the notion of an objective truth, outside of the process of the "knowing and the known," as they call it. Winthrop (1959) who protests against Scientism, created the useful term "factophilia." Similarly, Sorokin (1956) deplores the widespread tendency to indulge in "quantophrania" and "metromania." He describes the present scientific situation well: "The younger generation of sociologists and psychologists explicitly claims . . . that the real scientific era in these disciplines began only in the last two or three decades with the publication of their own researches and those of members of their clique. Claiming to be particularly objective, precise, and scientific, our sociological and psychological Columbuses tirelessly repeat this delusion as scientific truth. . . . The new and growing belief is that when one masters routine statistical methods, he becomes competent to do research on any problem, in any field."

The tragedy lies not merely in the fact that so much time and money is wasted in useless research which only satisfies the scientific demand for a "tight design." Money is available for research regardless of its significance or lack of it, as long as the project conforms to the accepted scientific standards of investigation.

Much worse is the actual interference with progress by scientifically and experimentally oriented sociologists and psychologists. They look askance at anyone as being "naive" when he dares to express any opinion in regard to social and psychological phenomena without any "proof" through research.

Polanyi (1957) points out the danger of science becoming a dogma. "In the days when an idea could be silenced by showing that it was contrary to religion, theology was the greatest single source of fallacies. Today, when any human thought can be discredited by branding it as unscientific, the power previously exercised by theology has passed over to science; hence, science has become in its turn the greatest single source of error."

At another time, Polanyi (1958) has this to say about the hazard of moving in an unaccustomed direction: "When a new system is sought, is at issue . . . those who reject it . . . will inevitably regard it as altogether incompetent and unsound. . . . Formal operations relying on one framework of interpretation cannot demonstrate a proposition to persons who rely on another framework. Its advocates may not even succeed in getting a hearing from them, since they first must teach them a new language, and no one can learn a new language unless he first trusts that it means something."

The foregoing quotations, expressing apprehension or even open rejection of present scientific endeavors, can be multiplied manyfold. Important is the fact that these objections to science do not come from mystics, from naive and uninformed laymen, but from highly respected and sophisticated professionals, seriously concerned with epistemology. This is an appalling predicament of our contemporary cultural epoch. We are in the midst of fundamental changes, brought about by the democratic revolution which ushers in a new cultural era and brings to an end the autocratic tradition of 8,000 years of civilization. It is more than an accident that the tremendous power of the individual, limited in time and space as he is, and the immense energy within the heretofore insignificant minute atom were discovered at the same time. The changes in basic scientific concepts coincide with equally monumental changes in human relationships on the social and political scene. While the physical sciences have adjusted rather quickly to the new scientific procedures, putting them to good use, and bringing about highly beneficial and previously unimaginable technical advances, the situation is different in the social and behavioral sciences. It is in this realm that the fallacies of our present research methods become obvious and lead to the increased critical denouncement of science.

Does this mean that we should disregard the scientific method? Of course not. It is even doubtful that criticism of "Science" as such is justified. What is objectionable is the abuse of the scientific method, the deification of scientific findings, the disregard of scientific limitations, and the dependency on science as the only source of knowledge. In other words, it is Scientism which is under attack, "psychologism" and "sociologism" as Frankl (1955) calls them.

"Psychologism" and "Sociologism"

Considerable and very fundamental changes in our scientific concepts and methods will be necessary before we can eliminate the objectionable features in scientific research. We are only just beginning to translate revolutionary epistemological concepts into practical approaches within the social and behavioral sciences.

One obstacle to progress is the fact that the social sciences are still in a pre-scientific state (Argyle, 1957). Most social scientists would object to this statement because they are just beginning to apply the methodology of classical physics, which they consider to be the basis for all scientific endeavors.

No scientific research is yet available to explore the complexities of groups and societies (Frank, 1957), the "organized complexities," as Weaver (1948) calls them.

We have no scientific tools to validate any personality theory, for example. But we need and already have personality theories to deal effectively with individuals and groups. This indicates clearly that "knowledge" is available without waiting for quantification and statistical analysis to support any personality hypothesis. The same situation exists even in physics, where important discoveries like super-conductivity are made without a full scientific explanation of observable phenomena. The physicists cannot yet scientifically determine the relationships of more than two particles at a time; and yet our sociologists try to manipulate variables scientifically in such complexities as groups, societies, and individuals.

The first requirements, therefore, are a clear definition of what can and cannot be explored with present scientific methods, and a clear realization that much more can be known and is known other than through these methods. We have an overabundant literature on the assumed causes of maladjustment; scientific research has "proven" the importance of the psychosexual development of the child, the dangers of too early toilet training, the need to have the mother's heartbeat simulated in the nursery, the importance of physical closeness to mother or father figure, and innumerable other theories, all sufficiently "proven" by various investigators, and equally denounced by those with other orientations.

The split in ideologies has fractionated the fields of sociology and psychology into camps that have little in common with each other and little communication among them. The written output is too abundant, and the interest in acquainting oneself with material which does not reflect one's own view is too little to allow benefits to accrue from the results of the immense investments of time and efforts in "scientific" research within the social and behavioral sciences. Very little is produced which is of value to those on the firing line, who deal practically with the social and psychological problems of our time. It will be necessary to consider seriously whether the time, money, and effort spent on such research is justified and whether it should be continued.

THE SIGNIFICANCE OF THE OBSERVER

Even of more significance, but at the same time more difficult to implement, is another issue which has been brought forth by a new realization in theoretical physics: the significance of the observer. In present research one assumes that in a properly designed project the researcher is dealing with facts, is objective, and his findings could be duplicated by other researchers. This, of course, is not true. It is not true that we are evolving one body of knowledge. It is not true that in the social and behavioral sciences the findings of one are supported by everybody else. All research findings reflect the subjective bias of the researcher. To accept this means a fundamental change in our scientific endeavors. New methods and approaches are needed to establish the bias of each researcher and to take it into account in the evaluation of the data which he has collected. The development of such new and unprecedented methodologies seems to be the prime task of contemporary science.

Eric Dreikurs developed an intricate system which he calls "transaction feed-back." Through taping all interactions in a research, and through ingenious new ways of retrieving the material, it is possible to take a look not only at the findings, but also the observer. The first prerequisite for any research project is to identify the orientation of the observer and the model of man which is the basis for his operations. This will require major efforts, since most professionals involved in social and psychological research not only fail to realize their own biases, but are inclined to deny their existence. To demand that they declare their biases would almost automatically interfere with customary investigative tradition.

The pressure of such a request on anyone who is asking for financial support for his research is bound to stop immediately the tremendous and mostly futile output. Adopting such a standard would require a change in our general outlook, on man, on society, and on science. But without such a change, science will not be able to free itself from its present state of scientism.

SOME BASIC TENETS

The process of identifying one's bias depends on the clarification of existing complimentarities. We recognize today three fundamental differences in concepts and methodology dealing with human problems. Maslow (1954) and others speak of the "Third Force" in psychology, the other two being psychoanalysis and experimental psychology, both of which have exerted and are exerting a commanding influence. However, we find within the existential-phenomenological field of the Third Force as many complimentarities as in each of the other two. The most important is the distinction between holism and reductionism. The holistic approach implies the recognition of the whole, which is more than the sum total of its parts; in contrast, in the reductionistic approach one examines partial phenomena and processes in order to understand the whole. At the present time, there is relatively little research based on the holistic approach; the vast majority of research studies in psychology and social sciences are reductionistic.

Other complimentarities, fundamentally different concepts from which the researcher must choose are:

Is man a product of forces from within and from without, or is he a self-determining organism?

Is behavior the result of causes or of purpose, indicating movement toward a goal?

Can man be understood as an isolated organism or is he to be seen operating in a social field?

Is he driven by emotions, or are cognitive processes the basis for his operation and behavior?

Is he a product of past experiences or is he motivated by decisions made in the given moment?

Are human conflicts primarily the expression of intra-personal dynamics, or are the intra-personal conflicts the result of conflicts with others?

These are some of the opposing assumptions which cannot be reconciled. Everyone dealing with human beings, scientifically, clinically, educationally, is operating on one or the other of these basic tenets, even if he believes himself to be "broad-minded" and eclectic and tries to incorporate whatever is "good" in each proposition.

Since the examiner is by necessity biased, all his findings will reflect his bias and will be valid only within his frame of reference. This cannot be avoided. However, the biased investigator is least qualified to analyze his data objectively, all claims of statistics notwithstanding. For this reason, it will be necessary in future research to submit all data to a board of judges with varying orientations. The need to broaden the scope of research has been reflected in the search for an interdisciplinary approach. However, this usually has meant the participation of professional workers of different disciplines but with the same orientation. What is needed is the participation of workers with different fundamental orientations, presenting their perceptions of what has been observed and how it can be evaluated. This approach would serve to eliminate any preconceptions of what is right or wrong, true or false, and the present need for objective verification through measurement would not be satisfied. But do we need to know what is right and wrong? More important are the results of such studies, indicating what can be seen and what possibilities for action can emerge from the various interpretations of observable events. It is not difficult to imagine how stimulating and motivating such research results would be, in contrast to the futility, insignificance; and sterility of most contemporary research.

Such research studies would be able to handle not only experimental research findings, but also the clinical observations and practical experiences of workers in the fields of sociology and psychology who could present their ideas and reports for study and evaluation. Then there would be no schism between the presently haughty "scientists" who use the traditional methods of research, and those whom they ridicule as "arm-chair psychologists." Until many more of these so-called arm-chair philosophies are tested, we will not be taking advantage of the many resources which already exist in our midst and are presently ignored.

A new form of science is in the state of being born. Let us hope that it will escape the criticism to which science is exposed today.

REFERENCES

ARGYLE, M. The Scientific Study of Social Behavior. New York: Philosophical Library, 1957.

BOHR, NIELS. Atomic Physics and Human Knowledge. New York: John Wiley and Sons, 1958.

DAC. ANDRADE, E. N. An Approach to Modern Physics. Garden City, N.Y.: Doubleday, 1957.

DEWEY, JOHN. Logic: The Theory of Inquiry. New York: Henry Holt, 1938.

DEWEY, JOHN and BENTLEY, ARTHUR F. Knowing and the Known. Boston: Beacon Press, 1949.

DREIKURS, ERIC AND RUDOLF. The Quantum Revolution and Scientific Research on Individual Behavior. Unpublished paper.

DREIKURS, RUDOLF. "The Psychological Uncertainty Principle." In *Topical Problems of Psychotherapy.* Basle: Karger, 1963, IV, pp. 23–31.

FRANK, L. K. "Research for What?" *Journal of Social Issues,* Suppl. 10, 1957.

FRANKL, VIKTOR E. *The Doctor and the Soul.* New York: Knopf, 1955.

FRAZER, JAMES. *The Golden Bough: A Study in Magic and Religion.* New York: Macmillan, 1951.

HAYAKAWA, S. I. *Language in Thought and Action.* New York: Harcourt, Brace & World, 1939.

KORZYBSKI, K. *Science and Sanity: An Introduction to Non-Aristotelian Systems and General Semantics.* Lancaster, Pa.: Science Press, 1933.

LONDON, F. *Superfluids.* New York: John Wiley and Sons, 1950.

MASLOW, A. H. *Motivation and Personality.* New York: Harper, 1954.

MATSON, FLOYD W. *The Broken Image.* New York: George Braziller, 1964.

POLANYI, MICHAEL. *Personal Knowledge.* London: Routledge & Kegan Paul, 1958.

POLANYI, MICHAEL. "Scientific Outlook: Its Sickness and Cure." *Science,* V. 125, 1957, pp. 480–484.

SMUTS, J. C. *Holism and Evolution.* New York: Macmillan, 1926.

SOROKIN, P. A. *Fads and Foibles in Modern Sociology and Related Sciences.* Chicago: Henry Regnery, 1956.

WEAVER, W. "Science and Complexity." *American Scientist,* V. 36, 1948, pp. 536–554.

WINTHROP, H. "Scientism and Psychology." *Journal of Individual Psychology,* V. 15, 1959, pp. 112–120.

WHITEHEAD, ALFRED N. *Adventures of Ideas.* New York: Macmillan, 1933.

WHITEHEAD, ALFRED N. *The Function of Reason.* Princeton, N.J.: Princeton University Press, 1929.

7. Philosophic Aspects of Counseling Communication

Herbert Stroup

It was a philosopher, George Berkeley, who lamented that philosophers "have first raised a dust, and then complained we cannot see" (Berkeley, 1955). But, unfortunately there are times when the dust has settled and still one cannot see. This state may be as true of the counselor as of the philosopher. In fact, the common task of both counselor and philosopher, as well as others, is both to raise the dust and to see through it.

Counseling and philosophy are not unconversant allies on the current intellectual scene. Thus, in the spirit of their interdependence, three

Herbert Stroup, "Philosophic Aspects of Counseling Communication," from *Personnel and Guidance Journal,* June, 1966, pp. 1020–24. Copyright © 1966 by the American Personnel and Guidance Association, Inc., Washington, D.C. Reprinted by permission.

philosophic aspects of counseling communication will be explored briefly: (1) private *versus* public; (2) present *versus* past; and (3) content *versus* structure. These three themes are arranged in antithetical relations in order to heighten their philosophic complications.

PRIVATE VERSUS PUBLIC

The counselor regularly distinguishes between private *versus* public knowledge concerning his client. The client who says "I feel generally unhappy" is expressing private knowledge. His expression may be termed "subjective." But the client who says "I got all B's in my courses" is expressing public knowledge or what is commonly called "objective" knowledge.

Another aspect of the private knowledge of the client is the psycho-analytic expression, the "unconscious." The unconscious, however, is a more delimited word than private. But, according to Freud the unconscious and the conscious are both relatively undependable sources of knowledge. Thus, he writes: "The unconscious is the true psychic reality; *in its inner nature it is just as much unknown to us as the reality of the external world, and it is just as imperfectly communicated to us by the data of consciousness as is the external world by the reports of our sense-organs*" (Brill, 1938b).

Private expressions appear to depend upon inner states of being concerning which there is admittedly no externally dependable way of providing certification. Yet counselors and others place considerable reliance upon such utterances. By definition, however, private experiences are accessible only to those who have them. Attempts may be made to communicate them to others, but the experiences themselves cannot be transferred from one person to others; it is merely information regarding the experiences that can be conveyed. (The Vienna circle of philosophers at one time argued that experiences as such are incommunicable; see, for example, Schlick (1918) and Carnap (1928).)

In fact some philosophers have gone so far as to undermine firm belief in any kind of permanent and self-identifying self, as seemingly did David Hume when he spoke of the self as a "bundle of perceptions" (Hume, 1951). It was Hume who said that when he looked for an impression of his self, he failed to find one and that he always found instead some particular perception of himself (Hume, 1951).

Descartes (1955) thought that it might be possible for an evil force to deceive him even with regard to those matters of which he was most certain. All communicable meaning of private experience was thus incapable of validation, according to Descartes. But he went on in his reasoning to claim that there was one proposition that can be asserted that necessarily is beyond the reach of any demon or any other limiting power. That proposition is the famous *cogito ergo sum:* I think, therefore I am (Descartes, 1955). So, in Descartes' reasoning that which appears to be the least reliable, verifiable, and communicable, namely private experience, is in actuality self-evident and, therefore, in need of no proof.

Public knowledge at first blush seems to be on a different ground. Being "objective," this kind of knowledge seems not to require extensive validation. If the client relates that he is one of five members of a family or describes the day-by-day itinerary of last summer's trip he is communicating regarding what most people would consider to be objectively verifiable experiences. Such statements are in the realm of public knowledge.

Yet, in this connection, it is significant to note that oftentimes public knowledge is the least significant knowledge pertaining to a client. Thus, for a client to refer to his space occupancy by saying "I was in the gym at one o'clock" may in itself be highly unimportant. Mere space occupancy is like that. Similarly a person's fingerprints, social security number, army number, and similar objective means of personal identification are for most counseling relationships relatively unimportant. Even the proper names of persons, that are used so widely in human communication as Mill (1930) noted, carry no particular connotations in themselves of an objective reality. He called them "unmeaning marks."

Public knowledge, moreover, is dependent usually and to some degree upon private knowledge. Public knowledge seldom is as "hard" or "objective" as it appears to be. It too is "accepted" in the form in which it is presented or else one would need to be like the man who bought several copies of a newspaper in order to assure himself that what one said was also said by the others. This degree of skepticism would lead one to buy or view every copy of a newspaper's printing (Wittgenstein, 1958).

Carnap (1934) dealt at length with private *versus* public knowledge. Carnap used the term "protocol language" to designate that class of statements which ostensibly refer to one's private experiences and "physical language" to designate that class of statements that ostensibly refer to physical objects or occurrences. While Carnap appreciates the distinction between private and public knowledge, he maintains that these languages are interrelated. He believes that any use of physical language requires that protocol language be included in it. Carnap reasons that protocol statements are necessarily bound up in physical statements, otherwise "physical statements would float in a void disconnected, in principle, from all experience." Carnap may not be sufficiently aware of the contradictions that are involved in any effort to merge the two kinds of languages, but he is clear in wanting to interrelate the two. The counselor can do no less.

PRESENT VERSUS PAST

Both the counselor and the client tend to intermingle the present and the past in the counseling process without a critical appraisal of what the "present" and the "past" should properly mean. Ayer illustrates the complexity of this philosophic dilemma in a non-counseling context:

It was one and the same man, Napoleon Bonaparte, who won the battle of Austerlitz and lost the battle of Waterloo, but in what sense was he the same? What is it that makes a set of descriptions, which are logically independent of one another, into descriptions of the same person? (Ayer, 1956).

The problem of present and past experience is even more complicated, in reference to the above quotation, if one were to ask for a report by Napoleon himself in contrast to a report on Napoleon by an observer. Present experience seems to be "objective," while past experience seems to be "subjective."

The client who says "I feel a headache now" infers that he has had headaches before with which he is able in the present to make comparisons. His statement about the present is open to some degree of confirmation. But what can one say with certainty about his inference from the past? Admittedly one can be in different places at different times, but the idea of being at different times at the same time is illogical. There appears to be no known way by which past experience can be reclaimed with anything like the objectivity of present experience. Does this fact, then, invalidate past experience? Does it place past experience into a secondary or inferior realm of knowledge regarding the client's experience of himself?

The relation of the present to the past raises, of course, the question of causation. Is the present directly and necessarily related causally to the past? If so, in what way is the relation determinative? Can the counselor draw a direct line, so to speak, between any particular instance of the present and any particular instance of the past? If he cannot, should he claim that he is scientific in any significant sense of that term? If he cannot, what does such a conclusion mean for his dependence upon client content derived from the past?

Surely the question of the relation of the present to the past in counseling communication is related to that which is assumed to exist in the physical sciences. There the notion of "functional dependence" is widely held, especially among modern physicists. This view holds that phenomena are so correlated in nature that, "when one measurable quantity, characterizing a certain physical state (say, the Earth's distance from the sun) varies, this corresponds to a change of another (say, the

Earth's acceleration towards the sun) according to a simple mathematical rule" (Waismann, 1961).

Yet, the fact that there is a "functional dependence" evident in physics does not necessarily mean that it is apparent in counseling. The "functional dependence" of present and past, in parts and in whole, is not fully understood for counseling communication.

The knowledge of such relationships in physical nature leads to the possibility of prediction, securing the future from the present. It suggests that the unknown can be known from the known. But, it also provides the physicist with an ability to understand the past through an understanding of the present. Thus, information about the present state of the solar system can be used to calculate the condition in which it was at any past moment of its history. The reason for this is that the equations of dynamics are insensitive to a change in the direction of time. But, the question remains: Does the counselor have the same or anything like the same method of apprehending the past through an understanding of the present? Does the present in itself provide the counselor with an adequate means for appropriating the factual nature of the past? The answer seemingly is negative.

Russell (1921) claims that an image is a *memory* insofar as it is accompanied simply by a feeling of familiarity. But "familiarity" is not a sufficient validation of past experiences. I may be able to recall an image from childhood, but mere recall or familiarity with the image gives me no assurance that my present impression of the image is identical with or even similar to the one I held in childhood.

But there can be no denying that whatever memory image a person may have of past experience is for him in the present the only image that he has available to him and to others. Alexander (1920) puts it: "the pastness of [a remembered] object is a datum of experience, directly apprehended." Alexander means, of course, that no one can experience a past event, since experience is necessarily confined to the present. But one can remember a past experience and by the reconstitution of the past experience in memory possess a present experience. Thus, the seeming antithesis between present and past knowledge is lessened to some degree.

Philosophers also may be helpful to counselors by their recognition of two classes of memory: (1) "habit-memory," and (2) "factual-memory." By habit-memory philosophers generally refer to those instances of knowing how to do things in which it is not necessary that the performer should know that anything is the case. Factual-memory refers to those instances of knowing in which the knowledge displayed is classified as knowledge of fact. If I write a letter, walk on the sidewalk, fine-tune my television set, I am involved in habit-memory. But when I tell when Columbus discovered America, relate the proof of the existence of irrational numbers, or recall that the Republican party was founded in Ripon, Wisconsin, I am engaged in factual-memory. Habit-memory (knowing how) calls for direct past participation, while factual-memory (knowing that) obviously in many cases cannot even permit past participation in what is recalled. So, for the counselor as well as for the philosopher, a different sort of knowledge is secured according to the class of memory assertion involved in declarations regarding the present and the past. "How-to-do memory" (habit-memory) commonly involves no sense-data or images for present communication, but "I-recall-that memory" (factual-memory) depends essentially upon sense-data and images that are much more readily communicable.

CONTENT VERSUS STRUCTURE

The contrast between "content" and "structure" in counseling communication refers philosophically to the two principles which Hume (1951) admitted that he could neither renounce nor reconcile. He states "all our distinct perceptions are distinct existences." In contrast he also stated "the mind never perceives any real connection among distinct existences." For the counselor the contrast may be stated in a somewhat different language. The counselor, like others, is intent on acknowledging the face-value of direct and verbal communication. This is the "content" of counseling communication. On the other hand, the counselor also recognizes the validity of the organized forms by which the content in counseling communication is expressed. This is "structure."

Freud (Brill, 1938a) had to face this dilemma in his efforts to account for the various forms of mistakes in speech, memory, erroneously carried-out actions, and so forth, in his account of the psychopathology of everyday life. But, necessarily he faced the problem of dealing with the philosophic implications of "chance" and "determinism." As a stimulant he received a criticism of his version of name-forgetting by "a colleague of a philosophical turn of mind." Freud asked himself the question: "Does the solution given for faulty and chance actions apply in general or only in specific cases, and if only in the latter, what are the conditions under which it may also be employed in the explanation of the other phenomena?" Interestingly for a person of the intellectual scope of Freud, he commented upon his own question, saying: "In answer to this question, my experiences leave me in the lurch . . ." (Brill, 1938a). Apparently Freud could not solve the dilemma of content *versus* structure, at least for the phenomena under review.

The client regularly infers or states that he "knows." Yet knowing takes many forms. It may involve, as Locke (1959) stated, both "simple" and "complex" ideas. Locke believed that the mind is capable of "simple ideas" among which are its ideas of the qualities of objects. The mind, however, constructs "complex ideas" from these "simple ideas." Complex ideas are ideas of the objects which possess qualities. The objects in Locke's view are "substances." The traditional language of "perception" and "conception" also expresses the contrast between the two kinds of knowing.

The counselor then must distinguish, in Locke's terms, whether a client is expressing a simple or a complex idea and he must be in a position to evaluate the significance of each. It is not sufficient for him to rely in the spirit of empiricism upon the sheer words which are communicated by a client. He also must take into account the relationship of the client's communication of simple ideas to the client's assumptions regarding the nature of complex ideas.

This means, furthermore, that no person is capable of restricting himself only to expression derived from the empirical sphere. Every person who makes sense in his communication rests his declarations upon assumptions regarding reality that the rational enterprise makes available. The role of reason may be inadequate for the transfer of valid information from one person to another, but its existence and importance cannot be denied. Simple ideas secure their meaning within the shared context of complex ideas, or as Ryle (1954) says: "There can be false coins only where there are coins made of the proper materials by the proper authorities." Thus, a perception that is not consonant with conceptions that are veridical is by nature illusory. Content, both for the counselor and his client, must be related to structure if reliability and meaningfulness are to be achieved.

In summary, it is apparent that counseling communication involves philosophic implications that are worthy both of exploration and of the development of precise understanding. Three such elements have been described briefly to illustrate the task: (1) private *versus* public; (2) present *versus* past; and (3) content *versus* structure. Arranging the three as "contraries" illustrates the complexity of the philosophic aspects of communication in counseling.

REFERENCES

ALEXANDER, S. *Space, time & deity.* London: Macmillan, 1920, Vol. 1, 113.
AYER, A. J. *The problem of knowledge.* Baltimore: Penguin Books, 1956, 187.
BERKELEY, G. "The principles of human knowledge." Chicago: *Encylopaedia Britannica,* 1955, Introd. Sect. III, 405.
BRILL, A. A. "Psychopathology of everyday life." In *Basic writings of S. Freud.* New York: The Modern Library, 1938, 171.(a)

BRILL, A. A. "The interpretation of dreams." In *Basic writings of S. Freud*. New
    York: The Modern Library, 1938, 542. (b)
CARNAP, R. *Der logische aubau der welt*. Berlin, 1928.
CARNAP, R. *The unity of science*. London: K. Paul, Trench, Trubner, 1934, 82.
DESCARTES, R. "Meditations on the first philosophy." Chicago: *Encyclopaedia
    Britannica*, 1955, Meditation II, 1952.
HUME, D. *A treatise of human nature*. Oxford: Clarendon Press, 1951, Book 1,
    Sect. VI, 252, App. 636.
LOCKE, J. *An essay concerning human understanding*. New York: Dover, 1959.
MILL, J. S. *A system of logic*. London: Longmans, Green & Co., 1930, Chap. 2,
    Sect. V, 20.
RUSSELL, B. *The analysis of mind*. London: G. Allen & Unwin, 1921, Lect. IX.
RYLE, G. *Dilemmas*. Cambridge: University Press, 1954, 95.
SCHLICK, M. *Allegemeine erkenntnislehre*. Berlin, 1918.
WAISMANN, F. "The decline and fall of causality." In *Turning points in physics*.
    New York: Harper Torchbook, 1961, 86–87.
WITTGENSTEIN, L. *Philosophical investigations*. Oxford: Blackwell, 1958, I,
    265, 93.

8. Counselors Seek to Understand Themselves:
A Philosophical Inquiry

Martin H. Astor

Counselors frequently confuse role definition with professional self-understanding. The role-definition approach is misleading because it is only after we
achieve professional self-understanding will we be able to define ourselves in
our unique situations. Too strict a position on counselor role is not desirable
as it leads to arbitrary, dualistic choice models. Sigmund Freud and Carl Rogers
have already provided us with a basis for perceiving alternatives to static,
dualistic absolutes. Using an existential model, this paper seeks new direction
through subject-object "bridge building" for achieving deeper professional self-
understanding in guidance and counseling. The five subject-object bridges are
concerned with: (a) ideals and reality, (b) being and becoming, (c) tentativeness and commitment, (d) the individual and society, (e) freedom and
responsibility.

Counselors should no longer be asking, "Are we or are we not a
profession?" They should be asking instead, "What is the meaning of our
professional being?" In the first question we focus attention upon role-
definition; in the second, we are in quest of a professional self-concept.

Martin H. Astor, "Counselors Seek to Understand Themselves: A Philosophical
Inquiry," from *Personnel and Guidance Journal*, June, 1965, *43*: pp. 1029–33. Copyright © 1965 by the American Personnel and Guidance Association, Inc., Washington, D.C. Reprinted by permission.

Just as the "semantic accident" (Lloyd-Jones, 1962) concerning the title of "counselor" and the function of "counseling" has created confusion in the past, now the question of role-definition threatens to divert us further from our search for deeper professional self-understanding. It is this author's contention that role-definition evolves logically and clearly, following clarification of the meaning of our professional existence. Our professional behavior as counselors will be determined by professional self-concept and not the other way around.

Using a philosophical existential frame of reference, the main effort of this paper serves as an inquiry into the meaning of our professional existence as counselors. Rollo May (1963) provides us with a shorthand definition of existentialism—as a cutting below the subject-object cleavage. This would suggest that *man has more than only two choices*, the choice between subjective self-determination on the one hand and objective fatalistic-determinism on the other. The role-definition approach forces us to choose between black or white absolutes. *Either* we are a profession *or* an occupation. *Either* we are generalists *or* specialists. *Either* we are faculty *or* administration. The role-definition approach compels us to make "either-or" choices, which is nothing more than an extension of subject-object dualism. Through use of an existential model, the building of subject-object bridges, we seek to achieve a higher degree of self-awareness as a profession.

FREUD AND ROGERS REJECT DUALISM

Both Sigmund Freud and Carl Rogers have demonstrated that one need not be trapped into accepting the limitations of arbitrary, dualistic choice models. They have succeeded in providing new approaches and strategies that have contributed greatly toward our further understanding of psychology and psychotherapy. Their theories cut under the subject-object cleavage!

Freud showed us that psychology was complex-dynamic, not simple-mechanistic. He outlined the organization of the psyche, not as a single, simple absolute, but as a complex psychodynamic involving continuous interaction between ego, id, super-ego and reality (Freud, 1955). Freud (1953) also established that human development was continuous, harmonious, and progressive. He stressed concepts of balanced interaction of opposites: Eros-Thanatos; introjection-projection; love-hate; conscious-unconscious; and so on. Freudian psychology focuses upon cause-effect determinants of behavior through rational analysis. Static givens and arbitrary absolutes are non-existent in the psychoanalytic system. Although Freud is not usually identified with philosophical existentialism, one can argue that he was able to make his great contribution to psychological theory because he was able to undercut the traditional subject-object split. Freudian psychology is both dynamic and progressive.

More recently Carl Rogers addressed himself to the subject-object controversy. He too declined the either-or position; instead, he stressed the importance of utilizing and understanding interrelationships between subject and object. In discussing research in psychotherapy he notes the paradox:

. . . That to advance in our understanding of the field the individual must be willing to put his most passionate beliefs and firm convictions (the subjective) to the impersonal test of empirical research (the objective); but to be effective as a therapist, he must use this knowledge (the objective) only to enrich and enlarge his *subjective* self . . . (Rogers, 1961, p. 269) [Parenthetic notes and italics were added to give emphasis].

Here we have an extremely clear statement noting both interdependence and interaction between subject and object. As Gordon Allport points out, subject and object are not necessarily opposites of each other. In fact, they are sometimes so closely related that it is difficult to distinguish the difference between them: ". . . a human person is both structure and process, a being both biological and neotic, a being who changes his identity even while he retains it" (Allport, 1962).

Rogers's non-directive or client-centered approach is closely related to existential philosophy. He even uses existential language when he refers to the therapeutic relationship as an "interpersonal encounter" (Rogers, 1962). Rogerian psychotherapy places central emphasis upon the quality of the therapeutic relationship; and it is here that Rogers succeeds at cutting below the subject-object cleavage. He nearly does away completely with the client-counselor (subject-object) dichotomy with his emphasis upon congruence, empathy, and unconditional positive regard. He speaks of the counselor as being ". . . genuine and without 'front' or facade, openly being the feelings and attitudes which at that moment are flowing in him" (Rogers, 1962, p. 417). He speaks of the need "To sense the client's inner world of private personal meanings as if it were your own" (Rogers, 1962, p. 419). And finally, the counselor ". . . feels an *unconditional* positive regard for this person." How does this differ from the Buberian existential "I-Thou" relationship? There can be no question that Rogerian psychotherapy in its stress upon relationship rejects the either-or dualistic choice model of traditional Western European philosophy.

It seems that Freud and Rogers have already provided us with a basis for perceiving alternatives to the subject-object approach relative to psychoanalysis and psychotherapy. For the remainder of this article we shall examine other alternatives to the subject-object issues that are directed specifically to the profession of guidance and counseling. Consider these but beginning efforts at the construction of subject-object bridges for our field.

BETWEEN THE IDEAL AND THE REALITY

The guidance and counseling profession must come to the realization that idealism and realism go hand in hand. In a sense we must all be the kind of idealists who are willing and able to face the facts of life. As idealists we continually dream of what we can do to make a better world tomorrow; but as realists we are actively involved in the present working with concrete specifics of the daily jobs. *We need both,* the never-ending dream and the ability to get on with a job that needs doing. Effective guidance counselors are dreamers with shovels:

There are some who dream great dreams but never feel this urgency "to do something about it." . . . But the dreamers with shovels want only a job that is magnificent enough, room enough to stand in, and a chance to make a start (Lilienthal, 1945).

This applies to counseling as well as any other phase of guidance work. The counselor always strives to assist others to achieve their ideals. But, implicit in this "idealistic" guidance process, we are always helping the client to focus upon the realities of life. While we seek to broaden his horizon of present and future environments, in the very same process we help the individual to sharpen his sense of personal reality (Wrenn, 1962).

Guidance counselors need to be able to understand, tolerate and work with the constant tension that exists between ideals and reality. This does not mean that they compromise ideals, values, and professional standards to accommodate situational realities. It means that they have learned to take as well as to give. That they have learned to navigate through rough straits with appropriate calmness, sensitivity, and reasoned understanding.

BEING AND BECOMING PROCESSES

Counselors and guidance workers must come to understand that "being and becoming" are inextricably related in time, form, and process. In other words, although we know who we are now, we are continually in process of growth towards something else. We are an ever-maturing profession. For this reason we must be careful not to seek absolute, inflexible professional role definitions. If we create too much super-structure for ourselves in the present we run the risk of over-determining our roles in the future.

In order for us to know who we are and what it is we do as guidance counselors, it is extremely important that we continue to seek clarification of our various roles. But because there are no blueprints or finished products of our work we can never really hope to achieve any kind of final judgment as to the efficacy of our efforts. In this respect ours is an ever-frustrating profession. We work in a continuum for which there is no end, and therefore we are forever involved in continuous self-examina-tion. The sooner we do a job the more we have to do. While we must do what is needed to be done today, we must be prepared to change our roles if necessary in relation to the future. Gilbert Wrenn (1962) defines maturity as ". . . the ability to live productively and with a sense of personal satisfaction in regions of tension. . . ." Counseling and guid-ance is an ever-maturing profession. Mature counselors must be people with a good amount of frustration tolerance who are capable of respond-ing positively to challenge and change.

"Twin Virtues" of Tentativeness and Commitment

Gordon Allport (1962) suggests counselors must learn to cultivate the "twin virtues" of tentativeness and commitment. Anyone familiar with the scientific method knows full well the relationship between these two concepts. While truth in science is tentative and relative, the method of science requires commitment and consistency. Scientific "truths" should always be subject to question and possible change. At the same time the method of science insists upon logical laws, rules, and standards.

Applied to counseling, we need flexibility in our work but we must also have purpose and direction. We are sensitive to changing client moods, needs, and feelings, but we must also be consistent in our acceptances and understanding. As a "talking profession" we place great stress on qualitative interpersonal relationships, but we must also be able to provide concrete and specific services when needed. While we may disagree about different counseling theories, our ultimate treatment goals and counseling methods cannot be too dissimilar. There are many "in-tangibles" in good counseling, but very definite skills and disciplines in the technology of counseling are also important. Whereas tentativeness is desirable in some aspects of our work, we cannot profess to be able to accomplish anything without our being committed to important funda-mentals.

We might need to be tentative with respect to certain aspects of our work, but there is no reason why we cannot learn to live with ambiguity provided we are committed to meaningful professional beliefs and values.

RELATIONSHIP TO INDIVIDUAL AND SOCIETY

We need to consider the nature of our responsibility both to the individual and to society. In accordance with dualist dialogue man is usually placed in conflict with society. The fact remains, however, that man and society are integral with each other. They share in a total, continuous relationship with each other. One could not exist without the other. It is erroneous to think that man and society could be arbitrarily separated and pitched against each other as if they were enemies from opposing camps.

In relation to counseling, we believe that as we help the individual to function better we contribute toward the betterment of our society. As the individual achieves a fuller sense of self awareness he begins to see himself better both as subject and as object. He not only learns to understand himself, but he also begins to understand how other people see him. It is an old Freudian truism that the individual achieves ego identity only as he is capable of responding to society—as he is able to distinguish himself from others. As Rollo May (1963) phrases it, ". . . the more awareness of self, the more awareness of world, and vice versa." Gilbert Wrenn (1962) sums it up in *The Counselor in a Changing World,* ". . . The counselor must respond to individual need and societal need, not either one to the exclusion of the other. . . ."

ON FREEDOM AND RESPONSIBILITY

Finally we must come to terms with the issue of freedom and responsibility. Responsibility is really a dualistic concept. It can refer to self-determination or to logical determinism. Self-determination suggests that man is free to determine his own destiny. He is the master of his own fate. Logical determinism relates to cause-effect theory. It suggests a fatalistic outlook on life, as if everything were predetermined. There is a cause for everything, or the cause is responsible for the effect. Since man is able to control some things and other things are determined for him, is it not possible to consider both aspects of responsibility as part of the same problem? Responsibility implies a certain amount of freedom, and freedom implies responsibility.

Freedom without responsibility equals anarchy!
Freedom with responsibility equals democracy!

In a democracy we need this combination of freedom *and* responsibility
or else we would have neither choice of self-determination nor law and
order.

Counselors seek to encourage individual self-expression, free choice
and self-determination. We do this through counseling and guidance
work. As counselors we seek to help the client to make important educa-
tional-vocational decisions. As guidance workers we help to create flexible
environments in keeping with individual needs and interests.

Encouraging individual self-expression and free choice is not the
same as encouraging license and abandon (Pierson, 1962). We are
careful not to confuse the therapeutic doctrine of permissiveness with
arbitrary personal irresponsibility. As counselors we seek to help others,
but ultimately the responsibility for self-help remains with the client. The
individual is free to act—to choose, decide, behave—but he must also be
prepared to accept the consequences of his actions. Such are the rules
when freedom and responsibility go hand in hand.

IN CONCLUSION

The main purpose in attempting to build subject-object bridges was
to demonstrate that role-definition follows and evolves from self-understanding processes. The illustrations used in this article are only beginning efforts as "bridge building" in order to stress the importance of
relationship as opposed to choice.

Instead of phrasing questions "either-or," forcing us to choose one or
the other, hopefully we can develop new and more meaningful alternatives for action. Opposites can be compatible and it is possible to live
constructively with contradictions. Instead of becoming a fragmented
profession, there is no reason why we cannot achieve "another way" or
"other ways" and thus preserve the unity and identity of our profession as
guidance counselors.

The existential model presented here is not offered as a final solution
or panacea; it merely serves as a useful vehicle for thought. Hopefully,
we may be able to construct better models in the future. For the time
being, the existential approach frees us to achieve a higher degree of self-
awareness and it allows us to establish new forms of relationships to old,
"unsolvable" problems.

REFERENCES

ALLPORT, GORDON W. "Psychological models for guidance." *Harv. educ. Rev.*, 1962, 32 (4), 373–381.

FREUD, SIGMUND. "Three essays on sexuality (1901–1905)." In standard edition of the *Complete psychological works of Sigmund Freud.* Vol. 7. England: The Hogarth Press, 1953.

FREUD, SIGMUND. *The origin and development of psychoanalysis.* Chicago: Henry Regnery, 1955.

LILIENTHAL, DAVID. *TVA: democracy on the march.* New York: Pocket Books, 1945.

LLOYD-JONES, ESTHER. "Implications of the Wrenn report for counselor education." *Couns. Educ. Supv.*, 1962, 2 (1), 17–25.

MAY, ROLLO. "Freedom and responsibility reexamined: development." In Lloyd-Jones, Esther, & Westervelt, Esther, eds., *Behavioral science and guidance; proposals and perspectives.* New York: Bureau of Publications, Teachers College, Columbia Univ., 1963.

PIERSON, GEORGE A. "Position paper—administration relationships." In joint publication of ACES and ASCA, *Counselor education—a progress report on standards.* Washington, D.C.: American Personnel and Guidance Association, 1962.

ROGERS, CARL R. *On becoming a person.* Boston: Houghton Mifflin, 1961.

ROGERS, CARL R. "The interpersonal relationship: the core of guidance." *Harv. educ. Rev.*, 1962, 32 (4), 416–429.

WRENN, C. GILBERT. *The counselor in a changing world.* Washington, D.C.: American Personnel and Guidance Association, 1962.

9. Metaphysics, Religion, and Psychotherapy

Orville S. Walters

In the physical sciences, the swing from a thesis of prescientific speculation to the antithesis of a cocksure empiricism has been followed by a wholesome heuristic humility in search of a synthesis. The resurgence of an attitude that is willing to acknowledge aspects of reality beyond the reach of science has been recognized both by its opponents and its advocates.

Hook (1943), in describing this trend, comments: "In the schools, the churches, and in the literary arts the tom-tom of theology and the

From: Orville S. Walters, "Metaphysics, religion, and psychotherapy," *Journal of Counseling Psychology*, V, No. 4, 1958, 243–252. Copyright by the American Psychological Association, and reproduced by permission.

bagpipes of transcendental metaphysics are growing more insistent and shrill." He contends that "the refurbishing of theological and metaphysical dogmas about the infinite as necessary presuppositions of knowledge about the finite" indicates a latter-day "failure of nerve."

Flewelling (1953), on the other hand, declares that "the traditional abrogation of metaphysics by science has been brought to sudden pause." Citing the philosophical implications of relativity, indeterminacy and the new significance of the observer in physical phenomena, he concludes, "The positivistic philosophies, in faithful obedience to the dogmas of a discarded science, still 'hold the sack' waiting for the materialistic rabbit, while contemporary science approaches a new personalism."

METAPHYSICS AND THE SCIENCE OF MAN

The sciences of man have been slow in reflecting this change. The pendulum has swung from psychology's early identification with metaphysical philosophy to an extreme empiricism. As Borow (1956) has expressed it, "When psychology joined the company of the experimental sciences, it embraced empiricism with a vengeance." There is increasing conviction that an ultimate synthesis will require recovery of some of the elements that were rejected by psychology in the process of achieving recognition as a science.

Psychology becomes most deeply involved in metaphysical issues when it turns to the treatment of personality ills. Contemporary psychotherapy is confronted by a question that has far-reaching theoretical and practical implications: What is to be the place of metaphysics in psychotherapy? At opposite poles are those who are trying to "exorcise the metaphysical gremlin," (Borow, 1956) and those who hold that "at the bottom of every neurosis there is a metaphysical problem" (Allers, 1955).

Some of psychology's reluctance to modify an empiricistic rigidity is traceable to the influence of Freud. In his lecture, "A Philosophy of Life," Freud (1933, p. 203) asserts the adequacy of science to achieve a full understanding of personality. While acknowledging that the world view of science is incomplete, he disdains and disparages the constructs of philosophy that would offer a more complete tentative picture of the universe. He denies any validity to philosophy and religion, and stakes out "the whole field of human activity" as the exclusive province of science.

Much of the psychotherapy now being taught and practiced has its roots in the Freudian system. Freud's personal philosophy has often been tacitly regarded as a part of psychoanalysis, although there is evidence that he himself acknowledged the separability of the two (Ostow, 1955).

Because they are frequently interwoven, Freud's reductive naturalism and the principles of psychoanalysis have had widespread influence upon American psychology and psychiatry.

Some of the present-day protests against this influence are voiced by Stern (1954) and Maritain (1957), who see Freud's reductionism currently producing a devaluation of man, contempt for the spirit and a loss of the metaphysical sense. Stern states that when divested of its Freudian positivism, psychoanalysis contains a movement toward personalism.

Freud's renunciation of metaphysics in favor of science has been continued and reinforced by some contemporary theoreticians. Feigl (1953) lumps theology and metaphysics with magic, animism and mythology and describes them as "remnants of and regressions to . . . prescientific thought patterns." He condemns the "something more" philosophy as a "seductive fallacy" and rejects the assertions of transcendent theology and metaphysics as "largely emotive."

Psychotherapy as Applied Science

The practice of psychotherapy plunges psychology into metaphysical issues. There is general agreement that science cannot determine values. The function of science is to observe, describe and classify what *is*, but not to decide what *ought to be*. Psychology, as long as it remains a pure science, does not make judgment of value. It is when turning to treat maladjustments of human personality that psychology moves away from the canons of scientific precision and ventures into the realm of values.

The transition from a pure to an applied science involves a value judgment of major consequence. Such a judgment presumes to differentiate between illness and health, and proposes to use scientific knowledge to displace the one, the servant of the ethical judgments and, in some measure, the value system, in favor of the other. In psychotherapy, psychology as a science thus becomes the servant of the ethical judgments and, in some measure, the value system of the therapist. As a healer, he seeks the recovery of his patient, sacrificing the neutrality and objectivity of the scientist for a stake in the outcome.

The application of psychological knowledge by one person to modify the attitudes and ideas of another involves the formation of further value judgments as to the need, the goal and the method of therapy. The counselor may be called upon, for example, to assist a person who is troubled by conscience. Is this illness or health? Is *any* trouble with conscience compatible with health? If so, how much? And if too much is present, how is the pressure of conscience to be abated? How much sensitivity of conscience should be left when the end-point of treatment has been reached?

In an effort to stay close to its scientific base, psychotherapy has concentrated upon technics of uncovering the patient's conflicts, upon analysis of interviews and upon theories of personality organization. The patient, on the other hand, is struggling with metaphysical concerns: What is the good life? Where does it lead? How much freedom does man have? Are the claims of religion illusion or are they insight into transcendent reality? Before these questions science stands silent, claiming no competence in matters of ethical discrimination, moral responsibility, and ultimate destiny.

Not everyone is willing to concede this inherent limitation in the nature of science. There is confidence that science will ultimately be able to provide a full explanation of the phenomena of the universe, including human behavior. This faith is responsible for most of the opposition toward permitting metaphysics to complement the incomplete world view that science now offers.

Freud proclaimed his loyalty to "the scientific *Weltanschauung*," not only staking out "the spirit and the mind" as proper objects of scientific investigation, but specifically rejecting religion and philosophy as collaborators in truth-finding. In this broad repudiation of philosophy, Freud was merely electing a different metaphysical viewpoint and enunciating an impassioned *credo* in the philosophy of scientism.

Feigl (1953) similarly scorns "the sham completeness metaphysicians procure for their world pictures by verbal magic" and declares that it is a sign of maturity to be able to live with an unfinished world view. To proclaim such an affirmation of faith in the ultimate adequacy of science is to close the gaps in a science-centered *Weltanschauung* by philosophical scaffolding and to crystallize a unique value system. The unfinished world view is an abstraction. Commitment to something is necessary to existence. Even to repudiate metaphysics is to affirm a significant metaphysical position.

There are many who doubt that science will ever be able to offer a complete world view. Conant (1955) expresses this viewpoint:

As to the unifying, materialistic World Hypothesis, my doubt stems from its manifest inadequacy. As a conceptual scheme attempting to account for everything in the whole universe, it seems to me unsatisfactory because it is incomplete. It fails to provide for the altruistic and idealistic side of human nature.

Freud declared that since psychoanalysis is a part of science, it has no concern with judgments of value. It is no less valid to say that psychoanalysis, psychotherapy and counseling cannot be purely scientific, even though they are grounded in an empirical psychology, since they inescapably involve human values. The limitations of science are apparent wherever human autonomy becomes a variable in a problem.

Zilboorg (1956) recognizes that the therapist cannot avoid encounter with philosophical, ethical and moral issues:

> Suffused with anxiety . . . man again is forced to contemplate what it is that he is, what it is that he wants, what it is that he ought to want, and what his place is in relation to his fellow man individually, to society, to himself as an autonomic person. These are ontological, metaphysical and fundamentally religious questions. A psychoanalyst, more than any other professional man, must cultivate a philosophy of values.

NEUROSIS AND WELTANSCHAUUNG

The scientific framework in which any exploration of neurosis and anxiety begins is soon found to be inadequate to encompass all the phenomena, implicating as they do the values and the world view of the patient.

Masserman (1955, p. 458) who has produced what he calls "experimental neurosis" in animals, cautions against the drawing of sweeping identities between his experiments and "the almost incomparably more complex dynamics of clinical psychotherapy." In the treatment of neurosis, Masserman (1955, p. 488) departs widely from the experimental approach to recommend that the therapist enter into the patient's "personal universe of desires, meaning, values and actions."

Rioch (1957), in a review of "experimental neurosis" acknowledges that the degree of complexity, modifiability and variability of human behavior is of a different order of magnitude than that in lower forms and refers to Harry Stack Sullivan's contention that anxiety is limited to human beings.

Efforts to understand neurosis apart from an ontology of anxiety have been disappointing. Even after the creation and unrestricted manipulation of his metapsychological constructs, Freud (1936, p. 92) concedes:

> We find ourselves abruptly confronted, once again, by the oft-repeated riddle: What is the source of neurosis, what is its specific, underlying principle? After decades of analytic effort this problem rises up before us, as untouched as at the beginning.

Shoben (1953) formulates a theory of neurosis based upon experimental findings and learning theory. His view of neurosis as a consequence of defective social learning fails to deal with the concept of conscience and superego, and identifies guilt with anxiety.

Mowrer (1950, p. 483) draws upon both learning theory and Freudian concepts to elaborate his concept of neurosis, concluding that neurotic persons suffer because they have repudiated their own moral strivings. This makes the undoing of repressions preeminently a moral enterprise.

A similar view was advanced by Pfister (1931):

> . . . The repressed conscience plays a still more troublesome role than the known conscience . . . There consequently remains nothing but to purify the known, and, very often, too, the unknown conscience. In every psychoanalytic transaction deserving of the name, it is of great importance to replace the ill-advised with a clear and noble-piercing voice of conscience.

Stekel (1950), another of Freud's early pupils, described neurosis as "the disease of a bad conscience" and recognized that somatic complaints could have a similar origin:

> Important is the fact that the voice of conscience may find bodily expression, this being what we call somatization. . . . The psychotherapeutist, taking his patients by the hand, must help them to restore the ideals which, deliberately, or under compulsion, they have destroyed (Stekel, 1940).

May (1950, p. 191), after a detailed examination of the various concepts of anxiety offered by Freud and by the deviant schools of psychoanalysis, formulates a broad definition of anxiety as "the apprehension cued off by a threat to some value which the individual holds essential to his existence as a personality." He concludes, "The system of value on the basis of which one confronts normal anxiety . . . broadly speaking . . . is the person's religious attitude toward life" (May, 1950, p. 230).

Winkler (1956) argues the inadequacy of the leading psychological doctrines of man. Freud saw man as a natural organism, Adler viewed him as a social being and Jung emphasizes him as an individual. "In addition to this," Winkler continues, "he is also a person in the philosophic and theologic sense, and he related as an individual to the transcendental reality. He can also fail in this regard, producing that which may be labelled 'existential neurosis.' "

Frankl (1955) believes that every man has a will-to-meaning, the frustration of which produces existential neurosis. His logotherapy aims to revise the defective world view in terms of meaning and value. "Patients themselves bring us philosophical problems," Frankl writes. ". . . The proper diagnosis can be made only by someone who can see the spiritual side of man."

Progoff (1956) traces the progressive emergence of this recognition through Freud, Adler, Jung and Rank. He writes,

> Their psychological investigations led them to a realization of the fundamentally spiritual nature of man. . . . They came in other words, to the

metaphysical foundation of life that underlies psychology. . . . Psychological work fulfills itself only when it goes beyond psychology.

While psychological theory is moving to recognize the necessity of active encounter with the patient's value system, a parallel current is influencing the practice of psychotherapy. Pumpian-Mindlin (1957) traces the ten-year evolution of practice in a mental hygiene clinic through various stages during which different emphases were found inadequate and dropped, one after another. The expression of hostility by the patient, the giving of love and affection by the therapist, the offering of psychodynamic interpretations and, finally, attempts at ego-integration, were all pronounced "not enough." In the continuing search for a more adequate approach, Pumpian-Mindlin concludes, "We must examine our culture and our values and those of our patients. We must see how these affect the 'self,' the total person."

A similar awareness is apparent on a social scale. Schindler (1956) holds that many personality disturbances are caused by "confusion on a spiritual level," growing out of cataclysmic events in the past few decades that have brought the fundamental questions of human existence to the psychiatrist's attention. May (1950, p. 109), in applying Mowrer's concept of neurosis, observes: "The repression of guilt feelings, with its concomitant generation of neurotic anxiety . . . in some ways is pervasive of our culture as a whole." This view is supported by Riesman (1954) who comments:

Increasingly today, this new type of analytic work with people who are not obviously ill—whose "symptom" is their malaise, their whole way of life— people who are troubled about moral issues, or who ought to be troubled about them, forces analysts to become concerned with problems of casuistry, of values, as part of the very task of therapy.

Tillich (1952) finds that the common denominator in all theories of anxiety is the awareness of conflict between structural elements of the personality. Only in the light of an ontological understanding of human nature, he believes, can a consistent and comprehensive theory of anxiety be formulated. In the interpretation of human existence, the psychotherapist can benefit by collaboration with the philosopher and the theologian. Tillich views existential anxiety as basic, growing out of the threefold ontological threat of death, meaninglessness and guilt. These belong to existence and cannot be eliminated. Existential anxiety is properly the object of priestly concern, while pathologic anxiety is the concern of the psychotherapist. The goal of both professions is to help the patient achieve full self-affirmation. They may collaborate fruitfully, but neither should try to replace the other.

FREUD, PSYCHOTHERAPY, AND RELIGION

Although he emphatically denies its validity, Freud (1933, p. 206) acknowledges that religion possesses a philosophy of incomparable strength and consistency, that has successfully resisted severe criticism. Religion, he concedes, exerts power over the strongest human emotions. A religious view of the universe adds strength and stability to personality, Freud acknowledges, even while he is trying to refute religion's claim to truth by arguments from psychoanalysis.

Freud's attacks have undoubtedly contributed strongly to the reluctance of psychotherapy to appropriate and apply the insights of religion. This unwillingness to deal with religion is discussed by Gordon Allport (1950). Noting that "psychologists write with the frankness of Freud or Kinsey on the sexual passions of mankind but blush and grow silent when the religious passions come into view," Allport argues that the psychologist has no right to retire from the field, since two-thirds of the adults in this country regard themselves as religious people and nine-tenths affirm belief in God. Seventy per cent of the 500 college students questioned by Allport felt that they needed some form of religious orientation or belief in order to achieve a mature philosophy of life. Seventy-five per cent of the women and 65 per cent of the men acknowledged praying, many every day.

In spite of Freud's professional atheism and his violently anti-religious writings, Zilboorg (1955) believes that he had "unconscious, intense, positive religious leanings." There is a note of wistfulness in one of his letters to Oskar Pfister, a Swiss Protestant clergyman who was one of the earliest practitioners of psychoanalysis. In the letter, Freud complained about the kind of patients who came for analysis, describing them as "often very poor material." "You, on the other hand," he wrote, "have young people with recent conflicts who are attached to you personally, and who are in a suitable state for sublimation and indeed for its most convenient form—religious sublimation . . . You are in the fortunate position of leading them on to God and reconstructing the conditions of earlier times, fortunate at least in the one respect that religious piety stifles neurosis" (Jones, 1955).

Freud's observation that religion can give strength and stability to personality and can "stifle neurosis" is not bound to the hypothesis that he devised to explain the fact. By "genetic analysis" he arrived at the conclusion that "the religious *Weltenschauung* is determined by the situation that subsisted in our childhood" (Freud, 1933, p. 210). Religion provides ethical precepts and a sense of protection, Freud decided, by preserving childhood attitudes.

This explanation has two flaws: Freud's defective understanding of religion, and his neglect of one of the most significant aspects of personality, purposive striving.

Freud's anti-religious writings indicate a lack of any real acquaintance with religion. Immediately after the appearance of *The Future of an Illusion,* Pfister (1928) replied with a paper giving effective answer to Freuds' criticisms of religion. Dalbiez (1941) has offered a comprehensive criticism of the logic and philosophy inherent in Freud's position. In biographies and critiques, friend and foe alike have referred to the evidence for unconscious bias in Freud's anti-religious pronouncements.

Allport (1955, p. 92) warns against "the trivial view that holds adult religion to be merely a repetition of the experiences of the child," adding, "The most comprehensive units in personality are broad intentional dispositions, future-pointed." This aspect of universal human experience, largely unrecognized by an empiricism that sees man as a passive being responding only to forces outside himself, is illuminated by the insights of religion. "While religion certainly fortifies the individual against the inroads of anxiety, doubt and despair," Allport continues, "it also provides the forward intention that enables him at each stage of his becoming to relate himself meaningfully to the totality of Being."

The stability of personality and resistance to neurosis that Freud observed and acknowledged in religious people thus has an alternative explanation more inclusive than Freud's hypothesis, because it articulates with major aspects of personality that he failed to include. Poverty in representing the future, in Allport's opinion, is the chief shortcoming of American psychology. Leo Alexander (1955) also comments, "The concepts of ego and superego must be widened to include the will and the purpose as the key to responsibility. There is undeniable historical and social evidence for the existence of will and purpose in human affairs." Limitations set by the canons of scientific method and by the philosophies derivative from science have prevented psychology from recognizing or adequately studying these facets of personality.

THE THERAPIST'S VALUE SYSTEM

Every psychotherapist is a philosopher of sorts. When the psychologist turns away from his measurements and statistics to deal with troubled individuals on a one-to-one basis, he leaves pure science behind. Becoming a participant in the healing process draws him inescapably into the realm of values. At this point, as Allport (1953) has pointed out, "Whether he knows it or not, every psychologist gravitates toward an ontological position. Like a satellite he slips into the orbit of positivism, naturalism, idealism, personalism." Refusing, as Freud did, to acknowledge commitment to a basic philosophy, is to defend it less effectively than if it were consciously avowed.

Furthermore, the therapist's own value system is deeply involved in the process of psychotherapy. Developments in ego psychology have not abated metaphysical involvement. The therapeutic goal of psychoanalysis is described by Gill (1954) in these terms:

A progressive analysis from the surface to the depth; analysis of the defenses and the motives for defense; the development and analysis of the transference neurosis; a resolution of symptoms, and as complete a "structural" alternation of the neurotic aspects of the personality as possible.

The process is further elaborated with the statement, "The gross major decision is whether the defenses of the ego are to be strengthened or broken through as a preliminary toward a reintegration of the ego."

This view of psychotherapy makes it a prerogative of the therapist to decide what aspects of personality shall be dismantled, as well as the form and content of the restorative process. Here the personal philosophy of the psychotherapist may determine the pattern of reconstruction. Reorganization of his patient's personality cannot help but implicate the therapist's own value system.

Even apart from active intervention in the reintegrative process the therapist's value system exerts its influence. Wolff (1956) in his survey found some therapists contending that treatment should consist of reshaping distorted value concepts, while others advocated exclusion of the therapist's values from psychotherapy as far as possible. Wolff (1954) also reported that while only 6 per cent of 43 therapists regarded change of values as a goal of therapy, 48 per cent believed that therapy does in fact directly transmit or develop value concepts in the patient. An additional 24 per cent thought that values have an indirect effect in therapy.

Rosenthal (1955) commented after his study upon the changing of moral values in psychotherapy:

It may be that the therapist communicates his values to the patient in many unintended, subtle ways, even when trying to avoid doing so. The patient, who is often sensitized to the therapist's every word and inflection, may be able to receive these communications, and because of his trust, admiration and respect for the therapist, may permit himself to be influenced by them.

The world view of the counselor apparently exerts its influence in ways unrecognized by either the patient or the therapist himself—in the selection of subject matter for response or discussion, in nonverbal cues if not by verbal expression. This was true even of Freud in the analytic situation. The account of Wortis (1954) describes frequent manifestations of his misanthropy and pessimism. If only in subtle, inadvertent expression, the therapist's value system appears to be a constant factor in the relationship.

The therapist usually conceives of himself and is often represented as the detached, dispassionate scientist. A more realistic view would see him as an involved participant with an interest in the outcome, following a sectarian psychotherapeutic doctrine or combination of doctrines, the selection and practice of which are tinctured by his own basic philosophy of life.

The Therapist and Religion

Recognition of the role of the therapist's philosophy of life raises questions fundamental to the success of therapy. Can a therapist who denies the importance of supra-empirical factors in neurosis achieve an empathic relationship with a patient who is burdened with a sense of sinfulness? To reassure such a patient that "this is not a moral problem but can be understood only with impersonal, objective, scientific attitudes" (Thorne, 1955) may lead in a direction opposite to improvement and insight.

If metaphysical concerns are at the bottom of many neuroses, to avoid the discussion of religion in psychotherapy as Wolberg (1954) recommends may be to bypass the most significant area of conflict. Masserman (1955, p. 494) advises assuring the patient that his philosophic or theological faith will not be challenged, confessing that "only in the early years of his inexperience and defensive dogmatism did he think it necessary to explore, let alone attack, the patient's religious beliefs or practices." This calculated inattention to an area of frequent personality conflict may easily overlook a greater difficulty for a lesser.

To ignore or minimize the field of metaphysical concern in favor of sexual conflict or any other predetermined framework may leave untouched the most important cause of difficulty. Reider (1955), for example, tells how a patient called him ten months after treatment had ended to say, "I just wanted you to tell me that there is no such thing as hell where people go for their sins." He complied with a pontifical negative, giving no recognition that the patient's request expressed anxiety growing out of a metaphysical concern that had been presented at the beginning of treatment, and that had obviously remained unresolved.

The responsibility for determining what religious attitudes are healthy or neurotic is a crucial one, certain to be colored by the therapist's own basic orientation toward religion. This is well illustrated by Casey's (1943) citation of an analyst whose own unconscious resistance to religious appeal led to his opposing any religious adjustment by his patient. In the presence of such an attitude, the question of Arnold (1954) is pertinent, "whether the therapist can correctly evaluate the resistance of a patient with whose philosophy of life he cannot agree."

Many psychoanalysts believe that religious beliefs and practices have a sexual origin and represent infantile emotions. Others regard religious concepts as benign but delusional. Can a therapist with such views enter into the personal universe of a religious patient's meanings and values to establish empathy on any other basis than as the discerning possessor of truth communicating with the naive victim of error?

The frequent concern of the religious-minded patient and his family over the therapist's attitude toward religion is not without relevance. The naturalistic orientation not only includes certain beliefs, but excludes others. In providing himself with one variety of philosophical stuffing "to stop up the gaps in the universe," (Freud, 1955) the naturalistic psychotherapist at the same time rejects those philosophies that are open-ended toward a reality beyond science. The patient's concern is whether such a counselor can be tolerant toward a world view that he regards as error, and can leave such faith undisturbed during treatment. How many therapists will recognize and acknowledge the error of attacking the patient's religious beliefs, as Knight (1937) did in his analysis of a minister?

DOCTRINES OF MAN

The inability of science to provide a complete view of the universe is most apparent in its apprehension of the nature of human personality. There is no mature science of man; there are only doctrines of man. Science at its best provides a truncated view of man. Every doctrine of man includes a substantial body of theoretical assumptions. These doctrines vary from the biological emphasis of Freud with its destructive death instinct, though the deviant psychoanalytic schools that stress social and cultural factors, to those that postulate an inherent upward drive in man toward self-enhancement.

Somewhere between these extremes is the Jewish-Christian doctrine of man that recognizes both the potential for good and the tendency to evil in man's nature. In contrast to the relatively scant empirical data and unilateral focus characterizing most of the neonate doctrines of man, the insights provided by religion are supported by centuries of observation and experience, and deal with the full sweep of human existence.

The psychotherapist is not offered a choice between a scientific and an unscientific doctrine of man. Rather, the choice is among different views of man that are corollary to various philosophies. Most of today's psychotherapy is set in a context of naturalism or positivism. The empirical findings of scientific psychology are not bound inseparably to either of these basic faiths. Such a context is a psychology-plus-philosophy; there are other philosophies equally compatible with the science of man that may lead to a clearer understanding of the patient who is troubled by metaphysical concern. To quote Outler (1954), for example:

> The Christian faith is at least an equal option for the thoughtful man.
> . . . It is at least as intelligible a faith, resting on at least as much experimental evidence and exhibiting a capacity to interpret the inescapable issues of human life in a fashion both more meaningful and truly profound. The truth claims of the Christian faith cannot be "proved." . . . But they can be tested by those who place themselves inside the circle of faith. . . . Moreover, the Christian faith can be an ample and hospitable context for the scientific enterprise, in all its proper dimensions and concerns.

The Thomistic affirmation is similar: "A truly comprehensible and tenable view of man is achievable within the Christian ideology" (Braceland, 1955).

Among others, two factors have contributed to the growing congeniality between psychotherapy and religion. The first is an increasing insistence on the part of religionists that "psychiatry cannot adequately perceive the whole man without taking into account the contributions religion has made available for the search" (Steinbach, 1956). Coupled with some acceptance of this claim by psychotherapy is a measure of recognition that the synoptic view of man offered by religion is both comprehensive and penetrating, its validity being supported by an impressive empirical background and maturity. As a consequence, the offices of the minister are being more widely utilized to augment the skill of the psychotherapist in the recognition of metaphysical concern as contributory to neurosis, and in the resolution of that concern through the resources of religion.

REFERENCES

ALEXANDER, L. "Moralism and morality from the viewpoint of the psychiatrist." in I. Galdston, ed., *Ministry and medicine in human relations* New York: International Universities Press, 1955, p. 97.

ALLERS, R. "Psychiatry and the role of personal belief." In F. J. Braceland, ed., *Faith, reason and modern psychiatry*. New York: P. J. Kenedy & Sons, 1955.

ALLPORT, G. *Becoming*. New Haven, Conn.: Yale Univer. Press, 1955.

ALLPORT, G. *The individual and his religion*. New York: Macmillan, 1950.

ALLPORT, G. "The psychological nature of personality." *Personalist*, 1953, 34, 347.

ARNOLD, M. B. "The theory of psychotherapy." In M. B. Arnold & J. A. Gasson, eds., *The human person*. New York: Ronald Press, 1954, p. 529.

Borow, H. "The logic of counseling research." *J. counsel. Psychol.*, 1956, 3, 292.

Braceland, F. J. "Clinical psychiatry—today and tomorrow." In *Faith, reason and modern psychiatry.* New York: P. J. Kenedy & Sons, 1955, p. 27.

Casey, R. P. "Religion and psychoanalysis." *Psychiatry*, 1943, 6, 291.

Conant, J. B. *Modern science and modern man.* New York: Doubleday Anchor, 1955.

Dalbiez, R. *Psychoanalytical method and the doctrine of Freud.* New York: Longmans Green, 1941.

Feigl, H. "The scientific outlook: naturalism and humanism." In H. Feigl & M. Brodbeck, eds., *Readings in the philosophy of science.* New York: Appleton-Century-Crofts, 1953.

Flewelling, R. T. "The metaphysical predicament of science." *Personalist*, 1953, 34, 117.

Frankl, V. *The doctor and the soul.* New York: Knopf, 1955.

Freud, S. "A philosophy of life." In *New introductory lectures on psychoanalysis.* London: Hogarth Press, 1933.

Freud, S. *The problem of anxiety.* New York: Norton, 1936.

Freud, S. "Letter to Jung in Ernest Jones." *Sigmund Freud life and work, vol. II.* London: Hogarth Press, 1955, p. 488.

Gill, M. M. "Ego psychology and psychotherapy." In R. P. Knight, ed., *Psychoanalytic psychiatry and psychology.* New York: International Universities Press, 1954, p. 77.

Hook, S. "The new failure of nerve." *Partisan Review*, 1943, 10, 2.

Jones, E. *Sigmund Freud, life and work, vol. 2.* London: Hogarth Press, 1955, p. 489.

Knight, R. P. "Practical and theoretical considerations in the analysis of a minister." *Psychoanal. Rev.*, 1937, 24, 350.

Maritain, J. "Freudianism and psychoanalysis—a Thomist view." In Benjamin Nelson, ed., *Freud and the 20th century.* New York: Meridian Books, 1957.

Masserman, J. H. *The practice of dynamic psychiatry.* Philadelphia: Saunders, 1955.

May, R. *The meaning of anxiety.* New York: Ronald Press, 1950.

Mowrer, O. H. *Learning theory and personality dynamics.* New York: Ronald Press, 1950.

Ostow, M. Review of "The third revolution." *Psychoanal. Quar.*, 1955, 24, 448.

Outler, A. C. *Psychotherapy and the christian message.* New York: Harper, 1954, p. 255.

Pfister, O. "What transformations does psychoanalysis require in ethics and moral education?" *Psychiatric Quar.*, 1931, 5, 407.

Pfister, O. "Die illusion einer zukunft." *Imago*, 1928, 14, 149.

Progoff, I. *The death and rebirth of psychology.* New York: Julian Press, 1956, p. 250.

Pumpian-Mindlin, E. "Changing concepts of therapy in a veterans administration mental hygiene clinic." *Am. J. Psychiat.*, 1957, 113, 1095.

Reider, N. "Psychotherapy based on psychoanalytic principles." In J. L. McCary & D. E. Sheer, eds., *Six approaches to psychotherapy.* New York: Dryden Press, 1955.

Riesman, D. *Individualism reconsidered.* New York: Doubleday, 1954.

Rioch, D. McK. "Experimental aspects of anxiety." In J. H. Masserman & J. L. Moreno, eds., *Progress in psychotherapy, Vol. II Anxiety and therapy.* New York: Grune & Stratton, 1957.

Rosenthal, D. "Changes in some moral values following psychotherapy." *J. consult. Psychol.*, 1955, *19*, 431.

Schindler, R. "The development of psychotherapy in Austria since 1945." In F. Fromm-Reichmann & J. L. Moreno, eds., *Progress in psychotherapy 1956*. New York: Grune & Stratton, 1956, p. 267.

Shoben, E. J. "Some observation on psychotherapy and the learning process." In O. H. Mowrer, *Psychotherapy theory and research*. New York: Ronald Press, 1953.

Steinbach, A. A. "Can psychiatry and religion meet?" In Simon Noveck, ed., *Judaism and psychiatry*. New York: Basic Books, 1956, p. 174.

Stekel, W. *Conditions of nervous anxiety and their treatment*. New York: Liveright, 1950, p. 22.

Stekel, W. *Technique of analytical psychotherapy*. New York: Norton, 1940.

Stern, K. *The third revolution*. New York: Harcourt Brace, 1954.

Thorne, F. "Directive and eclectic personality counseling." In J. L. McCary & D. E. Sheer, eds., *Six approaches to psychotherapy*. New York: Dryden Press, 1955.

Tillich, P. *The courage to be*. New Haven, Conn.: Yale Univer. Press, 1952, p. 70.

Winkler, W. T. "The present status of psychotherapy in Germany." In F. Fromm-Reichmann & J. L. Moreno, eds., *Progress in psychotherapy 1956*. New York: Grune & Stratton, 1956, p. 288.

Wolberg, L. R. *The technique of psychotherapy*. New York: Grune & Stratton, 1954, p. 033.

Wolff, W. *Contemporary psychotherapists examine themselves*. Springfield, Ill.: C. C Thomas, 1956.

Wolff, W. "Facts and value in psychotherapy." *Am. J. Psychotherapy*, 1954, *8*, 466.

Wortis, J. *Fragments of an analysis with Freud*. New York: Simon & Schuster, 1954.

Zilboorg, G. "Psychoanalytic borderlines." *Am. J. Psychiat.*, 1956, *112*, 706.

Zilboorg, G. "Some denials and affirmations of religious faith." In F. J. Braceland, ed., *Faith, reason and modern psychiatry*. New York: P. J. Kenedy & Sons, 1955, p. 99.

10. Conceptions of Man and the Helping Professions

C. Harold McCully

Any discussion of the professions that lends itself to clear and precise communication is difficult at best. A major source of interference to

C. Harold McCully, "Conceptions of Man and the Helping Professions," from *Personnel and Guidance Journal*, May, 1966, pp. 911–17. Copyright © 1966 by the American Personnel and Guidance Association, Inc., Washington, D.C. Reprinted by permission.

C. Harold McCully, who was a Specialist in Counseling and Guidance with the U.S. Office of Education, died October 13, 1965.

communication stems from the privileged status Western society accords the members of recognized professions. Privileged status yields prestige. Our society seems to value prestige more than it does wisdom. Thus the urge to status and prestige may lead to rationalization and the clouding of rational processes. This is particularly true among occupations aspiring to professionhood. Another interference with clear communication may stem from failure to recognize what it is that makes a vocation a profession. The term "profession" first appeared in the *Oxford English Dictionary* in 1541. The current definition in that dictionary is ". . . a vocation in which a professed knowledge of some department of learning or science is used in its application to the affairs of others or in the practice of an art founded upon it." Of central significance to the definition are two ideas. The "professed knowledge of some department of learning or science" can be acquired only through a prolonged period of specialized training; and that which is applied "to the affairs of others" is intellectual in nature. All operational elaborations of the distinguishing characteristics of a profession stem from these central concepts (McCully, 1962).

It is emphasized that a vocation may involve specialized knowledge of a department of learning or science, but unless this specialized knowledge yields an intellectual technique that is applied to the affairs of others, the vocation is not a profession. Likewise, a vocation may apply a technique to the everyday affairs of others, but unless the technique is an intellectual one that is based upon specialized knowledge of a department of learning or science, the vocation is not a profession.

The fact that a profession applies an intellectual technique to the everyday affairs of others implies at once an obligation. This obligation is to apply the intellectual technique to the affairs of others only in ways that will benefit and not injure them. This obligation is basic to the essential altruism that, theoretically at least, has characterized the professions in Western society, i.e., placing the welfare of the client and, hence, of society, above the advantages, monetary and others, which may accrue to the practitioner. It is because of this central obligation that protective devices, particularly codes of ethics and licensure, have been employed.

HELPING PROFESSIONS DEFINED

Among the professions is a group of undetermined number that have been referred to as the "helping professions." In the absence of any authoritative definition of the helping professions, one will be attempted. In a broad sense, all professions are by definition helping professions. But in a narrower, more precise sense, some professions plus some vocations aspiring to professionhood can be distinguished as helping professions in the sense here used. A helping profession is defined as one which, based upon its specialized knowledge, applies an intellectual technique to the existential affairs of others toward the end of enabling them to cope more effectively with the dilemmas and paradoxes that characterize the human condition. Immediately, it is contended that this definition does not limit the helping professions to those that practice psychotherapy in the traditional sense. The notion that all people who need help in coping better with existential problems are sick people is rejected. Existential problems are defined as those which imply the need for choice or decision, but for which there is no sure external guide to the answer or solution. Obviously, valuing is central to coping with the dilemmas and paradoxes that characterize the human condition. Of necessity, then, the practitioner in a helping profession must recognize rather than deny the centrality of valuing in his clients' coping with existential problems. It is emphasized, as well, that existential problems as here used are not limited to profound and ultimate questions. They also include the mundane to which there is no sure external guide, such as the suitability of an occupation for an individual, whether to go to college, marriage versus career, etc.

Under the foregoing definition it appears that among the helping professions are counseling psychology, social work, and two aspiring to be a profession—school psychology and the vocation of school counselor; and in certain settings clinical psychology and psychiatry. This is not necessarily an all-inclusive list, and any vocation listed is granted the prerogative to exclude itself.

Two inferences of far-reaching significance can be drawn from those characteristics that distinguish the helping professions from other professions.

The first is that in the application of his intellectual technique to the existential affairs of others, the practitioner cannot do so completely as scientist. To assume that science yields a sure external guide to the resolution of existential problems is scientism, not science. This is a ready trap for practitioners of the helping professions. There are forces which nudge the practitioner in the direction of attempting or pretending to operate completely as scientist. One of these forces is the prestige of science in modern society. It is prestigeful to be viewed by others as scientist. Also it is possible that the cultural echoes of his ancient forebears are still resounding in the subconscious mind of the practitioner. It seems safe to conjecture that those forebears in distant primitive societies were the shaman, the medicine man. They were the ones who helped people cope with existential problems, with the paradoxes and dilemmas of the primitive human condition. To be sure, they relied on magic, on presumed supernatural powers, on sorcery and divining. In understandable rejection of these primitive practices, perhaps the practitioner of the

helping profession strives to become completely a scientist so as vehe-
mently to deny this ancient lineage.

The second inference is that in the case of the helping professions
the obligation to benefit and not to injure is a much heavier obligation
than it is in other professions. This is true because the potential consequences of the application of his intellectual technique to the existential
affairs of others are more sweeping. The situation is further complicated
because what is beneficial and what is injurious may in individual cases
be ambiguous and somewhat indeterminate. This places an inescapable
and heavy responsibility upon the practitioner of the helping profession.
How can he prepare himself to cope with this dilemma?

Preparing To Help

A necessary part of this preparation is to ground himself in what is
known about man through scientific study of him, of his development
and his behavior. For this he turns to the biological and behavioral
sciences. But while knowledge of the science of man is necessary, it is
insufficient. It is insufficient because man is still in part a mystery, and in
applying his intellectual technique to the existential affairs of others, the
practitioner inevitably must cope with the mystery as well as utilizing
what is known through science. Failure by the practitioner to recognize
this, or to deny it, may lead to reckless and irresponsible practice. Coping
with the mystery as well as using the science of man leads the practitioner inescapably into values and valuing as he applies his intellectual
technique to the existential affairs of others. Thus, he needs a fundamental base for valuing which he can explicate to himself and to others,
and by which he lives. Hence the need of the practitioner in the helping
professions for a formulated conception of man.

It is contended that a consciously formulated conception or image of
man can serve as one's fundamental basis for valuing. Apart from man,
there is no basis for valuing in nature. The rock does not say to the
mountain, "I prefer you to the stream below." Valuing falls exclusively in
the human domain. The basis for valuing, therefore, must respond to the
age-old question, "What is man, and what is his destiny *in terms of his
potential?*" The phrase "in terms of his potential" is emphasized because
this helps to distinguish the basis for valuing in the sense used here from
theology or institutionalized religion. Since man remains in part a mystery, it follows that a basis for valuing that rests on a particular image of
man must consist at least in part of postulates. Such postulates, as I shall
try to show later, need not depend for their support either on mysticism
or primitive supernaturalism. Such postulates can be inferred from the

"hints" nature, as examplified by man, constantly keeps throwing at us. The implications of these hints are perceived and proposed by men of unusual sensitivity and insight. These insights are revealed in great myths, in philosophy, in fiction, in the drama, and in great works of art as well as in the social sciences. Once formulated, however, any set of postulates as to the image of man will have to be updated over time in the light of new information about man supplied by ongoing science. So long as man remains in part a mystery, it obviously will be impossible to replace all postulates with the facts of science.

IMAGE OF MAN

Let us now illustrate what is meant by postulates as to the image of man. The illustration used is a personal formulation. Some years ago I felt a strong need to identify a fundamental basis for valuing. I have arrived at a tentative formulation for myself. This was done in reaction against mysticism and against what William James termed the "crasser form of supernaturalism." I needed a basis transcending these and transcending simple piety. I was, and am, disturbed by the encapsulation of logical positivism, and the resulting deterministic points of view in psychology, in education, and in guidance that seem based upon the image of man as a robot.

The superordinate postulate in my formulation as to the image of man is that he is born with the potential of becoming a free and responsible agent; that he not only reacts to his environment, but also that he enters into dialogue with his environment and transforms and transcends it. What is there to support such a sweeping postulate?

The clue to an answer was yielded by the traditional fascination of behavioral and biological scientists with the similarities between man and other forms of life, particularly the other primates. The classical behaviorist Watson, for example, held that there was no dividing line between man and brute (Watson, 1961). This has been the party line of behaviorists in psychology. Some scientists have expressed a contrary view. Solly Zuckerman, an authority on the great apes, has pointed to the "enormous gap between the intelligence of man and any other primate" (Eiseley, 1957). Eiseley has written that "The profound shock of the leap from the animal to human status is echoing still in the depths of our subconscious minds" (Eiseley, 1957).

The clue here is that the more valid image of man may be reflected not by the many similarities, but by certain characteristics which distinguish him as an organism from all other known forms of life. Contrary to Watson, I believe man does differ from the brute in profound ways that need not rest for their explanation either on supernaturalism or mysticism. They lend themselves to validation through direct observation and research. What are some of these distinguishing characteristics?

1. Man is born without the set of genetically imprinted behaviors possessed by other forms of life, particularly mammals, that see them through infancy and early life in the struggle for survival. His early survival does not depend upon tooth and claw, but upon care, affection and protection. At birth, his brain is roughly equivalent to the brain of a baby gorilla. But, in the first three years of his life, a unique and dramatic thing occurs. His brain spurts in growth—almost trebles in size. Divested of most instinctive responses, his fabulous brain permits him to ". . . receive, store, and utilize" what it receives from others (Eiseley, 1957). But this brain is not his mind. He is not born with the mind he comes to possess. This he develops through interaction with the social world about him. His mind is of social origin.

2. Man has a surplus of energy that exceeds that possessed by other organisms. Play and the quelling of hunger do not lead man to repose. Dostoevski caught this when he said man was an engineer that had to build roads irrespective of where they lead (Dostoevski, 1961).

3. Man has the capacity for pause between stimulus and response—he may choose among alternatives in responding (May, 1963). *This is the taproot of individual freedom.* This is not to deny the reality of limits. A necessary condition to the exercise of freedom is to recognize limits and to see in the intervening space between limits the ever present and often vast opportunity for choice among alternatives.

4. Man is the only living organism that can capture the time stream —i.e., take into account the past as well as the present and project both into the future. He is the only organism that can transcend the eternal now, and presumably is the only organism that knows he shall die.

5. Through use of gesture and symbol, primarily language, man is able to take the role of the other (Pfuetze, 1961). No distinguishing characteristic of man is more profound in its implications. By taking the role of the other, man is able to separate self from other selves, and *to become aware that he is aware.* This clearly distinguishes him from all other living organisms. Furthermore, his taking the role of the other, and thus differentiating self from other selves, enables him to experience himself both as subject and object. This makes possible inner discourse between self as subject and self as object, namely, thought. It is highly probable also that man's capacity to take the role of the other is fundamental to his singular capacity for love.

6. Through ability to capture the time stream thus projecting himself into the future, and ability to take the role of the other, man is able to estimate the consequences of the choice he makes, both for himself and for others. *This is the tap-root of individual responsibility.*

7. In the exercise of freedom within the limits of necessity, man has a *reason* for the choice he makes among alternatives. This "reason" when consciously held is for him a value. Thus man inescapably is a value-creating organism. This too distinguishes him from all other forms of life.

Consequence of Commitment

What inferences for the helping relationship can be drawn from this image of man? First, two premises: all men at birth possess the potential for these distinguishing characteristics; and, second, the environmental conditions the individual experiences from birth on may either nourish or suppress their realization. In the light of these premises, I am presently able to accept this image of man as my fundamental basis for valuing man. Since these distinguishing characteristics illumine the uniquely human in man, I accept them as *good;* and, I hold as *evil* anything which interferes with their development. But if one is so committed, there will be far-reaching consequences.

If one is so committed, he will accept all human beings at birth as equal in the sense that each possesses the potential for the development of those characteristics that distinguish him from all other forms of life. The accident of being born black or white, in a ghetto or in the suburbs, on this side of the iron curtain or the other, would make no difference in terms of the infinite value of the individual.

If the practitioner in the helping profession were so committed he would accept the nurturance and development of individual freedom and responsibility as his primary goal. Those practitioners within education, school psychologists, school social workers, and school counselors, would accept the nurturance and development of individual freedom and responsibility as the primary goal of education. To do so, in my perception, would be revolutionary. If the nurturance of individual freedom and responsibility were to become the primary goal of education, the conditions of the learning environment would be radically changed. The entire environment of the school, classroom and counseling room, activity room and playing field would be strategically ordered so as to face the student with the constant necessity of making choices within limits, of experiencing the process of becoming free and responsible. And I do not mean vapid "permissiveness." Freedom can be exercised only within limits or it will dissolve into license. Rather than robbing the student of the opportunity to examine values for fear of controversy, the student actually would be encouraged to examine, and himself accept, reject, and create values—else how could he become free and responsible. These are some of the axial changes in education that could be expected to follow commitment to the image of man which is proposed.

But there are other inferences as well for the practitioner in the helping profession.

One inference can be drawn from the postulate that man is not born with the mind he comes to possess. The mind is of social origin. This postulate would challenge the assumption that human intelligence is fixed by genetic inheritance. It would challenge the assumption that individual differences in mental ability are normally distributed and essentially immutable. It should be noted that these assumptions were initially made and gained credence during a period when Social Darwinism was flourishing in Europe and particularly in America. These assumptions were convenient bedfellows to Social Darwinism, which was used to support the notion that European social aristocracy and laissez-faire capitalism in America were justified on the basis of natural law (Hofstadter, 1955). These assumptions have been challenged recently by Schwebel (1965). He examined three major positions on the theory of the development of mental process, that of the Swiss psychologist, Piaget, the Russian psychologist, Leontiev, and the American psychologist, Hunt, and found them in agreement on the central proposition that the mental structures are developed during the course of experience; or in the pointed words of Hunt ". . . the assumptions that intelligence is fixed and that its development is predetermined by the genes is no longer tenable." This challenge cannot be viewed neutrally by the practitioner of the helping professions as a mere academic debate. Taking the challenge seriously should lead to axial change in attitude as well as in practice on the part of the practitioner.

An inference of great significance to the practitioner of the helping profession can be drawn from the postulate that through taking the role of the other, man is able to separate self from other selves, and to become aware that he is aware. Implicit here is the notion that this is also the fundamental avenue to regard for the other. Perhaps this is the capstone of distinction between man and all other known forms of life. It appears central to learning and the development of a mind; it is basic to choice among alternatives and to estimating the consequences of choice—hence central to individual freedom and responsibility. No claim is made of understanding this characteristic fully. But that the phenomenon exists, and that it has long been noted is indisputable. In the seventeenth century Descartes employed the method of pushing doubt to its ultimate extremity in a test to determine whether there was any proposition that could not be doubted. He imagined further a profound deception perpetrated by a malignant Being of supreme power and cunning. But as a result of the exercise he concluded: "Even then, if I am deceived, I must exist. No deception can bring it about that I am nothing, so long as I am aware of myself as a conscious being" (Hocking, 1959). There are a number of implications here for the practitioner. Perhaps the primary task of the practitioner in applying his intellectual techniques to the existential affairs of others is to help them become consciously aware of increasingly wider sectors of their experience. Allied to this is the need to help the client to take the role of the other, and thus come to distinguish self from other selves. There are alarming signs in our society of loss in reflective awareness of experience with a consequent threat of the eclipse of the individual (McCully, 1965). A number of social forces are at work to reduce reflective awareness of experience. A primary force is that of mass communications media, particularly television. The child that spends hours daily before a television screen is being fed vicarious experience at the expense of direct experience. To the extent that he becomes consciously involved, he can only react. He has no opportunity for interaction, for dialogue. Another force working against reflective awareness of experience is that of bureaucracy which pervasively affects the lives of increasing numbers of adults. Bureaucracy is not confined to government. It exists in big business and big education as well. Bureaucracy is the collectivization of man into organization based on the model of the machine. Proper functioning calls for ever closer integration and nicer adjustment of the parts—the reduction and elimination of friction. Hence, the products of reflective awareness of experience—variation, spontaneity, divergence and creativity—tend to be eliminated. Negative reinforcement is used against these.

The postulate concerning man's ability to take the role of the other, and through doing this to become more human, has still another implication of great significance to the practitioner of the helping profession. It should be obvious that the social barriers, the iron curtains so to speak, which separate groups from each other in our society, and cut off communication and dialogue between their members tend to depress if not to obliterate that which is most human. A notable example is the iron curtain between the upper-middle-class suburbs and the cancerous core of poverty-ridden slums in many metropolitan areas. Another is the psychological distance which separates racial groups from each other, and perpetuates the outworn myths of race, and stokes the smoldering fires of hate and prejudice. Still another example is the deliberate establishment of academic ghettos within schools through a track system or similar device, which tends to cut off communication and dialogue between groups of students in the same school. Before leaving this point, it must be emphasized that when social barriers cut off communication and dialogue, prevent the taking of the role of the other, between groups, be they suburb and slum, colored and white, or basic track and college preparatory, the members of both groups suffer some loss of opportunity to realize their human potential.

1984 AND ALL THAT!

Reference was made earlier to applications in education of deterministic points of view in psychology that seem clearly based upon the image of man as a robot. These deterministic points of view obviously stem from radical behaviorism. The classical behaviorist, Watson, viewed psychology as a "purely objective branch of natural science." "Its theoretical goal," he wrote, "is the prediction and control of human behavior." He held that there was no dividing line between man and brute, and that consciousness was not a fit phenomenon for psychological inquiry. To be sure, Watson was reacting to the barrenness of introspection as a method in psychology. But this reaction denied the existence of man as subjective inner being. Rather, he viewed man as an object, stating that when his system of psychology had been worked out "given a response, the stimulus could be predicted" (Watson, 1961).

The modern counterpart, of course, is that of operant conditioning, which holds that behavior is acquired, maintained, or eliminated solely on the basis of its environmental consequences. According to the dogma of operant conditioning, whether a behavior is acquired, or maintained, or eliminated depends upon the nature, timing, and frequency of reinforcing events associated with it. This approach to a science of behavior led Skinner in 1953 to deny man's potential for freedom and in 1963 to deny purpose in human behavior (Skinner, 1953, 1963). It is emphasized that the danger here is not that of employing such hypotheses in the scientific study of human behavior. The scientist should be free to use any premise or hypothesis he desires in connection with his scientific inquiry, operating solely as scientist. The grave danger occurs when the radical behaviorist steps out of his role as scientist, and proposes to make application of his so-called behavioral system to the affairs of others—to assume, if you please, the responsibilities of the professional but in the role of scientist. When this is done, the behavioral system becomes a dogma—for example the dogma that operant conditioning is the prototype of all human learning. Or the dogma proposed by Michael and Meyerson that " . . . the only channel open to counselors for influencing behavior is through changes in the environment," and

further their candid though frightening statement that "Under appropriate environmental conditions which man can create, almost anyone can
be motivated to do anything" (Michael & Meyerson, 1962). The grand
epitome of this dogma is that the behavioral system can be used to
engineer a better world, as proposed in *Walden II*. I see no essential
difference between Skinner's *Walden II* and Orwell's *1984*, except that
the former had a benevolent master manipulator, and the latter a malevo-
lent one. Both portrayals suppress and obliterate man's potential for freedom and responsibility.

There are two reasons why practitioners of the helping professions at
this time need to be particularly sensitive to the implications of the
dogma of operant conditioning when applied as an intellectual technique
to the existential affairs of others. First, it extends the invitation for the
practitioner to assume the role of scientist in disguise and to change his
practice to a technology of human engineering. And, second, it may cause
the practitioner to abandon his grave responsibility to benefit and not to
injure. There is no present assurance that indiscriminate application of
the behavioral system to the affairs of others will not suppress or obliterate man's potential for freedom and responsibility.

SUMMARY

In this paper a definition of the so-called helping professions has
been proposed. This definition would differentiate them from other professions. Implicit in the definition is an added obligation on the practitioner in the helping profession to apply his intellectual technique to the
affairs of others in ways which will benefit and not injure. This obligation
is heavier in the helping professions than it is in other professions because
what will benefit and what will injure does not always have objective
clarity, and the consequences of the intervention may be more sweeping.
Since there is no sure external guide to the resolution of existential problems, the practitioner of the helping profession cannot escape or deny the
centrality of valuing in helping his clients cope with the paradoxes and
dilemmas that characterize the human condition. This requires him to be
something more than scientist in his practice. He must have a fundamental basis for valuing. To be a responsible practitioner he must have a
conception of man which he can explicate to himself and communicate to
others. One formulation as to the image of man has been proposed. This
carries no implication that it should be accepted as is by others. A conception of man cannot be put on and worn as a garment. To be functional
it must emerge as the personal formulation of the individual practitioner.

REFERENCES

DOSTOEVSKI, F. M. "Notes from underground." In Kaufman, W., ed., *Existentialism from Dostoevski to Sartre*. New York: Macmillan, 1961.
EISELEY, L. *The immense journey*. New York: Vintage, 1957.
HOCKING, W. E. *Types of philosophy*. New York: Scribner, 1959.
HOFSTADTER, R. *Social Darwinism in American thought*. Boston: Beacon Press, 1955.
MAY, R. "Freedom and responsibility re-examined." In Lloyd-Jones, Esther, & Esther M. Westervelt, eds., *Behavioral science and guidance*. New York: Bureau of Publications, Teachers College, Columbia Univ., 1963.
McCULLY, C. H. "The school counselor: strategy for professionalization." *Personnel Guid. J.*, 1962, *40*, 681–689.
McCULLY, C. H. "The counselor—instrument of change." *Teachers Coll. Rec.*, 1965, *66*, 405–412.
MICHAEL, J., & MEYERSON, L. "A behavioral approach to counseling and guidance." *Harv. educ. Rev.*, 1962, *32*, 382–402.
PFUETZE, P. E. *Self, society, existence*. New York: Harper Torch Books, 1961.
SCHWEBEL, M. "Learning and the socially deprived." *Personnel Guid. J.*, 1965, *43*, 646–563.
SKINNER, B. F. *Science and human behavior*. New York: Macmillan, 1953.
SKINNER, B. F. "Operant behavior." *Amer. Psychologist*, 1963, *18*, 503–515.
WATSON, J. B. "Psychology as the behaviorist views it." In Shipley, T., ed., *Classics in psychology*. New York: Philosophical Library, 1961.

SECTION THREE

Some Empirical Concerns:
Statistics, Research, and Evaluation

AFTER the generally negative attitude toward the suitability of Newtonian research models displayed in Section Two (and again in Sections Four and Five), the reader may question the study of "obsolete" methodology. Suffice it to say that while the editors share the opinion that currently available research methodology and assumptions are an insufficient means by which all dimensions of the human enterprise can be studied, there is no need to discard all information thus obtained. More specifically, valuable knowledge has resulted and will continue to result from careful research based on traditional models of behavioral science investigation.

One point needs to be distinguished in understanding the criticisms referred to previously. Criticisms of research models as a function of particular presuppositions such as an Aristotelian logic system and a Newtonian epistemology are quite apart from the criticisms of "good" and "bad" research within these broad systems. More simply, the bone of contention evidenced in other sections of this book rests primarily with the assertion that such traditional tools of inquiry are the *only* or the *best* way to discover knowledge, and not that they are not *a* way. On the contrary, with some exceptions it is generally and legitimately held that traditional research models are *an* appropriate method of inquiry in virtually all areas of interest to the practitioner of the guidance function. Stroup's argument in Section Two is relevant here.

For the reader interested in the former body of criticism, the editors suggest David Bakan's collection of his own essays in *Psychological Method: Toward a Reconstruction of Psychological Investigation* (San Francisco: Jossey-Bass, 1967).

The principle scientific methods currently in use in the broad field of guidance consist essentially of using the statistical, research, and evaluation tools of psychology. As in the case of substantive content, tools of inquiry from a broader disciplinary base seem to have an untapped potential for numerous problems of interest to practitioners of the guidance function. Thus analysis of trends, prediction models from econometrics, systematic historical analysis, and a host of other means of gathering and systematizing knowledge seem potentially productive, although they are virtually unused in current research.

The selections in this section contain only bare mention of the general methods of *multivariate analysis*,[1] a set of investigatory techniques of current and increasing use. It seems likely, moreover, that the principle means of analysis in research reported in journals of standard interest to personnel workers will be multivariate techniques of one kind or another. This course of likely events makes it necessary for even the consumer of research to have a somewhat sophisticated knowledge of the assumptions, proper use, and interpretation of methods such as discriminant analysis, canonical correlation, and multivariate analysis of variance.

An introduction to multivariate methods *per se*, however, will not be presented at this point primarily for two reasons. First, multivariate techniques are simply extensions of the techniques and principles discussed in the articles of Millman and Kerlinger. Second, the complexity of *interpretation* of such methods is beyond the scope of this brief section and requires of the reader a thorough familiarity with the basic principles and terminology

---

[1] So called because the systems of analysis deal with more than one variable taken at one time. For example, a researcher might compare two variables with each other. This is an example of univariate analysis. He might, however, wish to compare the same two variables, *taken as a whole system,* with two others, also taken as a whole. The latter would be a case for multivariate methods.

of the predominantly univariate methods described. The editors are not aware of a suitable source which surveys multivariate methods with respect to their conceptual applicability to research problems in the social-behavioral sciences and which is written with the beginning student in mind. The text that is the source of the present selection by Kerlinger contains a suitable introduction to some multivariate techniques such as factor analysis. Additionally, an article by Maurice Tatsuoka and David Tiedeman, "Statistics as an Aspect of Scientific Method in Research on Teaching," in the *Handbook of Research on Teaching* (Chicago: Rand McNally and Company, 1963) also is of value, although it assumes that the reader has already reached a high level of sophistication. A more comprehensive reference, though again requiring sophistication, is the *Handbooks of Multivariate Experimental Psychology* (Chicago: Rand McNally and Company, 1966).

The initial article in this section is a successful attempt by Jason Millman to provide a brief, straightforward, and easily understood introduction to elementary statistical terminology and analysis. It is designed to familiarize the beginning student with basic terminology and analysis necessary to understand much of the current literature.

Where Millman's article is limited to a succinct focus on statistical terminology of both a descriptive and inferential nature, Fred Kerlinger in the following selection broadens the scope to discuss in detail some of the methods and assumptions of both the analytical and the interpretative process in research. Kerlinger's internal references to other chapters of the book from which the present selection was reprinted give a hint of the thoroughness of treatment in *Foundations of Behavioral Research* (New York: Holt, Rinehart & Winston, 1965). The text is generally regarded as one of the best of such introductory books, and contains an excellent exposition of a wide range of indispensable knowledge for both the consumer and producer of research in the behavioral sciences.

In the initial selections, which deal with methodology, neither Millman nor Kerlinger makes explicit the difference between "experimental and correlational" research, a useful distinction originally proposed by Lee Cronbach. Simply stated, experimental research involves the use of comparison groups, thereby attempting to control the influence of all the variables that may affect the findings except the one or more dependent variables under study. By contrast, correlational or regression research seeks to ascertain the amount of significant relationship among variables of interest, although no attempt is made to manipulate the variables to determine an antecedent-consequent effect. A large number of research studies in the behavioral sciences are correlational or quasi-experimental in nature. The difficulties in carrying out a rigorously controlled experimental study under field conditions are many—both in a practical and a theoretical sense. Bergin, for example, after an extensive review of the literature concluded that conditions of an adequate research design to test the effectiveness of psychotherapy had rarely been met. A perusal of relevant journals today will find many of Bergin's criteria still unsatisfied. It is equally apparent, however, that the methodological quality of counseling research is now of a generally higher level of sophistication than it was at the time of Bergin's review.

Beginning with Bergin's article, the rest of this section focuses on other than methodological tools in research and points out design flaws resulting in the typical "no-mean-difference" findings of counseling outcome research.

Carkhuff and Truax, who have in recent years published a large number of counseling research studies, summarize their attempts to deal with outcome research. They conclude that though no significant mean differences usually appear between counseled and noncounseled groups, there is a pronounced trend toward significantly greater variability in the post-counseling measures of the counseled groups when compared with those of the control groups. This finding is in agreement with those of numerous other researchers and suggests that a client may be hurt as well as helped in intensive counseling. A recent publication, *Toward More Effective Counseling and Psychotherapy* by Carkhuff and Truax (Chicago: Aldine, 1967) summarizes and discusses the implications of the research findings of their important and startling work.

In the final selection, Thomas Edgar examines the implications of assumptions underlying the "Standards for Counselor Education . . . ," published by the Association for Counselor Education and Supervision in 1964. He presents a lucid and concise case for the necessity of specifying precisely desired outcomes in both counselor education and counseling. The reader will again recognize the Aristotelian logic framework.

Earlier writings dealing with research in the helping professions often seemed to reflect a somewhat apologetic tone in calling for "more and better research." As will be observed, however, less concern is presently evident with "proving" the effectiveness of the enterprise than with "improving" practice.

Additionally, more fundamental questions regarding the nature and appropriateness of research methods based on a traditional and dated definition of the "scientific method" have been raised.

11.   An Introduction to Statistical Analysis and Terminology

Jason Millman

One of the characteristics of a social science such as educational psychology is that it reports in its professional literature the results of its researches quantitatively. Phenomena are measured and counted, but only a portion of such data is presented. Averages and other statistical indexes and techniques are used to reduce the data to forms like the ones found in the readings in this book. A major purpose of the present article will be to discuss these indexes and techniques so that the readings can be followed with greater understanding.

MEASURES OF CENTRAL TENDENCY

The most frequently used index in these readings is the *mean*. The mean of 3, 4, and 8 is 5; that is, 15 (the sum of the numbers) divided by 3 (the number of values added). Characteristic of the mean is that the *deviations* of the numbers above it balance the deviations of the numbers below it. Thus in the example above, the deviation of 8 from 5, or 3, is

Pp. 1–7, "An Introduction to Statistical Analysis and Terminology" by Jason Millman in *Readings in Learning and Human Abilities*, edited by Richard E. Ripple. Copyright © 1964 by Richard E. Ripple. Reprinted by permission of Harper & Row, Publishers.

equal to the sum of the deviations of 3 and 4 from the mean. For this reason, the mean is considered as that value which is at the center of gravity of the numbers.

The *median,* another widely used type of average, is that value above and below which an equal number of values lie. The median of the numbers 3, 4, and 8 is thus 4.

It is possible to compute both a mean and a median for any set of numbers, regardless of what the numbers signify. In the readings in this volume, means or medians represent test scores, correlation coefficients, ages, number of trials, and so forth.

The means or medians of two or more sets of data are frequently compared. For example, Ausubel (1960, Table 1, p. 270) reports the mean retention score of experimental and control groups to be 16.7 and 14.1 respectively. The experimental group has, on the average, greater retention than the control group. Although every member in the first does not necessarily have a greater retention score than every member in the second group, there is an average difference between the groups of 2.6 points.

Measures of Variability

The *range* is a single numbered index which indicates the spread of values from one extreme to the other. For example, a day's temperature range might be 15°, from 50° to 65°. Since the calculation of the range depends upon only two numbers, and is therefore highly unstable, most investigators prefer to use *standard deviation* and *variance* as measures of the spread or dispersion of a set of numbers. These statistics depend upon all the values.

One way to compute a standard deviation and variance is to first calculate the square of the deviations of each number from the mean of all numbers considered. The variance is the mean of these squared deviations; the standard deviation is equal to the square root of the variance. Hence the greater the deviations, the greater the spread of the numbers, and the greater the value of the standard deviation and variance.

In the Ausubel study cited previously, the standard deviation of retention scores for the experimental group was 5.8 and for the control group 5.4. Thus, the spread of scores for the experimental group was greater than it was for the control group. To put it another way, the experimental group had more heterogeneous retention scores than the control group. In this example, the experimental group had both the higher mean and the greater standard deviation. This is not always the case, however, and the group with the higher mean may have the smaller standard deviation.

One characteristic of the standard deviation which aids in its interpretation is that, for most sets of data, 55 to 75% of the numbers are within one standard deviation of the mean. Thus for Ausubel's experimental group, which had a mean retention score of 16.7 and a standard deviation of 5.8, approximately two-thirds of the subjects can be expected to have retention scores between 10.9 and 22.5.

Sometimes investigators wish to compare the performance of an individual on several *variables* (attributes possessing two or more values), each variable having a different mean. A crude procedure is to indicate on which variables the individual was above the mean, and on which he was below. A more precise procedure is to determine how many standard deviations above or below its respective mean is each score. Scores based on such standard deviation units are called *standard scores*.

MEASURES OF RELATIONSHIP

The primary aim of most of the research articles in this volume is to determine the existence and magnitude of relationships between variables. Some variables such as sex have only two values (male or female) and are called *dichotomies*. Individuals can be divided into two groups on the basis of which value they possess on a dichotomous variable. The relation between two variables, one of which is a dichotomy, can be then provided by a comparison of each group's mean value on the second variable. For example, in the study noted previously, Ausubel (1960) reported a relation between type of group (experimental or control) and retention scores. That is, there was a difference between the mean retention scores for the two groups. Had there been virtually no overlap in the distribution of retention scores for the two groups, that is, had almost all of the highest scores been made by subjects in the experimental group, the relation would have been close to perfect.

An index which indicates the amount of straight-line or linear relationship between two variables is the *Pearson product-moment correlation, r*. To compute a correlation coefficient, two values are needed for each of several subjects. If the subjects who have high values on one variable have also high values on the second variable, the correlation coefficient is positive. If the tendency is the reverse, that is, if high values on the first variable are associated with low values on the second, the coefficient is negative. The closer to plus or minus 1.00, the stronger the relation. A correlation coefficient of either plus or minus 1.00 indicates a perfect relationship and therefore perfect prediction. A correlation coefficient of .00 represents no relation. For example, the height of a group of subjects, when measured in feet, would correlate 1.00 with their height when measured in inches, since an individual's height in feet could be perfectly predicted from knowledge of his height in inches. High-school and colleges grades correlate approximately .50. Shoe size and intelligence would be expected to correlate approximately zero.

When Feldhusen and Klausmeier (1962) correlated anxiety and reading scores for students of average intelligence, they obtained a correlation of −.31. This negative correlation indicates a tendency for the *more* anxious students to have *lower* reading scores. The corresponding correlation for students of high intelligence was +.15. In this case, there was a slight tendency for the more anxious students to have better reading scores.

Although correlation coefficients may look like percentages, it is incorrect to interpret them as such. In terms of predictive efficiency, a correlation of 1.00 is more than twice as good as a correlation of .50, which in turn is more than twice as good as one of .25.

The *biserial correlation* is also a product-moment correlation and may be interpreted similarly. The *rank order correlation, rho,* is the product-moment correlation r between the ranks of the values rather than between the actual values themselves. A slightly different measure of relation is the *tau coefficient.* It too has limits of plus and minus 1.00, and in the special case when both variables are a dichotomy, the tau coefficient is numerically equal to r. *Epsilon* is a measure of curvilinear relation. For example, over the entire life span of a person, age and strength, if graphed, would form a curve. The epsilon correlation coefficient between age and strength would therefore be much higher than a measure of straight-line relation such as r. Only in the special case when the curve which best fits the data is a straight line, would epsilon be as low as r.

Often students mistakenly believe that the size of a correlation depends upon the number of cases used. If this were true, one could obtain a near perfect relation or prediction between two variables by measuring a large number of people. In fact, increasing the number of cases does not necessarily result in higher correlations, although it does tend to bring the computed correlation closer to the true correlation.

Throughout this volume, *reliability* of the measuring instruments being employed is reported. An instrument possesses reliability to the extent that the same individuals have the same relative standing on two testings with the same instrument or on two equivalent instruments. This is expressed numerically as a correlation coefficient. Most carefully made standardized tests have reliability coefficients of over .80; however, the reliability coefficients of short, experimental measures of personality constructs are often much lower.

When a large number of variables are correlated with each other, *factor analysis* is sometimes used to reduce the data. Instead of indicating the correlation of each variable with each other one, factor analysis provides correlation coefficients between each variable and each of a fewer number of hypothetical variables, called *factors*. Each factor represents what is common to several variables. The correlations between the variables and the factors are called *factor loadings*. For example, the first factor loading in Table 1 of an article by Ryans (1961) is .07. There is a .07 correlation between pupil behavior on the apathetic-alert dimension and a hypothetical variable, Factor A.

Tests of Statistical Significance

A frequently asked question is whether chance alone can account for the size of certain statistical indexes or for the magnitude of the difference between corresponding statistical indexes of two or more groups.

If a coin were tossed in the air ten times, chance alone could account for it landing heads seven times. The question is: how many of the tosses must be heads, or how large must be the difference between the number of heads and tails, before the likelihood or *probability* of chance alone operating is so low that one is led to believe the coin or the process of flipping is biased?

A researcher may ask whether the difference of two means is sufficiently large so that chance alone could no longer be expected to account for the difference; or, he may want to know whether an observed correlation of .31 is sufficiently greater than the chance correlation of .00 to conclude that the two variables are truly related.

To answer such questions, the researcher determines the probability that the observed statistical values (or ones more extreme) could occur *if* chance alone were operating. If this probability is low—traditionally five chances in a hundred (.05), or less—he rejects the hypothesis that chance alone accounts for the results and considers them *statistically significant*. The lower the probability, the less likely it is that the results could be caused solely by chance, and the more statistically significant are the findings. If the probability of results in only one direction are considered, the test is known as a *one-tailed test*.

Such statements as, "significant beyond the .05 level," "significant at the 5% level," "reliable beyond the .05 level," "significant beyond the .05 level of confidence," "probability less than five chances in one hundred," and "$p < .05$" are synonymous. If the probability of obtaining results if only chance were operating were greater than .05, the results would not be considered statistically significant.

Whether a particular result is statistically significant depends upon the size of the sample. While 70% heads landing in ten coin tosses may not be considered unusual, even 55% heads in 10,000 tosses could virtually never happen by chance alone. Thus, it is possible for a small difference (55% vs. 50% in the example just given), or a low correlation computed on a large sample to be statistically significant, but not be very large in an absolute sense. The distinction between statistical significance and practical significance, or importance must be remembered.

If, to vary the original example, ten coins were welded to each other with the same side up, a toss of the ten coins at once would have to result in either all heads or all tails. In this situation, an event of 10 out of 10 heads would not be surprising, whereas if the ten coins were tossed independently, 10 out of 10 heads would be highly significant. Technically, then, it is the number of independent cases, called *degrees of freedom*, rather than the actual size of the sample, upon which significance most directly depends.

Depending upon the statistics and the type of data with which he is working, as well as the assumptions he is willing to make, the investigator can often determine both theoretical distributions of possible results and the probabilities of those results occurring, were chance alone operating. The statistical test that the investigator is using is often named after the theoretical distribution appropriate for his set of circumstances. The *t*, normal, *F*, and chi-square distributions are most frequently employed. This volume includes selections using *Fisher's t* and the *normal-curve critical-ratio test* (when testing the significance of the difference between two means), the *F test* (when testing the significance of the difference between two or more means), and the *chi-square test* (when testing the significance of the difference between percentages or frequencies). For a

	Relevant	None	Irrelevant
Age 4			
7			

given number of degrees of freedom, the larger the value of the *t*, critical-ratio, *F*, or chi-square statistic, the more significant the results.

Other statistical tests included in this volume are the *Mann-Whitney test*, which indicates essentially the significance of the difference between two medians: the *Tukey gap test*, the *Dunnett procedure*, and the *Duncan range test*—all of which test the significance of the difference between the means of specific groups when several groups are being compared. *Analysis of variance* makes use of the *F* distribution and can test in one process the significance of the difference between several means. *Analysis of covariance* is similar to the analysis of variance, except that the means to be compared are first adjusted to account for differences between the groups on one or more uncontrolled variables.

To illustrate additional statistical terms used in this book, consider the situation where children are grouped on two independent variables, as shown in Figure 1. This diagram is a 2 × 3 *table* or, if the six *cells* contained the number of children involved, a 2 × 3 *contingency table*. The analysis of variance technique, which uses an *F* test, can test the significance of the difference between mean scores of the two age groups on the dependent variable (in this case a measure of learning), the significance of the difference between the mean scores of students receiving the three types of verbal condition, and the *interaction* between age and type of verbal condition received on the learning measure. An interaction would exist if the superiority, on the learning measure, of the 7-year-old children over the 4-year-old children was different for groups of children receiving different verbalization conditions. Figure 7 in Kendler and Kendler's (1962) article clearly shows this interaction. The younger children profited more from one type of verbal condition, and the older children from another. Since both some younger and some older children received each type of verbal condition, this is an example of a 2 × 3 *factorial design*.

Statistical Symbols and Abbreviations

Symbol or Abbreviation	Meaning	Selection Where Used
C.R.	critical ratio	(5)
df	degrees of freedom	several
M	mean	several
Mdn.	median	(5)
MS	mean square; an intermediate value calculated during an analysis of variance	(6, 16)
N	number of cases	several
ns	not significant, statistically	(22, 28, 37)
p	probability	several
r	Pearson product-moment correlation coefficient; sometimes a reliability index	several
r_{bis}	biserial correlation	(5)
s	standard deviation	(28)
SD	standard deviation	several
SS	sum of squares; an intermediate value calculated during an analysis of variance	(20)
$\bar{x}$	mean	(28, 36)
x or X	by; examples: 2 × 3 is read two by three; A × B is read A by B or the interaction of variables A and B	several
z	a value to which correlations are transformed before being averaged	(29)
z	the end calculation of a critical ratio test	(29)
<	less than	several
≦	less than or equal to	(20)
>	greater than	(22)
χ^2	chi-square	(15, 17, 33, 37)
∂	a corruption of the more frequently used symbol for standard deviation, σ	(36)

REFERENCES

AUSUBEL, D. P. "The Use of Advanced Organizers in the Learning and Retention of Meaningful Verbal Material." *J. of Educ. Psych.*, 1960, 51, 267–272.
FELDHUSEN, J. F. & KLAUSMEIER, A. J. "Anxiety, Intelligence, and Achievement in Children of Low, Average, and High Intelligence." *Child Development*, 1962, 33, 403–409.
KENDLER, H. H. & KENDLER, T. S. "Vertical and Horizontal Processes in Problem Solving." *Psychological Rev.*, 1962, 69, 1–16.
RYANS, D. G. "Some Relationships Between Pupil Behavior and Certain Teacher Characteristics." *J. of Educ. Psych.*, 1961, 52, 82–91.

12. Principles of Analysis and Interpretation in Research

Fred N. Kerlinger

The research analyst breaks down data into constituent parts in order to obtain answers to research questions and to test research hypotheses. The analysis of research data, however, does not in and of itself provide the answers to research questions. Interpretation of the data is still necessary. To interpret is to explain, to find meaning. In most cases it is difficult or impossible to explain raw data: one must first analyze the data and then interpret the results of the analysis.

DEFINITIONS

Analysis is the ordering, the breaking down of data into constituent parts in order to obtain answers to research questions. A researcher hypothesizes a relation between methods of teaching and pupil achievement. He plans an experiment, executes it, and gathers data from his subjects. Then he must so order, break down, and manipulate the data that he can obtain an answer to the question: Do the methods affect pupil achievement? Actually, ordering and breaking down the data should be planned very early in the research. The researcher should lay out analysis paradigms when working on the problem and the hypotheses. Then, in the actual analysis phase of the research, only mechanical analytic manipulations are required.

Interpretation takes the results of analysis, makes inferences pertinent to the research relations studied, and draws conclusions about these relations. The researcher who interprets research results searches them for their meaning and implications. This is done in two ways. (1) The relations *within* the research study and its data are interpreted. This is the narrower and more frequent use of the term interpretation. Here interpretation and analysis are closely intertwined. One almost automatically interprets as one analyzes. That is, when one computes, say, a coefficient of correlation, one almost immediately infers the existence of a relation and draws out its significance for the research problem as one orders, breaks down, and manipulates the data.

(2) The broader meaning of the research data is sought. This is done by comparing the results and the inferences drawn within the data to theory and to other research results. One seeks the meaning and implications *between* one's research results and conclusions either of one's own or of other researchers (Jahoda, Deutsch & Cook, 1951). More important, one compares one's results with the demands and expectations of theory.

An example that may illustrate these ideas is the perception of teacher characteristics research described earlier. Reasoning from so-called directive-state and social perception theory (Allport, 1955; Maccoby, et al, 1958), we might predict that perceptions or judgments of desirable characteristics of effective teachers will in part be determined by the attitudes toward education of the individuals making the judgments. Suppose, now, that we have measures of attitudes toward education and measures of the perceptions or judgments of the characteristics of effective teachers. We correlate the two sets of measures: the correlation is substantial. This is the analysis. The data have been broken down into the two sets of measures, which are then compared by means of a statistical procedure.

The result of the analysis, a correlation coefficient, now has to be interpreted. What is its meaning? Specifically, what is its meaning within the study? What is its broader meaning in the light of previous related research findings and interpretations? And what is its meaning as confirmation or lack of confirmation of theoretical prediction? The first and last questions usually have to be considered together, since the meaning of a finding can ordinarily be interpreted only by relating the internal data to theoretical expectation. If the "internal" prediction holds up, one then relates the finding to other research findings which may or may not be consistent with one's present finding.

The correlation was substantial. Within the study, then, the correlation datum is consistent with theoretical expectation. Directive-state theory says that central states influence perceptions. Attitude is a central state; it must therefore influence perception. The specific deduction is that attitudes toward education influence perceptions of the effective teacher. We measure both variables and correlate the measures. From the correlation coefficient we make an inferential leap to the hypothesis: since it is substantial, as predicted, the hypothesis is upheld. We then attempt to relate the finding to other research and other theory. In this case the finding is consistent with much of the research on directive-state and social perception theory, though it may be a far cry from laboratory experiments on perceptions of sizes of coins and perceptions of food objects to measurement of educational attitudes and perceptions of desirable teacher characteristics.

FREQUENCIES AND CONTINUOUS MEASURES

Quantitative data come in two general forms: frequencies and continuous measures. Although we have earlier seen that it is possible to view both types of measure in the same frame of reference by our definition of measurement, in practice it is necessary and useful to distinguish them.

Frequencies are simply the numbers of objects in sets and subsets. Let U be the universal set with N objects. Then N is the *number* of objects in U. Let U be partitioned into A_1, A_2, $\cdots$, A_k. Let n_1, n_2, . . . , n_k be the numbers of objects A_1, A_2, . . . , A_k. Then n_1, n_2, $\cdots$, n_k are called frequencies.

It is helpful to look at this as a function. Let X be any set of objects with members $\{x_1, x_2, \cdots, x_n\}$. We wish to measure an attribute of the members of the set; call it M. Let $Y = \{0, 1\}$. Let the measurement be described as a function:

$f = \{(x, y)$; x is a member of the set X, and y is either 1 or 0 depending on x's possessing or not possessing $M\}$

This is read: f, a function, or rule of correspondence, equals the set of ordered pairs (x, y) such that x is a member of X, y is 1 or 0, and so on. If x possesses M (determined in some empirical fashion), then assign a 1. If x does not possess M, assign a 0. Obviously this works very well with attributes like sex, religious preference, social class membership, and so on. It can also be adapted to variates (continuous measures) by definition and convention, as we learned earlier. To find the frequency of objects with characteristic A, count the number of objects that have been assigned 1.

With continuous measures or variates, the basic idea is the same. Only the rule of correspondence, f, and the numerals assigned to objects change. The rule of correspondence is more elaborate and the numerals are generally 0, 1, 2, . . . and fractions of these numerals. In other words, we write the measurement equation:

$$f = \{ (x, y) \, ; \, x \text{ is an object, and } y = \text{any numeral} \}$$

which is the generalized form of the function. This digression or review is important, because it helps us to see the basic identity of frequency analysis and continuous measure analysis.

THE FIVE RULES OF CATEGORIZATION

The first step in any analysis is categorization. Categorization is merely another word for partitioning, that is, a *category* is a partition or a subpartition. If a set of objects is categorized in some way, it is simply partitioned according to some rule. The rule tells us, in effect, how to assign set objects to partitions and subpartitions. If this is so, then the rules of partitioning we studied earlier apply to problems of categorization. We need only explain the rules, relate them to the basic purposes of analysis, and put them to work in practical analytic situations.

Five rules of categorization are given below. Two of them, (2) and (3), are the exhaustiveness and disjointedness rules discussed earlier in the book. Two others, (4) and (5), can actually be deduced from the fundamental rules, (2) and (3). Nevertheless, we list them as separate rules for practical reasons.

1. Categories are set up according to the research problem and purpose.
2. The categories are exhaustive.
3. The categories are mutually exclusive and independent.
4. Each category (variable) is derived from one classification principle.
5. Any categorization scheme must be on one level of discourse.

Rule 1 is the most important. If categorizations are not set up according to the demands of the research problem, then there can be no adequate answers to the research questions. We constantly ask: Does my analysis paradigm conform to the research problem? Does the analysis scheme enable me to test my hypotheses adequately? Suppose the hypothesis were: Religious education enhances the moral characteristics of children. Religious education has been defined as "parochial school education," moral characteristics as "honesty." The hypothesis is, therefore: Parochial children are more honest than public school children. (We ignore the great difficulty in designing an adequate test of this and related hypotheses.) Whatever data are gathered, whatever analysis is used, both data and analysis must bear directly on this hypothesis.

The simplest type of analysis is a frequency analysis. We randomly sample parochial and public schools, randomly sample n children from each school, and measure their honesty. Let us suppose that the best we can do is to label each child as *honest* or *not honest*. The paradigm for the frequency analysis would look like this:

	Honest	Not Honest
Parochial		
	FREQUENCIES	
Public		

If we had continuous measures for the *honesty* variable, then the paradigm would be different:

Parochial (1)	Public (2)
.	.
. Y Measures	.
.	.
.	.
M_{Y1}	M_{Y2}

It is obvious that both paradigms bear directly on the hypothesis: both enable the researcher to test the hypothesis, albeit in quite different ways. The point is that an analytical paradigm is, in effect, another way to state a problem, a hypothesis, a relation. That one paradigm uses frequencies while the other uses continuous measures in no way alters the relation tested. In other words, both modes of analysis are logically the same: they both test the proposition that the type of education affects honesty.[1] They differ in the data they use, in statistical tests, and in sensitivity and power.

There are several things a researcher might do that would be irrelevant to the problem. If he included one, two, or three variables in the study with no theoretical or practical reason for doing so, then the analytic paradigm would be at least partly irrelevant to the problem. To take an extreme example, suppose a researcher collected achievement-test data from both types of schools and tested the achievement differences. This would probably have no bearing on the problem, since the researcher is interested in the moral differences and not the achievement differences between the two types of schools and, of course, between

[1] (Editor's note) More precisely, the two paradigms test the proposition that children in public and parochial schools differ in honesty, a condition which may be due as much to the selection system of the two types of schools as to the type of education. Kerlinger alludes to this and similar qualifications in the following paragraphs.

religious instruction and no religious instruction. He might bring other variables into the picture that have little or no bearing on the problem, for example, differences in teacher experience and training or teacher-pupil ratios. If, on the other hand, he thought that certain variables, like sex, family religious background, and perhaps personality variables, might interact with religious instruction to produce differences, then he might be justified in building such variables into the research problem and consequently into the analytic paradigm.

Rule 2, on exhaustiveness, is quite familiar to us.[2] To repeat briefly, it simply means that all subjects, all objects of U, must be used up. All individuals in the universe must be capable of being assigned to the cells of the analytic paradigm. With the example just considered, each child either goes to parochial school or to public school. If, somehow, the sampling had included children who attend private schools, then the rule would be violated because there would be a number of children who could not be fitted into the 2×2 paradigm. If the research problem called for private-school pupils, then the 2×2 paradigm would have to be changed to a 3×2 paradigm, the rubric Private being added to Parochial and Public.

The exhaustiveness criterion is not always easy to satisfy. With true attributes, there is no problem. If sex is one of the variables, any individual has to be male or female. Suppose, however, that a variable under study were religious preference and we set up, in a paradigm, Protestant-Catholic-Jew. Now suppose some subjects were atheists or Buddhists. Clearly the categorization scheme violates the exhaustiveness rule: some subjects would have no cells to which to be assigned. Depending on numbers of cases and the research problem, we might add another rubric, Others, to which we assign any subjects who are not Protestants, Catholics, or Jews. Another solution, especially when the number of Others is small, is to drop these subjects from the study. Still another solution is to put these other subjects, if it is possible to do so, under an already existing rubric. Other variables where this problem is encountered are political preference, social class, types of education, types of teacher training, and so on.

Rule 3 is one that often causes research workers concern. To demand that the categories must be mutually exclusive means, as we learned earlier, that each object of U, each research subject (actually the measure assigned to each subject), must be assigned to one cell and one cell only of an analytic paradigm. This is a function of operational definition. Definitions of variables must be clear and unambiguous so that it is unlikely that any subject can be assigned to more than one cell. If reli-

---

[2] It is familiar to the reader as an example of the "law of the excluded middle" referred to by Dreikurs in Section 2 and by Edgar in a subsequent article, in the present section. (Editor's note)

gious preference is the variable being defined, then the definition of membership in the subsets Protestant, Catholic, and Jew must be clear and unambiguous. It might be "registered membership in a church." It might be "born in the church." It might simply be the subject's identification of himself as a Protestant, a Catholic, or a Jew. Whatever the definition, it must enable the investigator to assign any subject to one and only one of the three cells.

The independence part of Rule 3 is often difficult to satisfy, especially with continuous measures—and sometimes with frequencies. *Independence* means, as we have seen before, that the assignment of one object to a cell in no way affects the assignment of any other object to that cell or to any other cell. Random assignment from an infinite or very large universe, of course, satisfies the rule. Without random assignment, however, we run into problems. When assigning objects to cells on the basis of the object's possession of certain characteristics, the assignment of an object now may affect the assignment of another object later.

Among the five rules, Rule 4, that each category (variable) must be derived from one classificatory principle, is sometimes violated by the neophyte. If one has a firm grasp of partitioning, this error is easily avoided. The rule means that, in setting up an analytic design, each variable has to be treated separately, because each variable is a separate dimension. One does not put two or more variables in one category or one dimension. If one were studying, for instance, the relations between social class, sex, and school achievement, one would not put social class and sex on one dimension. If one were studying the relations between methods of teaching, types of motivation, and school achievement, one would not lump together methods of teaching and types of motivation on one dimension. Such an error might look like one of the following designs:

(*a*)

	Method 1	Method 2	Type *a*	Type *b*
High School Achievement				
		FREQUENCIES		
Low School Achievement				

(*b*)

	Method 1	Method 2	Type *a*	Type *b*
		ACHIEVEMENT SCORES		

It is clear that both paradigms violate the rule: they have one category derived from two classificatory principles. Correct paradigms might look like those of [c] (frequency analysis) or [d] (continuous measure analysis). If the student will use different letters for each variable, A, B, C, · · · , with breakdowns A_1, A_2, · · · , B_1 B_2 · · · , he is not as likely to make this error.

(c)

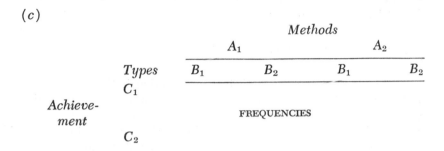

Rule 5 is the hardest to explain because the term "level of discourse" is hard to define. It was defined in an earlier chapter as a set that contains all the objects that enter into a discussion. If we use the expression "universe of discourse," we tie the idea to set ideas. When talking about U_1, do not bring in U_2 without good reason and without making it clear that you are doing so.

(d)

	Methods	
	A_1	A_2
Types B_1	ACHIEVEMENT	
B_2	SCORES	

In research analysis, it is usually the measures of the dependent variable that are analyzed. Take the problem of the relations among methods, intelligence, and achievement in an analysis of variance frame work. Methods and intelligence are the independent variables; achievement is the dependent variable. The objects of analysis are the achievement measures. The independent variables and their categories are actually used to structure the dependent variable analysis. The universe of discourse, U, is the set of dependent variable measures. The independent variables can be conceived as the partitioning principles that are used to break down or partition the dependent variable measures. If, suddenly, we switch to another kind of dependent variable measure, then we may have switched levels or universes of discourse.

STATISTICAL PRESENTATION AND ANALYSIS

There are a number of types of statistical presentation. In this section, we merely glance at the main types in order to put them into perspective. We do not go into the presentation and analysis of statistical data, since these topics are well covered in almost any elementary statistics text (Tate, 1955).

FREQUENCY DISTRIBUTION

The simplest type of statistical presentation is the *frequency distribution,* which is, as the name indicates, the numbers of cases, or distribution of cases, falling into different categories. More specifically, a frequency distribution is a tabulation of quantitative data in classes. The classes can be the partitions of a variable or they can be frequency intervals.

There are two general types of frequency distribution: primary and secondary. *Primary presentation and analysis* is descriptive. One tells the reader how many cases of the sample or universe fall into each class. Here is a simple example. I tossed four coins 20 times. The frequency distribution of numbers of heads that turned up in each of the classes 4 Heads, 3 Heads, 2 Heads, 1 Head, 0 Heads is as follows:

Number of Heads	f
4	1
3	6
2	11
1	2
0	0
	20

More elaborate frequency distributions are mainly variations on this simple theme. Though the purpose of primary analysis is mainly descriptive, sometimes hypotheses can be tested with it. For example, we might be testing observed frequencies against frequencies expected by chance.

Secondary analysis consists of comparing frequencies and percentages. Analyzing the data of an $m \times n$ frequency or percentage table is secondary analysis. We have already seen examples. The basic idea is that variables—actually the categories of variables—are juxtaposed so that relations can be studied. Primary analysis is not concerned with relations; secondary analysis is. The simplest example of secondary analysis is the 2×2 crossbreak which is in essence the same as a double frequency distribution. If we had two columns of frequencies in the little distribution above, one for men and one for women, and proportions in the table, we might be able to say something about sex and coin-tossing behavior. Any crossbreak is in effect a frequency distribution, then, though we ordinarily do not use the two terms interchangeably.

It is possible that measures of central tendencies, statistical averages, are used more than any other measures. The reason is not hard to find. Groups of measures are too many and too complex for the eye and understanding to grasp. To compare groups of measures and to represent all the measures of a group with indices, and to interpret individual measures, measures of central tendency are used. They accomplish these purposes succinctly and efficiently.

The three principal measures of central tendency are the mean, the median, and the mode. They are averages by definition. The *mean* is the arithmetic average of a set of measures and is the most important and most used central tendency average. The mean is the staple statistic of statistics, because of its reliability and its useful algebraic properties. There are three or four other kinds of means, but they will not be discussed here.

The *median* is the midmost measure of any set of measures. It is a useful average when there are only a few very high or very low measures. The mean is unduly affected by such measures; the median is not. Compared to the mean, however, its usefulness is limited. It is a nonalgebraic measure that lacks the manipulative flexibility of the mean. Lately statisticians have been working out statistical tests that require the use of the median. Perhaps its most frequent use in social scientific and educational research is to help split a group into two equal parts, high intelligence and low intelligence, high anxiety and low anxiety, for instance.

The *mode* is the most frequently occurring measure of a set of measures. Modes are sometimes important in describing distributions. For example, it may be important for an educational investigator to know that a distribution of achievement scores is bimodal, a distribution with two points at which many similar scores cluster. In fact, such an occurrence may indicate that important factors, unknown to the investigator, are operating.

It is perhaps superfluous to mention here that the variability of any set of scores is one of its most important characteristics. In earlier chap-

ters variability was discussed rather thoroughly; a few practical words
will suffice here.

Research data reports should contain measures of variability. Generally speaking, a mean should not be reported unless a standard deviation (and the N) is also reported. The reader of a report should be able
to interpret the data, always difficult or impossible without variability
measures. In addition, some readers may wish to reanalyze the data of
research reports. To do so they need variability measures.

The measures of variability in most use are the range, the standard
deviation, the variance, and the semi-interquartile range. In most behavioral research, the standard deviation and the variance are used. If
the median is used as a measure of central tendency, as it must be with
certain kinds of data, the semi-interquartile range, or more briefly, the
quartile deviation, is used. One quartile deviation above and below the
median includes 50 per cent of the cases. This measure is independent of
extreme values, unlike the range and the standard deviation, but, because
of its nonalgebraic properties, it is useful mainly as a descriptive measure.

Until recent years the *range*, the difference between the highest and
lowest measures of a set of measures, had little usefulness. Lately, however, it has come into research use, particularly in statistical tests with
small samples (with N about 20 or 15, or less). For example, there are
one-way and two-way analysis of variance methods that use the range as
a measure of variability (Mosteller & Bush, 1954). The range can also be
used for quick estimates. Rough estimates of the standard deviation can
be obtained by taking fractions of the range. If samples are small, say 30
or less, divide by 4; if larger, divide by 5 or 6. More useful, perhaps, a
good estimate of the standard error of the mean can be calculated easily
and quickly with the range. If the sample size is 15 or less, simply divide
the number of cases (N) into the range; t tests are also possible with the
range (Mosteller & Bush, 1954).

MEASURES OF RELATIONS

There are many measures of relation in use. In this book we have
already examined the product-moment coefficient of correlation (r), the
rank-order coefficient of correlation (p), and the distance measure (D).
All coefficients of relation, no matter how divergent in derivation, appearance, and use, do the same thing. They express the extent to which the
members of the pairs of a set of ordered pairs vary concomitantly. It
should also be pointed out that there is no essential and basic difference
in purpose between a coefficient of correlation, a crossbreak frequency or
percentage table, and an F or t test. They all have the same essential
purpose: to tell the researcher whether a relation exists. Some of them,
coefficients of correlation or association, tell the degree of the relation.

Coefficients of correlation usually vary in value from –1.00 through 0 to +1.00, or from 0 to +1.00, −1.00 and 1.00 indicating perfect negative and positive association, respectively, and 0 indicating no discernible relation. Whether the student is going to do research or read research reports, he will need a rather thorough knowledge of correlation and measures of correlation. Fortunately there are good references on the subject (Tate, 1955).

ANALYSIS OF DIFFERENCES

The analysis of differences, particularly the analysis of mean differences, was discussed in detail in Part III. We merely need to add that analysis of differences is by no means confined to measures of central tendency. The variances of different groups can be compared. An investigator might predict, for example, that a certain method of teaching social studies will make groups of pupils more heterogeneous than some other method. In such a case the variances or ranges of two or more groups can be compared and the differences tested for statistical significance. (An F test is appropriate.)

A very common form of the analysis of differences is the analysis of frequencies and percentages. The differences studied are those between obtained frequencies and percentages and those expected by chance. If these differences are found to be statistically significant, the existence of a relation between independent and dependent variables is inferred.

The differences between coefficients or correlation often have to be analyzed. One might predict on the basis of theory that a relation between A and B is stronger than between C and D. Say that $r_{AB} = .62$ and $r_{CD} = .51$. We compare the two: $.62 - .51 = .11$. Is this difference significant? A statistical test exists to answer this question (Edwards, 1954; Tate, 1955).

PROFILE ANALYSIS

Recent developments have expanded the possibilities of analysis of profiles. A *profile* is a set of different measures of an individual or a group, each of which is expressed in the same unit of measure. An individual's scores on a group of different tests, if all scores have been converted to a common measure system (like percentiles, ranks, standard scores), constitute a profile. Although profiles are used mostly for diagnostic purposes, they are becoming increasingly important in psychological research. The scores yielded by the semantic differential and by Q sorts are profiles, for example. Factor analysis is partly concerned with profiles.

Important analytical problems are the assessment of the similarities of profiles and the related problem of how profiles cluster to form homogeneous groups of profiles. [Previously] the cluster problem was considered in some detail. In [one table], for instance, one subject's responses to five concepts on six semantic differential scales were given. The scores on the six concepts formed profiles. The cluster analysis of these profiles was given in [the next table], where D measures, measures of the similarity of the six profiles, were given. We might also have correlated these data using r. Thus r can also be called a measure of profile similarity.

Another simple but instructive example of profile data was given in [a table], where the scores of four persons on one Q sort were given. These profiles were intercorrelated with r.

There are a number of interesting possible applications of profile analysis to psychological and educational research problems. A child's meaning space, as well as the meaning spaces of groups of children, can be studied through profile analysis. We might ask: How do the meaning spaces of a child change over time? Is this child's meaning space similar to those of other children of his age and grade? Is the meaning space of the children of Group A similar to, or different from, the meaning space of the children of Group B?

We might be interested in the different perceptions of educational ideas and practices of educators and laymen, of teachers and administrators, of administrators and board of education members. Profile analysis can aid in the solution of these and many other research problems.

Profile analysis has special problems that require careful consideration. One of these problems is that similarity is not a general quality of persons. As Cronbach and Gleser (1953) point out, similarity is similarity only with respect to specified dimensions or complexes of characteristics. Therefore it behooves the researcher to specify and define just what characteristics or complexes of characteristics are similar.

Another difficulty, or rather, set of difficulties, lies in what information one is willing to sacrifice in computing indices of profile similarity. Such decisions, of course, depend on the research problem. When one uses the product-moment coefficient of correlation (r), one loses level, that is, differences between means are sacrificed. This is loss of *elevation*. Product-moment r's take only *shape* into account. Further, *scatter*, differences in variability of profiles, is lost when computing, for instance, Q correlations. Obviously, much information is lost (Cronbach and Gleser, 1953). A measure that preserves these differences is the distance measure, D (Cronbach and Gleser, 1953; Nunnally, 1962).

Index can be defined in two related ways. One, an index is an observable phenomenon that is substituted for a less observable phenomenon or for a phenomenon that cannot be directly observed. A thermometer, for example, gives readings of numbers that stand for degrees of temperature. The numerals on a speedometer dial indicate the speed of a vehicle. Test scores indicate achievement levels, verbal aptitudes, degrees of anxiety, and so on.

A definition perhaps more useful to the researcher is: An index is a number that is a composite of two or more other numbers. An investigator makes a series of observations, for example, and derives some single number from the measures of the observations to summarize the observations, to express them succinctly. By this definition, all sums and averages are indices: they all include in a single measure more than one measure. But the definition also includes the idea of indices as composites of different measures. Coefficients of correlation are such indices. So are F and t ratios. All of these combine different measures in single measures or indices.

IQ is an index: mental age divided by chronological age. (Mental age is itself an index since it is a composite of more than one measure.) There are indices of social-class status. For example, one can combine income, occupation, and place of residence to obtain a rather good index of social class. Sociometric indices were discussed [previously]. They are based on the expression of choices by single numbers. An index of cohesiveness can be obtained by asking members of a group whether they would like to stay in the group. Their responses can be combined in a single number.

Indices are most important in scientific analysis. They simplify comparisons. Indeed, they enable research workers to make comparisons that otherwise could not be made or that could be made only with great difficulty. Raw data are usually much too complex to be grasped and used in mathematical and statistical manipulations. They must be reduced to manageable form. The percentage is a good example. Percentages transform raw numbers into comparable form.

Indices generally take the form of quotients: one number is divided by another number. The most useful such indices range between 0 and 1.00 or between −1.00 through 0 to +1.00. This makes them independent of numbers of cases and aids comparison from sample to sample and study to study. (They are generally expressed in decimal form.) There are two forms of quotients: ratios and proportions. A third form, the percentage, is a variation of the proportion.

A *ratio* is a composite of two numbers that relates one number to the other in fractional or decimal form. Any fraction, any quotient, is a ratio. Either or both the numerator and denominator of a ratio can themselves be ratios. The chief purpose and utility of a ratio is relational: it permits the comparison of otherwise noncomparable numbers. In order to do this, it is perhaps best to put the larger of the two numbers of the quotient in the denominator. This of course satisfies the condition mentioned above of having the ratio values range between 0 and 1.00, or between −1.00 through 0 to +1.00. This is by no means absolutely necessary, however. If, for example, we wished to compare the ratio of male to female high school graduates to the ratio of male and female graduates of junior high school graduates over several years, the ratio could sometimes be less than 1.00 and sometimes greater than 1.00, since it is possible that the preponderance of one sex over the other in one year might change in another year.

Sometimes ratios give more accurate information (in a sense) than the parts of which they are composed. If one were studying the relation between educational variables and tax rate, for instance, and if one were to use actual tax rates, an erroneous notion of the relation could be obtained. This is because tax rates on property are often misleading. Some communities with high *rates* actually have relatively low levels of taxation. The assessed valuation of property may be low. To avoid the discrepancies between one community and another, one can compute, for each community, the ratio of assessed valuation to true valuation. Then an adjusted tax rate, a "true" tax rate, can be computed by multiplying the tax rate in use by this fraction. This will yield a more accurate figure to use in calculations of relations between the tax rate and other variables.

Newcomb (1961) in his study of the acquaintance process, invented an interesting ratio index. As an index of agreement, Newcomb counted the issues among a large number of issues on which pairs of individuals agreed and disagreed. For each pair of subjects, the following ratio was computed:

$$\frac{\text{Number of agreeing responses to items of importance to both members}}{\text{Number of disagreeing responses to items of importance to both members}}$$

As an index of "reality-irreality" of the perceptions of group members of themselves and each other, one could use a sociometric index: the number of perceived choices by other members (on some appropriate criterion) divided by the number of actual choices. Such a ratio might be called an index of perceived acceptance or perceived rejection.

A *proportion* is a ratio, a fraction, but it is a special kind of ratio. It is a fraction with the numerator one of two or more observed frequencies and the denominator the sum of the observed frequencies. The probability definition given earlier, $p = s/(s + f)$, where s = number of successes and f = number of failures, is a proportion. Take any two numbers, say 20 and 60. The ratio of the two numbers is 20/60 = .33. (It could also be 60/20 = 3.) If these two numbers were the observed frequencies of the presence and lack of presence of an attribute in a total sample, where $N = 60 + 20 = 80$, then a proportion would be: $20/(60 + 20) = 20/80 = 1/4 = .25$. Another proportion, of course, is $60/80 = .75$.

A *percentage* is simply a proportion multipled by 100. With the above example, $20/80 \times 100 = 1/4 \times 100 = 25$ per cent. The main purpose of proportions and percentages is to reduce different sets of numbers to comparable sets of numbers with a common base. Any set of frequencies can be transformed to proportions or percentages in order to facilitate statistical manipulation and interpretation.[3]

A word of caution is in order. Because they are often a mixture of two fallible measures, indices can be dangerous. The IQ is a good example. The numerator of the fraction is itself an index since MA, mental age, is a composite of a number of measures. A better example is the so-called Achievement Quotient: $AQ = 100 \times EA/MA$, where $EA =$ Educational Age, and $MA =$ Mental Age. Here, both the numerator and the denominator of the fraction are complex indices. Both are mixtures of measures of varying reliability. To make matters worse, they are now thrown together. What is the meaning of the resulting index? How can we interpret it sensibly? It would be hard to say. In short, while indices are indispensable aids to scientific analysis, they must be used with circumspection and care.

THE INTERPRETATION OF RESEARCH DATA

Scientists, in evaluating research, can disagree on two broad fronts: data and the interpretation of data. Disagreements on data focus on such problems as the validity and reliability of measurement instruments, the adequacy and inadequacy of research design and methods of observation, and the adequacy and inadequacy of analysis. Assuming a certain degree of competence and adequacy, however, we find that major disagreements ordinarily focus upon the interpretation of data. Most psychologists, for example, will agree on the data of reinforcement experiments. Yet they disagree vigorously on the interpretation of the data of the experiments. Such disagreements are in part a function of theory. In a book like this we cannot labor interpretation from theoretical standpoints. We must be content with a more limited objective: the clarification of some common precepts of the interpretation of data *within* a particular research study or series of studies.

[3] Percentages should not be used with small numbers, though proportions may always be used. The reason for the percentage computation restriction is that the relatively larger percentages give a sense of accuracy not really present in the data. For example, suppose 6 and 4 are two observed frequencies. To transform these frequencies to 60 percent and 40 percent is a bit absurd.

One of the major themes of this book has been the appropriateness of methodology to the problem under investigation. The researcher usually has a choice of research designs, methods of observation, methods of measurement, and types of analysis. All of these elements must be congruent; they must all fit together. One does not plan, for example, a factorial design with nominal data, nor does one use an analysis appropriate to frequencies with, say, the continuous measures yielded by an attitude scale. Most important, the design, the methods of observation and measurement, and the statistical analysis must all be appropriate to the research problem.

An investigator obviously must carefully scrutinize what might be called the technical adequacy of the methods, the measurement, and the statistics. The adequacy of data interpretation crucially depends upon such scrutiny. A frequent source of interpretative inadequacy, for example, is randomness. Investigators frequently interpret ex post facto research data as though they were experimental data in which random assignment has been used.

Another frequent source of interpretative inadequacy is neglect of measurement problems. It is urgently necessary, in all social scientific and educational research, to pay particular attention to the reliability and validity of the measures of the variables. Simply to accept without question the reliability and validity of psychological measuring instruments is a gross error.

The researcher must be especially careful to question the validity of his measures, since the whole interpretative framework can collapse on this one point alone. If an educational investigator's problem includes the variable anxiety, and the statistical analysis shows a positive relation between anxiety and, say, achievement, the investigator must ask himself and the data whether the anxiety measured is the type of anxiety warranted by the problem. He might, for example, be measuring test anxiety when the problem calls for general anxiety. Similarly, he must ask himself whether his measure of achievement is valid for the research purpose. If the research problem demands application of principles but the measure of achievement is a standardized test that emphasizes factual knowledge, the interpretation of the data can be quite erroneous.

In other words, we face here the obvious, but too easily overlooked, fact that adequacy of interpretation is dependent on each link in the methodological chain, as well as on the appropriateness of each link to the research problem and the congruence of the links to each other. This is clearly seen when we are faced with negative or inconclusive results.

Negative or inconclusive results are much harder to interpret than positive results. When results are positive, when the data support the hypotheses, one interprets the data along the lines of the theory and the reasoning behind the hypotheses. Although one carefully asks critical questions, upheld predictions are evidence for the validity of the reasoning behind the problem statement. In addition, positive results are evidence that the methodology, the measurement, and the analysis are satisfactory.

This is one of the great virtues of scientific prediction. When we predict something and plan and execute a scheme for testing the prediction, and things turn out as we say they will, then the adequacy of our reasoning and our execution seems supported. We are never sure, of course. The outcome, though predicted, may be as it is for reasons quite other than those we fondly espouse. Still, the fact that the whole complex chain of theory—deduction from theory, design, methodology, measurement, and analysis—has led to a predicted outcome is cogent evidence for the adequacy of the whole structure. We make a complex bet with the odds against us, so to speak. We then throw the research dice or spin the research wheel. If our predicted number comes up, the reasoning and the execution leading to the successful prediction would seem to be adequate. If we can repeat the feat, then the evidence of adequacy is even more convincing.

But now take the negative case. Why were the results negative? Why did the results not come out as predicted? Note that any weak link in the research chain can cause negative results. If the design and the observation methods are not appropriate to the problem, clearly positive results can only be fortuitous or erroneous. If the measurement lacks reliability, inconclusive results will almost necessarily follow. If the statistical analysis is unsuited to the data, the results can easily be inconclusive. If, for example, a weak nonparametric test is used when a strong parametric one is needed, an actual relation can go undetected. But which of these possible causes of inconclusiveness, if any, is the true cause? Or are the theory and hypotheses at fault? It is an extremely difficult if not impossible task to answer these questions. Why?

Negative results can be due to any one, or several, or all of the following: incorrect theory and hypotheses, inappropriate or incorrect methodology, inadequate or poor measurement, and faulty analysis. All these factors must be carefully examined in turn. All must be scrutinized and the negative results laid at the door of one, several, or all of them. If we can be fairly sure that the methodology, the measurement, and the analysis are adequate, then negative results can be definite contributions to scientific advance, since then and only then can we have some confidence that our hypotheses are not correct.

The testing of hypothesized relations has been strongly emphasized in this book. This does not mean, however, that other relations in the data are not sought and tested. Quite the contrary. The practicing researcher is always keen to seek out and study relations in his data. The unpredicted relation may be an important key to deeper understanding of theory. It may throw light on aspects of the problem not anticipated when the problem was formulated. Therefore researchers, while emphasizing hypothesized relations, should always be alert to unanticipated relations in their data.

Suppose we have hypothesized that the homogeneous grouping of pupils will be beneficial to bright pupils but not beneficial to pupils of lesser ability. The hypothesis is upheld, say. But we notice an apparent difference between suburban and rural areas: the relation seems stronger in the suburban areas; it is reversed in some rural areas! We cross-partition the data using the suburban-rural variable. We find that homogeneous grouping seems to have a marked influence on bright children in the suburbs, but that it has little or no influence in rural areas.[4] This would be an important finding indeed.

But such unpredicted findings must be treated with more suspicion than predicted findings. Before accepting them, they should be substantiated in independent research in which they are specifically predicted and tested. Only when a relation is deliberately and systematically tested with the necessary controls built into the design can we have much faith in it. The unanticipated finding may be fortuitous or spurious.

PROOF, PROBABILITY, AND INTERPRETATION

The interpretation of research data culminates in conditional probabilistic statements of the "If p, then q" kind. We enrich such statements by qualifying them in some such way as: If p, then q, under the conditions r, s, and t. Ordinarily we eschew casual statements, because we are aware that such statements cannot be made without grave risk of error.

Perhaps of greater practical importance to the research interpreting data is the problem of proof. Let us flatly assert that nothing can be "proved" scientifically. All one can do is to bring evidence to bear that such-and-such a proposition is true. Proof is a deductive matter, and experimental methods of inquiry are not methods of proof. They are controlled methods of bringing evidence to bear on the probable truth or

[4] I am indebted to Dr. Bernard Bryan, Superintendent, Second Supervisory District, New York State, for suggesting this hypothesis.

falsity of relational propositions. No scientific investigation ever proves anything, in short. Thus the interpretation of the analysis of research data can never use the term proof in the logical sense of the word. Interpretation, rather, must concern itself with the evidence for or against the validity of tested hypotheses.

Fortunately, for practical research purposes it is not necessary to worry excessively about causality and proof. Evidence at satisfactory levels of probability is sufficient for scientific progress. Causality and proof were discussed in this chapter to sensitize the reader to the danger of loose usage of the terms. The understanding of scientific reasoning, and practice and reasonable care in the interpretation of research data, while no guarantees of the validity of one's interpretations, are helpful guards against inadequate inference from data to conclusions.

REFERENCES

ALLPORT, F. *Theories of Perception and the Concept of Structure.* New York: Wiley, 1955.
CRONBACH, L. & GLESER, G. "Assessing Similarity Between Profiles." *Psychol. Bull.*, 1953 L.
EDWARDS, A. *Statistical Methods for the Behavioral Sciences.* New York: Holt, Rinehart and Winston, 1954, pp. 304–307.
JAHODA, M., DEUTSCH, M. & COOK, S. *Research Methods in Social Relations,* Part 1. New York: Holt, Rinehart, and Winston, 1951, pp. 252 ff.
MACCOBY, E., NEWCOMB, T. & HARTLEY, E., eds., *Readings in Social Psychology* (rev. ed.), New York: Holt, Rinehart, and Winston, 1958, pp. 85–94.
MOSTELLER, F. & BUSH, R. "Selected Quantitative Techniques." In G. Lindsey, ed., *Handbook of Social Psychology,* Vol. I. Cambridge, Massachusetts: Addison-Wesley, 1954, pp. 304–307.
NEWCOMB, T. *The Acquaintance Process.* New York: Holt, Rinehart and Winston, 1961, pp. 281–282.
NUNNALLY, J. "Analysis of Profile Data." *Psychol. Bull.*, LIX, 1962, 311–319.
TATE, M. *Statistics in Education.* New York: Macmillan, 1955.

13. The Effects of Psychotherapy: Negative Results Revisited

Allen E. Bergin

The questions raised by Eysenck (1952) ten years ago regarding the effectiveness of psychotherapy when compared with the effects of no-

Allen E. Bergin, "The Effects of Psychotherapy: Negative Results Revisited," in *Journal of Counseling Psychology,* X, No. 3, 1963, 244–249. Copyright 1963 by the American Psychological Association, and reproduced by permission.

treatment can be re-phrased today in much more sophisticated and scientific terminology, but they are still questions. For Eysenck, and perhaps others, there is in fact no longer a question; psychotherapy is *not* effective in ameliorating psychopathology. Indeed, in his most recent and depressing review we find Eysenck (1960, p. 697) expressing his pessimism by quoting Galen thusly:

All who drink this remedy recover in a short time, except those whom it does not help, who all die and have no relief from any other medicine. Therefore it is obvious that it fails only in incurable cases.

For the rest of us who require more persuasive evidence before believing that a null hypothesis has been thoroughly confirmed, there remain questions regarding the validity of this challenging, but seemingly unrefuted, assertion.

Let it be recognized that this conclusion, and the question which stimulated its derivation is highly simplified and ignores essential underlying complexities in outcome research; nevertheless, let us consider first of all the current validity of the challenge embodied in the general proposition that psychotherapy has no unique effect upon personality change.

Controlled Studies of Therapeutic Effects

On the basis of an extensive review we are forced to conclude that the requirements for an adequate test of this proposition have rarely been fully met. It is unusual to find independent pre-, post-, and follow-up measures as well as the use of equivalent treatment and nontreatment control groups all in the same study. I wish to discuss with you six of these more adequately designed studies representing the major findings to date with regard to the main point at issue.

The Chicago study of client-centered therapy edited by Rogers and Dymond (1954) was once considered the epitome of good research design in studying the effects of psychotherapy; however, its presumed demonstration of positive change for psychotherapy subjects and not for control subjects is subject to important limitations. First of all, the study utilizes a normal rather than a neurotic control group. The neurotics in therapy *do* change significantly but the study provides little evidence on "spontaneous" changes in control neurotics over time which was the point Eysenck originally raised. Would an equivalent group of neurotics tested over an eight-month period as was the case with the experimentals, show as much change as the experimentals? The two-month pretherapy testing of the experimentals offers evidence on the basis of own-control data that neurotics do not change spontaneously over time while waiting for psychotherapy; nevertheless, we do not know whether or not they would have changed if the testing had been done at an eight-month interval rather than at a two-month interval. The data are conclusive with respect to normals and are indeed suggestive with regard to neurotics; but they do not conclusively demonstrate that psychotherapy has an effect upon neurotically disturbed persons which does not occur with equal potency outside of psychotherapy.

Another major project, the Cambridge-Somerville Youth Study of delinquency prevention (Powers & Witmer, 1951) was an impressive, well-designed study of 650 boys, 325 experimentals and 325 controls, over approximately a ten-year period. The results were utterly negative; in fact, if anything, the controls may have been slightly better off than the experimentals at the conclusion of the experiment. However, there are serious problems with this study also, one upon which Eysenck leans heavily in support of his current, more pessimistic position regarding the effects of psychotherapy. First, the treatment cannot be truly said to have been what most of us would term psychotherapy. It consisted of a variation of social casework which involved primarily the counselor's being a warm, interested friend of the boy—in fact, the intent of the study was to determine whether boys would model themselves after a positive figure who was simply warmly and humanly interested in them. Second, we have no assurance in this nor any other instance where a control group of disturbed persons is used, that the controls are genuine controls.

Perhaps, here, as in other cases, neurotic persons seek counsel and advice from a variety of sources including friends, relatives, clergymen, and physicians or in other ways informally seek out resources for promoting change. In this case, parents or other environmental figures may have been agents promoting such contacts. It is known, for instance, that at least 10 per cent of the control boys had contacts with other treatment centers. We cannot be assured, either, that the effects of such extra-therapeutic contacts are randomized across experimental and control groups for it is unlikely that persons already in a psychotherapy or counseling relationship will be strongly motivated to seek additional help from other sources. Thus, we cannot say that the only difference between the experimental and control groups is the administration of the treatment.

Two other studies utilizing control groups provide interesting data in the present context. The Barron and Leary study (1955) utilizes an outpatient waiting list control group and the Cartwright and Vogel study (1960) utilizes an own-control design. Both studies meet the requirement of equal time periods between testings for experimental and control groups. Both studies provide evidence of change in the experimental group which is matched by a similar amount of change in the control group; thus the data are negative in both instances with regard to the proposition at issue. It has been noted, however, that the experimentals in both of these instances manifested significantly greater variability in criterion scores at the conclusion of psychotherapy than did the controls. The Cartwright and Vogel study provides interesting additional data which appear to explain this result. It was found that when therapists were divided into experienced and inexperienced groups that the experienced therapists produced positive change whereas the clients seen by inexperienced therapists actually got worse. This is striking and requires further analysis. We shall return to it in a moment.

Shlien, Mosak, and Dreikurs (1962) report a fascinating research comparing time-limited client-centered and Adlerian psychotherapy on the basis of pre-, post-, and follow-up self-ideal Q sorts. The data indicate very similar and statistically significant changes in both experimental groups after 20 sessions of therapy and no change in two equivalent control groups, one a group of normals, the other a group of neurotics. Of the six studies we are reporting, this is the only one which provides unequivocally positive results.

The final study is as yet unpublished, but the quality of design and the results, which have been privately circulated, require inclusion in our own survey because of their importance. This large program of intensive research with schizophrenics underway at Wisconsin (Gendlin, 1962; Rogers, 1959, 1961; Truax, 1962) has begun to yield its results, some of which pertain directly to the question at issue. The study involves unusually thorough matching of experimental and control groups and an extensive program of outcome evaluation. It is, at least in design, a paradigm for all research addressed to the basic, simple question of whether psychotherapy has any effect at all. Since the treatment studied was applied to schizophrenic subjects, many of them severely regressed, we hesitate to include these data in our analysis; nevertheless certain aspects of the results provide an interesting comparison with the work already cited by Cartwright and Vogel.

In the present instance, preliminary data show no significant differences between experimental and control subjects; however, when experimental subjects are divided according to qualities of the therapist it was found that patients of therapists who provided high therapeutic conditions (high empathy, positive regard, and congruence) improved significantly whereas patients of therapists who provided low therapeutic conditions (low empathy, positive regard, and congruence) became significantly worse. The effectiveness of the one group of therapists is cancelled out by the negative effects of the other group when the two are combined into a single experimental group and compared with the controls. This clearly shown result is an exciting breakthrough. It confirms what was suggested in the Cartwright and Vogel and perhaps the Barron and Leary study, that change does indeed occur in psychotherapy, but in two opposite directions, the direction depending upon therapist qualities.

This may indeed be the answer to the series of negative findings on the generalized effectiveness of psychotherapy. The positive results in the Shlien study and the partially positive findings in the Rogers and Dymond study may be explainable in this context on the basis of good therapist selection.

IMPLICATIONS OF THE DATA FOR NEW RESEARCH FRONTIERS

There are no simple generalizations which derive readily from the foregoing studies or the class of studies which they represent. They provide many stimuli for further theorizing and for further research exploration and in this sense are eminently fruitful. Let us pursue for a moment three interesting directions from among those which these data lead us to consider.

CONTROL GROUPS NOT CONTROL GROUPS

One of the most provocative implications of the series of negative findings cited here and the additional ones cited in the two Eysenck papers is that neurotics change positively with time without the benefits of psychotherapy. Many of the studies using adequate control groups and reporting negative results show significant changes in the tested subjects. The fact that the changes are of similar degree among both experimental and control subjects should not prevent us from noting the significant fact that change *does* occur! This finding has now reached the stage of being a repeatedly replicated fact. What is going on in these control groups? Why do these people change? The fact is that we have little knowledge whatsoever as to what goes on in these control groups. It is tacitly assumed that since they do not receive formal psychotherapy that they are controls equal in every other way with the experimentals. But are they? I know of no controlled study which has provided sampling of the subject's daily life experiences which might affect his adjustment or personality disturbance. It should be recalled here that we have no reason to assume that outside experience effects should be randomized across therapy and no-therapy groups.

I would like to propose the following solution to this puzzle. The control groups in these studies are not control groups; they are therapy groups! We have substantial evidence from two independent and thoroughly done studies that anxious or disturbed people seek help but not from psychotherapists. Jerome Frank (1961) reports that during a 4½ year follow-up period of the cases which had been seen for six months in an experimental therapy design, *one-half* of them had contacts with a medical or nonmedical "help-giving person that was more than casual and lasted some time." He states that "In light of the help-seeking activities of the patients in this study, their progressive improvement in social effectiveness probably represents the average effect of non-specific help" (p. 212). One of the many projects stimulated by the Joint Commission on Mental Illness and Health involved a survey of how *Americans View Their Mental Health* (Gurin, Veroff, & Feld, 1960). One of the striking findings in the study was the report that when people became seriously upset they sought help but with significantly greater frequency from clergymen, physicians, friends, teachers, etc. than from mental health professionals. Perhaps, then, the changes occurring in control groups can be attributed to this type of help-seeking. If this is so it suggests that what may actually be the effective ingredient in the psychotherapeutic process is not specific to psychotherapy.

THERAPEUTIC CONDITIONS AMONG PROFESSIONALS AND NONPROFESSIONALS

This brings us to the second deduction which can be made from our brief analysis of outcome research. It was noted in several instances that a negative outcome, that is no difference in amount of change between experimentals and controls, could be accounted for by the mutually cancelling effects of two different kinds of therapists having provided treatment—one kind apparently promotes positive change and the other kind promotes negative change. The evidence regarding exactly *who* produces which kind of change is not altogether clear. This ability appears to have some relationship to amount of experience, but the more impressive data concern attitudinal qualities of the therapist. Truax (1962) reports from the Wisconsin project that among these qualities are empathic understanding, congruence, and unconditional positive regard. Additional information is provided in the studies by Whitehorn and Betz (Betz, 1962) in which therapists who were successful in treating schizophrenics were clearly distinguishable from those therapists who were unsuccessful. The more effective therapists were measurably more democratic, nonauthoritarian, noninterpretive, and personal in their approach and were especially perceptive of the "individualistic inner experiences of the patient" (however, McNair, Callahan, and Lorr demonstrate that the picture may be more complex than this, 1962).

It is interesting to consider the thought that these qualities could very likely characterize the experienced client-centered and Adlerian therapists in the Shlien study which is the only report demonstrating an unequivocally positive outcome. The deduction to be drawn from this reasoning is obvious. The therapists who produce positive results are those who have certain personal qualities and ways of responding to others rather than a well-trained armamentarium of techniques; therefore it is no vain stretch of the imagination to hypothesize that our so-called control subjects who change in spite of being controls are seeking help from and being influenced by people who have the same personal qualities as those therapists who produce positive personality change. The proposition tendered for consideration here suggests that not only have our control groups not been control groups, but that what we have called psychotherapy is not in fact the psychotherapeutic agent. Future research, then, calls for greater precision in specifying controls, the dimensionalizing of therapist qualities in order to better specify our antecedent variable, and, finally, experimentation with new forms of psychotherapy based upon newly hypothesized change agents.

STIMULI TOWARD THE ASSESSMENT OF VALUED OUTCOMES

This stage of our argument leads to the third and final observation which derives from the survey of outcome studies. It does not pertain directly to research results, but rather to broader conclusions about the direction and meaning of therapy outcome research. The studies reviewed here and the larger number which they represent exemplify the fact that subjective value judgments underlie the selection of all outcome criteria. This fact has presented an enduring problem in specifying the effects of psychotherapy. Disagreement regarding the acceptability of criteria on both theoretical and practical levels is pervasively commonplace and is undoubtedly traceable to issues of personal values. The present studies are suggestive of how such a state of affairs produces great diversity in indices of psychotherapy's effect. The outcome measures in these reports include self-ideal discrepancy, a TAT index of adjustment, social effectiveness, personal comfort-discomfort, MMPI indices, number of arrests or court appearances, behavior rating scales, and therapist judgments.

It is no longer original to conclude from such evidence that outcome can mean many things, that different and important outcome criteria tend to be uncorrelated, and that discrepant research results are to be expected under such conditions. All this is well demonstrated and simply punctuates the need for as much specificity with regard to measured consequences as is needed with regard to antecedent conditions of therapeutic promise. In fact, it should be noted that neither the term "psychotherapy" nor the term "outcome" are denotative and that they refer neither to a specified antecedent variable nor a specified consequent. There are dozens of now precisely specified variables, which could serve as referents for these terms, but there is little agreement as to which ones are the most relevant and useful. In an attempt to remedy such an unseemly condition, the problem of outcome has been minimized in favor of process analyses and experimental analogues of psychotherapy (Astin, 1961). Let us discover, it was heralded, what leads to what! That is true science! Once we know what conditions lead to what results, then we or someone else can worry about whether the results are desirable or not. The psychotherapy situation became, then, a laboratory for the study of interpersonal processes and the problem of outcome was often set aside, not because outcome analysis was a scientifically unfertile field, but because the valuational issues presented were something that modern psychology was ill-equipped to deal with.

It is clear that this solution has side-stepped, rather than resolved the problem of determining the quality of therapeutic results. As an alternative, I would like to propose that psychotherapy research will become most fruitful when it is not only scientifically correct but is socially sensitive, when research and practice are geared toward the discovery and application of means toward accomplishing specifically valued goals. We never have and, I believe, never will strictly agree upon the goals or outcomes to be strived for, but to me it is folly to suppose that the research enterprise in psychotherapy will become optimally fruitful until it includes an enlarged devotion toward valued ends. The folly lies, in part, in the implicit and inhibiting notion that we ought to have culture-free criteria. There are no such phenomena as culture-free or values-free people; consequently it seems inevitable that specific attention and action is required on the part of both practitioners and researchers with regard to these facts. This involves becoming explicit about the values to which we are committed, doing all we can to specify their meaning in precise psychological terms, and finally, devoting ourselves to developing ways of achieving those ends. Our research frustrations in this area can be alleviated only by studying how specifically valued goals can best be achieved as consequences of therapeutic regimes organized to accomplish such purposes. It seems axiomatic to me that we cannot escape this requirement and that to do so would necessarily undermine the potential contribution of the psychotherapy research enterprise.

Summary

To sum up, we find that the question of the effects of psychotherapy has led to a series of researches which has raised a number of alternative questions or problems. These vexations of the scientific spirit appear on the verge of stimulating important breakthroughs in the analysis of psychotherapeutic effects even though the majority of findings are negative with regard to the global question of the effects of psychotherapy.

First, the studies reviewed appear to have demonstrated that control groups may actually represent a test of the effectiveness of nonprofessional therapeutic conditions, that these conditions may very well exist in professional psychotherapy as well, but that they are found primarily among a selected group of therapists and that the remainder of therapists have a negative effect which accounts for the unimpressive results among experimental groups. We have noted also the need for additional precision in specifying both antecedents and consequents in psychotherapy, and have suggested that in particular the problem of specifying therapeutic consequences can only be addressed in terms of values, that this should then be the basis for positive action with regard to promoting what we value rather than dilly-dallying in midstream because we are afraid to assert openly what we believe and act upon privately.

Finally, perhaps we can all feel at one with Jerome Frank (1961, p. 207) when he cited Alice in Wonderland as having a true kinship with the psychotherapy researcher:

. . . the croquet balls were live hedgehogs, and the mallets live flamingoes, and the soldiers had to double themselves up and stand on their hands and feet to make the arches—Alice soon came to the conclusion that it was a difficult game indeed.

Received November 12, 1962.

REFERENCES

ASTIN, A. W. "The functional autonomy of psychotherapy." *Amer. Psychol.,* 1961, *16,* 75–78.

BARRON, F., & LEARY, T. "Changes in psychoneurotic patients with and without psychotherapy." *J. consult. Psychol.,* 1955, *19,* 239–245.

BETZ, BARBARA J. "Experiences in research in psychotherapy with schizophrenic patients." In H. H. Strupp & L. Luborsky, eds., *Research in psychotherapy,* vol. 2. Washington, D.C.: American Psychological Association, 1962, pp. 41–60.

CARTWRIGHT, ROSALIND DYMOND, & VOGEL, J. L. "A comparison of changes in psychoneurotic patients during matched periods of therapy and non-therapy. *J. consult. Psychol.,* 1960, *24,* 121–127.

EYSENCK, H. J. "The effects of psychotherapy: An evaluation." *J. consult. Psychol.,* 1952, *16,* 319–324.

EYSENCK, H. J. "The effects of psychotherapy." In H. J. Eysenck, ed., *Handbook of abnormal psychology.* New York: Basic Books, 1960, pp. 697–725.

FRANK, J. D. *Persuasion and healing.* Baltimore: Johns Hopkins Press, 1961.

GENDLIN, E. T. "Client-centered developments and work with schizophrenics." *J. counsel. Psychol.,* 1962, *9,* 205–211.

GURIN, G., VEROFF, J., & FELD, SHEILA. *Americans view their mental health.* New York: Basic Books, 1960.

McNair, D. M., Callahan, D. M., & Lorr, M. "Therapist 'type' and patient response to psychotherapy." *J. consult. Psychol.*, 1962, *26*, 425–429.

Powers, E., & Witmer, Helen. *An experiment in the prevention of delinquency.* New York: Columbia Univer. Press, 1951.

Rogers, C. R., & Dymond, Rosalind F. *Psychotherapy and personality change.* Chicago: Univer. of Chicago Press, 1954.

Rogers, C. R. *The process of personality change in schizophrenics and normals during psychotherapy: A research investigation.* Unpublished manuscript, Univer. of Wisconsin, 1959.

Rogers, C. R. *Introduction to the Symposium.* Paper read at a symposium: Therapeutic and research progress in a program of psychotherapy with hospitalized schizophrenics. Amer. Psychol. Assn. Convention, New York, 1961.

Shlien, J. M., Mosak, H. H., & Dreikurs, R. "Effect of time limits: A comparison of two psychotherapies." *J. counsel. Psychol.*, 1962, *9*, 31–34.

Truax, C. B. "Effective ingredients in psychotherapy: An approach to unraveling the patient-therapist interaction." *J. counsel Psychol.*, this issue.

14. Toward Explaining Success and Failure in Interpersonal Learning Experiences

Robert R. Carkhuff and Charles B. Truax

A decade ago Eysenck (1952) and Levitt (1957) drew and substantiated conclusions that the helping professions were not effective in producing improvement in their clients at all developmental levels. A careful review of carefully controlled research exploring the efficacy of various therapeutic, counseling, and guidance activities established no significant average differences in the outcome indices of persons who were treated and persons who were not treated. In spite of the fact that so many have devoted so much in the anticipation of positive change, this challenge has gone unanswered for years. That such a challenge has not been specifically leveled at parents and teachers, coaches, ministers and personnel workers is attributable not to the absence of this same interpersonal phenomenon in those spheres, but rather to the absence of any substantial body of research investigating the outcome criteria of these relationships.

Robert F. Carkhuff, and Charles B. Truax, "Toward Explaining Success and Failure in Interpersonal Learning Experiences," from *Personnel and Guidance Journal*, March, 1966, pp. 722–28. Copyright © 1966 by the American Personnel and Guidance Association, Inc., Washington, D.C. Reprinted by permission.

A Response to the Challenge

The findings from a program of intensive research with hospitalized schizophrenics (Rogers, 1962; Truax, 1963; Truax & Carkhuff, 1964) found similarly: no overall *average* differences between patients receiving more traditional forms of counseling and psychotherapy and matched control patients; however, and this is an important "however," the patients receiving counseling and psychotherapy showed significantly greater variability on a variety of change criteria at the conclusion of the therapeutic process than did the controls. More therapy patients demonstrated positive behavioral change and more demonstrated negative behavioral change than did control patients who received no therapy.

A view of the chronically mentally ill patient as the deteriorated consequence of a progression of particular kinds of relationships dictates that we trace back along his developmental path in an attempt to explicate the interpersonal processes contributing to his negative change—an outcome certainly unintended by the number of people interested in facilitating his positive development and learning. Studies of the effects of counseling and psychotherapy with outpatient, neurotic-type populations have yielded data of startling consistency to that of the research with schizophrenics (Barron & Leary, 1955; Bergin, 1963; Cartwright & Vogel, 1960): (a) there are no overall outcome differences between "traditionally" treated groups and their controls; (b) the patients receiving counseling and psychotherapy show significantly greater variability on change indices at the conclusion of the processes than did the controls. Thus, encounters in counseling and psychotherapy with less disturbed clients may also have a positive or negative outcome on indices of behavioral change. Some clients appear to improve and some appear to deteriorate.

We might have expected similar findings in other studies but most often such analyses were not conducted. Eysenck (1960) based some of his later and stronger conclusions upon such research as the extremely well-designed study of 325 potentially delinquent boys and their controls over approximately a 10-year period (Powers & Witmer, 1961; Teuber & Powers, 1953). Forms of supervised treatment varying from a "big-brother" approach, in which the case-worker *attempted* to be a warm, interested friend who offered the youths a positive model, to the more traditional psychotherapeutic approaches yielded no significant differences.

Even here, while the project was neither designed nor the data analyzed in such a way as to provide the necessary information, one critical, if not systematic, finding emerged: certain caseworkers tended to form less effective relationships with the youths in terms of the intended goals, i.e., keeping the potential delinquents out of court and jail; other caseworkers tended to form more effective relationships in achieving the goals of the project. The inference may be drawn, then, that the variety of therapeutic approaches as implemented by the individual caseworkers might have been facilitative or retarding. Here the evidence, while more sparse, is supportive of the thesis presented. Mink and Isaksen (1959), working with nearly 100 junior high school students who were divided into a group receiving guidance and a group receiving no guidance, found no significant differences in adjustment outcome. Further, the students' actions taken as a result of guidance counseling of both the more traditionally clinical and the nondirective variety did not differ from those not counseled. However, again the variability on the change indices was significantly greater for the counseled group than for the non-counseled group, that is, significantly more improvement as well as regression in social adjustment was in evidence in the treated groups. Thus, the findings seem to support the suggestion that even with shorter-term guidance counseling with a younger, relatively non-pathological population, the interpersonal encounter may have a positive or a negative impact.

In general, then, the relevant findings seem to offer an explanation for the puzzling mass of data already existing concerning the overall lack of efficacy of the "helping" relationship. Together these studies suggest one very consoling and one very distressing message to those of us who have dedicated our lives to "helping" others. First, *we have an impact!* Second, the findings force us to take a long, hard view at this impact for clearly the impact may be in a constructive or deteriorative direction. *Counseling may be "for better or for worse"!*

Thus, at a variety of different developmental stages we find that "helping" relationships may be facilitative or deteriorative. The problem then becomes one of looking at outcome and then tracing back through the process (and this makes out a case for some form of the all-too-often neglected recording of the process) in an attempt to explicate those process variables that facilitate positive movement and those that inhibit this goal or even contribute to individual deterioration. "How can we incorporate the multitude of potentially significant variables into one meaningful system?" becomes a critical question to which we must address ourselves.

Some Dimensions Are Discerned

In spite of the bewildering array of theories and practice in counseling and psychotherapy, there have been many recurring themes. Psychoanalytic, client-centered, and various eclectic theorists alike have emphasized: (a) the importance of the counselor's ability to sensitively and accurately understand the patient in such a manner as to communicate this deep understanding; (b) the importance of nonpossessive warmth and acceptance of the client by the counselor; (c) the necessity for the counselor to be integrated, mature, and genuine within the counseling encounter. These three elements of the counseling relationship are aspects of the counselor's behavior that cut across the more parochial theories of effective "helping" processes and appear to be common elements in a wide variety of interpersonal approaches.

When rating scales of adequate reliability were used with hospitalized schizophrenic patients (Rogers, 1962; Truax, 1961; Truax, 1963; Truax & Carkhuff, 1964) to divide them according to the level of these conditions provided by the therapists of differing orientations, patients receiving high levels of empathy, positive regard and genuineness demonstrated significant process movement and constructive personality and behavioral change. Patients who received low therapeutic conditions did not become engaged in positive therapeutic process movement and actually deteriorated on the outcome criteria. The very significant and exciting counseling outcomes experienced by chronic hospitalized mental patients when they interacted with hospital attendants trained only in operationalizing the dimensions of empathy, positive regard, and genuineness in the counseling encounter (Carkhuff & Truax, 1965 a; b) provide an additional source of supportive evidence. Thus, even in the case of the severely regressed schizophrenic, the presence or absence of certain relationship variables may act to facilitate or retard the learning or relearning process.

Such is also the case with less pathological populations. Working with neurotic-type populations, Bergin and Soloman (1963) at Teachers College found evidence that accurate empathic understanding was significantly related to predominantly psychoanalytically trained therapists' efficacy. An analysis of substantial samples of a number of recorded counseling cases from the University of Chicago and Stanford University indicated that accurate empathy ratings were significantly higher for the more successful than for the less successful cases (Truax, 1963). In addition, the works of Halkides (1958) and Barrett-Lennard (1962) have strongly supported the relevance of the counselor characteristics of empathy, warmth, and genuineness for success with counseling center cases. Further, in the aforementioned Cambridge-Somerville study (Powers & Witmer, 1961; Teuber & Powers, 1953), the results of which were not analyzed very systematically for our present purposes, it was found that ineffectual relationships between the caseworker and the delinquents were characterized by such factors as "mutual misinterpretation" which continued throughout the case. Thus, increasing evidence has established the efficacy of the facilitative conditions for a variety of populations in a variety of different settings such as Wisconsin, New York, Kentucky, Massachusetts, Illinois, and California.

SOME GENERALIZATIONS ARE MADE

The findings that certain counselor-offered conditions are related to the likelihood of progress or retardation has direct relevance to teacher-student and parent-child relationships. If the current evidence is reliable and a lack of such elements as empathy, warmth, and genuineness tends to impede or retard positive movement, while the presence of higher levels of these conditions leads to constructive gain, then the model for interpersonal processes may be a reversible one: the model can be used to predict positive movement and gain as well as to predict negative movement or deterioration. The absence or low levels of facilitative conditions in relationships with parents, teachers, and other significant figures in all likelihood contributes to the development of the difficulty or psychopathology in the first place. It makes sense that counselors offering a continuation of these same conditions will continue to produce further deterioration.

There is today a growing body of literature directly supportive of the presence of related conditions in teacher-student relationships. (Davitz, 1964; Isaacson, McKeachie, & Milholland, 1963; Pace & Stern, 1958; Thistlewaite, 1959). It is significant, for example, that Willis (1961), in *The Guinea Pigs after 20 Years,* points out that the value of the secondary school program most frequently and spontaneously mentioned by graduates 20 years later was the "warmth and human atmosphere" communicated by the school teachers and administrators, i.e., "the friendly relations of the students with each other and with the teachers; the homelike feeling of the school; the school was living as well as learning; there was freedom, but the abuse of freedom was handled in a firm but friendly manner, the classes were small, the atmosphere informal. . . . " The next two categories spontaneously emitted included "learning as a process of discovery (perhaps highly related to the process of exploration in counseling and therapy)" and the genuine concern of the school teachers and administrators for the individuals.

At the primary and preschool level there is additional evidence for the effectiveness of high levels of facilitative conditions and the ineffectiveness resultant from the absence or low levels of these conditions. In a more rigorous study of the school setting, extensive support was found for the role of the teacher's positive regard and warmth for her students in effecting positive changes in the preschool adjustment of the children

(Truax, 1960). Partial, yet extremely promising, support was discerned for the relationship between the teacher's empathic understanding of her students and the student's improved adjustment. Even on non-adjustment indices the results are very exciting. Christensen (1960), for example, found the warmth of teachers to be significantly related to the vocabulary and arithmetic achievement of primary grade pupils.

The suggestion here is, then, that those teachers who are facilitative, who "hook" the students in a lifelong learning and growing process involving or leading to self-exploration, self-direction and dependence and self-realization, creativity, democratic living, social sensitivity, and the method of intelligence, and the variety of other goals that have been prescribed by and for our educational system, are not unlike the effective counselors, those who provide the highest levels of these facilitative conditions. This is not to negate the critical nature of knowledgeable and "quality" faculty, although only 10 per cent of the former students designated this category as having been particularly meaningful in terms of their constructive development in Willis' work. (In this regard, the finding by Feifel and Eells (1963) that clients tend to focus on the opportunity to talk over problems and emphasized the "human" characteristics of the counselor while the counselor focused upon the successful implementation of his technique is relevant and stimulating.) A "quality faculty" might instead didactically bring to bear in an alterable form that accumulated knowledge that has proved to be of value in the past in a relationship based upon conditions of genuineness, warmth, and understanding, conditions that elicit the value of a potentially heretic present in the form of the student's openness of his current experiencing and their expression.

Similarly, there is a growing body of evidence in the child-rearing province to suggest that the absence or low levels of these facilitative conditions in the parent-child relationship often seems to lead to the development of problems and/or psychopathology as discerned by our present change indices. An inordinate degree of interpersonal conflict, and lack of warmth, for example, has been found in the homes of schizophrenic patients (Frazee, 1953; Lidz, Cornelison, Fleck, & Terry, 1957); the parent-child relationships have been variously described as ingenuine, distant, stereotyped, defensive, and unsatisfying (Baxter, Becker, & Hooks, 1963; Bowen, 1960; Lidz & Lidz, 1949; Wynne, Ryckoff, Day, & Hirsch, 1958) and the entire family has been described as tending to use styles of communication that are unempathic, inefficient, contradictory and conflict arousing (Bateson, Jackson, Haley, & Weakland, 1956; Weakland, 1960). In addition, the backgrounds of children who display a great amount of social maladjustment (Cass, 1953; Montalto, 1952) and overt hostility (Chorost, 1962) are characterized by higher levels of parental authoritarian control and lower levels of parental warmth and awareness of their needs than is the case with children who are better adjusted socially.

Toward Failure or Fulfillment?

While the present effort is only a beginning attempt to explicate some of the critical dimensions of interpersonal learning processes, it takes a step toward demonstrating that these interrelationships may indeed facilitate or retard functioning in a variety of areas. Let us turn again for a moment to the severely and chronically (perhaps permanently) disturbed patient. He is the negative consequent of a succession of relationships which have in no way facilitated his efforts. At almost each significant encounter (and each encounter may become more significant for the individual moving in a negative direction) he has demonstrated negative outcome.

Thus, our subject is a failure in life. More importantly, perhaps, he may have been failed. He may have been failed by the numerous significant people who have not provided those conditions that would appear to be conducive to his constructive growth. Indeed he has often been provided with the reverse of facilitative conditions—retarding conditions where the persons involved with him have been almost totally unconcerned or have lacked any real comprehensive understanding of him. He has been failed by his parents, his teachers and his counselors. Such failure, especially by teachers and counselors, may be preventable for, unlike the case with parents, we can say something about who they will be and what they will do.

There may, of course, be variations on this theme. While the evolution of the severely disturbed might include a series of failing relationships, less severely disturbed or moderately distressed may be seen as the consequents of some relationships that have been facilitative and some which have been retarding. Thus, the less severely disturbed individual may be seen as the end product of a succession of deteriorative relationships interrupted by possibly one important facilitative relationship. Similarly, the moderately distressed case may be the result of a number of relationships of varying degrees of facilitation or retardation while the healthy case results from a succession of essentially successful relationships, which significantly outweigh the potentially negative direction which might otherwise be dictated by those important figures offering low condition relationships.

It has yet to be systematically determined which of these relationships are of greatest consequence. It may be that early relationships are most significant and give the basic directionality for life. Then again, it may be that with each failing relationship, the next relationship comes to be more critical. By the time, for example, that the hospitalized patient encounters his therapist it may be that there is no "next relationship" to which to look forward. How critical is the therapist standing before him! Not to be understood at this point is to be doomed to eternal confusion.

The task of further discerning, understanding, operationalizing and implementing facilitative conditions in human encounters looms large before us. The knowledge that all interpersonal processes have the potential for constructive or deteriorative consequences impels us onward to this task.

REFERENCES

BARRETT-LENNARD, G. T. "Dimensions of therapist response as causal factors in therapeutic change." *Psychol. Monogr.*, 1962, 76, No. 43 (Whole No. 562).

BARRON, F. & LEARY, T. "Changes in psychoneurotic patients with and without psychotherapy." *J. consult. Psychol.*, 1955, 19, 239–245.

BATESON, C., JACKSON, D., HALEY, J. & WEAKLAND, J. H. "Toward a theory of schizophrenia." *Behav. Sci.*, 1956, 1, 251–264.

BAXTER, J. C., BECKER, J. & HOOKS, W. "Defensive style in the families of schizophrenics and controls." *J. abnorm. soc. Psychol.*, 1963, 66, 512–518.

BERGIN, A. E. & SOLOMAN, SANDARA. *Personality and performance correlates of empathic understanding in psychotherapy.* Paper read at American Psychological Association, Philadelphia, September, 1963.

BERGIN, A. E. "The effects of psychotherapy: Negative results revisited." *J. counsel. Psychol.*, 1963, 10, 244–250.

BOWEN, M. "A family concept of schizophrenia." In D. Jackson, ed., *The etiology of schizophrenia.* New York: Basic Books, 1960, 346–372.

CARKHUFF, R. R. & TRUAX, C. B. "Training in counseling and psychotherapy: An evaluation of an integrated didactic and experiential approach." *J. consult. Psychol.*, 1965, 29, 333–336. (a)

CARKHUFF, R. R. & TRUAX, C. B. "Lay mental health counseling." *J. consult. Psychol.*, 1965, 29, 426–431. (b)

CARTWRIGHT, ROSALIND D. & VOGEL, J. L. "A comparison of changes in psychoneurotic patients during matched periods of therapy and no therapy." *J. consult. Psychol.*, 1960, 24, 121–127.

CASS, LORETTA K. "Parent-child relationships and delinquency." *J. abnorm. soc. Psychol.*, 1953, 47, 101–104.

CHOROST, S. B. "Parent child-rearing attitudes and their correlates in adolescent hostility." *Genet. Psychol. Monogr.*, 1962, 66 (1), 49–90.

CHRISTENSEN, C. M. "Relationships between pupil achievement, pupil affect-need, teacher warmth and teacher permissiveness." *J. educ. Psychol.*, 1960, 51, 169–174.

DAVITZ, J. R. *The communication of emotional meaning.* New York: McGraw-Hill, 1964.

EYSENCK, H. J. "The effects of psychotherapy: An evaluation." *J. consult. Psychol.*, 1952, 16, 319–324.

EYSENCK, H. J. *The handbook of abnormal psychology.* New York: Basic Books, 1960.

FEIFEL, H. & EELLS, JANET. "Patient and therapist assessed the same psychotherapy." *J. counsel. Psychol.,* 1963, *27,* 310–318.

FRAZEE, H. E. "Children who later become schizophrenic." *Smith Coll. stud. soc. Work.,* 1953, *23,* 125–149.

HALKIDES, GALATIA. *An investigation of therapeutic success as a function of four variables.* Unpublished doctoral dissertation. Univ. of Chicago, 1958.

ISAACSON, R. L., MCKEACHIE, W. J., & MILHOLLAND, J. E. "A correlation of teacher personality variables and student ratings." *J. educ. Psychol.,* 1963, *54,* 110–117.

LEVITT, E. E. "The results of psychotherapy with children: An evaluation." *J. consult. Psychol.,* 1957, *21,* 189–196.

LIDZ, T., CORNELISON, ALICE, FLECK, S. & TERRY, DOROTHY. "The intrafamilial environment of schizophrenic patients: II. Marital schizm and marital skew." *Amer. J. Psychiat.,* 1957, *114,* 214–248.

LIDZ, RUTH W. & LIDZ, T. "The family environment of schizophrenic patients." *Amer. J. Psychiat.,* 1949, *106,* 332–345.

MINK, O. G. & ISAKSEN, H. L. "A comparison of effectiveness of non-directive therapy and clinical counseling in the junior high school." *Sch. Counselor,* 1959, *6,* 12–14.

MONTALTO, F. D. "Maternal behavior and child personality." *J. Proj. Tech.,* 1952, *16,* 151–178.

PACE, C. R. & STERN, G. G. "An approach to the measurement of physiological characteristics of college environment." *J. educ. Psychol.,* 1958, *49,* 269–277.

POWERS, E. & WITMER, HELEN. *An experiment in the prevention of delinquency.* New York: Columbia Univ. Press, 1961.

ROGERS, C. R. "The interpersonal relationship: The core of guidance." *Harv. rev.,* 1962, *32,* 416–429.

TEUBER, H. L. & POWERS, E. "Evaluating therapy in a delinquency prevention program." *Proceedings of the assoc. of res. in nerv. ment. Dis.,* 1953, *31,* 138–147.

THISTLEWAITE, D. L. "College press and student achievement." *J. educ. Psychol.,* 1959, *50,* 183–191.

TRUAX, C. B. *Conditions relevant to constructive personality change in preschool children.* Unpublished manuscript, Univ. of Iowa, 1960.

TRUAX, C. B. "The process of group psychotherapy: relationships between hypothesized therapeutic conditions and intrapersonal exploration." *Psychol. Monogr.,* 1961, *75,* No. 7 (Whole No. 511).

TRUAX, C. B. "Effective ingredients in psychotherapy: an approach to unraveling the patient-therapist interaction." *J. counsel. Psychol.,* 1963, *10,* 256–263.

TRUAX, C. B. & CARKHUFF, R. R. "For better or for worse: the process of psychotherapeutic personality change." Chapter in *Recent advances in the study of behavior change.* Montreal, Canada: McGill Univ. Press, 1964.

WEAKLAND, J. H. "The 'double-bind' hypothesis of schizophrenia and three-party interaction." In D. Jackson, ed., *The etiology of schizophrenia.* New York: Basic Books, 1960.

WILLIS, MARGARET. *The guinea pigs after 20 years.* Columbus, Ohio: Ohio State Univ. Press, 1961.

WYNNE, L. C., RYCKOFF, J. M., DAY, JULIANA, & HIRSCH, S. J. "Pseudomutuality in the family relations of schizophrenics." *Psychiatry,* 1958, *21,* 205–220.

15.   Wistful Wish: Evaluation Without Values

Thomas E. Edgar

All too commonly in professional groups, statements of principle are offered by leaders in the field. All too commonly such statements have no apparent basis in experience or in fact. Given enough time, however, these statements are sometimes accorded the credence of a God-given pronouncement—not subject to testing or to critical questioning. School counseling as a profession has a generous share of such chestnuts. Those in the field often hold that teaching is the best preparation for school counseling, that the ideal ratio of students to counselor is three hundred to one, and that, in order to be effective, a counselor must be accepting. The educators of counselors, through their professional organization, seem to be adding a few more questionable principles that seem to warrant careful study.

In its *Standards for Counselor Education* (1964), the Association for Counselor Education and Supervision (ACES) recognizes the importance of a clearly stated philosophy of education for counselors-to-be. It would seem that education without an underlying philosophy is unthinkable. For in acting in any way, one must act upon a set of accepted assumptions about the nature of the reality with which he is confronted, about what is likely to follow from a given act. Without these assumptions, behavior cannot be either rational or directed. Our assumptions do grow in part from what we do, from what we observe. However, once made, these assumptions help to determine what we will do in the future.

While ACES does not provide a statement of general philosophy for the educators of counselors to follow, it seems that much of what is written in the *Standards for Counselor Education* does, in fact rest upon some clear postulates or assumptions about counseling. The assumptions are generally unstated and need to be abstracted. Space limitations do not permit more than a few selected passages to be considered and analyzed in this paper.

Two passages have been drawn from the ACES report, and the underlying assumptions upon which they seem to rest are explored. One is the statement that counselor candidates should be prepared with the necessary tools for conducting research through the education provided them. The other passage considered is the statement that counselor candidates should be selectively admitted and selectively retained, and at the end of the successfully completed regimen, should be endorsed as counselors.

Thomas E. Edgar, "Wistful Wish: Evaluation Without Values," from *Personnel and Guidance Journal,* June, 1966, pp. 1025–29. Copyright © 1966 by the American Personnel and Guidance Association, Inc., Washington, D.C. Reprinted by Permission.

Assumptions Underlying Counseling Research

Now if research is to be done—the methods of science applied to this business of counseling—certain basic assumptions must be made. One of the most obvious is that counseling is an orderly and lawful process. This assertion seems to be basic to the entire philosophy of science. In order to function as a scientist, one must also make some assertion about a consistent relationship between antecedent events and certain subsequent conditions. It may not be necessary to speak of a cause and effect relationship, but to function as a researcher, one must assume that what one does must have a reliable and consistent subsequent effect on the world about him.

Further, the experimental scientist must find the subsequent events anchored in the world outside his system. What he hypothesizes must be testable in the external world. The assumptions one makes must lead to theories which in turn must generate hypotheses leading to predicted outcomes. The scientist cannot be content to merely claim logical validity while ignoring the truth or falsity of his findings.

The truth of any statement may be said to follow from its consequences, while logical validity follows from its antecedents. Logical validity is established by following logical steps, building step by step from basic assumptions to higher order statements and conclusions.

The syllogism, for instance, has the strongest kind of logical validity, the validity of identity. We can say:

All X are Y
All Y are Z
Therefore: All X are Z

However, if statements are inserted instead of the letters, the syllogism may lead to a conclusion that is not true. If one would say:

All men are evil
Evil things should be punished
Therefore: All men should be punished

the syllogism would be logically or internally valid, but the truth of the conclusion is subject to serious doubt because the premises are of questionable truth. Given the premises, though, the conclusion follows logically. In a sense, the assumptions examined in this paper are the premises of counselor educators, from which they may deduce a set of philosophical beliefs.

In order for the counselor-scientist to function in a meaningful way, he must push beyond the mere validity of the counseling situation. He must step outside his neat little system and anchor the consequents of counseling in the real, social world. In order to function as an experimental scientist, the counselor must make testable predictions growing from his theoretical system. Freud was not, in this respect, an experimental scientist because he did not attempt to make specific, verifiable predictions following from what he did. He attempted to construct a system to explain what he observed, true, but he did not extend his theory to generate predictions to be tested.

An assertion is operationally true only if all three of the following conditions are satisfied:

1. The assertion implies some predictions to be tested by conceivable operations.
2. The operations have been carried out to test the predictions.
3. The predictions have been verified by the operations performed.

If condition three fails, the assertion is said to be false. If condition two fails, the assertion is indeterminate. If condition one fails, that is, if no conceivable operations have been suggested, the assertion is said to be operationally meaningless. The counselor-scientist must eventually make some assertions about counseling that may be tested by conceivable operations. Until he does, most of the assertions he makes about counseling are really meaningless.

Most all the counseling theories that have been offered to date seem to be designed to comfort the counselor, not to yield predictions to be tested operationally. Shoben (in Farwell & Peters, 1961, pp. 574–579) points out that Carl Rogers' "self-actualization" is really a way of telling the counselor not to worry about not taking a very active part in counseling. All the counselor must do is to set up the right conditions and the client is capable of doing the rest. The concept of "self-actualization" does not lead to operations or to predictions that may be tested by these operations. Self-actualization is therefore operationally meaningless to one who would hope to do research in the field. Freud's "transference" seems to serve much the same purpose. It reassures the counselor when things get a little emotional and trying in counseling. Transference, too, is operationally meaningless for the researcher.

In summary, then, counselor educators by their emphasis on research in the field of counseling have assumed that counseling is lawful and orderly, and that there is something like a cause and effect relationship within counseling. Also implied is the assumption that the counseling relationship must be studied as a part of the whole context of the client's life. A counseling theory, to be useful to a researcher, must include statements about the conditions antecedent to counseling, the counseling process itself, and about the conditions of the client's life after counseling. The theory must yield predictions about the outcomes of counseling —and these predictions must be operationally testable. The outcomes must extend beyond the counseling situation and be firmly anchored in the reality outside the counseling situation, both antecedent to and subsequent to the act of counseling.

ASSUMPTIONS UNDERLYING SELECTION AND RETENTION

The ACES report on standards also recommends that counselor candidates be selectively admitted and selectively retained. At the end of a successful educational experience, they are to be endorsed for certification to practice their art. Underlying the belief in the efficacy of selection and endorsement procedures are some assumptions about counseling. Some are defensible, but some seem subject to serious doubt at this time.

One of the assumptions that may be most easily understood and defended is the assumption that the counselor is some kind of an influence within the counseling process.

Another assumption presupposed by the recommendation of selection, retention, and endorsement is that some kinds of influences are better than others. However, this assumption, in the light of our present inability or unwillingness to either predict or define the good or desirable goals of counseling, seems highly questionable. How else can we define the good counselor or the better counselor except by saying that what he does leads to good or better results?

At this point, researchers in the field of counseling and educators of counselors have been very much like a hypothetical group of dress buyers visiting a factory in order to make purchases for their respective stores. Some have looked only at the morale factors within the plant (researchers call this *relationship* within counseling); some have studied only the production lines, watching the flow of materials and pieces from person to person (counselor educators call this *process* in counseling); and some of the buyers have studied only the materials used in the production of dresses, noted the colors and the finish (called *content* by researchers and counselor educators). However, almost none of the buyers have looked closely at the finished product, the garment as it comes off the line. Almost none of them have judged its beauty and utility. Strange, isn't it? For *this* is the product that they must sell to the public. Counseling, too, must be judged by the end product.

Some have been unwilling to define the goals of "good" counseling, for this is placing a value judgment upon human behavior. However, not even the aseptic physicist in his gleaming laboratory is free of the social implications of his work.

Other counselor educators and researchers feel that they are unable to define the proper goals of counseling in social behaviors. If they cannot, then they cannot make judgments about the "good" counselor, and certainly not about the "good" counseling technique or "good" counseling. And yet they do. And the judgments are solidified by implication in the selection and the selective retention of counselors, and by the endorsement of some to practice, the rejection of others.

If one intends to make judgments about "good" counseling, he must move beyond the counseling situation to find the basis for the judgment, for counseling is only one aspect of the total situation that must be understood.

What one knows, or thinks he knows, is a function in part of the scale of observation. To illustrate this point, consider this example. Suppose a man, standing on the corner of the street, sees a car go by. He may assume that the car is traveling in a straight line. Now suppose this man can suddenly be whisked from his street corner and thrust into the coldness of outer space. We will see something quite different. The earth is spinning on its own axis. In turn, the earth is racing along its orbit about the sun. The entire solar system is moving with blinding speed toward the constellation Hercules. To the man who is able to see more, the car is clearly traveling in a corkscrew-like path.

Counselor educators and researchers in the field are typically standing on the street corner, looking at only one aspect of all the forces at work. Just as education must be judged finally by the end product, so must counseling, or an industrial process, or a new law, or a cancer cure.

By their provision of courses of study and certain experiences for the counselor candidates, counselor educators seem to assume that the counselor should have an influence of a *certain* kind. Most people in the field accept that the client learns something through the process of counseling. Many terms are used to describe these learnings—new responses, new views, gaining insight, restructuring of the perceptual field—but that the client learns something seems to be accepted by all.

Now if the counselor is to have a certain kind of purposeful influence on the learning of the client, is not the counselor a teacher of sorts? In order for one to function in the role of a teacher, one must have an orientation for the proper direction in which to move and some level of acceptance of an adequate goal for the process.

To be consistent, then, it seems that counselor educators must say that counselors must make value judgments about acceptable ways in which the client ought to move. Counselors must then work to bring about the goals they have specified.

The client hopefully learns to make more effective responses or more effective choices in the problem situations of his life after counseling has ended. But even to use the words "more effective" is to apply a strictly social value to the behavior of the client. "More effective" as applied to vocational choice, for example, can only make sense if judged according to the counselor's view of the client's abilities, aptitudes, interests, and needs.

Summary

By their works and by their words, educators of counselors may be judged to hold certain beliefs about counseling. Behind these general beliefs are certain assumptions. Counselor educators seem to believe in the value of research in counseling. They must then accept the basic assumptions of the scientist as those assumptions apply to a study of counseling. They must hold that the process of counseling is an orderly and lawful process. What happens in counseling must lead to verifiable and predictable outcomes. To be operationally meaningful, judgments made about the effectiveness of counseling must be anchored in conditions beyond the counseling process. The predicted outcomes of counseling must be verified by conceivable operations or remain essentially meaningless.

Counselor educators believe in the selection of counselor candidates. They believe in selective retention of candidates and in final endorsement for practice. This complex of beliefs rests upon other assumptions: (1) There are some influences in counseling that may be judged to be "more effective" than others, or some influences lead to "more effective" outcomes than do others; (2) These "more effective" outcomes must be judged by the conditions in the social context of the life of the client before and after counseling. Pepinsky & Pepinsky (1954) have said:

Depending upon whether the inferred feeling aspects of the interaction are judged to further or to impede the progress toward the "desirable" client changes, the relationship will be labeled "good" or "poor."

Counselors and counselor educators are social agents, like it or not. And whether they like it or not, counselors and counselor educators will need to define health and ill health, good adjustment and poor adjustment, effective behavior and ineffective behavior, behavior that is desirable and behavior that is not. The ultimate goal of research is better prediction and/or control. Neither group can be asocial if what they do will, in time, lead to predictable social outcomes.

Counselors or counselor educators cannot seek to escape the social implications of what they do any more than any other group of researchers. If they seek through the application of research and the purposeful selection of agents of change, to find ways to deliberately bring about certain, specified changes, they cannot escape the responsibility for also specifying the directions for that change.

If counselors are to be purposeful and effective agents of change, they simply cannot remain directionless. "Good" counseling must be judged in relation to "good" outcomes. There is no other way.

REFERENCES

Association for Counselor Education and Supervision. "Standards for counselor education in the preparation of secondary school counselors." *Personnel Guid. J.*, 1964, 42, 1061–1073.

FARWELL, G. F., & PETERS, H., eds., *Guidance readings for counselors*. Chicago: Rand McNally, 1961.

PEPINSKY, H. B., & PEPINSKY, PAULINE N. *Counseling theory and practice*. New York: Ronald, 1954.

ROGERS, C. R. *Client centered therapy*. Boston: Houghton Mifflin, 1951.

SECTION FOUR

Psychological Foundations

Psychology has always been the favored mistress of guidance. Perhaps because clinical and counseling psychology are ready models for the school counselor, he easily borrows their conceptual framework and methodology. Although some professionals apparently look to the counseling-psychology model as the one most viable for personnel workers in general, the editors regard the model as perhaps an insufficient vehicle for the full implementation of the guidance function in an educational setting. Engel expands upon this point in this section in an article entitled "Psychological Theory and Guidance."

Traditional subject matter of psychology—the study of human behavior in terms of learning, personality, motivation, perception, and development—is necessarily a part of the education of professional personnel workers. The wide and deep interchange between professionals of the two fields will continue as a matter of course in their common concern for the understanding and facilitation of optimum human behavior as a function of an individual's needs, attitudes, past experiences, and future aspirations.

Allport, in a widely quoted article reprinted here, portrays with admirable insight both the strengths and weaknesses of a psychology based upon three prescientific[1] assumptions about

---

[1] "Prescientific" is used in the sense that the truth of the statement is, by definition, not demonstrable through scientific methods.

the essential nature of man: man seen as (1) a reactive being, (2) a reactive being in depth, and (3) a being in the process of becoming. His article provides a cogent summary of the differing assumptions and consequent theory, practice, and research that constitute the underpinning of three major forces in psychology today.

For the reader with a more limited background, Paul Bruce provides in the next selection a broad and general survey of the same three forces in psychology, and offers some of the common implications of a literal interpretation of each. Bruce's article, while perhaps oversimplified and containing therefore some dubious conclusions, is nevertheless valuable if only because of its ample sprinkling of significant detail—names, terms, concepts, and titles—related to these major forces.

The article which follows is a lucid and erudite account of theories of Freud and Rorschach, in which Mary S. Engel demonstrates the untapped richness for guidance of little known developments in these and other classical theoretical positions in psychology. Whereas classical psychological theories do hold a largely unexploited wealth of suggestions and explanations of value to the guidance movement, Engel points out the necessity for guidance to develop theory of its own. In this way she anticipates the last article of this section, in which Blocher calls for a science of human effectiveness as a viable model upon which to build guidance theory.

Robert Watson's delineation of "prescriptions" (enduring assumptions that constitute parameters of definition) is a sweeping and insightful account of both the history and scope of psychology as a discipline. Parenthetically, the article is an excellent sample of the use of systematic analysis as a methodological technique of history conceived of as a social science instead of a chronicle of events. Watson traces the roots of his parameters of definition to antecedent philosophical issues—a course which leaves the article replete with both standard vocabulary and major issues of classical philosophy. The inclusion of this particular article was predicated on the assumption that predominance of philosophical belief in a particular direction on a scale between the opposing pairs of Watson's prescriptions must result in the differential practice of guidance. The counselor who operates consistently within a belief framework of *molecularism* as opposed to *molarism* may be expected to favor the use of extensive batteries of tests, be concerned virtually exclusively with specific behaviors, and in general emphasize discrete and concrete steps, which in total have the effect of defining more globally stated goals such as "better decisions."

In the penultimate selection Allen Bergin surveys the conceptual development of psychology. He finds indications that psychology is returning to issues that are more basically significant to a comprehensive science of human functioning. Bergin's analysis gives full credit to the monumental contribution of a more rigorous methodology of the mainstream of American psychology—the operational-behavioristic movement that began in the early 1920's. Bergin concludes that objective analysis of subjective experience is and always has been present in great amounts in psychological research. Following the revolution begun in the 1920's, a traditional reluctance to conceptualize psychology as a science of inner experience has resulted in the avoidance of investigating many significant problems which are excluded by definition from scientific study in an operational-behavioristic framework.

The "intellectual diet (of counseling psychology) is too often gleaned from the garbage can of other specialties, most notably, of course, clinical psychology." In answer to this frequent charge, Donald Blocher has proposed a model for a possible science of human effectiveness as an underlying discipline for counseling. Blocher offers a set of constructs exemplified by concepts such as commitment, competence, consistency, creativity, and control. That such constructs are seen potentially as products of a set of human behaviors should obviate the likely objection that such a science is "unscientific and operationally meaningless." A three-dimensional model consisting of social roles, coping behaviors, and developmental tasks is depicted as a potential way of organizing the study of the etiology of human effectiveness. Blocher's article is representative of much recent attention to the relative lack of systematic study in psychology of hygiolic or optimal human functioning as contrasted with the wealth of such study of pathological functioning. The value of studying the former kind of counselors, whose clientele typically function in predominantly nonpathological ways, is obvious: an approach of this kind assumes that "mental health" is more than the absence of pathology.

16.   Psychological Models for Guidance

Gordon W. Allport

However excellent his natural eyesight may be, a counselor always looks at his client through professional spectacles. It could not be otherwise. After all, he has invested time and money in his psychological training. Of what use is it unless it adds special prisms to his own unaided eyesight?

The lenses we wear are ground to the prescription of our textbooks and teachers. Even while we are undergraduates a certain image of the nature of man is fitted to our eyes. We grow accustomed to the image and when we become practitioners or teachers we may still take it for granted.

But every so often comes a time for optical re-examination. Perhaps the image we have is still the best fit we can get; perhaps it is not. We can tell only by examining alternative lenses. In particular I believe that three are worthy of special scrutiny:

1) *Man seen as a reactive being.* Under this rubric I would include outlooks known as naturalism, positivism, behaviorism, operationism, physicalism; these are also sometimes called—mistakenly, I think—"scientific psychology."

2) *Man seen as a reactive being in depth.* Here I include what is variously called psychoanalysis, psychodynamics, depth psychology.

3) *Man seen as a being-in-process-of-becoming.* This label covers recent trends known as holism, orthopsychology, personalistics, existential psychology.

These three images provide a focus not only for guidance practices, but for all other professional psychological activity whether it be teaching, research, counseling or therapy.

MAN: A REACTIVE BEING

One hundred years ago in his *Beiträge* Wilhelm Wundt mapped a program for the newly conceived science of psychology. His own view of the proper development of this science was broad and permissive, especially in the field of social psychology. But what has taken hold in the Anglo-American tradition is the experimental outlook of his *Physiologische Psychologie*. Fusing with Darwinism, Machian positivism, the quantitative outlook of Galton and his successors, as well as with tech-

Allport, Gordon W., "Psychological Models for Guidance," *Harvard Educational Review*, Vol. 32, No. 4, Fall 1962, 372–381. Copyright © 1962 by President and Fellows of Harvard College. Reprinted by permission.

niques invented by Binet, Pavlov, Hull and others—this experimental outlook prevailed and has ground the lens that is fitted to the eyes of almost all undergraduate students of psychology. Many of us who continue in the profession feel no need for further correction in this image of man.

Seen through this lens man is no different in kind from any other living reactor; and therefore, like the paramecium or pigeon, may be studied biologically, behaviorally, mathematically. To be sure a few special concepts need to be devised to take care of the vast complexity of human behavior, but all these concepts—among them habit hierarchy, secondary reinforcement, input and output of information, and the like—are consistent with the postulates of physicalism and naturalism.

If we ask, "What does it mean to be a human being?" this school of thought replies, "Man is one more creature of nature; his behavior though complex is predictable in principle. His present state is determined by his past state. A man's consciousness is unreliable and must be distrusted, preferably disregarded altogether. We seek the general laws of nature, not personal uniqueness. We study man, not men; objective reality, not subjective."

In principle this broad positive tradition, which we all know so well, puts a desirable end to psychological naïveté. It cautions us not to believe every verbal report that comes to our ears; it warns us to be skeptical of our own naked eyesight; and from it we learn to check ourselves for observer reliability. It teaches us to use precise and repeatable methods. Because of its stress on reliable methods this favored tradition in psychology has become known as "scientific psychology." Its methods are indeed scientific; but its primary postulate—that man is simply a reactive organism—is no more scientific than any other postulate.

It is here that the counselor encounters his first difficulty. Trained in tests, statistics, and experimental design, he may think, quite mistakenly, that to employ these useful aids he must also view his client as a reactive being—an exclusive product of stimulus impact, homeostasis, drive-reduction and re-inforcement learning. The term "scientific" has spread like a grease spot from method to theory. Just because most of our methods evolved through the positivistic tradition does not mean that the postulates of this tradition concerning the nature of man are the only acceptable postulates for scientific psychology.

A counselor whose theoretical spectacles disclose a merely reactive being, is likely to think of his client in terms of past conditioning and potential re-conditioning; in terms of reinforcements, in terms of environmental determinism. He will assume that his client's basic motives are drive-reduction or second-order conditionings which in some shadowy way are supposed to account for all his adult interests and vocational ambitions.

The vocabulary emanating from this type of postulate is replete with terms like *reaction, response, reinforcement, reflex, respondent, reintegration*—all sorts of *re*-compounds. The reference is backward. What *has* been is more important than what *will* be. Terms such as *proaction, progress, program, production, problem-solving,* or *propriate* are characteristically lacking. One would think that the client seated opposite would *protest*, for the language of response negates the subject's immediate certainty that his life lies in the future.

The positivistic view of man as a reactor has performed a good service, shaking us out of common sense naïveté, endowing us with useful methods, and correctly informing us that man is, in *some* aspects of his being, a simple respondent to simple pressures. Its postulates are, however, questionable. It sees reality as ordered but not as personal; it sees consciousness as a nuisance; it looks at man as reactive, not proactive.

It is probably true that no counselor fully follows this creed in his daily practice. Indeed he could not do so. It is too impoverished a view of real life. When a convinced positivist attempts to fit his image of man to concrete human situations, as B. F. Skinner has done in *Walden Two*, the result strikes many of us as threadbare, even pitiable.

Probably for this reason many behaviorists (starting even as far back as E. B. Holt in *The Freudian Wish and its Place in Ethics*) attempt to combine stimulus-response with psychoanalysis. Neal Miller and John Dollard in their *Personality and Psychotherapy* offer a good example. Man as a reactive being is combined with man as a reactive being in depth.

Man: A Reactive Being in Depth

So influential is this image of man that we find it everywhere: dominant in literature, in social work, in guidance, in therapeutic practice, and in the market place. There is no need today to describe this image to any educated, or even semi-educated, American adult. Freudianism, like positivism, is our daily dish.

What I should like to do is to make clear that Freudianism (in spite of its less reliable methods) is a close kin of traditional positivism. The only change in the image of man lies in adding the depth dimension. To the long psychological vocabulary of *re*-compounds, depth psychology adds *repression, regression, resistance, abreaction, reaction formation,* and many others.

Like other simple naturalistic views of man, psychoanalysis puts its chief weight upon the press of pleasure and pain. This pressure produces in the organism a tendency to seek an equilibrium between the force of his drives and the circumstances of reality. The fact that Freud maximizes the role of sex and locates the whole constellation of reactive forces chiefly in the unconscious does not alter the essential similarity.

For Freud causation lies in the past history of the individual just as it does for the conditioned-response theorist. Both have a dismaying disregard for the person's phenomenology of the future, for his sense of personhood and sense of freedom. The ego is a reactive agent, having no energy of its own, but borrowing from the unsocialized Id.

Central to depth psychology, and important for guidance, is the doctrine of *recall* and *recovery* (two more *re*-compounds). Therapy, and presumably guidance, proceeds by disclosing to the client some buried motive, or a troublesome and repressed psychic trauma. The client's salvation, if indeed he has any, lies in this vital recall. A troublesome memory is brought to cognizable form. Presumably the result is helpful to the individual in solving his conflicts. The theory, however, does not allow for any interaction between the person and the recovered memory. Simple re-instatement is itself, as Freud says, the "pure gold" of psychoanalysis. What values a client should live by when once the re-instatement has taken place is not the "pure gold" of psychoanalysis. That all adult values are simply sublimated aim-inhibited wishes, is the central doctrine. Freud never allows for the individual's capacity to disregard his past or to reshape it freely. Indeed, since the structure of the Id never changes, the future can at best be a redirection, never a transformation, of one's purposes. What one becomes is essentially what one is, and what one was.

Among the valid portions of psychoanalysis of special use to all counselors, is the brilliant account given us by Freud and by his daughter Anna, of the defensive mechanisms of the ego. In dealing with our client we do well to follow the advice of psychoanalysis and watch for rationalizations, denials of reality through repression, and displacements of aggression. All these, and other, ego-defenses belong to the nature of man, and therefore must find a place in any theory of human personality.

But what perplexes me is why so many of the ego-processes described by psychoanalysis should be merely protective strategies. Are there no ego-processes that lead to a transformation of what is recovered? To a creative cognition? To a revised sense of personhood and a new phenomenology of the future? To Freud the person seems never to be truly proactive, seldom even active. Almost always he is seen as reactive to early fixations—perhaps to some castration threat that occurred years ago, or to some other unsocialized infant complex, especially to Oedipal fantasies. My difficulty with this image of man is summed up most tersely by the late satirist, Max Beerbohm, who said, "They were a tense and peculiar family—those Oedipuses."

There is, I am well aware, a large group of theories that derive from the psychodynamic tradition but at the same time deviate considerably from the orthodox view of reactivity-in-depth. All these theories, in my judgment, move in a desirable direction. Here I shall mention only some of the relevant authors: Adler, Jung, Hartmann, Horney, Erikson, Fromm. Still more deviant from Freud are Goldstein, Maslow, Rogers, and Robert White. These and other writers offer a type of theory that views man as a being in the process of becoming. Many of them ask the pivotal question differently from the reactivist schools of thought. And it makes a good deal of difference just how a question is asked.

A story is told about two priests. They were arguing whether it was proper to smoke and to pray at the same time. One said "Yes," the other "No." To settle the matter they decided that both should write to the Holy Father for his opinion. Sometime later they met and compared notes. Each claimed that the Holy Father had supported his view. They were perplexed. Finally one asked, "How did you phrase your question?" The other replied: "I asked whether it was proper to smoke while one is praying; and the Pope answered, 'Certainly not, praying is serious business and permits no distractions.' And how did you phrase your question?" "Well," said the other, "I asked if it were proper to pray while smoking, and the Pope answered, 'Certainly, prayer is always in order.' "

Instead of asking Aristotle's question, "What is the place of man in Nature?" many authors today are asking St. Augustine's question, "Who am I?" This question, rephrased in the 20th Century, has opened the floodgates to a new theorizing of the broad type often labeled *existentialist*.

Man: Being in the Process of Becoming

Seelye Bixler, former president of Colby College, tells of a student who recently remarked, "I can't tell you how much satisfaction I take in my existential despair." In some student circles despair has always been popular. To label it "existentialist" makes it doubly attractive, in fact irresistible.

But overlooking the fashionable flavor of existentialism it is surely necessary for the modern counselor to take seriously the present-day anxieties of the younger generation. No longer can youth contemplate its future under the protection of the great social stabilizers of the past. No longer can one counsel within the framework of Victorian decorum, theological certainties, or the Pax Britannica. It is obvious to us all that some sort of shattering transformation is under way. The comfortable stabilities of culture, caste, the gold standard, and military supremacy are no longer ours.

Nor are the comfortable stabilities of traditional psychology adequate. Of what use is it to invoke an impersonal theory of learning, a biological theory of motivation, and a late Victorian formula for the unconscious, when youth's problems today are acutely conscious, intensely personal, and propelling him like an unguided astronaut into an unknown future? A counselor is not equipped for his job unless he can share in some degree the apprehensions of modern youth, and sense the swampy underpinning on which youth treads. Over his desk the counselor might well tack the wisdom of the Spanish writer Unamuno, "Suffering is the life blood that runs through us all and binds us together." While not every youth who comes to the counselor is at that moment a sufferer, it is a safe assumption that he comes for guidance that will fortify him for the inevitable suffering that he will encounter in his course of life.

TENTATIVENESS AND COMMITMENT

From the existential point of view the ideal counselor will strive to develop two attitudes in his client. Taken separately they seem antithetical; but fused into a world-view they provide strength for the future. One attitude is *tentativeness* of outlook. Since certainties are no longer certain, let all dogmas be fearlessly examined, especially those cultural idols that engender a false sense of security: dogmas of race supremacy, of naïve scientism, of unilinear evolutionary progress. Let one face the worst in oneself and in the world around him, so that one may correctly estimate the hazards.

Taken by itself such tentativeness, such insightfulness, might well lead to ontological despair. Yet acceptance of the worst does not prevent us from making the best of the worst. Up to now psychologists have not dealt with the remarkable ability of human beings to blend a tentative outlook with firm commitment to chosen values. The poet Tennyson perceived the point.

> There lives more faith in honest doubt,
> Believe me, than in half the creeds.

A commitment is, as Pascal has said, a wager. One may lose it, but one may also win. Cardinal Newman warned us that our religion can never be a matter of certainty. It is at best a subjective condition of certitude which he defined as "probability supported by faith and love." Yet a mature religion, thus defined, can be infinitely sustaining and heroically motivating. Existentialism, whether theistic or atheistic, makes the same point. We have the freedom to commit ourselves to great causes with courage, even though we lack certainty. We can be at one and the same time half-sure and whole-hearted.

William James, probably America's greatest thinker, tried to teach us this lesson, but fifty years ago we were not ready for it. It is surely noteworthy that, writing as he did in a period of social stability, James saw clearly how ultimately uncertain are our foundations of value. Wealth, he saw was a false god, leading us into a national disease that has recently been called "galloping consumption." The more we build up our material resources, the more we fear poverty. In religion, James knew, there was no certainty; yet, like Cardinal Newman, he recognized the constructive power of a mature religious commitment. Whatever ideal leads to long-range constructive consequences is psychologically sound. It is also pragmatically true. And who is to say that we have a test for truth more absolute than our own commitment in so far as it is validated by fruitful consequences?

Neither positivistic nor psychodynamic schools of thought allow for the fact that our psychological constitution permits both total tentativeness and total commitment. Such a paradox reminds us of the electron that is able to go in two opposite directions at the same time. Taken by itself tentativeness is disintegrative; commitment is integrative. Yet the blend seems to occur in personalities that we admire for their soundness and perspective. Presumably through teaching and guidance we may develop both attitudes in our youth.

Whenever the two attitudes coexist in a life we find important desirable by-products from the fusion. One is a deep sense of compassion for the lot of the human race in general and in each separate social encounter that marks our daily life. The other by-product is likewise graceful; it is the sense of humor. Humor requires the perspective of tentativeness, but also an underlying system of values that prevents laughter from souring into cynicism. As Meredith said, humor is a capacity to laugh at the things you love and still to love them.

RATIONALISM VS. IRRATIONALISM

The chief criticism made of existentialism is that it leads away from reason and exalts irrationalism. While this charge may apply to certain literary and theological trends in the existential movement I doubt that it jeopardizes the future of scientific psychology. The attitudes of tentativeness and commitment of which I speak are perfectly sound concepts— call them "intervening variables" if you wish. Indeed in so far as they reflect important states in human personality, and thus lead to improvement in understanding, prediction, and direction of human behavior, they are sounder scientific concepts than many of those we have been using.

And just what is rationalism? We venerate the ancient Greeks for their exaltation of human reason; and as psychologists we venerate Aristotle for asking the question, "What is man's place in nature." But Greek rationalism was broader than the limited, method-centered, scientism into which it has degenerated. The Greeks themselves saw a place for tentativeness and commitment within the scope of reason. The case is beautifully stated in an ancient inscription found somewhere on the coast of Greece:

> A shipwrecked sailor buried on this coast
> Bids you set sail.
> Full many a bark, when we were lost,
> Weathered the gale.

The dead sailor urges us to make the wager, take the risk, although we cannot be sure of coming through to our destination.

IMPLICATIONS FOR THEORY

What does all this mean in terms of psychological theory, and in terms of guidance? First of all it means that in order to achieve a more realistic image of man and his potentialities, we need to revise our current theories of learning and growth, of motivation and personality structure. Elsewhere (in *Pattern and Growth in Personality*, 1961) I have discussed some of the needed changes in detail, and so shall say only a few words about each.

The trouble with our current theories of learning is not so much that they are wrong, but that they are partial. They fit best the learning of animals and young children. The concepts of conditioning, reinforcement, identification, seem a bit hollow when the counselor tries to apply them to his work. They are not very helpful, for example, in explaining how a youth may learn both tentativeness of outlook and firmness of commitment. Supplementary theories in terms of organizational, biographical, and propriate learning are needed.

Except in the sense of physical maturation the concept of *growth* scarcely exists in psychology at all. Nor will it have its proper place until we have agreed upon normative standards for the maturity of personality. Up to now normative problems, except in the sense of statistical norms, are much neglected.

As for motivation and personality structure psychologists are in a state of turmoil and disagreement. That the past stages of a life do not fully explain the motivational "go" of the present, I for one am firmly convinced. Therefore we need a concept (*functional autonomy*, I think will do) to represent that portion of a life that is oriented toward the future and not toward the past. Also we need a theory of personal structure (of *personal dispositions*) to represent the important cleavages and foci of a given, concrete personality. Such a theory will, I am convinced, carry us much further than a conception of uniform variables to which every client is forcibly ordered, whether we call these variables factors, needs, dimensions, or common traits.

Most of all we need to surrender the models that would compress human personality into the routine homeostatic situation that we find in quasi-closed systems. Human personality is a wide-open system, responsive to tangible and intangible culture, on the look-out for new ideas, and capable of asking an altogether new type of question—asked by no other creature in nature, viz., "Who am I?"

There are, I am glad to say, many psychologists who feel as strongly as I that these various types of improvement need to be made before the counselor will have a fully fashioned science of psychology to undergird his practice.

IMPLICATIONS FOR GUIDANCE

Guidance is not a matter of gimmicks, nor of rules of thumb. A guide, like a philosopher and friend, is a person who loves wisdom and loves his fellow men. True, he has skills to mark him off from the professional philosopher or the untrained friend. To some extent the counselor's present-day skills are useful. Standard tests and measurements are helpful; so too achievement records and focused interviews. Most of our devices come from researches conducted under the positivistic outlook, or (in the case of projective techniques) under the psychodynamic. While many of them are serviceable I look forward to the invention of new instruments still better suited to the study of the central or propriate aspects of single personalities.

Most important, of course, are the spectacles the counselor wears. The image should no longer be borrowed from the tradition of simple naïve reactivism. Just as centimeters, grams, seconds are outmoded in modern physics so too are simple stimulus-response connections in modern psychology. In psychology, even more than in physics, we need theory capable of dealing with fluid becoming.

The plain fact is that man is more than a reactive being, more even than a reactive being in depth. If he were comfortably fixed at these levels we could with confidence apply a uniform stencil in studying his nature. But the life process is no less paradoxical than the processes of modern physics. How can one deal with space that is both finite and unbounded, with light that is both wave and particle, with electrons that pass from orbit to orbit without traversing the space between? Similarly, a human person is both structure and process, a being both biological and noetic, a being who changes his identity even while he retains it. Small wonder that at the end of his life, the famous physicist, P. W. Bridgman, said, "The structure of nature may eventually be such that our processes of thought do not correspond to it sufficiently to permit us to think about it at all."

We need not, I think, be quite so pessimistic. Our first duty is to affirm a new and wider rationalism; that is to say, to redouble our efforts to find a more adequate image of man to guide us in fashioning a more suitable science of personality.

And what about our personal attitudes as guidance specialists or teachers? Should we not cultivate the same twin virtues that we recommend to client and student: tentativeness and commitment? We can hold our own present image of man on trial, reviewing our own past psychological training in critical perspective. At the same time we can embrace courageously our task of interpreting the wisdom of the past in such a way as to make it most available to the youthful personality who is facing an uncertain, but not uninviting, future. Tentativeness and commitment are twin ideals for both counselor and client. To my mind they lie at the heart and center of guidance, of teaching, and of living.

17. Three Forces in Psychology and Their Ethical and Educational Implications

Paul Bruce

Practically all strands of our society are being influenced by theories and research from the field of psychology. Probably the most blatant example of this influence is seen in the women's magazines which month after month headline lead articles by "experts" advising and analyzing the psychological problems of our day: sex, marriage, child-rearing, narcotics, alcoholism, etc. Even more significant than this is the more subtle influence psychology is having in such fields as advertising (à la Vance Packard's *The Wastemakers*), human engineering in industry, psychotherapy and counseling, and, of course, in our schools. Maybe one measure of this impact is the amount of critical attention psychology (in the name of mental health) is getting from the ultra-conservative elements who, indeed, find the influence from psychology to be threatening the status quo of a bygone era.

The point I want to make is that if through psychology humans can be influenced in certain directions, then the ethical problem arises of evaluating these directions in terms of their being desirable or not. And if through psychology the process of education toward certain goals becomes more effective, then it becomes imperative that these goals and the determination of these goals be carefully evaluated.

Now, the typical psychologist (or I might better say the typical scientific psychologist) does not like to admit the ethical implications of his discipline; he prefers to don the robes of scientific impartiality and limit his consideration to the quest for truth as he finds it. But I don't think we should let him get away with this. We need to face up to the ethical implications ourselves, and we need to ask the psychologist to face up to the ethical implications of his theories and research and even to take a stand regarding them.

To illustrate and further define this issue, I want to discuss three forces or schools of influence in psychology today and indicate the ethical and educational implications of their formulations as I see them. These are associationism—particularly as represented by reinforcement (S-R) theory; Freudianism or classical psychoanalytic theory; and the third force which is relatively new and has no consistent label as yet, but goes under the names of humanistic psychology, perceptual psychology, existential psychology or neo-Freudianism. I will present these three schools of thought briefly as theoretical models and ask the reader to realize, as with everything else, that the adherents and practitioners who represent these models modify the theory to fit their own needs and perceptions.

ASSOCIATIONISM

Associationism in psychology developed during the latter part of the nineteenth century out of the thinking of such philosophers as Herbart, who described the mind as a complex of isolated sensations, ideas, thoughts, decisions, and feelings bound together by the process of association. With the aid of a new interest in the use of animals for observation and experimentation, psychologists, first under the leadership of E. L.

Thorndike, developed theories of behavior most familiarly represented by the stimulus-response formula. Thus, Thorndike proposed that every new idea, every new feeling or sensation is a response to a preceding idea, feeling, or sensation. Under this system, memory or learning was explained as a series of stimulus-response connections, particular stimuli calling forth the specific responses. Various laws or principles of learning were developed which explained the establishment of a bond or association between stimulus and response. For example, reward or punishment, repetition, need satisfaction, reinforcement, conditioning, etc., were postulated as effecting learning and could be used to elicit certain desired behavior patterns.

This school of thought has persisted though modified and developed, and today it remains the most popular theory (at least among scientific and academic psychologists) and perhaps the most influential force representing psychology in society today. In our schools and colleges, the prevalent use of repetition as in drills (e.g., write each spelling word five times); the use of workbooks and tests which provide the stimulus and require the student to provide the "right" response which is subsequently approved or disapproved; the extensive use of a system of rewards and penalties (as in the way grades are typically given); all of these reflect the influence of this school of thought. More recently a whole new medium has been developed and is currently being promoted—that of programed learning or more popularly termed teaching machines. Based primarily on B. F. Skinner's reinforcement theory (a refinement of associationism), programed learning involves the careful presentation and division of the subject matter into extremely small units so that the student is frequently rewarded by correct answers and can move along independently at his own pace.

In advertising, political campaigns, public relations programs, etc., the principle of conditioning is used very effectively. Briefly, the principle of conditioning states that if a stimulus and response are associated enough times together, this association will be learned. Thus, if you hear a brand name associated with a product enough times, you will automatically think of the brand whenever you think of the product; and if the terms "liberal," "socialist," "civil libertarian," "progressive education," "life adjustment," are associated with the concept of the Communist menace enough times, then these labels and those to whom they apply become tainted with the same attitudes ascribed to Communism.

Thus, when addressing themselves to the problems and issues of our times, these psychologists, believing that people's behavior to be a result of the forces exerted upon them, find their answers in terms of the manipulation of these forces. The ethical problem implicit in this system, of course, is that somebody, other than the persons affected, must decide the desired direction the behavior is to take. This necessarily calls for a "great man" philosophy of dealing with people—somebody who knows where the people should go. This system calls for leaders who are supermen of a sort, skilled in the manipulation of forces to get people to behave in the ways desired by the knowing few.

And so in schools, for example, we have developed specialists and experts who are determining what the children should learn in the various subject areas, and other experts who are predigesting what will be programed in the teaching machines. In the Midwest they now have airborne educational television by which one *expert* teacher can serve schools in six states (7000 school districts; over five million children); meaning that where used, all the children are getting the *same* presentation of the *same* curriculum at the *same* time!

One of my students wrote the following, which perhaps overstates the kind of teaching which follows from this system wherein learning is thought to result from having students respond to well-ordered stimuli:

Teaching too often becomes the process of carrying, pulling, showing, and assisting pupils along to the end of the course. *Teachers* do the reading, the explaining, the thinking, the talking, the appreciating, the devising, the planning; the problems are *teacher*-worked, the reasons are *teacher*-thought-out; the beautiful is *teacher*-selected. All the pupils do is to remain passive, to listen, to copy, to memorize, and finally to recite or to write at a stated time what they have managed to cull out of an extended dictation!

B. F. Skinner (1948), a prominent scientist from this force in psychology, wrote a novel some years ago entitled *Walden Two* in which he gives a fictional account of what he regards as a Utopian community in which the learnings of the behavioral sciences are fully utilized in all aspects of life—marriage, child rearing, ethical conduct, work, play, and artistic endeavor. Skinner's conception of paradise is a large rural colony where democracy is replaced by behavioral engineering. The common theme of this novel and of some of his other treatises is that the psychologist possesses the means of social control and must use these means effectively for the welfare of society. Let me quote what Skinner has his hero say in this novel:

Well, what do you say to the design of personalities? Would that interest you? The control of temperament? Give me the specifications, and I'll give you the man! What do you say to the control of motivation, building the interests which will make men most productive and most successful? Does that seem to you fantastic? Yet some of the techniques are available, and more can be worked out experimentally. Think of the possibilities! . . . Let us control the lives of our children and see what we can make of them. . . . (Skinner, 1948)

In another paper Skinner elaborates the implications of his theories; he states,

We must accept the fact that some kind of control of human affairs is inevitable. We cannot use good sense in human affairs unless *someone* engages in the design and construction of environmental conditions which affect the behavior of men. . . . (Skinner, 1955)

As you can see, Skinner's projection of his system is garbed in benevolence; however, the ethical question still remains as to who is to determine the *desired* direction behavior should take. And presumably this molding of human behavior would be the function of the schools, and we ask if this is the function we want education to perform.

CLASSICAL PSYCHOANALYSIS

If associationism is the most popular force among academic and scientific psychologists, Freudianism (classical psychoanalysis) has been the most influential among the clinical psychologists, and psychotherapists and counselors. Although few accept the theories exactly as Freud postulated them (which would be impossible anyway, since Freud modified and even contradicted his own theories throughout his lifetime), yet the main tenor of his system remains and poses some ethical questions.

Psychoanalysis originated in the field of medicine as a result of attempts to find some cure for the neuroses and in revolt against the dominant somatic or physiological explanations which were popular in the nineteenth century. Some psychiatrists were becoming convinced that such causal factors as brain lesions were not to be found in their patients, and they began to substitute such factors as emotional stress, weakness of will, suggestibility, and irrational habits as explanations. Soon hypnotism was introduced and accepted by some elements of the medical profession particularly when dealing with such neurotic conditions as hysteria. It was on this medical scene with an interest in neurology that Freud began his productive but controversial practice in Vienna. Influenced by the French schools in Paris under Charcot and later in Nancy under Janet, Freud built up a practice dealing primarily with hysteric patients, experimenting with hypnosis and eventually, giving this up, developing his own techniques and corresponding theoretical formulations.

The point I want to bring out in this very brief historical sketch is that psychoanalytic theory originated and was developed as a result of studying and treating mentally disturbed, upper-class Europeans during a period referred to as the Victorian era. In other words, Freud's sampling from which he drew his conclusions was anything but representative of the human race.

With his medical background, it is not surprising to learn that Freud believed that the nature of man is essentially biological; man is born with certain instinctual drives which can (though they frequently don't) work themselves out as a person grows. Freud classified the instincts under two main headings: the *life* instincts (*Eros*) and the *death* instincts (*Thanatos*). The life instincts include hunger, thirst, and sex, the latter being considered the most driving. The principle operating here is the pleasure principle or self-gratification. The death instincts include hate, aggressiveness, and self-destruction.

According to Freud, the *psyche* is divided horizontally into *conscious* and *unconscious;* and vertically into what he labels the *id, ego,* and *superego.* Gradually the child's unconscious fills with things forgotten or suppressed because they are unpleasant, and more importantly, with emotions and drives which are too painful to be tolerated in the consciousness. The *id,* entirely unconscious, is the most primitive and concerned only with the gratification of drives. The *ego,* almost entirely conscious, develops from experience and reason, interacts with the environment and acts as a check on the *id.* The *superego,* largely unconscious, is the restraining force, the conscience, and consists of the attitudes and moral codes absorbed unwittingly in childhood. Neuroses, then, result from a lack of harmony among the *id, ego,* and *superego.* Neuroses can develop as a result of lack of gratification of the instinctual drives (the *id*), or as a result of a weak *ego* structure and thus poor reality contact, or as a result of a too severe *superego,* which is the product of too strenuous socialization of the child at the hands of harsh, punitive parents.

In spite of the magical, fable-like quality of the theory, its distinctive, widely-accepted contribution to our understanding of human behavior is the significance the theory attributes to the unconscious.

The ethical implications of this theory are of greater or lesser significance depending on how literally we accept its assumptions and principles. Probably the most crucial implication stems from the proposition concerning the instinctual drives. Freud wrote,

. . . Men are not gentle, friendly creatures wishing for love, who simply defend themselves if they are attacked, but . . . a powerful measure of desire for aggression has to be reckoned as part of their instinctual endowment. The result is that their neighbor is to them not only a possible helper or sexual object, but also a temptation to them to gratify their aggressiveness, . . . to seize his possessions, to humiliate him, to cause him pain, to torture and to kill him; . . . who has the courage to dispute it in the face of all the evidence in his own life and in history? (Freud, 1930)

According to this view, man's *finer* sentiments and strivings are only sublimations of animal instincts which lurk beneath the surface of his civilized veneer.

If this be the nature of man, then we cannot look to nature to provide us answers to our ethical question—the definition of good and evil. Traditional Christian doctrine provides an out with its supernatural definition of good and evil. But Freud rejected religion and referred to it as the "mass obsessional neurosis," and deplored society's religion-based concept of morality. Furthermore, denial, or even worse, restriction of man's nature (as viewed by Freud) leads to mental illness indicating we cannot look to the antithesis of the Freudian assumption for a solution.

Interestingly enough, much of the recent clamor against permissiveness and "life adjustment" in the schools (neither of which ever existed to any great extent in actual school practice) has been misdirected when "Progressive education" and John Dewey are blamed. (Dewey argued for an experimental, experience-centered, activity, problem-solving approach to education.) Actually the permissive, life adjustment emphasis stems largely from the Freudian influence whereby parents and teachers are admonished not to thwart or deny the expression of a child's instinctual drives or else his *psyche* will become crippled and pave the way for adult neuroses.

On the other hand, acceptance of the Freudian notion of the inherent primitive, animalistic, aggressive nature of the child leads many teachers and administrators to be preoccupied with the problem of control and discipline sometimes to the exclusion of concern over the learning process.

Another implication derives from the deterministic nature of the theory. The underlying causal factors of behavior are primarily unconscious and irrational. Man's motives are something other than they appear on the surface, and his thinking is easily distorted by inner desires and passions of which he is not aware. How then, with the minimizing of man's rational powers, with the denial of free will, can the individual be held responsible for his actions or behavior? Anna Russell catches the spirit of the problem posed by Freud's psychic determinism when she sings in her "Psychiatric Folksong,"

> At three I had a feeling of
>   Ambivalence toward my brothers,
> And so it follows naturally,
>   I poisoned all my lovers.
> But now I'm happy; I have learned
>   the lesson this has taught;
> That everything I do that's wrong,
>   Is someone else's fault. (Russell, 1960)

This view (shared with associationism) that man is the product of forces beyond his control, undercuts the basic convictions underlying democracy and democratic relations among men. Democracy just doesn't make sense (and wouldn't work) unless man is basically free, and active (and not just reactive), and capable to some degree of making rational choices and decisions and being responsible for his actions.

THIRD FORCE: HUMANISTIC PSYCHOLOGY

Throughout the development of psychology as a formal discipline during the past 60–75 years a number of psychologists have started rebellions of some importance against what they considered the dominant deterministic and analytic trends in psychology represented by associationism and psychoanalysis. Until recently, these psychologists did not represent a unified system or school. In the last few years, however, these various groups have been coalescing into an increasingly comprehensive theory of human nature, into what Abraham Maslow (1954) calls a "Third Force." This group includes the so-called neo-Freudians who emphasize man's nature as being primarily social and cultural rather than biological or instinctual; the Gestalt or field theorists who emphasize man's interaction with his environment as a unitary function which cannot be understood in a piecemeal fashion, as they claim the associationists would have us do; the organismic psychologists who, like the Gestaltists, insist on considering the individual as a whole; the perceptual psychologists and existential psychologists who emphasize the uniqueness and integrity of the individual and of his very personal and unique interpretation of his life and environment. As all of these movements place great significance on the individual human being and on distinctively human qualities (as opposed to animalistic or mechanistic qualities of the other two forces discussed above) the label *Humanistic Psychology* seems appropriate.

In contrast to the other two forces, many of the propositions of this third force stem from a study of man (as opposed to animals) and a study of psychologically healthy (rather than neurotic or sick) men. For example, A. H. Maslow, although beginning his career in the study of abnormal psychology, developed his present theories while studying psychologically healthy people and while studying the healthiest experiences and moments (which he called peak experiences) in the lives of average people.

Basic to this humanistic force in psychology is the conviction that man is essentially *good* if permitted to develop his natural humanistic qualities. Only when his nature is distorted by pathological conditions, rejecting parents, constant failure and rebuff, or a repressive culture does man become aggressive and cruel. *Good* in this context is equated with *nature,* thus anything conducive to bringing out man's inner nature is desirable. *Bad* or abnormal is anything that frustrates or blocks or denies the essential nature of man. Putting it another way, Maslow equates what we *ought* to be with [what] we *can* be, and he states further that by substituting the concept of what one *can* become for the term *ought* or *should*, the matter becomes open to empirical, scientific investigation (Maslow, 1954).

Space does not permit me to be more definitive regarding the inner nature (and thus what would be defined as desirable) in man. Writers such as A. Combs, A. Maslow, and C. Rogers do this well in their writings. Suffice it to say that research being done in anthropology, psychiatry, sociology as well as psychology is coming up with some consistent findings. For example, there is wide-spread agreement that the following are characteristics of psychologically healthy (self-actualized) people: they can be described as loving, self-accepting, well integrated, fully functioning, creative, autonomous, reality-centered, adaptable, among other characteristics.

The other two forces we have discussed have built systems describing man as he *is*. Humanistic psychology has added the dimension of looking at what man can *become*—a look at not only the *actualities* but the *potentialities* as well. Also in contrast to the other two forces which look upon man as *reactive* to the forces in the environment or to the *psyche,* humanistic psychology looks upon man as being active and having the capacity, at least to some degree, to evaluate and choose. While agreeing that human behavior is influenced by the environment and culture, humanistic psychology emphasizes that the ultimate effect of the environment and culture is in large part determined by the individual's unique view and attitudes of these external factors. That is, I am influenced by my world as I see it, not as you or anyone else sees it nor as the world may *really* be.

This view of man as having a large potential for freedom is consistent with the democratic conviction that the ordinary man given access to factual information *can* evaluate public issues with some degree of objectivity and rationality rather than as a robot conditioned to think and behave in certain ways. It is assumed that the freedom granted by democracy to the individual to make decisions is not just an illusion.

Similarly, the view of man as free and active is basic to a philosophy of education which emphasizes the development of young adults capable of rational problem solving, creativity, and critical evaluation. Applying the insights of this force in psychology (compared to those of associationism), teaching would involve facilitating learning rather than directing learning; it would involve uncovering new vistas rather than covering what is already known; it would involve asking pertinent questions rather than telling what is already thought out; it would involve helping chil-

dren learn rather than making children go through the motions of learning (Combs & Snygg, 1959).

Obviously, the ethical implications of this third force are part and
parcel of the system it proposes. Unlike the other two forces, it does not
beg the question of values. A commitment to a criterion for determining
value—that which corresponds to basic human nature—underlies the
entire movement. Some will claim that this takes the movement out of
the jurisdiction of science. Maslow argues otherwise. He claims that the
scientific approach can and should be used to develop greater understanding of man's basic nature, and thus a science of values *is* possible.
Erich Fromm writes:

> The thesis is that values are rooted in the very conditions of human existence;
> hence that our knowledge of these conditions, that is of the "human situation,"
> leads us to establishing values which have objective validity; this validity exists
> only with regard to the existence of man; outside of him there are no values.
> (Fromm, 1959)

In summary, let me make this observation. The diverse views of
human nature as neutral, evil, or good have important ethical and educational implications. Whichever view one accepts, it is apparent that man
is a highly educable creature and that his development for good or evil
can be greatly influenced by environmental conditions. But here agreement ends. If man is by nature hostile and aggressive, society through the
school must shape him by exerting stringent controls; if, on the other
hand, man's natural tendencies are for good, society through the school
can best achieve its purposes by structuring the environment in such a
way as to allow the child considerable freedom for creativity and self-
development.

REFERENCES

Combs, A. W. & Snygg, D. *Individual Behavior* (Rev. Ed.). New York: Harper
and Row, 1959, pp. 401–402.

Freud, S. *Civilization and its Discontents*. London: Hogarth Press, 1930, pp.
85–86.

Fromm, E. In A. H. Maslow, ed., *New Knowledge in Human Values*. New
York: Harper and Row, 1959, p. 151.

Maslow, A. H. *Motivation and Personality*. New York: Harper and Row, 1954,
p. 344.

Russell, A. "Psychiatric Folksong." Cited by O. H. Mowrer, "Sin the Lesser
of Two Evils." *Amer. Psychol.*, 1960, *15*, p. 301.

Skinner, B. F. *Walden Two*. New York: Macmillan, 1948, p. 243.

Skinner, B. F. "Freedom and Control of Men." *American Scholar*, 1955–56,
Winter, p. 56.

18. Psychological Theory and Guidance

Mary S. Engel

The topic assigned to me necessitates delimitation because it bears the burden of riches; one can find relevance to guidance in all psychological theories. In what follows, I shall ask you to consider some general comments about the role of theories in practice and discovery. I shall use as examples certain psychological theories, with the qualification that these are not the only ones relevant to guidance.

Theories may be regarded as more than a collection of testable hypotheses and concepts, more than abstractions poured into words which facilitate communication about human behavior. Theories, particularly in psychology, represent systems of belief about the nature of man, largely because they contain assumptions about the extent of his modifiability through experience, the qualities of his baseness, and the limits that must be placed upon his aspirations. Theories are at the same time blinders and field glasses. They define the most appropriate position of the observer and determine the fate of the data he gathers from his observations. Because in our interrogation of nature theories dictate the questions and determine if there can even be an answer, theories deserve our most painstaking scrutiny.

Theories are not the rare luxuries of academicians. To the extent that each of us holds within himself an implicit or explicit system of belief about the nature of man, to that degree we operate on some kind of theoretical basis in making decisions about children. Implicit theories about human behavior come to expression in clinical action. When we provide psychotherapeutic help within the school, we are operating on the conviction that there is "something" about two people talking that will make life better for at least one of them. Probably, each of us has some idea about what that "something" is—that which distinguishes psychotherapy from baby-sitting. Each of us has some name for the forces that make children a nuisance on rainy days. Similarly, regarding diagnosis, each of us holds a preference for categorizing people as stupid or intelligent, as creative or commonplace, as more or less in touch with publicly shared reality. On some level of explicitness we repeatedly describe and categorize people. These processes are called diagnostic when they are aided by certain clinical methods, that is, when description and categorization of people are carried out with the formal accoutrements of professional functioning.

While in clinical work theories may remain implicit, research demands a greater degree of explicitness of assumptions. To the extent that we gather observations and then cannot assign them a theoretical home, to that extent data remain like useless bricks on an empty lot, and do not contribute to the construction of a cohesive image of reality.

It is profitable then to raise the question: What are the most powerful psychological theories that have already affected the field of guidance and how are the postulates of these theories used and how might they be? It is here that I will need to be selective and to ask you to turn your attention to two names, that of Sigmund Freud and that of Hermann Rorschach. To me, both of these names stand for some of the misunderstandings of ideas. The theories of both of these men grew out of the seeds of brooding, fed on introspection and tortured self-appraisal, were laboriously tended by doubt, the obsessions of clinical unrest, and by the never-ending, inward-looking talmudic dialogue of a man with himself. These giant minds gave forth with two methods not at all unrelated and yet different in their aims of cure and diagnosis, and then their ideas were transferred from one soil to another, and it is in this process of transplanting that we must seek the answer when we ask: why does guidance not make full use of the vast and powerful implications of these unfinished theories?

It is my thesis that guidance has not made use of the potentialities of either of the theories of Freud and Rorschach and that only certain aspects of these theories are even recognized as existing, while the most challenging and also the most unfinished aspects of them are, as far as guidance and much of clinical psychology is concerned, left unused. It is my impression that when guidance talks psychoanalysis, it talks the language of the libido theory which, to be sure, is a very important aspect of psychoanalysis, but may perhaps not be its most useful aspect for guidance. Most guidance counselors' understanding of psychoanalytic theory is that it talks of the developing child in terms of certain phases that mark the shifting of sexual and aggressive energy from one zone of the body to the other, and that this development reaches a culmination both in the Oedipal phase and also in adolescence, after which, if the unworkable attachment to the parent of the opposite sex has been given up *more* than it is being clung to, then the person is on the road towards good mental health, whatever the definition of that term happens currently to be. There are other conceptions of psychoanalysis that appear in the guidance literature as well as in professional parlance. The concept of the unconscious has been made use of, and most of us would today agree that there is an aspect of motivation that is not under the intentional control of the person and that one road towards understanding it is through dreams. But I do not think that these conceptions of psychoanalysis are the most useful ones for guidance. There are others which demand our attention because they are so directly applicable and because we need them so much when we undertake the cultivation of creativity, the reexamination of the curriculum and teaching methods in light of child psychology, and when we take upon ourselves the task of educating in special classes children who are so ill that we have to teach them in groups of five or ten.

It is not sufficiently appreciated that one of the major interests of contemporary psychoanalytic theory is in the process of thought. Particularly, those who research on the frontiers of contemporary ego theory concern themselves with processes of thought as these relate to character structure. (Gardner, R., et al., 1959.) It appears indeed that there is an important relationship between larger aspects of personality organization, what we might call character, and the styles of thought that people are capable of, and which they prefer. All this has to do with delay because psychoanalysis construes the origins of thinking to reside in that infantile experience which occurs between the time of need for the mother and her eventual appearance. This temporal delay, invitable and necessary, brings with it a vague re-creation of the presence of the physically absent mother, through primitive mental processes, so that the infant, in Erikson's language, "can tolerate her absence through experiencing the sensation of her presence." Psychoanalysis says that this is how thinking begins. That is, through frustration of the need and through an initial and primitive mental activity which becomes the groundwork for memory, for fantasy, and upon which other aspects of the thought process are later built.

It is said that the continued development of mental activity that takes place during the temporal delay gives rise to certain psychological structures. These structures include not only patterns of thought—if not the very act of thinking itself—but also patterns of defense against anxiety, and habits; in other words, those recurrently present aspects of people by which we know them and *with* which or *against* which we have to teach or cure. So that when we speak of delay we do not just mean temporal delay, and we do not just mean the ability to wait until we get what we want, but we speak of structural delay—the kind of delay that the structure of a breakwater or a dam represents. The difference between temporal and structural delay may be illustrated by the example of an angry person who instructs himself to count to ten before he reacts, then he discharges his anger in the same unmodified way as if he had not waited. In this case temporal delay is ineffective because there are not sufficient structures in the personality to divert or modify the force of the discharge.

An example of the use one can make of the concept of delay comes from the treatment of a very impulsive ten-year-old, who engaged in that time-honored psychotherapeutic activity: building airplane models. While he was extremely bright and agile, he was unable to be successful with his models because his impulsivity made it impossible for him to wait until the glue dried. The therapist undertook to teach him delay, recognizing that he had little in his repertoire with which to achieve delay on his own. So when the pieces were adequately glued together, he suggested to the child a number of activities—simple ones, like going to the water fountain or coloring, activities that would make delaying easier for him and which would harness the child's energies in such a way that the repeated failures with models would turn into success and make delay worthwhile. This same child was not without structures, in the sense in which I use the term here, because he had unfortunately taught himself that when his anxiety reaches unbearable heights he must help himself by going around parking lots, making long and useless lists of license plate numbers. These lists then became precious to him in a way that no one could understand, not even the therapist, until one day the child told him that in case of war, he would defend himself by waving his list of license plate numbers at him. This habit of his provided delay, that is, it harnessed quantities of unmanageable anxiety, but from the point of view of others it seemed wasteful, annoying and even bizarre.

The clinical example above talks the language of the concept of defense mechanisms. This is an instance of obsessive-compulsive defenses having grown out of proportion, while the thought processes remained primitive to such an extent that the child could not multiply because some numbers reminded him of snakes and others of swords, and as he told us after a year and a half of psychotherapy, when you bring a sword together with a snake you make a bloody mess.

To be sure, there is a lot about this youngster that can be understood in terms of libido theory. But there is still more about him that can be helped in terms of ego theory. I would just like to restate that I think in guidance it is libido theory which is most well known, and that it is ego theory which is most useful. To put this in terms of the history of psychoanalysis, it is as if guidance tries to use the yields of a theory before the 1920's. It is as if guidance were not making an acquaintance with the gains that were made in the third and fourth phases of the theory, with the possible exception of Erickson's contributions around 1937. That is, the contributions of ego psychology, the development of which began around 1923, have remained unexploited and largely unknown in our circles. Perhaps the reason is that we do not like to know that Freud has changed his conceptualizations a number of times, about some of the most basic propositions pertaining to his most spectacular discoveries—perhaps there are some other reasons.

It is worth knowing that the emphasis of psychoanalysis upon reality, external reality, in relation to unconscious mechanisms underwent a thoroughgoing reappraisal when Freud discovered that many of the early experiences reported to him by his patients did not *happen* to these patients, but were made up by them, and that they *believed* these experiences to have occurred, until the spotlight of treatment turned itself upon these experiences and found them to be made of fancy. With this discovery, there was an understandable shifting of interest to those processes that constructed imaginary realities with such incredible conviction. It was not until the third phase of the history of this theory, particularly with the publication of the *Problem of Anxiety* in 1926, and with a reevaluation of the role of anxiety in relation to defenses, that aspects of ego functioning of most interest to us came to the foreground.

Until about 1926, Freud believed anxiety to be a toxic product, as it were, of repressed sexuality, that is, anxiety was seen as a product, or a penalty, if you will, for the non-expression of the sexual drive. But in the *Problem of Anxiety* (Freud, 1926) it was recognized that anxiety itself is a sufficiently unpleasant experience to mobilize the defense mechanisms. In other words, the role of anxiety in the theory changed from that of a product of defensive functioning to that of an agent in the operation of defenses. This change marked then the beginning of the interest in the defense mechanisms, that is, in the variety of intrapsychic ways, in the variety of structures with which people manage anxiety. With the opening up of the whole vast area of the defense mechanisms and of the thought processes we have the basis upon which ego psychology is built. In fact, the simplest way to define ego psychology is to say that it concerns the study of the defense mechanisms and of the thought processes. (Rapaport, D., 1959.)

No doubt you have recognized much similarity between some of what I have said and conceptualizations of learning theories. The rapprochement of ego psychology and learning theory, the examination of their differences and the spelling out of their similarities, was the purpose of the last years of David Rapaport's existence and because of his untimely death this reconciliation has not been accomplished.

I have said that theories deserve our most careful scrutiny and earlier I invited you to turn your attention to the names of Sigmund Freud and Hermann Rorschach, in the hope of illustrating that in guidance we do not make sufficient use of either the potentialities or the unfinishedness of these imported theories, one pertaining to treatment the other to diagnosis. In the remaining time I should like to review what has happened to Hermann Rorschach's work, as another illustration of my point. You might find it of interest to have it retold that Hermann Rorschach (1922) was actively involved in the psychoanalytic movement, particularly between the years 1909 and 1913, and that his major work, *Psychodiagnostik*, was not published until 1922. This volume, presenting us with what is now known as the Rorschach test, was woven out of a multitude of delicate threads in this man's life. One of his favorite pastimes was to try to predict people's reactions to paintings in art galleries. This is one of the threads. He wrote extensively about one of his patients who recounted how she derived pleasure from looking at the humidity spots on the ceilings. Working in a Swiss hospital, he made systematic observations of the reactions of patients to movements of a monkey—this is another thread. That he himself was an artist and that as a child he was nicknamed by his school fellows "Klecks"—which in German means inkblot—is another one of the threads. The influence of the Norwegian philosopher Vold upon Rorschach is also important because Vold studied dreams (In those days philosophers were free to study dreams and psychologists were free to study philosophy). In any event, Vold found that when he restrained the feet of his subjects, they dreamt of movement more than when not restrained, and so he began some formulations of the relationship between muscular movement and kinesthetic perception. All these threads were joined in the formulation of the Rorschach method. (Ellenberger, H., 1954.) It was meant as an avenue to the study of personality, *as an instrument for discovery*. Many this day are careful not to refer to the Rorschach as a test, but as an experiment, and although the personality theory that Rorschach evolved with the help of his ink blots certainly lends itself to classification of people, the Rorschach blots were not designed to predict college grades or to be correlated with overt behavior in complex situations. The difference between an instrument that is a *test*, and therefore has to prove its accuracy, and a *method for the study and discovery of a personality functioning* is such an enormous one, that one can only marvel at the rapidity with which we have taken the Rorschach method and turned it into a group test. All the reasons of statistical convenience are not sufficient to make up for the loss of a method that led to conceptualizations such as those concerning the variations of capacity to resonate to internal experience, optic perceptions and kinesthetic experience in relation to creative introversion, as opposed to the tendency to turn outwards to reproduce what the world has already presented. May I just remind you that until 1935 no papers on the Rorschach method appeared at Swiss professional meetings, and that it was only during the last years preceding World War II that Samuel Beck brought the Rorschach method to the United States, and that it was only in 1936 that publications concerning the Rorschach began to appear in a journal which is now called the *Journal of Projective Techniques*. So that in less than thirty years a personality theory with a brilliant start, which happened to use ink blots to facilitate observations, has now to stand up to our demands of reliability and normality of distribution of scores, and I rather doubt that the ease of handling of data that will arise from our modifications of the Rorschach method will make up for the inventions which are being cast aside.

To sum up then what I have tried to say, it would appear that there is no scarcity of psychological theories that are applicable to the business of guidance, albeit the applicability has in many cases not been worked out. I have tried to illustrate the ways in which powerful psychological theories undergo modification and re-emphasis when they are transplanted from one soil to another, and in all this there is an implicit plea not to search for newer and better theories or even to try to do without them, but to scrutinize the theories of this century more carefully, before we either dismiss them or discard them. The task of guidance is so gigantic and ranges over the entire business of the school that it cannot, because of an urge to get things done, afford to proceed to premature closure regarding psychological theories.

While guidance will find a wealth of suggestions, explanations and conceptualizations of human nature in the basic writing of Freud, or Rorschach, or many others (Werner, Spitz, Escalona, Piaget, to mention only a few), I do not think that any of these existing theories will hold an answer to some of the major dilemmas of the field. There are some confusions which beset all clinical professions, but there is one *most* crucial to guidance. This is the problem of matching services with children, the question of the demarcation of boundaries or, if you will, simply the question: where do guidance services stop? Which guidance services will be offered to whom or by whom has already been considered by Professor Landy in a recent publication. (Landy, 1963.) My point touches on some of his.

There is a group of children upon whom schools spend, on the average, over $700 per year—these are the psychotic and borderline psychotic children. (Engel, 1963.) The severity of their illness leaves little choice; if the schools are going to help them, this has to be an intensive, highly specialized help, the purpose of which is to relieve them of their psychological suffering, so they can re-enter society. And then there are other children who do not need us directly, but whom we can benefit indirectly, through interpreting scientific discoveries to curriculum builders, to teachers and to parents. But there is a large middle group, to whom guidance services are rendered with the same uncertainty with which these children are referred. We counsel them, but precisely to what purpose? For greater use of their potential? For better self-actualization? No one has yet adequately conceptualized these terms, much less has anyone been able to measure the effect of guidance upon the degree of use of potential, for we cannot even measure potential. Guidance services rendered to this middle group have few if any theoretical underpinnings.

Thomas Szasz, the Hungarian psychoanalyst, has recently accused our culture of making a myth out of mental illness. (Szasz, 1961.) He says that silently we have reclassified a host of behaviors as sick, while previously they have been seen as bad, naughty, obstreperous, immoral, or illegal. He points out that we have stretched the definition of mental illness to such width that it now includes just about all problems in living: theft, cheating, stupidity, marital discord and even malingering. Because, he says with tongue in cheek, isn't anyone who is healthy but wishes to appear sick, a candidate for psychotherapy?

It is here that guidance needs a theory of its own. Perhaps it will be hewn from what is known about child development, about the problems of instruction, and the larger realities of the school. With adequate conceptualization of what kind of help should be given to what purpose, guidance will contribute not only to its own growth, but also it will enrich all those neighboring disciplines which now feed into guidance.

REFERENCES

ELLENBERGER, H. "Hermann Rorschach, M.D., 1884–1922." *Menninger Clinic Bulletin*, 1954, *18*, 173–213.

ENGEL, M. "Public education and the 'emotionally disturbed' child." In press, *J. of the Amer. Acad. of Child Psychiat.*

FREUD, S. *The Problem of Anxiety*. New York: Norton, 1926.

GARDNER, R., et al. "Cognitive control." *Psychological Issues*, Part IV. New York: International University Press, 1959.

LANDY, E. "Who does what in the guidance program." *School Counselor*, 1936, *10*, 112–118.

RAPAPORT, D. "A historical survey of psychoanalytic ego psychology." *Psychological Issues*, Part I. New York: International University Press, 1959, 5–49.

RAPAPORT, D. "Toward a theory of thinking." In: Rapaport, D., trans. and ed., *Organization and Pathology of Thought*. New York: Columbia University Press, 1951.

RORSCHACH, H. *Psychodiagnostik*. Bern: Hans Huber; New York: Grune & Stratton, 1922.

SZASZ, T. S. *The Myth of Mental Illness*. New York: Harper and Row, 1961.

19. Psychology: A Prescriptive Science

Robert I. Watson

In a recent analysis of the dynamics of the history of the older, more mature sciences Kuhn (1962, 1963) holds that each of them has reached

From Robert Q. Watson, "Psychology, A Prescriptive Science," *The American Psychologist*, June, 1967, pp. 435–443. Copyright 1966 by the American Psychological Association, and reproduced by permission.

the level of guidance by a paradigm. In one of its meanings a paradigm is a contentual model, universally accepted by practitioners of a science at a particular temporal period in its development. With this agreement among its practitioners, the paradigm defines the science in which it operates. In a science where a paradigm prevails, one recognizes that a particular paradigm concerns chemistry, astronomy, physics, or the biological science. Illustrative in astronomy is the Ptolemaic paradigm which gave way to the Copernican paradigm, and in physics is the Aristotelian paradigm which gave way to the Newtonian dynamic paradigm, which, in the relatively recent past, was superseded by the paradigm provided by Einstein and Bohr. The great events of science which occur when a new paradigm emerges Kuhn calls a revolution.

The historical sequence Kuhn holds to be as follows: As scientists go about the tasks of normal science, eventually an anomaly, i.e., a research finding, which does not fit the prevailing paradigm, is obtained. A normal science problem that ought to be solvable by the prevailing procedures refuses to fit into the paradigm or a piece of equipment designed for normal research fails to perform in the anticipated manner. Failures in science to find the results predicted in most instances are the result of lack of skill of the scientist. They do not call into question the rules of the game, i.e., the paradigm, that the scientist is following. Reiterated efforts generally bear out this commitment to the accepted paradigm that Kuhn calls a dogmatism. Only repeated failure by increasing numbers of scientists results in questioning the paradigm which, in turn, results in a "crisis" (Kuhn, 1963). The state of Ptolemaic astronomy was a recognized scandal before Copernicus proposed a basic change, Galileo's contribution arose from recognized difficulties with medieval views, Lavoisier's new chemistry was the product of anomalies created both by the proliferation of new gases found and the first quantitative studies of weight relations. When the revealed anomaly no longer can be ignored, there begin the extraordinary investigations that lead to a scientific revolution. After sufficient acceptance of this anomaly is achieved from the other workers in the field, a new paradigm takes the place of the one overthrown and a period of normal science begins. Since a paradigm is sufficiently open-ended it provides a host of problems still unsolved. In this period of normal science the task of the scientist is to fill out the details of the paradigm to determine what facts, perhaps already known, that may be related to the theory, to determine what facts are significant for it, to extend to other situations, and in general to articulate the paradigm. In short, it would appear that the activities of normal science are a form of "working through" in a manner somewhat akin to that task which occupies so much time in psychoanalytic psychotherapy.

When a new anomaly appears and is given support, the cycle then repeats.

The bulk of Kuhn's monograph is taken up with a historical account of the events leading up to scientific revolutions, the nature of these revolutions, and the paradigmatic developments thereafter, with many familiar facts of the history of astronomy, physics, and chemistry cast in this particular perspective. It is here that the persuasiveness of his point of view is to be found. The test of the correctness of Kuhn's views rests upon the fit of his data with the available historical materials. Kuhn uses the key concept of paradigm in several degrees of breadth other than contentually defining and it is difficult to know precisely what differentiates each of the usages. Fortunately, I can leave to the specialist in the history of the physical sciences the evaluation of the correctness of his reading the details of their history and the various meanings of paradigm, for I am more concerned with what can be drawn from what he has to say about other sciences that he contends lack a contentually defining paradigm.

In all of its meanings, a paradigm has a guidance function. It functions as an intellectual framework, it tells them what sort of entities with which their scientific universe is populated and how these entities behave, and informs its followers what questions may legitimately be asked about nature.

What are the consequences in those sciences that lack a defining paradigm? Foremost is a noticeable lack of unity within a science, indications of which Kuhn (1962, p. 4) acknowledges as one of the sources for his paradigmatic concept, which arose in part from his being puzzled about "the number and extent of the overt disagreement between social scientists about the nature of legitimate scientific methods and problems (1962, p. X)" as compared to the relative lack of such disagreement among natural scientists.

That psychology lacks this universal agreement about the nature of our contentual model that is a paradigm, in my opinion, is all too readily documented (Koch, 1959, Chaplin & Krawiec, 1960). In psychology there is still debate over fundamentals. In research, findings stir little argument but the overall framework is still very much contested. There is still disagreement about what is included in the science of psychology. In part, at least, it is because we lack a paradigm that one psychologist can attack others who do not agree with him as being "nonscientific" or "not a psychologist," or both. Schools of psychology still have their adherents, despite wishful thinking. And an even more telling illustration, because it is less controversial, is the presence of national differences in psychology to such an extent that in the United States there is an all too common dismissal of work in psychology in other countries as quaint, odd, or irrelevant. National differences, negligible in the paradigmatic sciences such as physics and chemistry, assume great importance in psychology. A provincialism in psychology in the United States is the consequence, provincialism on a giant scale, to be sure, but still a provincialism which would and could not be present if a paradigm prevailed.

Before its first paradigm had served to unify it and while still in "the preparadigmatic stage" each physical science was guided by "something resembling a paradigm," says Kuhn. Since it was outside his scope, Kuhn said hardly more than this about the matter.

Psychology has not experienced anything comparable to what atomic theory has done for chemistry, what the principle of organic evolution has done for biology, what laws of motion have done for physics. Either psychology's first paradigm has not been discovered or it has not yet been recognized for what it is. Although the presence of an unrecognized paradigm is not ruled out completely, it would seem plausible to proceed on the assumption that psychology has not yet had its initial paradigmatic revolution. The present task is to answer the question—if psychology lacks a paradigm, what serves to take its place?

It would seem that it follows from Kuhn's position that whatever provides the guidance could not have the all-embracing unifying effect of defining the field in question since if it did so, a paradigm would exist. What seems to be required is some form of trends or themes, numerous enough to deal with the complexity of psychology and yet not so numerous as to render each of them only narrowly meaningful. Those which I have isolated follow:

THE PRESCRIPTIONS OF PSYCHOLOGY ARRANGED IN CONTRASTING PAIRS

Conscious mentalism-Unconscious mentalism (emphasis on awareness of mental structure or activity—unawareness)

Contentual objectivism-Contentual subjectivism (psychological data viewed as behavior of individual—as mental structure or activity of individual)

Determinism-Indeterminism (human events completely explicable in terms of antecedents—not completely so explicable)

Empiricism-Rationalism (major, if not exclusive source of knowledge is experience—is reason)

Functionalism-Structuralism (psychological categories are activities—are contents)

Inductivism-Deductivism (investigations begun with facts or observations—with assumed established truths)

Mechanism-Vitalism (activities of living beings completely explicable by physicochemical constituents—not so explicable)

Methodological objectivism-Methodological subjectivism (use of methods open to verification by another competent observer—not so open)

Molecularism-Molarism (psychological data most aptly described in terms of relatively small units—relatively large units)

Monism-Dualism (fundamental principle or entity in universe is of one kind—is of two kinds, mind and matter)

Naturalism-Supernaturalism (nature requires for its operation and explanation only principles found within it—requires transcendent guidance as well)

Nomotheticism-Idiographicism (emphasis upon discovering general laws—upon explaining particular events or individuals)

Peripheralism-Centralism (stress upon psychological events taking place at periphery of body—within the body)

Purism-Utilitarianism (seeking of knowledge for its own sake—for its usefulnesɔ in other activities)

Quantitativism-Qualitativism (stress upon knowledge which is countable or measurable—upon that which is different in kind or essence)

Rationalism-Irrationalism (emphasis upon data supposed to follow dictates of good sense and intellect—intrusion or domination of emotive and conative factors upon intellectual processes)

Staticism-Developmentalism (emphasis upon cross-sectional view—upon changes with time)

Staticism-Dynamicism (emphasis upon enduring aspects—upon change and factors making for change)

The overall function of these themes is orientative or attitudinal; they tell us how the psychologist-scientist must or should behave. In short, they have a directive function. They help to direct the psychologist-scientist in the way he selects a problem, formulates it, and the way in which he carries it out.

The other essential characteristic is that of being capable of being traced historically over some appreciable period of time. On both counts, the term *prescription* seems to have these connotations (Leibniz, 1949). It is defined in the dictionaries as the act of prescribing, directing, or dictating with an additional overtone of implying long usage, of being hallowed by custom, extending over time (Cousin, 1829; Morell, 1862; Lewin, 1935; Brunswik, 1956; Murphy, 1932; Bruner and Allport, 1940; Murray, 1961).

It is for the reason of persisting over relatively long periods of time that prescriptions can be of historical moment. In fact, in choosing the particular prescriptions with which I deal the presence of historical continuity over at least most of the modern period was a major decisive factor. If an instance of some conception serving a directive function was of relatively short temporal dimension, it was not considered a prescription. It is for this reason that some prominent trends in psychology today do not appear as prescriptions. Physicalism and operationalism are very much part of the current *Zeitgeist* in psychology but because they are relatively new upon the psychological scene, they are not considered prescriptions. Instead, they serve as challenges to utilize the prescriptions for their explanation. It is characteristic of prescriptions that modern, more specifically formulated versions of the more general historically rooted ones may appear. Empiricism-rationalism have modern descendents in environmentalism-nativism.

To arrive at a reasonably complete and appropriate categorization of the prescriptions, I carried out two separable, although actually intertwined steps. I considered the present scene, for example, in a paper on national trends in psychology in the United States (1965), in order to ascertain what seemed to characterize psychology today, and then turned to the very beginning of the modern period in the history of psychology in the seventeenth century to see if these themes were then discernible in recognizable form. In the 300-page manuscript that I have so far prepared, I can say that I find encouraging indications of the historical roots of these prescriptions somewhere in the contributions of Bacon, Descartes, Hobbes, Spinoza, Leibniz, Locke, and Newton, and in those of the lesser figures of the seventeenth century.

Turning to its directive-orientative function, it will be remembered that this theory of prescriptions is more than a classificatory system, more than a convenient means for a particular historian to order his account. These prescriptions were and are part of the intellectual equipment of psychologists. Psychologists are always facing problems, novel and otherwise. They do so with habits of thought, methodological and contentual, which they have taken from the past. This applies today with just as much force as it ever did in the past. In short, they are dynamic because psychologists accept, reject and combine prescriptions, thus thinking in certain ways, and not in others.

In the above list, prescriptions have been presented in one of the ways they function—as contrasting or opposing trends (Woodger, 1929; Jones, 1961; Brunswik, 1956). At some point in their history most of these prescription pairings have been considered as opposed, even irreconcilable for example, naturalism as opposed to supernaturalism, and empiricism as opposed to rationalism.

A summarization, such as the list gives, inevitably distorts its subject matter. Especially pertinent here is the false impression of tidiness this arrangement of antithetical isolated pairs gives. Consider the dichotomy, mechanism-vitalism. Does this oppositional way of presenting them exhaust the matter? By no means, mechanism bears relation to molecularism, and molecularism may come in conflict with supernaturalism, which in turn, relates to certain forms of dualism.

Prescriptions are by no means simple, dominant, isolated themes moving monolithically through history. In a recent analysis of the history of mathematical concepts in psychology, George Miller (1964) warns expressly against this kind of oversimplification. His treatment of what he calls the "varieties of mathematical psychology" (Miller, 1964, p. 1), that I consider to bear considerable relation to the quantitavistic prescription, is further subdivided into several categories and subcategories. As he indicates, a more extensive treatment would require still others.

Their oppositional character does lead to explication of another characteristic of prescriptions. At a time, past or present, when both of the opposed prescriptions had or have supporters, it is possible to make some sort of an estimate of their relative strength; in other words, we may speak of dominant and counterdominant prescriptions. Rationalism dominated in seventeenth-century England; Locke was nearly alone in advocating empiricism. Nomotheticism dominates today in the United States; an idiographic prescription is sufficiently viable to make itself heard in protest against the prevailing state of affairs. Hence, idiography is counterdominant.

The presence of dominant and counterdominant prescriptions helps us to see how competitions and conflict may result. Whether purism or utilitarianism dominates in American psychology today, I would be hard put to say, but we can be sure of one thing—both prescriptions have sufficient protagonists to make for a prominent conflict. Dominance may shift with time; at one time supernaturalism dominated decisively, there followed centuries of conflict and today naturalism dominates almost completely.

Although important, their oppositional nature is not always present. Empiricism-rationalism has been presented as a contrasting pair, yet at least to the satisfaction of some psychologists and philosophers of science, they have been reconciled today at a higher level of synthesis. Induction and deduction were also considered antithetical once. In actual practice today, the scientist often sees them as aspects of an integrated method which permits him to weave them together. Sometimes prescriptions, rather than being contradictory, are contrary; there may be gradations, or relationships of degree as seems to be the case with methodological subjectivity-objectivity.

Reinforcing its directive character is the fact that prescriptions sometimes are "prejudgments," presuppositions or preconceptions that are acted upon without examination, that are taken for granted (Whitehead, 1925; Lovejoy, 1936). Some prescriptions are characterized by their being tacit presuppositions taken as a matter of course and even operating without explicit verbalization. What psychologist today says to himself that the problem he is considering is one that I must decide whether I should or should not quantify; instead he immediately starts to cast the problem in quantitative terms without further ado. Similarly, most psychologists are monists. That many psychologists would react to being called monists with a sense of incredulity and even resentment nicely illustrates my point. We think monistically without using the term. Similarly we are apt to follow empiricistic and naturalistic prescriptions without much thought to the fact that we do so. But there was a time when the issues of quantitativeness-qualitativeness, of monism-dualism, of empiricism-rationalism, and of naturalism-supernaturalism were very much explicit issues, occupying the center of the psychological stage. Often their implicit character seems to have come about when one became so dominant that the other no longer stirred argument. Sometimes no clean-cut agreed-on solution was verbalized, instead they were allowed to slide into implicitness. A shift of interest, rather than resolution with a clear-cut superiority of one over the other seems characteristic. Old prescriptions never die, they just fade away. Naturally, at some times and to some extent a prescription became less relevant to psychology, but these are matters of degree.

Much of psychology's early history is, of course, a part of philosophy. Many of these prescriptions had their roots in philosophical issues, and are even still stated in what is current philosophical terminology as in monism-dualism and empiricism-rationalism to mention the two most obvious. I do not hesitate to use philosophical terminology because psychology cannot be completely divorced from philosophy either in its history or in its present functioning. This state of affairs is cause for neither congratulation nor commiseration. Psychology is not the more scientific by trying to brush this sometimes embarrassing fact under the rug as do some of our colleagues by teaching and preaching psychology as if it had no philosophically based commitments. They are psychology's Monsieur Jourdaines who deny they talk philosophical prose. Denying there is need to consider philosophical questions does not solve the problem. The very denial is one form of philosophical solution.

Since they were originally philosophical issues, it will be convenient to refer to some prescriptions as "contentual" problems. To bring home this point, the areas of philosophy in which certain of the prescriptions fall might be identified. Rationalism and empiricism have their origins in epistemology, monism and dualism in ontology (nature of reality), and molarism and molecularism in cosmology (structure of reality).

A major task in the history of psychology is to trace how the field individuated from the philosophical matrix. In this process, the prescriptions that served as major guidelines in the emergence of psychology as a separate discipline originally had a philosophical character, which took on a general scientific character with the emergence of the physical sciences in general, and psychological science in particular. It is in this sense that they can be referred to as philosophically contentual in character. Moreover, consideration by psychologists and others in the sciences transformed them sometimes in ways that only by tracing their history can one see the relation to their parentage.

Often the traditional terminology used herewith, for example, its dualistic and mentalistic locus has had to give way to objectivistic and monistic terminology. Confused and confusing though these terms might be, they still referred to something relevant to psychology. As they are formulated, psychologists may be repelled by "old-fashioned" air of the statement of many of the prescriptions. Justification is found in the fact that these are the terms in psychology's long history until a short 50 years ago.

Lacking a paradigm has meant that psychology looked to other scientific fields for guidance. It is characteristic of prescriptions that borrowing from other fields has taken place. Psychology's heritage from philosophy could be viewed in this manner. But there are other forms of borrowing which have entered into prescription formation. There has been noteworthy borrowing from biology, physiology in particular, signalized by Wundt's calling his work "physiological psychology" in deference to the methodological inspiration it was to him. But physics, highest in the hierarchy of the sciences, has just as often served as the model science. Psychology has had its dream of being a changeling prince. The rejected child of drab philosophy and low-born physiology, it has sometimes persuaded itself that actually it was the child of high-born physics. It identified with the aspiration of the physical sciences, and, consequently, acquired an idealized version of the parental image as a superego, especially concerning scientific morality, i.e., the "right" way for a scientist to behave.

Psychologists looked to these other sciences for methodological guidance.[1] This methodological cast is particularly evident in the prescriptions concerned with nomothetic law, inductivism-deductivism, quantitativism-qualitativism, methodological objectivism and subjectivism, and determinism-indeterminism. It follows that these prescriptions apply in varying degrees to other sciences. So, too, does the puristic-utilitarian prescription, and working through the naturalistic-supernaturalistic problem.

Some of the contentual prescriptions have counterparts in other sciences. Salient to all biological sciences are developmentalism-statisticism, functionalism-structuralism, mechanism in its various guises, and molecularism-molarism. It is also at least possible that many of these prescriptions would be found to have counterparts in other non-scientific areas of knowledge, such as literature, religion, and politics. After all, man's reflective life, as the "Great Ideas" of Adler and Hutchins and their cohorts show, has much more interpenetration into the various compartmentalization of knowledge than is customarily recognized. But to explore this further would be to extend discussion beyond the scope of the paper.

In the preparadigmatic stage of a science, a scientist may also become an adherent to a school, that is to say, he may accept a set of interlocking prescriptions espoused by a group of scientists generally with an acknowledged leader. Functionalism, behaviorism, Gestalt psychology, and psychoanalysis are representative.

The orientative character of prescriptions is also present in a school.

---

[1] It should be noted that this looking to other sciences and finding evidences for prescriptions implies that paradigmatic sciences are not denied the presence of prescriptions. Exploration is, however, outside of the scope of this paper.

As Marx and Hillex (1963) recognize, each school seems to follow a directive—you should be primarily concerned with the study of the functions of behavior in adapting to the environment and the formulation of mathematical functions relating behavior to antecedent variables: *functionalism*—you ought to study the stimulus-response connections through strict methodological objectivism; *behaviorism*—you can arrive at useful formulations of psychological principles through consideration of molar units of both stimulus and response, i.e., configurations or fields; *Gestalt* —you should be concerned with the interplay and conflict of the environment and native constituents of the disturbed personality with special attention to its unconscious aspect, *psychoanalysis*.

Salience or nonsalience of particular prescriptions characterize schools. Behaviorism is both contentually objectivistic and environmentalistic (empirical). However, the former is salient; the latter is nonsalient. Contentual objectivism is central and indispensable, environmentalism is not crucial to its central thesis. Behaviorism would still be behaviorism even if all behaviorists were nativistic in orientation.

In broad strokes based on salient prescriptions, functionalism is functionalistic, empiricistic, quantitativistic and molecularistic. Behaviorism has as salient orientative prescriptions, contentual objectivism, and molecularism. Gestalt psychology may be said to make salient molarism, subjectivism, and nativism. The salient directive prescriptions of psychoanalysis seem to be dynamicism, irrationalism, unconscious mentalism, and developmentalism.

The differing patterns of salient prescriptions of the schools serve also to make more intelligible their differing research emphases upon particular contentual problems—the functionalists with their empiricistic salience upon learning; the behaviorists with their peripheralism upon motor activity (including learning); Gestalt psychology with its molarism and nativism upon perception; and psychoanalysis with its dynamicism and irrationalism upon motivation.

There is an even broader level of prescriptions, that of national trends exemplified by the Symposium on National Trends at the XVIIth International Congress to which reference already has been made (Watson, 1965). Here greater diversity than that of the schools is expected. Instead of patterns, it is most meaningful to couch their discussion in terms of dominance and counterdominance.

Immersion in the current scene as a participant-observer, adds immeasurably to the already complicated task of the historian who is apt therefore to approach the present with a great deal of trepidation. What will be hazarded is inclusive broad, therefore, crude overall characterization of the current scene of psychology in the United States. It will serve as another exercise in the application of the prescriptive approach. Although couched in terms of a somewhat different array of prescriptions

than now is being used, for reasons explained earlier, I will quote from
the concluding summary of my paper on this Symposium:

It has been seen that national trends in modern American psychology follow
certain dominant prescriptions. Determinism, naturalism, physicalism and
monism, although very much operative, are judged to incite relatively little
opposition. Functionalism, operationalism, quantification, hypothetico-deductiv-
ism, environmentalism, and nomotheticism are likewise dominant, but there
are counterprescriptions which tend to oppose them. As for the schools of psychology, psychoanalysis, very obviously, and Gestalt psychology, less firmly,
still stand apart. Serving as counterprescriptions to those dominant in psychology are those calling for increased complexity in theorizing, for an increased
attention to philosophical matters, for general acceptance of phenomenology,
for increased attention to existential psychology and in a somewhat amorphous
way almost all of the areas of personality theory calls for counterprescriptions
of one sort or another (Watson, 1965, p. 137).

It is important to note that most national prescriptive trends have
been stated in terms of dominance and counterdominance, which reflects
diverseness, not integration. Indeed, the highest level of integration in
psychology is still that of the schools, not that of the nation. Different
patterns of dominance and counterdominance are present in different
countries. For the sake of brevity, but at the risk of oversimplification,
methodological and contentual objectivity, particularly in the form of
operationalism, prevails in the United States, while methodological and
contentual subjectivity, especially in the form of phenomenalism, does so
in large segments of Continental Europe.

It follows that patterns of dominant prescriptions characterize a
given temporal period and geographical area. When we wish to emphasize the then current intertwined pattern of dominant prescriptions as
having a massive cumulative effect, we refer to the *Zeitgeist*. The *Zeitgeist* in itself is empty of content until we describe that which we assign
to a particular *Zeitgeist*. The strands that enter into the *Zeitgeist* include
the dominant prescriptions of that time. So the *Zeitgeist* and prescriptive
concepts are considered complementary. One of the puzzling facets of the
Zeitgeist theory is just how to account for differential reaction to the same
climate of opinion. The prescriptive approach may be helpful in this
connection. Plato and Aristotle, Hobbes and Spinoza, Hume and Rous-
seau, each experienced the same *Zeitgeist* but also had idiosyncratic, non-
dominant prescriptive allegiances.

What I have said about prescriptions by no means exhausts this
complexity. Prescriptive trends fall and rise again, combine, separate, and
recombine, carry a broader or narrower scope of meaning, and enter into
different alliances with other prescriptions, change from impliciteness to
explicitness and back again, and concern with different psychological
content and its related theories. Beyond this, I hesitate to go, except to

say I am confident there are probably other as yet unrecognized ramifications. Prescriptions endure while the psychological facts, theories, and areas which influenced their acceptance are ephemeral and ever changing.

If I have stressed the directing and guiding phase of the effect of prescriptions on a scientist's thinking, it is not because of blindness to the other side of the coin, the originality of the scientist. A scientist not only is guided by but also exploits both paradigms and prescriptions. He does so in terms of his originality, and other factors that make for individuality.

My enthusiasm for prescriptions may have left you wondering whether this is all that I can see in the history of psychology. Let me reassure you at this point. The usual contentual topics of psychology, most broadly summarized as sensation, learning, motivation, and personality and the hypotheses, laws, and theories to which their investigations give rise are still considered very much a part of its history. As differentiated from philosophically oriented contentual prescriptions, it is these and related contentual topics which show that a concern for psychology is the subject matter of historical investigation. These contentual topics are the vehicles with which all historians of psychology must work. Even here there is another point about prescriptions that I might mention. There seems to be some historical evidence of an affinity between certain prescriptions and certain contentual topics, e.g., dynamicism with motivation, developmentalism with child and comparative psychology, personalism, idiographicism, and irrationalism with personality, and empiricism with learning. Individual psychologists who have been strongly influenced by particular prescriptions are apt to reflect them in their work. Although the evidence has not yet been sought, it is quite plausible to believe that, reciprocally, choice of problem area may influence allegiance to certain prescriptions. In similar vein, I suspect that prescriptions tend to cluster in nonrandom fashion. Offhand, acceptance of supernaturalism seems to have an affinity for teleology, indeterminism, and qualitativism; naturalism with mechanism, determinism, and quantitativism; nomothesis with determinism; rationalism with deduction; empiricism with induction.

To return to extraprescriptive aspects of psychology, the methods of psychologists—observation and experiment—cannot be neglected in a historical account. Psychologists' use of these methods are an integral part of that history. However, certain prescriptions, particularly those identified earlier as methodological in nature, allow casting considerable historical material in the way that has been sketched.

Any adequate history of psychology must reconsider the personality characteristics of individual psychologists and the extrapsychological influences, such as social circumstance, which have been brought to bear upon each psychologist. Can one imagine that Hobbes' psychological views were independent of his detestation of organized religion, adoration of a strong central government, and fear of the consequence of political disorders?

I would like to summarize briefly some of the functions that I consider prescriptions to serve. They provide classification and summarization through a conceptual framework which can be applied historically. Prescriptions provide principles of systematization which are related to, and yet to some extent are independent of, the particular contentual or methodological problem of the individual psychologist. They are also mnemonic devices which make it possible to summarize and convey a maximum of meaning with a minimum of words. Going beyond anything even hinted at in the paper, prescriptive theory might also help to make history a tool for investigation of the psychology of discovery, and also serve as a framework for studies using content analysis applied to historical documents.

Prescriptions are characterized by an oppositional character manifested in dominance and counterdominance, an implicit as well as explicit nature, a philosophically based contentual character, a methodological character borrowed from the other sciences, a presence in other fields, an interlocking in schools of psychology with some salient and others non-salient, a clash of prescriptions at the national level and a participation of prescriptions at the national level, and a participation of prescriptions in the *Zeitgeist*. Since psychology seems to lack a unifying paradigm, it would seem that as a science it functions at the level of guidance by prescriptions.

REFERENCES

ALLPORT, G. W. "The psychologist's frame of reference." *Psychol. Bull.*, 1940, 37, 1–28.

ALLPORT, G. W. "European and American theories of personality." In H. P. David & H. von Bracken, eds., *Perspectives in personality theory*. New York: Basic Books, 1957, pp. 3–24.

BRUNER, J. S., & ALLPORT, G. W. "Fifty years of change in American Psychology." *Psychol. Bull.*, 1940, 37, 757–776.

BRUNSWIK, E. "The conceptual framework of psychology." In O. Neurath et al., eds., *International encyclopedia of unified science*. Chicago: University of Chicago Press, 1955, pp. 655–760.

BRUNSWIK, E. "Historical and thematic relations of psychology to other sciences." *Scientific Monthly*, 1956, 83, 151–161.

CHAPLIN, J. P., & KRAWIEC, T. S. *Systems and theories of psychology*. New York: Holt, Rinehart & Winston, 1960.

COUSIN, V. *Cours de l'histoire de la philosophie*. 2 vols. Paris: Pichon & Didier, 1829.

JONES, W. T. *The romantic syndrome: Toward a new method in cultural an-thropology and history of ideas.* The Hague: Nijhoff, 1961.

KOCH, S., ed. *Psychology: A study of a science.* Study 1. *Conceptual and sys-tematic.* New York: McGraw-Hill, 1959.

KUHN, T. S. *The structure of scientific revolutions.* Chicago: University of Chicago Press, 1962.

KUHN, T. S. "The function of dogma in scientific research." In A. C. Crombie, ed., *Scientific change.* New York: Basic Books, 1963, pp. 347–369.

LEIBNIZ, G. W. *New essays concerning human understanding.* Trans. by A. G. Langley. La Salle, Ill.: Open Court, 1949.

LEWIN, K. "The conflict between Aristotelian and Galilean modes of thought in contemporary psychology." In, *A dynamic theory of personality.* New York: McGraw-Hill, 1935, pp. 1–42.

LOVEJOY, A. O. *The great chain of being.* Cambridge: Harvard University Press, 1936.

MARX, M. H., & HILLIX, W. A. *Systems and theories in psychology.* New York: McGraw-Hill, 1963.

MILLER, G. A., ed. *Mathematics and psychology.* New York: Wiley, 1964.

MORELL, J. D. *An historical and critical view of the speculative philosophy in Europe in the nineteenth century.* New York: Carter, 1862.

MURPHY, G. *An historical introduction to modern psychology* (3rd rev. ed.). New York: Harcourt Brace, 1932.

MURRAY, H. A. "Historical trends in personality research." In H. P. David & J. C. Brengelmann, eds., *Perspective in personality research.* New York: Springer, 1961, pp. 3–39.

WATSON, R. I. "The historical background for national trends in psychology: United States." *J. of the History of the Behavioral Sciences,* 1965, *1,* 130–138.

WHITEHEAD, A. N. *Science and the modern world.* New York: Mentor, 1925.

WOODGER, J. H. *Biological principles: A critical study.* New York: Harcourt, Brace, 1929.

20.   Psychology As a Science of Inner Experience

Allen E. Bergin

The field of psychology originally grew out of concerns with inti-mately human and ultimately philosophical issues. The natural history of its development from philosophy and theology (Boring, 1950) hardly requires further documentation, but central to the present thesis is the

Reprinted by permission of the publisher from *The Journal of Humanistic Psy-chology* (Palo Alto, Calif.), IV, No. 2, Fall 1964, 95–103.

assumption that psychology, indeed, came into being partly in response to the desire to explain and guide the most profound and practical qualities of human experience.

There has been a significant period of estrangement from such involvements which is indelibly marked in our history by the behavioristic revolution against the subjective and experiential (Hebb, 1960). No matter how the future may evaluate it, behaviorism and its descendants have been the life-blood of American psychology. Regardless of our current preoccupations or our investments in new pathways, it is this fact that has made the following facetious remark such a poignant commentary upon our scientific past: "American psychology first lost its soul, then its mind, and finally its consciousness, but it still behaved" (Waters, 1958).

Because of a continuing commitment to the essentials of this behavioristic trend, academic American psychology has had a tendency to turn away from issues of significance for a comprehensive science of man. It seems that the field moved away from those issues perhaps with due cause, but like the prodigal son is now returning with its hard won independence and sophistication to the basic issues of human living it once left. While an estrangement from the weightier dimensions of human experience may have been a temporary necessity during the operational-behavioristic revolution, it is unacceptable as an enduring trait if we are to treat systematically the basic problems which have been spurned as mentalistic and, therefore, misleading for an objective science. Fortunately, the repercussions of the behavioristic revolt have settled and their positive contributions have been absorbed into the main stream of psychological science. Psychology now seems able, and has shown some evidence of being willing, to move on from quarrels about proper subject matter to become a more comprehensive science of human functioning.

There is no intention here of minimizing the great contributions made by S-R psychology, but it is important to clarify their basic qualities. The primary contributions of the behavioristic and logical-positivistic traditions have been the bringing of objective, operational, and fertile theoretical *methods* into psychology. The tools of inquiry thus provided can now be applied to the problem areas long ago staked out as the province of psychology. Earlier attempts to attain objectivity by emphasis upon physiology, motor movements, or animal research has produced an objective psychology which has had great difficulty coming to terms with the major problems of a comprehensive science. Evidence is now accumulating, though not often recognised, that it is possible to have both the kind of objectivity that behavior theory strived for *and* significance at the same time *if* we accept the inner life of man as not only personally real but as subject to adequate observational methods.

THE RETURN TO THE GREAT ISSUES

While an important minority within psychology (Allport, 1961; Murray, 1959; Rogers, 1959) have stressed, for decades, the significance of subjective, inner experience, it is only recently that psychology, as a science, has begun to move again in that direction. It appears that we are on the frontier of a new breakthrough in the measurement, manipulation, and conceptualization of intrapsychic phenomena. The natural history of the field reveals periods of peak activity in areas where significant change is occurring and where the potential energy for a sustained impact is being accumulated. The rise of behaviorism and subsequent theories of learning is an obvious example. The *Zeitgeist* appears to be again on the march—toward the re-inclusion of the subjective within the explicit framework of psychology.

An even cursory review of recent theoretical statements in the areas of motivation and personality reveals an impressive contingent of proponents favoring both the elimination of methodological codes for scientific endeavors and the bringing of significant human experience within the realm of objective analysis. Unambiguous commitments to these purposes are salient features of the first three volumes of the monumental *Psychology: A study of a science:*

The results of Study I set up a vast attrition against virtually all elements of the Age of Theory Code . . . for the first time in its history, psychology seems ready . . . or almost ready . . . to assess its goals and instrumentalities with primary reference to its own indigenous problems . . . the more adventurous ranges of our illimitable subject matter so effectively repressed or bypassed during recent decades, are no longer proscribed. (Koch, 1959, p. 783; also quoted in Jessor, 1961.)

Independently of the Study I authors, many others have voiced serious concern that psychology has not attended sufficiently to its basic subject matter and that its problems demand new methods generating from its own soil. Jessor (1961) argues compellingly for an objective study of experience, an avoidance of traditional reductionism and definitions of S and R in psychological and meaningful terms (1961). Colby (1960) proclaims with equal assertion the irrelevance of most behavior-laboratory derived methods for analyzing the psychoanalytic process. Blum's (1961) substantive and conceptual work provide a stimulating example of the objectification of the subjective. It is not often that an experimentalist offers a conceptual model of the *mind* and research which stresses ". . . mental functions occurring *between* stimulus and response . . ." studied, in part, by means of *introspection*. Tomkins (1962) has creatively reformulated vast domains of psychological data and theory via a conceptual framework centered significantly upon "private" experience. His opening statement that: "The empirical analysis of consciousness has been delayed by two historical developments, Behaviorism and Psychoanalysis," could not have been more timely nor, perhaps, more significant. Holt's (1962) recent interpretation of the history of research on imagery (1962) gives strong reinforcement to this position as does Arnold's (1960) creative review of the field of emotion (1960). The mind, consciousness, imagery, emotion, all of these are the subject of renewed and vigorous attack which is depending largely upon objective operations for obtaining reports of inner, subjective experiences. All of the foregoing and more are considered by Koch (1961) in his bold recipe for a future psychology which would unify the sciences and humanities by coming to terms with the great issues of human concern within an objective framework.

The Need for a Methodology of Introspection

Perhaps the most important and at the same time most difficult problem of this increasing trend in psychological science concerns the objective study of what a person privately experiences. Thus far, it appears that there is no way of approaching this problem psychologically save via some type of introspective report. However, the most immediate association one is likely to have to this is: "Look what happened to introspection!" But what did happen to introspection? Ordinarily we think of Titchenerian introspection in this context and we must recognize that the failure of this method, its unreliability, was due more to the way in which it was used than to the method itself. The fatal assumption was that correct observation produced immediate experiences which did not differ from individual to individual. It seems clear that the re-introduction of introspection need not bring with it the attendant fallacies of the older method as we apply it to new problems. Personality inventories are a good example of such a modern application.

Historically, the quest for objectivity coupled with the unreliability of introspective reports of the Titchenerian variety served to focus attention away from direct experiencing and upon phenomena correlated or concomitant with the internal, subjectively sensed processes. This eventually led to the development of more reliable, but external, measures based upon physiological changes or motor movements which are indirect approaches to the old problem of inner experience. The failure of these methods to adequately solve the problems they were devised to attack is becoming increasingly obvious (Lacey, 1958) and is representative of the more general failure of behavioristic techniques to cope with the subjective.

Other approaches have emphasized methods similar to introspection but without acknowledging the fact. This is indicated by Boring (1953) when he asserts that the basic principle of introspection remains with us today under various aliases which range from psychophysical perceptual responses to patients' protocols. If he is correct, we might assume that it is so because the principle deals with phenomena of essential concern to a science of man and because it yields data thus far unobtainable in any other way.

The importance of reconsidering the value of introspection is attested to not only by Boring but by a great variety and an increasing number of psychologists. This can be illustrated specifically at a research level, but first let us consider the more sweeping observations being made of this particular issue. Koch (1959) notes in his Epilogue to the three volumes of the APA's Study I that "an important and quite general trend of the essays is an increased recognition of the role of direct experiential analysis in psychological science." These are psychology's systematists speaking. Carnap (1956) evaluates the method by asserting that while ". . . many of the alleged results of introspection were indeed questionable, a person's awareness of his own state of imagining, feeling, etc., must be recognized as a kind of observation in principle not different from external observation, and, therefore, as a legitimate source of knowledge." Feigl, in his comments upon the philosophical embarrassments of psychology notes this new trend with optimism if not with delight:

The reintroduction of introspection, the new concern with the phenomenal field, the clinical attention to subjective experience, the studies in social perception, etc., seem to me to indicate, not indeed a regression to an obsolete psychology, but rather an advance along the spiral . . . of the evolution of the scientific outlook (Feigl, 1959, p. 123).

Thus, an historical view reveals how the early philosophical psychology was concerned with the problems of inner experience but that it lacked empirical precision. It also reveals how the introspectionists retained formal interest in the problem but did not deal with meaningful material and did not obtain objective reliability; and finally how the behavioristic reform brought objectivity but left out the historically meaningful content. Now that objectivism is solidly part of our discipline the possibility of moving on to a fruitful psychology of experience via a modernized introspective methodology seems feasible, if we but attend to it.

The problem of measuring and manipulating experiential phenomena is not simple, however, and we must recognize, as Skinner does, the exceptional difficulty involved in coming to terms with this problem:

Behaviorism has been at least to most behaviorists nothing more than a thoroughgoing operational analysis of traditional mentalistic concepts . . . but behaviorism too stopped short of a decisive positive contribution . . . and for the same reason: it never finished an acceptable formulation of the verbal report. The conception of behavior which it developed could not convincingly embrace the use of subjective terms (Skinner, 1945, p. 271).

Skinner's (1957) own contribution to this problem does not, however, convincingly account for subjective experience either, but in fact avoids it by focussing upon verbal behavior as behavior without reference to the experience associated with it. Acting as though the inner processes do not exist does yield substantially different approaches to research and theory than if one assumes their existence and that verbal behavior has direct reference to them.

It is perhaps at this juncture that the crucial issue of this paper stands out. We do not disagree with the conviction that the only things a science can use are overt observables. Our point is a matter of emphasis, an emphasis stressing the notion that verbal behavior refers to actual phenomena and that centralizing our concern on these referred-to phenomena is more crucial than centralizing our concern on the verbal behavior, or any other reporting behavior, per se. The significance of that emphasis should not be underestimated with regard to its potential impact upon the entire domain of psychological work.

As an example, a currently important research area deriving from Skinner's position concerns the manipulation or shaping of verbal responses by selectively reinforcing them. In some research contexts, the changes in verbal behavior thus produced have been considered psychotherapeutic (Bandura, 1961; Lindsley, 1962). Let us contrast this for a moment with the research by Rogers (1960), Truax (1961; 1963), and others at Wisconsin. They have been concerned with the relationship between a number of therapist attitudes or feelings and associated therapeutic change in Schizophrenic clients. They have found significant relationships between variables such as therapist genuineness (or congruence), understanding, liking, etc., and therapeutic change as measured by indices of inner experience in the patients. Their approach utilizes both ratings which infer inner feeling states from verbal behavior and measures of the relationship as subjectively perceived by client and therapist (Truax, 1963; VanderVeen, 1961). The procedures involved and the functional relationships arrived at differ markedly from a verbal behavior analysis of the Skinnerian variety simply by virtue of acting as though inner experiences do exist and that they have a significant effect upon the functioning of both participants in an interaction. This clearly suggests that intrapsychically oriented research can add significantly to the variance accounted for in personality functioning.

It should be noted here that the therapeutic interaction is somewhat unique in that the most significant human experiencings are most salient and the need for such an analysis is thus most apparent. In fact, it should be noted that clinical psychology in general has had a significant role in the changing orientation of the whole science (Bakan, 1956). *It is possible, however, that behavior theory has been able to thrive without including inner experiences within its framework precisely because the research problems selected have been ones where such variables are not salient.*

Osgood's (1957) contribution to the measurement of subjective meaning via the semantic differential is a further illustration of the explanatory power which can be generated by applying a rigorously objective approach to the analysis of inner experience. His has been a boldly imaginative and scientifically fertile grappling with the difficulties of adequately operationalizing introspective report, an unexpected but gratifyingly fruitful response from one identified with an S-R tradition.

Psychology's New Look

The extent to which introspective reports such as those just specified are utilized in psychology is not often fully recognized. It is common practice in studies of stress, attitude change, and inter-personal perception to demonstrate that the experimental manipulation was successful by obtaining a report of whether the subject actually experienced the intended antecedent condition. It would not do, for example, to test the effects of differing levels of communicator prestige upon the amount of attitude change on communicatees without being certain that subjects would actually perceive the prestige differences as intended. This amounts to no less than a perceptual or experiential definition of the stimulus condition. Interestingly, in many of these studies the criterion or dependent variable is equally experiential and its measurement equally dependent upon introspective reports. Reports by subjects of their attitudes is just this kind of a procedure. On this basis, it is easy to see that a great portion of social psychology consists simply of the analysis of experiential factors.

The entire range of personality tests from the MMPI to the Rorschach represents attempts to sample inner experience in the hope of developing adequate predictive equations for complex behavior. Most studies of achievement motivation and of anxiety are similarly crucially dependent upon overt indices of inner referents. The entire field of perception from psychophysics to "new look" perception is related to the same problem. The objective measurement of physical stimulus intensities does not, in principle, differ from the reliable estimation of the *meaning* of social stimuli as it pertains to personal predispositions, and, in both instances, the crucial dependent variables are indexed by overt responses that refer directly to private experiences. Many other existing areas of study focus more explicitly on analyses of experience: Studies of the self, of feelings and emotions, and many experimental explorations of psychoanalytic concepts (Klein, 1958; Rapaport, 1959) can all be conceived within this framework. Self-related Q sorts are indeed, like the semantic differential, nothing more than an objectified approach to the subjective and private in one's experience.

It is not difficult to see that much of psychology has addressed itself to and is dependent upon the study of personal phenomenology. The incongruous and surprising thing is that this research is not seen in that light. If it were, it is very likely that, as the psychotherapy research cited or in the recent work of Blum (1962), some new dimensions of investigation would be added and some new concepts developed. It is conceivable, in fact, to envision much of psychology becoming re-oriented around the task of a science of inner experience simply by a change in emphasis. The groundwork is already laid in the vast research enterprises just cited.

The Need for Further Change

As psychologists have addressed themselves to basically phenomenological subject matters, even though they have been behavioristically oriented, the subject matter they have been dealing with has forced them to utilize methods dependent upon subjective reports and has forced the stretching of old theories or the developing of new concepts that are indeed very similar to the tradition of phenomenological theory building. Unfortunately most researchers have continued implicitly to operate within a behavioristic theory which is inappropriate to what is really a phenomenological subject matter.

An important re-orientation could easily come about (a) by a further attenuation of the behavioristic influence upon psychological thinking which has made it so difficult to fully realize just what we have in actuality been doing, and (b) by the explicit recognition that the data of psychology can consist of experiences, that they are primary phenomena and that overt observables can be a means of measuring them rather than that the overt observables are the only subject of study in and of themselves.

The imminent possibility of such a consummation is overwhelmingly testified to by the numerous contributions to theory and research noted above. That this is so and that it is desirable should in no way minimize or undermine the distinctive contributions of behavioristic and neo-behavioristic approaches to human and animal phenomena.

Whether one considers the rising status of concerns with inner experience in terms of developing a two-factor theory of behavior or in terms of an integration of the neo-behavioristic and phenomenological traditions, it is stimulating to realize that the acknowledgement of either as an important and substantively feasible alternative casts psychology, as a science, in a modified perspective, one which may indeed signify a movement towards increasing comprehensiveness and social significance.

REFERENCES

ALLPORT, G. W. *Pattern and growth in personality.* New York: Holt, Rinehart & Winston, 1961.

ARNOLD, MAGDA. *Emotion and personality.* New York: Columbia Univ. Press, 2 vols. 1960.

BAKAN, D. "Clinical psychology and logic." *Amer. Psychol.*, 1956, *11*, 655–662.

BANDURA, A. "Psychotherapy as a learning process." *Psychol. Bull.*, 1961, *58*, 143–159.

BLUM, G. S. *A model of the mind.* New York: Wiley, 1961.

BORING, E. G. *A history of experimental psychology.* New York: Appleton-Century-Crofts, 1950.

BORING, E. G. "A history of introspection. *Psychol. Bull.*," 1953, *50*, 169–189.

CARNAP, R. "The methodological character of theoretical concepts." In H. Feigl & M. Scriven, eds., *Minnesota studies in the philosophy of science.* Vol. II. Minneapolis: Univ. of Minnesota Press, 1956, 38–76.

COLBY, K. M. *The viewpoint of the psychoanalyst.* Paper presented at the American Association for the Advancement of Science meetings. New York, December, 1960.

FEIGL, H. "Philosophical embarrassments of psychology." *Amer. Psychol.*, 1959, *14*, 115–128.

HEBB, D. O. "The American revolution." *Amer. Psychol.*, 1960, *15*, 735–745.

HOLT, R. R. *Imagery—The return of the ostracized.* Presidential address presented to Division 12 at the meetings of the *Amer. Psychol. Assn.* St. Louis, August, 1962.

JESSOR, R. "Issues in the phenomenological approach to personality." *J. Indiv. Psych.*, 1961 (Spring).

KLEIN, G. S. "Cognitive control and motivation." In G. Lindzey, ed., *Assessment of human motives.* New York: Rinehart & Co., 1958, pp. 87–118.

KOCH, S. "Epilogue." In S. Koch, ed., *Psychology: A study of a science.* New York: McGraw-Hill, Vol. III (1959), pp. 729–788.

KOCH, S. "Psychological science versus the science-humanism antimony: Intimations of a significant science of man." *Amer. Psychol.*, 1961, *16*, 629–639.

LACEY, J. I. "Psychophysiological approaches to the evaluation of psychotherapeutic processes and outcome." In E. A. Rubinstein & M. B. Parloff, eds., *Research in psychotherapy.* Washington, D.C.,: *Amer. Psychol, Assn.*, 1958, pp. 160–208.

LINDSLEY, O. R. *Direct behavioral analysis of psychotherapy sessions by conjugately programed closed-circuit television.* Paper presented at the meetings of the Amer. Psychol. Assn. St. Louis, September, 1962.

MURRAY, H. A. "Preparations for the scaffold of a comprehensive system." In

S. Koch, ed., *Psychology: A study of a science,* New York: McGraw-Hill, Vol. III (1959), pp. 7–54.

Osgood, C. E., Suci, G. J., & Tannenbaum, P. H. *The measurement of meaning.* Urbana, Ill.: Univ. of Illinios Press, 1957.

Rapaport, D. "The structure of psychoanalytic theory: a systematizing attempt." In S. Koch, ed., *Psychology: A study of a science.* New York: McGraw-Hill, Vol. III (1959), pp. 55–183.

Rogers, C. R. "A theory of therapy, personality, and interpersonal relationships, as developed in the client centered framework." In S. Koch, ed., *Psychology: A study of a science.* New York: McGraw-Hill, Vol. III (1959), pp. 184–256.

Rogers, C. R. "Significant trends in the client-centered orientation." In D. Brower & L. E. Abt, eds., *Progress in clinical Psychology.* New York: Grune & Stratton, Vol. IV (1960).

Skinner, B. F. "The operational analysis of psychological terms." *Psychol. Rev.,* 1945, 52, 270–277.

Skinner, B. F. *Verbal behavior.* New York: Appleton-Century-Crofts, 1957.

Tomkins, S. S. *Affect, imagery, consciousness.* New York: Springer, Vol. 1 (1962).

Truax, C. B. "Effective ingredients in psychotherapy: An approach to unraveling the patient-therapist interaction." *J. Counsel. Psychol.* (In press).

Truax, C. B. "The process of group psychotherapy: relationships between hypothesized therapeutic conditions and intrapersonal exploration." *Psychol. Monogr.,* 1961, 75, No. 7 (Whole No. 511).

Van Der Veen, F. *The perception by clients and by judges of the conditions offered by the therapist in the therapy relationship.* Paper read in a symposium on "therapeutic and research progress in a program of psychotherapy with hospitalized schizophrenics" at the meetings of the *Amer. Psychol. Assn. Convention.* New York City, September, 1961.

Waters, R. H. "Behavior: Datum or abstraction." *Amer. Psychol.,* 1958, 13, 278–282.

21. Wanted: A Science of Human Effectiveness

Donald H. Blocher

In 1955 Donald E. Super, writing in the second volume of the *Journal of Counseling Psychology,* described the transition "From Vocational Guidance to Counseling Psychology." Super discussed the way in which the new field of counseling psychology had developed out of the vocational guidance movement and described some of the problems facing this emerging profession. In the almost 10 years that have elapsed

Donald H. Blocher, "Wanted: A Science of Human Effectiveness," from *Personnel and Guidance Journal,* March, 1966, pp. 729–33. Copyright © 1966 by the American Personnel and Guidance Association, Inc., Washington, D.C. Reprinted by permission.

since the publication of that paper, counseling psychology has continued to emerge, but unfortunately has not developed into the full-grown specimen foreseen by those who attended its birth. In many respects it is not unfair to say that counseling psychology has remained a promising development in the field of professional psychology for the past 15 years.

Super pointed out in 1955 that counseling psychology had not succeeded in establishing its own uniqueness. Other older groups, including clinical, educational, and industrial psychology, tended to view counseling psychology as intruding into peripheral areas of their own domains. Unfortunately, the events of the past decade have apparently done little to change the fundamental perceptions of our psychological breathren in this regard (Brigante, Haefner & Woodson, 1962; Granger, 1959; Pepinsky, Shoben, & Berg, 1960).

NEED FOR AN UNDERLYING DISCIPLINE

At least one basic factor can be identified for the failure of counseling psychology to come of age as a full-blown psychological specialty. In many ways counseling psychologists must plead guilty to the charge of intellectual vagrancy. Counseling psychology remains in large part an applied field with little visible means of support. Its intellectual diet is too often gleaned from the garbage cans of other specialties, most notably, of course, clinical psychology.

This situation arose at least in part because as counseling psychology, the field apparently outgrew the basic body of knowledge that had sustained it as vocational guidance. The goals and purposes that counseling psychology espoused went considerably beyond that which was attempted in the name of vocational guidance.

A document on the training of counseling psychologists makes the following statement regarding the goals of the counseling psychologist.

The counseling psychologist wants to help individuals toward overcoming obstacles to their personal growth, wherever these may be encountered, and toward achieving optimal development of their personal resources. Therefore, this psychological specialist is found to be working in the full range of social settings, e.g., school, hospital, business or industry, or community agency. The counseling psychologist may help individuals in their personal development while they are progressing through school, suffering the effects of illness or physical disability, changing jobs, or attempting to cope with marital situations or problems of parent-child relationships. (Thompson & Super, 1964, p. 136.)

Unfortunately, the transition into counseling psychology was not accompanied by a corresponding extension of its underlying body of theory and research. As vocational guidance, the field had employed a fairly distinct and well-organized body of knowledge about occupations and the individual differences that were associated with success or satisfaction in them. This body of knowledge in vocational behavior was generally accepted as the more or less definite province of the vocational guidance movement.

With the transition to counseling psychology, however, the field has not succeeded in broadening its foundations much beyond the former boundaries. The most important body of research produced in relation to counseling psychology has been that on vocational development. While this research has served to reorganize and reorient much of the thinking in vocational psychology, it has also emphasized the need for a broader basis that can integrate concepts in personality development, social psychology, and counseling theory.

Part of the failure to extend and enlarge its boundaries has been the inability of counseling psychology to obtain consensus about its own goals and purposes. Counseling psychology has been, as Brayfield (1961) states, a field seeking an identity. Lacking this identity, the field has been unable to organize existing knowledge or focus research to generate new knowledge in effective ways.

The same statement on preparation of counseling psychologists cited above contains this statement of purpose for counseling psychology.

At the present time the specialty of counseling psychology is approaching a state of balance among emphases upon contributions to (a) the development of an individual's inner life through concern for his motivations and emotion, (b) the individual's achievement of harmony with his environment through helping him to develop the resources that he must bring to this task (e.g., by assisting him to make effective use of appropriate community resources), and (c) the influencing of society to recognize individual differences and to encourage the fullest development of all persons within it. (Super & Thompson, 1964, p. 135.)

Considerable question seems to exist around whether a statement as vague and general as this can really provide a basis for professional identity. These goals seem equally appropriate for social workers, teachers, ministers, physicians, and others.

When pushed to define their field, counseling psychologists typically repeat certain characteristic statements. They tend, for example, to state that they want to work with normal people (whoever they are). The rehabilitation counselor, when confronted with the basic paradox of this, takes refuge in saying that he works with the normal problems of abnormal people, as though this clarified the situation. Counseling psychologists also tend to state that they wish to work with the assets rather than the liabilities of people (who doesn't?) or that they are concerned with decision-making rather than personality change. None of these ideas really seems to have provided a satisfactory basis on which counseling psychology can establish its uniqueness or around which it can organize a body of knowledge. At least it is obvious that these statements have not yet generated either a theoretical system or a body of research uniquely suited to the accomplishment of these goals.

THE CONCEPT OF HUMAN EFFECTIVENESS

Perhaps a more central idea that could more fully embrace the work of the counselor is the concept of maximizing human effectiveness. The term "human effectiveness" is, of course, a value-loaded concept. Effectiveness will undoubtedly be defined in different ways by different individuals with different value systems.

One relevant concept of human effectiveness is simply the ability to obtain long-term control over environment. From this standpoint, the effective person is able to control those aspects of his environment that are subject to control and to control his own affective responses to those aspects of the environment that are essentially uncontrollable.

Psychology at present has only a very primitive understanding of human effectiveness. Because of its preoccupation with abnormality, psychology has very few constructs that are of value even in conceptualizing the development of human effectiveness. One possibly useful set of constructs in analyzing human effectiveness would be to view it as the product of a set of behaviors that are described best in terms of constructs like *commitment, competence, consistency, creativity,* and *control.*

In this framework, the effective person is seen as being able to *commit* himself to projects, investing time and energy and being willing to take appropriate economic, psychological, and physical risks. He is seen as having the *competence* to recognize, define, and solve problems. He is seen as reasonably *consistent* across and within his typical role situations. He is seen as being able to think in divergent and original, i.e., *creative,* ways. Finally, he is able to *control* impulses and produce appropriate response to frustration, hostility, and ambiguity.

Through some such schema the concept of human effectiveness can be rooted firmly in behavior.

Final decisions about what constitutes effective behavior in specific cases will always be made by individual counselors working with individual clients. The developmental contract or meeting of the minds that results in counselor and client working toward a common set of goals to which both are committed is a fundamental condition for the establishment of a counseling relationship under any circumstances.

THE ETIOLOGY OF HUMAN EFFECTIVENESS

In a broader way, however, the general concept of human effectiveness can be used to organize a body of knowledge that can extend the boundaries of the underlying discipline in ways helpful to counselors of all value orientations. The counselor is uniquely interested in the *etiology of human effectiveness,* in the study of those causes that underlie effective living. His interest is just as fundamental as that of the psychiatrist who is interested in the etiology of pathological behavior.

A THREE-DIMENSIONAL MODEL

One way of organizing a discipline around the etiology of human effectiveness involves a three-dimensional model.

SOCIAL ROLES

The first dimension of this model relates to social roles. Every human being is confronted with a set of social roles in which he engages. He is a worker, a husband, a parent, a friend, a colleague, a subordinate, a supervisor, etc. A study of individual lives reveals the obvious fact that a person may vary greatly in the effectiveness with which he meets the varying demands of these roles. The effective worker, for example, may be a less effective friend or leader. The business executive who exercises control over the operations of a giant corporation may be totally ineffective as a husband and father. The movie star who commands the adulation of millions may be unable to perform adequately in any of a series of marital relationships.

Social roles are usually seen as structured expectations for an individual's behavior set forth by others. To a great extent this is true. It is possible, however, as Allport (1961) points out, to view the way in which an individual *interprets* and *accepts* these expectations as part of his role. The effective personality is not an "other-directed" person who merely conforms to external demands. He interprets role expectations in ways that permit self-actualization. Examples of such interpretations are those that result in opportunities for *leadership, creative or original contributions, helping relationships,* and *unusual levels of accomplishment.* Almost every person has some chance to interpret role situations in ways that give rise to these kinds of opportunities.

COPING BEHAVIORS

The situations produced by social role expectations and interpretations produce the second dimension of the model. Each such role elicits certain coping behaviors by which the individual attempts to function in the role situation. These coping behaviors may be classified in various ways according to their consequences. Those which are self-defeating or punishing are typically termed neurotic. Psychology has done a fairly good job of describing and explaining these self-defeating behaviors. Because of its relative preoccupation with the sick or neurotic, however, psychology has not adequately analyzed those coping behaviors that are reasonably effective. Studying the effective ways in which people cope with social role situations may provide an opportunity for counseling to demonstrate uniqueness. Organizing existing knowledge and generating new knowledge about effective coping behavior can extend the discipline underlying counseling into new and relatively unexplored areas.

DEVELOPMENTAL TASKS

The third dimension of this model intervenes between the first and second. It is concerned with the ways in which effective coping behaviors are acquired. This is the dimension of *developmental tasks.* Typically, clients come to counselors when *discontinuities* exist between the social role situations with which they are confronted and the coping behaviors which are available to them. The unique role of the counselor is as an expert in the nature and characteristics of developmental tasks. Some of these developmental tasks may be mastered in the counseling relationship itself. Examples of these would be, of course, those developmental tasks that involve primarily self-understanding, self-acceptance, and personal problem-solving ability. Other developmental tasks with which the client is faced must be mastered outside the counseling relationship itself. In these situations the counselor becomes an expert consultant to the client in helping him find the best setting in which he can master the relevant developmental tasks. Such situations, of course, may include the choice of a college or career, a course or a club.

The kinds of dimensions, concepts, and constructs that seem most relevant to a human effectiveness emphasis in counseling do not appear to be those which are particularly prominent in counseling psychology as the field is represented by current theory and research. The needed concepts are actually more relevant to fields such as sociology, anthropology, or social psychology. Perhaps counselors will have to look outside counseling psychology as presently constituted if they are to develop an applied science of human effectiveness.

Summary

It is possible within this point of view to conceive of an underlying discipline for counseling based upon the study of human effectiveness and organized around dimensions such as social roles, coping behaviors, and developmental tasks. These dimensions could provide boundaries within which research efforts could be focused and findings interpreted.

Much of the knowledge needed to provide the outlines for this new discipline may already exist in other behavioral science fields, particularly in sociology and anthropology. By approaching these fields with the focus supplied by such new models, counseling may be able to abstract and organize much that is significant. It may be just as relevant to consider counseling sociology or counseling anthropology as being an appropriate base for counselor education as to use counseling psychology as the appropriate umbrella. What is needed for counselor education is an organized body of knowledge about the development of human effectiveness. The pursuit of this knowledge will take the counselor wherever it leads, whether that domain be called counseling psychology or something else. For counselor educators, if this be treason to counseling psychology, let us make the most of it.

References

ALLPORT, G. *Pattern and growth in personality.* New York: Holt, Rinehart, and Winston, 1961.

BRAYFIELD, A. H. "Counseling psychology: some dilemmas in the graduate school." *Journal of counseling Psychology,* 1961, 8, pp. 17–19.

BRIGANTE, T. R., HAEFNER, D. P. & WOODSON, W. B. "Clinical and counseling psychologists' perceptions of their specialties." *Journal of counseling Psychology,* 1962, 7, pp. 225–231.

GRANGER, S. G. "Psychologists' prestige ratings of twenty psychological occupations." *Journal of counseling Psychology,* 1959, 6, pp. 183–188.

PEPINSKY, H. B., Shoben, E. J., & Berg, I. A. "The current status of counseling psychology." *Report to A. P. A. Education and Training Board.* 1960, Mimeographed.

SUPER, D. E. "From vocational guidance to counseling psychology." *Journal of counseling Psychology,* 1955, 2, pp. 3–9.

THOMPSON, A. & SUPER, D. *The professional preparation of counseling psychologists.* Report of the 1964 Greyston Conference. New York: Teachers College, Columbia University, 1964.

SECTION FIVE

The Social Sciences,
Anthropology and Sociology

THIS section begins with an article that surveys the scope of the social sciences. In the remaining selections, two specific social sciences—anthropology and sociology—are examined, with one more—economics—as the focus of Section Six. Whether or not the personnel worker perceives social reconstructionism as part of his role, the study of the social sciences is important, because each client[1] carries with him his unique set of social learning acquired as a human being functioning within a given social system.

Sociology as a distinct social science is barely more than a century old. As such, it examines, for example, how changes in social structure affect human behavior, how conflicts between the values and mores of a society reflect and influence social change, and how man invents and adapts to systems of social organization. For obvious reasons, the professional with responsibility for performance of the guidance function has an obliga-

[1] And counselor, we might add. For an excellent exposition of the influences of culture upon counselors, see Norman Kagan's "Three Dimensions of Counselor Encapsulation," in *Journal of Counseling Psychology*, 11, No. 4 (1964), 361–365; and C. Gilbert Wrenn's "The Culturally Encapsulated Counselor," in Mosher, V. *et al. Guidance: An Examination* (New York: Harcourt, Brace, and World, 1965), pp. 214–224.

tion to study the methodology of sociology and to be aware of its assumptions and major findings. Hansen and Jones, in their respective articles, explore in detail the potentially profitable interchange between guidance and sociology.

The sociologist assumes the existence of causal relationships between variables of social systems and the behavior of groups of individuals. Thus, he is not concerned with why one individual becomes a juvenile delinquent except insofar as that individual is representative of a sub-population in which conditions maximize the possibility of the development of a delinquent sub-culture. Similarly, only to the extent that a particular client's problems represent the influences of certain social *patterns* or other variables will sociological knowledge be appropriate and useful.

In the initial selection Kenneth Boulding explores the interrelationships of several disciplines in the social sciences and humanities. He asks whether the existing structure of the division of the social sciences into fields such as sociology, anthropology, political science, economics, and the like may not operate to hinder seriously the study of the social system as a totality. The question is relevant to the point raised in the introduction to Section Two regarding the assignment of articles to sections in the present book. The somewhat arbitrary overlapping nature of the distribution of areas of study over the current structure of "disciplines" may also be a major factor in what seems to be irresponsibility on the part of some practitioners of the helping professions when they disavow either "emotional" or "learning" problems because "That's not my area of concern."

In his vice-presidential address to the American Association for the Advancement of Science[2] Boulding also decrys maintaining the myth of nonparticipation of the scientist in the empirical world he studies[3] and calls for explicit recognition by the social scientist of the changes he brings about in the social system as a consequence of studying it. The presence of much relatively accurate folk knowledge is, further, a blessing in disguise for the

[2] The American Association for the Advancement of Science is the body that commissioned C. Gilbert Wrenn's monumental *Counselor in a Changing World* (Washington, D.C.: American Personnel and Guidance Association, 1962). A postscript to this book, "A Second Look," written by Wrenn several years later is included in Section One.

[3] Compare this with Dreikur's description of the psychological uncertainty principle in Section Two.

social scientist—a blessing because of the potential sustenance for the sciences and an impediment because every man then is an "expert" on social structure and problems.[4]

> If we want to navigate a satellite or produce a nuclear weapon, we do not call in the old wives. In social systems the old wives, or at least their husbands, are called in all the time. Creating a peaceful world, abolishing slums, solving the race problem, or overcoming crime and so on are not regarded as subjects for scientific technology but are regarded as fields where a pure heart and a little common sense will do all that is really necessary.

Ruth Landes relates school counseling to the total cultural indoctrination of the child in a brief article entitled "An Anthropologist Looks at School Counseling." The problem of incomplete or incompatible learning among minority groups in different subcultures is examined as it relates to the role of the counselor. She offers nine practical suggestions on this subject which are derived from the assumptions of cultural anthropology.

Cultural anthropology is the branch of that science probably most relevant to counseling. The subject matter of the cultural anthropologist is culture, "that complex whole which includes knowledge, belief, art, morals, law, custom, and any other capabilities and habits acquired by man as a member of society." Landes speaks from an anthropological point of view, where counseling is seen as part of the social apparatus that transmits culture to the younger or maladaptive member of society and thereby assimilates them into the mainstream of functional adult life. The counselor is culturally bound, and the service he performs is the very pragmatic one of assisting members of society to prepare for and adjust to the existing social arrangements and to internalize certain critical social values and behavior patterns. Such a view of counseling may not win wide acceptance in the face of the humanistic contention that counseling is a liberating process and facilitates the transcending of culture. Nevertheless, a glib denial should not be made of the powerful and subtle conformity-inducing elements in the very structure and process of counseling. The selection by Hansen, which follows Landes' article, speaks to the point cogently.

[4] A perfect illustration of this impediment is evidenced in the composition of President Lyndon Johnson's committee to study the etiology of violence. There was not a practicing social scientist in the group!

In many ways, anthropology is the most ambitious of all the social sciences. It seeks to explain all human activity, including philosophy and science, in terms of its function for the preservation and continuation of the society in which it is found. In examining the myriad variations of social patterns and customs existing in human societies, anthropology provides the perspective necessary for transcending culture and for understanding phenomena such as racial and national differences in human behavior. For the counselor in an urban, pluralistic society such as ours, the perspective and insights of the anthropologist can be of considerable assistance.

The title of Donald Hansen's article, "The Indifferent Intercourse of Counseling and Sociology," implies that personnel workers barely have begun to expand their perspectives and promise by borrowing from sociology's wide store of concepts. Hansen seeks to remedy this by proposing the beginnings of a "counseling sociology" and a "sociology of counseling." The former would focus on the counseling relationship as a social process, while the latter would study the impact of counseling and guidance on society and vice versa. By proposing specific applications of sociological concepts to the client-counselor relationship and posing significant questions about the function *and* possible *dysfunction*[5] of counseling in modern society, Hansen convincingly demonstrates that indifference to sociology is costly to any counselor. The reader will be interested in another of Hansen's articles, "The Responsibility of the Sociologist to Education" (*Harvard Educational Review*, Vol. 33, p. 312–325), which is in large part a repetition of the selection printed here, but which includes an excellent comparison and synthesis of interactional theory in sociology with existential philosophy in terms of their common implication for the fields of guidance and education.

In the next to last selection, Carl Weinberg reiterates the charges made by Hansen and goes on to sketch briefly five areas in which applied sociology can make significant contributions to educational and guidance practices. By analysis of demographic factors and individual adjustment, role expectations and role conflict, the adolescent subculture and the social structure of the

---

[5] Carkhuff and Truax, in their article in Section Three, discuss empirical evidence for the negative effects of counseling.

school, sociology has a highly important and long neglected place in the preparation of the educator and the counselor. Carl Weinberg has recently published a book, *Sociological Aspects of Guidance* (New York: Free Press of Glencoe, 1968), which appears to be one of the best attempts thus far to cross-fertilize the fields of sociology and guidance on a systematic basis.

Jones, an eminent sociologist, offers an analysis of aspects of the sociology of guidance and makes the point—often overlooked by critics of the helping professions—that guidance had developed as an institutionalization of historically omnipresent helping-functions that were carried out in large part on an informal basis by parents, friends, clergy and others. The development of a body of professionals to perform the guidance function is a logical and necessary concomitant of the shift from a *Gemeinschaft* to a *Gesellschaft* society. These terms represent roughly the concept of change from a folk-rural-sacred to an industrial-urban-secular society. Jones makes an excellent case for the fusion of sociology to guidance on the basis of the importance of the social systems under which we live for the individual life organizations of all of us. He points out the dangerous tendency to assume that all maladaptive behavior is a product of individual defect, when in fact much maladaptation is exhibited behaviorally precisely because individuals *are* "average or normal" and thus are ready to accept the reassurances about reality offered by the system during the process of socialization. Maladaptation occurs when the very reassurances are discovered to be unrealistic. The importance of this phenomenon in understanding student activism, for example, can hardly be minimized. The counselor should be the last to ask the question, "What's wrong with those kids?" without asking at the same time, "What's wrong with the social system?"

22.   Dare We Take the Social Sciences Seriously?

Kenneth E. Boulding

The title of this paper is a rhetorical question, designed to arouse specific expectations in the hearer. It is not couched in the language of science, but the language of oratory. It is indeed as inappropriate to this august gathering as a chorus girl at the first Thanksgiving dinner. I chose it deliberately, however, because it illustrates in its very form and style the problem with which I wish to struggle.

Science is one subculture among many in our society. That is a statement in the rhetoric of science itself. The concept of a subculture is a concept of the social sciences, not of the world of literature and oratory. I would find it hard to preach a fiery sermon or make a rousing political speech addressed to a subculture. It is an ugly word and in some sense an ugly concept. It involves what might be called a Copernican stance on the part of man, standing off from his own activities and his own society and observing them in Olympian detachment. I once happened to be with a group of anthropologists at a conference on the fourth of July. In the evening the fireworks were beginning to go off in the local park and one of them said, "Let's go down and see the tribal rites." The implications of this remark are profound. The anthropologist stands apart even from his own culture. The ordinary citizen probably never thinks of the fourth of July celebrations as tribal rites, any more than a tribe thinks of tribal rites as tribal rites. The citizen is unself-conscious about his national holidays and his national allegiance. The social scientist begins to see these as special cases of general principles. He participates in his own society as a participant-observer and so inevitably begins to have values different from a participant.

All the sciences are themselves a part of the system which they study. All scientists are participant-observers in their own systems. In the physical sciences, and to a somewhat lesser extent in the biological sciences, it is possible for a time to maintain the myth of nonparticipation, and to suppose that the scientist simply studies an empirical world which is not affected by the fact that he is studying it; even in the physical sciences, however, this myth has had to be abandoned, in the justly famous Heisenberg principle. Increasingly the scientist is creating the universe which he studies. Physicists are producing particles unknown in nature. Chemists have produced elements unknown in nature and innumerable new compounds. The biologist produces new hybrids, new

From: Kenneth E. Boulding, "Dare We Take the Social Sciences Seriously?," *The American Psychologist*, Nov., 1967, pp. 879–887. Copyright by the American Psychological Association, and reproduced by permission.

genetic arrangements and may shortly begin to intervene in genetic evolution on a massive scale. Our knowledge of ecology is likely to change
the whole ecological system of the earth.

Social sciences are dominated by the fact that the social scientist and
the knowledge which he creates are themselves integral parts of the
system which is being studied. Hence the system changes as it is studied
and because it is studied. There can be no myth of an unchanging universe with the scientist acquiring abstract knowledge about it. Economists are no longer interested in merely observing and predicting the
course of the business cycle, they are interested in controlling it, even in
abolishing it. The development of polls and sample surveys has profoundly changed the political system and the way in which political
decisions are made. Anthropologists unquestionably have contributed
substantially to the downfall of empire by revealing the cultural and
artistic achievements of so-called primitive peoples. Aesthetically, indeed,
in the twentieth century one might almost say that Africa has defeated
Greece, and for the first time in human history, as a result of the spread
of communication, a world style is emerging. The peace researchers are
aiming not merely to understand the international system but to transform it through the explicit understanding of it, as economists have transformed the economy.

If science is a subculture it must have a value system. What characterizes and distinguishes one subculture from another is its value system,
that is, a set of legitimated preferences. A subculture consists of a set of
people having something in common. They may have certain physical
characteristics in common. They may have certain technologies in common. Each person in the set may have a common body of knowledge and
skill. There may be a common language, a common vocabulary, and
certain common life experiences. All men, however, or nearly all, have
two legs, reproduce with approximately the same technology, communicate with each other through some sort of language, have a common age
pattern from birth to babyhood, childhood, adolescence, adulthood, old
age and death, and grow up in some kind of a kinship structure. What
differentiates the cultures and subcultures of mankind is uncommon
knowledge, knowledge which is common to the members of the subculture but which is not common to the rest of mankind, and uncommon
values, that is, sets of preferences which members of the subculture have
in common which differ from those outside it. Americans like raw power,
masculinity, democratic institutions, coffee, hot dogs, and french fries,
whereas the Japanese like ceremony, technical skill, green tea, and raw
fish.

Every subculture, furthermore, has an ethic, that is to say, a value
system for evaluating and legitimating preference systems. It is the possession of a common ethic more than any other characteristic which

differentiates one culture from another and even one subculture from another. It is not enough that throughout the subculture there should be a wide preference, shall we say, for beef as over against ham. To a considerable extent, what creates the common preference is an ethic, that is, preference for preference systems in which beef is preferred to ham, and a feeling that those preference systems in which ham is preferred to beef are not themselves to be preferred. When there is an ethic there is a strong tendency for the preferences of different individuals to converge. Whether there is a dynamics of convergence which itself produces the ethic or whether the ethic produces the convergence we need not now inquire.

A scientific subculture is like all others in that its constituent members share certain preferences and likewise an ethic. Again, whether the ethic came first and created the preferences, or whether the preferences, by converging, came to be common and so implied an ethic, is hard to determine. Probably both processes have been at work. Thus, in its European origins the scientific subculture can well be regarded as a mutation from reformed (and counterreformed) Christian culture, and one which took over many of the ethical preferences of the culture out of which it grew. Without denying the debt of modern science to the Greeks, to Islam, to the Chinese, and to the Jews, and without implying any ethnocentric superiority, for the random element in these processes is strong, the fact remains that it did not grow up as a separate subculture producing a self-sustaining expansion of knowledge either in Athens or in Baghdad, or in Peking or in the medieval ghettoes. Its founding fathers, Galileo, Copernicus, Kepler, Newton, Boyle, and so on, were products of a predominantly Christian culture and themselves for the most part accepted an ethic which was derived from it. More than that, it was Christian culture in its more puritan aspects, a culture in which Luther had challenged successfully traditional outward authority and in which innumerable writers hymned the praises of veracity, simplicity, purity, and the testing of truth in experience. This may be one key to the mystery of why science originated in Europe and not in China, which is still a major mystery of history.

Thus it can be argued that the ethic of the scientific subculture in considerable measure originated outside it. Just as Christianity as a cultural phylum may properly be regarded as a mutation out of Judaism, with some hybrid qualities, but inheriting the ethical system out of which it grew, so science can be regarded as a mutation out of Christianity, again inheriting in part the ethic of its parental matrix. Once a subculture gets under way, of course, it differentiates itself as a social species from its surroundings and it begins to develop ethical systems of its own. Science is no exception to this rule. The idea that the scientific culture is exempt from ethical principles is one which will not stand up to a moment of examination. These ethical principles, however, are fairly simple. There is, in the first place, a high preference for veracity. The only really unforgivable sin of the scientist is deliberate deception and the publication of false results. The career of any scientist who has destroyed his credibility in this way is virtually over.

Along with the preference for veracity goes also a strong preference for truth. These are not the same things. Veracity is the absence of deceit and truth is the absence of error. There is a profound epistemological difference between these two phenomena. The deceiver usually knows that he is deceiving, although there is, of course, the phenomenon of self-deception. The man whose image of the world is in error obviously does not know this, for if he knew it he would not hold this particular view. The testing of error, therefore, is a much more difficult problem than the testing of deceit, and most of the aspects of the technology of science are methods that we might almost call the rituals for the detection of error. Error is detected by the falsification of predictions. This involves the comparison of two images. An inference of the future derived from the basic image of the world which is to be tested is then compared with an image of how the future turned out once it had become past. If there is no disappointment, that is, if the two images coincide, no error is detected, so the failure to detect error does not necessarily imply that no error exists. If the two images do not coincide, that is, if there is disappointment, then error of some kind is detected. The error might be, of course, in either of the two images and a large part of the technology of science is devoted to insuring that the error is not in the image of the past. This is done by refinement of instrumentation, careful recording, quantitative measurements and so on. There must also be defenses against error in inference, that is, in the way in which the image of the future is derived from the basic image of the world. If both these sources of error have been eliminated and there is still disappointment, the scientist is forced to revise his basic model or theory. It has been by this means fundamentally that science has progressed.

It should be pointed out, however, that the method by which the scientific subculture discovers error is not different in essence from the method by which error is detected in the folk culture, that is, in the ordinary business of life. We find our way to a meeting by folk knowledge, not by scientific knowledge. We had an image of where it was in our minds, we had an image of the future in which a meeting was happening, and if we had gone to the wrong place, or the right place at the wrong time, error would very soon have been revealed. It is by this kind of elimination of error that we find our way around town, that we find our way around in our personal relationships, and even how we learn to drive or to ski. The thing which differentiates science from folk culture is not the method of eliminating error, but the complexity of the systems which are imagined, the refinement of the expectations and the refinement of the records by which disappointment is tested.

The social sciences differ from the natural, even the biological sciences, in that there is a good deal of quite accurate folk knowledge about the system which they study, that is, the social system. Our folk knowledge of physical or biological systems is accurate as far as it goes. In finding our way around town there is no necessity to know that the earth is a sphere, and the flat earth, which is the folk image, is quite adequate. Similarly, it is folk knowledge which enables us to procreate children without any necessity for knowing about the details of fertilization and mitosis. In these areas, however, the scientific subculture is sharply differentiated from the folk culture. If we want to navigate a satellite or produce a new drug or a new hybrid, or even explode a nuclear weapon, we do not call in the old wives. In social systems the old wives, or at least their husbands, are called in all the time. Creating a peaceful world, abolishing slums, solving the race problem, or overcoming crime and so on, are not regarded as suitable subjects for scientific technology but are regarded as fields where a pure heart and a little commonsense will do all that is really necessary. Either we have no really explicit concept of social systems at all, or we regard knowledge about social systems as something which can be achieved in the ordinary business of life. In the case of simple social systems, this is true. In the case of complex systems, unfortunately, it is totally false, and many of our failures and difficulties arise from this fact. We have very little concept of what might be called social astronautics. Social astronauts who have to operate the complex social systems are sent into social space with what is the equivalent of the image of a flat earth.

There is a certain implication in the title of this paper that we do not take the social sciences seriously. This seems like rather a brash assertion when we reflect, for instance, that economics has a good claim to be the second oldest of the sciences (after physics), having reached its fundamental theoretical formulation in 1776 at the hands of Adam Smith at a time when chemistry was still floundering in the phlogiston theory, biology and geology had not gone beyond taxonomy, the theory of evolution was 100 years off, and sociology, psychology and anthropology as separate sciences were hardly thought of. Economics, furthermore, has had a substantial impact on economic policy, not all of which has been necessarily good, but in which one can detect a continual increase in the sophistication with which the economy is guided. The English Poor-Law of 1834 may have been unnecessary and a false deduction under the circumstances of the time from what were essentially sound principles. The record of free trade is fairly impressive even if it is somewhat ambiguous, and the Keynesian economics has undoubtedly scored resounding victories. One has only to compare the miserable failure of the 20 years after the First World War with the at least moderate success of the 20 years after the Second World War to see what difference a more sophisticated approach to economics and to economic policy has been able to make.

Judged by their impact on society, the other social sciences do not look so good. The record of industrial psychology, for instance, is not one in which one can put unbounded confidence. It has been naïve about the more subtle aspects of the social system; it is not altogether exempt from the accusation of having corrupted its principles for the sake of its masters (Baritz, 1960). Even here there has been a learning process at work, and the surprises and the disappointments, such as the "Hawthorne effects," have at least detected a certain amount of error and contributed to an overall learning process. Clinical psychology and psychiatry likewise can only be counted as minor successes. There is not much evidence that recovery from mental illness is markedly affected by any kinds of treatment. Psychoanalysis, whatever its virtues, is much too expensive to deal with the mass problem. Our knowledge of the learning and maturation processes in the human being is still extremely primitive. It is quite possible, for instance, that child-rearing practices based on Watsonian behavioral psychology may have actually done a great deal of damage both to individuals and to the society. The alternative methods of Dr. Spock are much more agreeable, but again we really know very little about their overall impact. All the experimentation with animals, important as it is, has not thrown much light on the complexities of the learning process when it involves the use of language and symbols. One may certainly be permitted to doubt whether all the rat psychology of the last 50 years has contributed anything toward the improvement of social policy even in the field of education. This of course is not to say it should not have been done. In exploring the tree of knowledge every promising limb should be followed at least to the point where its end is clearly in sight. One cannot help the impression, however, that in this matter we have not found the main trunk and that until we do so we will continue to be frustrated.

In even hinting that we do not take the social sciences seriously I have no intention of belittling the large mass of important work which has gone on in them and which continues to go on which has already produced a major impact, as I have suggested in a recent essay (Boulding, 1966). Nevertheless, there are legitimate causes for dissatisfaction, both with the organization of the social sciences, with the amount of work which goes into them, with the quality at least of some of its work, and by the absence of an adequate vision of the future.

The disciplinary and departmental organization of the social sciences at the moment has unquestionably arisen in response to need. There is nothing intrinsically wrong with specialization; it is, indeed, a necessity.

The days of the Renaissance man are over and no one could be expected to cover even a small part of the field of the social sciences. Nonetheless, there are good reasons for raising the question as to whether the existing types of specialization and especially the existing departmental structure is not now a handicap rather than a convenience. One reason for raising this question is that the social sciences are not really separated from each other by different levels of systems in their subject matter. Crystallography is separated from physiology by a very sharp difference in the level of the systems which are being studied, even though there no doubt may be fruitful interaction between them. Sociology, economics, political science, and anthropology, however, are not distinguished by any great difference in the level of the systems which constitute their subject matter. In a real sense, they are all studying the same thing, that is, the total social system. The only real distinction of systems levels seems to be the difference between small systems and large. The social psychologist and the psychologist, for instance, are concerned more with the study of small systems, the sociologist and the economist more with the study of larger systems. Even this distinction, however, cuts across the existing fields and departments.

There is, of course, a difference between the disciplines in the social sciences in what might be called the focus of abstraction. The basic abstraction of economics is the phenomenon of exchange, and economics could well be defined as the study of how society is organized through exchange and how commodities and other exchangeables are produced and consumed. In dividing up the study of particular social institutions those tend to go to economics which operate mainly in an exchange environment, such as banks, corporations, businesses, and the exchange aspects of the household as a spending unit. The political scientist focuses on the abstraction of the threat, more or less legitimated. He studies how society is organized through threats, legitimated by political institutions. In apportioning for study particular institutions and organizations the political scientist tends to concentrate on organizations which have the tax power, and which can obtain revenue by a legitimated threat system. Of these, of course, the national state is the chief, and so the study of the international system as the interaction of national states likewise usually falls in political science. Sociology has a less clear focus of abstraction, but in practice there is a tendency for it to concentrate around those aspects, institutions, and organizations of the social system which are concerned primarily with what I call the integrative system, that aspect of society which deals with status, identity, legitimation, loyalty, love, and their opposites, in which society is organized through the common recognition of status and community. In dividing up the institutions among the disciplines, sociology tends to get things like the family, the church, philanthropic and welfare organizations, informal groups, and so on, which are primarily institutions of the integrative system. Sociologists themselves will probably dispute this characterization, arguing that they deal mainly with the social and organizational structure of all social institutions. In some sense, however, each science can study any particular object from the point of view of its focus of abstraction.

The status of psychology in the social sciences is somewhat confused. It is a loose collection of largely unrelated disciplines, ranging from physiology of behavior on the one hand to clinical psychology and psychiatry on the other. Its relation to the other social sciences is rather like that of physics to chemistry. The person is in some sense an "atom" of the social system, and psychology has the task both of describing the imput-output relationships of the person as a black box, but also perhaps of opening the lid of the box to some extent and increasing knowledge about the system which is inside. Social psychology is more clearly a social science. Its basic abstraction is that of role rather than of the person, the role being thought of as a node in a system of inputs from other roles and outputs to other roles. The role occupant does not even have to be a person, it may be a machine or an animal, though roles which are occupied by persons have centrality in the social system which other roles do not.

Anthropology is the aristocrat of the social sciences and somewhat aloof from the others. Traditionally it has studied small societies in their totality which has meant in practice for the most part the study of primitive societies. Its methods are looser, it has less theory, in some ways it stands closer to the humanities than to the social sciences, and acts as a bridge between the two. It has some ambition to study complex total societies. Here, however, it runs into a difficulty that it does not have a methodology complex enough to deal with the complexities of advanced societies.

We should not leave this very brief survey without noting the place of history, geography, and linguistics, and perhaps the field of communications, all of which also stand a little uneasily between the social sciences and the humanities, and perhaps in consequence are undergoing certain transformations. The business of history is to build up an image of the past by the study of the deposits of the past. In a broad sense it straddles all the sciences, as it reaches back into cosmology, palaeontology, archeology, and so on into the history of literate societies. Geography likewise straddles all the sciences, as it studies the relations in space through geomorphology, through plant and animal ecology, through human ecology. Communications science is again a growing field with one foot in art and literature on the one side and coming through linguistics, semantics, into the physiology of speech and hearing. Running like a horizontal line through the whole spectrum we have philosophy, general systems, epistemology, ethics, and so on, which stand on a somewhat different systems level from the particular disciplines.

When one looks at the disciplines in terms of their subject matter it is clear that physiology, for instance, is a study in a very different kind of system from economics, but it is not clear that economics is studying a very different kind of system from sociology or even from political science. One does not have to jump from this proposition to the conclusion that departments of economics, sociology, and political science, and so on, should be abolished, and their respective professional associations merged. Nevertheless, the question must be asked whether the existing structure does not at many points seriously hinder the study of the social system as a totality, and whether it does not operate to prevent the development of that general social theory which the nature of the system itself would seem to require.

It is when we look at the overall information collection processing apparatus of the social sciences, and the theory-testing procedures which depend on this apparatus, that we find the greatest source of dissatisfaction. The situation is best, perhaps, in economics, where in the last 30 years or so we have developed a system of economic statistics and carefully collected sample data, which is at least adequate for gross purposes, such as economic stabilization. Even here, when we come to such problems as the impacts of changing technology of the economy we find that the overall data are very poor indeed and we have to rely on what is essentially journalism or interesting stories about fancy machines. We also do not know enough about the distribution of income or about the impact on distribution of overall government policies at all levels. Compared with the information systems of the other sciences, however, these are relatively minor defects. A recent work (Bauer, 1966) has spelled out in considerable detail the deficiences of our present information system, even on the national level.

At the international level the situation is much worse. The information collection and processing apparatus of the international system is not only inadequate, it is corrupt; it is not merely a zero, it is a minus. It is an enormous apparatus designed, in fact, to produce misinformation and to prevent feedback from inadequate images of the world so that the whole organization of the international system becomes organizationally schizophrenic, that is, the existing images of the world are confirmed no matter what happens. Information is collected without any precautions about sampling, it is processed by a system which has strong value filters which tend to filter out anything which challenges the prevailing image of the world. The one possible exception to this gloomy picture is the information apparatus of the United Nations and the related agencies, where at least the representatives of national states are exposed to each other's points of view, and where an international secretariat collects and processes information with at least a world bias. The United Nations, however, is a pitifully small organization, and though we get a lot out of it for what we put in, what we put in is so little that it cannot achieve major changes in the system. It is not surprising, therefore, that the international system is by far the most costly and the most dangerous element in the whole world social system. It costs about $150 billion a year and it produces a positive probability of almost total disaster.

One can cite many examples of policies of government in which the failure to recognize that what was involved was essentially a social system has led if not to disaster at least to gross inefficiency. Flood control is a famous example where the attempt to treat floods as a purely engineering and physical problem instead of as a parameter in the social system has led to what may be disastrous interference with the whole ecological system of the river basins and has built into the system positive probabilities of very large-scale disasters. Floods are not a problem of a river but are indeed part of its normal way of life. They are a problem only to people and the absurd attempt to "conquer" the rivers is likely to lead to increasing disasters as people build on flood plains which cannot be protected from a hundred-year flood.

One could extend the list substantially of areas of social policy where we have made serious mistakes because we have neglected the social systems aspects of the problem, and treat social systems as if they were physical systems. Urban renewal has been thought of in primarily physical terms, and as a result has broken up communities and may easily have worsened the problem of poverty. Road building has been done largely in terms of cement, not in terms of people. Agricultural policy has been designed in terms of commodities, and while its byproducts have been favorable, from the point of view of technical development, it has done very little, again, to solve the problem of agricultural poverty. Even welfare policies, like social security, though they are obviously a part of the social system, have not been designed with any overall concepts of the dynamics of society in view, but are designed rather as measures to relieve immediate problems rather than to develop a long-range program of social change. The critics of society, unfortunately, do not seem to be much better informed than its defenders. They have romantic notions about revolutions or about how to change the existing power structure. They tend to preach and lament rather than to develop accurate and testable images of social dynamic processes. It is not surprising that under these circumstances social reform has so often proved disappointing. The prohibition movement is perhaps the most striking example of a large grass roots movement for social reform which failed of its objective and perhaps even made the problem worse than before because of its naïveté about social change. Whether the current reform movements are really much better only the future will show. They may be luckier than the prohibitionists, but one wonders if they are really more sophisticated.

I have suggested elsewhere almost as a kind of fantasy to illustrate the magnitude of the problem that if we made a study of the "sociosphere," that is, the total sphere of the world social system, with the same degree of seriousness with which we study the atmosphere we would need a world network of social data stations analogous to the network of weather stations. These social data stations would be engaged in a constant collection of data from their local areas by carefully sampled statistically significant methods and would transmit this data to a central agency for processing in the form of maps, indices, distributions, and other statistical images. The need for this is particularly great in the international system. It is great also however in many aspects of social policy. The information processing capability of the modern computer opens up a whole new epistemological field. It is by no means absurd to suppose, for instance, that all the records of the human race might be codified in a single computer and then searched to reveal hitherto unsuspected patterns. What we are looking for in all the sciences is repeatable patterns. We can think of the social system as if it were a four-dimensional structure, three dimensions of space and one of time, a structure which may have strong random elements in it but in which also non-random patterns can be perceived. In a structure of such complexity, however, the pattern requires complex images, complex inferences, complex predictions, and complex instruments of perception if predictions are to be compared with reality. At the moment neither our theoretical structures, nor our inferences, nor our predictions, nor our perceptual apparatus and instrumentation in the social sciences are in any way adequate to measure up to the complexity of the social system. In this sense we do not take the social sciences seriously. We are using salt spoons to clear away snow drifts and reading glasses to study the structure of molecules. It is not surprising that up to now our results have been ambiguous.

We are still left with two further questions: One, could we take the social sciences seriously, and two, should we do so. I would answer both these questions with a cautious affirmative. There certainly seems to be no reason why our theoretical structure, our inferences, and our perceptual apparatus should prove intractable to improvement, if we set our best minds on the problem and if we were prepared to devote economic resources to the kind of instrumentation which, say, the nuclear physicist now demands. The network of social data stations which I suggested above would probably not cost more than a billion dollars a year and the return for this investment might be enormous in terms of disasters avoided, stable peace established, and development fostered. By and large, the social sciences have not been ambitious enough to want to study the sociosphere as a totality. They have been content with the kind of professional advancement which comes from the adequate processing of small pieces of information. They have not had the larger vision of the study of the sociosphere as a totality. Economists have perhaps come closest to this but they are handicapped by the limitations of their own abstraction, and as a result have been unable to deal satisfactorily even with such problems as the process of world development.

That we could develop much more realistic images of the sociosphere can hardly be denied. The question whether we should develop such images or how far we should develop them is not so easily answered. We cannot assume in any of the sciences that the development of more realistic and complex images of the world leaves the human value structure unchanged. Our image of value and our image of fact are symbiotic. They are part of a single knowledge structure and it is naïve in the extreme to suppose that they are independent. The view that science or any other knowledge process is simply the servant of existing folk values is doomed to disappointment. Science is corrosive of all values which are based exclusively on simple epistemological processes. The natural sciences have created an image of the world in which ghosts, witches, and things that go bump in the night are so little valued that they have withered and died in the human imagination. Biology has created a world in which the folk ideas of racial purity can no longer survive. Similarly, the social sciences are creating a world in which national loyalty and the national state can no longer be taken for granted as sacred institutions, in which religion has to change profoundly its views on the nature of man and of sin, in which family loyalty and affection becomes a much more self-conscious and less simple-minded affair, and in which, indeed, all ethical systems are profoundly desacralized. There is a deep and seemingly unresolvable conflict between the ethic of science on the one hand, and the ethic of the American Legion, the United States Department of Defense, the Communist Party, the John Birch Society, the Jesuits, and the Jehovah's Witnesses on the other hand. One method by which these conflicts have been resolved in practice has been the remarkable human capacity for holding two incompatible images in the head at the same time. Up to a point these incompatibilities are even creative. It is hard, however, for an astrophysicist to be a Jehovah's Witness or for a biologist to be a racist, and it may become hard for a social scientist to be a good Russian Communist or even a 100% American liberal without strong mental reservations.

The real problem of the impact of the social sciences on the folk culture or even on the literary culture that is dominant in the international system, is that it operates in the same system as that of the folk or literary culture in which it is imbedded. Social science presents much more of a challenge and a problem to the politician than do the physical or biological sciences. In the case of the latter it is possible to maintain the fiction that the scientist should be on tap but not on top. The scientist, in other words, gives power but not values. He is merely a servant of values which are derived from other parts of the social system. In the case of the social sciences this myth is harder to maintain. It is not without reason that southern senators and the patriotic societies distrust the social scientist, for at this point there may be deep conflict between the values which are created and sustained by folk images of the world and the values which both create the social sciences and are fostered by them. It is true, I think, of all scientists that when they become the servants of power they lose an essential element of the ethic of science itself. Here lies the fundamental dilemma. The power structure pays for the sciences, and if the sciences are to survive in any society they must find a niche in the power structure, either purchasing power or political power. How, however, do we find a niche in the power structure which does not confine or corrupt its occupant? The classical answer to this problem has been the concept of the university, a niche, as it were, specially designed to protect its occupants against the very power structure which has created it. In earlier days the church or the monastery provided such a niche. Whether niches like this can be created within the structure of government itself is one of the unsolved problems of our day. The National Science Foundation, the National Institutes of Health certainly represent an attempt to find an answer to this problem. Whether we should institutionalize the social sciences still further within this framework and create, say, a National Social Science Foundation, as is proposed (Carter, 1966), is a problem which troubles the judgment and consciences of a great many who are concerned. The cloud of the "Camelot" fiasco hangs heavily over the relations between Government and the social sciences, and foreshadows all too clearly the possible shape of things to come. It could well be that the kind of knowledge which would result from taking the social sciences seriously would turn out to be more threatening to traditional values and institutions even than the H bomb and bacteriological weapons. The folk knowledge itself, however, will be quite incapable of dealing with this problem, simply because it would itself represent a social system of enormous complexity. It looks therefore as if only the social sciences themselves could solve the problems which they themselves might create, which looks suspiciously like the principle that another little drink will cure drunkenness. Until we have drunk deeper of this particular spring, however, the dangers of a little learning may be all too apparent.

References

BARITZ, L. *The servants of power.* Middletown: Wesleyan University Press, 1960.

BAUER, R. A., ed. *Social indicators.* Cambridge: Massachusetts Institute of Technology Press, 1966.
BOULDING, K. E. *The impact of the social sciences.* New Brunswick: Rutgers University Press, 1966.
CARTER, L. J. "Social sciences, where do they fit in the politics of science?" *Science,* 1966, 154, 488.

23.   An Anthropologist Looks at School Counseling

Ruth Landes

The social anthropologist's sphere of study is the entire culture of any given society, and analytic comparison of it with others to deduce generalizations about social behavior and development of the human race. In this perspective, formal education in the United States is one institution and set of traditions that mesh into the whole patterned civilization of American society; and counseling is a special mode of education.

Then, how does an anthropologist view a school counselor's job of fostering pupils' "normal development"? What is this normality? What goals are the proper pursuit of school guidance?

To social anthropology it is logically improper to conceptualize a "normal person" but it is proper to conceptualize traditional or prevailing standards of normality and of deviation in particular societies, which are carried by members of these societies. Members carry them upon being taught to do so by authoritative persons, with the knowledge and the responsibility defined by the parent culture. In anthropological theory, personality is shaped by the dynamics of a particular culture interacting with genetic potentials of the newborn, the whole mediated by indoctrinated adepts called parents, teachers, clergy, police, friends.

This means that the "child," conceptually, is a novice in culture who progresses towards adeptness or maturity as specified by the culture, meaning, by the determinations of parents and other teachers. By this system of thought, only adepts or adults are responsible for "normality," not the child as is suggested by phrases about "normal and abnormal children."

According to these concepts, children may learn well or ill. Since

From: Ruth Landes, "An Anthropologist Looks at School Counseling," *Journal of Counseling Psychology,* X, Spring 1963, pp. 14–17. Copyright by the American Psychological Association, and reproduced by permission.

learning is shaped preeminently by the culture or social environment (viewed both as external and as internalized in thoughts, emotions and habits), it is possible to hypothecate that much bad learning results from improper exposure to particular standards of normality. Learning, in the comprehensive sense of acquiring a culture, is measured by established norms of channeling success and failure, by the achievement and maintenance of status and by its loss, by neurosis, physical disease and creativity. Normative emphases and appearances vary around the globe. The theoretical position is expressed classically in Ruth Benedict's *Patterns of Culture* and in Alfred L. Kroeber's *Configurations of Culture Growth*. These studies argue that each people's tradition evolves upon a limited base of selected human potentialities in temperament and talent, inferred from analytic comparisons of many human societies; and that each selection follows a particular culture's bent that integrates aspects of the total life into a characteristic "pattern" (in Benedict's term) or "style" (in Kroeber's term). Kroeber goes on to reason that not more than 2 or 3 per cent of human creative potential is given opportunity by any culture; but that without culture there would be no realization of human gifts at all.

Supported by biological and behavioral sciences generally, anthropologists hypothesize that human potentials for learning are practically limitless, if learning conditions are suitable. To the anthropologist, learning conditions include all of life's circumstances in a given society, around the clock, education in formal public schools being only one set of circumstances.

Studies of school performance, initiated in the classic work of Otto Klineberg and continued by Allison Davis and others, show that Negro and Indian pupils fall below American "middle-class" norms in discriminatory surroundings, like the Jim Crow South and the tribal reservation, but improve markedly in favorable surroundings, as after moving from rural to urban schools and from southern to northern schools. Similar reasoning can be applied to learning by women. Women resemble a minority in our society because demands of our traditional equality conflict with other values and practices in women's lives and reduce women's incentives for public achievements. Yet now the equality principle affects ever more profoundly the lives of females so that more girls and women must foster appropriate ambitions, though the only choices of prestige are in men's careers.

SUGGESTIONS ON SCHOOL COUNSELING

Practical suggestions for school counseling programs flow from assumptions of cultural anthropology.

1. Since norms of conduct are taught a child first by his parents, who continue to teach through daily living, the school must develop active associations with parents, on school grounds and *out* in their neighborhoods and homes, through teachers, counselors and school social workers. California and New York schools find that, for instance, Spanish-speaking children can be taught more readily when their parents are school-taught, though this has nothing essential to do with so-called "bilingualism." It has to do with the fact that the school world is already familiar to the elders, though usually under conditions of segregation. California teachers, who complained of Mexican-American pupils generally, made the point that the satisfactory ones were children of former pupils, who thus had a head start in the school culture. New York City's Board of Education releases school personnel as field coordinators for work with Puerto Ricans and American Negroes in their home areas. The writer completed 2 years of training educators, under one California school system, in how to reach Mexican-American parents; the fortunate results included parents' soaring participation in school conferences, PTA programs and school bond issues. When school activities reach beyond buildings and grounds, all parties learn about opportunities, responsibilities and needs; and the gains mount among pupils and teachers.

2. Counselors and teachers must learn carefully the subcultures and perhaps the languages of the groups they counsel and teach. Even the English spoken at home by low-status groups, like rural Negroes and Okies, is in great part a foreign language. It voices an alienated subculture that must be understood before it can be led to support educational communication. Details of each family must be known, regarding education, occupations, marital status, religion, regional origins, for these determine a child's responses to school.

3. Individual counselors and other educators should each learn his own cultural background and family antecedents in systematic detail, in order to understand his own behavior with those of other origins. The writer has worked with many educators and social workers in this connection—all parties observed that such knowledge clarified disturbed exchanges with pupils and parents when the disturbances rested on differences of cultural origin. Thus, "apathy," for example, gets understood as a *creative* social mechanism in *particular* situations of prejudice rather than as personal insolence or stupidity. This training requires access to a cultural specialist, especially in sections of sociocultural variety, high transiency, desegregation and integration. Schools in southern California, for example, may have annual pupil turnovers of up to 70 per cent, showing different ethnic strains, and teacher turnovers of 30 per cent or more.

4. The interests of the child *and* of his parents should be observed carefully in school recommendations, whether the proposals concern

study programs or something else. "Observed" includes literal watching, even silently. People tell a great deal apart from, or despite, words. Words that come from authority can be alarming to any group. What is communicated through such observation marks useful guide-lines. For example a high school counselor complained of his distress that a Mexican-American girl refused to transfer to the enrichment program he recommended. He had directed her to get the approval of her father, an unschooled man with a flourishing taco stand. When she failed to report, the counselor asked the girl why and she answered, "My father says he doesn't know and that I don't have to transfer anyway." A house visit revealed that neither the parents nor the girl welcomed the emotional isolation that the scholastic advance would create; parents and juvenile peers felt they would be unable to talk with the girl afterwards, and she felt the same.

This does not mean that school standards should not prevail. It does mean that fresh tactics are demanded for showing all parties the extent to which the recommendation is of general benefit.

5. School staff should be clear about boundaries and modes of evincing responsibility as these are defined by the group from which the pupil comes. The frequent counseling device of asking a child, "Now, what shall we do?" to correct some wrong, falls flat with a Mexican, Negro or Okie boy. These children are accustomed to sharp demarcations of authority by generation, sex and status. In none of these groups does an adult ask a *child* to make a decision, though such a query may be proper among some American Indians in particular connections. To the receiving group of low or minority status, such school action is suspect and irresponsible. It arouses confused behavior which is recognized at school under rubrics like "hostile . . . apathetic . . . ," etc. Knowing the boundaries of authority and responsibility, and the modes of enacting their ranges in particular cultural groups, are vital for these cultures differ so significantly in details as to determine success or failure in school relationships.

6. Provide or demonstrate models of work and action for the desired ends offered to pupils, parents and school staff. Limitations of time and staff mean heavy reliance on printed materials; these should include novels, poems and reproductions of fine works in arts, sciences and other humanities. Such models stir emotionally charged convictions that inspire counselors and teachers to carry on. One integrated California junior high school trained its Mexican-American pupils (in a traditionally segregated town) to teach conversational Spanish to classmates, who were almost entirely Anglo-American whites. This provided so effective a model of competence, decency, and respect that parental and adolescent gang hostilities vanished, local newspapers carried unprecedented stories of appreciation, and the school won a national award.

7. The conceptual "normal curve of distribution" should be forgotten in counseling pupils of backgrounds unfamiliar to the particular counselor. This is because the curve sets a negative frame that cues counselors' expectations, and the expectations inevitably reach pupils and parents. New York City's "higher horizons" programs among Puerto Rican pupils, originally scored very low on standard tests and curves, report the superior achievements of the pupils under judiciously enriched guidance of these pupils and their parents.

8. Counselors must attempt to personalize and individualize the educational relationship. Teaching is more than putting information into a brain or machine and waiting to see the outcome. Teaching, like loving, must nurture the desire to carry on. This is what educators call motivation. Our mass industrial society and our massive professionalization carry grave liabilities of depersonalization and anonymity. The human creature does not flower without strong specific social orientations and recognition; the pupil of minority or alien status is often confused anyway as to what school and he can do together. Responsible personalizing elicits surprising responses in teacher and pupil, which carry enthusiastic and creative solutions to questions like what job or study course should be advised or to questions about how delinquent symptoms can be redirected.

If we consult simpler societies, including 19th century pre-industrial ones, we find that personalizing was extended responsibly and fruitfully to treating even such divergent and eccentric personalities as we now consider neurotic and psychotic. Innumerable independent reports over centuries document how American Indians kept their berdaches (respectable male homosexuals or male transvestites) and their extreme visionaries in the community, putting on them responsibilities of their divergencies, and so permitting them to be useful, content and "adjusted." Berdaches cultivated arts and other male visionaries cultivated war and hunts. Russians provided similarly for the so-called village idiots, as recorded in novels of Tolstoi, Dostoievsky, Turgenev. All persons hunger for respect and status, and this is what honorable social usefulness allows.

9. A final suggestion is that counselors and teachers be trained to assume responsibility towards pupils and to manifest this without expressing hostility. As the adolescent approaches the adult generation, at high school and junior college, many counselors and teachers show him strong competitiveness. Teachers and counselors so driven are often unaware of their actions, but pupils are amply aware of the sexual and sadistic overtones. Doctrines of permissiveness in child-rearing have questioned firm assumption and disciplines of responsibility by adults. The counselor's or teacher's uncertainty about his own responsibility does

not advance teenagers' learning and motivation but actually injures the trust needed to advance learning and ambition. Dependence on a competent teacher, at any age, characterizes man's genius. Want of this responsibility wastes school facilities and destroys the goal of education.

24. The Indifferent Intercourse of Counseling and Sociology

Donald A. Hansen

The words "counseling" and "psychology" go together like pubescent lovers; they are seen linked together in all the acceptable places, and even in some of the shadier. Counseling is nothing if it is not psychological.

"Counseling" and "sociology," however, are almost strangers: less incompatible than indifferent, they seem happily unconcerned with one another's comings and goings.

But counseling is carried on within dynamic social networks; counselor and counselee each brings, to their private hours, meanings and values that cannot be understood apart from social contexts. If the counseling process is to be fully comprehended, these meanings and values cannot be ignored, any more than society can be ignored if the individual is to be understood. Without social perspective it is impossible to fathom the counseling situation, the counseling movement, and even counseling techniques and theories.

Yet sociology and counseling remain strangers when they meet. For its part, sociology (using concepts rather than glass) is ever busy grinding and polishing new lenses to look at the world. Each new focus reveals intricacies and excitements in places before grown dull: new fields need not be sought, for those already examined with less perfect lenses provide new variety and reward.

Counseling, for its part, is myopic: It can scarcely see beyond psychology. Other behavioral disciplines are rarely discerned, and then only as sources of information to be used in predicting client behavior and development. The information is useful—but it is only one of many contributions social sciences can make to counseling; it is useful, but too often by the time the information reaches the counselor, it is distorted or drained of vitality (Warner, 1949; Hollingshead, 1959).

From: Donald A. Hansen, "The Indifferent Intercourse of Counseling and Sociology," *Journal of Counseling Psychology*, X, No. 1, 1963, 3–13. Copyright by the American Psychological Association, and reproduced by permission.

Sociologists, for example, have discovered many ways in which families from laboring classes usually differ from white-collar families, and have specified ways in which an individual will behave differently in various groups. Such discoveries could be valuable to counselors, but the unfortunate fact is that sociology is passive in offering this information; the sociologist appears little interested whether counselor or client benefits from his findings. He lets others carry his ideas, and pays little attention to the way they are carried; he allows the insensitive, but articulate, typewriters of the popularizers to deliver his message. The result is shabby, and counselors are left to feed on second- or third-rate sociology.

Counseling needs sociologists who are their own interpreters, who pursue the counseling implications of their findings and theories. The need is for those who know what they are talking about, and who know where their knowledge is weak, to *tell* what they know and don't know. To meet the need counselors must induce the word-bound sociologist to speak his mind and to speak it clearly.

The need is not totally unrecognized. Miller's (1961) significant volume is strongly devoted toward sociology in its portrayal of the cultural foundations of the school guidance movement. The 1960–62 Commission on Guidance in American Schools included sociologists as well as educators, and stimulated Wrenn's (1962) incisive analysis of *The Counselor in a Changing World*. But Wrenn's book is small, and the problem he tackles is a giant; a good deal of help, from many quarters, will be needed to bring the giant down (Barry & Wolf, 1957; Humphreys and Traxler, 1954; Warters, 1960; Rogers, 1951; Mathewson, 1962; Skinner, 1948; Rogers, 1961). Other counseling theorists must become aware that sociology can do far more than tell of the world outside counseling offices. If encouraged, it can intimately study counseling itself.

From one perspective, sociology can focus *within* counseling, turning its lenses on counseling relationships, processes and evaluation. With such focus, sociology would perform much as counseling psychology does today; it is appropriate, then, to call this approach "counseling sociology."

From another perspective, sociology can focus *on* counseling, and attempt to understand counselors and the counseling field in their social contexts. This "sociology of counseling" would turn its lenses on the relationship between counseling and society: it might examine counseling's influence on society; the social functions of counseling; the influence of social movements and change on the counseling movement; the effects of the social milieu on counseling perspectives and theories.

In brutally simple terms, sociology, from the one perspective (counseling sociology) might ask counseling, "What can I do to serve you?" From the other perspective (sociology of counseling) it might ask, "What, in the name of society, *are* you, and what are you up to?"

This paper suggests only a few dimensions of the broad fields that might be surveyed by these two eyes of sociology.

COUNSELING SOCIOLOGY

One of the pressing themes in the sociological tradition is the relationship of the person to other persons and to the collective society. This theme is similarly crucial to counseling. Even though sociology seeks generalization where counseling seeks causal explanation in a *specific* case, the sociological perspective is highly pertinent to counselors' theories of human behavior, and even to theories of counseling practices and relationships. Indeed, underlying this paper is the idea that the counseling theorist and researcher who is sophisticated in sociology will generate practice and theory that are more adequate to the real world and more easily operationalized and tested. This idea is supported by at least the following three facts of counseling.

The client in his daily life is involved in social situations. He brings elements of these diverse social situations to counseling sessions, and may switch from one social referent to another in making his responses. In switching social referents, the client also switches frames of conceptual reference. Though psychologists are greatly talented in perceiving this switch of reference, and though they have made idiographic studies of this switch, sociology has developed an array of concepts which might be used in nomothetic studies, to gain insight into the general counseling processes. Particularly useful is the array of concepts developed in interactional role analysis, as represented by E. Goffman (1959), and Arnold Rose (1958) and brought to maturity by George Herbert Mead (1934).

The client returns to his normal social life while much of the therapy of counseling is still at work. Perhaps the greatest changes in the client occur after the counseling session, as the individual interacts with others in his normal daily life. Sociology can serve counseling well through analysis of the individual's outside life, particularly through insights about interaction with significant others and significant social structures.

Sociology can help evaluate the therapeutic effect of changing the individual's social situation or removing the individual to another situation. The work of the counselor might indeed be extended outside the walls within which it is confined by current counseling theory. Milieu therapy, in which the individual is placed in an entirely new social situation which is controlled by the therapist, is one of the most promising developments in current therapy, from a sociological perspective. It might be just as fruitful to explore the potentials of structuring the individual's environment to a lesser extent, through change of jobs, change of family relationships, counseling with entire families and change of significance groups. Though counselors are moving in some of these directions today, many move in ignorance of the substantive and conceptual riches sociology has gathered in the past thirty years; riches that might help counselors to make the move more successfully, and to determine success or failure of their efforts (Bell & Vogel, 1961; Cavan, 1959; Faber, 1960; Hill, 1959; Hill & Hensen, 1962; Parsons & Fox, 1952; Tizzard & Grad, 1961).

The counseling situation is not just a one-to-one relationship between "counselor" and "client," but is indeed a full-fledged social situation. Meanings and values are shared by the two persons, each a complex human being rooted in social situations beyond that in which he is engaged. This fact is recognized to some degree, in most counseling theories, especially that of Rogers. Rogers' system possesses genius in treatment of the individual as a whole, semi-autonomous being, and in placing the individual in the most simple of social situations without taking his social reality away from him. (Yet, Rogers, as other theorists, fails to account for the individual as a *social* being, in the full sense of the word. At the close of the relationship, the individual may be left without awareness of his *social* responsibility, and without being sensitized to the social consequences of his behavior. He may be fairly at ease with himself, but completely inept or immature socially (Green, 1946).

These factors of the counseling relationship underline the importance of social perspectives to the counselor's work and theory (Cicourel & Kitsuse, 1960). Counseling is not just a relationship of socially insulated individuals—it is an interpersonal relationship, and both persons are *social* beings, each carrying a world in his head and heart.

SOCIOLOGICAL CONCEPTS AND COUNSELING RESEARCH

Sociology is pertinent to theories and practices of counseling, and is no less important to counseling research and evaluation. It possesses, in varied states of development, numerous conceptual frameworks, concepts and propositions, that offer counseling a wealth of ideas and methodology; perspectives that might help counselors move away from the simplified cause-effect relationship they apparently seek in evaluating their work.

Examples: Promising Concepts. Space will allow description of only a few of the applicable concepts. The listing is incomplete, and the description not exhaustive, for each concept deserves more than one full paper. Most quickly:

1. The concept of "functional autonomy" (from social groups) suggests the importance of systematic investigation into the significance groupings of the individual client. The concept is an old one in sociology (and, with somewhat different referents, in psychology), but has been reworked most adequately by Gouldner.

2. The concept of "covert culture," borrowed from psychoanalysis, and modified by sociology (Rose, 1958), can return to counseling with new sensitivity. It suggests there may be substitutions, not only at an individual level, but also at the social level. If the individual is unaware of the social substitution, he may feel greatly out of tune with society, even though, in reality, he is closely attuned.

3. A similar false sense of being out of tune with society may be identified with the concept "pseudo-mores," which refers to mores that are subscribed to verbally, but not in action (Rose, 1958). The individual in modern society, for instance, feels guilty about masturbating, even though it is a most common practice among his contemporaries.

4. Disaster research suggests the concept of "emotional room" (Hill & Hansen, 1962), which refers to the opportunity within a family or group for an individual to express emotional disturbance. If one member of a family, for instance, is severely upset following a crisis, another individual may postpone his expression of disturbance until the first one heals. Then the second one may "suddenly" fall ill.

This concept is highly related to the insight in sociology that roles are situational and that an individual may be allowed new strength through assignment of a new role. This new strength, however, might be temporary, and might help the individual only within his new situation. Evaluation of the effect of counseling on an individual, then, is necessarily a long-term process and must be made of the individual in a number of social roles, and not only the role which immediately follows his release from the counseling relationship (Foote, 1951).

Disaster research also suggests a lack of responsible roles outside the counseling situation may be the precipitating factor in bringing on disturbed behavior (Hill & Hansen, 1962).

5. The same body of research suggests the concept of "therapeutic community," or the "thereapeutic family," in which the individual sufferer is in a "healing milieu." Indeed this healing milieu may even be a society of fellow sufferers who help him out of his own difficulties by sharing his hardships (Fritz, 1961).

Example: Group and Structure. One final concept deserves particular attention in both sociology and counseling. This is the distinction between "structural" and "group" (or "personal") relationships. This distinction was first made in sociology almost a century ago, but only recently received the insight that renders it relevant to the counseling situation.

The full pertinence of this insight for counseling is not yet obvious, but it seems the distinction might apply throughout the counseling process. That counselor and client react both to structural and interpersonal situations is recognized implicitly in the concept "rapport." "Rapport" generally evades precise definition, but attempts to conceptualize it suggest that it is a movement from a highly structured relationship (doctor-counselee) to a group or an interpersonal relationship (benevolent and competent friend-needy friend). According to this conception, the pair moves along a continuum, from a structural relationship to an interpersonal (group) relationship.

Recently, Francis and Stone (1957) suggested that this distinction between group and structure refers not to a continuum, but rather to two continua, composed of a duet of ever-present variables. If both group and structure operate in a relationship, at the same time, it is quite possible that high rapport be established, even though the structural aspects of the relationship are predominant. For example, brothers who are army officers act in one structural relationship when enlisted men are present and in another structural relationship when they are alone. Yet, at the same moments, the most profound personal relationship may flow between them. Or, when a young man talks with a young woman at a cocktail lounge, certain actions are expected in the structural relationships imposed by the physical and social setting. He sits attentively forward, smiles his best, keeps his body and legs in pose, and touches no more than her hand or shoulder. The structural expectations he responds to are quite different from those held when they are drinking in the young man's apartment—yet the personal relationship may not vary between the two situations.

It may be obvious that a client may react quite positively to structural as well as personal relationships with his counselor. A girl in treatment for two years said, "I know my therapist likes me as a person. I can tell him everything and accept him as a friend. But I want somebody to talk to that I'm not *paying*." This girl wasn't referring to the cost of the treatment, but to her awareness that he was a professional man, dedicated to working with people who need him. She wanted another situation which was less structured. Yet, within her counseling situation, she claimed, there was great rapport.

Another girl, under therapy for two years, said she would not be able to talk to her doctor were it not for the structural aspects of the situation. Indeed, she could not meet him outside his office, on any occasion, without extreme embarrassment and feeling of great dread. The counselor must be liked; there must be personal relationship. Yet the structural relationships are crucial. This insight has been held in counseling for a long time, but has not been conceptualized in such a way that rapport might be *investigated*.

The distinction between structural and group relationships also may be fruitfully applied to communications during the counseling session. *The client, as well as the doctor, may refer to structural or group aspects of a relation which is being investigated.* For example, in response to the doctor's question, "How did your father feel about your being arrested?" a boy may respond:

(1) "Well, he's a *father,* after all, I guess he was pretty mad because I'm his son and I let him down." (Responses emphasizes structural elements of father-son relationship.)
(2) "He was really mad, and I could see that he felt hurt, and that made me feel bad too. I guess he didn't think I'd do something like that." (Response emphasizes group elements.)

These responses may reveal a great deal about the child's relationship to his father. Just as pertinent, *the client may respond within the structural line or group lines of communication.* For example:

(1) "Well, Doc, I suppose you want to know what he did and how I felt about it. He was mad, but I don't see that's got anything to do with this counseling." (Response within structural lines of communication between counselor and client.)
(2) "He was mad, but I don't feel like talking about it now." (Response within group lines.)

Structural communication can facilitate the counseling process, and, equally possible, structural communications can be used as a protective device by the client, serving to block the movement of the counseling process. In these cases, as in those mentioned above, content analyses might stimulate valuable insights.

However useful the distinction might be to the counselor (especially the group counselor), its greatest potential lies in research, for it helps conceptualize aspects of relationships which traditionally elude research definition.

SOCIOLOGICAL INSIGHTS AND THE COUNSELOR'S PROFESSIONAL PROBLEMS

In its journals and books, sociology holds profound and penetrating insights for many practical problems in counseling; problems such as how professional demands affect personal development (Dubin, 1951; Hughes, 1958; Waller, 1932; and Weber, 1946), how individuals develop professional identities (Becker & Strauss, 1956; Goffman, 1959) and what importance work holds in the life of modern man (Stein, Vidich & White, 1960). Problems of vocational analysis (Weber, 1946; Martindale, 1960) and even problems of how best to implement a guidance or counseling program can be spotlighted by sociology. The latter problem really is one of how to bring social change, a favorite topic of many sociologists. Particularly interesting is the discussion by Katz (1960), which brings together the research on social change in the two fields of rural sociology and mass communications.

Sociology has another, most practical potential: Counseling is at that point in its history in which it is attempting to move from the status of a somewhat maverick practice into full professionalization equal to that of medicine and law. How does it make the transition? What does the current emphasis on professionalization mean for counseling's future? What are the effects of current trends on the nature of the movement? Sociology already holds some answers to these questions, gained in study of the professionalization of other vocations.

Sociologists would be less interested in helping counseling gain status than in studying counseling as a changing movement. Thus the questions are properly posed not by counseling sociology ("How can I serve you?") but by the sociology of counseling ("What, in the name of society, *are* you, and what are you doing?").

THE SOCIOLOGY OF COUNSELING

THE INFLUENCES OF COUNSELING ON SOCIETY

Perhaps the most pressing question sociology of counseling can ask is: What are the social functions *and dysfunctions* of the counseling movement? (Corwin, 1962) Since its inception, the movement has been critical of its consequences, but the criticism has been directed only toward the *immediate* effect on a *particular* client. Counseling also has long-term effects on the individual client, and these, too, are crucial.

Even more important, counseling has long-term effects on the entire social structure within which the client and every fellow human operate. Counseling does not mold society, but it does have the power to further or fight the trends of the time. *How* the power is used has been ignored; indeed, some counselors may be unconsciously working toward conditions they despise. Huxley's message in *Ape and Essence* seems all too appropriate: two armies, led by baboons who keep Einsteins as mascots, have just destroyed one another, and the world as well. With dying breath, the Einsteins ask how such a thing could happen. The answer is clear:

> Surely its obvious.
> Every schoolboy knows it.
> *Ends* are ape-chosen,
> Only the *means* are man's.
> (Huxley, 1948)

A sociological perspective alone cannot save man from domination by the ape within him; but it can help man resist. Such perspective not only takes a broad (and, at best, historical) view of men as individuals and in social groups, communities and nations, it also attempts to view social movements and individual behavior both for their functions and dysfunctions. Such a perspective views the effect not only on the individual but on the entire social situation. This broad perspective might be shown on a 2 x 2 table, with appropriate questions identified.

In short, counselors today focus attention on the immediate, social function, and now and then discuss the dysfunctions of their particular experience. Counselors are fully aware that their actions may have ill effects as well as desirable effects, and that the two may occur at the same time. But counselors virtually ignore the *latent* functions and dysfunctions of the counseling movement, except in occasional discussions of whether counseling is suppressing individuality. They too easily and glibly reject the arguments that counseling serves forces that move toward a *Brave New World* or *The Rise of the Meritocracy* (Young, 1958), that counseling is but a tool of the *status quo*, that counseling is but a manipulative agent of the greater social forces that mold the individual.

These arguments also are made too easily and glibly by the critics of counseling. Neither counselor nor critic has adequately considered the questions, and there is little pressure for them to do so: on these questions persons react emotionally, dulling their intellects and blinding their imaginations. Dispassionate analysis with penetrating and sweeping perspective is needed, but only cheap bromides are offered—and accepted.

THE INFLUENCE OF SOCIETY ON COUNSELING

Perhaps the most profound potential of sociology, then, lies in its capacity to evaluate counseling in its broad social context. Such evaluation views counseling's influence on society; it asks, in essence, "What are you doing to the world?" Counseling might also be asked, "What influence does the world have on you, and how adequate are you to meet the complexities of modern social life?"

EXAMPLE:COUNSELING THEORY.

For instance, a sociology of counseling might attempt to discover the relationship (if any) between the theory developed by a man and his social and educational background and situation. How important to his theory was it that Rogers worked only with persons who sought him out, only with persons who were mentally alert and perceptive? How

Table I

Some Categories of Effects of Counseling:
Immediate and Latent Functions and Dysfunctions*

	Functions	Dysfunctions**
I M M E D I A T E	Examples: A Has counseling achieved what it set out to do for the client? Is the counseling program improving the functioning of the group or organization (school, hospital, community)?	Examples: B Have there been any negative effects from counseling on the client, his family or friends? Do counseling and testing lead to unfair or inaccurate "typing" of individuals or groups? Are individuals biased against themselves or rendered psychologically unable to accept promising possibilities? Does the counseling program upset the functioning of the community and its members?
L A T E N T	Examples: C Is counseling part of an effective movement toward profitable use of our nation's human resources? Does counseling exert any lasting influence on an individual; on his attitudes, self-conception, levels of aspiration, etc.? Does counseling contribute to a general growth of social responsibility and maturity?	Examples: D Is counseling suppressing individuality and encouraging nation-wide conformity? Does testing lead to violation of individual freedom and lessening of free choice? Is counseling contributing to *The Rise of the Meritocracy* or to a *Brave New World*? Are counselors unthinking tools of the status quo?

When counselors worry about their effect, they traditionally focus on questions such as those in cell A: Immediate functions. Cell B questions are now and then discussed, and the individual counselor is aware of occasional dysfunctions resulting from his efforts. Little systematic research or thought is attempted, however, and virtually no attention is paid to the questions of cells C and D.

* Questions are only illustrative.
** The questions under "Dysfunctions" reflect a number of the author's personal biases and assumptions about man and society. Another person may consider such possibilities as functional. A careful sociologist, in speaking of "dysfunctions," refers to "a *designated* set of consequences of a *designated* pattern of behavior, belief, organization that interfere with a *designated* functional requirement of a *designated* social system. Otherwise, the term social dysfunction becomes little more than an

important to his theory was it that Robinson worked only in the college situation, only with people who desired his help; that Williamson worked out his theory while administering personnel work in a mushrooming university; that Freud was a medical doctor? And how important to all of these men that they are rooted in Western culture?

The last question is a large one: Will counseling as we know it ever be applicable in non-Westernized countries. How successful would a Rogerian be in a highly authoritarian government? How successful would a strict Freudian be in a culture in which physical desires and emotions are freely and openly expressed? Such questions could intrigue the sociologist if once they drew his attention.

EXAMPLE: THE SOCIAL VALIDITY OF TESTS

A sociology of counseling might also bring some light to the controversy over the usefulness and fairness of testing and evaluation; the fire that has been drawn by the entire testing movement might be placed in perspective. Is testing really as unfair as claimed by its critics?

Sociology has little to contribute to the traditional quest for "reliability and validity" in tests; this is purely the realm of the psychologist and psychometrist. Sociology could have a great deal to say about social validity, however, for a test can be valid without being of any use whatsoever socially. A test can consistently measure exactly what it sets out to measure and yet be a worthless instrument, because it measures things unimportant or irrelevant to human experience. And if it leads persons to believe these trivia are crucial to human life, a test is worse than worthless: it is a force for ignorance and injustice. Sociologists can help evaluate the *social* validity of a test; they can help determine whether a test seeks information that is indeed needed and useful. For example, the effort to construct a battery of intelligence tests to determine college aptitude may be desirable, for counseling purposes, but it may also suffer from tunnel vision. The social facts of our society and our colleges point up that intelligence is only one necessary (but not sufficient) condition, *sometimes,* for success. Continued efforts to derive predictive instruments may well have blinded educators to the possibility that they don't yet have the foundation on which to build predictors. More attention may be

epithet of disparagement or a largely vacuous expression of attitude." Robert K. Merton (p. 732). It must be emphasized that the sociological approach is (ideally) purely empirical—but at the same time it is not *incompatible* with normative judgments. If we hold that our nation (designated social system) requires a populace of independent, creative individuals each exercising free and responsible choice (designated functional requirement), then we have a criterion for assessing the actions, beliefs and organization of counselors and counseling. The assessment will be empirical, even though normative evaluation of the conclusions will likely follow.

needed to criteria and components of success in a social order (Fishman, 1961). Prediction is desirable, but it may be we are not ready for it; a sociology of counseling could help discover the questions and answers on which predictions must build.

Sociology, then, might help the testing movement lift its eyes from the confusion on the ground, and to look about it; it might help the testing movement discover where it stands and what it is doing in a social world.[1]

EXAMPLE: COUNSELING AND SOCIAL PROBLEMS

The counseling movement has traditionally shown concern with individuals whose problems are intimately involved with society, such as juvenile delinquents and alcoholics. But what are the potential and actual influences of counseling on the social problems of a community? Counseling certainly has helped many individual delinquents, but does it have any effect on a community's delinquency problem, or on the juvenile subcultures of a city? Similarly, is marital counseling effective and has counseling curtailed alcoholism or drug addiction? More important, *can* counseling, as it is today developing, have any noticeable effects on these social pathologies?

Such questions are highly important. They must be asked, and the sociologist is in an excellent position to do the asking.

THE LIMITS OF PROMISE

Sociology is no panacea for all counseling ills. It is not possible nor desirable to develop a counseling theory based only on data and logic, and if it were, the data and logic of sociology would not suffice. For, above all, counseling remains an art—a human art, to which sociology can be only a supplement.

But it can be a most useful supplement, indeed. With interest and effort, sociology can help counseling understand its place in a complex world, it can help assess uniformities of counseling behavior; it can help counseling realize that, while continuing idiographic research, it must move to nomothetic research. Sociology, in short, can help counseling develop by offering new concepts, propositions, techniques and, most importantly, new perspectives.

The relationship would not be all give and no take, however. In turn, counseling offers the researcher intriguing social situations, programs of social change, and experimental settings which occur in everyday life.

---

[1] (Editors' note) This example is explored in more detail by Goslin in Section 7.

The counseling process is pregnant with problems which sociologists might consider crucial to an understanding of man and society, and, for the student of social change, professions, or social action, counseling presents a recent and rapid development of a movement that is peculiar to modern times.

But potential is not realization; the intercourse between counseling and sociology remains indifferent. This indifference gives the sociologist few pains, for, like a joyous adolescent, he sees a world filled with exciting opportunities, from which he must only choose which to tap and which to leave to the future.

The counselor, also, feels few pains. Unfortunately, his indifference is costly. The future is not soon enough to begin the steps toward more socially adequate theory and practice.

If he is interested in his profession and his society, the counselor must make the first move; he must encourage communications with sociologists, suggest shared projects, entice with research funds. Once attention is won, and efforts supported, the sociologist will find that counseling holds research questions at once fascinating and urgent.

Received June 6, 1962.

REFERENCES

BARRY, RUTH, & WOLF, BEVERLY. *Modern issues in guidance and personnel work*. New York: Bureau of Publ., Teachers College, 1957.

BECKER, H. S., & STRAUSS, A. "Careers, personality and adult socialization." *Amer. J. Sociol.*, 1956, 62, 253–263.

BELL, N., & VOGEL, E., eds. *The family*. New York: Free Press, 1961. Selected chapters.

CAVAN, RUTH S. "Unemployment: Crisis of the common man." *Marr. & Fam. Living*, 1959, 21, 139–146.

CICOUREL, A., & KITSUSE, J. *The social organization of the high school and deviant adolescent careers*. Unpublished manuscript, 1960.

CORWIN, R. G. *An alternative to the search for talent*. Paper delivered to the Ohio State University Counseling and Guidance Training Institute, April 1962.

DUBIN, R., ed. *Human relations in industry*. Englewood Cliffs: Prentice-Hall, 1951. Especially chapters 7–9.

FARBER, B. "Family organization and crisis: maintenance of integration in families with a severely mentally retarded child." *Monographs of the Society for Research in Child Development*, Vol. 25, No. 1, 1960.

FISHMAN, J. A. "Social-psychological theory of selecting and guiding college students." *Amer. J. Sociol.*, 1961, 66, 472–484.

FOOTE, N. "Identification as the basis for a theory of motivation." *Amer. sociological Rev.*, 1951, 16, 14–21.

FRANCIS, R. G. "The relation of data to theory." *Rural Sociol.*, 1957, 22, 258–266.

FRITZ, C. "Disaster." In Robert K. Merton and Robert A. Nisbet, eds., *Contem-*

porary social problems. New York: Harcourt, Brace & World, 1961, 651–694.

GOFFMAN, E. *The presentation of self in everyday life.* Garden City, New York: Doubleday, 1959.

GOULDNER, A. "Reciprocity and autonomy in functional theory." In Llewellyn Gross, ed., *Symposium on sociological theory.* Evanston, Ill.: Row Peterson, 241–270.

GREEN, A. "Sociological analysis of Horney and Fromm." *Amer. J. Sociol.,* 1946, *51,* 533–540.

HILL, R. "Generic features of families under stress." *Soc. Casewk,* 1959, *39,* 139–150.

HILL, R. & HANSON, D. A. "Families in disaster." In George Baker & Dwight Chapman, eds., *Man and society in disaster.* New York: Basic Books, 1962.

HOLLINGSHEAD, A. *Elmstown's youth.* New York: Wiley, 1959.

HUGHES, E. C. "The study of occupations." In Robert K. Merton *et al.,* eds., *Sociology today.* New York: Basic Books, 1958, 442–458.

HUMPHREYS, J. A., & TRAXLER, A. E. *Guidance services.* Chicago: Science Res. Associates, 1954.

HUXLEY, A. *Ape and essence.* New York: Harper, 1948.

KATZ, E. "Communication research and the image of society: convergence of two traditions." *Amer. J. Sociol.,* 1960, *65,* 435–440.

MARTINDALE, D. *American society.* New York: Van Nostrand, 1960. (a)

MARTINDALE, D. *The nature and types of sociological theory.* Boston: Houghton Mifflin, 1960, pp. 383–393. (b)

MATHEWSON, R. H. *Guidance policy and practice* (revised edition). New York: Harper, 1962.

MEAD, G. H. *Mind, self and society.* Chicago: Univer. of Chicago Press, 1934.

MERTON, R. K. "Social problems and sociological theory." In Robert K. Merton & Robert A. Nisbet, eds., *Contemporary social problems.* New York: Harcourt, Brace & World, 1961, 697–737.

MILLER, C. *Foundations of guidance.* New York: Harper, 1961.

MILLS, C. W. *White collar.* New York: Oxford Univer. Press, 1951.

PARSONS, T., & FOX, RENEE. "Illness, therapy and the modern urban American family." *J. Soc. Issues,* 1952, *8,* 31–44.

ROGERS, C. R. *Client-centered therapy.* Boston: Houghton-Mifflin, 1951.

ROGERS, C. R. "The place of the person in the new world of the behavioral sciences." *Personnel guid. J.,* 1961, *39,* 442–451.

ROSE, A. *The institutions of advanced societies.* Minneapolis: Univer. of Minnesota Press, 1958, Preface.

ROSE, A. *Theory and method in the social sciences,* Minneapolis: Univer. of Minnesota Press, 1954. Especially chapter 1.

SKINNER, B. F. *Walden II.* New York: Macmillan, 1948.

STEIN, M., VIDICH, A. J. & WHITE, D. M., eds. *Identity and anxiety.* New York: Free Press of Glencoe, Inc., 1960.

TIZZARD, J., & GRAD, J. C. *The mentally handicapped and their families.* London: Oxford, 1961.

WALLER, W. *The sociology of teaching.* New York: Wiley, 1932. Especially pp. 375–409.

WARNER, W. L. *et al. Social class in America.* Chicago: Science Res. Associates, 1949.

WARTERS, JANE. *Group guidance: principles and practices.* New York: McGraw-Hill, 1960.

Weber, M. In Hans Gerth and C. Wright Mills, eds., *From Max Weber: Essays in Sociology*. New York: Oxford Univer. Press, 1946.
Wrenn, C. G. *The counselor in a changing world*. Washington: APGA, 1962.
Young, M. *The rise of the meritocracy*. London: Thames & Hudson, 1958.

25. Sociology: A Missing Ingredient in the Educational Process

Carl Weinberg

Institutions of higher education are now, more than ever before, recruiting to their schools and departments of education psychologists, sociologists, and anthropologists to assist in a national program to translate knowledge uncovered in their separate disciplines into meaningful educational terms. The skills of these individuals are largely incorporated into the research interests of institutions. As a group, however, they have yet to make a dent in the officially designated programs of teacher, counselor, or administrator certification. Psychology, as a theoretical discipline, has done the most to ensure its place in the field of education, and because of its long association with the field of education it has been able to dictate a place for itself in the organization of formal requirements. Sociology and anthropology have yet to secure recognition for themselves in the educational program on any consistent or extensive basis. It is the purpose of this paper to support the contention that the understandings, concepts, and procedures of sociology are as crucial to the working knowledge of the educator functioning in a highly complex technological society as are the psychological tools and techniques that have to date constituted the bulk of his training.

The Current Emphasis in Training and Accreditation

Guidance counselors, for example, have been traditionally accustomed to associating their task with that of the clinical psychologist. Only recently, in the wake of a movement towards self-inspection in the field of guidance, accompanied by a simultaneous increase in sociological interest

From: Carl Weinberg, "Sociology: A Missing Ingredient in the Education Process," *The Clearing House*, Sept., 1965. Reprinted by permission of *The Clearing House*.

in education and problems of adolescents, has the profession begun to take account of the social forces which contribute to the school and career orientations of youth. This ferment may be observed at institutions of higher learning, but there is no indication that policy makers are ready to extend the dimensions of training to the socio-cultural areas. Thirty-eight states and the District of Columbia designate certification requirements for the credentialing of guidance counselors. Of these states, 31 specify that some work in psychological foundations is required. In eight of these states, some work in psychological foundations appears to be optional. (This information, as well as the data presented in the following paragraph, was derived from the booklet *Guidance Workers Certification Requirements*, a publication of the U.S. Department of Health, Education and Welfare, Washington, D.C., 1960.)

A search of the requirements revealed that sociology as a field of study related to the certifying of guidance workers was significantly less represented. Only two states (Hawaii and New Mexico) fully expect that guidance counselors shall have taken some work in the sociological foundations. Twelve states indicate that one or two courses will be accepted as electives towards fulfilling the certification requirements. Twenty-five states make no mention whatsoever of sociology courses, suggesting that, since requirements must be attained from mentioned areas, there is no room for sociology in the program.

The modern teacher in America is conceptually defined by most educators as a "guidance" kind of teacher, a person concerned with instructional materials only as these can be incorporated into the individual interests and proclivities of the individual student. Like its parent discipline, the field of guidance itself, guidance teaching orients itself almost exclusively to psychological data. In an educational world that is suddenly becoming familiar with such terms as "cultural deprivation," "urban renewal," "suburbanization," and "cultural enrichment," it is naive and perhaps presumptuous to assume that psychology can carry the ball for the behavioral sciences.

SOCIOLOGY'S DILEMMA

The lag that has characterized the omission of sociology as a discipline from educational programs is partly a function of what has been going on in the field of sociology itself. On the one hand it has not been until relatively recently, at least in comparison with the development of psychology as a method of investigation, that sociology has turned with confidence to empirical research. Not until the Fifties, for example, have we had any sophisticated sociological concepts applied to major areas

such as the family, the church, and the school. With the development of
tools and techniques of investigation, accompanied by a staggering increase in the number of Ph.D's produced by various departments of
sociology in the last decade, sociological analysis has emerged as a reliable means for coming to grips with actual theoretical problems, particularly of the sort with which the educator must be concerned.

A second factor which has come from the discipline itself to retard
its making a contribution to educational theory has been the apparent
lack of concern that sociology has shown in the solution of social or
educational problems, at an ameliorative level. Since sociology has been so
long associated with the business of social work, a concentrated effort has
pervaded the ethos of the discipline in the direction of establishing itself
as a basic science. Only as it has gained confidence in itself has the field
begun to realize that contributions to its body of knowledge can be
accomplished by working in laboratories such as educational institutions
where applied interests might also be served.

A Contribution to Education

Students in education usually take no more than one course in
sociology. Such a course can ordinarily do no more than introduce the
students to general categories which have been of working interest to the
sociologist. These students do not get the chance to see how research and
empirical analysis might be an effective procedure of dealing with real
problems facing the school.

Sociological analysis has turned a systematic eye upon many problems which constitute logical facets of the educator's knowledge, but such
knowledge is not frequently made available through courses of instruction. The student is attempting to function in an environment both external and internal which has been and will continue to be a subject for
social research. The secondary student is constantly maneuvering to survive in a climate of incompatible forces which he cannot always reconcile.
The awareness of and knowledge about these forces cannot continue to
be absent from the working knowledge of the educator. Five such forces
which must be taken into account in any complete analysis of student
motives or conflicts are outlined below. These are only examples of the
kinds of contributions sociology can make and has made to the applied
interests of education.

1. *Demographic factors and individual adjustment.* The size and
structure of the family unit, the size and structure of the neighborhood or
community, the organization and distribution of community resources,
occupational backgrounds and educational level of parents, ethnicity, and

a number of other such variables have been shown to bear some relationship to such factors as delinquent behavior, school dropouts, career choice, scores on intelligence, achievement, and personality tests, school grades, participation in extracurricular activities or voluntary associations, and mental illness.

Sociologists, in work situations such as colleges and universities, departments of urban affairs and urban planning, and research divisions of national, state, and local government, are constantly attempting to identify demographic factors that will provide an explanatory base for social dynamics. The wisdom of certain vocational choices might hang on an understanding of complex trends in such areas as urban renewal, rural stability, and occupational status.

Too many misconceptions take the form of generalized beliefs as factors are categorized too quickly as salient causes of the educational problems of youth. Broken homes, working mothers, slum living, father's occupation, high physical mobility, too frequently jump to the attention of teachers as "of course" explanations, while the specific relationships, many untested, rest in the journals.

Factors antecedent or extrinsic to the school are slowly gaining recognition as motivating and impinging forces which influence the adjustment individuals make to that institution.

2. *Role expectations and role conflict.* Whether we are focusing upon the student role or the role of the teacher in the school, the problem of conflicting expectations is relevant to the work of the educator. The question of how decisions are made in the face of such conflicting expectations has occupied the attention of sociological analysis. Samuel Stauffer (1949), Neal Gross (1958), and Melvin Seeman (1953) have made significant beginnings in this area. The range of possible roles to be subjected to this kind of analysis has not neared being exhausted. Of most significance in this regard would be an investigation into the conflicts in expectations held by students, administrators, parents, teachers, and counselors themselves about the role of the teacher and how she typically resolves these ostensibly incompatible demands.

Students live in a world of separate institutions, all of which demand of them separate and often conflicting loyalties. The home, the school, the church, the peer group, and the social class system present a complex network of allegiances. When two or more come into conflict a choice must be made. Sociological analysis is constantly attempting to isolate the factors which explain the direction of the choice. In our time, when the formal expectations of the school conflict with the informal expectations of the peer group, the conflict has frequently resulted in decisions leading to deviation and delinquency. An understanding of the complex base of these supposedly incompatible forces could result in a restructuring of the expectations which would allow survival in both systems. Students may comply with the expectations of both the school and the peer group if the teacher understands the social structure which produces the conflict.

3. *The adolescent subculture.* Of recent theoretical import, Albert Cohen's (1955) *Delinquent Boys* has concerned itself with exploring the nature of the values and attitudes of delinquent adolescents. Other authors such as James Coleman (1961) and Albert Reiss (1959) have conducted research attempting to derive some consistent system of adolescent values that might constitute a subculture.

The adjustment of youth to the institution of the school has been shown by sociological investigation to hinge on the concept of status. The status system fostered by the school around such criteria as achievement, participation, and cooperation is not a system that all can serve equally. Opportunity to attain status in the school is differentially distributed throughout the student population. Lacking one avenue for status in the adolescent subculture, many members set up a competing status system in which their chances for success are greater. As new status systems arise, whole sets of values become reorganized to support the system. Many of these are contradictory to success goals such as education and occupational stability and supportive of deviation.

It seems unlikely that teachers can escape the fact that much motivation for educational and career decisions is highly related to the nature of the subculture of which the student is a member.

4. *The social structure of the school and classroom.* Sociological theories of organization have focused upon the structure of the school. Social system analysis employs such useful sociological concepts as norms, values, sanctions, formal and informal systems, bureaucracy, and role in a new kind of look at the organization of the school and the classroom. Wayne Gordon (1956), Talcott Parsons (1959), and W. W. Charters, Jr. (1952), have appeared in the socio-educational literature with themes on this subject. The way in which external norms are mediated and translated into paths of achievement and career orientation is crucial to the applied interests of educational theory.

Coleman has made a beginning in introducing educators to the notion that achievement in school is related to the informal value system of the school in which the achievement is being measured. The informal influence of the school student body was earlier noted by Wayne Gordon (1957) in *The Social System of the High School.* The compromise that arises out of the interaction of the formal requirements of the school with the student perception of and adjustment to these requirements is seen to establish a climate for learning that is uniquely that of neither the formal nor the informal organization.

The crucial position of the teacher with respect to this system and the means for educational and occupational allocation makes it incumbent upon him to understand the dimensions of the approach to the organization of the school.

5. *Social mobility through educational guidance.* The following statement appeared in the abstracts of papers delivered at the Fifty-Seventh Annual Meeting of the American Sociological Society:

Samuel A. Stauffer, late professor of Sociology and Director of the Laboratory of Social Relations at Harvard University and Past President of the American Sociological Association, conducted basic and applied research on the process of social mobility for over a decade prior to his death. . . .

In the course of his basic research, Stauffer became deeply concerned over the denial of opportunity and waste of human talent which he saw in the great career sorting, much of which occurs in the elementary and secondary school years. In order to help school personnel—especially guidance counselors —in their efforts to reduce the individual and social loss involved, Stauffer developed a unique school guidance questionnaire machine reporting system (Shea, 1962).

The means by which individuals gain or are denied access to the upper strata of the occupational hierarchy are of real concern to the educational enterprise. Sociological analysis *has* turned its tools, as the above comment suggests, to the applied interests of education. A search for a better system of personnel allocation by which a greater proportion of the talent loss to our society can be averted may be the consequence of basic sociological research on social mobility.

THE TEACHER AS PREDICTOR

The teacher is in a position, either formally or informally, of needing to hypothesize that the specific direction taken in the teaching situation will be successful. She bases this hypothesis upon assumptions that arise from her organization of the data which are relevant to the individual case. She proceeds on the assumption that the data are meaningful and directing and hopefully as complete as she can have them. She molds her instructional materials around the conclusions she has made regarding the nature of the particular child she is to teach. If she should fail in her endeavor—if the hypothesis is not demonstrated by achievement of the educational goal—the fault may not lie with the relevance of the collected information or the skill of the teacher. It could conceivably lie in the ignorance of the social context of the data. Aggressive behavior, for example, may be either a reaction to a deeply felt frustration or simply a play for status amongst a significant group of peers. Sociological data as well as sociological context need to be considered as a useful adjunct to the working knowledge of the teacher. It cannot help but improve the predictive efficiency of her decisions and consequently the attainment of the students' goals.

The contribution of applied sociology to the problems of American education has only made a small beginning. The horizons are unlimited. The five subject matter areas sketched above are only examples of the kinds of material that could prove an invaluable increment to the body of knowledge reserved for the educator. As relationships between the social dynamics operating in and out of the school and success and failure in school are discovered, sociological analysis will be making a major contribution to this discovery. It behooves those who are concerned with the adjustment of youth to the school to consider the importance of sociological analysis in the entire educational enterprise.

REFERENCES

CHARTERS, W. W., JR. "The School Class as a Social System." *Rev. of Educ. Res.*, 1952, Vol. 22, pp. 41–50.

COHEN, A. *Delinquent Boys.* New York: Free Press of Glencoe, Inc., 1955.

COLEMAN, J. *The Adolescent Society.* New York: Free Press of Glencoe, Inc.; 1961.

GORDON, W. "Role of the Teacher in the Social Structure of the High School." *J. of Educ. Sociol.*, 1956, Vol. 29, pp. 21–29.

GORDON, W. *The Social System of the High School.* New York: Free Press of Glencoe, Inc., 1957.

GROSS, N. *Explanations in Role Analysis: Studies in the School Superintendency Role.* New York: John Wiley & Sons, 1958.

PARSONS, T. "The School Class as a Social System." *Harvard Educ. Rev.*, Fall 1959, Vol. 20, pp. 297–318.

REISS, A. J. & RHODES, A. L. "Are Educational Goals of Conforming, Truant, and Delinquent Adolescents Influenced by Group Position in American Society?" *J. of Negro Educ.*, 1959, Vol. 28, pp. 252–267.

SEEMAN, M. "Role Conflict and Ambivalence in Leadership." *Amer. Sociol. Rev.*, 1953, Vol. 18, pp. 373–380.

SHEA, P. Paper presented at the meeting of the American Sociological Society, September, 1962.

STAUFFER, S. "An Analysis of Conflicting Social Norms." *Amer. Sociol. Rev.*, 1949, Vol. 14, pp. 707 ff.

26. Aspects of the Sociology of Guidance

Marshall E. Jones

We assume here that sociology may be adequately defined as "the study of the influence of social systems on human behavior" or in some similar way. Obviously, we are taking a "functionalist" approach to sociology instead of a "symbolic interactionist" approach, though some mixture of the two is almost inevitable in any theoretical discussion of sociology. From this viewpoint, sociology is a behavioral science; it is a social science only in its emphasis on social systems as a primary influence on human behavior. This definition relates itself to the guidance enterprise in at least two ways: (1) Since people who practice the profession of guidance counselors are "behaving," presumably changes in social systems would account for some of the changes in the guidance enterprise; (2) People who seek the services of guidance counselors, or who at least are now coming to recognize guidance as a legitimate enterprise, are also "behaving" in the course of their search or acceptance. We are not suggesting that system-changes account for *all* changes in the guidance enterprise; some such changes are self-generated in the course of professional development. And we are not suggesting that the relationship between social system and guidance enterprise is mechanical or automatic. Rather, we are viewing changes in the system as stimuli towards developments in the enterprise and we regard those developments themselves as responses to the stimuli. Under such circumstances we expect a lag between stimulus and response rather than a mechanical following of one by the other.

A first point to make is that some kind of guidance, in the sense of a "helping relationship" among people, has existed as a *function* in most social systems with which we are familiar. Certainly it existed as function in the social system of our immediate past in America, though it was not explicitly designated as a formal guidance relationship. Carl Rogers says:

I have long had the strong conviction—some might say it was an obsession— that the therapeutic relationship is only a special instance of interpersonal relationships in general, and that the same lawfulness governs all such relationships (Rogers, 1961).

Thus in the past the "helping" aspects of relationships was often a "side effect" rather than the explicit goal of the relationships. It is also true that much of the "helping" was done by parents, elders, friends, associates in

Printed by permission of the author, Dr. Marshall E. Jones, Professor of Sociology, University of Wyoming, Laramie, Wyoming.

general rather than by professionals. But regardless of its more or less incidental character and its nonprofessional status, the helping relationship did exist as a function in our past social system.

What has happened over the years in America has been the development of a professionalized *structure* of a more or less sophisticated kind, to perform the same *function* which was incidentally performed in the past. Because the structure is new, it appears to some people that a new function has also been developed. This mistaken perception of the facts has led to some opposition to the guidance enterprise on the grounds that it "babies" people, it does not permit them to grow up, it channels their lives into stylized paths, and so on. Much of the social-work enterprise in America suffers from the same criticism based on the same mistaken view of the facts. The mere visibility of these new structures has drawn attention to them, whereas the incidental nature of the older function concealed its existence.

From the viewpoint of a sociologist, it becomes important for guidance people to emphasize this matter of old function and new structure in order to offset some of the popular criticisms of guidance and thereby to further its acceptance as a legitimate part of our social structure performing a significant and long-recognized function.

But beyond this practical application of theory, it is useful to examine the changes that have taken place in our collective way of life which make the emergence of the guidance structure an expectable and itself functional growth. Our purpose here is to offset the belief that guidance is merely an elaboration of techniques nurtured by a growing bureaucracy of self-interested practitioners. On the contrary it is a necessary result of existing social arrangements.

Perhaps the most obvious change in our way of life has been that which Toennies called the change from *Gemeinschaft* to *Gesellschaft* and which has been noted by other writers under such terms as the change from a *folk* to an *industrial* society or from a *sacred* to a *secular* society (Toennies, 1957). Whatever term is used, the essential change is a shift from a social system based on personal, intimate, kinship relations involving trust and confidence in one's associates to a system based on impersonal, indirect, bureaucratic relations involving stylized approaches to one's associates. In *Gemeinschaft* society, the familial kind of relationship extended beyond one's immediate family to a sense of kinship with all the other members of the group. Both a "helping" attitude and the assurance of readiness to help were inherent in the very type of social system.

We must, of course, be careful not to romanticize *Gemeinschaft*. It could be, and often was, repressive of individual development in areas beyond those accepted by the system. Control was strict and strictly imposed. Intimacy of contact often led to such unhappy results as vendettas, bitter quarrels, and other kinds of disordered relationhips.

But, in spite of these drawbacks, the security of individual position in the structure, the assurance of help in times of necessity, the opportunity to help others, were all present. The results of *Gemeinschaft* for individual, if conformist, adaptation to the facts of life were constructive. As Rieff points out,

> . . . in the classical tradition of social theory, the sense of well-being of the individual was dependent on his full, participant membership in a community (Rieff, 1966, p. 71).

He also points out that the opposite theory—that men must free themselves from binding attachments to communal purposes in order to express more freely their individualities—is also powerful and, by now, equally venerable. But, as deviant groups in our own system have discovered, the free expression of individuality is meaningless unless such expression takes place in association with some kind of a community. Hippie and similar deviants create communities of their own, a fact which is entirely expectable in view of the socialization towards some kind of collective behavior which is common in our own and other social systems. It is interesting that the new communities created by those who feel themselves outsiders in the normal community all show a search for *Gemeinschaft* relationships.

In *Gemeinschaft*, the "helping" relationship would grow out of the very nature of the social organization, but the development of a specialized structure to implement a helping relationship would simply be unthinkable.

In *Gesellschaft* types of social system, the community as a meaningful pattern certainly declines in importance and eventually tends to disappear (Stein, 1960). The sense of common group-identity, entwined with occupancy of a specific geographical location, loses its force as an influence on human behavior. A social life marked by an established, if simple, social structure imbedded in tradition, the usual concomitant of such a geographically based identity, ceases to exist. It is replaced by a congeries of associations perceived as meeting specialized individual needs, often geographically remote from the "home base" of the participants, and often of such selectivity in choice of membership that members of one family are "split" among their own separate associations. The basis of these associations, as of an increasing number of relationships in *Gesellschaft*, is contractual and therefore limited in both extensity and intensity (Sorokin, 1947).

But a contract, explicitly stated or implicitly understood, is a rational technique because it is perceived as an efficient means for attaining specified goals. In *Gemeinschaft* society, both goals and means for attaining goals were specified by tradition, and both means and goals were equally important. In *Gesellschaft* society, goals are to some extent individualized but the social definition of goals ("success," to be accepted, and so on) is still overwhelmingly the important definition, especially in our social system in which subtle means of mass influence are predominant. Since the means by which the socially defined goals are to be attained are no longer defined by strong tradition, stress on means tends either (1) to be neglected to a large extent or (2) to be left to the rationality of a con-tractual means-ends emphasis (Merton, 1957). The cultural legitimacy of means becomes of secondary importance. Of primary importance is the "efficiency" of the means, and, in turn, efficiency is tested by pragmatic, "rational" procedures.

As this process continues, the system becomes characterized by *anomie*, that is, by a state of "normlessness" especially with respect to the means which are legitimately usable to attain the ends desired. Older traditional norms lose their influence and either no new norms are estab-lished or, if they are established, they are accepted only by specialized groups, not by the majority of the population. One of the immediate results of anomie is a decline in the "trust" in one's associates which characterized *Gemeinschaft*. We cannot regard other people as trust-worthy if the means they use to attain goals are self-centered, rational, and (possibly) involving procedures which will harm us. Relationships then tend to become characterized by elements of suspicion and doubt.

It is not surprising, then, that *alienation* from system and from as-sociates should become commonplace. Here we understand *anomie* to be a condition of social systems, and *alienation* to be a condition of individ-uals. The condition of alienation carries with it a feeling of "estrange-ment" and of being a stranger to one's surroundings and to one's associ-ates. Thus associations, relationships, the social structure in which one lives, all become progressively meaningless. A sense of loyalty to system or to people tends to disappear, though this fact does not preclude loyalty to individuals or to groups which are perceived as satisfying. Indeed, it is difficult to feel loyal to, or "at home" in, systems in which norms have disintegrated, traditions have been weakened, relationships have become disorganized, and problem-behavior is apparently becoming the domi-nant form of social expression. Doubtless these ills need not necessarily appear in a *Gesellschaft* system. We are saying only that they have ap-peared in our own system. Anomie and alienation are two of the root causes of the behavior with which guidance counselors deal. We stress again that these two factors may, and do, affect seriously numbers of people who are not in any sense inherently defective. The normal person as well as the abnormal person are alike subject to their influence.

To summarize this portion of the discussion: The major change in our social system over the past century has been a shift from a *Gemein-schaft* to a *Gesellschaft* type of social system. This shift has been accompanied by an increasing degree of anomie and alienation, both of which have appeared with the decline of community and of the personalized kind of "trust" relationships which were characteristic of the past. All of this is reflected in the disordered behavior evident in our own times through the ease with which culturally illegitimate means are becoming acceptable ways of attaining goals. And all of this, of course, is clear evidence of the need for a structured, professionalized guidance enterprise. This need is obvious not only because we do observe a significant amount of disordered behavior but also because there is no reason to believe that any informally functioning helping relationships will develop as they developed from the different system of the past.

But thus far the discussion has been somewhat oversimplified because we have made it appear that individuals are directly affected by anomie and other forms of social disorganization. This is not the fact. The various aspects of the social system mediate between individuals and the influences of their associates. But if the system itself becomes disorganized, then the results of disorganization for individual behavior are multiplied (Buckley, 1967). This topic merits some further discussion.

For our purposes here, we consider *culture* to consist of patterns for living which are to some extent idealized and which are perceived as adaptive to a total environment. Culture is, in other words, a blueprint on the basis of which various environmental facts can be used for effective group-maintenance and therefore for effective individual life-organization. By contrast with culture, a *social system* is a more or less organized and integrated series of *instruments* by the use of which the ideal patterns of culture can be made operative in the life of the groups and individuals concerned. Social systems, then, consist of such things as institutions, roles, statuses, norms, prescriptions, expectations and proscriptions, all of which are intended to be usable by groups and individuals in manipulating for their advantage the total environment in which they live. No social system is ever perfectly integrated nor is any system entirely realistic in its estimates of the utility of its instruments. And, while both patterns of culture and institutional arrangements are perceived as adapted to existing conditions, the perception is often inaccurate. Also, arrangements adaptive to conditions of the past at a given time may become unadaptive because of changes in the conditions, yet the perception of the utility of existing arrangements may not change with the changed conditions. We then have the familiar phenomenon of cultural "lag."

This mediation of systems between individuals and the realities of life is advantageous if the system is realistically functional. If it is not, the mediation exacerbates problems of adaptation to reality by individuals. By processes of socialization, we come to rely on existing social-system arrangements to provide acceptable patterns for living and usable instruments by which those patterns can be applied to personal situations. A life-organization is built up on this kind of expectation. Then, if we find that the very instruments and ideals on which we have relied do not meet realistically the problems of adaptation to situations we face, the shock may be disastrous. It is more than a personal disappointment: it raises doubts about the whole system in which our lives have become embedded. We become increasingly puzzled when "the rules don't fit the game."

A common mistake, as we suggested earlier, is to assume that the disordered behavior resulting from the impact of all of these things appears only in people who are in some way inherently defective. By a process of circular reasoning, we find it easy to believe that observed behavioral results in some way demonstrate that failure to adapt is based on an inherent inability to adapt. As an illustration of this kind of attitude, note that tendency of the medical profession and other biologically oriented professions to assume that "pot-smoking," the use of LSD and similar patterns of behavior occur only in those individuals who are predisposed towards such habits by a biopsychological defect. There is certainly no evidence that this is true. The fact appears to be that in some cases inherent defect operates to inhibit adaptive behavior. But it is equally a fact that in other cases essentially average ("normal") individuals fail to adapt precisely because they are average and therefore are ready to accept the reassurance about reality offered by the system during processes of socialization. Maladaptation then occurs when the very reassurances are discovered to be unrealistic. In such instances, the search for individual defect and attempts to correct individual defect are quite beside the point. It is the behavior which requires correction, not an assumed defect in ability to behave normally. Corrective measures should move in the direction of realistic assessment of the social system and of the social situations in which the maladjusted individuals are involved. These facts are increasingly recognized by therapists of many varieties, but the assumption that individual inherent defect is prepotent in explaining disordered behavior is still very common outside professional circles (Menninger, 1963).

An implication of all these facts for the guidance enterprise is that guidance must accept a strong infusion of the sociological outlook into what has been a preponderantly psychological and psychotherapeutic outlook. No doubt professionals in the field of guidance will hesitate to agree to some of the convictions of the sociological fraternity, but this one conviction—especially now when, through mass communication, the influence of system-patterns is very subtle—must be accepted. All of this is intended to indicate the importance of the social systems under which we live for the individual life-organizations of all of us. But it is certainly *not* to imply that professional guidance personnel should change their *prac-*

tices and become social reformers! Guidance practice involves working primarily with individuals and with small groups and guidance personnel must continue that vital involvement. It is the *theory* on which practice is based that must change in the direction of including much more recognition of the disordering effect of a disordered social system on quite "normal" individuals. As this fact is recognized and therapeutic measures include a greater understanding by the patient of his relation to social systems, and of his own essential normality, more constructive and realistic readaptations become possible.

One final area of discussion should engage our attention: the question of the relationship between the *self* and social systems. Again, the importance of this matter from a sociological viewpoint lies in the fact that life-experiences are organized and integrated into a self, or personality, or character—the terms vary somewhat with the outlook of those who use them but they all describe in a general way the fact that what happens to us does not affect only the surface layers of existence, it penetrates to the deeper layers. Thus a disorganizing experience has not only immediate effects; its effects are multiplied by the remote effects it has on the organization of the self. Since the days of Cooley, Mead, and Baldwin, the significance of social definitions of situations and of other aspects of social systems on the formation of the self have been recognized and to some extent accepted (Martindale, 1960). As we play social roles, establish social relationships with other people, learn to follow culturally accepted patterns, we form a concept of our selves as able to do all of these things, and others, well, poorly, about as well as most people, in an inferior manner, and so on. Once the concept of a self is established—and this concept is a changing thing, influenced by new experiences and new interpretations of old experiences—it becomes a powerful influence on behavior. If we regard ourselves as inferior, for example, we will avoid even attempts at certain tasks. If we belong to a minority group which has been labeled by the system as inferior, this label attaches also to our selves and we tend to accept structured positions of inferiority. On the other hand, a "strong" self can act as an "insulator" against delinquency and can in other ways be an asset in meeting life-situations (Reckless, 1956; Coates and Pellegrin, 1957; Empey, 1956).

All of these things are generally acknowledged today by professionals in the field of guidance, but among non-professionals there is the same tendency to reason in a circle we mentioned before in another connection. It is easy to believe that the self which actually develops in an individual is the only self which could develop because, in some way, this kind of self was inherent in his constitution. There is no evidence for this point of view. On the contrary, the evidence is in favor of a maximum of plasticity in the potential for developing many different kinds of self. The self which does emerge is a compromise among a number of potentials, the compromise brought about by the weight of varying life-experiences which individuals undergo. And, in turn, the weight of these experiences depends very largely on social-system definitions of the experiences. We are not suggesting that all individuals are, or need be, completely passive towards social-system definitions or other patterns. We are suggesting that *most* individuals in our own social system *are*, in fact, very largely passive towards their system. Perhaps part of the function of guidance is to decrease this passivity and increase individual evaluations of the system.

If, for some large proportion of our people, the self is a reflection of their social system, we can understand better the selves with which we deal if we examine some of the current social-system definitions. The predominating definition of the appropriate self we should develop, for example, is that of consumer, an essentially passive definition. Not only does the weight of persuasive advertising pressure us in the direction of consuming; it is also true that consuming has become attached to many other facets of life. Thus, possession of goods--which is, of course, the end-product of consuming—is equated with success, with high status, with favorable evaluations by associates, and with assurances that we are worthwhile human beings. All of these goals are common in all social systems. It is the concentration on one means of attaining these goals which typifies our own social system, and some others in the past and present. To repeat, the means are essentially passive, especially since our system makes consuming as easy as possible through extension of credit and similar devices.

The definition of the human being as consumer is functional for the social system in which we live. That system is founded on mass production; but obviously mass production demands mass consumption if it is to operate profitably. The only possible way of making expensive machinery pay for itself is to produce as many units as possible by the use of the machinery. In reality, no machine is used to its full capacity in our ordinary economy, hence "as many units as possible" really means "as many units as can be sold." The pressure therefore is on consuming.

Is the definition also functional for the individuals involved? Up to a point, yes—up to the point at which life becomes meaningless in spite of the plethora of possessions because acquiring new possessions is simply a repetition of a familiar pattern with little variation in meaning. Perhaps it is the adolescent and the young who are most troubled by this fact, not that they have a plethora of possessions but that they see their elders bored and irritable in spite of their acceptance of the social definition that success consists in an abundance of things. Perhaps, also, the enabling of the young to channel their questions and to examine without guilt their doubts about the validity of social definitions is one of the important functions of guidance.

On this basic concept of the self as passive consumer, other facets of passivity are easily developed through the mechanical efficiency of mass influence. Spectator sports, moving pictures, television, radio—all involve the passive acceptance of what is offered for most of the patrons of these enterprises (Larsen, 1968). It is unrealistic, then, to expect as a *typical* "self" one which is active and creative; just as it is unrealistic to criticize segments of our population for being "apathetic" about politics, world problems, and other incidents which seem to a minority of people to be important and vital. Perhaps, again, it is part of the function of the guidance counselor in his personal contacts with clients to bring the client to an understanding of the social-system influences which are operative and to enable the client to come to his own balance with the social definitions to which he is subjected. Unfortunately, especially among younger people, the feeling that system definitions are inevitably right and that any criticism of them is in some way wrong can easily induce guilt feelings at their own doubts about the system. We should help them to be realistic about the total situation in which they find themselves in relation to their social system.

To summarize the several viewpoints presented in this paper:

1) The erection of a new and professional structure to perform the traditional function of guidance is expectable in our social system and the utility of such a new structure should be emphasized to counteract criticisms of guidance which allege that the whole *function* is new and in some way degenerative of people.

2) The shift from *Gemeinschaft* to *Gesellschaft* has reduced the number of meaningful personal contacts available to many people, thereby leaving an unsatisfied "hunger" for such contacts. The guidance process can introduce to its clients both explanations for the existance of that hunger and suggestions as to how it can be satisfied.

3) The existence of anomie and alienation as common patterns in our society is traceable to social changes. Individuals suffering from alienation and other results of anomie are not thereby demonstrated to be inferior as individuals. On the contrary, they may be "normal" in the sense that they have responded to socialization processes and have accepted social definitions. It is the definitions which are inadequate and unrealistic and, in that sense, defective rather than the individuals being defective.

4) Much the same thing may be said of the defective "self" which troubles some people. It is the social definitions of an appropriate "self" which are at fault and those who find these definitions inadequate are not thereby demonstrated to be "abnormal." Neither is the behavior (disordered behavior in general) evidence of inherent defect in the people so

behaving. Rather, it is evidence of a "normal" learning process—but the material presented by the system to be learned is defective. Presentation of this kind of fact to the clients of guidance should be helpful to them in re-orienting their lives.

5) Finally, a much closer rapprochement between the traditionally individualistic field of guidance and the traditionally collective field of sociology will further development both of sociology and of guidance. It is hoped that this symposium will be a contribution towards such a rapprochement.

REFERENCES

BUCKLEY, W. *Sociology and Modern Systems Theory.* Englewood Cliffs, New Jersey: Prentice-Hall, 1967.

COATES, C. H. & PELLEGRIN, R. J. "Executives and Supervisors: Contrasting Self-Conceptions of Each Other." *Amer. Sociol. Rev.,* April 1957, 217–220.

CLOWARD, R. A. "Illegitimate Means, Anomie, and Deviant Behavior." *Amer. Sociol. Rev.,* April, 1959, 164–176.

EMPEY, L. T. "Social Class and Occupational Aspiration." *Amer. Sociol. Rev.,* Dec. 1956, 703–709.

LARSEN, O. N., ed. *Violence and the Mass Media.* New York: Harper and Row, 1968.

LEE, D. *Freedom and Culture.* Englewood Cliffs, New Jersey: Prentice-Hall, 1959, pp. 5–14.

MARTINDALE, D. *The Nature and Types of Sociological Theory.* Boston: Houghton Mifflin, 1960, pp. 313–317, 344–347, 353–359.

MENNINGER, K. *The Vital Balance.* New York: Viking Press, 1963.

MERTON, R. K. *Social Theory and Social Structure* (Rev. Ed.), New York: Free Press of Glencoe, Inc., 1957.

RECKLESS, W. C., *et al.* "Self Concept as an Insulator Against Delinquency." *Amer. Sociol. Rev.,* Dec., 1956, pp. 744–746.

RIEFF, P. *The Triumph of the Therapeutic.* New York: Harper and Row, 1966.

ROGERS, C. "The Characteristics of a Helping Relationship." *On Becoming a Person,* Boston: Houghton Mifflin, 1961, pp. 39–58.

SOROKIN, P. A. *Society, Culture, and Personality.* New York: Harper and Row, 1947, pp. 102–106.

STEIN, M. *The Eclipse of Community.* New York: Harper and Row, 1960.

TOENNIES, F. *Community and Society.* East Lansing, Mich.: Michigan State University Press, 1957.

SECTION SIX

Foundations in Economics

IN the previous section Boulding commented that "economics has a good claim to be the second oldest of the sciences [after physics]," and that it existed in its major theoretical formulation "before sociology, psychology, and anthropology as separate sciences were hardly thought of." Economic determinants of man's style of life and personal development are paid little heed in most formal personality theories, yet it is an obvious truth that occupational choice will play a large part in determining both the style and quality of an individual's life. Economics, the scientific study of the business cycle and related phenomena in social systems, is thus of far reaching import to the definition and practice of the guidance function.

Numerous areas of study in economics (manpower development, labor force and structure, unemployment, occupational change and automation, for example), are of direct concern not only to the practice of the guidance function, but also to the very development of the professional work force. A specific instance of the latter was the influence of federal support resulting from the National Defense Education Act (NDEA) of 1958, which provided a major impetus to the increased professionalization and growth of school counseling. A prime motive for the passage of NDEA was the perception of critical manpower needs following the public furor crystallized by the precipitous orbiting of the Russian "Sputnik." Manpower development, especially the development of a greater body of scientific personnel to overcome the "space gap," received much attention, and school counselors were needed to help "guide" qualified youth into the critical fields of mathematics and science. Much heat was generated with respect to the issue of whether the major focus of guidance was more properly conceptualized as manpower selection or human development.

Ralph Berdie's selection makes a strong case that economic development and social survival are both closely tied to effective manpower utilization, yet he sees no inherent conflict between effective manpower utilization and human development.

Obviously, personal adjustment and productivity, mental health and manpower are intimately related . . . [and] . . . almost everything said [about manpower development] with a slight twist can be made to refer directly to the mental health functions of the counselor.

Specific implications for counseling, Berdie concludes, are (1) that the counseling process should be continuous and not restricted to choice points only and (2) that counseling should take into more consideration factors related to the family.[1]

The present era is often referred to as the "human resources era," a slogan which represents the continuing economic concern for the conservation and development of manpower resources. One of the primary purposes of the guidance function, in the words of the present Executive Secretary of the American Personnel and Guidance Association, is "to supply the highest quality of service to society in the broad area of human resources and their full development" (Dugan, W., 1966, p. 668).

Broadly conceived economic information about occupational structure and trends has long been part of the standard arsenal of vocational counselors in the schools, in the United States Employment Service, and in Vocational Rehabilitation Centers. Examples of this information include the *Dictionary of Occupational Titles, The Occupational Outlook Handbook*, and numerous other publications of the Departments of Labor and Commerce.

In the selection following Berdie's, economist Louis Buckley surveys changes in the composition of the labor force and job

[1] Compare this with Hansen's brief discussion of milieu therapy in Section Five.

structure. He reiterates the often-made point of the radical rate of change and its implications for the fulfillment of the guidance function.

Buckingham portrays the rampart change in American occupational structure in startling detail and explores implications for educational practice. Other selections dealing with automation are included in Section Eight, *The Information Function*.

In an article that appeared as part of a symposium devoted to manpower problems, Robert Overs relates the economic system to sociological structure and discusses the interaction of vocational counseling with the American economic system. He concludes with a series of propositions connecting vocational counseling and labor economics to the problems of vocational choice and adjustment.

27. The Counselor and His Manpower Responsibilities

Ralph F. Berdie

Within the broader educational purposes of the school, the counselors' tasks broadly conceived concern, first, mental health and, secondly, manpower. Just as education is concerned with the welfare of the individual and the welfare of the community, so is counseling. Both mental health and manpower are concepts that directly reflect upon the welfare of the individual and also upon the status of the society in which he lives, but when counselors talk about mental health, emotional stability, personal adjustment, or happiness, they usually are thinking about the way the individual feels and the behavior that is a direct cause or result of his feelings. On the other hand, in discussions of manpower, the referent usually is the productivity of the worker in terms of his contribution to his fellow men. Obviously, personal adjustment and productivity, mental health and manpower are intimately related, and when we discuss the manpower responsibilities of the counselor, as we will here, we must remember that almost everything said with a slight twist can be made to

Ralph Berdie, "The Counselor and His Manpower Responsibilities," from *Personnel and Guidance Journal*, February, 1960, pp. 458–63. Copyright © 1960 by the American Personnel and Guidance Association, Inc., Washington, D.C. Reprinted by permission.

refer directly to the mental health functions of the counselor. Here, however, we will be concerned with this particular aspect of counseling—the manpower implications.

Much has been written and said during the past decade concerning the manpower problems we face. Our population in the United States is increasing in a quite unusual way. We have a great increase in the number of persons in the country but no proportionate increase as yet in the number of workers in their productive years. Due to the relatively low birth rate prior to World War II, the number of persons in the age range from 20 to 40 is quite small compared to the very large number of persons in the younger age range and to the increasingly large number of persons in the older ages. Thus, we have a larger population and greater demands for production and services, and at the same time we have no proportionate increase in the number of persons who are to make these products and services available.

The kinds of workers needed also have changed during recent decades. The proportion of workers who are in highly trained professional occupations has increased perhaps 25 per cent, but the need, and the demand, has been unmet in such occupations as medicine, teaching, nursing, engineering, mathematics, chemistry, physics, psychology, and management. Simultaneously, the proportion of workers required for jobs calling for little or no special training has declined, and this decline is continuing or even accelerating.

UNDERLYING ASSUMPTIONS

Those who have been concerned with manpower research have made a few rather explicit assumptions:

1. Every individual should be given the opportunity to obtain training at the maximum of his capacity.

2. Every person should be given an opportunity to have full knowledge concerning his capacities and potentialities and to decide for himself the extent to which these will be utilized.

3. The community must make available to an individual those experiences and situations which will give him full opportunity to appreciate his own potentialities and to realize the satisfaction that can be derived from their fulfillment.

4. A "well-manned" society must provide education and training to persons at all levels of abilities and skills, not only to a few selected leaders.

5. Society must encourage within its members broad diversity of talents and skills and eventually provide equal opportunities to persons developing skills in the sciences, the arts, humanities, and government and the social studies.

These assumptions throw much light upon the role of the counselor as it relates to both his responsibilities to the individual and to society. Certainly, they stress the fact that the counselor cannot achieve his goals by working in an interviewing room alone with a counselee, but rather in addition to working with individuals he also must assume his social responsibilities as he works with the schools, the universities, and other broad aspects of society. The effective counselor must be not only an effective educator and a competent psychologist but also a practicing citizen.

In order to maximize the probability of happiness for the individual and production and protection for society, two general approaches are available. The first approach would involve the identification of social objectives and the distribution of individuals, upon the basis of their abilities and potentials, into pursuits that lead to these social objectives. For instance, a government could decide that a given number of engineers, mathematicians, accountants, and nurses would be required within a certain period of time to obtain the objectives of that government. Children then could be analyzed, diagnosed, studied, and assigned to training programs in proportions that would result in the desired number of persons in each occupation. The second alternative would provide each individual with the greatest possible opportunity to become acquainted with his own potentials and possibilities and then allow each individual, within broad limits, to select the kind of training he wished to pursue. During his education, each student would be provided ample opportunity to review his own potential and to become acquainted with changes and developments as they occur in his abilities and personality. A maximum of opportunity would be provided for an individual to transfer from one training program to another and to continually revise his educational and occupational objectives in light of changes of ability, interests, and opportunity. Social objectives thus in part would be determined by the number of persons in different occupations and the number of citizens expressing various types of interests as shown by both educational and occupational activities.

The first alternative is a planned approach based on the assumption that men and communities can foresee and predict their own needs with some degree of accuracy and that persons can be used to attain social objectives in this way. The second alternative rests on the assumption that each man should have the opportunity for self-fulfillment and that the nature of society and the organization of the community must depend upon the ways individuals seek and find such fulfillment.

These two alternatives, obviously, are two extremes and the actual practice in most of our societies falls somewhere between. Usually the community possesses some control over the attractiveness of occupations. Through means of monetary, social, and other rewards, subsidized training through scholarships and other grants, and increases in status and prestige, society influences the numbers of persons entering occupations. The publication and dissemination of labor market and occupational information serve this same purpose. Job requirements can be changed and incentives manipulated to gain social control in a system of free choice.

Counseling also can be an instrument for filling manpower complements, but most counselors will not happily accept this assignment. The counselor is not responsible for providing the appropriate number of workers needed to fill the jobs society wishes filled, but rather, he can best serve the community and the individual by assisting each individual to find his own potential, to become acquainted with his own self, to accept himself as a person, to exploit his social and psychological environment in order to attain the desired fulfillment, and to constantly seek for new opportunities that will help him become a person. When he does this, the jobs most likely will be filled, but if they are not, then this is a much broader problem that touches on all of the values of our society.

IDENTIFICATION OF TALENT

The counselor has begun to play an important role in our schools in identifying individuals with rare and exceptional talents and calling these individuals to the attention of others in positions to help the person take advantage of these abilities. Thus, competent counselors in junior and senior high schools and in colleges and universities are in positions to identify students who eventually will become productive, if not great, authors, musicians, chemists, engineers, cabinet makers, designers, teachers, and statesmen. Equally as important as this job of identifying students with exceptional talents, however, is the job of helping each individual study his own abilities and aptitudes in order to determine which of these abilities can be utilized to the best advantage, which perhaps should be by-passed or ignored.

For each student with exceptional talent, there are many students with only average abilities, and the significance of any social contribution made by the rare individual who happens to be in the appropriate occupation is matched by the sum of the significances of the contributions made by the many mediocre persons each of whom is in an appropriate occupation. Perhaps more important than the social contribution made by the individual or the group of persons is the satisfaction and the feeling that can be derived from the ability to perform well in the work of one's choice.

Perhaps the one generalization that can be made is that the probability of identifying talent is increased if a systematic program is established for this purpose. Teachers and counselors, as well as parents and others, are able in many instances to find children who have unusual abilities or to help children determine what are their outstanding abilities, but if this is left to chance, in many, many cases students will be overlooked unless a school and a community provide systematic opportunity for the study and review of each individual.

CULTIVATION OF TALENT

The counselor's responsibility for the use of human resources does not end when the exceptionally talented individual has been identified and when the talents of all have been properly evaluated. The counselor and the school must find and know the abilities of students, but it is equally important that the student and his family also know about these abilities. The process of acquainting the student and his family with the potential of the student is an important counseling function, and here we all must agree that simply to make known the existence of these abilities is not sufficient; further steps are necessary. To give the student and his family information about abilities is not the same as to lead these persons to a point where they are able to accept the reality of this information and to understand its implications. Even acceptance and understanding are not enough to lead to a person's developing his own personal resources. The student must have opportunities to acquire the education and training appropriate for him, and also he must have the desire.

Let us look for a moment at the problem of the high-ability student who terminates his education upon graduation from high school. Fortunately, most bright students, at least in the United States, at present wish and seek education beyond high school. Among very bright students, perhaps between 90 and 95 per cent go on to higher education. These consist of the upper one to five per cent of the population in terms of abstract or academic ability. Thus, almost all exceptionally bright persons now at least are obtaining some higher training. If we become less selective and look only at the upper one-third of high school graduates (the upper third in terms of ability as shown both by college aptitude tests and high school achievement), we might safely generalize and say that approximately one-half of these students are now attending colleges and universities. We are failing to send on to continued education only a very small proportion of our exceptionally bright youngsters, but we are failing to educate beyond high school a rather large proportion of persons quite capable of completing college work, even in one of our more demanding institutions.

Certain groups can be identified that contribute more than their share to the noncollege-going, bright student. For instance, the female sex perhaps is the most delinquent group here. In almost every study reported, a far larger proportion of men than women drawn from comparable populations continue in college. One slight exception sometimes is noted; that is, among rural groups sometimes more women than men are found attending college. The rural group itself perhaps is the second most delinquent group. The sons and daughters of farmers are less prone to go to college than are children of equal ability whose parents are city folks. Economic and occupational groups also vary greatly in the frequency with which children attend college. Considering Minnesota high school seniors who had college aptitude test scores that placed them in the upper 10 per cent of their class, of the children of fathers in top-level occupations, 90 per cent planned to attend college; but of the children of factory laborers, only 55 per cent planned to attend college. Considering the children of different occupational groups and disregarding ability, differences, of course, were even larger. For instance, 81 per cent of all of the sons of professional workers planned to attend college, as compared to 30 per cent of all of the sons of factory workers. Although the relationship of college attendance to occupational status of parents is marked, we must remember that in almost every occupational group studied in Minnesota more than 50 per cent of the high-ability students were planning to attend college. College certainly is not restricted to the occupationally or economically privileged.

Certain religious, racial, and national groups fail to send their share of students to college. In the entire country, relatively few Negroes attend college. In Minnesota, if the same proportion of Indians as of non-Indians attended college, more than 200 Indian students would be in college instead of the less than 20 now enrolled. In some communities college attendance is strongly influenced by attitudes related to church and religion. The influences of race, nationality, and religion are difficult to isolate from those of economic status, ability, and family attitude, but nevertheless their effects are disturbing.

All-Important Attitudes

When we consider the reasons why high-ability students do not attend college, we obtain some clues in general as to why persons fail to develop their potentials and what might be done about this. The most frequently given reason as far as both students and speculators are concerned is an economic reason. It is assumed that if students had more money, more of them would attend college or university. The general acceptance of this reasoning is evidenced by the great pressure for the establishment of scholarship and financial aid programs. On the basis of studies done both in Minnesota and elsewhere, we can conclude that this is a reason for many persons not attending college. Many persons, if they had more financial help, would change their plans and go to college. Most people, however, overestimate the number whose plans would so be changed. In Minnesota, when we asked high school seniors what they planned to do during the year following graduation, almost one-third said they planned to join the labor force with no additional training. Of these 9,000 students who planned to go to work, one-third or 3,000 said they would go to college if they had more money. About 50 per cent of this one-third said they would need enough money to pay all of their expenses. About 10 per cent of these 9,000 students said they could easily afford to go to college if they wanted to, and another 20 per cent said they could barely afford it. Thus, about one-third could afford to attend college if they wanted to, but they were not planning to. Of the high-ability students in this study who were not going to college, fewer than 10 per cent indicated that they could easily afford college, and approximately an additional 25 per cent indicated they could barely afford college.

These figures suggested that lack of money was not the only important factor in determining whether or not high-ability students attend college. Many of the students who were not planning on college immediately after high school graduation had plans for eventually entering college. For instance, 24 per cent of the 96 metropolitan boys of high ability planning to work the year after graduation said they eventually planned to enter a profession. There were 711 high-ability students in this total group who planned to work, and of these, 58 per cent said they would attend college if they had more money. Thus, all of the evidence appeared to indicate that although lack of money was an important reason for students failing to continue their education, there were other reasons.

Information obtained in studies from questionnaires, interviews with students, case histories, and interviews with parents suggested that as important as any other reason is the attitude of the parent. A surprisingly large number of students reply when asked when they decided to attend college, that they had never made such a decision, that they simply always had assumed they would. A family apparently talks about college and education when the child is still small, and it is this type of conversation and related attitudes that determine in large part what the student does when he matures. Some interesting items related to college going can be found. For instance, the number of books a student reports in his home is closely related to whether or not he attends college. The education of the parents naturally is closely related to college attendance, and interestingly enough, the education of the mother seems to be a more potent variable than does the education of the father. This might make those persons think who contend it more important to educate our men than our women. Evidently, one of the ways for us to obtain more educated men is to have more educated mothers.

The types of organizations and the types of recreational activities families participate in are related to college attendance. When an attempt was made to isolate the relationship between economic conditions and college attendance and social-cultural conditions and college attendance, the latter correlation was slightly higher. In general, the conclusion seems justified: development of one's potential appears to be as much a function of one's attitudes and desires as it does a function of one's opportunities.

COUNSELING IMPLICATIONS

What does all of this mean for the counselor? First, it suggests that those processes that result in decisions to develop one's talents and abilities occupy long periods of time, and counseling that is to help students make these decisions must also be extensive. Counselors cannot be optimistic about the effects of counseling interviews conducted in the senior year; for instance, in many schools each graduating senior has only one or two interviews with a counselor. Counseling must extend not only through the senior year but through the junior and the sophomore year and the freshman year, and more and more recognition must be given to the need for counseling at least from grades seven on. Just as the decision-making process is a continuous one, so must be the counseling process.

Another implication is that counseling must, in the future, take into consideration factors related to the family more than has ever been done in the past. Just as teacher-parent conferences are becoming increasingly prevalent in our elementary schools, so must counselor-parent conferences increase in our junior and senior high schools. Parents can learn and accept what counselors can tell them regarding their children through counseling; the chances of this learning or acceptance occurring through the means of a single counseling report, either a written one or an oral one, is small.

Another implication derived only indirectly from the data at hand, can be stated in this way. In our concern over manpower and the development of the individual, we often have acted as if students were not motivated for college or for appropriate training and our job were to provide such motivation. We have seemed to assume that in the absence of motivation for college there was no motivation at all. We had better look at this assumption for when we talk with individual students it frequently appears that these students have strong motivations for things other than college. We are faced not with the problem of developing a motivation for college but rather with the job of helping the student understand his present motivation, consider the desirability of that motivation, and then if the student appears willing, stimulating whatever motivation is present for college so that the student arrives at a decision appropriate for him.

In conclusion, the counselor's responsibilities do not end when he has the student's abilities identified and the student rolling along on what appears to be an appropriate educational and occupational highway. The counselor is concerned with the student's obtaining the maximum benefit from his education. Many students lack certain basic educational skills that cause them trouble in college or in whatever training they select. Some college students do not read well enough to do college work, and counselors can help remedy this situation. Some college students do not have the other learning skills college requires, and the counselors can understand and help in this way. Many students of superior academic ability find difficulty in their school work and even fail in their work, as a result of personal frustrations, family difficulties, feelings of social inadequacy, or minor or even major mental diseases. The counselor, as one author has said, has a major responsibility for delivering to the classroom the student in an optimum condition for learning.

A student's educational and occupational plans are not completely formed when he begins his training. Periodically, a student should review his plans, consider the appropriateness of these plans in light of his progress, take into account changes in opportunities and new opportunities that have developed, and review his felt satisfactions with the kind of activity in which he is engaged. The counselor's function here is an important one.

In all of this, the counselor's role is not to advise the student or to make the student dependent upon a presumed authority. Rather, the counselor is neglecting his major responsibility if he does not help the student ever seek increasing independence, develop new skills in making decisions, learn how to explore problems, and acquire evidence needed in the solution of these problems. In this sense, the counselor is an educator. His greatest role perhaps is to help students apply to their own personal lives those same processes that concern others in the academic enterprise. When students can sense when they have problems and needs, when they can adequately understand the nature of these problems, when they can explore possible solutions and evaluate evidence relevant for these solutions, when they know how to solve personal problems just as they know how to solve more abstract or impersonal problems, then the educational role of the counselor is fulfilled.

The manpower role of the counselor is best fulfilled when he provides the counselee with the type of help that will allow the student to understand himself, his abilities, his interests, and his personality, that will lead to the student's acquiring information about the many opportunities that surround him, both educational and occupational, and that will enable the student to arrive at the unique solution that best fits him individually. When individuals are able to make these decisions and influence their behavior accordingly, then our manpower problem can be solved.

28. Economics and Guidance

Louis F. Buckley

Margaret Mead has observed that "we have a right to demand that guidance workers draw effectively upon all that the modern life sciences can give them." It is significant that economics is represented in this book as a related discipline in addition to five of the behavioral sciences, as well as philosophy and theology. Economics as a base for counseling has been strangely neglected. Gilbert Wrenn, in a study made for the American Personnel and Guidance Association, observed that the school counselor cannot afford to be a graduate student in psychology and a second grader in economics (Wrenn, 1962, p. 42). Since vocational choice in our democratic society is free, within the limits of certain determining factors, those who are in a position to influence vocational choice occupy a special position in relation to the economic system. The more specialized the society, the more important the guidance function (Overs, 1964, p. 213).

The origin of vocational guidance in the early years of the present century has been traced to the problems arising from the industrial revolution with its creation of new and specialized occupations in contrast to the agricultural era where the son followed in the occupation of his father. The resulting confusion, uncertainty, insecurity, and readjustment, according to Harold Goldstein, "cried out for some form of order in the chaos and, in our rational, pragmatic society, vocational guidance was the inevitable answer" (Goldstein, 1963, p. 227).

The economic revolution, which we are now experiencing, is likely to change the occupational structure more drastically than did the industrial revolution. The year 1950 is often referred to as the break between the period of rapid change and that of radical change. What is different now

Louis F. Buckley, "Economics and Guidance," in Thomas C. Hennessy, S.J., ed., *The Interdisciplinary Roots of Guidance* (New York: Fordham University Press, 1966), pp. 1–22. Reprinted by permission of the publisher.

is the pace of change. David Sarnoff of RCA predicts that science and technology will advance more in the next thirty-six years than in all the millennia since man's creation.

THE LABOR MARKET

I would like to center my attention on the labor market aspects of economics which are of particular significance to the counselor. Emphasis will be placed on the important changes which are taking place in the demand for and the supply of labor which are indicative of what we may expect in the future. The following thought from Abraham Lincoln might be considered as a text for this approach: "If we could first know where we are and whither we are tending, we could better judge what to do and how to do it."

CHANGES IN INDUSTRY

The nature of the demand for labor has changed in many respects during the past fifteen years. Within the overall pattern of increase in demand for labor, some industries, like agriculture and mining, have shown a steady decline. Demand for labor in contract construction grew at a rapid pace during the first decade of the postwar period, but has changed very little in the past several years. In the largest industry sector—manufacturing—the demand for labor has had wide fluctuations between industries without a discernible overall trend of increase or decline.

A significant change in demand for labor took place about 1950, when, for the first time in history, the number of workers in service industries, which include trade, transportation, public utilities, finance, insurance, real estate, government and other services, surpassed the number in the production or goods-producing industries, which include manufacturing, agriculture, construction and mining. The proportion of all workers in goods-producing industries declined from 51 per cent in 1947 to 46 per cent in 1957, and fell to about 40 per cent in 1963. The rate of decline in the proportion of goods-producing employment in the economy in the last six years has been almost two times greater than in the previous decade. The United States is the only country in the world in which the jobs in services outnumber the jobs in goods industries.

The principal reason why the demand for the majority of our workers is in the service-producing sectors of the American economy is because of the extraordinary increases which have taken place in output per man hour in the goods-producing industries. As a result, we simply need fewer people to put out the enormous complex of goods that we have available to us. Underlying the productivity gains are a number of factors, including technological advances, improvements in the quality of the labor force, increases in capital investment, and investments in research and development.

The major buying sectors which determine the demand for goods and services and the ultimate demand for labor are individual consumers, business, government and export. Purchases by government have shown a far greater tendency to rise over the last several decades than those by other sectors. Wars, international tensions, and depressions, along with population growth, have all provided the impetus at one time or another to increase purchases by government agencies—federal, state and local. During the postwar period the trend continued, with government expenditures more than doubling in real terms. Although there has been a substantial slackening in the rate of growth of federal purchases since 1957, state and local spending continued their steady rise resulting from increased demands for community services mainly related to population growth and the critical problem of expanding urban communities. Gains in employment have been especially rapid in education, health and hospital and sanitation services.

Purchases by individuals, which have grown steadily, account for the largest share of national demand for goods and services. However, outlays for services showed the most persistent increase. Families tend to spend relatively less of their income for goods, such as food, but more for health and recreation, housing, transportation and financial services. Expenditures on business plant and equipment and on residential construction have varied widely. While investment spending is much smaller in total volume than consumer expenditures, the role of investment is crucial to increased labor force productivity.

OCCUPATIONAL CHANGE

The changes in labor demands, from the viewpoint of industries which we have discussed, are reflected in changing occupational demands for labor. The divergent industry employment trends have brought with them, inevitably, marked changes in the demand for workers in different occupations. The decrease in the demand for farmers and farm labor which was part and parcel of the overall decline in agricultural employment is an obvious illustration. In addition, the emergence of new industries (television and atomic energy, for example) has given rise to wholly new occupations.

Within industries, the occupational composition of the work force has been affected by a great variety of factors, of which the most pervasive is technological change. As a result of technological innovations, new occupations have emerged while others have expanded, contracted or even disappeared. The new *Dictionary of Occupational Titles* will contain about 22,000 jobs of which 6,000 will be new to the Dictionary. Many of these new jobs are also relatively new in the economy.

A shift in employment toward white-collar occupations (professional, managerial, clerical and sales) and a relative decline in blue-collar groups (craftsmen, operatives, and laborers) has been evident since the beginning of the century. In 1956, for the first time in our history, professional, managerial, clerical, and sales employees outnumbered employees in manual occupations. These trends reflect the increased demand in service industries where more white-collar workers are employed and the slower employment growth in goods-producing industries which have relatively large numbers of blue-collar jobs.

In addition to the workers in white-collar and blue-collar occupations, there are two broad occupational groups—farm and service workers—which do not fit neatly into either category because they include workers of both types. The persistant decline in employment of farm workers has been interrupted in only three of the fifteen postwar years. Employment of service workers, on the other hand, has increased notably. In 1953, for the first time, the number of workers employed in service occupations—cooks, janitors, barbers, etc.—exceeded that of farm workers, and the differences have widened fairly steadily since then—providing one more indication of the shift in employment from goods-oriented jobs to service-oriented jobs in our economy.

The fastest growing demand for occupational groups during the decade 1950 to 1960 was for professional, technical and kindred workers. This group includes all the recognized professions—teaching, engineering, law, the ministry, the various health professions, the natural and social sciences, and many others. It also includes a large number of technical and kindred occupations—for example, the many types of technicians who work with engineers and scientists and with members of the health professions. Such occupations typically require less education than is needed for fully professional work, although many experienced technicians have jobs demanding considerable technical training.

Employment demand for professional and technical workers as a group increased by 47 per cent between 1950 and 1960—a rate of growth more than three times the average for all occupational groups. However, employment demand grew much faster for some professions than others. The number of engineers, for example, increased by about 64 per cent over the decade; among engineers, the aeronautical group grew fastest, increasing by 193 per cent.

Although there has been a decline in the number of self-employed proprietors, the number of managers and other salaried officials required by private industry and government increased by more than a third during the past decade. Clerical workers increased 34 per cent between 1950 and 1960. Despite the strides made in the automation of many clerical functions, the demand for certain types of clerical workers has continued to rise—due partly to the substantial expansion of industries such as finance, insurance and government. Demand for secretaries and typists increased about 70 per cent during the 1950's. Other clerical occupations showing rapid increases in demand were office machine operators, receptionists, cashiers, and bank tellers. The number of workers required in wholesale trade and other industries increased by 33 per cent in contrast to only a 10 per cent increase in retail trade.

Turning now to the demand for blue-collar workers, we find only an increase of 12 per cent in the 1950's. More than two-thirds of the increase occurred among foremen, mechanics and repairmen. Construction craftsmen, who constitute one-fourth of all skilled workers, had only a small increase in employment over the decade. Skilled workers who decreased in numbers during the decade included locomotive firemen and engineers, railroad mechanics, furriers, jewelers and shoemakers. The operative or semi-skilled group as a whole did not change significantly in absolute numbers during the 1950's. Machines have been substituted for the more routinized operations performed by semi-skilled workers. Such changes have permitted great expansion in production without commensurate increases in the demand for machine operators. Demand for drivers and deliverymen rose by almost 20 per cent between 1950 and 1960.

Another major effect of changing technology has been the declining need for industrial laborers. Employment in laboring jobs dropped by almost 10 per cent between 1950 and 1960. Requirements for laborers have decreased primarily because of the increasing substitution of machinery for unskilled labor in the handling and moving of heavy objects, in unloading and in excavating. In contrast, demand for service workers has increased almost twice as fast as employment generally during the 1950–60 period. The increase in employment of hospital attendants and practical nurses was very sizable. Other types of service workers who had substantial increases in employment were waiters, cooks and counter workers in restaurants.

GEOGRAPHIC TRENDS

The shifts in the industrial demand for manpower which we have discussed have also contributed to changes in the location of employment. The older industrial areas of the Northeast and Great Lakes have grown at a much slower pace than the nation as a whole, while the southern and western regions experienced a much faster growth. In California, Oregon and Washington, employment rose 61 per cent in the past 15 years. Along the South Atlantic coast it increased by 41 per cent. In contrast, employment in New England rose by only 13 per cent and actually declined in West Virginia and Rhode Island.

EMPLOYMENT OF WOMEN

The greatly increased demand for women in the labor market has been a most striking recent development and reflects the trend toward white-collar occupations and the expansion of industries which normally employ a large number of women, such as trade. The greatest increase in demand for women has been in the professional group where 58 per cent more women were employed in 1962 than in 1950. Teaching is the largest occupational group in the professional employment of women. There have been increases of over 50 per cent also in the employment of women in clerical work and as service workers such as waitresses. About 30 per cent of women workers are employed part-time. The demand for part-time workers exists most frequently among private-household workers, sales workers and waitresses.

NEGRO EMPLOYMENT

There have been increases in the demand for Negro workers in some of the professional, technical and clerical fields and in other white-collar occupations. The largest relative gains made by Negroes between 1955–62 were in professional services, such as hospital, medical, and other services, and in welfare and religious institutions. Negroes also have experienced relatively sharp gains in the growing fields of educational services and public administration. Howard University recently reported that 319 companies had visited their campus in 1964 recruiting their graduates. This is an increase of 300 over 1963. A recent report by the President's Equal Employment Opportunity Committee, (1963–64) based on data from 4610 companies with a total of 2,404,253 employees, indicated that white-collar employment of Negroes increased 17.4 per cent from 1962 to 1963 while total employment in these occupations rose by only 1.9 per cent. The Negroes started from so small a base, however, that the gain increased their percentage of total white-collar employment in the companies from 1.2 per cent to only 1.3 per cent.

Despite this limited progress in the shift of the Negro to white-collar and skilled occupations, it must be recognized that in 1962 only 17 per cent of all employed Negroes were in white-collar occupations, compared with 47 per cent of white workers. White workers in this group outnumbered Negroes 28 to 1, in marked contrast to their comparative representation in the civilian labor force (10 white for each Negro worker). Unless there is a substantial acceleration of the trends noted, the percentage of Negro workers in white-collar employment will be substantially below that of white workers for many years. The rate of increase in Negro employment in the white-collar occupations must be expedited as these are the occupations which will show the greatest rate of growth in the future.

The future is even bleaker than the present for the Negro worker in many respects because the gap is widening between the occupational distribution of Negro workers and the nature of the demand for workers in the labor market. Forty-three per cent of Negroes compared to 25 per cent of white workers are in semi-skilled or unskilled occupations. These jobs tend to be concentrated in those goods-producing and related industries which are quite sensitive to the business cycle. Moreover, the demand for this type of labor has diminished steadily during the post-war period as a result of automation and other technological developments. On the other hand, less than 10.0 per cent of Negro workers compared to over 3 per cent of white workers are employed in professional, technical, managerial and sales occupations where the demand for workers is expanding.

RISING EDUCATIONAL REQUIREMENTS

The most rapidly expanding occupations, professional, technical, managerial, clerical and skilled, are those which require the most education and training. The average years of school completed by those in the professional and technical occupations now exceed four years of college and in clerical and sales they exceed four years of high school. A high school diploma is generally required now for entrance into skilled jobs and to an increasing extent even in the operative occupations. As Secretary of Labor, Willard Wirtz, has stated: "The machines now have, in general, a high school education—in the sense that they can do most jobs that a high school education qualifies people to do. So machines will get the unskilled jobs, because they work for less than living wages. Machines are, in the most real sense, responsible for putting uneducated people out of work."

SUPPLY OF MANPOWER

The growth in the country's labor force over the past two decades has been very substantial. From 56 million in 1940, the number of workers grew to 73 million in 1960. This gain of 17 million workers was the largest ever experienced in this country in any 20-year period. Between 1957 and 1962, the net annual increase in the labor force averaged about three-quarters of a million. In 1963, with improved employment conditions and with the first large group of the postwar baby boom reaching working age, the labor force rose sharply by 1.1 million.

Women have accounted for about three-fifths of the entire labor force increase over the 1947–62 period. This recent rise in women's employment has occurred almost entirely among married women. For women, labor force participation reaches a peak in the late teens and early twenties, as they leave school, and then drops in the middle twenties as marriage and motherhood bring withdrawals from the work force. After they reach 35 or thereabouts and their children reach school age, the proportion employed outside the home rises. It reaches a new peak at ages 45 to 54 and then tends to drop off, since many women stop working at a younger age than is customary for men.

A substantial rise in the educational attainment of American workers has been achieved. The relative numbers of workers who are college graduates have risen especially fast in the past 10 years—from 7.9 per cent in 1952 to 11 per cent in 1962, for those 18 years old and over. The increase in the proportions that have had at least a high school education is also noteworthy. This proportion rose from 42.8 to 53.8 per cent over the past decade, a gain of more than 25 per cent. At the lower end of the educational ladder, the proportion of workers with less than 5 years of school fell from 7.3 to 4.6 percent.

IMBALANCE IN THE LABOR MARKET

Maladjustments in the forces of supply and demand in the labor market have resulted in a serious and persistent problem of unemployment. Despite a lengthy period of expansion in economic activity, the 1962–63 unemployment rates stubbornly remained between 5½ and 6 per cent. The year 1963 marked the sixth consecutive year in which unemployment rates failed to return to the 4 per cent level which prevailed during most of the 1955–57 period. Moreover, the trend in unemployment has been getting progressively worse. In each of the last few business booms, the unemployment rate has failed to decline to a level as low as that reached at the peak of the previous expansion. The unemployment rate for non-white workers is more than double that of white workers.

Teenage unemployment rose in 1963. An average of nearly 1 million teenage boys and girls were unemployed in 1963, compared with 800,000 during 1962. At 15½ per cent, the 1963 teenage unemployment rate was close to those recorded in the recession years of 1958 and 1961, and higher than in any other postwar year.

About 1.1 million or 26 per cent of the unemployed in 1963 had been seeking work 15 weeks or longer. In terms of skill levels, unskilled workers, service workers and semi-skilled operatives together represented more than three-fifths of the experienced unemployed in 1963, while they accounted for only two-fifths of all employed persons.

A major factor which accounts for the imbalance in the labor market, thus resulting in unemployment, is that the great increase in demand for labor has been concentrated in occupations at the top of the ladder in terms of education and skill at a time when there is not a sufficient supply of labor available to meet the qualifications of the so-called "knowledge" occupations. And even in occupations where the supply of workers may approximate the demand on a nationwide basis, local shortages can and do develop, owing to sudden increases in local demand, to lack of worker mobility, and to other frictions and inefficiencies in the operation of the labor market.

Other important factors which explain imbalance include the inability of the labor demand growth to absorb the increases taking place in labor supply and the workers displaced because of technological improvements. These two factors alone—labor force and productivity increase—required a growth in employment opportunities equivalent to about 3 million jobs between 1962 and 1963 if a rise in unemployment was to be prevented. Unfortunately this amount of growth was not achieved in 1963 or in recent years.

FUTURE MANPOWER TRENDS

The major industrial and occupational changes during the past fifteen years which we have discussed are likely to continue during the next ten years. We may expect a continuation of the more rapid growth of the so-called white-collar group of occupations, a smaller growth in the blue-collar occupations and a faster-than-average growth among service workers and a further decline among farmers and farm laborers. The direction of employment demand is clearly for workers with more education and greater skill. The occupational outlook also is assuming an increasingly international aspect. More people will have jobs abroad in the next decade. An uncertain element on the demand side of the labor market is the possible decrease in the defense budget which accounts for expenditures of $51 billion dollars a year. We are now feeling the effect of the recent decrease in this budget.

The dramatic technological developments which we have witnessed during the past fifteen years are but the beginning of fundamental, industrial and occupational changes which will continue at an accelerating rate as far ahead as we can see. The application of this new technology will extend outside the factory and major industries will probably develop that do not exist now as was the case of computer production in the last fifteen years.

Demand created by replacement needs is of equal importance to net employment growth. In fact, the number of persons who will be required to replace workers who retire, die or leave the work force for other reasons between 1960 and 1970 will exceed the 13.8 million net growth in employment projected for the economy as a whole during that period.

Another aspect of impending manpower adjustment relates to changes in the pattern of labor supply stemming from growth in the labor force. During the next twelve months 1 million more young people will be reaching age 18 than in the last twelve months, or an increase of over 35 per cent. This large growth results from a sharp increase in the birth rate during the postwar period. Although fortunately a large number of these young people will not enter the labor market until later, the number of new young workers entering the labor force annually will increase from two million in 1960 to three million in 1970. This increase represents a far greater number than the economy has ever had to absorb in a single decade.

The sheer number of workers who will be entering the labor force to seek work next year and in the years immediately ahead represents only one aspect of the problem. The adequacy of their education and training to meet the rising job requirements of a fast growing economy reflects another of the problem's dimensions.

LABOR MARKET IMPLICATIONS FOR GUIDANCE

The changing industrial and occupational structure, the changing geography of American industry, the changing educational prerequisites of employment and the changing size and educational attainment of the work force which we have discussed are major factors with which the counselor must cope. These changes should be considered a prelude to even more rapid and extensive change which we must anticipate in the future. Seymour L. Wolfbein of the U.S. Department of Labor emphasizes that change will continue to be a surpassingly important dimension in the field of counseling. He has redefined the concept of the education and guidance process as helping the individual to withstand the onslaughts and, in fact to take advantage of the inevitable changes which will occur in the world of work (Borow, 1964, p. 171).

The counselor must recognize that safe and secure occupations of the present may be obsolete in the future. Margaret Mead has observed, "No one will live all his life in the world in which he was born, and no one will die in the world in which he worked at maturity." This situation emphasizes the need to look at long-run employment prospects rather than at the immediate situation in career planning. It indicates that overemphasis on specific skills should be avoided at the expense of developing basic capabilities. Those preparing to enter the world of work must acquire a broad-based background which will equip them with maximum ability to adjust to change. John Diebold, head of a consulting firm, and a recognized authority on automation, maintains that counselors should no longer emphasize the choice of one career as a lifetime pursuit (Diebold, 1962, p. 1). Young people must also recognize that additional education throughout adult life will be increasingly necessary as occupational skills need constant refurbishing. Similarly, guidance must be considered to be a developmental process over the lifetime of the individual.

Louis Levine, Director, United States Employment Service stresses that "employment counselors must consciously and deliberately think in terms of change. They must think in terms of long-range projections and must adopt an attitude of anticipation of a preparation for change. They must think 'future' and keep abreast of information on new job fields, or they will be counseling for a world of work that no longer exists."

IDENTIFICATION AND CULTIVATION OF TALENT

The counselor can make an important contribution toward reducing the imbalance between the abilities of our labor force and the labor demand requirements of the new technology which we have discussed. By 1970, the experts predict industry and government will have a deficit of at least 20,000 physicists—about one-third of the total number required. The Engineering Manpower Commission of the Engineers Joint Council cited with alarm the increasing advantage the Soviet Union is establishing in the production of engineers. It noted that the Russians are outproducing the United States better than 3 to 1. During 1961, the Red Chinese turned out 19,000 engineers—five times as many as in 1950. In the same period, engineering graduates in this country declined from 42,000 to 36,000. As individuals and as a nation we are engaged in a competitive struggle to maintain a position of world leadership. Albert S. Thompson of Columbia University points out that "just as the passing of the frontier in the late 1800s meant that we could no longer be so profligate with our natural resources, so the current challenge to our world leadership in social and technical developments means that we cannot afford to waste our human resources" (Borow, 1964, p. 488).

The counselor can play an increasing role in identifying individuals with rare and exceptional talent and in helping these individuals analyze their abilities and aptitudes in order to determine which of these abilities can be utilized to the best advantage. The counselor also has a function in the cultivation of talent as the student must have opportunities to acquire the education and training appropriate for him and also he must have the desire to do so.

THE POTENTIAL DROPOUT

Since our analysis has indicated that most of the expanding job opportunities require an educational background, it is essential that more of our young people are motivated to remain in school. The extent to which school dropouts find difficulty in fitting into the labor market is indicated in that the rate of unemployment for 1962 school dropouts in October was 29 per cent, about twice as high as the rate for the June high school graduates despite the higher proportion of dropouts in farm areas, where unemployment is less common. The situation for dropouts can be expected to worsen in the coming years, because little growth or some declines are expected in occupations with low educational and skill requirements and workers without at least a high school diploma will have increasing difficulty entering expanding occupations where educational and training qualifications are high. They will constitute a new disadvantaged minority group in the American labor force—increasingly handicapped in competing for jobs because of the greater availability of graduates and decreasing opportunities for partly-educated workers.

Seymour Wolfbein, of the U.S. Department of Labor, has pointed out that many, if not most, of our potential dropouts have neither the predilection nor the aptitude for academic, college-preparatory courses of training. But a very large group is composed of manually-talented boys for whom meaningful courses of instruction in the vocational area would make the difference between dropping out of school and achieving a high school diploma. This is an opportunity to build meaningful pathways which will help the young person realize his potential and at the same time help fill our needs for skilled personnel.

THE SKILLED WORKER

As an increasing proportion of the brighter than average young people go on to college, as the percentage rises from one-fourth to one-third of our population, we are running the risk of starving the skilled and service occupations of competent workers. We have seen that among blue-collar workers, the craftsmen, foremen and kindred workers will continue to have the most favorable employment outlook. Because of the mounting need for mechanics and repairmen to install and maintain the ever-increasing amount of complex equipment used by industry, government agencies and private households, employment of these workers will continue to increase rapidly.

It is of major importance that guidance and counseling personnel familiarize themselves with the need for skilled workers. It is important for them to know and impart the fact that the crafts represent one of the best fields for young persons. These occupations rank near the top of the earning scale. About three out of every four who are employed are year-round full-time workers. They enjoy greater-than-average job security. Their unemployment rate is only half that of the unskilled workers.

It is essential that all of us help to endow the craftsman with the stature and status he deserves. Seymour Wolfbein has observed that too often, the young person pursuing a non-academic course, preparing himself for a trade, is considered to be at the bottom of the totem pole, down in the ranks of the untalented. This is an entirely false impression. The skills and aptitudes may be different from those of professional or other personnel, but they can be just as difficult to acquire, just as complex in their concepts and techniques, and they are just as strategic to the growth of our economy.

GUIDANCE OF SPECIAL GROUPS

The counselor must assume an increasing role in the war on poverty by providing disadvantaged groups of young people with the guidance needed to assist them in preparing themselves for a place in the complicated and changing labor market we have discussed. Young people who come from low-income families and suffer from social deprivations must be given special consideration and attention by the counselor. The report of the Senate Committee on Labor and Public Welfare (1960) in considering amendments to the Manpower Development and Training Act summarized this problem as follows: "Dropouts leave school for many reasons not necessarily related to their intellectual capacity or potential. Their reasons are rooted in the poverty, discrimination, and social chaos in which they have been reared. Their motivation has been corroded by a hostile society."

Unless we are more successful in making young people appreciate that the lack of a high school diploma is rapidly becoming an impassable barrier to entrance into the labor force and to stable employment and unless we succeed in motivating young people to complete their education, we are committing them to economic suicide. Secretary of Labor Willard Wirtz expanded on this matter recently when he said the nation is stacking up young boys and girls just out of school on an economic slag heap at a rate of a quarter of a million a year.

The current Negro situation would not be so serious if all of us, educators, counselors and the public, had done a better job of preparing young Negroes for the shortage occupations in the professional and technical fields which are opening to them today. The National Urban League did outstanding pioneer work in this area by encouraging, motivating, and assisting young Negroes to obtain the kind of education needed for work in the technical and scientific fields while many counselors were thinking in terms of continued entrance of Negroes only in the unskilled and least desirable service occupations where they formerly could find work.

Another group that requires special mention are girls. Our analysis of labor market trends indicates that nine out of ten women are likely to work outside of their home during the course of their lives. An increasing number of women will make significant contributions in vocations in the world of work as well as in the home as wife and mother. This is another situation where the counselor has contributed to the restrictive concept of limited occupational choice because they are women.

There is need for particular emphasis on the counseling of talented girls. Because of the current pattern of early marriage, many girls take it for granted that they will work for only a few years at most, and so fail to take seriously their educational and vocational planning. Yet, as indicated earlier in our analysis, women in their 30's are going to work in rising numbers after their children reach school age. By helping girls to realize that they may spend many years at work, even if they marry, and assisting them to plan their education accordingly, counselors can contribute to the later job satisfaction and income of many women. If you can stimulate bright girls to think more seriously about their professional potentialities, you may also help to relieve the national shortage of creative personnel.

An interesting by-product of the education of women is that studies of college students indicate a closer relationship between the education of the mother and college attendance than does the education of the father. As one author commented, this might make those persons think who contend it more important to educate our men than our women. Evidently, one of the ways to obtain more educated men is to have more educated mothers (Berdie, 1960, p. 462).

OCCUPATIONAL INFORMATION

Counselors, in order to give meaningful guidance, must keep abreast of the rapidly changing world of work. They must be able to help young people acquire an accurate picture of the hard facts of the American job market in relation to their interests, aptitudes and abilities, that they may be better able to make an intelligent choice of occupational goals.

I am sure you are familiar with the basic occupational information available in the following Department of Labor publications: *Occupational Outlook Handbook, Occupational Outlook Quarterly, Job Guide for Young Workers* and *Dictionary of Occupational Titles.* Many state public employment services have occupational guides and area skill surveys available in localities which are helpful in becoming better acquainted with local labor market conditions.

Annual reports are required under the Manpower Development and Training Act of 1962, on manpower requirements, resources, utilization and training. I relied on these reports issued in March, 1963 and 1964 for much of the basic information used in my analysis of the labor market in this discussion. There are other developments which will assure us of even more comprehensive and adequate occupational information. Under the Manpower Development and Training Act, local public employment agencies must determine whether or not manpower shortages exist and the probable opportunity for placement of trainees in various occupations. Furthermore, the Vocational Education Act of 1963 places the responsibility upon state public employment agencies to inform the State Board of Education about job opportunities and job requirements for which training is needed. In carrying out this assignment, public employment services are directed to collect information not otherwise available about jobs in fields of work for which vocational training is deemed practicable.

I would urge that the interdisciplinary approach which is stressed in this book[1] be followed by counselors in establishing working relations with the agencies in the community which can assist in keeping the school counselor familiar with the present and future employment needs of the community. Such information and working arrangements should include in addition to the local state employment office, groups representing employers, labor unions, religious organizations and professional organizations. In areas where local manpower committees have been formed to advise the state employment service, counselors may want to discuss with the local committee chairmen their need for being advised of current labor market developments.

All individuals planning to leave school should be made aware of services provided by state employment offices. School guidance personnel should take advantage of the referral, testing, vocational counseling, and placement services provided by state employment offices for both part-time summer opportunities and for entry job placement. Cooperative arrangements have been developed in many communities whereby potential dropouts, particularly those without definite job prospects, are referred to the local public employment office prior to actually leaving school.

[1] The author refers to the book for which this selection was written originally.

I was impressed during a visit to Germany with the practice followed there of having attractive calendars in each classroom which carry pictures of various occupations. Time is spent each week discussing one of the occupations so that students at an early age obtain a knowledge of the nature and requirements of the jobs. Emphasis is placed on every type of occupation including, in particular, the manual or blue-collar jobs. I believe we could do much more and begin at an early age (grade school) in this country to develop an interest and to provide information which will be helpful to the student when he is ready to make a vocational choice. It must be recognized that vocational choice and adjustment is a long-time process which is never completely finished.

I also liked the emphasis placed by counselors in Germany on meeting with parents to discuss vocational choice. A program of this nature might serve a purpose in this country in dealing with parents who fail to provide children with the proper incentive for achievement. It might also serve to deter parents who drive their children into academic programs beyond their abilities and thus into failure and frustration.

Conclusion

That the need for guidance and counseling services will mount sharply in the years ahead and will assume a greater, more important and more decisive role is one of the findings which emerges most clearly from our analysis of our rapidly changing occupational structure. Counselors will be called upon to guide unprecedented numbers of young people in a vocational adjustment likely to present difficult problems. Moreover, the vocational aspects of counseling including the providing of occupational information, are likely to assume steadily increasing importance in view of the competition for available jobs and the shifts in occupational requirements which will occur in this period of rapid technological change.

Our democracy is now engaged in a world-wide struggle with a totalitarian system, in which the government can direct the education and training of the people in a manner designed to achieve an allocation among occupations in accordance with its concept of national needs. In our country, we face the much more difficult task of meeting the nation's needs for specialized personnel without impairing freedom of choice for the individual.

What is needed and is evolving to meet this challenge is the cooperation and the effective working relationships of all groups who have any bearing on education, counseling, training, employment and the job market process. The pattern of cooperation is similar to the interdisciplinary approach being used so effectively in this book. Each discipline and each interested group will contribute its special training and background to work as an effective team in achieving a solution to these challenging manpower problems based on the total acceptance of the dignity and worth of each individual as a human being.

REFERENCES

BERDIE, RALPH F. "The counselor and his manpower responsibilities." *The Personnel and Guid. J.*, February, 1960, 458–463.
BOROW, HENRY, ed. *Man in a world at work*. Boston: Houghton Mifflin, 1964.
DIEBOLD, JOHN. "Automation: its implications for counseling." *Occupational Outlook Quarterly, 6*, No. 3, September, 1962, 1–3.
GOLDSTEIN, HAROLD. "Economic setting for vocational guidance." *The Vocational Guidance Quarterly, 11*, No. 4, Summer, 1963, 227–231.
OVERS, ROBERT P. "The interaction of vocational counseling with the economic system." *Amer. J. of Econ. and Sociol.*, 23, April, 1964, No. 2, pp. 213–221.
President of the United States. *Manpower report of the President and a report on manpower requirements, resources, utilization and training*. Washington, D.C.: Government Printing Office, 1963 and 1004.
U.S. Department of Labor, *Manpower Challenge of the 1960s*. Washington, D.C.: Government Printing Office, 1960.
WOOD, HELEN. "The manpower future—its challenge for vocational guidance." *The Personnel and Guid. J.*, December, 1959, 300–304.
WRENN, C. GILBERT. *The counselor in a changing world*. Washington, D.C.: American Personnel and Guidance Association, 1962.

29.   Educational Implications of Our Changing Occupational Structure

Walter Buckingham

Because of technological changes, over 200,000 production jobs have been eliminated in recent years in the aircraft industry alone, even though the industry's total business has continued to increase. Productivity (or output per man-hour) in the soft coal industry has doubled since World War II, but employment has fallen by nearly 300,000 people, or approximately two-thirds. Railroad productivity increased 65 per cent during this same period, but employment dropped by 540,000. Total steel

From Walter Buckingham, "Educational Implications of Our Changing Occupational Structure," in Max Abbott and John Lowell, eds., *Change Perspectives in Educational Administration* (Auburn, Ala.: School of Education of Auburn University, 1965), pp. 17–26. Reprinted by permission of the publisher.

production remains about the same as a decade ago, but employment has declined over 80,000. Employment in the manufacture of refrigerators and washing machines fell 18 per cent and employment in instrument production fell 15 per cent, while total production of these products was increasing. In transportation, not one new net job has been added since 1929 in spite of the enormous increase in our population. True, the demand for professional people, such as scientists, engineers, and teachers, has exceeded the supply, but all of the professional people put together are only about 11 per cent of the labor force. If displaced coal miners could immediately become nuclear physicists this would not be the solution.

A leading business executive, President John Snyder of U. S. Industries, Inc., estimates that the rate of disemployment, or "silent firing," is 40,000 persons per week. "Silent firing" refers to those who are never hired because their potential jobs were eliminated. A more conservative estimate by the U.S. Labor Department is that we now need 158 new jobs per day, compared with 100 jobs needed daily in the 1950's. Many experts now estimate that for every job created by automation, or new technology, five jobs will disappear. New job openings, due to limited economic growth, have prevented the labor force from feeling the full impact.

The children of our poverty-stricken people may be able to work in the many new industries, which are being created so rapidly, if we rise to the challenge of educating or training them. The most serious part of this program is that most of the parents of these children need help of a positive nature. Although private industry has done a good job in this area, and is planning to do more, this will not be enough. The federal, state and local governments must provide help where private industry or labor unions are not planning to re-educate or retrain.

Ignorance, poverty, and unemployment breed on each other. Many studies have shown that the greatest cause of both poverty and unemployment is lack of education. R. Sargent Shriver recently reported that forty per cent of the people rejected from our military service come from families where the head of the household did not complete grade school. Unemployment and ignorance tend to be passed on from one generation to the next.

Furthermore, the rates of unemployment vary inversely with education at all levels. Few people with any college education are out of work. A slightly higher percentage of high school graduates need jobs. But one-third of all people under age 24 with no high school education are unemployed. The average income of those people at work in all fifty states, and even by counties within states, varies inversely with their education. Studies of this have shown that when per capita income, per county, in a state is compared with the level of education a difference of one year in average education accounts for about $200 income per year.

Most American cities, towns and rural areas have a large economic underworld of uneducated people who are unemployed, under-employed, or poverty stricken though employed. Of those who are working, millions are employed in hotels, restaurants, hospitals, laundries, as housemaids, or at other jobs not considered in interstate commerce. In retailing jobs alone there are about 7 million workers. The workers in all of these areas typically earn from 50 to 75 cents an hour and some have had to join unions to be allowed to earn this. Being ignorant and poor they are easy prey for racketeers in labor or management, and are easily exploited by loan sharks, used car dealers, etc. They are quickly fired for numerous illegal reasons, such as trying to organize the workers into a union or for just "not staying in their place." The rate of those rejected from employment or laid off is in almost direct proportion to their lack of education or training. These people seem almost immune to help.

Within ten years automation has made such gigantic inroads that there is no longer much of a market for uneducated or unskilled people. Yet, a million American youngsters drop out of school every year. If present trends continue they are destined to lives of unemployment and poverty. Relief, for millions, has become a way of life.

At the same time that hundreds of thousands of jobs are being wiped out, new ones are being created in areas unknown only a few years ago. Some of these new jobs have titles that defy easy understanding and pronunciation. Included here are data telemetry, gyrodynamics, micro-miniaturization, transistorized circuitry, and ferret reconnaissance. Although many of these jobs are going begging the number of people displaced vastly exceeds the number of new jobs created. The answer to this enormous obsolescence of skills and displacement of labor lies in re-education, retraining, keeping more students in school at all levels for longer periods of time, and, most of all, in greater international trade and economic growth.

Education has the particular characteristic of being a product which enriches both the buyer and the seller. Those who do not invest in education lose much, as in the case of the parable of the talents. In addition, *college* education often has the peculiar characteristic of enticing customers who pay for the product and then seem to take away as little as possible.

There is a tidal wave of students propelling American education today. This is due to three things; first, an explosion in knowledge and population; second, a burst of technological advancement together with a worldwide uprooting of old cultures; and, third, an unparalled change in occupational structure. All three of these lead to a corresponding need for better education.

The total number of people in the United States has doubled in the last fifty years and births have more than doubled in the last twenty years. The 17 million students in school in 1900 have now grown to over 50 million. The best estimates based on children already born indicate that there will be over 6 million students ready for college by 1970—about double the enrollment in 1960. College students were less than 5 per cent of college age people in 1900. They are over 30% today. High school enrollments, which were only 15 per cent of the 14–18 age group in 1900, have shot up to over 90 per cent nationally today. Yet only 37 per cent of our total population has finished high school and only 8 per cent has completed college. There is a direct relationship between the age of children who drop out of school and the level of education of their parents. Furthermore, we are producing fewer engineers and scientists than the Russians and fewer than we produced ourselves in 1950.

The return on education is not only proportional to the expenditure on it but actually is multiplied several times. Education brings a more rapid increase in inventions, new processes, and innovations; all of which increase the nation's income. But new income circulates through being spent and becomes the income of other people who in turn spend a large portion of it so that it becomes the income of still additional people. The total new income which is created from one dollar's worth of new expenditure is over three dollars after allowing time for circulation. Therefore government spending on education would not be wasting our money but rather would be investing in a profit-making enterprise. Every successful student would move from a low to a high demand sector of the economy, and would pay back in taxes much more than was invested in his education. It has been estimated that the creation of knowledge through education accounts for 29 per cent of all national production and that it is growing two-and-one half times faster than the industries that produce all other goods and services.

Yet in spite of these enormous advantages what happens to our students? If present trends continue during the next ten years one-third of all high school students will quit before graduation. Although some of these will lack the ability to finish, nearly three-fourths will quit because the chance of a temporary job in order to buy a car or new clothes or go to parties seems more important to them at the time. Very few dropouts ever return to school.

In the next ten years more than 26 million new young workers will enter the job market, according to the U. S. Department of Labor. This is not based on any theoretical projection of population growth. These people are already in school. If current trends continue, 7.5 million will not complete high school and 2.5 million will not finish elementary school. About 12 million of those who are displaced by automation or who enter the job market for the first time in the next ten years will have no high school diploma. About 4 million will not have finished elementary school. In some areas 70–80 per cent of our young people will be unemployed.

Today there are over a million young people of ages 16–17 who are not enrolled in a school of any kind. They will be most ill-fitted for the highly technical jobs that will open up in the coming years of rapid technological advance.

The National Planning Association has estimated the same level of production can be maintained this year as in 1961 with 1.8 million fewer workers. The 26 million new workers who will enter the job market will average 2.6 million a year. Adding these together we get about 4.4 million people who will be added to the nation's jobless rolls every year. This rate of unemployment is costing the nation about $40 billion annually in goods and services.

We must train people to work for themselves or we will have to support them out of profits and taxes. The only economically sound thing to do is to think in terms of capital investment in people. Education must place central emphasis on developing students' thought processes so that after graduation they will be able to learn for themselves and utilize the tools of analysis which they have mastered during their formal education. This will require that primary attention be given to developing (a) mental flexibility, (b) skills for thinking logically, analytically, and often quantitatively, (c) ability to think creatively, (d) receptiveness to new ideas, and (e) emotional maturity. Furthermore it will require a revolution in our thinking about education.

Apparently as a people, we have relatively little genuine regard for education. We lavish much more generous applause on superior physical endowment (as in the athletic and theatrical arts) and on outstanding commercial abilities (as witness the enormous salaries and prestige of businessmen) than on any form of scholastic distinction. Americans annually spend more money for liquor and tobacco than for all forms of education. We go on buying fancier and gaudier automobiles, appliances, and all the other superficial, glittering attributes of our modern age. It is fair to inquire if we in the United States have put luxury above the values of cultural living.

More and better education is far more important to our national security than national defense, and uneducated population is unemployable, so education must become our major occupation in the years ahead. We must produce a population that can improve itself and anticipate with equanimity the many changes which face us. In the next ten years we will need five million new skilled workers. At present we are training only about a fifth this many.

We are entering a new phase of world history with primary emphasis on economic competition. Particularly, we are competing to assist the underdeveloped areas, most of which are politically neutral and which together hold the balance of power in the world. The efficient, economical, and perceptive application of technology to the broad human problems in these areas can alone tip the scales toward peace and democracy in the world; but a broader and deeper understanding of world tensions will be required than we have demonstrated so far.

Modern educators must recognize that we live in an age of uncertainty and that their efforts should be directed toward turning cocksure ignorance into a thoughtful recognition of the uncertainty with which we are faced. In this complex and rapidly changing world we must educate for uncertainty. We are in the midst of an explosion of knowledge that threatens to run over us. If we are to adjust to the world of the future it will be "knowers" and not "doers" who will make the important decisions. It follows from this that the future will demand a far greater commitment to education than we have ever made in the past.

Since Sputnik raised doubts concerning our technological supremacy, there have been some urgent demands for a crash program in science. But science for what purpose? The stern scientific discipline of German schools did not prepare a generation to resist Hitler. The spectacular Russian scientific education has not transformed communism, though it may in time. Emphasis on science must be matched by emphasis on social sciences and humanities. Virtually all leading scientists and educators have urged this balanced approach. We already have a serious cultural lag; technology is far ahead of our ability to adjust psychologically to it and make wise use of its tremendous power.

The Russians have proven that some educational bottlenecks can be broken by massive quantitative efforts alone. Sputnik may be the greatest technological achievement since the airplane, but it was not a victory for communism. It was the ability of focusing attention and developing a sense of national purpose that led to this triumph for technological education. The pioneering conquest of outer space began in the classroom. The German scientists led the Russians to this achievement. (We have some, and one, notably, is our top missile expert, Wernher van Braun.)

The average Russian high school student gets about 40 per cent more mathematics and science than the average American student. Five thousand American students are studying Russian compared with ten million Russian students studying English. While we spend about 3 per cent of our national income on education the Russians spend 10 per cent. This is a world where the great struggle is for men's minds, and the principal weapon is words.

The Russians probably work their students harder than we do, leading to considerable emotional erosion and probably excessive narrowness of outlook from specialization. In fact, it was necessary for the Soviet government to pass a law recently to prevent homework from being assigned 7 days a week. Nine prominent Soviet physicians complained that Russian students were suffering from "chronic overexhaustion, frequent headaches, weakened memory and vision, and proneness to infectious diseases with various complications." These were blamed on the stiff curriculum and discipline. But Soviet college students in good academic standing receive state grants equal to half an average factory worker's pay (they they usually have no dependents to support), so they need not work at part-time jobs as so many of our college students must do. Russian college students are also exempt from military service. If they fail in their studies, they may still pursue college education at night although they lose their government subsidies.

In Russia, education ranks high in prestige and in the aspirations of parents for their children. This may be due partly to the negative incentive that education is one of the few avenues whereby a person can advance on his merit with minimal compromise of his ethical principles or involvement in political intrigue. It is also due, however, to the high-prestige value that the government places on educational achievement and which is translated into high pay and special privileges.

It has been estimated that the United States must obtain an additional $50 billion over the next 10 years, over and above what we are now spending for public elementary and secondary education, if we are to keep up with the needs of the times. Thirty-eight billion dollars of the $50 billion should be used for teachers' salaries and there is no question but that a substantial portion of the $50 billion must come from the federal government. Compared with defense, however, education is cheap. All of the degree-granting colleges in the United States have estimated their *combined* annual needs for the next decade will be $800 million in addition to their present income sources. This is less than the cost of four aircraft carriers of the *Saratoga* class.

Our unemployment rate has been about 5 per cent for eight years. The percentage of unemployed in Western Europe has averaged less than half that of the United States during this period. During the same period that we have had four recessions Western Europe has experienced none. The Europeans seem to have repealed old-fashioned business cycles. Furthermore, Western Europe's economic growth rate has been about two-and-one-half times that of ours.

What are the reasons for this great difference between Europe and the U.S.A.? One is the attitude in Europe toward government spending. The ultra-conservative German government devotes 40 per cent of its annual national product for social needs; the conservative government of France, 32 per cent; the Tory government of Great Britain, 30 per cent; and the moderately conservative government of Italy, 28 per cent. American public spending—local, state, and national, is less than 20 per cent. At the other extreme, poverty-stricken "socialist" India devotes only 7 per cent of its national income to government spending.

To finance the major programs that have maintained full employment and rapid economic growth, Western Europe's "conservative" governments do two things. First, they tax at a higher rate than the U.S. Yet, incentives have not been dulled and risk capital has not dried up; both have increased enormously. Second, they don't try to balance their national budgets every year, but only over the long run. They are able to make surpluses in good times to offset deficits in times of excessive unemployment.

The explanation of all this is that Germany, France, and Great Britain, consider true conservatism to mean the conserving of the essentials of free enterprise through the kind of government collaboration that builds social services and public projects to provide for fiscal flexibility and economic expansion. They, like all other Western European conservative governments, including England, consider the role of government as one of partnership with industry and labor in pursuit of a common national goal.

With genuine full employment private firms would find it to their advantage to finance most of the necessary retraining, as they have done before, during full employment periods. Furthermore, nothing less than full employment is going to establish our political and ideological leadership in the world.

A combination of legislation and governmental policy could now be effective in setting up a national planning program for stimulating a much more rapid rate of economic growth and maintaining full employment and production with no loss of private initiative or incentive. Every Western European country has such a program. Japan has one that is programmed entirely on electronic computers.

The teachers and school administrators who are closest to educational problems have generally contended that state and private educational support must be supplemented by more direct federal assistance. They are not alone in this belief. Many national organizations support federal aid for schools, such as the Committee for Economic Development which is composed primarily of presidents of large corporations and university economists. There have been the inevitable objections that federal aid leads to federal control, but many forms of federal educational aids have been in existence for a long time without any noticeable tendencies toward federal control of any kind. Under the Jackson administration $47 million of federal money was distributed to states for schools. The federal government's system of land-grant colleges was begun almost a century ago. Under the GI Bill of Rights and the present aid to impacted areas program, colleges and public schools have been large recipients of federal aid without any noticeable loss of autonomy. In Great Britain, schools and universities are wholly supported by the national government and yet they are well known for their academic freedom and independence from government domination. Even in this country, academic freedom is as secure in state colleges as in private colleges. Freedom is no less secure under federal government control than when subject to control by state, private, alumni, or church interests.

Many other activities in the United States that are similar to education have been almost entirely supported by federal funds without interference with local administration. The Hill-Burton hospitals, the Smith-Hughes vocational schools, the $800 million retraining act, social security, and public housing are among many examples of federal aid without dictatorial federal controls. In these cases, there is not even any especially bureaucratic or centralized administration. The federal government also spends billions of dollars annually to aid farmers, businessmen, military training, hospitals, highways, pensions, and money-leading institutions. Ironically, we voted $40 million in federal aid to stamp out hog cholera. In this space age is education less important?

It is even possible that federally supported schools would be free and more democratic than the present state-supported systems. Almost every state government is dominated by a rural minority which is able to impose on schools all sorts of restrictions and controls that are not approved by a majority of the people in the state. Typical examples are censorship of textbooks and intimidation of teachers who mention subjects considered "controversial." The federal government, which rests on a far broader political basis, is less likely to interfere in matters of this kind than are state governments. The principal effect of federally supported education could well be higher and more uniform academic standards throughout the nation.

We are going to have to decide what is imperative to the welfare of this country and should therefore demand financial support. We might consider the emotionally disturbed 5 per cent to 10 per cent of our population, and the fact that the total cost of rehabilitation is higher than the cost of prevention. As for the unemployed, the cost of retraining is a small fraction of the total loss to the economy through unemployment or underemployment.

Investment in education pays the highest dividends at all levels. The average college education costs about $6,000, yet the average college graduate today can be expected to earn nearly $250,000 more in his lifetime than a high school graduate. This is well over a 50 per cent return on his investment, compounded annually. The average high school graduate earns nearly $80,000 more in his life than a high school dropout and, more important, he can expect a fairly well-paid and secure job. Furthermore the dropout, if hired, is the first fired, is the lowest paid, and has the least chance for advancement. Roughly 18 per cent of our unskilled workers are now unemployed. This is about double the rate for semiskilled workers. Eighty per cent of those now unemployed did not finish high school.

In 1900 the government spent one dollar on education for every two dollars spent for other purposes. Fifty years later, despite the fact that the importance and complexity of education was greater than ever before, the government at all levels was spending only one dollar out of every six dollars for education.

One form of education which should not be overlooked is that of experience. Undoubtedly there are some things that can be learned best, even exclusively, by experience. But one of the purposes of formal education, both technical and academic, is to substitute other forms of learning for experience, since experience is usually a slow and costly teacher. It has been said that experience may be the best teacher, but it is also the toughest because you get the test first and the lesson afterward.

When a famous college president was asked how he accounted for the vast store of knowledge at his university, he replied that it was because the freshmen brought so much with them and the seniors took so little away. Several years ago a student asked the late Harvard economics professor, Sumner Slichter, if we dared leave the future of our country to brain trusters. "To what other portion of the anatomy would you entrust it?" was his reply. If this was an appropriate answer then, it is infinitely more so now. The future will belong to those who are prepared to accept its responsibilities, and we have no place to look except to our schools and colleges for this preparation.

30. The Interaction of Vocational Counseling with the Economic System

Robert P. Overs

Sociologists are interested in the structure of a society which encourages, sustains and supports a certain type of economic system. A recent analysis by Talcott Parsons (1960) is of significance here. He points out that in an industrial society the economic system either is given or has been given special emphasis. Greater concern has been shown with handling the external environment than with values internal to the society. Western industrial civilization obviously differs widely from

From *The American Journal of Economics and Sociology*, XXIII, April 1964, No. 2, pp. 213–221. Reprinted by permission of the publisher.

other civilizations in this respect. To meet the needs of an industrial economy, labor as a commodity must be emancipated from the demands of other structural areas of society. In order that labor might be sufficiently mobile to meet the rapid changes in an industrial economy, the family structure had to change. The small, mobile family replaced the large kinship group. In a similar manner, the geographical and political limitations on the worker under feudalism gave way to permit a more mobile labor supply.

Parsons emphasizes the importance of a value commitment to exploiting the external environment as essential for the development of an industrial society and traces this to the Judaeo-Christian tradition (Parsons, 1960, p. 138). The internalization of this high valuing of the conquest of the outside environment provides the motivation for workers to meet the complex work demands of an industrial system. In Parsons' words:

. . . (1) people must be motivated to serve the goal of *production* beyond the levels previously treated as normal, desirable, or necessary in the society, and (2) they must perform such tasks to a far higher degree than before, in organizations specifically differentiated from other, nonproductive functional contests, *i.e.*, labor must be "alienable" (Parsons, 1960, p. 140).

This fundamental valuing of work within the industrial framework is substantially different from the economic hedonism postulated by the economists.

One of the institutional bases necessary for the development of an industrial society is the substitution of a legal system supporting universalism and specificity for primary group controls. This permits the contractual relationships necessary for industrial enterprise. Characteristic of this legal system is a definition of what could be contracted, what was illegal in securing the other party's agreement to the contract, how unforeseen events should be handled under the contract and the nature of society's interest in the contract (Parsons; 1960, p. 145).

Another institutional base necessary for industrial society is the concept of authority. This is defined as the ability to make decisions within the economic framework. It permits whoever is exercising the leadership to make disposition of material and labor in a rational way to maximize production. This is clearly at odds with nonindustrial civilizations where such authority is weakened by the coexistence of other and frequently nonrational authority systems.

The concept of regulation is different from that of authority. Some occupational activities cannot be successfully carried on under direct authority. That is to say, such professional activities as are carried on in universities, hospitals and industrial research laboratories require some independence from authority in order to maximize production (Parsons;

1960, p. 153). A system of regulation or setting outer limits of performance is operative here in lieu of direct authority.

In understanding the place of government in industrial society, Parsons notes that "government must be sufficiently stable and also sufficiently *differentiated* from institutionalized structures in the society which are incompatible with industrialization. . . ." Government support of other institutional patterns interfering with the industrialization process must be withdrawn. We turn now to a more detailed consideration of vocational counseling within this structure.

I
INTERRELATION OF THE VOCATIONAL COUNSELING AND LABOR ECONOMICS THEORY SYSTEMS

By definition, any occupation interacts with the economic system. However, vocational counseling has a special relationship because of the significance of vocational choice. Since vocation choice in our democratic society may be generally regarded as free, within the limits of certain determining influences, those who are in a position to influence vocational choice may be said to occupy a special position vis-à-vis the economic system. The more specialized the society, the more important the process. In sacred societies, the assigning of vocation was accomplished through social inheritance of jobs, status and skills. Such a system, aside from other considerations, would not meet the needs of a secular society such as ours. American society is, within limits an open society. Who enters what occupation is influenced, however, by the social-class position of the parents (Hollingshead, 1949). This, in turn, is strongly affected by the father's occupation (Warner *et al;* 1944). There is an intervening variable of the educational ladder which children of the middle and upper social-class families find easier to climb (Mills; 1951, pp. 266–268). In any event, the individual has considerable latitude in choice of occupation, probably greater than in any other than frontier societies.

One aspect of labor economics is signified by the label "manpower." The study of manpower needs and problems has drawn together an assortment of labor economists, educators, business executives, union representatives, government officials and occasionally vocational counselors (usually as consultants). Most vocational counselors would not quarrel with the following ambitions of manpower organizers:

1. To maintain a high-level employment economy which can provide job opportunities for all those willing and able to work.

2. To build and maintain a stable work force which is, at the same time, sufficiently mobile to adapt to the changing needs of a dynamic economy.
3. To utilize the labor force efficiently through proper matching of jobs with people, effective management, and the appropriate education, training and development of people, and thus to raise the productivity of labor and the general standard of living through the nation.
4. To provide reasonable security against the hazards of illness, unemployment, disability and old age.
5. To preserve and enhance the freedom, dignity and worth of the individual both as a member of the labor force and as a citizen.
6. To provide the proper and necessary distribution of manpower between our armed forces and civilian work forces in order to maintain adequate national defense and a healthy economy (Haber; 1954, p. x).

Vocational counselors are critically interested, however, in how and to what degree these statements are implemented in the lives of individual clients. In a statement such as the following they see the possible neglect of client needs:

Manpower policy, therefore, should be conceived of as one aspect of total public policy in economic affairs and not as a separate or unique problem (Harbison and Rees; 1954, p. 213).

Vocational counseling as a practicing profession has sought a theoretical base for its practice primarily in psychology, to a far lesser extent in sociology. Economics as a possible theoretical base has been strangely neglected. Only occasional concern with the theory of manpower needs has maintained a minimum cross fertilization (Berdie, 1960; Bray, 1955; Mitchell, 1956; Olshansky, 1956; Reutter, 1957; Super, 1954; Winthrop, 1959). While Freud is well known to most counselors, the name of Keynes or Galbraith might not even be recognized. This is not to say that writers in other fields have not been concerned with this problem of cross fertilization. A body of relevant literature is accumulating (Clark, 1956; Hickman and Kuhn, 1956; Katona, 1951; Lauterbach, 1954). There has been marked dissatisfaction among economists themselves with their own concepts pertaining to human motivation (Galbraith, 1952; Dahl and Lindblom, 1953). Nevertheless, a textbook published as late as 1952 describes economic incentives in terms of instincts (Suranyi-Unger, 1952). Since the power elite supports the older assumptions in respect to the motivations of men in the functioning of the economic structure, legislation passed or not passed is generally enacted or defeated within the framework of these traditional assumptions. Therefore, in analyzing the economic concepts which impinge on the practice of vocational counseling we are concerned with the older doctrine which is still dominant in the actual decisions made. Vis-à-vis orthodox economics as a theoretical science, vocational counseling as a practicing profession is still accepting such basic assumptions as "economic man," "competition," "laws of suppy and demand" in a naïve fashion. It follows that vocational counseling is operating on a very shallow theoretical base in respect to the institutional arrangements of society in the world of work. To press the matter further, we suggest a series of propositions to place in juxtaposition the separate approaches of vocational counseling and labor economics to the problems of vocational choice and vocational adjustment.

II
SOME CONNECTING PROPOSITIONS

PROPOSITION 1

Vocational Counseling	*Labor Economics*
Vocational counseling insists on the freedom of individual choice and the fullest development of the capacities of each individual (Hoppeck, 1957).	Labor economics is concerned with the utilization of manpower in the most effective way to further the maximum production for the economy as a whole (Tyler, 1953; Thomas, 1956).

Both vocational counseling and labor economics pay lip service to the goals of the other. Labor economists disclaim any authoritarian tinge to their proposals. They believe that if counselees are given the facts about the manpower needs of the country they will elect suitable choices. They want vocational counselors to bring these facts to the attention of the counselees.

PROPOSITION 2

Vocational Counseling	*Labor Economics*
As a psychological base, vocational counseling, for the most part, uses the phenomenological personality theory as a base (Snygg and Combs, 1949).	As a psychological base, labor economics, for the most part, still uses the "economic man" theory as a base (Scitovsky, 1951; Hicks, et al., 1955).

Schism between the two is perhaps clearest in the concept "competition." The pertinent use of the word in labor economics means competition for work among workers. This is the normal operation of the market mechanism, and presumed to motivate workers to look for jobs and to motivate them to work hard once they have a job. Psychological research indicates that a moderate amount of anxiety may be motivating but that greater amounts of anxiety are incapacitating rather than motivating. Clinical experience suggests that for many people the anxiety involved in competing for a job is so overwhelming as to be incapacitating rather than motivating. If this is true, the economic model breaks down for those individuals who are incapacitated by this amount of anxiety. The concept "competition" (competition among workers for jobs) is not an operational concept until it is restated to exclude the potential job seekers immobilized by anxiety.

PROPOSITION 3

Vocational Counseling	*Labor Economics*
As a philosophical base, vocational counseling accepts the inalienable right of the individual to life, liberty and pursuit of happiness. What is good for the normal individual is good for society.	As a philosophical base, labor economics accepts the inalienable right of the individual to life, liberty and pursuit of business. The individual in this case is defined as the entrepreneur and subsequently the corporation. "What is good for General Motors is good for the country." The discrepancy between the rights of the entrepreneur (corporation) and the rights of the worker is glossed over semantically by considering all workers potential entrepreneurs.

The basic conflict here is that vocational counselors experience the work which people do through the client's perceptual field. The labor economist views the work which people do as a commodity. The commodity construct is divorced of psychological and sociological meaning. Boulding defines it this way:

The basis of the economists' system is the notion of a commodity. The economist sees the world not as men and things, but as commodities, and it is precisely in this abstraction that his peculiar skills reside. A commodity is anything *scarce*. That is, in order to get more of it a quantity of some other commodity must be relinquished (Boulding, 1958).

The orthodox economist has assumed that large-scale movements of labor as a commodity could be profitably discussed without recourse to any psychological or sociological referents. It is this gap with which we are primarily concerned.

PROPOSITION 4

Vocational Counseling	*Labor Economics*
Work is considered psychologically desirable for the fulfillment of intrinsic needs for achievement, craftsmanship and to provide earned income with which to satisfy extrinsic desires (Darley and Hagenah, 1955).	Work is considered economically desirable to maximize productivity. But productivity is defined within the special circumstances of the price-profit system. Work outside this system has no legitimate status:
a. In government as with work within the price-profit system, both intrinsic needs and extrinsic desires may be met. There is some evidence that intrinsic needs may be more fully satisfied and extrinsic desires less fully satisfied, although with some people and some jobs the reverse may be true.	a. In government—a necessary evil and a tax drain on the price-profit system—to be reduced to the minimum (Galbraith, 1958; Sutton, et al., 1956; Scitovsky, 1951).
b. In cooperatives the intrinsic needs are apt to be more fully satisfied than the extrinsic desires.	b. In cooperatives—an unfair (socialistic) threat to the price-profit system.
c. In prisons, the satisfaction of intrinsic needs is the primary concern.	c. Prison Labor—an unfair threat to the price-profit system (unless farmed out through the price-profit system).

Work, in the eyes of the vocational counselor, is meaningful for certain intrinsic satisfactions it brings to the client as well as for its contributions to the productiveness of the country. Thus, work outside the price-profit system is valued equally by the vocational counselor, provided that he is not too strongly influenced by the business ethos. The labor economist experiences difficulty with the concept "productiveness." To group all activities which are measured in the calculation of Gross National Product as productive and exclude all others creates many dilemmas. For instance, under this definition, the man who distributes advertising handbills (most of which blow into the street) is productive; the street cleaner who cleans up the handbills is not (Galbraith, 1958).

PROPOSITION 5

Vocational Counseling	*Labor Economics*

Unemployment in "normal" times is considered a pathological state against which the entire armamentarium of counseling techniques will be deployed. Three separate views are held of unemployment:
 	
    a. It is dysfunctional to *family organization.* Failing to fulfill the breadwinning role, the head of the household loses status and friction develops.
 	
    b. It is dysfunctional to the social security of the wage earner and his dependents. For lack of funds they are unable to fulfill their usual social roles.
 	
    c. *Morale* of the wage earner and significant others is threatened. This in turn is dysfunctional to mental health, and support of primary, associational and community activities.
	Unemployment is considered a market mechanism, essentially normal at certain stages of the business cycle. Three separate views are held of unemployment:
	
	    a. The *practical-administrative view.* Being unemployed is a temporary status, and besides, the needs of the unemployed are met by unemployment insurance and public welfare (Galbraith, 1952).
	
	    b. The *"bird dog"* (and guilt-relieving) *view.* They need not be unemployed if they had the initiative to become entrepreneurs (mow lawns, shovel snow, wash windows) at prices people would be willing to pay.
	
	    c. *Labor as a commodity view.* The price-profit system requires a surplus labor pool to prevent inflation. This is based on the concept "competition" (for jobs) (Galbraith, 1952).

The vocational counseling concept of unemployment as a pathological state is at odds with the practical-administrative view of unemployment. Clinical experience suggests that for a substantial group of the unemployed, being unemployed is not a temporary status. It also affirms that for few workers is the status of receiving unemployment insurance a satisfactory way of life (Miller, 1954). Finally, existence on public welfare is so unsatisfactory that it creates secondary problems of social disorganization highly costly in the long run to the price-profit system.

In contrast to the "bird dog" view, the clinical experience of vocational counselors gives evidence that the unemployed do a great many odd jobs (primarily the repair and painting of homes of relatives and friends). A secondary pattern is for the husband to stay home and baby-sit while the wife secures a part-time job as clerical worker, waitress or nurse's aide. The unemployed as a group lack the capital, initiative and know-how required to become successful entrepreneurs.

The concept of unemployment held by vocational counselors is diametrically opposed to the labor-as-a-commodity view. Should it be true that the price-profit system requires a surplus labor pool to prevent inflation, then the efforts of vocational counselors to help the unemployed reenter employment are either:

    a. futile: for every worker employed, another must be laid off;

or

    b. dysfunctional: to the operation of the price-profit system.

PROPOSITION 6

Vocational Counseling	*Labor Economics*
Vocational counselors accept the forecasts of economic activity and manpower requirements promulgated by the labor economists and reformulate them for use in counseling individuals.	These forecasts are rarely geared to the problem of producing the exact number of workers required. Implicit in most of them is the assumption that a surplus of skilled manpower is desirable.

From the point of view of the vocational counselor's client, the situation of being trained for an occupation and unable to secure placement in it is as frustrating as not being trained for an occupation in which there are openings (Harris, 1949, Kotschnig, 1937). Economists speak frequently of the high cost to industry of a "tight" labor market; little or no attention is paid to the economic waste of producing more workers with particular skills than are required. The employer is interested in a reservoir of skilled labor sufficient so that he need neither incur any costs for recruitment nor make any concessions to nonrational standards in respect to age, color, religion, etc. There is a strong suspicion that the forecasters of manpower needs adhere rather closely to the employer's point of view. Were the concept of labor as a commodity to be followed in all its implications, this utilization of trained manpower would be in sharp contrast to current operations of large corporations in respect to materials inventories. Here, to reduce inventories means cutting costs (within the framework of the accounting system of the individual corporation), and materials are scheduled to arrive to supply assembly lines in the nick of time. The formula seems to be that it is no longer desirable to stockpile inanimate commodities but it is desirable to stockpile animate commodities, since the latter cost the employer nothing.

A quotation from Professor Hathway applied to social work may be equally applicable to vocational counseling.

Either we accept professional responsibility in relation to the environment and follow the road to the control of forces which threaten to destroy human personality or we admit that the problems are insoluble and become, in the oft-quoted words of Roger Baldwin, "merely stretcher bearers of industry" (Hathway, 1942).

The vocational counselor is ideally situated to appraise the exact manner in which the economic structure is functional or dysfunctional in the case of the individual worker or would-be worker. He is able to supply the worm's eye view of the human situations in which the meaning of broad economic concepts are spelled out in the lives of individuals. He is able to bring to this analysis relatively keen tools from psychology with which to appraise in clinical situations the meaning of broad concepts in microeconomics. A similar orientation is expressed in the introduction to *Manpower in the United States.*

The editors can hope that the reader will bring to the sixteen essays comprising the volume what might be termed the humanist approach to manpower. Simply stated, that is the realization that the proper study of manpower is man. To assist in achieving this recognition of manpower as a collection of individual, sentient human beings in a social milieu of economic activity and to dispel the concept of a mobile mass statistic, it is sometimes helpful to contemplate the obvious in a sharper focus (Haber, 1954).[1]

PROPOSITION 7

Vocational Counseling	*Labor Economics*
Vocational counseling makes no value judgment as to the inherent usefulness of respective vocations. Counseling philosophy explicitly precludes the counselor from favoring one choice over another in terms other than that of client self-fulfillment.	For his part, the orthodox labor economist makes no value judgment as to the social desirability of one set of goods or services over another.

Vocational counselors and labor economists merge on this point: neither make any value judgment as to the social desirability of the goods or services involved. For the counselor, as an ideal type, the predatory occupations and the social service occupations are of equal worth. To what extent in actual counseling a sense of valuing is communicated implicitly to the client is unknown. The labor economist makes no honorific distinctions among the various goods and services produced so long as they are produced within the price-profit system.

[1] The author refers to an issue of *The American Journal of Economics and Sociology* which deals with manpower development.

In summary, it has been the attempt of this article to compare and contrast the conceptual bases on which the science of labor economics and the practice of vocational counseling are founded, with the hope that eventually solutions may be found to the current ambiguous conflicting positions.

REFERENCES

BERDIE, R. F. "The Counselor and His Manpower Responsibilities." *Personnel and Guid. J.*, Feb., 1960, No. 6.

BOULDING, K. E. *The Skills of the Economist*. Cleveland: Howard Allen, 1958, pp. 9–10.

BRAY, D. W. "Vocational Guidance in National Manpower Policy." *Personnel and Guid. J.*, Dec., 1955, No. 4.

CLARK, J. M. "Economics and Psychology." *Journal of Political Economy*, 1956, No. 5.

DAHL, R. A. & LINDBLOM, C. E. *Politics, Economics and Welfare*. New York: Harper, 1953, pp. 219–220.

DARLEY, J. G. & HAGENAH, T. *Vocational Interest Measurement*. Minneapolis: University of Minnesota Press, 1955, p. 10.

GALBRAITH, J. K. *The Affluent Society*. Boston: Houghton Mifflin, 1958.

GALBRAITH, J. K. *American Capitalism*. Boston: Houghton Mifflin, 1952.

HABER, W. *et al.*, eds. *Manpower in the United States*. New York: Harper, 1954, p. x.

HARBISON, F. H. & REES, A. "Manpower Mobilization and Economic Controls." In W. Haber *et al.*, eds. *Manpower in the United States*, New York: Harper, 1954, p. 213.

HARRIS, S. E. *The Market for College Graduates*. Cambridge: Harvard University Press, 1949.

HATHWAY. "Social Action or Inaction: The Challenge." *Training For Social Work in the Department of Social Science*, University of Toronto, 1940, p. 35. Cited by E. L. Brown, *Social Work as a Profession*. New York: Russell Sage, 1942, p. 186.

HICKMAN, C. A. & KUHN, M. H. *Individuals, Groups and Economic Behavior*. New York: The Dryden Press, 1956.

HICKS, J. R., HART, A. G. & FORD, J. W. *The Social Framework of the American Economy*. New York: Oxford University Press, 1955, pp. 74–82.

HOLLINGSHEAD, A. B. *Elmstown's Youth*. New York: Wiley, 1949.

HOPPOCK, R. *Occupational Information*. New York: McGraw-Hill, 1957.

KATONA, G. *Psychological Analysis of Economic Behavior*. New York: McGraw-Hill, 1951.

KOTSCHNIG, W. *Unemployed in the Learned Professions*. London: Oxford University Press, 1937.

LAUTERBACH, A. *Man, Motives, and Money: Psychological Frontiers of Economics*. Ithaca: Cornell University Press, 1954.

MILLER, G. "The Effect of Social Security on Manpower Resources." In W. Haber, *et al.*, eds. *Manpower in the United States*. New York: Harper, 1954, pp. 59–64.

MILLS, C. W. *White Collar*. New York: Oxford University Press, 1951, pp. 266–268.

MITCHELL, J. P. "Vocational Guidance and Skills of the Work Force." *Personnel and Guid. J.,* Sept., 1956, No. 1.

OLSHANSKY, S. S. "Guidance and the Labor Market." *Personnel and Guid. J.,* May, 1956, No. 9.

PARSONS, T. *Structure and Process in Modern Societies.* New York: Free Press of Glencoe, Inc., 1960.

REUTHER, W. "The Crisis Before Us." *Personnel and Guid. J.,* Sept., 1957, No. 1.

SCITOVSKY, T. *Welfare and Competition.* Chicago: Richard D. Irwin, 1951, pp. 94–104, 339–341, 426–427.

SNYGG, D. & COMBS, A. W. *Individual Behavior.* New York: Harper, 1949.

SUPER, D. E. "Guidance: Manpower Utilization or Human Development?" *Personnel and Guid. J.,* Jan., 1959, No. 5.

SURANYI-UNGER, T. *Comparative Economic Systems.* New York: McGraw-Hill, 1952, p. 176.

SUTTON, F. *et al. The American Business Creed.* Cambridge: Harvard University Press, 1956, p. 195.

THOMAS, L. G. *The Occupational Structure and Education.* Englewood Cliffs, New Jersey: Prentice-Hall, 1956, pp. 11–12.

TYLER, L. *The Work of the Counselor.* New York: Appleton-Century-Crofts, 1953, p. 3.

WARNER, W. L., HAVIGHURST, R. J., & LOEB, M. G. *Who Shall Be Educated.* New York: Harper and Brothers, 1944.

WINTHROP, H. "Automation and the Future of Personnel and Industrial Psychology." *Personnel and Guid. J.,* Jan., 1959, No. 5.

PART TWO

Major Functions

Part Two is organized around four interrelated sets of activities commonly subsumed in the implementing of the guidance function. The pattern of organization was chosen both for efficiency and to stress the commonalities of job performance among personnel workers irrespective of their particular work setting. The most common alternative to this organizational pattern is a listing of guidance services, a choice which may tend to stress differences between settings. Thus, for example, a counselor working in vocational rehabilitation setting would not necessarily recognize the "individual inventory" service of the counselor in the secondary school as being essentially the same activity as the "psychological evaluation" service he offers.

The four sets of interrelated activities that are discussed in the following section are (1) the appraisal function, (2) the information function, (3) the counseling function, and (4) the organizational and administrative function. In keeping with the rationale of the book more attention is given to development and conceptual elements than to specifics of operation.

SECTION SEVEN

The Appraisal Function

THE appraisal function in guidance derives directly from the branch of psychology known as differential psychology, or the psychology of individual differences. The broad purpose of appraisal or assessment is to gather relevant information about individuals for two major reasons: (1) to allow for comparision with similar individuals along the dimension under consideration; (2) to provide data useful for comparison of the individual with himself at different points in time or in different characteristics. Appraisal data may be subjective and impressionistic, or they may be objective. Objective means such as standardized psychological tests are perhaps the most common means of fulfilling the appraisal function in guidance, yet not all uses of standardized tests are necessarily guidance uses. Specifically, in a secondary school setting the administration and analysis of results of an educational achievement test for a particular class are not necessarily tasks for the school counselor, though his expertise in the area of testing may be solicited in a collaborative relationship with the teacher of the particular class.

Many nontest techniques of appraisal are available to the counselor. Structured observations, rating scales, autobiographical reports, anecdotal reports, questionnaires, sociometric techniques, and the like are common means of gathering information about the individual. The selections which follow do not deal specifically with nontest techniques; however, the rationale, use, and limitations of such information are essentially the same as those discussed for standardized tests.

In the initial selection Anne Anastasi, a psychologist well known in the field of testing, traces the courses of the scientific study of individual differences. Her survey points out influences of numerous disciplines—physiology, genetics, astronomy, and biology—on the development of differential psychology. It was an interest in individual differences that led to the early development of numerous fundamental statistical concepts[1] which are in use in assessment today. C. E. Alexakos continues in the next selection by highlighting the development of standardized testing.

White discusses assumptions and limitations, both procedural and philosophical, of the use of appraisal data by the counselor. He stresses that anyone responsible for the professional use of appraisal data must be careful to use them within the confines of the instruments and procedures yielding them. Prediction of individual human behavior is a hazardous enterprise, yet appraisal instruments apparently do have potential value in contributing to improvement of judgments, assuming that they are carefully used. White concludes with an examination of the tendency of counselors and educators in general to overestimate their powers of prediction—an integral part of effective educational and vocational planning.

David Goslin cites relevant research dealing with the general social impact of testing to identify four major problem areas. First, what is the objective influence of test scores on opportunities open to individuals? Second, what part do test scores play in influencing the direction deemed "appropriate" for the individual by various agencies and personnel? Goslin's third area is the effect of objective information about the person on the person himself. Finally, Goslin poses several questions about the ultimate effects of objective selection methods on the society that employs them wholeheartedly.

In the last article of the section, "Standards for Test Users," George Hill takes a broader view of the use of tests as they relate to individual development. While Hill's article is addressed to the school setting, the concerns and standards he raises are equally appropriate to the industrial arena or to the counseling agency in general.

[1] The normal distribution and the coefficient of correlation are examples.

Each of the authors of the last four selections stresses the need for those who use appraisal data to be both competent and judicious with such data. Such caution reflects the very real potential harm resulting from inept or illegitimate uses of appraisal data. For example, an approach to assessment which regards the person as an object to be studied rather than a partner in the studying process is antithetical to the purposes of counseling. Similarly, if the only concern in using test results is to make as few mistakes as possible in selecting students for college admission, for example, the broader purposes of guidance are thwarted. The counselor cannot afford, then, to be satisfied with mere technical competence in the uses of appraisal data. He must be continuously aware of and committed to the broader purpose of the enhancement of human development—the implicit rationale for the guidance function.

31. Sources of Differential Psychology

Anne Anastasi

Although it is likely that in practical dealings with his associates man has always been aware of individual differences, the scientific study of such differences is of relatively recent origin. Several developments in related fields and in psychology itself contributed to the rise of differential psychology—a field of psychology concerned with individual and group differences in behavior.

Curiously enough, it was in astronomy that the systematic collection of data on individual differences in a behavioral characteristic was first undertaken. In 1796 there occurred in the Greenwich Astronomical Observatory an incident that has been immortalized in the history of psychology. In that year Maskelyne, the astronomer royal at the Greenwich Observatory, discharged Kinnebrook, his assistant, because of what he regarded as excessive observational errors. Maskelyne found discrepancies of nearly a second between the times of stellar transits reported by himself and by his assistant. At that time, astronomers used what was

"Sources of Differential Psychology," from Anne Anastasi, *Individual Differences*. John Wiley & Sons, Inc., Publishers, Copyright 1967, pp. 1–11. Reprinted by permission.

known as the "eye-and-ear" method to make such observations. The observer read the time to the nearest second on a clock and then began to count seconds with the beats of the clock, at the same time watching the star as it crossed the field of the telescope. He noted the position of the star at the last beat just before it reached the critical line in the field and again at the first beat after it had crossed this line. From these observations, he estimated in tenths of a second the time when the star crossed the critical line. This procedure was generally assumed to be accurate to about one-tenth of a second. Kinnebrook's estimates, however, varied by as much as seven-tenths of a second from those of Maskelyne.

In 1816 Bessel, astronomer at Königsberg, read of the Kinnebrook incident in a history of the Greenwich Observatory and decided to look further into such observational errors. He sent to England for Maskelyne's complete report, studied the records of Kinnebrook's "error," and set out to discover whether such personal differences could be found among more experienced astronomical observers. He began by comparing his own observations with those of other well-known astronomers who recorded the time of transit of the same star. Finding even larger discrepancies than those between Maskelyne and his assistant, Bessel published his results in the form of a "personal equation" for every pair of observers. These equations gave the difference in seconds between the estimates of any two observers and could be used to "correct" the observations and make them comparable from one observer to another.

Other astronomers computed similar personal equations, not only for stellar transits but also for other astronomical observations. With the introduction of chronographs and chronoscopes in the second half of the nineteenth century, it became possible to obtain an absolute measure of each observer's personal equation, without reference to any other observer. By means of an artificial star whose transit could be automatically recorded on the chronograph, each observer's performance could be checked against "true values" and his absolute error recorded. Astronomers also became interested in the various conditions that affected the magnitude of the personal error, such as visual-versus-auditory modality, rate of movement of the stimulus, and the like. It was these questions, rather than the measurement of individual differences, that were followed up by the early experimental psychologists in their studies of reaction time.

In 1879, Wilhelm Wundt established the first laboratory of experimental psychology at Leipzig. Before this time, some psychological experiments had been performed by such well-known investigators as Weber, Fechner, and Helmholtz. But Wundt's laboratory was the first to be devoted exclusively to psychology and to provide facilities for training students in the methodology of the new science. Consequently, it played a major part in the development of early experimental psychology.

Students from many nations were attracted to Wundt's laboratory and, after earning their doctorate at Leipzig, often established similar laboratories of experimental psychology in their own countries.

The first experimental psychologists had received their own training chiefly in physics and physiology. The influence of these sciences is clearly apparent in the nature of the problems investigated in the early psychological laboratories. Visual and auditory sensations, reaction time, and psychophysics were by far the principal areas of study. In their emphasis on general laws and uniformities of behavior, early experimental psychologists also reflected the approach typical of physicists and physiologists of their time. It was characteristic of these early psychologists either to ignore individual differences or to treat them simply as chance errors. The greater the individual variation in a phenomenon, the less accurate would be the generalizations regarding its nature. The extent of individual differences was therefore regarded as the margin of error to be expected in the application of general laws of psychology.

The rise of experimental psychology thus seemed to shift interest away from—rather than toward—the study of individual differences. Nevertheless, experimental psychology made some noteworthy contributions to the development of differential psychology. By investigating the many factors that influence even the simplest sensorimotor responses, experimental psychologists focused attention on the importance of controlling extraneous variables in measuring individual behavior. The standardization of testing materials and procedures undoubtedly owes much to these early experiments. An even more basic contribution is to be found in the demonstration that psychological phenomena are amenable to objective and quantitative investigation. Such a step was required before subjective speculation about individuals and groups could give way to empirical measurement of individual differences.

Several developments in the biological sciences during the late nineteenth century also helped to shape modern differential psychology. One of the by-products of Darwin's doctrine of evolution was the emergence of the comparative viewpoint, involving the observation of similar phenomena in different species. In the attempt to test some of the implications of evolutionary theory, Darwin and some of his contemporaries amassed the first large body of data on animal behavior. Beginning with anecdotal material and field observations, this search led eventually to the highly controlled animal experiments of the twentieth century. Differential psychology has profited in many ways from such investigations of animal behavior. An outstanding example of pertinent research is provided by the many controlled experiments on the effects of early experience on subsequent behavior development.

Another prominent influence in the history of differential psychology is found in the rise of modern genetics. The rediscovery of Mendel's laws

of heredity in 1900 led to extensive research on the mechanisms of
heredity. The investigation of the inheritance of physical traits in animals,
as illustrated by the highly successful work on the fruit fly Drosophila,
has contributed to differential psychology from several angles. First, it
helped to clarify and refine the concept of heredity. Second, it provided a
variety of genetic models in terms of which behavioral data could be
examined. Third, it led directly to animal experiments on selective breed-
ing and crossbreeding for behavioral traits. Finally, the development of
human genetics suggested methods for the statistical analysis of family
relationships that have been extensively applied to psychological data.

Of particular relevance to differential psychology is the work of Sir
Francis Galton, an English biologist. It was Galton who first undertook to
apply the Darwinian principles of variation, selection, and adaptation to
the study of human populations. Galton's scientific pursuits were mani-
fold, but they were unified by his underlying interest in heredity. . . . He
published a book entitled "Hereditary Genius" (1869) in which, by the
application of the now well-known family history method, he tried to
demonstrate the inheritance of specific talents in various fields of work.
This was followed . . . by a similar book on "English Men of Science"
(1874). In a still later book, entitled "Natural Inheritance" (1889), Galton
applied the same techniques to a sample of the general population. Data for
this study were gathered through a published offer of cash prizes to
persons submitting the best reports on their own family records. Usable
records on approximately 150 families were received in response to this
offer.

Many of Galton's activities were concerned with the direct measurement of physical and mental traits of large numbers of persons. For this
purpose he devised several ingenious tests and measuring instruments
and tried a variety of schemes for obtaining data. Among his best-known
efforts was the establishment of an anthropometric laboratory where, for
the payment of a small fee, the visitor could be examined in sensory
discrimination, motor capacities, and other simple traits.

Arguing that all the information we receive about outward events
reaches us through the senses, Galton regarded the measurement of
sensory capacities as a promising method of gauging intellectual level.
For this reason, tests of sensory discrimination were relatively prominent
in his series of measuring instruments. Examples include the Galton bar
for measuring visual discrimination of length, the Galton whistle for
ascertaining the highest audible pitch, and a set of weights to be arranged in order of heaviness as a test of kinesthetic discrimination. In
addition, the series included tests for measuring strength of movement,
speed of simple reactions, and other sensorimotor functions. Galton also
initiated the use of free association tests, a technique that was subsequently adopted and further developed by Wundt. Galton's extensive

study of individual and group differences in mental imagery was another of his pioneer efforts. Utilizing questionnaire and rating procedures, this investigation forershadowed many of the methodological problems now familiar in the use of these instruments.

Galton was keenly aware of the need for specialized statistical techniques for processing his data on individual differences. Accordingly he set out to adapt several mathematical procedures for this purpose. Chief among them were those dealing with the normal distribution curve and correlation. In connection with the latter, Galton carried out much of the spadework and evolved a measure that eventually led to the coefficient of correlation. It was his student and ardent admirer, Karl Pearson, however, who later worked out the mathematical details of correlation theory and proposed the correlation coefficient that bears his name. Pearson, in fact, was responsible for developing and systematizing what for many years constituted nearly the whole field of statistics.

Of equal importance with statistics as a tool of differential psychology is psychological testing. We have already identified the early beginnings of the testing movement in the pioneer work of Galton with simple sensorimotor tests. Another outstanding contributor to the development of psychological testing was the American psychologist, James McKeen Cattell. In Cattell we can see a convergence of two parallel movements: the rise of experimental psychology and the measurement of individual differences. For his doctorate at Leipzig, under Wundt, Cattell prepared a dissertation on individual differences in reaction time. Later he spent some time in England, where his interest in individual differences was strengthened by contact with Galton. Following his return to America, Cattell was active both in the establishment of psychological laboratories and in the development of the testing movement.

In an article published in 1890, Cattell introduced the term "mental test" to the English psychological literature. The article described a series of tests that were being administered annually to college students in an effort to measure their intellectual level. The series included tests of muscular strength, speed of movement, sensitivity to pain, keenness of vision and hearing, weight discrimination, reaction time, and memory, among others. In his choice of tests, Cattell shared Galton's view that an estimate of intellectual functioning could be obtained through tests of sensory discrimination and reaction time. Cattell's preference for such tests was further supported by his conviction that simple functions could be measured with precision, while the more complex, "higher mental processes" could not.

Cattell's tests were typical of those found in several test series developed during the last decade of the nineteenth century. Some of these series did, however, try to tap more complex processes by including tests of reading, word association, memory, and simple arithmetic. Such tests were administered to school children, college students, and random samples of adults. At the Columbian Exposition held in Chicago in 1893, for example, Joseph Jastrow set up an exhibit at which visitors were invited to take tests of sensory, motor, and simple perceptual functions and then compare their skill with the norms. A few attempts to evaluate these early tests yielded discouraging results. The individual's performance showed little correspondence from one test to another, and it exhibited little or no correlation with independent estimates of intellectual level derived from teachers' ratings or school grades.

Similar test series were assembled by several European psychologists of the period, notably Oehrn, Kraepelin, and Ebbinghaus in Germany, and Guicciardi and Ferrari in Italy. In an article published in France in 1895, Binet and Henri criticized most of the available test series because of their overemphasis on sensory functions and their undue concentration on simple and narrowly specialized abilities. They also argued that, since individual differences are larger in the more complex functions, a high degree of precision is not needed in the measurement of these functions. Binet and Henri then went on to describe their own test series, which covered such functions as memory, imagination, attention, comprehension, suggestibility, and esthetic judgment. In these tests we can recognize the forerunners of the famous Binet intelligence tests.

In 1904, the French Minister of Public Instruction appointed a commission to study the problem of retardation among public school children. As a direct outgrowth of his work for this commission, Binet, in collaboration with Simon, prepared the first intelligence scale designed to yield a global index of intellectual level. Their first revision of this scale, in which tests were grouped into age levels on the basis of empirical data, appeared in 1908. For example, in the four-year level were placed all tests that normal four-year-olds could pass, in the five-year level all tests passed by normal five-year-olds, and so on. A child's score on the scale could then be expressed as a mental age, that is, the age of normal children whose performance he equaled.

Even before the publication of the 1908 revision, the Binet-Simon scales were enthusiastically adopted by psychologists throughout the world. Translations and adaptations soon appeared in many countries. In America, several revisions were prepared, including the well-known Stanford-Binet developed by Terman and his associates at Stanford University. First published in 1916, the Stanford-Binet was revised in 1937 and brought up to date and further refined in 1960.

Another important milestone in the mental testing movement was the development of group tests. The Binet scales and their revisions are individual tests, that is, they can be given to only one person at a time. In addition, these tests are of such a nature that they require a highly trained examiner to administer and score them. They are thus unsuited for large-scale testing and are now used chiefly as clinical instruments for the intensive study of individual cases. The advent of group intelligence tests was undoubtedly a major factor in the popularization of psychological testing. Group tests are not only designed for the simultaneous examination of large groups, but they are also relatively easy to administer and score.

The immediate stimulus for the development of group tests was provided in 1917, when the United States entered the first World War. At that time, the American Psychological Association appointed a committee, under the chairmanship of Robert M. Yerkes, to consider ways in which psychology could help in the conduct of the war. The committee recognized the preeminent need for the rapid classification of the million and a half recruits with respect to their general intellectual level. Such information was required for many administrative decisions, including rejection or discharge from military service, assignments to different types of service, and admission to officer training camps. The tests developed by the Army psychologists to meet these needs were the Army Alpha and the Army Beta. The Army Alpha was designed for general routine testing; the Army Beta was a nonlanguage test employed with illiterates and foreign-born draftees who were unable to take a test in English. Both tests were suitable for administration to large groups.

So far we have identified the antecedents of differential psychology in the growing interest in individual differences manifested in such diverse fields as astronomy and biology, as well as in the development of experimental psychology, genetics, statistics, and mental testing. By the turn of the century, differential psychology had begun to take definite shape. The previously cited article by Binet and Henri, published in 1895, was entitled "La psychologie individuelle." Besides describing their own test series, Binet and Henri presented therein the first systematic analysis of the aims, scope, and methods of differential psychology. Their opening sentence reflected the status of this field of psychology at the time. It read, "We broach here a new subject, difficult and as yet very meagerly explored" (Binet and Henri, 1895). They went on to discuss what they regarded as the two major problems of differential psychology. The first dealt with the nature and extent of individual differences in psychological functions. The second was concerned with the interrelationships of mental processes within the individual whence one may arrive at a classification of traits and establish which are the more basic functions.

In 1900 appeared the first edition of William Stern's book on differential psychology, "Uber Psychologie der individuellen Differenzen." Part 1 covered the nature, problems, and methods of differential psychology. Within this field, Stern included differences among individuals as well as among racial and cultural groups, occupational and social levels, and the two sexes. He considered the fundamental problem of differential psychology to be threefold. First, what is the nature and the extent of differences in the psychological life of individuals and groups? Second, what factors determine or affect these differences? In this connection he mentioned heredity, climate, social or cultural level, training, and adaptation, among others. Third, how are the differences manifested? Can they be detected by such indices as handwriting, facial conformation, etc.? Stern also discussed the concepts of psychological type, individuality, and normality-versus-abnormality. Under the methods of differential psychology, he considered introspection, objective observation, the use of material from history and poetry, the study of culture, quantitative testing, and experiment. Part II contained a survey of data on individual differences in various psychological traits, from simple sensory capacities to more complex mental functions and emotional traits. Stern's book appeared in a revised and enlarged edition in 1911, and again in 1921, under the title of "Die differentielle Psychologie in ihren methodischen Grundlagen."

In America, national organizations were becoming cognizant of the problems of individual differences. At its 1895 meeting, the American Psychological Association appointed a committee "to consider the feasibility of cooperation among the various psychological laboratories in the collection of mental and physical statistics" (Cattell and Farrand, 1896). The following year, the American Association for the Advancement of Science established a standing committee to organize an ethnographic survey of the white population of the United States. Cattell, who was a member of this committee, urged the inclusion of psychological tests in this survey and suggested that its work be coordinated with that proposed by the American Psychological Association.

Investigators were also beginning to administer the newly devised tests to various groups. R. L. Kelly in 1903 and Naomi Norsworthy in 1906 compared normal and mentally defective children in several sensorimotor and simple mental tests. Their findings highlighted the continuous gradation in ability between these groups, suggesting that mental defectives do not represent a distinct category. In 1903 appeared Helen B. Thompson's "The Mental Traits of Sex," the result of several years' testing of men and women with a variety of tests. This study was the first comprehensive investigation of sex differences in psychological traits.

Tests of sensory acuity, motor capacities, and a few simple mental processes were also being employed for the first time in the comparison of different racial groups. A few scattered investigations were conducted before 1900. In 1904, R. S. Woodworth and F. G. Bruner tested members of several racial groups at the St. Louis Exposition. Their findings called into question the prevalent belief that "primitive" man excelled "civilized" man in sensory capacities. Later research dispelled many other popular notions about racial differences. It was not until the 1920's, however, that the role of cultural factors in the mental test performance of different groups was systematically investigated. Studies of the intellectual development of culturally deprived groups—such as children reared in orphanages, gypsy camps, isolated mountain communities, and city slums—focused attention on the effects that early experience has upon intelligence test performance. These studies, together with research on the influence of schooling and other experiential factors, helped to clarify the results of the many comparative investigations of racial, national, and cultural groups conducted in the 1920's and 1930's.

From its inception, differential psychology has been concerned with the nature of intelligence and the identification of mental traits. An important landmark in this area of research was the publication . . . of an article by the British psychologist, Charles Spearman (1904). In this article, Spearman proposed his Two-Factor theory of mental organization and introduced a statistical technique for investigating the problem. He thereby launched the empirical, quantitative study of trait relationships and opened the way for the modern techniques of factor analysis.

REFERENCES

BINET, A. & HENRI, V. "La psychologie individuelle." *Anne' psychologie*, 1895, 2, p. 411.
CATTELL, J. McK. "Mental Tests and Measurements." *Mind*, 1890, *15*, pp. 373–380.
CATTELL, J. McK. & FARRAND, L. "Physical and mental measurements of the Students of Columbia University." *Psychol. Rev.*, 1896, *3*, p. 619.
SPEARMAN, C. "General intelligence objectively determined and measured." *Amer. J. of Psychol.*, 1904, *15*, pp. 201–293.

32.   Highlights of Standardized Testing

C. E. Alexakos

Informal testing and evaluation must have existed in all ages. It is likely that primitive man selected his leaders and heros by some kind of informal assessment of their skills and competencies. Ancient civilizations

Printed by permission of the author, Dr. C. E. Alexakos, College of Human Resources and Education, West Virginia University, Morgantown, West Virginia.

used tests of both mental and physical traits for the selection of new members for important functions of the state. China had a national system of examinations for selecting public officials as early as 2000 B.C. These early tests do not conform to current ideas of standardized testing, but tend to support the hypothesis that some criteria of evaluation are necessary for all organized societies.

The "first" written examination was given at Cambridge University, England, in 1702. Oxford and other English schools, realizing the advantages of a written test, adopted it shortly afterwards. The system of written examinations was well established in England and other European countries long before it was introduced in the United States. Horace Mann, Secretary of the State Board of Education in Massachusetts, encouraged replacing oral with written examinations, the first of which was administered to pupils in the schools of Boston in 1845. Mann believed firmly that the written examination marked a new era in educational measurement. His convictions were so strong that he exhorted all school committees ". . . never to relapse into the former inadequate practice."

During the last decade of the 19th century several attempts were made in the United States to apply psychological tests to the prediction of college grades. Wissler, a student of Cattell, administered a large number of the early sensory tests and correlated the scores with grades in various subjects at Columbia University. He found that most of the correlations clustered around zero, the highest being .19. Gilbert in a similar study at Yale in 1894 found similarly disappointing correlations between test scores and grades. These disappointing results made many American educators aware of the limitations of early psychological tests and to some degree helped in the enthusiastic acceptance of the Binet scale soon after its publication.

Although a few "psychological" tests had been used in various experimental studies in the 19th century, it was not until 1905 when Binet devised the first intelligence scale that the movement of standardized testing gained momentum. Earlier Binet and Henri (1895) had criticized most of the test series of that time as emphasizing only sensory functions and concentrating unduly on the measurement of very simple abilities. Binet observed that his own test of intelligence measured memory, imagination, comprehension, problem solving, and other complex mental functions. In collaboration with Simon, Binet revised his scale in 1908 and 1911. A third revision was discontinued because of Binet's death.

Binet's concept of intelligence was a generalized or global one integrating a child's ability to judge correctly, to reason clearly and logically, and to comprehend effectively. His definition of intelligence emphasized that "maintaining a definite direction, choosing appropriate means to ends, and evaluating one's actions are the major parts of a unitary mind whose over-riding function was effective adjustment to environment."

Shortly after its publication the Binet-Simon scale was translated into other languages or adapted for use in other cultures. In America the first translation into English was undertaken by Goddard at the Vineland, New Jersey, Training School for the Feebleminded. Goddard's translation was used in institutions for the mentally retarded, in prisons, reform schools, and juvenile courts. The obtained results indicated that Goddard's translation of the Binet-Simon scale was a rather poor instrument for the measurement of intelligence of American children.

In 1910 Terman undertook an extensive revision and adaptation of the Binet-Simon scale to meet the needs of the American culture. Terman's first revision was published in 1916 and became known as the Stanford-Binet scale.

In 1937 Terman in collaboration with Merrill published a second revision of the Stanford-Binet scale. The new edition was a considerable enlargement of the 1916 revision. It contained two scales designated as L and M. Each scale consisted of 129 items, more than twice the number of the original Binet-Simon scale. The items were selected from more than 600 items administered to a representative sample of the United States white population. Other improvements of the L and M scales included: (1) statistical analysis of item data to screen the best items and also [to] divide them equivalently between the two forms, (2) carefully written instructions for administration and scoring of the items, and (3) compilation of norms and other statistics from large numbers of representative populations of all ages. The new scales also corrected some deficiencies in the very low and very high ranges of IQ that were found in the 1916 revision. The two scales could be administered interchangeably, providing a safeguard against practice effects in cases where it became necessary to test the same subject more than once. The work of Terman and Merrill revised and enlarged the Binet Scale to such an extent that it hardly resembled the original Binet-Simon test of intelligence. It was only out of respect to Binet's original idea that the name Stanford-Binet was retained for the 1937 scales.

A third revision of the Stanford-Binet was published in 1960, after Terman's death. The new revision combined the two 1937 scales into a single form designated L-M. The combined form incorporated the best items of the two scales on the basis of data collected on 4498 subjects ranging in age from 2½ to 18 years.

Two types of changes were introduced in the 1960 revision: content and structure. Content changes involved elimination of unsatisfactory items, relocation of satisfactory items to other age levels to satisfy the criterion of difficulty, and clarification of directions for administration and scoring that had been found to cause ambiguity or misinterpretation to different examiners. Structural changes involved a statistical adjustment to make the ratio of the *average* mental age to the *average* chronological age equal to unity for all age levels and construction of IQ tables with built-in adjustments purported to eliminate certain extreme variabilities of IQ scores observed at some age levels and to assure the comparability of IQ scores at all age levels. The 1960 revision also extended the maximum chronological age from 16 to 18 years, since many experimental studies had demonstrated that the intellectual development of the average human being does not cease at the age of 16 as Terman had believed.

The monumental work of Terman inspired an enormous amount of research concerning both the theory of testing and measurement and the practical application and interpretation of the scores obtained by the Stanford-Binet. The Stanford-Binet scale has been in the past 50 years and still remains the most reliable and the most valid test of general intelligence.

Testing gained momentum after World War I. Prior to the war Otis had compiled items for testing and ability to comprehend. He contributed these items to the development of Army Alpha (intended for literate English speaking recruits) and Army Beta (based on graphic or pictorial items and intended for illiterate or foreign born recruits) scales. The army scales were administered to more than one and a half million recruits. The data gathered through their administration constituted the largest amount of measurements ever collected on adult intelligence. After the war, Otis re-allocated his items and constructed the well known Otis Alpha, Beta, and Gamma scales for civilian use. The post-war construction of tests was so rapid that in 1928, just a decade later, approximately 1300 standardized or semi-standardized tests were competing in the American market.

The fever of activity in both intelligence test construction and field testing continued throughout the second decade of the current century. From this fervor a few new well-constructed tests came into being. In 1921 Thomson devised the Northumberland Mental Test, which proved very useful in the identification of bright rural children who were adversely affected by the ordinary tests of intelligence because of impoverished background, ill-health, or inadequate school training. The Northumberland Mental Test enjoyed so much popularity in the British Isles that by 1930 a new version of it was published annually for the prediction of the educational success of underprivileged children.

In 1923 Kohs devised the Block Design Test, the first test of performance to be used successfully for the measurement of general intelligence. Other performance tests came into existence shortly thereafter. For a while they gained an advantage over verbal tests because they were thought to be less culturally biased. The period after 1930 produced the following main trends: (1) Performance tests gained such popularity and prominence that Wechsler balanced his scales with an equal number of verbal and performance tests, computing separate verbal and performance IQ scores; (2) Much attention was focused on the objective achievement test. Achievement batteries testing the major school subjects and skills were standardized on nationwide samples; (3) Vehement attacks, led primarily by Thurstone, were leveled against the concept of general intelligence. These were followed by voluminous experimentation with multi-factor batteries, the component parts of which were designed to measure different aspects or different ingredients of intelligence.

Wechsler devised his first intelligence scale in 1939 while working as a psychologist at the Bellevue Psychiatric Hospital of the city of New York. The original scale was known as the "Wechsler-Bellevue" Scale: Form I and was used extensively by psychologists and psychiatrists in military hospitals during the Second World War. A revised version of the Wechsler-Bellevue appeared in 1946, but was never standardized. It soon was replaced by the improved forms of WISC (Wechsler Intelligence Scale for Children), published in 1949, and WAIS (Wechsler Adult Intelligence Scale), published in 1955. A new form, the Wechsler Preschool and Primary Scale of Intelligence (WPPSI), was published in 1967. The age levels for each scale are as follows:

WAIS: ages 16 and above,
WISC: ages 5 to 15, and
WPPSI: ages 4½ to 6½.

Wechsler's original purpose was twofold: (1) to devise an intelligence scale for adults, since he believed that adult intelligence differed from the intelligence of children, and (2) to construct a scale that, besides measuring general intelligence, would provide information as to which mental functions were impaired in psychiatric patients. Paradoxically, his scale became most popular as a measure of general intelligence in children. His WISC scale was used in many studies of children intelligence after its publication and became the first serious competitor of the Stanford-Binet. His second purpose of identifying the mental disfunctions of psychiatric patients was hardly fulfilled. The diagnostic profiles published by Wechsler proved to have very little validity for clinical diagnosis.

Today the Wechsler scales are used primarily as tests of general intelligence. Wechsler, too, although he introduced a few innovations in individual intelligence testing, adhered to the generalized concept of intelligence proposed by Binet and subscribed to by Terman. He defined intelligence as "the aggregate or global capacity of the individual to act purposefully, to think rationally and to deal effectively with his environment." (Wechsler, 1944; p. 3).

The main innovations introduced to testing of intelligence by Wechsler are as follows: (1) he included the best available performance tests in all versions of his scale. In the latest tests—WISC, WAIS, and WPPSI—the number of performance subscales is equal to the number of verbal tests. Separate IQ scores are computed for the verbal and performance parts in all Wechsler scales in current use. (2) The same items were administered to all subjects in contrast to the Binet-Simon and Stanford-Binet scales where testing began at the age where the testee passed all items and ended at the age where he failed all items of a particular year. Discontinuation of testing in each sub-scale of the Wechsler tests is effected when the testee fails a certain number of consecutive items. The number of items that must be failed varies from subtest to subtest. (3) Wechsler did away altogether with the concept of mental age, introducing instead a statistical deviation IQ with a mean of 100 and a standard deviation of 15. Standardized verbal, performance, and total (sum of verbal and performance) scores were then translated into z-scores and assigned IQ values in terms of probabilistic expectations with reference to the normal curve. (4) Wechsler demonstrated that mental ability continues growing up to the ages of 27–30 and then begins to decline gradually and slowly. He also found that mental ability as determined by performance tasks declines more rapidly than verbal ability. That is, ability to perform manual tasks deteriorates more rapidly than proficiency in language skills.

Generally, Wechsler's work is characterized by a greater statistical sophistication than either Binet's or Terman's. This may be due primarily to the fact that modern statistical theory and methodology was completely undeveloped at the beginning of the century when Binet devised his scale. Notwithstanding the statistical sophistication Wechsler found it necessary to validate his scale with reference to the Stanford-Binet. The correspondence between Stanford-Binet and Wechsler IQ scores was found to be very high, giving an average correlation of .82. Wechsler's severe criticisms against the concept of mental age were hardly justified, particularly since he used the Stanford-Binet to validate his own scale. The concept of mental age was based on equally sound statistical principles as his own deviation IQ. Certain of his advanced techniques and some of his findings, however, were used in the 1960 revision of the Stanford-Binet to correct minor deficiencies of the L and M scales.

The testing of American recruits in World War I encouraged experts to construct and try out objective test items intended to measure attainment in school subjects. Among the first to realize the value of standardized achievement testing were Tyler and Lindquist. Tyler's book *Constructing Achievement Tests* was published in 1934; Lindquist's efforts culminated in the publication of the Iowa Tests of Basic Skills for elementary school students in 1940 and the Iowa Tests of Educational Development for high school students in 1942. The main criticism against early achievement tests was that they encouraged children to accumulate

great quantities of unrelated facts which appeared to be a hindrance
rather than an aid to their intellectual development; however, in many
instances it was found that such tests predicted achievement at high
school and college much better than intelligence or other types of tests.

Since 1940 thousands of achievement tests have been published.
Batteries of achievement tests enjoyed the advantage that a student's
performance in one subject could be compared with his level of achievement in other subjects (*ipsative* comparisons). Since batteries could also
be standardized on nation-wide samples, they permitted comparisons
among students' performances in different schools of the country (*normative* comparisons). Batteries of achievement tests have been more popular at the elementary school level, covering most frequently the areas of
language usage (grammar, and syntax), reading, spelling, arithmetic,
and social studies (primarily, history and geography). In high school and
college the trend has been to rely on independent tests for each subject
area, although some comprehensive batteries are available today for high
school students. Such batteries have been found helpful in counseling
students to plan their course work in high school and college, on the one
hand, while, on the other hand, they have raised controversial issues
concerning the concepts of underachievement and overachievement of
certain students.

The surge in the development of achievement testing is associated
with Thorndike's work. In 1918 Thorndike published a significant paper
on educational measurement which began with the dictum: "whatever
exists at all exists in some amount." Thorndike subsequently was named
the father of educational measurement. The decade between 1920 and
1930 evidenced the rapid development of achievement tests intended for
the major academic subjects of high school curriculum. It also marked a
transitory period during which test-construction passed from amateur to
professional hands. By 1930 both the widespread application of "objective" measurement and the professionalization of the testing movement
were established. In 1929 the University of Iowa undertook a statewide
project to test every high school student attending Iowa public schools.
Five years later the statewide testing program was extended to all pupils
of the upper elementary grades. Three important organizations: the
American Council on Education, the Carnegie Foundation for the Advancement of Teaching, and the College Entrance Examination Board
were formed in 1930. Finally, in 1947 the Educational Testing Service
was formed, which took over most testing activities performed by the
three previous groups, thus encouraging further the professionalization of
test development and application.

Another area of testing greatly influenced by intelligence testing is
the so called personality testing. The roots of personality testing go back
to Galton's study of mental imagery conducted in the 1880's. Binet him-

self carried out a few rudimentary experiments in personality testing. Along with his standard procedures, Binet continually collected observations on each subject's reaction to different questions. Although his test was used primarily as a test of mental adaptation, it was also considered to be a standardized interview. Binet observed that two students performing at the same level of mental age, as measured by his scale, would often react differently to different items of the test and also achieve differently in different school subjects. The discrepancy between performance in school and on tests was thought to be caused by personality differences.

At the beginning personality testing progressed without a definition of what constitutes "personality." Attempts to define personality encountered more obstacles and complexities than efforts to define intelligence. A pragmatic definition of personality offered by test makers was that "personality is that which, when known, will enable one to predict future behavior and success." Such a definition, of course, was not acceptable to personality theorists. Later on, many test specialists favored a definition of personality given by Allport. According to Allport, "personality is an amazingly complex organization comprising man's distinctive habits of thought and expression, his attitudes, traits, and interests, and his own peculiar philosophy of life. . . . Personality . . . determines man's unique adjustment to his environment" (1938, p. 12).

Ignoring the lack of an adequate definition, early developers of personality tests proceeded in two main directions: (1) measurement of "traits" that were thought to make up personality, and (2) validation of their instruments as predictors of behavior. The main motive for the development of the personality inventory, as with the group intelligence test, was the need of the army during World War I. While the Army Alpha and Beta scales were being developed to facilitate classification of recruits on the basis of intelligence, it was realized by many psychologists that intelligence test scores alone could not predict success in important specialties of the army. Thus, Woodworth devised the "Personal Data Sheet," an inventory of neurotic tendencies and emotional maladjustments, which was easy to administer to large groups and could be used to screen recruits and officers unfit for combat because of personal idiosyncrasies or conflicts.

Further, the construction of measuring instruments of personality followed two distinct paths: one represented by such instruments as the Rorschach inkblots and the Thematic Apperception Test (TAT), which are based on a wholistic theory of personality with some proneness to favor the Freudian school of psychology in their interpretation, and the other composed of paper-and-pencil instruments, questionnaires, or personal data inventories intended to measure specific personality traits and dependent on a behavioristic approach in the interpretation of their results. In addition, some experiments have been conducted with performance tests, but such tests have been proved of little practical value for mass personality testing. The Rorschach and TAT, too, are of limited usefulness because they can be administered only individually by highly trained psychologists. Furthermore, interpretation of Rorschach and the TAT protocols is largely subjective, depending almost exclusively on the examiner's perception and judgment. For these reasons, the treatment of personality testing here will be confined to the paper-and-pencil inventories which tend to affect large populations of testees.

Woodworth's Personal Data Sheet contained 116 questions such as "Do your interests change quickly?," to which soldiers responded by "yes" or "no." Woodworth first tried out a larger questionnaire on both normal and psychoneurotic samples, and on the basis of his findings he determined the items that differentiated between normal and neurotic adults. A soldier's score on the questionnaire was the sum of his responses that resembled the responses of neurotic patients. Soldiers whose scores were high enough to raise doubts concerning their success in the army were sent for further psychiatric examinations.

Woodworth's questionnaire set the pattern for the majority of inventories that followed. During the 1920's a large number of such inventories was published for civilian use. Woodworth's own questionnaire was adapted for use with young children in 1923 by Mathews and for college students in 1927 by House (known as House's Mental Hygiene Inventory). Other inventories were developed to measure the degree of introversion-extraversion, ascendance-submission, self-sufficiency-dependency, and a multitude of other such traits. All these inventories shared not only common characteristics, but also common philosophical foundations. Freeman (1955) tried to justify their philosophical foundations by observing that both "behavior and personality are manifestations of certain traits, and that the strength of traits can be measured."

The *Bernreuter Personality Inventory* published in 1931 introduced an improved method of scoring questionnaires. Through experimentation it was discovered that the predictive efficiency of personality inventories could be improved by assignment of differential weights to responses to different questions. The method of differential weighting of items was further refined in the construction and scoring of the *Minnesota Multiphasic Personality Inventory* (MMPI). Also, the Bernreuter was the first inventory to produce a profile of four traits: self-sufficiency, introversion-extroversion, neuroticism, and dominance-submission. Weights were assigned to items, according to their discriminating power as determined by statistical methods, primarily biserial correlations of the items with the total score.

The *Bell Adjustment Inventory* published in 1934 followed the pattern of the Bernreuter. The main problem that these two inventories faced was inability to show that the traits they intended to measure did exist and did not overlap. Since no adequate statistical techniques were available at that time, the developers of questionnaires tended to group items together to form subscales by armchair judgment. In 1935 Flanagan demonstrated that the correlations among the Bernreuter scales made it possible to reduce the four scales to only two, which Flanagan named self-confidence and sociability. Cattell (1946) conducted a great number of actor analyses which showed that many personality scales which were thought to be independent were in fact correlated and overlapping.

The *Minnesota Multiphasic Personality Inventory* (MMPI) published in 1943 took advantage of a refined system of item weights. It consisted of 550 questions, not all of which were taken into account in constructing the clinical scales. Some items were used in deriving the validity and fakability scales; others were ignored altogether. The MMPI contains 9 clinical scales and 4 validation scales. Prior to the standardization of the MMPI the 550 questions were administered to two groups: a group of psychiatric patients and a matched group of normal adults. Only those items which clearly differentiated statistically between patients and nonpatients were included in the scoring scheme of the inventory. An improved version of the MMPI was published in 1951. The MMPI has been used more frequently than any other personality inventory for clinical research. In most instances, the MMPI proved to have some validity in screening mental patients and in predicting nonpatients who are likely to seek psychiatric help. However, its reliability has been questioned by many workers, both clinicians and researchers.

The *California Personality Inventory* (CPI) developed in 1957 in the pattern of the MMPI for use with normal adolescents and young adults proved very poor in terms of both reliability and validity. The lack of any evidence in favor of the CPI has raised additional questions concerning the predictive efficiency of the MMPI. Namely, if the MMPI predicts, it may predict too late for the patient to seek proper treatment.

The *Guilford-Zimmerman Temperament Survey* (GZTS) constructed in 1949 was the first inventory to be established on the basis of evidence provided by factor analytic studies. By means of factor analysis clusters of items were identified and separated into independent scales. The GZTS was an improved version of earlier personality scales constructed by Guilford. It is an easily administered instrument intended for both adolescents and adults. It contains ten scales: ascendance, emotional stability, friendliness, general activity, masculinity, objectivity, personal relations, restraint, sociability, and thoughtfulness.

The *Edwards Personal Preference Schedule* (EPPS) was the first inventory to deal with problems of testee honesty in responding to paper-and-pencil questionnaires. Edwards believed that subjects tended to answer questions in a manner they thought to be socially acceptable;

therefore, he tried out his items in a preliminary experiment requesting that testees rate each answer in terms of social desirability. Then, he matched pairs of items in his schedule so that subjects had to choose between two equally desirable statements. Edwards method is known as the "forced choice" method and proved to be more reliable than other nonforcing methods. The EPPS contains 15 scales measuring such needs as achievement, affiliation, order, and so on, derived from Murray's theory of personality. Murray's theory of needs, however, has never been validated.

Finally, mention will be made here of the *Vineland Social Maturity Scale* (VSMS). The VSMS, published in 1935, constitutes a unique adaptation of Binet's idea of mental age. It measures broad nonintellective characteristics from which the *social age* of the subject is determined. The obtained social age divided by the child's chronological age gives his social quotient. The social age of a subject is arrived at by both observation of the subject's behavior and completion of a checklist indicating what he should be doing (in some instances thinking) at each age level. The VSMS is considered a personality scale because it does not require knowledge of facts, neither does it depend on correct answers.

These are only a few of the multitude of personality inventories that have been devised since the appearance and use of the Woodworth Personal Data Sheet during the first World War. To enumerate even the major inventories in use today would be a taxing experience. The few that were described briefly in the foregoing paragraphs were selected in such a way as to illustrate the main improvements and the basic phases through which such instruments passed from their original conception to the present.

Almost all paper-and-pencil personality inventories have faced and still face the same basic problems and difficulties. The most disturbing of these problems are enumerated below: (1) The most obvious problem is that of faking. The subject can easily distort his responses to present a good or bad picture of himself at will. (2) Associated to some degree with the previous problem is the finding that many subjects tend to change opinions or attitudes in very short periods of time. In many occasions, a number of testees had never thought about some questions prior to taking the inventory. Deeper thought or refreshed memory is likely to cause alteration of a substantial number of responses by many testees. (3) Another problem is the tendency of many testees to give an affirmative rather than negative answer to doubtful or controversial items as well as to items they know very little about. (4) A fourth problem is the tendency of many people to take moderate rather than extreme, unusual, or uncommon positions on many issues. This difficulty is encountered primarily in rating scales where the subject is asked to check an item on a continuum extending from the least to the most favorable rating. (5) A fifth problem is the tendency of many testees to give answers which, according to their reasoning, are agreeable with the expectations of the examiner. That is, testees try to be obliging or "nice" to the tester. (6) All paper-and-pencil inventories face severe problems of reliability. The problem of reliability is twofold: (a) on the one hand, it involves linguistic or semantic differences. In some instances, very slight changes in the wording of a question may alter considerably the responses; (b) on the other hand, it involves situational or circumstantial changes of responses. In one situation the subject may give a positive answer, while under slightly different conditions he may give a negative answer to the same question. And (7) the most entangled and the most difficult to solve is the problem of validity. Many developers of personality inventories point to the personality theories on which their inventories depend; however, most of these theories are not proven theories as yet. No satisfactory outside criteria are available to validate the inventories, except in the case of mentally ill vs. normal subjects, but even on this criterion the "false-positives" and "true-negatives" are large enough to make the best inventory disrespectful in terms of validity. In addition, the problem of validity becomes further complicated by a lack of evidence concerning the stability of personality traits. Neither the degree nor the causes of change have been adequately explored. Research on the area of opinion and attitude changes seems to stumble against unsurmountable obstacles.

Closely related to the development of personality inventories is the development of interest inventories. The first to publish an interest inventory was Moore in 1921, although the Carnegie Institute of Technology held a series of graduate seminars on interests during the academic year 1919–20. The seminars stimulated the publication of several devices measuring interests, the most successful of which was the *Strong Vocational Interest Blank* (SVIB) published in 1927. The SVIB was based exclusively on empirical data that differentiated among different occupational groups in terms of preferences, hobbies, sports, and social activities. The SVIB explored a large number of such preferences by asking testees to respond with L (like), D (dislike), or I (indifferent) to 400 items covering a wide variety of activities.

The main purpose of the SVIB was to help young men and women make wise vocational choices by comparing their preferences with the typical preferences of persons engaged in certain occupations. Two forms of the SVIB have been in existence for many years: one for men, the other for women. The two forms were originally similar in structure and purpose, but differed in content. In recent revisions the blank for men provides information about 47 specific occupations, 6 occupational groups, and 4 vocational scales. The blank for women contains norms for 29 occupational scales, dealing primarily with occupations favored by women. In the newest revision, the best items were selected from five previous forms and incorporated into a single form, known as Form L.

The SVIB has been continually researched and revised since its inception in 1927. Controversy still flourishes concerning both the utility and the validity of the SVIB. Concerning its utility, many specialists observe that the time spent on administering and scoring the SVIB is wasted because subjects, if asked, are likely to state their occupational preferences directly and without reservations. Supporters of the SVIB, however, argue that younger subjects do not usually know what type of occupation they want to enter, neither do they possess information concerning the activities performed by workers in a specific occupational field. Concerning its validity, the main problem arises from the instability of vocational interests during adolescence and early adulthood. For mature adults vocational interests are satisfactorily stable and therefore the predictive validity of the SVIB is respectably high. However, no such claim can be made for younger subjects, among whom the need for vocational guidance is most critical.

The chief competitor to the SVIB, the *Kuder Preference Record* (KPR) Form C: Vocational, appeared in 1939. It was revised in 1951 and 1956. Items which in previous versions of Forms C and D proved effective in differentiating among occupational clusters were included in the currently used Form C. In contrast to the SVIB which was based exclusively on empirical evidence, the KPR depended on a theoretical scheme of occupational classifications, according to which the great majority of occupations were grouped into ten homogeneous clusters. Factor analytic techniques were used by Kuder to organize the items of his inventory into ten descriptive scales corresponding to the ten occupational fields. Another innovation introduced by Kuder was that, instead of asking testees to respond to each item by L, D, or I, he grouped his items into triads of which the testee was instructed to check one as the *most* preferred and one as *least* preferred, leaving, the third unmarked.

At the beginning evidence of validity concerning either the ten scales of the KPR or the theory on the basis of which they were developed was completely lacking, but gradually some evidence of predictive validity was accumulated as more and more students took the inventory. The ten scales of the vocational form are: Outdoor, Mechanical, Computational, Scientific, Persuasive, Artistic, Literary, Musical, Social Service, and Clerical. A student's scores on the ten scales were plotted on a sheet of paper to form the so-called "Kuder profile." Profiles which contained a mixture of high and low scores were found to be helpful in vocational counseling of high school students; therefore, the KPR gained more popularity among younger students than the SVIB. Also, in comparison with the SVIB, the KPR proved much easier to administer and score.

The SVIB and the KPR are the most frequently used interest inventories today. They, also, have faced the same problems as the personality inventories discussed previously. The most disturbing of these problems in the case of interest inventories was that of faking. It was found that many testees, particularly among those seeking employment in a specific field, could purposefully change their responses in such a way as to show a profile of interests congruent with their prospective occupation. To guard against extreme faking Strong developed a "lie" scale and Kuder a "validation" scale, but even with such precautionary measures sophisticated subjects can still fake interest inventories to their advantage.

The foregoing is a very cursory description of the historical development of standardized testing. Only the most significant phases and the most popular instruments were mentioned. To follow all the paths that testing took in the course of its development would require much more space than that provided here. To illustrate the rapid and diverse development of testing, it suffices to mention that by 1928, only one decade after the first large scale program was conducted in the United States Army, approximately 1300 different standardized or semi-standardized instruments had been constructed and distributed for use in the American public. By 1940 the number of standardized tests exceeded 2600, or twice the number of the first period. Today the number of available tests of all types is estimated to approximate 6,000. The bulk of these tests has been produced in the United States, a fair indication that standardized testing is a phenomenon of the American culture. Today more than 200 million tests are taken annually by school children alone. Adding to this number tests that are administered in employment centers, in private counseling or psychological clinics, in mental hospitals, in colleges and college counseling centers, the number will exceed the 300 million; that is, 1½ tests per member of the general population, or approximately an average of 3–4 tests per member of the test-taking population. Notwithstanding some recent attacks against industrialized testing, it seems that large scale testing will continue in the future.

CALENDAR OF MAIN EVENTS IN THE DEVELOPMENT OF TESTING

A calendar of main events leading to the development of standardized testing is as follows:

1702   Replacement of oral by written examinations at Cambridge University, England.
1845   Introduction of the written examination to the schools of Boston by Horace Mann.
1864   The Reverend George Fisher constructed a "scale-book" for evaluation of his students' performance on various school subjects.
1880s Galton used tests of sensory perception and discrimination as well as

a test of mental imagery to measure intelligence; however, with very little success.

1894 Rice constructed the first standardized test on spelling. It gained for him the title of "inventor of educational measurement."

1897 The first completion test intended to measure verbal comprehension and ideational fluency was devised by Ebbinghaus.

1901 The first test of achievement in elementary arithmetic was published by Courtis.

1905 Publication of the first Binet-Simon Intelligence Scale. The scale was revised in 1908 and 1911.

1909 Translation of the Binet-Simon scale into English by Goddard.

1910 Appearance of the Thorndike Handwriting Scale.

1910 Terman began his work on the revision of the Binet-Simon scale for the purpose of adapting it to the needs of the American culture.

1911 Ayres published his legibility of handwriting scale.

1912 Publication of the Hillegas Composition Scale.

1913 Buckingham constructed a spelling scale involving words of gradual difficulty.

1916 Terman published his first revision of the Binet-Simon and designated it the Stanford-Binet Intelligence Scale. He introduced the term IQ.

1917 The Army Alpha and Beta scales were constructed and used for classification of recruits by a committee of specialists headed by Yerkes.

1917 Woodworth devised the Personal Data Sheet for use in the army.

1918 Thorndike in an epoch-making paper on educational measurement pronounced that "whatever exists at all exists in some amount." The paper gained for him that eponym of "father of educational measurement."

1919 The beginning of professionalization of the testing movement.

1920 Otis' scales: Alpha, Beta, and Gamma and the Otis Quick Scoring Test of Mental Ability were distributed for civilian use.

1921 First concern with culture-fair tests. Development of the Northumberland Mental Test by Thomson.

1922 Publication of the Stanford Achievement Tests.

1923 Kohs devised the Block Design Test, the first performance test to measure intelligence.

1923 Mathews adapted the Woodworth Data Sheet for use with young children.

1927 A Mental Hygiene Inventory in the pattern of Woodworth's questionnaire was devised by House.

1927 Strong published the first viable Interest Inventory.

1929 Inauguration of the first state-wide testing program in Iowa.

1930 Formation of the College Entrance Examination Board.

1931 Publication of the Bernreuter Personality Inventory.

1934 Publication of the Bell Adjustment Inventory.

1934 *Constructing Achievement Tests* by Tyler.

1936 Second revision of the Stanford-Binet (Forms L and M).

1939 The first Wechsler-Bellevue Scale was published.

1939 Publication of the Kuder Preference Record.

1940   Organized testing programs were in existence in 26 states.
1940   Iowa Tests of Basic Skills.
1942   Iowa Tests of Educational Development.
1943   Minnesota Multiphasic Personality Inventory (MMPI)
1947   Formation of the Educational Testing Service.
1949   Wechsler Intelligence Scale for Children (WISC).
1955   Wechsler Adult Intelligence Scale (WAIS),
1960   Third revision of the Stanford-Binet (L-M scale).
1967   Wechsler Preschool and Primary Scale of Intelligence (WPPSI).

Prior to 1930:   Interest focused on the nature of intelligence.
1930–1940   Interest focused on cultural differences—culture fair tests.
1940 to present: Interest focused on nonintellective characteristics of students.

REFERENCES

ALLPORT, G. W. Personality: a psychological interpretation. New York: Holt, Rinehart, and Winston, 1938.
BINET, A. AND HENRI, V. La psychologie individuelle. Année Psychologique, 1895, pp. 441–463.
CATTELL, R. B. The description and measurement of personality. New York: World Book Publishing, 1946.
FREEMAN, F. S. Theory and practice of psychological testing. New York: Holt, Rinehart, and Winston, 1955.
GARRETT, H. E. AND SCHNECK, M. R. Psychological tests, methods, and results. New York: Harper & Row, 1933.
WECHSLER, D. The measurement of intelligence. Baltimore: Williams, 1944.

33.   Some Aspects of the Appraisal Function in Guidance

Arden White

Counselors deal with two major realms of information. The first is the environment, particularly its occupational, economic, general culture and subcultural components. The second is the individual, the idiosyncratic, personal, unique elements of a person's circumstances. Information about the environment, though complex, sometimes contradictory, and subject to interpretation with competing theories, is available in immense quantity, by and large.

Printed by permission of the author, Dr. Arden White, Professor of Guidance Education, University of Wyoming, Laramie, Wyoming.

Some of this environmental information may be relatively difficult to locate and difficult to acquire, because of either remoteness or expense. But even the most obtuse or obscure aspects of the environment seem to have been observed and recorded in some fashion by somebody. Therein lie two hazards, however. Much environmental information soon becomes dated and must be almost constantly replaced with new material. Additionally, this information always has an element of incompleteness or unrecognized inapplicability. Incompleteness sometimes appears to be the result of a deliberate attempt to slant the information in favor of some particular value, behavior, or judgment which is often not readily recognizable. The counselor bears some responsibility to serve as an evaluator of information about the environment, but this responsibility would seem to be met by regularly attending to sources of information and allowing time to maintain a regimen of reviewing occupational and educational information documents and other sources of information, such as community survey reports, statistical summaries, bibliographies, and the like. Parenthetically, one major way to maximize a counselor's effectiveness would be to provide him with assistants who could perform, with specific preparation and subsequent supervision, the tasks of attending to sources of information.

In his everyday work, the school counselor encounters multiple occasions demanding the appropriate individual use of information about students. Frank Parsons (1909) perhaps was the first writer formally to express the potential value of data about individuals in the guidance process. His specification of the relationship of information about the individual to other aspects of guidance remains viable today. The development of most significance in the sixty years since his book appeared is in the realm of philosophical rather than methodological or procedural concerns. Certainly methodological developments have occurred; and vast improvements have been wrought, such that the arsenal of tools available to the counselor is quite large presently. The increasing complexity of devices and procedures has produced ethical concerns (e.g., about the use of computers for central storage of data about individuals). But basic concerns presently stem primarily from philosophical rather than procedural issues.

Information about the individual seems to be available in lesser amounts than information about the environment, and interpretation seems to be a much more difficult matter. It is necessary, then, that competing models for interpretation be studied, and one selected. The values of the user of theory enter into the selection process and become an often covert and frequently unspecifiable factor in the total set of factors from which the final interpretation is made. In addition to the difficulties and hazards inherent in arriving at a model for data interpretation, the data are often minimal, incomplete and contradictory, often much more so than with information about the environment. The instruments and procedures used typically yield information that is internally correlated, though seldom perfectly. Lack of high relationship between sets of data poses a severe problem for the interpreter of information about the individual. He must make a judgment about which of two or more descriptions is to be used in a particular instance. And although some methodological guidelines are available, these procedural directives seldom are sufficient, and frequently are awkward to apply.

A second difficulty associated with the realm of information about the individual is the apparent inadequacy of sufficiently precise descriptions about all aspects of individual behavior. Based upon persistent results from prediction studies, the measurement devices lack either scope, or precision, or both. Lack of reliability is a continuing problem in developing specific, parsimonious descriptions about an individual. Predictions cannot approach perfection without precision in the basic, or raw, measurement descriptions. But a second issue poses an equal, if not greater, difficulty for the user of data about the individual. Apparently some of the realm is not being described with any of the instruments and procedures at hand, or by any combination of them. Such a statement is itself theoretical, however, because the models currently available for prediction yield a prediction equation of one or more independent variables in combination to predict a subsequent behavior, the dependent variable or criterion. That is, the predictor or predictors are known or thought to be related to the behavior to be predicted in some amount which would improve the precision of statements about the predicted behavior over what other statements devoid of the information would provide. Probably the concept of correlation is the most utilitarian expression of the relationship between a behavior one hopes to predict better than base rate occurrence and the information set employed to make the prediction. Typically, the goal of prediction is to identify one variable or set of variables which can be assessed and employed to forecast a second variable or set not directly measurable. Usually the school counselor is involved with attempting to forecast a behavioral outcome inaccessible because of time. He seeks to describe through prediction an event in time before it appears directly. This point may seem rudimentary, but variables can be employed to make statements about conditions, not directly observable, which occur simultaneously with those variables. Assessing the status of an automobile engine by its various emissions would be an example. Any diagnostic effort is essentially analagous.

Counselors frequently become involved in status descriptive efforts. They help teachers or administrators assess student levels of subject achievement. Students confer with them about social development. Parents seek descriptions from them about the developmental level of a child. But any time a present, or prior, characteristic is employed to forecast a subsequent event, whether of the same sort or of an apparently different sort, a prediction has been made. Counselors are deeply involved in predictions, sometimes in making them directly but perhaps more frequently in helping someone else arrive at a prediction. Even more likely, the counselor is assisting someone else to arrive at a series of simultaneous predictions, each with an implied probability attached such that a hierarchy among the predictions can be established and specified. The basic elements of the procedure seem evident, the present state of the art notwithstanding. These prediction sets are not perfect, however. They relate imperfectly to the behavior to be predicted. The difference between the obtained result and perfection commonly is referred to as "error," meaning that variation in the predicted behavior is not accounted for by the prediction set of information. A most difficult problem confronting the user of information, the individual himself, the school counselor, or any one else, is the separation of this "error" component into its two apparent parts.

One part is the result of imprecision in the basic data collection instruments and procedures, and these are legion. Kerlinger (1964, pp. 429–443) presents an excellent discussion of the problem of separating true individual differences from the effects of errors of measurement. A basic problem in developing appraisal instruments is to minimize errors of measurement. The user of data derived from imperfect appraisal instruments and procedures is faced with a different problem. He must allow for the imprecision of the data being used in arriving at his judgments. Quite frequently he has no means at hand to identify error in his data as a distinct entity. His approximations often cannot have a specific probability of correctness so that the risks attached to them are indistinct, even to the point of an apparent equality among data from several different sources. Such a state of apparent equality is most misleading since the counselor, and particularly, those with whom he is working may be lulled into selecting an alternative based upon its subjective value potential, which may be unrelated to the actual probability of achievement. A mundane example would be selection of a college. The student may have reasons extraneous to his probability of success in any given college for wanting to attend there. If the counselor is unable to assess with considerable differentiation his actual chance of success at that college compared to other possible colleges, the student will fall back on his subjective preferences in reaching a decision, having no better objective basis for selection. Counselors typically seem to be in such a circumstance. Either data are not at hand upon which to make differential statements, or the data does not fit into the system the counselor is prepared to use, or the imprecision of the data is so great as to yield useless results.

The other part of the "error" component in information is the unique or idiosyncratic nature of the individual himself. To the researcher involved in the development of measurement instruments, and to anyone interested in methodological research, such a reality is either untenable or a source of ultimate, unsolvable difficulty. Any unpredictable element necessarily would prevent qualification in prediction.

The problem is essentially a confrontation with the philosophical view one has of the nature of man. If one believes essentially that all behavior is caused in the reactive sense, i.e., of being confined to responses to stimuli, then one is likely to take the position that the "error" in one's predictions is due to methodological inperfections. The solution to the present state of imperfection would be to improve methodological procedures and instrumentation. But if one allows himself the view that individual behavior is at all spontaneous, not wholly reactive, then he must be willing also to live with condition of being unable entirely and completely ever to achieve perfection in his predictions.

On the one hand, to believe that one's predictions are less than perfect because of inadequacies in one's assessment procedures or instruments is a humbling condition, but one likely to lead to a feeling of caution and a sense of urgency in developing better procedures. On the other hand, to believe that perfection in predicting is unattainable could lead to a feeling that one need not seek to improve over the present state of affairs. Those who avail themselves of counselor services ultimately would be deprived of the best possible assistance.

The problem and the philosophical issue can be avoided at present from the methodological view, because even recognized, unsolved procedural and instrumentation difficulties appear unlikely to be solved in even the remote future. But the difference in how data must be used in the present state of imperfection would appear to be sufficient reason to consider the philosophical position one has about the nature of the individual in the society.

The counselor should be aware of a second apparent consequence of his basic view of human behavior. The view of man as basically not completely objectively predictable would seem to lead to temporizing of predictions and caution in expression of interpretations of assessment data. Responsibility for information usage probably would be shared with others involved in using the data. The counselor committed to the view that the individual is reactive would seem to be vulnerable to preempting responsibility for decision-making. He could be charged with the covert development of a procedural bias likely to result in a press structured against the selection of an alternative not at the top of the probability hierarchy, as he has construed it from his particular orientation. Although most, if not all, of the issues would seem to relate equally well to the entire gamut of tools and procedures, "tests," particularly the comparative devices in rather wide use, have been the focal points for criticism. The appearance and development of tests have been approximately contemporary with the emergence of counseling as formal humanistic activity.

The basic charge given to Simon and Binet was to improve judgments about individuals. That is, they were charged with the task of making better differentiations, (Anastasia, 1961, pp. 10–11). Those who use tests presently should continue to be sensitive to the basic product of "tests" of any sort—discriminating, differential, comparative data. With normed devices, this condition is rather more clear, though as easily forgotten or overlooked, perhaps, as with devices not normed where the user of the data, usually a clinician, counselor, or personnel worker, actually is employing a norm, sometimes even concealed from himself, and usually so from his subjects, Levy (1963, pp. 1–150) discussed this circumstance quite pointedly in his book *Psychological Interpretation*. Perhaps the most pointed, concise statement about the basic place of tests, which also would seem to apply to any device in the general domain, was made by Gardner (1961) in his lucid book *Excellence: Can We Be Equal and Excellent Too?*

As Gardner (1961, pp. 1–28) discusses so very well, a basic paradox is present in our view of ourselves resulting from our cultural heritage. We are confronted with the circumstance of attempting to live simultaneously with the notion that all men are equal and that individual differences in potential to perform do exist. Our society is confronted with the problem of attempting to emphasize individual differences in some circumstances, at some times, and for some purposes, while concomitantly attempting to establish and maintain restraints on individual performances in others. But we seem not to approach the situation directly, nor to educate people, particularly our young, about it. People have become concerned about appraisal of individuals, particularly through tests and testing. Gardner seems to have identified the view most people have of tests and the bases for their fears about tests.

To some degree, fear of the tests is a fear of the potentialities for social manipulation and control inherent in any large-scale processing of individuals. The tests bring vividly to mind the hazards of a society which deals with the individual as a statistic.
The tests are designed to do an unpopular job. An untutored observer listening to critics lash out at the imperfections of the tests might suppose that the criticism would be stilled if the tests were perfected. No at all. As the tests improve and become less vulnerable to present criticism, the hostility to them may actually increase [Gardener, 1961, p. 47].

Fortunately, Gardner (1963) also wrote a companion volume in which he develops possible behavioral remedies for the conditions he identified, testing among them. However, people who employ data about individuals must be careful to observe the intended differentiating nature of much of these data. Most of the criticism lodged against such data, and [against] those who use the information, seems to have been in the area of mis-application of the data, rather than with methodological problems. The difficulty seems to have two major causes. One appears to be an objection to the use of data from tests or any other devices for purposes of differentiating or discriminating. A second appears to be a criticism of the specific usages or applications of assessment devices. However, as Gardner observes, alternatives to present assessment procedures seem to be less workable and therefore more perilous.

It has been proven over and over again that the alternative methods of evaluating ability are subject to gross errors and capable of producing grave injustices. Whatever their faults, the tests have proven fairer and more reliable than any other method when they are used cautiously within the limits for which they were designed (Gardner, 1961, p. 49).

Anyone responsible for the use of appraisal data must be more careful to use those data within the confines of the instruments and procedures yielding them. By definition, anyone using such data is in a clinician role. The hazards and risks in clinical judgments have been pointed out by several writers, including Meehl (1954) and Thorne (1961). In any instance where a school counselor employs information of any kind to state or imply a prediction, he is functioning as a clinician. In the clinician role he faces risk. Levy succinctly expressed the hazards the counselor accepts when he makes predictions.

Because a decision is required, because the interpreter is aware that he is making a decision, and because this decision involves the disregarding of certain attributes in favor of others, the interpreter faces risk (Levy, 1963, p. 74).

Within limits of reliability and validity, appraisal instruments apparently do have potential value in contributing to improvement of judgments. Those who argue for deletion of appraisal information, particularly test and inventory data, from the decision-making process would seem to be flying in the face of a social reality. The legitimate need for reasonable, fair and promptly achieved appraisal data is increasing. To wish for return to a less complicated time when fewer judgments were needed is forlorn. To debate the quality of decisions made without appraisal data as presently gathered is purposeless as well, although evidence presently available seems preponderantly to indicate that quality of judgment increases as appraisal procedures are improved. Increasing opportunity, exemplified by the diversification of occupations, geographical mobility, and availability of preparation for a wide range of these opportunities, has led to the application of procedures to assist effective decision-making. The issue has become one of proper utilization of results from appraisal instruments and procedures. The question of using such results has been settled effectively. From the very beginning, instrumentation and procedures have been developed to meet a need of some sort, not the reverse. Thus, the counselor's view of the individual becomes critical when he assumes the role of clinician.

Hubert Bonner (1965) has made a cogent, impassioned statement about basic views of men as individuals. He argues the peril in attempting to reduce man to a statistical description. Reading Bonner's statement should sharpen one's awareness of the hazard inherent in many procedures of dehumanizing individual man, of reducing the individual to an objectively described thing bereft of any unpredictability, except for procedural, methodological error. Bonner's view of psychology would seem to have value for the school counselor who is presumably committed to aiding and assisting individual persons striving toward self-attainment.

A psychology that believes in man, fully aware that he is a remarkable phenomenon but not a masterpiece, is open to the vision of man as a perfectible personality and of an ideal society made up of perfectible human beings. It believes in man as a being capable of error and evil and cowardice, yet as a person who can transcend these human defects and create of himself a better person and of his society a better commonwealth. Each person can be, within the limits of the human condition, his own philosopher, the creator of his own personality (Bonner, 1965, p. 217).

If the counselor is to facilitate the development of the individuals, he apparently must posit his actions on the nature of man, an issue that has received remarkably little attention compared with the vast array of methodological writing. Although not comfortably acceptable because of the essential uncertainty injected into concepts of behavior, quantum theory has led to a restructuring of physical science and only recently has the theory been employed in discussions of models used to make predictions about human behavior. Dreikurs (1966, pp. 1–6) has presented a cogent argument counselors should have in their concepts of man.

Certainty of diagnosis and certainty of prediction have vanished.
Predictability has become merely a question of statistical probability (Dreikurs, 1966, p. 1).

Referring to concepts from quantum mechanics theory, Dreikurs[1] discusses the far-reaching consequences of these concepts as they apparently can be extended to apply to human behavior as well as to the behavior of physical particles and all realms of knowledge between.

[1] (Editors' note) Dreikurs' article appears in Section 2.

Truth is merely a statistical phenomenon. Absolute truth cannot be perceived since all our knowledge is only approximate. Attempts to find what is true or false is hopelessly snarled. . . . Interpretations of facts can contradict each other and yet both be correct (Dreikurs, 1966, p. 2).

Significantly, physics again has been the source of challenge to other disciplines. Finding accepted theory inadequate to explain information at hand, theoretical physicists found new concepts were required. Once expressed, these ideas were found to have explanatory value elsewhere, particularly in the realm of human behavior. Because new ideas quite slowly become infused into the thinking of individuals, the significance of quantum theory for conceptualizing human behavior has not yet been realized fully. Translation through various language systems requires considerable time. Even then, new ideas must await an open thought system for integration and subsequent improvement of that thought system. Man, the thinker, is not known for his ready openness to new ideas.

Writing about assumptions inherent in psychology, Van Kaam (1958, pp. 22–28) discussed the subjectivity in science and scientific models. He refers to the work of Planck, Bohr, von Weizsaecker and Heisenberg, particularly with regard to quantum physics. The ideal of absolute objectivity of man, the researcher, has been shown to be impossible of realization. Any view of the environment is necessarily and inherently restricted. Out of the many viewpoints that could be taken, one is adopted. Inherent in that view is judgment, often unspecified, about the concept one has of the nature of the world. The counselor engages in such a procedure just as surely as does the researcher. Being a practitioner he may be even more sensitive than his research colleague to the limitations of his particular approach to data collection, data analysis and judgment formation. Rogers (1955, pp. 267–278) expressed the importance of counselor perception of the individual and the system employed to explain behavior. He emphasized the subjectivity of knowledge and its utilization, which it seems must be reemphasized again and again.

Counselors must develop and then maintain an awareness that they do indeed have a particular view of the world and that the view is by its very nature a theory. Many counselors seem not to regard themselves as theoreticians, for they do not presume to communicate the model used to make judgments. Therein lies a hazard for such counselors. By definition, the presuppositions, assumptions and cognitive framework constitutes the model being used, and all models have subjectivity inherent in them, the idiosyncrasies of personal, private individuality. Nor is there any escape from these circumstances. Theory exists because certainty is unobtainable. Therefore, competing models will continue to exist simultaneously, one having predominance for a time, perhaps, only to be replaced by another and another as new knowledge is developed. Each counselor can be thought of as having a unique theory, because of the inherent, unavoidable subjectivity of individual existence. Levy (1963, pp. 1–29) has presented a useful view of theory as it involves the use of data about individuals. Each counselor should cultivate an awareness of himself and so of his theory-model. Doing so should result in the salutary effect of caution in his work and avoidance of an attitude of certainty.

Far from shattering the confidence of the counselor in his facility for collecting data and his skill in employing that information to advantage, he should proceed with an attitude of cautious optimism and an openness to the views of others, also subjective like his own, willing to accord them, whether counselees, colleagues or other adults, a place of significance parallel with his own. He need be responsible only for his own views, granting to others credence for the views they achieve, and sharing in decision-making, without pre-empting the responsibilities of others involved in judgment-making and the action that follows. A small compendium of statements, assembled by Severin (1965), is a ready source for reading related to the emerging re-statement of behavior explanation systems.

If the school counselor accedes to the concept of lack of certainty in efforts to predict individual behavior, he must have in his thinking another concept to apply to his information about individuals. The concept most essential to adequate usage of appraisal data within the limits of those data is the standard error of measurement. Awareness that any result from an appraisal instrument or procedure is only an approximation should lead to caution in application. Risk of error in interpretation and application of information can be minimized, though obviously never eliminated, through application of the standard error of measurement statistic to each bit of obtained, descriptive data.

A basic difficulty inherent in much data the counselor would like to use, or is asked to use, is that no numerical approximation of precision is available. Non-quantitative information is severely circumscribed by this lack of a relatively objective, readily applicable estimate of precision. The counselor is reduced to making a subjective, personal estimation. His own experience and his own values become the bases for the estimation. To the degree that those values and experiences are inappropriate, his resultant estimation will be faulty, perhaps without any realization of fault by anyone involved. An obvious alternative would be to disregard all information for which no quantified error term is available. Beyond the apparent impracticality of excluding all such data from consideration, since information of all sorts is brought to counselors for interpretation, any information could have contributory value to development of judgments. The skill needed by the counselor is to attach no more credence to a piece of information than is warranted (Levy, 1963, pp. 128–134). Information should be studied for consistency, relatedness, patterning and cross-validation. Those pieces of data with relatively imprecise or low credibility will be discarded when inconsistent with more credible data.

A risk is involved in discarding any data, regardless of the credibility of the data. Error can occur in either of two alternatives. Any piece of information that does not fit the model being employed may be discarded when, actually, the model is an unappropriate one. Had another model been chosen, the discarded data might have been judged appropriate and quite valuable. The opposite error is to assign undue credence to incongruent data that do not fit the model, calling into question the model and possibly leading to abandonment of an appropriate model (Levy, 1963, pp. 128–129). As noted earlier, no way to avoid this sort of risk-taking is at hand.

Even when an apparently adequate standard error of measurement is known, the data may be severely limited for lack of substantiating research appropriate to the use intended for the information. For example, predictive data developed in one college setting cannot be assumed to apply identically to another. An aptitude test developed to be predictive of assembling small parts must be shown to have predictive relationship to packing shipping containers. Not only is research incomplete, indeed probably can never be complete, in part, because of the dynamic nature of both individuals and the environment; but also learning about even the available research is virtually impossible for the individual counselor. Even with present attempts to collect and collate research findings for more ready access and utilization, individual counselors probably cannot be expected to have at hand all of the relevant findings for each problem with which he may be confronted. Much remains to be done in support of the counselor in need of relevant information for making applications. In the meantime, his best safeguard seems to be a sense of caution and care to stay well within the bounds of collection instruments and procedures.

A related concept of fairly recent emphasis has to do with the significance of the observer as an integral agent in the process of data collection.

Since the examiner is by necessity biased, all his findings will reflect his bias and will be valid only within his frame of reference. This cannot be avoided. However, the biased investigator is least qualified to analyze his data objectively, all claims of statistics notwithstanding (Dreikurs, 1966, p. 5).

Dreikurs here seems to be supported by Rosenthal (1966) who has made a rather detailed and penetrating study of the effects researchers seem to have on the very data they seek to collect and study. The concept would seem to apply to counselors who may be construed as researchers when collecting and interpreting data about individuals. The precepts of research should have equal applicability to counselors involved with making predictions. Basically, cross-verification from varying conceptual viewpoints would seem to be a highly advantageous procedure. In effect, the school counselor is practicing such an approach when he asks class-room teachers or others among a school faculty to evaluate his data for completeness and applicability and his judgments for relevance and apparent accuracy. Because of the commonly similar backgrounds of school personnel, the counselor should consider cross-verification with personnel of non-school backgrounds in instances involving predictions of a particularly critical sort. Care must be taken, of course, not to compromise the security of the individual when seeking cross-verification.

A recent research project was reported by Watley (1967, pp. 134–139) in which he studied apparent counselor style in relationship to prediction of college freshman grade performance. A sample of 66 counselors was formed. Twenty-six were college counselors and 40 held positions in high schools. Of the 66, 41 were men and 25 were women. All of the members had some graduate work and some had doctorates. All were experienced in counseling activities. They were asked to predict college performance of 100 male freshmen who entered an arts college in a university. The 100 students selected were chosen randomly from the entire entering group of freshmen who had complete data files. Counselors were asked to make a dichotomized decision of "C" or "less than C." Three conditions were established: (1) academic performance and aptitude information only; (2) data from (1) with SVIB and MMPI results; and, (3) data from (1) and (2) with biographic information. Counselor style was judged by how data were used in arriving at a decision. Four counselor style classes resulted: (1) no model building; (2) some model building; (3) considerable model building; and, (4) extensive model building. An analysis of variance was made of the correct predictions made by the counselors in the classes for the three conditions. A non-significant F ratio, at the .05 level, resulted. Evidently, whether a counselor was prone to use an apparent regression model (class 1) or an extensive, individualized approach (class 4), or something in between was unrelated to "success" in prediction for the 100 student files as the criterion. Both more accurate and less accurate counselors were sorted across all four style classes, apparently at random. The amount of case data was unrelated to counselor accuracy, as well. The total successful identifications ranged between 63.9 and 69.6 out of the possible 100 in each instance. The results of the study were not expected. The expectation was that counselors prepared in the use of assessment information would use a prediction formula of some sort and that such an approach would prove to be superior to other approaches. Within the limits of the data in the study, the results did not confirm but also did not invert the hypothesis. Assuming the results are characteristic of counselor behavior generally, and no evidence seems to be contradictory, the level of accuracy of counselor predictions may be regarded as suspect.

In a previous report, Watley (1967, pp. 62–67) discussed the confidence the sixty-six counselors seemed to have in their judgments. He found that the counselors over-estimated their prediction accuracy and predictive skills. In fact, students asked to make the same predictions as the counselors did quite well when compared to counselors. Neither counselors nor students were far removed from chance or base rate experience, however. Counselors seem vulnerable to committing a simultaneous double error—over-estimating their own power of prediction and under-estimating the counselee's facility for self-prediction and under-estimating the counselee's facility for self-prediction. As Watley so pointedly observed, counselors need to assess their own behavior, recognize the inaccuracies in their predictions, and then seek to improve their predictions and their prediction skills. The necessity for each counselor systematically collecting evidence about his predictions seems apparent. Only by so doing can he achieve self-evaluation and determine his level and realm of competency (Watley, 1967, pp. 62–67). He likely will find that predictions about some behaviors are quite good, others quite poor. Obviously, he should refrain from making predictions if he cannot improve much upon base rates, or chance.

An awareness of philosophical concerns seems to be increasing among counselors, but much thinking remains to be done and an extensive dialogue is needed among counselors and counselor educators. The importance of deepening philosophical understanding for counselor action must be understood. A trend in this direction seems to be evident, as does a need for counselor awareness of self. As the inaccuracy of counselor predictions becomes more widely known and accepted among counselors, a movement should develop and gain momentum to clarify the boundaries of counselor prediction efforts as well as to improve predictions within those boundaries. The limits of counselor prediction efforts are a function of ethical judgments as well as empirical efficiency. No assurance can be had that prediction efficiency will improve with specification of ethical bounds, of course; but counselors may exclude themselves, or possibly be excluded from, making predictions in some situations and for some purposes. Such possibilities are a separate concern, a sequel to the present discussion. As the philosophical knowledge that certainty is unobtainable spreads among counselors, each counselor should guard against the complacent view that he is doing well enough now. Certainly he is not. Even though perfection in predictions is the ideal apparently not to be realized, counselors do have the responsibility to employ data about individuals properly. They have the greater responsibility of sharing with others their awareness of a world not wholly predictable, one in which risks must be taken as responsibly as possible. If counselors are able to achieve this high level of competence and responsibility, they will be far removed from the role of technician to which many counselors-to-be were directed in the past and to which they aspired as the ideal.

REFERENCES

ANASTASI, A. *Psychological Testing* (2nd Ed.). New York: The MacMillan Company, 1961.
BONNER, H. *On Being Mindful of Man: Essay Toward a Proactive Psychology.* Boston: Houghton Mifflin, 1965.
DREIKURS, R. "The Scientific Revolution." *Humanist,* January/February, 1966, pp. 8–13.
GARDNER, J. W. *Excellence: Can We Be Equal and Excellent Too?* New York: Harper and Row, 1961.
GARDNER, J. W. *Self-Renewal: The Individual and the Innovative Society.* New York: Harper and Row, 1963.
KERLINGER, F. N. *Foundations of Behavioral Research: Educational and Psychological Inquiry.* New York: Holt, Rinehart and Winston, 1964.
LEVY, L. H. *Psychological Interpretation.* New York: Holt, Rinehart and Winston, 1963.
MEEHL, P. E. *Clinical vs. Statistical Prediction: A Theoretical Analysis and a Review of the Evidence.* Minneapolis: University of Minnesota Press, 1954.
PARSONS, F. *Choosing a Vocation.* Boston: Houghton Mifflin, 1909.
ROGERS, C. R. "Persons or Science? A Philosophical Question." *Amer. Psychol.,* July, 1955, 10, No. 7, pp. 267–278.
ROSENTHAL, R. *Experimenter Effects in Behavioral Research.* New York: Appleton-Century-Crofts, 1966.
SEVERIN, F. T. *Humanistic Viewpoints in Psychology.* New York: McGraw-Hill, 1965.
THORNE, F. C. *Clinical Judgment: A Study of Clinical Errors.* Brandon, Vermont: Journal of Clinical Psychology, 1961.
VAN KAAM, A. L. "Assumptions in Psychology." *J. of Individ. Psychol.,* May, 1958, *14,* No. 1, pp. 22–28.
WATLEY, D. J. "Counselor Confidence in Accuracy of Predictions." *J. of Couns. Psychol.,* Spring, 1966, *13,* No. 1, pp. 62–67.
WATLEY, D. J. "Predicting Freshman Grades and Counselors' Prediction Style." *Personnel and Guid. J.,* October, 1967, *46,* No. 2, pp. 134–139.

34. The Social Impact of Testing

David A. Goslin

During the last few years a great deal of attention, both public and professional, has been focused on standardized tests and, in particular, on their use in schools. This interest has been the result of a variety of

David A. Goslin, "The Social Impact of Testing," from *Personnel and Guidance Journal,* March, 1967, pp. 676–782. Copyright © 1967 by the American Personnel and Guidance Association, Inc., Washington, D.C. Reprinted by permission.

influences, the most important of which has probably been the growing competition for college admission and the consequent use of standardized tests both in counseling situations and in the admissions process itself. Up to now this concern with standardized tests has, for the most part, been directed toward two main questions: how accurate are tests as techniques for evaluating a student's potential, and how wisely are tests being used by admissions officers, guidance personnel, teachers and others? While it is clear that we have a long way to go before we have perfectly accurate tests (or, to be more precise, tests that are perfect predictors of whatever it is we are interested in predicting), or before everyone who uses standardized tests does so in a thoroughly sophisticated and professional way, the time has come to raise a "second generation" of questions about standardized testing, to wit, those concerned with the social effects of the use of tests, given whatever validity they have been demonstrated to have.

Some justification for ignoring the issues of validity and misuse is necessary at the outset. First, it has been demonstrated beyond any reasonable doubt that a great many standardized tests are in fact useful (if not perfect) aids in measuring the intellectual growth of individuals and in predicting their future performance, at least in certain situations (Lavin, 1965). Second, it is a fact that standardized ability tests are being used extensively throughout our educational system for counseling, for screening candidates for admission to schools and colleges, and for organizing groups of pupils at all levels according to their abilities (Goslin, 1963; Goslin, Epstein, & Hallock, 1965). The extent to which an individual's test score *really* influences decisions made about him or advice given to him is, of course, determined by a number of factors. From a research standpoint it is extremely difficult to evaluate the extent of this influence, even in specific cases or where formal policies and practices have been established. Nevertheless, that testing and some degree of reliance on test results is a fact of life in this country today will be confirmed by any college admissions officer, counselor, or parent. Finally, given the facts of wide test usage and even minimal validity, there exists a set of problems that are of major importance in their own right and that are likely to become even more significant as our testing technology improves. To phrase the question in extreme form, supposing our tests were perfect, what would be the effect of using such tests on the individuals involved and on the groups that used them?

Second Generation Testing Problems

Given the necessity and relevance of a concern with the social effects of testing, we may distinguish four major problem areas that seem to be of particular importance for those who are in the business of developing and using standardized tests. First, what is the objective influence of tests on the opportunities open to individuals? Everyone agrees that test scores play an important part in the process of getting individuals allocated to positions in our society, but there is very little hard data on the extent to which test scores make a real difference in the availability of opportunities, especially if we take into account situational factors such as class background, discrepancies between test scores and other indicators of ability, and the nature of the school or occupational setting. Second, what part do test scores play in influencing the kinds of advice given to young people in schools, counseling agencies, and the like? Relevant here is not only whatever explicit suggestions are given but also the subtler forms of advice conveyed by the personnel officer, counselor, teacher, or principal, who inevitably react to their counselees on the basis of previously formed opinions about that individual's capabilities and limitations. Test scores cannot help but influence the formation of such opinions. Third, does "objective" information about an individual's abilities have any special effect on the opinion the individual holds about himself? Obviously, individuals utilize information from many sources in arriving at estimates of their own capabilities. Nevertheless, because they represent, at least for some people, a somewhat more scientific and consequently, perhaps, more accurate source of information, it is reasonable to inquire into the special contribution to self-image that might be made by test scores under circumstances where the recipient places some faith in the validity of the information and where such information finds its way back to the individual. And, finally, we may pose several questions about the ultimate effect of the use of essentially objective criteria for evaluating the abilities of individuals on a society that commits itself wholeheartedly to the employment of such measures. In all of these cases, the validity of standardized tests is, of course, a relevant variable. But it is only one of a number of important things to be considered.

During the last three years, researchers at Russell Sage Foundation have been involved in a series of endeavors designed primarily to delineate the major dimensions of attitudes about standardized tests on the part of pupils, parents, teachers, counselors, and principals, as well as the general public. In addition, considerable data have been gathered on current testing practices, including uses of standardized tests, amount of reliance on test scores, the frequency of reporting of scores to pupils and parents, and the extent of coaching for tests. Most of the data come from questionnaire and interview surveys of relevant population groups. Specifically, the following research activities have been undertaken: (1) with the assistance of the National Opinion Research Center, a national interview survey of 1,421 adults concerning their experiences with and attitudes about standardized tests (Brim, Neulinger, & Glass, 1965); (2)

a survey of approximately 5,300 public high school pupils, 1,200 private high school pupils, and 2,600 parochial high school pupils concerning their attitudes toward and experiences with tests, as well as a variety of other relevant characteristics (Brim, Goslin, Glass, & Goldberg, 1965); (3) in the same public, private, and parochial schools, and in 36 additional public high schools, a survey of 1,754 tenth, eleventh, and twelfth grade teachers and 188 counselors concerning their opinions about tests and their uses of tests (Brim, Goslin, et al., 1965); (4) detailed information was obtained on school policies regarding tests from all of the high schools in which pupils, teachers, and counselors were surveyed and, in a separate study, a random sample of 800 elementary school principals in New York, New Jersey, and Connecticut reported on testing practices in their schools (Goslin, et al., 1965); (5) in 15 elementary schools chosen on the basis of characteristics of their testing programs, fifth grade children were interviewed, questionnaires were sent to their parents, sociometric and IQ data collected, and a questionnaire administered to teachers. In addition, a study of counselor use of tests conducted by David J. Armor at Harvard University was supported by the Foundation, which has also funded a major study of personnel selection procedures in business and industrial organizations with special reference to the use of standardized tests. As is apparent from this list, the focus of the research program thus far has been primarily on attitudes, opinions, and reported uses of tests rather than on direct experimental studies of the effects of testing. For this reason the conclusions reached must be viewed as inferential and suggestive of the kinds of problems in need of more systematic and detailed investigation in the future.

The data lead to two interesting propositions about testing and counseling. The first of these is whether counselors, along with other school personnel such as teachers, are cognizant of the extent to which standardized test scores influence decisions about and attitudes toward pupils. The second is the problem of arriving at some consistent and intelligent policy regarding the dissemination of test score information to pupils and their parents.

COUNSELOR USES OF TEST SCORES

All the research completed support this conclusion: that whatever opinions about tests might be formally expressed by a counselor or teacher, actual use of test scores may vary considerably from the reported view or practice.

On both the counselor and the teacher questionnaires, respondents were asked to express an opinion about the overall accuracy of standardized tests, in particular "intelligence or aptitude tests," as a measure of a pupil's intellectual potential. In addition, they were asked to give an opinion about how much weight should be assigned to several different kinds of indicators of a pupil's ability—including intelligence, achievement, personality, and vocational interest test scores, grade average, teacher recommendations, and family background—in a variety of specific decisional situations such as placement in fast- or slow-learning groups, writing a recommendation for college admission, allowing a student to take extra courses, and advising him about a choice of college. On all items considerable variation was found in the opinions expressed by both teachers and counselors on the accuracy of intelligence tests. (Incidentally, when it came to assigning weights to various measures the teacher sample gave the highest weight to recommendations of former teachers in every single use category.) General "good sense" was reflected in the mean responses of both groups to the weighting items. For example, family background got a much higher rating in the context of counseling about college choice than in the context of deciding whether a pupil should be admitted to a special class. And intelligence test score weight dropped sharply in the case of writing a recommendation for college scholarship aid, while the greatest consideration was given to overall grade average in deciding whether to allow a pupil to take an extra course. Modal responses appear to reflect a fair degree of sophistication with respect to the characteristics of tests and the way they should be used. But the question remains whether these opinions are translated into practice.

To get some indication of an answer to this question, teachers and counselors took a card sort test on which they had to make judgments about 28 fictitious students on the basis of test score data, grade averages, and subjective evaluations of former teachers and advisers. This test (Hastings, 1960) was specifically designed to measure tendencies of the respondent to rely either on subjective factors, such as teacher comments about each fictitious pupil, or on objective criteria, such as test scores, in deciding whether to place each pupil in a special advanced science class. In 14 of the 28 cases the subjective and objective indicators were in agreement with each other, and a judgment was relatively easy. In the other 14 cases, missing or conflicting information created a direct test of the respondents' inclination to give one type of information greater weight than the other. These 14 cards were used to generate an overall score for each teacher or counselor indicating his or her reliance on objective as opposed to subjective factors.

It was predicted that those teachers who expressed very great confidence in the accuracy of intelligence tests, and who felt that high weight should be given to standardized test scores in the various judgmental situations, would be considerably more likely to obtain high scores (indicating reliance on objective factors) on the card sort test. A moderate positive correlation between card sort scores and opinion about the accuracy of tests was found for both teachers and counselors; members of both groups who felt that intelligence tests were very accurate tended to rely more on objective criteria in the card sort test. But, while the relationship was clear, and statistically significant in the case of the larger teacher sample, it was far from an exceptionally strong relationship. In fact, a mean difference of *less than five* points on the 64-point card sort score scale separated those counselors who said that intelligence tests were *no better or slightly better* than other measures of a pupil's intellectual capacity from those who said intelligence tests *were much better than any other measure.* The same was true in the case of the teacher sample. Thus a sizable group of respondents, both counselors and teachers, who had previously stated the opinion that intelligence tests were much better than other indicators of intellectual capacity *consistently* ignored pupils' test scores in favor of such subjective comments as "Robert is a capable and hardworking student who does well in all his classes; his ability is well above average," on the card sort test. In addition, a significant number of respondents who felt that tests were no better than other indicators of ability consistently *relied* on test scores as opposed to subjective evaluations.

Inconsistency of response from opinion to real situation was even more striking when we considered the relationship between card sort scores and opinions about weights that ought to be assigned to IQ and achievement test scores in the various situations described above. No correlation at all was found between *teacher opinions* and their scores on the card sort test. Only a very small positive correlation was found between *counselor opinions* about test weights and their card sort scores.

What explanations can be given for these findings? First, the card sort test may not have been a "real" enough situation, although Hastings, in extensive pretesting, found no evidence that this was the case. Second, one could argue that the opinion questions were not worded carefully enough to differentiate clearly between respondents who in fact had different beliefs about tests and, conversely, there might not have been any real difference in opinion between respondents who expressed different opinions. While it is probably true that this factor accounts for some of the observed inconsistency, strong relationships found between the various opinion items and between opinion items and other variables, such as familiarity with tests and experience in administering and scoring tests, permit some confidence in the validity of the opinions expressed.

This leads to the conclusion that, in fact, inconsistency between behavior and expressed opinions on the part of teachers and counselors is a factor in the findings.

These data underscore the difficulty of obtaining accurate information from either counselors or teachers concerning how they use tests unless one contrives real situations in which the respondent's behavior can be directly observed. One clear implication is that while counselors and teachers may have been exposed to enough literature concerning tests and their proper use to make it possible for them to give the "right" answers on a questionnaire, when it comes to actually using test scores all bets may be off.

REPORTING OF TEST SCORES

One of the thorniest issues in the whole field of testing concerns the conditions under which scores or other information about the examinee's performance should be given to the examinee or his parents. An examination of this problem involves not only an analysis of the complex social psychological effects of such information on individuals, but also a consideration of the legal and moral responsibilities of those who possess the information.

The complexity of the problem is clearly reflected in our data concerning opinions and reported practices in this area. Greater differences of opinion are expressed by both counselors and teachers on this issue than on any other. For example, 10 per cent of the counselors felt that specific information, such as an actual test score or percentile rank, about a high school pupil's performance on an intelligence test ought to be reported *routinely* to his parents; while 18 per cent felt that such information should *never* be reported. (The remaining 75 per cent split almost evenly between "reported on request" and "reported only in special cases.") Similar differences of opinion were evident regarding reporting scores to pupils and reporting general information (not specific scores) to pupils and parents.

Teachers were also divided sharply in their opinions about providing pupils or parents with test data. Furthermore, when teacher reports of whether they had ever given such information to parents or pupils were compared with their opinions on the subject, 26 per cent of those who had expressed the opinion that *all* pupils should be given general information about their intelligence reported *never* having given *any* student such information. Thus there are not only extreme differences of opinion, but sizable discrepancies between opinion and practice.

Although one can legitimately ask for more-detailed data on school policies regarding the dissemination of test scores and additional data on the actual practices of both counselors and teachers, it seems to be a clearly established fact that there is great need for a more coherent and consistent policy throughout our educational system on this question. During the last few years we have seen some evidence of increased parental interest in finding out what information the school has about their children. The New York court ruling concerning parents' rights to information in their child's permanent record file is a case in point. Increased pressure from parents for such information can be expected as public awareness of school testing programs grows, as competition for college admission increases, and as civil rights groups take a more active interest in educational opportunities.

THE SOCIAL EFFECTS OF TEST USE AND THE REPORTING OF SCORES

Two general issues have been raised: first, the lack of awareness on the part of counselors and teachers of the extent to which they make use of scores, and second, apparent ambivalence about disseminating scores to pupils and parents.

The problem of directly measuring the effects of possessing information about a pupil's intellectual abilities on teacher or counselor attitudes toward pupils is an extraordinarily difficult one from an empirical standpoint. One recent study done at Harvard indicates that if first and second grade teachers are told to expect exceptional intellectual growth on the part of a randomly selected group of their pupils, real and dramatic IQ increases *actually take place* in those pupils in as short a time as a year (Rosenthal & Jacobson, in press). Thus, teacher expectations alone apparently can account for changes in pupil performance, even when measured by intelligence tests over relatively short periods of time. This study underscores the importance of the kinds of images counselors and teachers hold, either consciously or unconsciously, of students. If test scores play a part in the formation of such expectations about a pupil's abilities, the possession of test scores by teachers and counselors may actually contribute to the predictive validity of the tests themselves. And the data show that estimating the extent of influence of test scores on a teacher or counselor's perceptions of pupils is extremely difficult.

The immediate implications of this line of reasoning are twofold. First, more attention needs to be given to the problem of teacher access to test scores, i.e., under what conditions should teachers be given data about their pupils' abilities? And second, where test data are available to counselors and teachers, can any formal procedures or controls be established to reduce the self-fulfilling prophecy effect that possession of such information may produce, i.e., how can we use test data to provide more effective guidance, without, as a consequence of the guidance process *itself*, influencing the behavior of counselors in what may be negative ways? To phrase the issue differently, given the evidence that almost anything we do in this area is likely to affect our counselors, how do we deliberately manage our test data so as to *uniformly enhance* counselee performance?

Research data are needed on which to base a clear statement of policy on test score dissemination to serve as a guideline for school psychologists, counselors, teachers, principals, and others who use tests. Aside from calling for experimental research on this question, it may be helpful to outline briefly the dimensions of the problem. What are the possible effects on an individual of receiving, let us say, a test score or at least general information about his intellectual capacity? The following variables, among others, must be considered in estimating the impact of such information.

1. To what extent is the information different from the individual's already formed estimate of his abilities? Our evidence indicates that in most cases the test score will not be sufficiently different from the individual's private estimate to raise any problems in assimilating it. Nevertheless, there are substantial numbers of individuals for whom the score will be significantly different.

2. If it is different, is it higher or lower than the individual's private estimate? Only if it is lower are obvious motivational problems raised, although some might argue that telling a child that he is exceptionally intelligent can have a debilitating effect. Our data indicate that about three-fourths of the time the test score will in fact be lower than the individual's self-estimate.

3. If the information is different, what are the factors that will influence whether it will result in a change in the individual's self-image? These include: (a) the opinion of the individual about the accuracy of tests in general and this test in particular, as well as the credibility of the source of the information; (b) the strength of competing ability estimates; for example, what peers, parents, and others have said; (c) the availability of rationalizations in the event the score is lower, such as exceptionally poor performance due to anxiety or bad health.

To summarize, it may be assumed that even where the test information is different, change in self-perception is highly problematical except in those cases where (a) the information is higher and thus rewarding to believe, or, as will usually be the case, (b) the information is lower and a recipient who believes strongly in the test and the legitimacy of the source of the information cannot find any support for the rationalization that the test was in error this time, and, finally, cannot find counter-information to bolster his original self-estimate. The latter set of conditions is no doubt only rarely satisfied. And, further, we have yet to demonstrate that a downward (or upward) revision of an individual's self-estimate of his abilities is detrimental to motivation, aspiration level, or personality adjustment, *assuming that the movement is in the direction of a more accurate perception.* (Here is where the validity of the test becomes an important variable.)

Furthermore, what are the consequences of *not* providing pupils or their parents with information? Obviously, *some* children and parents *do* receive test scores or other information, either by chance or through deliberate actions of teachers, counselors, or principals. Does this give them any advantage over those pupils who do not receive information about their abilities? Can we really justify withholding information from some and giving it to others in the absence of data either about the effect of giving it or not giving it? Further, what legal rights do parents have to information possessed by the school about their children? (See Goslin, in press.)

These issues make it clear that the whole area of reporting test scores deserves more consideration by educators and, especially, by social scientists, who must provide the educator with the data on which he can reach a reasonable policy decision. The same may be said about the other issues raised by the use of standardized tests. It is hoped that the fragments of data and the concepts examined in this paper will help to get a much-overdue dialogue started.

REFERENCES

BRIM, O. G. JR., GOSLIN, D. A., GLASS, D. C., & GOLDBERG, I. "The use of standardized ability tests in American secondary schools and their impact on students, teachers and counselors." Technical Report No. 3 on the Social Consequences of Testing, New York: Russell Sage Foundation, 1965.

BRIM, O. G., JR., NEULINGER, J., & GLASS, D. C. "Intelligence tests and American adults." Technical Report No. 1 on the Social Consequences of Testing. New York: Russell Sage Foundation, 1965.

GOSLIN, D. A. "The search for ability: standardized testing in social perspective." New York: Russell Sage Foundation, 1963.

GOSLIN, D. A. "The social consequences of predictive testing in education." In H. M. Clements & J. B. McDonald, eds., *Moral dilemmas in schooling.* Columbus, Ohio: Charles E. Merrill, in press.

GOSLIN, D. A., EPSTEIN, ROBERTA R., & HALLOCK, BARBARA A. "The use of standardized tests in elementary schools." Technical Report No. 2 on the Social Consequences of Testing. New York: Russell Sage Foundation, 1965.

HASTINGS, J. T., *et al.* "The use of test results." Urbana, Ill.: Bureau of Educational Research, Univ. of Illinois, 1960.

LAVIN, D. E. "The prediction of academic performance." New York: Russell Sage Foundation, 1965.

ROSENTHAL, R., & JACOBSON, LENORE. "Self-fulfilling prophecies in the classroom: teachers' expectations as unintended determinants of pupils' intellectual competence." In M. Deutsch, et al., *Social class, race and psychological development.* New York: Holt, Rinehart & Winston, in press.

35. Standards for Test Users

George E. Hill

The point of view regarding the uses of tests in schools which is developed in this paper rests upon some assumptions regarding the objectives and the programs of our schools. To understand what the writer has to say about tests and their uses he must, then, first state briefly what he thinks schools are for and what he thinks should be the characteristics of a good school program. His attention is focused primarily upon the elementary and secondary schools. However, what he has to say is—in his opinion, at least—just as applicable to colleges and universities, with proper adaptations and emphases appropriate to the developmental levels of their students.

THE OBJECTIVES OF PUBLIC EDUCATION

Characteristically the purposes of free education in this country get badly twisted, especially when the layman is considering why his children are in school. What are commonly called the "fundamentals" of education are, actually, concomitant, or contributory, learnings. The really important things which children need to learn are not reading, mathematics, science, social studies, art, music and the like. Important as these learnings are they serve a worthy purpose in one's life only as they enrich and make more functional the true fundamentals of education. These are such matters as the following:

1. Children need to mature in their understanding of themselves, to grow up in the habit of self-examination and self-understanding which makes rational the life of feeling, the life of the spirit, which is the real heart of humane human existence.

2. Children need to mature in their sense of responsibility for themselves, to develop a sense of self-regard which puts pride and a feeling of concern for others behind his management of his own personal resources and the use of these for socially constructive ends.

An address delivered at the Michigan School Testing conference, March 6, 1968 and printed as a booklet by The University of Michigan: Michigan School Testing Service. Reprinted by permission of the author, Dr. George Hill, Distinguished Professor of Education, Ohio University, Athens, Ohio; and The University of Michigan Bureau of School Services.

3. Children need to mature in their understanding of human relations, of how human beings can best live together in our complicated society. The end sought in this development of understanding is, of course, to be found in a fourth learning.

4. Children need to mature in their skill in human relations, in learning the art of harmonious and happy relations with the many others in their lives.

5. Children need to learn—and this learning starts much earlier than most schools recognize—the significance of education in the life of modern man, the relation between education and employment, and the respect for gainful employment which will enable them to move gradually toward becoming productive workers in the American economy.

6. Children need to mature in their ability to make decisions, to solve problems, to meet the multiple exigencies of life with reasonable skill in the use of their intellectual and emotional resources.

7. Children need to mature in their ability to meet changing conditions and to adapt to the necessity for change in both their personal and their vocational lives. "Learning how to keep on learning," as some have put it, is one of the most important of the learnings fostered by our schools.

8. Finally, children need to mature in their sense of values, the ideals that pull their behavior toward goals of improved human relations, the conscience which guides their daily decisions.

These eight learnings apply with equal relevance to education in the kindergarten and to education in the graduate school. Life is going to be productive and it is going to be satisfying only if the learner begins early in life to achieve these learnings and keeps on maturing with respect to them into adulthood. Of course, it is recognized that explicit attention to such educational ends as are suggested by these learnings will differ in the primary grades as against the secondary school and college. The intellectual content of maturing in these learnings will become broader and deeper as the processes of growing up move along. But let it be noted that far more seekers of the Ph.D. fail because of immaturity with respect to one or more of these eight learnings than because of intellectual incompetence.

The use of tests in schools and colleges must take place within a framework of a well conceived set of principles which guide the instructional and pupil personnel program of the school. There are three principles which seem to us to be especially important (Hill and Luckey, 1968):

1. The educational program must be developmental. Teaching must, to be successful, start where children are and must then help them to move along in the achievements seen as essential for their fullest development. If we want a 16-year-old to read skillfully, we don't wait until he is 14 to start teaching him to read. Yet there is a great deal of what could be called "too lateness" about much of our educational effort. The most startling ground swell of educational change in America today is the burgeoning of formal educational efforts in the early years usually called "pre-school." (What a misnomer that term is!)

2. The educational program must be integrative. It must hang together. The various aspects of a given child's educational experiences must be reasonably harmonious. The pupil is a person, not a brain plus a heart plus a physical structure plus a social being. His schooling must, then, be viewed by all of his educational helpers as contributing to his development as a person, not just a mind, or a body.

3. The educational program must be relevant. This is the principle that causes the most debate because we deal now with the relation of formal education and life itself. Making education relevant entails both making schooling meaningfully contributory to the living of real life and making educational experiences in the schools sensible to the child because he can see their relationship to life as he is currently living it. The teacher seeks to mediate for the child between what she is expected by society to teach and what are the current and anticipated realities of living outside the school.

Thus good education not only helps the child grow up, it *insists* that he do so. Good education also helps the child remain and become a person whose life has integrity, whose life in and out of school makes sense because he sees where it is leading him. Good education also makes sense to the child because he sees that it is relevant to the realities of life, that it takes meaning from and adds meaning to his out-of-school life. It is moving him along toward the kind of life that he wants to live. Does all this mean that formal education must be completely attuned to, and never out of harmony with, life as children are already leading to? No. But good schools seek the achievement of goals which are attainable, provide learning experiences that have meaning to the children, and encourage children along developmental paths that have been planned with insight, compassion, and high idealism (Hill and Luckey, 1968).

STANDARDS FOR TEST USERS

A standard, we are told, is "something used by general agreement to determine whether or not a thing is as it should be . . . a level or grade of excellence regarded as a goal or measure of adequacy" (Webster's, 1421). If we accept this kind of definition, and I do, we are then talking about *excellence* in the use of tests, what *should* be in the use of tests, a *goal* toward which we strive in the use of tests to achieve the excellence in the practices of test users which might well be called true professionalism in these practices. In discussing such matters we naturally face the constant fact of current school practice, practice which is bound in some instance to fall below a recognizable standard of excellence. We are also bound to have to deal with practices that fail to meet our standard of excellence simply because the practitioner doesn't know any better. Perhaps no aspect of educational practice can better be used to illustrate both sub-standard and ignorantly inept practice than the field of testing.

With this rather critical and perhaps a bit pessimistic observation behind us, let us look more constructively at a series of what I have called "standards." These are arranged in no special order, although they begin with two standards that are, in this writer's opinion, fundamentally important. These first two standards color all the remaining statements and reflect the earlier formulations of this paper.

1. The most important user of tests in schools is the individual who takes them; therefore *all uses of tests should be geared to our primary concern for his best interests.* A test should never be administered to a student unless we can honestly show that the results will be in some way contributory to his total development. Note that the singular is used in these statements. This is because tests make sense only in terms of their relevance to the education of particular people. It has been said that all business is local. It is equally axiomatic that all education is individual. John Dewey once said that we might as well say we have sold when no one has bought as to say we have taught when no one has learned. He sensed more clearly than most of us the intensely individualistic nature of the learning processes.

2. Taking a test, or responding to an inventory, is a self-revelatory process; therefore *all testing and use of test results in schools must be done with a sharp insight into the understanding of the person being tested, his perceptions as to why he is being tested, his concerns about being tested, his ability to capitalize constructively upon the information which may come to him as a result of having been tested.* One of the most common ways in which we kid ourselves in school and college testing programs is that those being tested know the whys and the wherefores of what we are up to and that they willingly and whole-heartedly respond as best they can and with honesty. It is not too difficult to detect test weariness, test wariness, test fears, and test resistance. Many persons in schools have faced a group of youngsters who show in many ways that

they couldn't care less, or that they care too much, or that they are confused and fearful, of a test that is about to be administered to them.

It is the subtleties of test evasion, test dishonesty, and test goofing-off that escape us. Too often we are left with results on tests and inventories that are far from representative of what the person tested really could do, or that are far from representative of what he really thinks and feels, if the inventory is in the interest or personality area.

Let me now look at these first two standards together for a moment. We see tests as useful in contributing to the basic learnings we listed earlier, as well as to the contributory learnings more commonly called the "fundamentals" of schooling. But the whole testing and test using process is a very human process and it needs to be geared to the needs and to the view of things of the youngster we are trying to educate. First, then, we must be sure that he is willing to respond to the test or inventory before him with a reasonable degree of enthusiasm and with honesty. Unless he has been adequately prepared—both by instruction and by past experience with tests in his school—he will be neither enthusiastic nor honest. We may trick him at times. Gustad has made the preceptive comment, quoting Samuel Butler's famous exasperated statement, "I do not mind lying, but I hate inaccuracy" (Gustad, 1966). So also with the youngster who has developed some sense of desire to "do well"—whatever that may mean—when he faces a test he does not understand the "why" of and thus resents. Though he may try to goof-off he may be tricked into doing quite well because he too hates inaccuracy. Or we may lure the younger child into responding to a test simply because he trusts teacher, or because the "games" we invite him to play are appealing.

We face the hard fact of life that even children at a quite early age begin to develop ramparts of their person which you and I are not going to storm successfully unless they want us to. A counselor friend of mine, for example, asked a group of high school students in an urban district to write down the statement they would most like her to transmit to their school counselors. The most common, bluntly translated, was "Don't be so nosey." One boy added, "When the counselor starts talking about my family I break in and tell him I'm an orphan. That stops them!" The boy in question has two very live parents.

The one experience, more than any other, that will result in enthusiasm and honesty in test situations is the experience of finding that the results of tests and inventories are actually used conscientiously to help the youngster gain greater understanding of himself—his achievements, his abilities, his interests, his personal makeup. In a school which sees child study and individual appraisal as a process in which the student is a *partner* seeking to enhance his own self-understanding, rather than an *object* of study, testing can become a meaningful exercise seen by the students as important to them. This is not to gainsay the importance of teachers and counselors enhancing their understanding of their students. But we would like to insist that this is secondary to the more important purpose of seeking to help the youngster grow in understanding of himself. Need it be said that this emphasis in child study entails the provision of *many* experiences, besides those in the area of testing, that are intended to help the youngster gain insight into his own abilities, achievements and interests. The writer sat, one afternoon some years ago, with his wife, his second daughter's fourth grade teacher, and his daughter as we talked about Judy's nearly-completed fourth grade experience. Judy's teacher kept pushing her gently along as Judy described what she had achieved, some things she had not achieved, and how—in the fifth grade—she was going to attempt some further gains in educational development. Three people who loved her and were supportive of her were helping Judy through an important experience in self-examination and self-understanding. It was a great experience for all of us. Test results got mentioned; and their reinforcing evidences helped both Judy and her adult companions to see where she had been and where she might go.

So, test users must put self-understanding by the person tested as their primary objective and must gear all testing and test usage to the understandings, expectations, fears and attitudes of those being tested. Need it be said that this demands a lot of all of us? Classroom teachers in the elementary schools rarely talk today, as they once did, as if they were self-sufficient and needed no help from "outsiders" such as supervisors, counselors or school psychologists. It takes a team to apply these first two standards. This leads us to our third standard.

3. A lot of people are in the testing act—the child, his parents, his teachers, his counselor, his school psychologist, his principal, the system's superintendent, and a considerable public who are viewing school practices with a critical and increasingly perceptive eye; therefore *the test program of a school system should be coordinated and led by a person highly competent in both the technical and the human aspects of testing and test use.*

It is difficult to say how large a school system should be to require a full-time test expert in this position. Actually, relatively small school systems could well use such a person full time; but commonly they cannot afford him—or her. But, whether full time or part time, *all* school systems need such a staff member. Such a person would, at best, be both technically educated with respect to all aspects of testing and professionally educated in the broader aspects of instruction and guidance. He should be a person committed first of all to the best possible interests of children, willing to see the testing program as contributory to this end, and never as an end in itself or as only an administrative tool.

Not uncommonly such a standard as this would be viewed as acceptable, if for no other reasons than the complexities of selecting, administering, scoring and deriving meaning from the results of tests. Technical knowhow is generally recognized as essential for these tasks. But the coordinator of the school's testing program can make contributions which extend beyond these obvious tasks. It is interesting that the 1937 session of the invitational conference on testing problems stressed the responsibility of test program directors (in this instance state testing programs) for educating "teachers and administrators to a wiser and more effective use of test materials in dealing with the individual pupil" (The Invitational Conference, 1966). In fact it was urged that this be the director's major responsibility. This is just as necessary three decades later.

When one turns to one of the most useful of books on school testing programs he may be surprised to note how little attention is given by its writers (Findley, 1963; Ebel, 1964; Wrightstone, 1963) to this third standard in our list! Perhaps they take for granted the presence of effective leadership for the test program. Our point is that this essential ingredient of a good program can not be taken for granted.

4. *Effective use of tests in schools demands constant attention to upgrading the understandings and skills of all the staff in the area of testing and test usage.*

Many teachers, counselors and school administrators have had only minimal education in the tests and measurement aspects of education. A shocking number of teachers have had none. If only to make teachers more sensitive to what tests "do to them," to use Tyler's expression (Tyler, 1966, pp. 46 ff.), we need on-the-job programs of education. Dyer has insisted that "testing, taken in its broadest sense, is indispensable to teaching" (Dyer, 1967). Yet many teachers do not accept such a sweeping assertion. Perhaps this is in part because, again to quote Dyer, "in fact a considerable part of the testing that goes on in schools is divorced from teaching. It has become part of the mystique of the school psychologist and the guidance counselor, and usually yields only incidental information for use in the actual management of instruction. This may explain why many teachers perceive standardized tests as either threatening or irrelevant" (Dyer, 1967).

Also, it needs to be noted that many teachers, like many lay people, have read the blasts at testing which have been popularized by magazines and books written by persons who have developed exceedingly limited understandings of testing and exceedingly strong convictions about testing. Hoffman, for example, a physicist, can write a whole book about the evils of multiple choice tests (Hoffman, 1962) and give it a title that makes it very sellable. Many teachers have read this and similar books and their own professional preparation has not been such as to help them much in evaluating the validity of the critics' arguments. The "reformer" we are told, is a man who says "let my conscience be your guide." Those who would reform school testing find far too many educators quite willing to accept their conclusions, unsupported though they be, except by invective and vituperation.

One of the effective means of in-service education regarding tests and testing programs has been shown to be the occasional all-staff evaluation of the school's testing program (Hill, 1959; Hill, 1960). It has been shown that the whole staff of a system can be involved in careful assessment of the tests given, their uses, and possible changes in the testing program. Such an evaluation results not only in improved testing but also provides a good means of up-grading test understandings by the staff members. Again, we would like to emphasize that these in-service efforts apply to *all* the staff. As Hunt has said, "Perhaps the most effective assurance against abuse of tests would come from better training in psychometrics for school administrators, guidance counselors and teachers" (Hunt, 1965).

5. *Effective use of tests in schools requires careful attention to the education of parents and other lay people regarding tests and their use.* Such a standard stated two decades ago would have sounded a bit strange. Today it would be expected and missed, if not included. Educators today must know how to deal with the best fed, the best dressed, the best educated and the most anxious parents we have ever had in this country of ours. Test producers and others have tried hard to help parents come to understand what testing in schools is all about. Witness the bulletins published by the best publishers:

"On Telling Parents About Test Results," Test Service Bulletin, No. 54, The Psychological Corporation, New York City, December, 1960.
"How to Tell Parents About Standardized Test Results," by Walter N. Durost, Test Dept., Harcourt, Brace and World, New York City, Test Service Notebook, No. 26, 1961.
"Why Do We Test Your Children?" by Walter N. Durost, Harcourt, Brace and World, New York City, Test Service Notebook, No. 17, 1956.

Hunt's fine little pamphlet for the Public Affairs Pamphlet series (Hunt, 1965) and Hawes' more ambitious treatment, "Educational Testing for the Millions" (Hawes, 1964) have made constructive contributions to parental understanding.

These published resource materials mean little unless in the local school efforts are made to help the parents at hand to become enlightened regarding their school's testing. Some schools have found a good response when parents were given the opportunity to take samples of the ability, achievement and interest measures used with their children.

Schools which use the parent conference instead of the periodic grade card have found it possible to help parents grow in their understanding of their child's developmental processes by using growth charts to convey a picture of the child's development to parents. Such charts include the results of recurring ability and achievement tests.

Of one thing we are sure: The parents of a given child make significant contributions to that child's developing conceptions of himself. If these contributions are to be supportive and are to help the child to develop a true picture of his abilities and achievements, parents must be consulted and informed from the primary grades onward as they, with the teacher, seek to achieve a growing understanding of how this particular child is developing. Recurrent testing of ability and achievement, and later of interests, can contribute helpfully in this process. Needless to say, such a process also helps place test results in their proper perspective along with the many other facts about a child that the school should be gathering.

6. *The use of test results, interpretation of test scores, should always be kept within a framework of child study that is as comprehensive as possible.* Perhaps no more common abuse of test results is to be witnessed in schools and colleges than the use of a single score in isolation from all else that is known about the person. Years ago it was my privilege to hear Sidney Pressey talk about what he called "functional intelligence." He drummed away at the point that the usable intellectual ability of a student consisted of (1) his work habits, (2) his accumulated knowledge and understanding, (3) his drive, zeal, or motivation, and (4) his measurable ability. Many other specialists well versed in testing have told us the same thing. Bordin answers the question he uses for a journal article, "Will testing tell the story?" with the statement "tests by no means give us the complete picture, but they do make a contribution" (Bordin, 1965). Findley puts down as his number one recommendation regarding school testing that "Testing is an essential supplementary tool in the operation of schools but should never be a dominant one" (Findley, 1963, p. 4). Berdie admonishes counselors to "combine all relevant evidence in predicting student success . . . direct observation, reports and records, student self-descriptions, and psychological and educational tests" (Berdie, 1963, p. 134). Berdie makes the perceptive and entirely valid recommendation that "the counselor must face the paradox of defeating his predictions—when they are unfavorable—through counseling" by encouraging the student to take risks and thus sometimes succeed when the evidence is against success! (Berdie, 1963, pp. 153–154).

7. *The use of tests in schools must, as in the use of information not gained from tests, be rooted in the rigorous application of standards to this information.* All information used in schools to characterize children

or to draw conclusions about them, must be subjected to reasonable criteria. They can best be stated as questions, and they are worded so as to point to the major concern—the welfare of the individual child—

Is this information true? This is our familiar criterion of validity.

Is this information fresh? A test score from last year may mean little today.

An anecdotal record from last week may not tell us much about the child today.

The recorded occupation of a father, in the file folder, may have been determined a month ago. Today it may be questionable as to its accuracy.

Is this information developmental? Information from the child's yesterdays can enhance our understanding of him today if it can be seen in such a way as to tell us something about how this child is developing. The growth chart does this for us with recurring administrations of mental ability tests, achievement tests, physical measures and the like.

Is this information complete? This is our standard number six.

These criteria are applicable to anything we think we know about a child, and as applicable to test scores as to any other information. This means that there must be constant surveillance of the records we keep, the personnel folders we maintain regarding each student. These criteria must be applied to the information at hand by persons who are most knowledgeable. Probably the best way to apply these criteria to a given child's folder is to conduct a case conference involving several adults in this child's life. The sifting and discussion of what we collectively know about him is bound to raise questions regarding this information and to result in discarding some of the "facts" we have at hand.

8. *In testing and in the use of test results, persistent efforts must be extended to reduce the impact of tests in producing anxiety among children and to lessen the chances of undue competitiveness in testing.* One does not need to read the work of Sarason and his associates (Sarason, 1960) to know that test anxiety is a very real fact of life in the lives of children. Sarason tells us that they used test anxiety, from among several kinds of anxieties that they might have studied, because "both the tester and testee (be it an individual or group test situation) far more often than not perceive the testing situation to have an evaluative or assessment purpose and that it is important to do well, however differently 'well' might be defined by tester and testee" (Sarason, *et al.*, 1960, p. 8).

As one reads Brim, Neulanger and Glass's informative report of a study of the experiences of a sample of adults with intelligence tests there are several points at which one is inclined to ask: I wonder how these adults really *felt* about this? Was this a kind of experience which could produce anything but anxiety in adults? For example, it was reported that one third of these adults "said they had learned nothing about the tests their children had taken" (Brim, *et al.*, 1964, p. 42).

Test users should see, and I believe most of us do, that a test is, as Chauncey has put it "the most visible part of the pressure" (Chauncey, 1966, p. 150) that is brought to bear on children and youth as they are placed in the competitive scramble for marks, for admissions, for scholarships—for all the attainments which have both practical worth in our culture and high status value. Thus, one way we can reduce the competitive pressure is to make test results less visible. This requires that, both with groups of students and with them in individual counseling, we must constantly be relating test scores with the vast array of other informations which are relevant to the questions at hand.

Need it be said that this also entails programs of pre-test orientation for children and for their parents. It also entails insuring that those who administer tests maintain a poised and balanced approach to the testing experience. There is little doubt that a combination of such emphasis is required if testing is kept from becoming high-pressure in its impact. It is entirely correct, as Chauncey has said, that "tests can actually be a valuable tool in reducing pressure" (Chauncey, 1966, p. 150). What is needed is the use of tests from early childhood on a periodic basis, with adequate guidance for children and parents, so that they "grow up" together in the process of maturing self-understanding that we have already described. In short, undue competitive pressure can be alleviated best by helping children develop the self-assurance which is rooted in self-understanding.

9. *Test users should use all their ingenuity to develop ways which will help children both to understand and retain information from tests and to use this information wisely.* This touches on matters we have already discussed, but here I would like to emphasize test use by school counselors in elementary and secondary schools. First let me urge counselors—as I am sure many have already done—to read with care the highly critical discussion of testing provided by Rothney and his associates (Rothney *et. al.*, 1959). While we may cringe a bit at some of his blasts, especially his junking of interest measurement, we need this kind of an antidote for the rather heavy emphasis on testing most of us experienced during education for our positions. But let me also urge the reading of such discussions as Berdie's on the counselor's use of tests (Berdie, 1963). Here we find a rather hard-boiled treatment of tests for predictive purposes to which some of our Rogerian counselors need to pay more attention. In short, counselors should be the most critical and the most skilled users of tests on any school staff.

Since there is the most hope for children, from a developmental standpoint, while they are still in elementary school, I believe the increasing use of counselors in the grade schools is one of the most hopeful educational developments of our day. This can mean not only better guidance in these schools, but far better test usage, if these counselors function as they should. The most common expectation school staffs have of the elementary school counselor is that she will be an expert in child study. Every one of our first eight standards, therefore, has a *special* significance for the new elementary school counselor.

The information we have regarding how well pupils understand and retain information gained from tests is not encouraging. Ohlsen has provided us with the best summary in print of the several studies and discussions of this matter (Ohlsen, 1963). Interpretation is not enough; this must lead to improvement in self-understanding. Nowhere can this be so intimately and completely revealed as in the counseling relationship.

10. *Tests users should insist upon periodic evaluations of the school's testing program by all the professional persons involved in testing and test usage.* It has been demonstrated that it is both possible and profitable to do this (Hill, 1959; Hill, 1960). Hill has developed an inventory for evaluating school testing programs which has been used successfully in a number of systems. It is very important that these evaluations involve everyone in the system, or at least a representative cross-section of all staff members. Persons who at first say "I simply don't know enough about our testing program" can be encouraged to enhance their knowledge. Often they actually know a lot more—as consumers at least—than they think they do. The experience of working at the evaluation greatly increases their knowledge.

11. *Considerable attention should be given to the ethical standards regarding testing that have been promulgated by various professional groups,* especially the American Personnel and Guidance Association and the American Psychological Association (A.P.G.A., A.P.A.). In these statements of ethics, when testing is involved, the emphasis is upon protecting the child, seeing to it that test scores are made available only to authorized persons, that interpretation is professionally sound. The ethical statements also emphasize the need to view test scores in a context of the other relevant information about the child that can be so rich and so enlightening. Through these statements of ethical standards one senses a search for reasonable balance between our finding out what we can about the child—all for his own good, of course—and protection for this child from undue intrusion upon his privacy. The delicacy of this balance is amply illustrated by the problems faced, and the methods used, by the U.S. Office of Education's Bureau of Research (Conrad, 1967). They make no bones of the fact that ultimate authority for determining the methods we use in seeking to understand children rests with the people.

Conrad makes a plea that "social science must not become identified in the public mind with 'snooping' and 'prying'" (Conrad, 1967, p. 175). Need it be said that this problem, in fact the whole matter of ethical practices in testing, entails *both* areas of decision-making, as described by Mehrens: "Individual decisions, where a person, such as a student, is making a decision about himself on the basis of test information" (Mehrens, 1967, p. 62). The other area of decision-making is "where somebody else, such as an administrator or counselor, is making decisions about a person."

Whether we see this as an ethical problem—and to this writer it is certainly such—or as a problem of professional competence and skill, we test users must be constantly on the alert to avoid the four harmful consequences of test usage which Ebel has underlined. He points out that testing may:

. . . place an indelible stamp of intellectual status—superior, mediocre, or inferior—on a child and thus predetermine his social status as an adult, and possibly do irreparable harm to his self-esteem and his educational motivation.
. . . lead to a narrow conception of ability, encourage pursuit of this single goal, and thus tend to reduce the diversity of talent available to society.
. . . place the testers in a position to control education and determine the destinies of individual human beings, while, incidentally, making the testers themselves rich in the process.
. . . encourage impersonal, inflexible, mechanistic processes of evaluation and determination, so that essential human freedoms are limited or lost altogether (Ebel, 1964, pp. 132–133).

Ebel goes on to mention several other possible negative consequences of testing. These include individual competition as against social cooperation, conformity as against creativity, cultural bias, neglect of important intangibles, invasions of privacy, injustice to individuals and rewards for specious testing-taking skill.

Ebel's suggestions to us regarding ways in which we can avoid these possible negative consequences of testing are so sound that I repeat them verbatim:

1. We could emphasize the use of tests to *improve* status and de-emphasize their use to determine status.
2. We could broaden the base achievements tested to recognize and develop the wide variety of talents needed in our society.
3. We could share openly with the persons directly concerned all that tests have revealed to us about their abilities and prospects.
4. We could decrease the use of tests to impose decisions on others, and instead increase their use as a basis for better personal decision making.— (Ebel, 1964, p. 142).

FINALLY

In stating eleven standards for test users the writer ends both with feelings of encouragement and with a sense of deep concern. We know more today about how to build good tests than we have ever known. Test program management is greatly improved. Most teachers are being provided at least minimal preparation in tests and measurement before they start to teach. Counselors are present in more and more schools—including the elementary schools—and these counselors tend to be persons quite knowledgeable in testing and test usage; thus building staffs are in a better position to use tests better than was once the case. People turn out in considerable numbers for conferences on testing and read a voluminous literature on testing. Public interest in testing is high and criticisms from laymen have been helpful.

Concern, however, arises, as we note that, despite our increased knowledgeability regarding test construction, the range of educational objectives and of human characteristics dependably measured by tests is still woefully narrow. Far too many school systems still do not have capable test coordinators on their staffs. Teacher education programs are still, by and large, weak in the tests and measurement area; and they have been weakened in part because of the spineless way we have given in to the raucus demands of narrow academicians to "eliminate the methods courses!" Most of our elementary schools still do not have counselors; in fact only about a fourth have *any* pupil personnel worker in the school as much as one day a week. (American elementary schools are, in fact, shockingly and disgracefully under-staffed.) I won't comment on the impact of conferences and professional literature as means of up-grading our skills in the use of tests; that's getting too close to home. Public interest is still badly under-informed and often misinformed regarding testing.

May I add, while on this negative note, that our test experts disappoint us also. When I look, for example, at a "Test Giver's Self-Inventory" issued by a test publisher and find almost no attention in it to test usage and test interpretation, even in the section labeled "after the testing period," I wonder *why* they are publishing tests. Also when I examine an issue of the *Review of Educational Research* (February, 1965) and find in it only one and a half of its 101 pages devoted to "interpretation," I am discouraged. It is even worse to cull the issue and find no reference to actual research on interpretation, except as the improvement of tests themselves make for better interpretation, a hope, but not necessarily a reality.

Thus we have both hopeful and discouraging—yet challenging—prospects for test usage in our schools. Our standards started with a strong emphasis upon the child as the prime user of tests. We believe that all tests are self-revelatory devices and thus must be used, and especially must be interpreted, with the prime purpose of enhancing the child's growth in self-understanding. We believe that testing programs in schools and colleges need coordinating leadership of top-notch professionals who are both technically and humanely qualified for this work. We believe that all school staffs need constant assistance with their growth in sophistication regarding tests and test usage. We believe the parents and the general lay public need the same kind of help. We believe that child study and individual appraisal efforts in schools and colleges need the broadest possible base, that they require skillful use of a great variety of methods for enhancing self-understanding and staff understanding of the child. We believe that everything we think we know about a child requires the application of rigorous and exacting standards of validity, freshness, completeness, and developmental wholeness. We believe that testing and test usage can be managed with minimal emphasis upon pressure and competitiveness and must be, if tests are to serve their proper purposes in schools. We believe that the most significant use of test results is in individual counseling and in any other procedures which help the student to understand, to retain and to apply sensibly what tests tell him. We believe that school testing programs require periodic evaluations by the whole staff and that this is one of our best in-service activities. We believe that a sensitive understanding and application of ethical standards is needed in testing and test usage. Especially is it important always to remember that we work in social-service institutions, that the public has ultimate responsibility for these institutions and that we professionals must be able and willing to give proper regard to the public will.

While there are discouraging problems in our midst, as regards testing and test usage, my own conviction is that we are doing far better than we did two decades ago. Two decades from now we had better be doing far better than we are now.

REFERENCES

American Personnel and Guidance Association. "Ethical Standards, American Personnel and Guidance Association." *Personnel and Guid. J.*, October, 1961, *40*, 206–209.

American Psychological Association. *Casebook on Ethical Standards of Psychologists*. Washington, D.C.: American Psychological Association, 1967.

BERDIE, R. F. "Testing Programs and Counseling in Schools." In W. G. Findley, ed., *The Impact and Improvement of School Testing Programs*, 62nd Yearbook, N.S.S.E., Part II. Chicago: Univ. of Chicago Press, 1963. Ch. 7.

BORDIN, E. "Will Tests Tell the Story?" *PTA Magazine*, January, 1965, 59, 4–6.

BRIM, O. G., JR., NEULINGER, J., AND GLASS, D. C. *Experiences and Attitudes of American Adults Concerning Standardized Intelligence Tests*. New York: Russel Sage Foundation, 1964.

CHAUNCEY, H. "How Testing Can be Used to Cut Academic Stress." *School Management*, April, 1966, *10*, 148–150, 155–156.

CONRAD, H. S. "Clearance of Questionnaires with Respect to 'Invasion of Privacy' Public Sensitivities, Ethical Standards, etc.: Principles and Viewpoint in the Bureau of Research, U. S. Office of Education." *Sociology of Education*, 1967, *40*, 170–175.

DYER, H. S. "Needed Changes to Sweeten the Impact of Testing." *Personnel and Guidance Journal*, April, 1967, *45*, 776–780.

EBEL, R. L. "The Social Consequences of Testing." *Invitational Conference on Testing Problems*, Princeton, New Jersey: Educational Testing Service, 1964.

FINDLEY, W. G. "Purposes of School Testing Programs and Their Efficient Development." In W. G. Findley, ed., *The Impact and Improvement of School Testing Programs*, 62nd Yearbook, N.S.S.E., Part II, Chicago: Univ. of Chicago Press, 1963. Ch. 3.

GUSTAD, J. W. "Helping Students Understand Test Information." In A. Anastasi, ed., *Testing Problems in Perspective*, Washington, D.C.: American Council on Education, 1966, pp. 37–45.

HAGEN, E. "Staff Competency in Testing." In W. G. Findley, ed., *The Impact and Improvement of School Testing Programs*, 62nd Yearbook, N.S.S.E., Part II, Chicago: Univ. of Chicago Press, 1963. Ch. 11.

HAWES, G. R. *Educational Testing for the Millions: What Tests Really Mean for Your Child*. New York: McGraw-Hill, 1964.

HILL, G. E. *Evaluating the School's Testing Program*. Athens: Ohio University Center for Educational Service, 1959.

HILL, G. E. *The Staff Evaluate the School's Testing Program*. Athens: Ohio University, Center for Education Service, 1960.

HILL, G. E. AND LUCKEY, E. B. *Guidance for Children in Elementary Schools*. New York: Appleton-Century-Crofts, 1968.

HOFFMAN, B. *The Tyranny of Testing*. New York: Crowell-Collier Press, 1962.

HUNT, J. McV. *What You Should Know about Educational Testing*. Public Affairs Pamphlet, No. 375. New York: Public Affairs Committee, 1965.

MCCALL, J. N. "Trends in the Measurement of Vocational Interests." *Review of Educational Research*, 1965, *35*, 53–62.

MEHRENS, W. A. "The Consequence of Misusing Test Results." *The National Elementary Principal*, Sept., 1967, *47*, 62–64.

OHLSEN, M. M. "Interpretation of Tests Scores." In W. G. Findley, ed., *The Impact and Improvement of School Testing Programs*, 62nd Yearbook, N.S.S.E., Part II, 1963. Ch. 12.

ROTHNEY, J. W. M., DANIELSON, P. J., AND HEIMANN, R. A. *Measurement for Guidance*. New York: Harper and Bros., 1959.

SARASON, S. B. *et al.* *Anxiety in Elementary School Children*. New York: John Wiley and Sons, 1960.

"The Invitational Conference on Testing Problems," In A. Anastasi, ed., *Testing Problems in Perspective*, Washington, D.C.: American Council on Education, 1966, pp. 46–52.

TYLER, R. W. "What Testing Does to Teachers and Students." In A. Anastasi, ed., *Testing Problems in Perspective*, Washington, D.C.: American Council on Education, 1966, pp. 46–52.

WOMER, F. B. "Testing Programs—Misconception, Misuse, Overuse." *Michigan*

Journal of Secondary Education, Spring, 1961, 153–161 (Reprinted by Educational Testing Service, Princeton, New Jersey).

WRIGHTSTONE, J. W. "The Relation of Testing Programs to Teaching and Learning." In W. G. Findley, ed., *The Impact and Improvement of School Testing Programs,* 62nd Yearbook, N.S.S.E., Part II, Chicago: Univ. of Chicago Press, 1963. Ch. 3.

SECTION EIGHT

The Information Function

S OME of the major activities in implementing the guidance function are specifically designed to fulfill the need for relevant information. Among the organized activities of a secondary school guidance program, for example, are *orientation* (information programs at transition points between schools), *placement* ("helping students take the next step" after leaving school), and the *information service* (coordination of the development and dissemination of a library of occupational, educational, and personal-social information). The latter is a functional grouping of what are typically regarded as separate guidance "services" in the literature. Each of the services has in common with the other services the provision and dissemination of accurate and useable information related to vocational, educational, or personal-social concerns.

In the first selection of the Section, Vincent Calia draws from a wide survey of the literature to discuss a number of issues and assumptions in "Vocational Guidance: After the Fall." Calia refers in the title to a series of recent condemnations of vocational guidance, which are based primarily on arguments that (1) currently available occupational information is relatively useless; (2) a naive assumption is made that information *per se* is determinative of occupational choice; (3) vocational guidance ignores the developmental nature of man and is consequently largely ineffective; (4) no adequate theories of vocational development or of decision making are available to the counselor. While the above criticisms have a large measure of validity—particularly with respect to the lack of psychosocial data in occupational information—Calia concludes that "vocational guidance remains a viable pursuit whose most pressing need is for efforts in unearthing more crucial questions and answers and not in debunking its importance or utility value."

Joseph Samler explores the effects and implications of rampart technological change for vocational counseling. His lengthy article is replete with indications of the rapid change in the job structure, especially those due to technological development. Samler's carefully drawn conclusions about the role of the vocational counselor leave no doubt about the viability of the development of a truly professional role in this sphere.

Further, Samler develops the theme that psychological sophistication about the dynamics of human development is a needed dimension of professional vocational counseling not only because of the kaleidoscopic nature of "careers" in contemporary American society, but also because of the intrusion of values and affect into "rational" occupational choices. Thus, while work has not always been universally regarded as a dignified pursuit, the dignity of work is inherent in our Puritan heritage. This value is exemplified in folklore sayings such as "Idle hands are the devil's workshop." To achieve self-worth in the face of a labor market which may not need the services of a large number of individuals requires not only an optimal vocational development effort nationally, but also a societal shift in values that provide for rich and full lives in a society characterized by much more leisure than "work." The "vocational" counselor is thus a counselor who, as any other counselor, is concerned with needs of the individual which may be orthogonal to the immediate demands of the larger society.

In the final selection, Robert Morman traces the history of automation and draws implications for counselors. Although some economists would disagree, Morman concludes that "on a national level, automation should lead to a fuller, richer life and bring more happiness in the way of economic benefits and leisure pursuits than ever before." Mormon's theme is reminiscent of the often drawn analogy comparing imminent American society to the Golden Age in ancient Greece which was characterized by an exceptionally high creative output. The slave base, which made such pursuits possible in that Greek society, is replaced in contemporary society by a "technological slave base" by those who make the analogy.

The knowledge explosion necessitates the efficient ordering and updating of large masses of information. The guidance administrator must use effective systems of information storage and retrieval. Technological advances in data processing and computer applications are exemplary of useable systems. Some authorities have estimated that approximately 75 per cent of the work of the typical secondary school counselor could be automated, thus providing additional time for functioning in more professional role dimensions.

36.   Vocational Guidance: After the Fall

Vincent F. Calia

Vocational guidance, or more specifically, the practice of disseminating occupational information in the school setting, has fallen into considerable disrepute. It has been downgraded in importance (Ginzberg, Ginsburg, Axelrod, & Herma, 1951), depicted as an essentially perceptual process (Rusalem, 1954), buried (Barry & Wolf, 1962), deemed "destructive" (Lifton, 1963), and "junked" (Barry & Wolf, 1963). On the other hand, this Parsonian notion has been defended (Sayler, 1964), needed (Gaither, Hackman & Hay, 1963) and placed in its proper perspective (Borow, 1964; Calia, 1964; Tiedeman, 1963; Hackman, 1965). The issue, while complex, centers on the relative importance of occupational information in the guidance and counseling process.

The proponents of the vocational guidance view subscribe essentially to a rather simple-minded hypothesis, viz., that "persons with more information about occupational environments make more adequate choices than do persons with less information" (Holland, 1959, p. 42). Holland and his sympathizers are quite aware that this relationship needs qualifi-

cation, however, and proceed to develop a number of elegant elaborations. But this hypothesis is, nonetheless, pivotal to their contentions.
Opponents of this view underscore the importance of self-discovery, the
overriding influence of the mechanism of selective perception, and the
fallibility of occupational materials. The arguments, pro and con, have
been rather thoroughly promulgated. But there are aspects of the controversy that have been generally ignored and that bear importantly on
the prospects of attaining a meaningful resolution. It is time for an
attempt to uncover such phenomena and to contemplate their significance
for the theory and practice of vocational guidance.

A Reactionary Proposal

In perusing the contemporary literature, one is forced to the rather
striking conclusion that Parsons' (1908) superannuated formulations are
still very much alive today. More than half a century has passed since his
assertion that the choice of a vocation consists of three phases: ". . . (1)
a clear understanding of yourself, your aptitudes, abilities, interests,
ambitions, resources, limitations, and their causes; (2) a knowledge of
the requirements and conditions of success, advantages and disadvan-
tages, compensations, opportunities, and prospects in different lines of
work; (3) true reasoning on the relations of these two groups of facts."
While a good deal more is known now about Phase 1 and Phase 2, and
more sophisticated methods for "matching" (counseling?) have been
developed, the rationale remains essentially unchanged. Ginzberg, Super,
and Tiedeman have added the process dimension, but others persist in
perpetuating the earlier and more static notion of achieving a satisfactory
and ultimate marriage of youth and job. Let us attempt an examination
of the current status of knowledge within the Parsonian context as well as
a critique of the assumptions underlying the more dynamic constructs of
vocational guidance.

PHASE 1—STUDY-OF-THE-INDIVIDUAL TESTS AS VOCATIONAL PREDICTORS

The wholesale use of psychological tests as vocational assessment
devices has precipitated a rising tide of public censure. The critics' attacks have centered primarily on the serious deficiencies of these instruments and the ethics involved in their use in school and work settings.
The legitimacy of the criticism is heightened by the rather disconcerting
fact that psychological tests *have* proved to be disappointing predictors.
Thorndike (1963) suggests that perhaps the best one can hope for is the
prediction of performance in school and work training programs and not

much beyond that. Yet this is the very notion that Super rejects, viz., that of matching youth and job and assuming that "once the match is made, the young couple lives happily ever after" (Thorndike, 1964, p. 4). He argues that the vocational psychologist needs to "stay" with his clients until they are well established in their careers or until their careers have become stabilized. The difficulty with his career model (practical considerations aside) and vocational prediction generally is that "getting ahead" in a career is not only a function of the individual, as Super himself notes, but is also a function of the people around him and what happens to *them.* If an employee's supervisor should die or resign suddenly, the employee may find himself abruptly and unexpectedly elevated in rank. In this instance, rapid advancement is partially a function of the individual because he is selected over other prospects, and partially a result of factors beyond his control. These contingencies or chance factors defy prediction by definition and seriously complicate the problem of forecasting careers. There are, of course, other criterion problems that continue to plague the field of psychological measurement, but they have been treated exhaustively elsewhere (Ghiselli, 1955; 1956a; 1956b; Goldman, 1961; Super & Crites, 1962; Thorndike, 1963). The major difficulty with using tests as vocational predictors is that while tests can be useful for predicting normative behavior, i.e., where decisions regarding large numbers of candidates are to be made, they are woefully inadequate when applied to the problem of predicting the behavior of the individual. This is a shortcoming which the perceptual psychologists have been lamenting for years.

The likelihood is that despite the admonishments of the career theorists, the trait-and-factor model is likely to persist for some time to come. While clients should be encouraged to think in terms of lifelong career plans, the fact is that normative or probability data will continue to be useful, particularly at crises or decision points. The use of computers and multivariate methods of prediction augurs well for the continued utility of this antiquated model. While Super and his colleagues wrestle with the complexities of developmental criteria, practitioners will continue to find solace and value in the more traditional psychometric concepts and devices. It is well to note, however, that as the complexity of these developments increases, irrespective of the model employed, such as the design of new computer programs, the application of the results of multivariate analyses, or the identification and measurement of the metadimensions of the self-concept, practitioners are likely to become increasingly despairing in their efforts to assimilate and implement the significance of these awesome developments. Care must be exercised and responsibility delegated for making these developments intelligible and operational at the level of practice.

PHASE 2—STUDY OF OCCUPATIONS

Taxonomy of occupational environment. Generalities abound in occupational materials. Viteles' (1961) humorous illustration in which he cites the qualifications of a librarian and then proceeds to use precisely the same description for the workers employed in scraping celery in a soup factory makes this point clearly. If such generalizations are to be curtailed and if occupational materials are to acquire meaning and utility value, then, as Brayfield (Viteles, *et al.*, 1961) cogently argues, measures of occupational environments need to be developed. Rather than compile subjective and stereotypic descriptions of occupations, an effort should be made to identify specific, quantifiable dimensions of occupational experience. Vocational guidance practitioners tend to operate exclusively in terms of the psychological profile of the individual primarily because developments associated with the first phase of choosing a vocation have attained a level of sophistication which makes such analyses possible. Similar developments have not carried over into the second stage. As a consequence, practitioners are inclined to rely upon their own resources and ingenuity for organizing the complexities of the occupational world. Profiles of occupational environments are needed to complete the sequence. The well-publicized efforts of Roe, Super, Holland, and Fine represent a promising beginning to the enormous task of systematizing occupational data. In addition, Pace and Stern's (1958) study of the psychological characteristics of college environment holds promise as a prototype for future taxonomic endeavors. Undoubtedly some occupational environments will be easier to dimensionalize than others. For example, occupations that place a premium on task-oriented activities are likely to be more susceptible to definition and measurement than occupations stressing the importance of social interactions. In effect, some environments are likely to be relatively stable with little tolerance for deviation of working role while others will permit variation according to the initiative and machinations of their occupants. The worker in the assembly line is less able to indulge his whims than the company executive whose personal qualities dominate and modify the requirements of his role.

Despite the fluidity inherent in a wide variety of occupational roles, vocational psychologists may ultimately "factor out" basic dimensions of the occupational environment that are influential in giving substance to the limits and requirements of such roles. The task is obviously a monumental one but Fine's imminent nine-digit revision of the earlier *Dictionary of Occupational Titles* (DOT) scheme is certainly a laudatory and promising beginning. The task remains, however, to devise a comparable and intelligible scheme for pupil or client use. Psychometricians have developed schemata designed specifically for client consumption (e.g., centiles, stanines, IQ, percentile bands, expectancy tables, etc.). Vocational psychologists have been less resourceful in this respect. Future efforts must be directed toward increasing the accessibility of occupational information by developing schemata appropriate for client use.

The relative merits of primary versus vicarious experience. Vocational guidance authorities have been assuming for years that experiencing the occupation firsthand via actual involvement in full- or part-time work activities, i.e., *primary experience,* is distinctly superior to experiencing the occupation indirectly via reading, talking, listening, and observing through the use of such media as films, tapes, role-playing, field trips, occupational pamphlets, career conferences, etc., i.e., *vicarious exploratory projection.* This position is typified by Rusalem's assertion that "the more intimate and the more emotional the contact, the more valid will be its contribution to decision-making and to counseling" (Rusalem, 1954, p. 86). The point that such contenders overlook is that primary experiences can be as misleading as reading faulty occupational brochures. Intimate contacts are likely to be more *potent* but *not* necessarily *more valid.* Primary experience may have a more profound impact on career thinking and planning than reading an occupational pamphlet but this has nothing to do with its validity. Selective perception operates here, too, and if the work experience is atypical in some important respects, distortion of occupational requirements will inevitably be compounded. For example, Rusalem suggests that:

. . . the closer the proximity of the individual to the actual job of his choice the greater will be the helpfulness of the occupational information gained in aiding clients to select occupations, to confirm realistic choices, and to negate unrealistic decisions (Rusalem 1954, p. 88).

On the other hand, on-the-job exposure can have reverse effects too. The marginal student who aspires to a career as a surgeon and is employed as a part-time orderly may be moved to discard the "hard facts" of selective admission as a consequence of his exciting and vivid proximity to the surgeon's tasks. In addition, physicians are not adverse to nurturing the dreams of such aspirants by displaying special interest in them and indulging in some fatherly, if misdirected, "guidance."

Perhaps the nature of the experience is inconsequential, or at least less important than the student's reaction to it. But more than the phenomenon of selective perception is involved here. More specifically, *it is not only what the student selects out of the myriad of stimuli to which he is exposed that is important, but it is what he does with them after he has made his selection that is highly significant.*

Some students are inclined to ruminate a good deal about their experiences while others characteristically dismiss them perfunctorily. While the former are predisposed to assuming or projecting themselves into a variety of occupational roles prior to entertaining a course of action, the latter are more apt to respond to the pressures or feelings of the moment. This distinction has its counterpart in Ginzberg's, *et al.* (1951) "active versus passive" personality types, Riesman's (1956) "inner-directed versus outer-directed" persons, and Ryan and Krumboltz's (1964) "deliberative versus decision-making" behavior. The point is that some people use these experiences by personalizing them; others simply accumulate them. It would be an error to assume, however, that this is a dichotomous phenomenon. High and low fantisizers undoubtedly are best depicted as falling on two ends of a continuum rather than in mutually exclusive categories.

It seems likely that the student who is vicariously disposed through a rich imagination and is able to exercise it frequently, may be productively responsive to all manner of experiences, primary and otherwise. For this group, then, occupational information, regardless of its source, serves to enlarge and enrich one's vocational images. On the other hand, students who have little talent or appetite for vicarious activity are likely to "seek out" or respond more favorably to *primary experiences.* Because vicarious activities are not especially meaningful to them, secondary experiences are likely to be averted and ineffectual. In effect then, *the degree to which one is inclined to fantasize about occupations is a highly significant variable and is seen as relating to the kinds and frequency of vocational exposures one should have.*

Rather than disseminate information indiscriminately, high and low fantasizers should be identified and supplied with appropriate experiences. Vicariously disposed pupils need to be encouraged to think about ways of translating their musings into action and ultimately to commit themselves to action. By the same token, the action-oriented youngster needs to learn to contemplate the consequences of his action and to become aware of and ponder the significance of opportunities not immediately or intimately available to him. As Tyler aptly notes:

Most of us in the counseling profession value awareness. It seems better to us that a person move forward along a road he has chosen for himself than that he is propelled by circumstances (Tyler 1961, p. 48).

Krumboltz and his colleagues (Ryan & Krumboltz, 1964; Krumboltz & Thoresen, 1964) have had some success in effecting changes in behavior of the kind envisioned here. Their reinforcement counseling procedures, however, hardly exhaust the possibilities. Guidance practitioners should be resourceful in developing additional methods.

PHASE 3—"MATCHING" 1 & 2

Self-study: precursor or concomitant of vocational exploration.
Oddly enough, there is little agreement among authorities as to the
optimum sequence of steps to be pursued in the vocational selection
process. Brayfield (1951), Kirk and Michels (1964), and Samler (1965)
take the position that self-understanding *must* precede the study of occupations. In a highly provocative and intriguing article, Samler posits the
conviction that:

The guidance process inevitably aims at self-understanding by the client, by
definition a key aspect of mental health. This is a precondition for making mature choices; for the assumption of responsibility for self. This kind of learning,
perhaps the most important in the world, must start before the individual attempts to relate himself to the working world (Samler, 1965, p. 55).

On the contrary, Baer and Roeber argue that the study of self and
occupations are inextricably related. They contend that self-study in its
fullest sense is a lifelong process and therefore:

. . . the concept of self-study before all else is contrary to the concept of
career development as a lifelong process. If a person had to understand himself to the extent advocated by some authorities before he could try work and
educational explorations, he might never be ready to start finding out about
work. Indeed it is the thesis of this [text] that *information can provide a stimulant to self-study through occupational and educational exploration* (Baer &
Roeber, 1964, p. 428).

It seems difficult to conceive of self-study as an exclusively introspective process, void of all empirical influence. Super's notion of vocational
development as a process of testing the self-concept against reality and
Rusalem's (1954) discussion of the verification function of occupational
information in which aspects of the self-concept are retained or discarded
as a consequence of exposure would certainly vitiate the importance of
self-study as a precondition for admittance to Phase 2, the study of
occupations. One might, in fact, make a case for reversing the first two
steps of the Parsonian sequence. Any attempt to separate these activities,
however, would appear to be artificial and unproductive. Baer and
Roeber's assertion above might be expanded to include the notion that
steps one and two are mutually influential, the one serving as impetus for
study of the other. Choosing a vocation would certainly appear to be the
result of a reciprocal process, experience interacting with preconceptions
eventuating in change and vocational development.

Explorations of self and work: inhibitory phenomena. The frequent
reference to the significance of the individual's *autistic inclinations* for

vocational planning and development has some precedence in Beilin's (1963) discussion of the importance of concept formation for vocational research, Samler's (1965) understandably defensive treatise on the relevance of the interpretation of dreams for expediting self-exploration and understanding *in the school setting*, and Mathewson and Orton's (1963) study of the vocational imagery of adolescent pupils. Self-study is undoubtedly a function of the predisposition to autistic behavior. Students who rate low on this variable are not predisposed to indulging in Phase 1 and 2 activity. There is some evidence to indicate, for example, that autistic behavior is a cultural concomitant; Riesman (1956) reports that autistic behavior runs contrary to the style of the poor. Indigent youngsters are typically less introspective, less introvertive, and less preoccupied with the self. They tend to be more responsive to the outside, to action. The implications for vocational counseling are interesting. Calia notes for example, that:

The client's characteristic resistance to the contemplation of self and his tendency to ascribe his difficulties and concerns to forces outside himself, poses a perplexing practitioner's dilemma. Does the counselor teach his client to talk about feelings, to search for them, to label them, as preparation for counseling? In short, must the counselor instruct his client to redirect his interest inward upon the self, or does he work essentially within the context of the client's life style, assisting in the identification of external impediments and solutions to client progress? (Calia, 1966, p. 101)

The answer is obviously not a simple one. But if the client is to pursue a life's course he has selected for himself rather than float whimsically along in a sea of external forces, then the counselor's task seems clear. As noted earlier, such clients need to learn to think about themselves and their vocational destinies.

In practice, it is not unusual to find that autistic youngsters who fall on the high end of this continuum fixate at the stage one level of self-exploration with little regard for the requirements and demands of the world of work and stage one and two relationships. But it is an error to assume that their fantasies or fixations are easily altered by simple cognitive appeals. Cooley's (1964) recent defense, for example, of the relevance of a computer-measurement system for guidance is a highly reactionary proposal. Shifts in educational and vocational planning, or more specifically, aspiration level, may be amenable to probability data, but this is a naïve and antiquated view. Aspirations are primarily a function of the individual's need system and, while capable of being modified by experience, are also found to be tenaciously unyielding to data-dissemination techniques. Adherents of the cognitive view generally assume that inappropriate educational and vocational goals are due to informational deficits of some kind. The task, then, is to diagnose the

deficit and disseminate pertinent data. The assumption is that greater
congruity of potentiality and ambition will follow. The author's clinical
experience suggests that some clients are responsive to this approach but
that their responsiveness is a function of such manifest variables as age
and duration of commitment to choice. As the theories of vocational development would indicate, the vocational plans of preadolescents are tentative and amenable to the exigencies of occupational exposure. But the
student who has had such exposure and persists over a relatively long
period of time in aspiring to goals beyond his predicted capacity is likely
to resist such efforts to adjust his vocational sights. Aspirations of this
kind function as important security operations, and as a consequence, are
refractory to rational treatment methods.

There is some evidence to indicate, however, that long-term over-
aspirers may well be composed of two distinct subpopulations, each
having differential implications for practice. The amount of risk a person
is willing to assume appears to be a function of his personality (McClelland, 1956; Ziller, 1957; Kogan & Wallach, 1964). The risk-taker or
student gambler is sensitive to probability data; he knows what the odds
are but decides to push ahead *in spite of them or because of them*. A
perusal of the school records of such students frequently indicates the
existence of considerable drive and discipline. Extrapolating from such
data, one suspects that they are likely to do something about transform-
ing their dreams into reality. The *student dreamer*, on the other hand,
seems to have successfully insulated himself from the ministrations and
admonishments of others. An examination of his educational and vocational history would indicate that his behavior is characterized by in-
activity. He dreams and appears impervious to repetitive experiences of
failure or the discouraging odds of goal attainment. Obviously, students
falling in this latter category are more difficult and exasperating clients
than their high-aspiring and high-driving intellectual peers. Certainly,
imparting information will have little influence on the frequency and
content of their dreams. The forces responsible for the existence of their
fanciful preoccupations will need to be uncovered and considered, a
complex and lengthy process indeed.

The Use of Tests in Vocational Counseling. The earlier discussion of
tests (Phase 1) focused on their utility as assessment and predictive
devices, but the use of tests in a counseling context is quite another
matter. The practice of disseminating test information indiscriminately in
a group or individual setting can be a frightening or unnerving experience for some clients. In a recent study Hills and Williams (1965) found
that reporting test results in counseling had a negligible effect insofar as
altering the client's goals or self-images were concerned. But, more
importantly, they report that rather than producing positive changes in
self-concept, "test results which differed from clients' preconceived no-

tions of themselves had a negative effect" (Hills & Williams, 1965, p. 275). Goldman's (1961) excellent and comprehensive summary of the research in this field would indicate that results are frequently contradictory and inconclusive. Some studies suggest that the use of tests in counseling *is* beneficial to the client; others, like the Hills and Williams study, yield inconsequential or negative results. The same study (Hills & Williams, 1965) suggests that whatever positive outcomes accrue as a result of counseling may well be a function of the relationships and not the test data per se. In light of their rather serious deficiencies generally and the inconclusive and disquieting findings of research, counselors need to be extremely cautious and judicious in their use of test information in the counseling process. Certainly such information should not be communicated as a matter of common practice.

Theories of Vocational Development

Despite the weaknesses of self-study data and the taxonomic insufficiencies of the occupational world, the Parsonian tradition persists. Its underlying assumption is beguilingly simple and appealing. Following increased self-awareness and occupational acuity, the client will "move" in a vocational direction that is "best" for him. The client decides, of course, what that direction will be. The major difficulty with this approach is its assumption that choosing a vocation is a totally intellectual exercise conducted at a particular point-in-time in the life of the individual. Recent theories of vocational choice have attempted to take these shortcomings into account by describing the developmental process and the personality dynamics which undergird the making of vocational choices. While promising, contemporary formulations fall short in two important respects. A number of writers (Brayfield, 1961; Slocum, 1965; Wilensky, 1963; Super, 1964) underscore the need to tie vocational development theory to cultural determinants rather than to conceptualize exclusively in terms of a universally applied developmental psychology. In effect, existing theories are premised on middle-class phenomena and do not permit generalization to the vocational behavior of those living in marginal socio-economic circumstances. In addition, few theorists attempt to breach the gap between theory and practice by interpreting the significance of their thinking and research to the harried practitioner working in the school setting. Tyler (1961) is an exception to this rule and discusses some of the implications of theory for practice while citing the need for more attempts of this kind. Until persistent and concerted efforts are made to translate theory into practice, busy practitioners are likely to find the esoteric meanderings of the vocational theorists unfathomable, and will continue to subscribe to the familiar, if anachronistic, three-step Parsonian model.

A Final Plea

Rather than condemn the concepts and practices of vocational guidance to oblivion, the need is obviously for unearthing more crucial questions and answers and not for debunking its importance or utility value. Vocational planning and development is an immensely important aspect of the life of the individual, particularly the middle-class male. More knowledge is needed, therefore, in understanding the dynamics of this process. Certainly the complexity of the current state of knowledge in the field and the needs of a large segment of the pupil population clearly indicate that the school and/or vocational counselor has a large and demanding role to play in comprehending and enhancing the vocational behavior of his clients. For the moment, however, counselors will need to rely on their own resources and intuitions in assisting their less socioeconomically fortunate charges, at least until more appropriate and valid vocational concepts are generated.

References

BAER, M. F., & ROEBER, E. C. Occupational information: the dynamics of its nature and use. Chicago: Science Research Associates, 1964.

BARRY, RUTH, & WOLF, BEVERLY. Epitaph for vocational guidance. New York: Bureau of Publications, Teachers College, Columbia University, 1962.

BARRY, RUTH, & WOLF, BEVERLY. "Should vocational guidance be junked? Yes, it certainly should be." NEA Journal, 1963, 52, 31–32.

BEILIN, H. "New research in vocational development: discussion of the papers." Personnel and Guid. J., 1963, 41, 780–782.

BOROW, H., ed., Man in a world at work. Boston: Houghton Mifflin, 1964.

BRAYFIELD, A. H. " 'Dissemination' of occupational information." Occupations, 1951, 29, 411–413.

BRAYFIELD, A. H. "Vocational counseling today." In M. S. Viteles et al., Vocational counseling, a reappraisal in honor of Donald G. Paterson. Minnesota Studies in Student Personnel Work, No. 11. Minneapolis: Univ. Minnesota Press, 1961.

CALIA, V. F. Review of Barry and Wolf's Epitaph for vocational guidance: myths, actualities, implications. Educational and Psychological Measurement, 1964, 24, 434–437.

CALIA, V. F. "The culturally deprived client: a re-formulation of the counselors' role." J. of Couns. Psychol., 1966, 13, 100–105.

COOLEY, W. W. "A computer-measurement system for guidance." Harvard Educ. Rev., 1964, 34, 559–572.

GAITHER, J. W., HACKMAN, R. B., & HAY, J. E. "Should vocational guidance be junked? No, most people need this special help." NEA Journal, 1963, 52, 31–32.

GHISELLI, E. E. *The measurement of occupational aptitude.* Berkeley: Univ. California Press, 1955.

GHISELLI, E. E. "Dimensional problems of criteria." *Journal of Applied Psychology,* 1956, *40,* 1–4. (a)

GHISELLI, E. E. "Differentiation of individuals in terms of their predictability." *Journal of Applied Psychology,* 1956, *40,* 374–377. (b)

GINZBERG, E., GINSBURG, S. W., AXELROD, S., & HERMA, J. L. *Occupational choice.* New York: Columbia Univ. Press, 1951.

GOLDMAN, L. *Using tests in counseling.* New York: Appleton-Century-Crofts, 1961.

HACKMAN, R. B. "The problem of vocational choice in vocational guidance: an essay." In J. F. Adams, ed., *Counseling and guidance, a summary view.* New York: Macmillan, 1965.

HILLS, D. A., & WILLIAMS, J. E. "Effects of test information upon self-evaluation in brief educational and vocational counseling." *J. of Couns. Psychol.,* 1965, *12,* 275–281.

HOLLAND, J. L. "A theory of vocational choice." *J. of Couns. Psychol.,* 1959, *6,* 35–45.

KIRK, BARBARA A., & MICHELS, MARJORIE E. *Occupational information in counseling, use and classification.* Palo Alto, Calif.: Consulting Psychologists Press, 1964.

KOGAN, N., & WALLACH, M. A. *Risk-taking: a study in cognition and personality.* New York: Holt, Rinehart and Winston, 1964.

KRUMBOLTZ, J. D., & THORESEN, C. E. "The effect of behavioral counseling in group and individual settings on information-seeking behavior." *J. of Couns. Psychol.,* 1964, *11,* 324–333.

LIFTON, W. M. "Social forces and guidance in the elementary school." *Vocational Guidance Quarterly,* 1963, *12,* 89–92.

MATHEWSON, R. H., & ORTON, J. W. "Vocational imagery and vocational maturity of high school students." *J. of Couns. Psychol.,* 1963, *10,* 384–388.

MCCLELLAND, D. C. *Interest in risky occupations among subjects with high achievement motivation.* Unpublished manuscript, Harvard Univ., 1956.

PACE, C. R., & STERN, G. G. "An approach to the measurement of psychological characteristics of college environments." *J. of Educ. Psychol.,* 1958, *49,* 269–277.

PARSONS, F. *Choosing a vocation.* Boston: Houghton Mifflin, 1908.

RIESMAN, D. *The lonely crowd: a study of the changing American character.* New Haven, Conn.: Yale Univ. Press, 1956.

RUSALEM, H. "New insights on the role of occupational information in counseling." *J. of Couns. Psychol.,* 1954, *1,* 84–88.

RYAN, T. ANTOINETTE, & KRUMBOLTZ, J. D. "Effect of planned reinforcement counseling on client decision-making behavior." *J. of Couns. Psychol.,* 1964, *11,* 315–323.

SAMLER, J. "The school and self-understanding." *Harvard Educ. Rev.,* 1965, *35,* 55–70.

SAYLER, R. C. "In defense of vocational guidance." *Vocational Guidance Quarterly,* 1964, *13,* 66–69.

SLOCUM, W. L. "Occupational careers in organizations: a sociological perspective." *Personnel and Guid. J.,* 1965, *43,* 858–866.

SUPER, D. E. "A developmental approach to vocational guidance: recent theory and results." *Vocational Guidance Quarterly,* 1964, *13,* 1–10.

SUPER, D. E., & CRITES, J. O. *Appraising vocational fitness.* New York: Harper, 1962.

THORNDIKE, R. L. "The prediction of vocational success." *Vocational Guidance Quarterly,* 1963, *11,* 179–187.

TIEDEMAN, D. V. Review of Barry and Wolf's "Epitaph for vocational guidance: myths, actualities, implications." *Contemporary Psychology,* 1963, *8,* 331–332.

TYLER, LEONA. "The future of vocational guidance." In M. S. Viteles *et al., Vocational counseling: a reappraisal in honor of Donald G. Paterson.* Minnesota Studies in Student Personnel Work, No. 11. Minneapolis: Univ. Minnesota Press, 1961.

VITELES, M. S. "Psychological perspectives in vocational guidance." In M. S. Viteles, *et al., Vocational counseling: a reappraisal in honor of Donald G. Paterson.* Minnesota Studies in Student Personnel Work, No. 11. Minneapolis: Univ. Minnesota Press, 1961.

WILENSKY, H. L. "Orderly careers and social participation: the impact of work history on social integration in the middle class." *Amer. Sociol. Rev.,* 1963, *26,* 521–539.

ZILLER, R. C. "Vocational choice and utility for risk." *J. of Couns. Psychol.,* 1957, *4,* 61–64.

37. Technological Change and Vocational Counseling

Joseph Samler

In actuality we are concerned with the effects of more than automation. If nearly all work requires considerable skill, if the individual loses his job and has to find another kind of work, if he is out of work for long periods or faces permanent unemployment, it makes little difference to him whether the cause was the installation of automatic equipment, the introduction of a computer to control and make decisions for the automatic machinery, a science fiction-type of development in transmission of information for industrial processes, or the emergence of a new or different product or service.

TECHNOLOGICAL CHANGE: THREAT AND PROMISE

The literature on technological change and its effects is exciting and frightening. It is strange to come across the strong adjectives in the pertinent literature. Thus "the capabilities of these devices are unlimited. They contain extraordinary implications for the emancipation and en-

Joseph Samler, "Technological Change and Vocational Counseling," from *Automation: The Threat and the Promise,* edited by G. D. Miller and E. D. Swanson, pp. 57–78. Copyright © 1964 by the American Personnel and Guidance Association, Inc., Washington, D.C. Reprinted by permission.

slavement of mankind" (Michael, 1962). Wolfbein (1962), in whose writing it is usually quite difficult to find the emotionally loaded word, states, "From the public point of view the implications become enormous." A Presidential Advisory Committee (1962) refers to the "infinite promise of automation and technological advance."

THE WORLD'S GOODS BUT FEW JOBS

The conviction grows that these seeming hyperboles are not that at all, that they are much closer to specific description than exaggeration. The capsules verify this point.

Automatic machines, linked by transfer equipment, move engine blocks through a complete manufacturing process, performing 530 precision cutting and drilling operations in 14½ minutes as compared to 9 hours in a conventional plant (Seligman, 1962).

. . . an automatic lathe . . . which gauges each part as it is produced and automatically resets the cutting tools to compensate for tool wear. In addition, when the cutting tools have been worn down to a certain predetermined limit, the machine automatically replaces them with sharp tools. The parts are automatically loaded onto the machine and are automatically unloaded as they are finished. These lathes can be operated for 5 to 8 hours without attention, except for an occasional check to make sure that parts are being delivered to the loading mechanism (Michael, 1962).

In petroleum and chemicals, the story is almost ancient: as far back as 1949 catalytic cracking plants were turning out 41,000 barrels a day with instruments and only a few workers to watch gauges. In a Texaco refinery the computer controls 26 flow rates, 72 temperatures, 3 pressure levels, and 3 gas combinations (Seligman, 1962).

Ribbon machines make 800 electric bulb blanks a minute running without end, and requiring only one worker who stands by to make an occasional adjustment (Seligman, 1962).

The R. H. Macy Co. is trying out its first electronic sales girl. This machine is smart enough to dispense 36 different items in 10 separate styles and sizes. It accepts one- and five-dollar bills in addition to coins and returns the correct change plus rejecting counterfeit currency (Michael, 1962).

In the electrical industry, output increased 21 per cent between 1953 and 1961, while employment declined 10 per cent.

The following changes occurred in a large bakery after the installation of new automatic equipment: One man operates the equipment that moves 20 tons of flour an hour from railway cars to bins, compared with 24 men who used to move 50 tons of flour into the plant in 5 to 6 hours. In the bread-baking department, the number of workers on each shift was reduced 50 per cent and capacity was increased 75 per cent. Jobs in the wrapping department were cut 70 per cent while there was a 75 per cent rise in capacity (Krantz, 1964).

With the aid of an electronic-computer installation for the Bank of America's mortgage and installment-loan operation, 100 employees are now doing the work of 300.

In the assembly of television components at the Admiral Corp., condensers, resistors, wire jumpers and tube sockets are inserted mechanically. By using automatic insertion and printed circuits, over 400 hand-soldered connections are eliminated.

A completely automatic plant is producing mixed and ready-to-use concrete for the Cleveland Builders' Supply Company. Operated from an electronic control panel, the plant can produce and load into ready-mix trucks any one of some 1500 different mixing formulas that may be demanded. This automatic plant has a capacity of 200 cubic yards of concrete per hour and it uses no manual labor at any point in the process (AFL-CIO, 1962).

Aside from the doubtful miracle of agricultural productivity and farm labor, nothing is more compelling than what has happened in the coal mines. Fifty years ago 700,000 American miners were able to mine less coal than 140,000 dig today. The prospect is that by 1980 coal production may double without any increase in the number of miners (Caudill).

From these instances and many that are similar the conclusion seems clear that unemployment inevitably accompanies technological change. Although this seems to be the preponderant opinion the conclusion is too facile. Conservative economists, Brozen for example, urge that automation makes as many jobs as it does away with. Perhaps the considered attitude is Gross's, that the resulting unemployment is uncertain but it is certain that automation leads to displacement. When the assembly line worker in Des Moines loses his job as a result of technological change, it does not help him to know that in Chicago someone was hired as a programmer or computer serviceman. But the extent of such new employment is not known. Despite the many books and articles, hard data are not available. "The Manpower Revolution," states the Report of the Subcommittee on Employment and Manpower (1964), "like the industrial revolution, is first and foremost the product of technological change. The nature of this change, however, is little understood, even by those who have had most to do with it."

This is presumably why extensive research in this area is being financed by the Office of Manpower, Automation, and Training, and why a Presidential Commission outside government has been appointed to study the impact of automation on production and employment.

This is the frightening part of what is before us. The loss of job, the inability to find work, the assignment of fault by the individual to himself, the seeping away of self respect, the need to live on a minimum budget or to have to scrounge for food and shelter, these make up the fear.

A NEW AND DIFFERENT KIND OF LIFE

But it also holds infinite promise. Since the gates of Eden closed and man has had to earn his bread the hard way, he has longed for time and energy to explore his own humanity. Gross puts it epigrammatically in urging that the purpose of the machine is to free man from having to behave like a machine.

Technology is a most potent agent for social change. Yesterday's history relates what happened following a much milder form of what we now face. The industrial revolution put man into the factory and brought about mass production. Luxury was made possible for more than a limited few. The machine replaced the slave and the slave came closer to assuming the attributes of his humanity. Today's reduction in hunger, alleviation of disease, increase of the life span, are the results of science and technology. But, sociologists are quick to point out that the innovations of technology brought new problems to the fore. The incredible toll of human life on our highways resulted from the invention of the automobile; mass production resulted in the alienation of man from himself on the assembly line.

A tremendous portal is swinging open. And with its opening other doors further on are at least unlocked. What is the prospect? The child of today as a productive citizen will be trained to optimum capacity but will be employed for a twenty-hour week. He will travel to the furthest part of the world in hours at minimum cost. His inexpensive clothing, made of miracle fibers, will be discarded after being worn a few times. Away from home, he will communicate with family and friends by wristwatch receiver and transmitter. At his desk or from the public booth his telephone call will be visual as well as aural. He may still call it a library but in fact it will be a central information retrieval center and he will get the reading he wants at home through his viewer. If the family tires of this there is always TV, wall sized, in color and three dimensions. His world will use fuel cells for portable electric power; solar energy will be available; nuclear power will produce more than is put into it for a wide variety of purposes including travel at least to the moon. The incredible laser beam will have opened new fields of knowledge and will be widely applied. Through 24-hour a day satellites, no part of the world will ever be isolated again. The oceans will be farmed and the ocean bottoms mined. Micro-organisms will be used widely in industry. DNA will have begun to yield its secrets and the control of genetic characteristics will be on its way.[1]

Is this fantasy? Its beginnings are all around us. Moreover, since the rate of accretion of knowledge is increasing, the picture is modest; we cannot note what is around the corner; and we will yet turn many corners.

TO FIND OURSELVES

What then will confront man? The problem may be one of a leisure which will be unwelcome to many and which others will be unable to use productively. Nevertheless, the leisure will be there and with it the

[1] Most of these ideas come from Seaborg, G. T. Chairman, U.S. Atomic Energy Commission.

chance after all these centuries, to open yet a further door and for man to explore the illimitable areas within himself. These are ranges and depths as yet unexplored and unknown. What a leisured class built upon slave labor could do in ancient Greece in the arts and in philosophy, a society built upon machine labor, with greater resources and accumulated knowledge can emulate and perhaps surpass.

The hope is held out that far from being an aristocratic elite, the new leisure class will be democratic in composition and temper. With increasing time to himself, man is more than ever in need of improved taste, more diversified interests, more constructive social values, a more active sense of citizenship, and higher individual ideals. We have no measure of human potentialities for the use of leisure because they have never before had adequate consideration in mass education. The time has come for broader and deeper cultivation of the arts, sciences, and humanities. Imaginatively taught, they can help toward understanding urgent public questions and give a meaningful direction to the use of leisure.

The problem in at least one important area is self-fulfillment, and work is not necessarily the only way for this achievement. There is evidence that nearly all of us do not know how to believe in ourselves except through work for pay. Beyond a kind of satisfied complaining we do not believe it is right to use leisure for more than temporary relief from work. If we trace the connections through the centuries the man-made nature of these sancrosanct and deeply held beliefs becomes quite clear. Thus very many who are out of work feel guilty and unworthy. It is a by-word that many who retire from work feel useless and out of the stream of life.

The Emerging Labor Force

THE MANPOWER REVOLUTION

The primary function of the vocational counselor in performing his task is to help the individual relate to the working world. It has been carried out well in relatively few instances. For identifiable reasons duties in vocational counseling have become second class. The therapeutic function, involvement in personality dynamics, has become the preferred mode. Brayfield (1961), Tyler (1961), and the present writer (1964) have urged that close and constant appraisal and understanding of the working world is the core of the vocational counselor's contribution. This does not mean that this is not a psychological task. The view of the worker as more than an economic entity, as it is perfectly obvious he is, requires psychological insight and understanding at a sophisticated level.

In a relatively stable industrial setting, in which, for example, the blacksmith had a generation to adapt to the disappearance of his trade, it was possible for the counselor to pay pro forma attention only to the working world, its requirements, its satisfactions and the variability of both in different kinds of work. That world is fast disappearing. For the specific client, it will be critically important for the counselor to know that the work setting of the console operator is such that here and there he is requiring "lonesome pay."

The nature of the technological change is first on the list of counselor understandings. Chief among these is understanding of the impending manpower revolution. This is no longer a term used for its dramatic effect. It appears and reappears in the literature and is carried as a basic title in the ten volumes of the Hearings of the Sub-committee on Employment and Manpower (1963). The concerns of vocational counselors flow from these data.

This is a revolution with a history as the following data reveal (Wolfbein, 1961):

	Percent of Labor Force		
	1910	1950	1960
All workers	100%	100%	100%
White collar	22	37	43
Professional & Technical	5	9	11
Proprietary & Managerial	7	9	11
Clerical and Sales	10	19	21
Blue Collar	37	41	36
Skilled	12	14	13
Semi-Skilled	14	21	18
Unskilled	11	6	5
Service	10	10	13
Farm	31	12	8

The white collar worker's rise to a plurality position is clearly revealed. Also quite evident are the enormous inroads into unskilled nonfarm labor as well as into the farm labor force. The stability of the skilled craftsmen group as a whole (but not for all occupations in it) is a point important to counselors and their clients. Current observation and projections for the decade ahead measure this swift tide.

The President's Manpower Report (1964) carrying the Labor Departments revised interim estimates informs us that the total population is expected to increase from 181 million in 1960 to 226 million in 1975 with a concomitant increase in the labor force from 73 million in 1960 to 93 million in 1975. Professional, technical and kindred workers will increase from 7.5 million in 1960 to 12.4 million in 1975 for an incredible increase of 65 per cent. Laborers (except farm and mine workers) will decrease in their proportion of the total labor force from 5.5 per cent to 4.3 per cent. Agricultural workers, already the most outstanding example of technological change, will decrease a further 28 per cent. Service workers are projected to increase from 8.3 million to 12.5 million. The increase in operatives and kindred workers of only 18 per cent is considerably less than the increase in the total labor force. The same point, though less dramatically, can be made relative to salesworkers.

It is data of this character that impelled the President's Manpower Report (1964) to note that "important shifts of manpower are in process with forced readjustment for large numbers of workers and serious implications for the education and training both of the present work force and of young people still in school."

If, as is clear, mechanical means more and more will replace human muscles, what happens to unskilled and semi-skilled workers? The answer is that there will be fewer and fewer jobs for them. The pattern this group will follow is exemplified in the history of agricultural labor. Unlike the story of farm labor, however, much depends on whether the economy as a whole is in sound shape. If there is a comfortable margin of income, needs will emerge, very possibly leading to work opportunities for this group as waiters, bartenders, cooks, gardeners, home maintenance men, retaining wall builders, home carpenters, and the like.

THE HIGH PREMIUM ON TRAINING AND SKILL

At the other end of the distribution is the fantastic story of what has happened and will continue to happen to professional and technical personnel. The occupational pattern in 1900 which showed one of every three male workers employed as laborer on or off the farm required a relatively low degree of educational attainment by the labor force. This is contrasted with a job pattern that showed in 1960 one in three male workers engaged as either a professional and technical person or a skilled craftsman and, therefore, requiring a significantly higher degree of education in the labor force (Wolfbein, 1964).

The Labor Department (1964) reports that more training is required for the maintenance positions where technological changes have been made because a combination of electronic, electro-mechanical and sometimes even hydraulic operations are involved. For this reason many instrument repairmen and business machine servicemen need post-high school education in engineering fundamentals, mechanics, or electronics, in addition to intensive occupational training. The Report states that maintenance electricians and appliancemen will need more technical education in order to handle a growing number and variety of electronic devices. In the scientific and engineering professions, aside from accretions of knowledge in all fields, new specialties have come into being, for instance, cryogenics, bionics, ultrasonics, computer technology, and micro-electronics.

When in the new world of technological change the employment trend is analyzed occupation by occupation in terms of probable job requirements, or, and this should not be discounted, of employer predis-positions, the basic direction of the requirement for workers with more education and greater skill is quite, perhaps disconcertingly, clear. The point concerning employer predispositions is made at some hazard. In terms of job skills it is not really known that high school graduation is a necessity; it may be that properly or not employers have bought the idea that this is so. Perhaps many of these jobs could be accomplished by non-high school graduates. Looking at it the other way, the uncomfortable question arises whether if the 7,500,000 youth estimated to leave school in the decade prior to high school graduation, did indeed stay in school, where would their jobs come from?

Another way of opening up the relationship between training and skills and employment is through assessing the situation of the unem-ployed. The relationship is only too clear. For 1963 three quarters of male professionals worked an entire year at full-time jobs as did two-thirds of male white collar workers. However, this is true for only one-third of laborers. In 1963 the average unemployment rate for the nation was 5.7. For the 14–19 age group it was 15.6. The deficiencies in the education and training of Negroes is too well known to require comment. It should not be surprising, therefore, to find that the unemployment rate for this group, for 1963, is more than twice that of white workers. Comparison of unemployment rates between high school graduates and dropouts rein-forces the same unhappy point. The data reveal that only 8 per cent of the graduates but 14 per cent of the dropouts were unemployed. This group, The President's Manpower Report notes, are likely to form the nucleus of the future hard-core unemployed.

Wolfbein (1962) states that "whether it be the unskilled or semi-skilled, the young school dropout, or the older man who also has a high rate of long term unemployment, one of the great common denominators which ties them all together is lack of skill."

THE EMERGING COUNSELING PROBLEMS

THE MEANING OF OCCUPATIONAL INFORMATION

All of this is the new background for viewing the work of the voca-tional counselor. A number of issues will be presented that bear on his work and on the profession. The counseling issues selected for attention flow out of the special problems presented by technological change and the manpower revolution. Normal counseling activities—helping clients in their development toward self determination and in assuming responsibility for self—are taken as understood.

Counselors need labor market data about the changing occupational structure and authoritative analyses about the nature of the job. This means not only that they require the tried and true items reasonably well carried in the standard occupational brochures, but also psychological and social characteristics of various occupations.

For example, the informed commentators on the automated scene report a reversal of the trend to decentralize managerial decisions. Moreover, the range of determinations now made by middle management can be made more authoritatively and very much more quickly on the basis of computer treatment of data (Anshen, 1962). Its import for the counselor lies in the information he provides the bright young men heading for business and industry whose career lines include stages in junior executive and middle management echelons.

The data shows that the need for skilled craftsmen is stable and point to a projected net increase of 2.3 millions in skilled workers for the decade with a total need of 5 million, taking into account skilled men leaving the occupation (Wolfbein, 1961).

The outlook for most of the skilled worker occupations is optimistic. The same point may or may not be made, for instance, about the service occupations. It is demonstrable that jobs associated with eating out, the protective service, and health service occupations have been increasing. Will they continue to increase? Will technological change and automation affect these occupations? We do not know, we cannot be sure. What is certain is that in helping the individual evaluate the educational and occupational choices before him, the counselor must have available for him current and sound information, including identification of what is not known.

We are becoming aware of the need to identify the psycho-social aspects of work—for instance, the particular culture of the shop, the status characteristics of a given position, the way in which personality needs can be met in an identified work setting. It is important that these understandings be sought for the new range of occupations and work settings. The "lonesome pay" of the dial watcher referred to earlier is a case in point. The fact that the skilled maintenance worker will be relating much more to machines than to fellow workers is another. Another is the intolerance of the equipment to allow for the coffee or cigarette break or just plain goofing off for brief periods. All these and others may affect worker satisfaction as much or more than pay, hours, or advancement possibilities. With new work settings and work structure affected, the whole area of job satisfaction must be re-examined. With job change, according to some authorities, much more the rule than the exception, what happens to the personality-based drive for security by some clients? All of this is important to the counselor not only in terms of the considerations to be put before his client but also because a proportion of those who are dissatisfied and unhappy at work may turn up in his office.

TRAINING TO OPTIMUM CAPACITY

This issue has to do with the problem of optimum use of human potential. The need in the economy not only for skilled personnel but also for high level skills seems quite clear. Noting that automation requires trained and educated people in unprecedented numbers, Drucker (1955) estimates that the quantitative need alone will be so great that eight or ten million college students expected fifteen years hence will be barely sufficient. He cites a large manufacturing company which estimates that after it is automated it will need *seven thousand college graduates* a year just to keep going; today it hires three hundred annually. A current Bureau of Labor Statistics study for the National Science Foundation reveals that fewer than 765,000 newly trained scientists and engineers will become available to fill more than one million openings for them between 1960 and 1970.

That the economic rewards are there for the individual who uses himself truly to capacity seems reasonable to assume. This is reinforced, moreover, by psychological tenets that it is self-fulfilling for the individual to use his capacities as fully as possible.

The question for the counselor and the profession is to what extent this should become a value commitment held in awareness, put on the table with the counselee, and strongly supported by the counselor? Before this point is reached, should it be decided affirmatively, there is much that can be done in counseling. For example, when support of training is involved as in rehabilitation programs, budget tends to set limits on the extent of training to be provided, if training is to be provided at all. Minimum employment goals are set, at relatively low skill levels, for the perfectly understandable reason that in this way more people will be served. There is no problem here that increased budget will not solve. The same reasoning precisely is applicable to providing funds for scholarships and student loans. There are other and serious complexities here, to be sure, but this formal part of the problem at least is capable of solution.

The principle of realization of potential requires that the talented baccalaureate science major go on to his doctoral degree. It also calls for realization of maximum skills on lower levels. It is applicable on all levels, and for all groups. It has reference to youth with high potential who should go on to college but whose expectations are far different. It is pertinent with the members of special groups—women, the disabled, members of disadvantaged minorities. With all of these and others, there is the opportunity to increase our resource of manpower skills.

PLANNING WHAT CANNOT BE PLANNED

Another aspect of training to optimum capacity may be said to be training to diverse capacity, perhaps to capacity in each of a number of different lines. The point made by various observers in this context relates to the need to plan for change, as a result of technological innovations (Diebold, 1962; President's Manpower Report, 1964). One way of meeting this problem is to avoid emphasis on specific skills and to develop instead basic capabilities. To the extent that this means emphasis, for instance, on the underlying principles of science, on a wide acquaintance with the humanities, it is quite clear. If industry were to assume responsibility for more than vestibule training the schools could limit themselves to so-called basics. But how far industry is willing or able to go is indeterminate as are the difficult definitions of what is general training and what more specific. Also inevitability of change can be communicated as a matter of basic attitude, of mind-set and expectancy. However, we ought to be more certain at least of our thinking before we start to implement in program terms, which in any case may present more problems than are allowed for in the theoretical position. There is thinking which at its extreme seems to say that there is no sense in specific vocational planning, for instance, in adolescence, since we do not know what kinds of work will be available when training is completed. However, it is most doubtful that the change will be so great for the majority of work, as to make the occupational picture unrecognizable.

When there are few clear leads for training and eventual occupation it has always been sound practice in counseling to advise young counseling clients to delay any forced choice. When he is unable to decide which fork of the road to take, it makes good sense for the individual to stick to the main road as long as possible. The clear advantage here is that such persons can complete high school and go on to college, opening up new possibilities for them.

Stripped to its bare bones, counseling can be seen as helping the individual confronted with a problem to weigh the choices available to him for its solution. So regarded, it also ought to be clear that in any single problem situation: change of job, choice of "track" in high school, dropping out of school, choice of college, meeting seemingly inordinate parental demands, and many others, much more is involved than merely the solution for the immediate problem. If the experience is attended to in terms of the basic process, it becomes a learning situation for attacking other similar problems—it becomes the model. Probably we have not deliberately used counseling for choice-making to foster learning in how to make choices, but the need seems inescapable. This learning is in itself, and for obvious reasons, highly desirable. Thus, the individual helped initially with a choice-making problem can face the question of job change whenever it occurs, in travail to be sure, but at least knowing that there is a way to attack it and that he has the ability to do so. The immediate difference may be between despair and discomfort. The more important difference relates to personal growth and maturity. This exposure to learning choice making is also necessary because the alternative is very difficult: to provide counseling service at every job change, at every point where more than ephemeral problems are involved.

CLIENT DEVELOPMENT THROUGH TRAINING

The long-range solutions to the vocational adjustment problems facing underprivileged youth lie in prevention. While the counselor is greatly concerned, he has no mortgage on the problem. Indeed it is a heartbreaking problem, and to say that the schools need to change is to say very little. Basically, the community should change through achieving greater understanding, diminishing distrust, providing opportunity, and making the values it professes to offer to such youth capable of achievement. If these community changes are effected, the school's problems may prove to be capable of solution. In these circumstances, the counselor's role is perhaps mainly that of agent, presumably more specifically trained than are others in understanding the perceptions and protest of today's underprivileged and bitter teenagers. We may yet have to learn the hard way under the lash of riots, as has happened recently in a number of cities.

As an agent for change the school counselor can attempt to help others construct the educational experience which in terms of the need for basic social change, still seems a second best approach. In the absence of such change in orientation and values of Negro youth as will overnight help them to adjust to the school as it is now, systematic efforts should be made and are in fact being made, to adjust the educational situation to fit more closely the needs of disadvantaged youth.

One such important but neglected possibility is the work-study program. Long known and never sufficiently extended, this is a program that the counselor can initiate, push, and assist with. In addition to providing a better framework for learning, work assignments carefully selected may be for many the first specific instance of systematic assistance extended to disadvantaged youth by the major culture.

Whether it is through a work-study program, the array of training courses available under the Manpower Development and Training Act, the courses and experiences in the skill development centers under the Economic Opportunity Act of 1964, or the usual school program, one major role of the counselor is well established. This is to assist the client in his development by helping him select and enter that school or course of training most appropriate to his developmental level and needs. There is involved in this process a body of theory and a methodology on the basis of which the individual is helped to assess in his own interests the various choices available to him. This is a simple sounding statement, but trained personnel are aware of the complexities it carries. The least ambitious information the counselor must have is comprehensive knowledge of resources, in this case training resources. Since increasing the range of choices is part of the counseling task, and since the client cannot choose what he does not know about, not to have such information is inimical to the client's needs.

THE "UNMOTIVATED" CLIENT

The prescriptions for success explicit and covert in the culture—to achieve is to be respected, success follows hard work, to be "someone" one must be popular—are frequently enough unreal, even though education will continue to be a great highway for achievement and status for many. For others, many underprivileged minority group youth, the promises seem only false. It is essential to provide tremendous programs of the kind authorized in the 1964 Economic Opportunity Act and under MDTA. Many have been selected for classes under Manpower Development and Training and no doubt there will be considerable numbers of applicants when the recruiting offices are opened under the 1964 Act. But what of those who do not apply? On the face of it they are different from youth interested enough to apply, follow through, leave home if necessary, and subject themselves to a discipline of training.

Those who do not apply are in the situation of the unwilling client, a problem consistently and quite successfully ducked by counselors. In fact, one criterion for successful counseling is said to be the willingness of the client to seek help. It is difficult to separate the unwilling from the unidentified. These are not students who knock on the counselor's door. If seen at all, they are seen in the exit-interview, generally too late to do anything. Many in this group may not even reach the secondary school. Nearly all, in all probability, are in the two and a half million who in this decade will not complete the eighth grade. Whether it is part of counseling role actively to seek out proper applicants, pursue case finding, and be more than only responsive is a very important question. No pat answer to a most difficult problem is intended in these lines, only underscoring of the problem and the strong urging that it receive attention. Essentially this is a problem in motivation. Seen this way, its difficulties become more evident since we know that no person can be motivated for another. How then is motivation energized? How are the presumable threats to productive functioning removed? How can we help youngsters with no significant experience in the validity of planning for oneself make the sacrifices in the present which investment in the future may require?

Concern with the unmotivated person is by no means limited to youth. Two instances cited by Gross are salutary. In the first instance, 433 employees were made idle when Armour & Co. closed its Oklahoma City plant. We need to focus attention on the fact that of 433 employees, only 170 applied for retraining. That of the 170, only 58 qualified is especially important for us and will be discussed later.

The second disconcerting experience, and surely they can be multiplied many times, occurred in Bridgeport, Conn., when of a total of 2143 invited for interviews to select trainees, 1550 showed up, of whom 441 said they were not interested and 201 failed to appear for a qualifying test. Out of 2143, therefore, 1235 were not interested or did not follow through.

The individual's experiences with the agency offering the training opportunities are of moment here; at least his perceptions of his experiences with the agent are an important consideration. For example, if his relationships have been unhappy and hostile, lack of response to an offer would be understandable. If this is generalized to stand for the individual's life experiences and the meanings he has attached to them, a great deal (but not all) of the mystery of lack of motivation might be explicated. With the economically and socially disadvantaged, basically this is a societal problem but to an extent, counseling can help through group and individual procedures. Perhaps a beginning will be made under the Economic Opportunity Act through the Youth Advisor program. According to the official releases the Youth Advisor position was created to reach out "to young people in disadvantaged environments who have never been in a local employment office and whose aspirations and motivations do not include training for or holding a job." No doubt the interest, sincerity, even youth, of the Advisors will result in some good things. However, on the face of it, this is a job for personnel at a very high level of competence and training.

QUALIFYING FOR TRAINING: THE DOUBTFUL ABSOLUTES

Even with the best we are ready and, perhaps, able to do, the outcome is quite uncertain. Taking into account the skill requirements of the labor force thirty years hence, and contrasting the progress made by white and Negro in education, Bell believes and underscores the serious point (stating that he is perhaps overdramatizing in order to highlight the case) that class society in the U.S. will be predominantly color society. In supporting his fear, he pulls together data in part already reviewed in this paper concerning the great proportion of lower class jobs occupied by Negroes, the high rate of functional illiteracy in the group, the high proportion of Negroes among school dropouts, and their high loading among the unemployed. It is the possibility of this hazard that requires the utmost in efforts and expenditures, indeed, as Bell fears, if there is time to do so.

Of the 170 who applied for training when the Armour plant closed, only 58 qualified. In the Bridgeport, Conn. experience, of 388 that were tested, 140 qualified. In each case about two thirds failed to qualify. These instances should stand as thoughtful reminders of the qualification hurdles we have set up almost universally for entrance into training and for employment. They should stand as reminders for our orthodox professional living, wherein we hew to hypotheses as principles and to our ways of thinking as immutable. This issue can be made as dramatic as anyone wishes, the point being that more likely than not it is counselors who determine the qualification standards.

It is possible to be very discouraged at the manpower prospect. On the one hand, the new technological world will demand great capacity and much skill. This is encapsulation, of course, and inevitable variation will occur but let us accept it as generally true. On the other hand, there is the given distribution of capacities and abilities. In a world with few work outlets for the minimally talented, what is to happen with the lower end of the distribution? At any given cut-off point there are very sizable numbers involved. Those who were found not qualified in the Armour and Bridgeport instances presumably fall in this group. Their name may be legion.

These questions have been raised before, somewhat tentatively, for instance, by Auman (1962), Bell (1962), and Gross. As far as is known to the present writer, they have not been raised so to speak within the family or very directly.

The problem of training qualifications and standards should be put on the line. We say that youngsters in the IQ range of 60–75 generally cannot learn to read material beyond the third or fourth grade level. We really mean that given present teaching conditions and methods and our strong beliefs in the sanctity of the Wechsler or the Stanford-Binet, the boy so described will not learn to read beyond a given grade. This instance should stand for all situations where particular instruments or a given methodology instruct us about the appropriate prediction and serve to shut the admissions door. It is quite understandable that we tend to forget that the truths we have are provisional by definition.

The question (and Diebold asks it also in his paper) has to do with the extent to which a person can be retrained and what the critical variables are. Suppose in the case of the retarded we had classes of 3 or 4 rather than 10 or 12; suppose retraining was on an on-the-job basis rather than mostly in a classroom, what might happen then? We know too much now to defend the position that human capacities are fixed. McClelland's work on supplying achievement motives is well known although it does not yet seem to have caught on. Bruner (1960) feels that any subject matter can be taught effectively in some intellectually honest form to any child at any stage of development. Even if we discount the reports of education in Russia, the effects on children's learning of assigned role and implicit expectations cannot be dismissed.

The responsibility of counselors lies in the fact that very frequently we are the people who hold the keys. We unlock the doors. The comforting labels of "false positive" and "false negative" only express our doubt. None of our educational and counseling practices should be beyond questioning. The point is not that with different premises, new approaches, and other techniques we will accomplish miracles but that *some* change *can* be brought about. Aptitudes and capacities are trainable up to a point. Whatever it is, intelligence may or may not be genetic but its development is strictly a product of culture as are the instruments that measure its functioning. Even modest increases in aptitudes and capacities would greatly ease the training problem.

COUNSELING FOR THE SOCIAL STRUCTURE

Somewhere in his development the professional faces a difficult problem. Given a monopoly by society, a profession can address itself to its technical and professional problems: maintaining standards, furthering knowledge, policing itself, and serving its public. As it reaches maturity it begins to be concerned with the social context in which the work of the profession is done. This is the situation of the nuclear physicists with respect to nuclear discoveries or psychologists in international peace. Is counseling psychology approaching such a crossroad in its development? We do not hold a mortgage in worrying about manpower problems, the country's welfare, or its future. But our task has to do with the optimum use of potential in work, the opportunity to be productive, securing as great a measure of satisfaction from job and life as possible. Therefore, we are warranted in being particularly alert to what is going on in the economy and to offer considered opinion on social programs. There will be many who will disagree.

There is plenty of cause for worry. In addition to the profound effects of technological change, 26 million new young workers are coming into the labor force in this decade. Short of full employment and an unemployment rate a good two percentage points lower than it is now, where will these young people work? Should counseling personnel address themselves to this problem and make themselves articulate about it? Should we say, with advice from economists, that the private sector cannot do it all? Should we urge as a profession that government must cushion the effects of technological change and of this tremendous increase, 40 per cent more than in the last decade, in the number of young workers?

If we get into a bind as well we may, what should be our stand relative to women workers? One third of the labor force is made up of women and in many settings their work may be greatly affected by technological change. It is not unlikely that the major focus of retraining will be for men as the family breadwinners. In such an eventuality should we concur? Should our special awareness of the need for talent compel us to urge special provisions for marriage-career patterns for women? Would this mean that we should take a definite stand about basic preparation prior to child bearing? If and when the work-week is shortened, the problem of women at work will be easier to solve. But even now are there career patterns that might utilize the hours at home of trained and capable women? There must be such possibilities—art illustration and limited practice of medicine, come quickly to mind as possibilities.

There are other minority groups. The disabled, in the perceptions of employers and for a complex of reasons nearly always marginal workers, present a mixed picture. To the extent that work becomes more sedentary —e.g., console operator, quality controller, systems analysts, programmer—physically handicapped workers will be less disadvantaged. On the other hand the set convictions of many employers operating in a relatively free labor market may work against their employment. Presently rehabilitation programs which emphasize narrow training aiming at highly specific jobs will need revaluation. It also seems clear that those with histories of serious emotional problems as well as the physically handicapped who have made a more or less sound adjustment at work, may be quite troubled at the challenge of change and at change itself. It is hardly necessary to reiterate that in harvesting high skills we cannot afford to neglect a resource that has proved itself many times. This is as true of course, for women workers and racial or ethnic minority group members as for the disabled.

There is no problem brought about by technological change that cannot be solved under full employment. The question is, will we have full employment? Informed opinion is that we will not. The question for counselors is whether, from our very special position, we should add our testimony concerning the need for government intervention in extending employment possibilities. We can do a certain amount of table pounding or we can maintain a passive role. As a discipline we have come out of the school system, a sector not particularly articulate about social needs. It would be unfortunate if we maintained a dignified academic distance.

In taking a stand we will have to consider the nation's unmet needs at least in health services, recreation, housing, and education. Through government support these needs can be the basis for important employment programs. It is almost fortunate, Gunnar Myrdal (1963) states, that we have such tremendous amounts of work to be done in our economy. The idea has to be faced that these may be permanent or at least extended programs, and that they should take various forms, as part of ambitious work-study plans on a secondary, post secondary, and college level. They might be limited to particular age groups: the older, very young, minority groups, or disabled. They could be used for try-out purposes as part of long range motivational exposure, as an aspect of counseling and education.

THE TRUTHS WE DO NOT HAVE

Much of what we do in guidance and counseling, not only in the express train rush of the emerging programs, but also in our long term work in schools and hospitals, is based on hypothesis and supposition. This is not to tear our work down but to be realistic about it. Very much the same thing can be said about nearly all disciplines in the social services, for instance, psychotherapy and social work. The problem is that our sciences are young and unsophisticated and our object of concern is man in all his complexity. The fact is that many look to us for help. Clients do so by definition, but so do the policy makers.

All of this underscores our need for finding out what works, under what conditions, to what ends, and lest we get lost in empiricism—why it works, and how we can evolve methodology for ends we predetermine. The object in this, as in other sciences, is to learn how to control and predict, and to do all this, moreover, with freedom for the individual. This must be one of the most difficult tasks in the world.

Of the large charters and huge funds becoming available to us some part, relatively it will be very small, should be set aside for research. This need not mean that every worker, from newly appointed counselor-aide to head of program, should be engaged in research some part of his time. The opinion is ventured that it will be enough if they maintain a scientific spirit about what they do and how they do it. The job of research should be done by personnel qualified to do so, conversant with the problems of counseling, skillful and ingenious in methodology, and aware of problems in most urgent need of attention. There are parallels for this kind of orientation in medicine and psychotherapy.

THE PROBLEMS OF BEING IN CHARGE

Support of guidance and counseling has become national policy. It is evidenced in hearing the Assistant Secretary of Labor say so in a public address (Moynihan, 1964), or the Secretary of Labor making a comprehensive manpower policy depend in part on "an effective vocational guidance and counseling program beginning in the elementary school," or even the President of the United States making the same point in an official communication to the Congress.

Looking back it becomes easier to see that we have been traveling along this road for some time. Financial support for guidance on a federal level has been available since 1938 when the Commissioner of Education ruled that Smith-Hughes and George-Dean funds could be used for partial support of state supervision of guidance services. However, support for guidance in the Office of Education has been something less than constant as is revealed by the abolition of the then Occupational Information and Guidance Service in 1952 and its re-establishment only under considerable pressure from APGA and APA. It is hardly possible to recognize the unit these days (now the Guidance and Counseling Program Branch) in terms of its growth in staff, added responsibilities, and presumable influence.

Legislation affecting veterans benefits in a federal, centralized, program operated in a countrywide network of regional offices and university guidance centers reveals a straight line progression with respect to counseling requirements. In 1943 in the Vocational Rehabilitation Act (for service-connected veterans) the need for vocational counseling was inferred. In successive laws, the GI Bill, the rehabilitation legislation for veterans of the Korea Conflict, and the War Orphans Educational Assistance Act, reference to vocational counseling became more and more explicit and direct. In the last law cited, educational and vocational counseling is mandatory but with considerable wisdom the counselee is not required to follow the counselor's recommendations.

More recent legislation is better known and brings us up to date. Starting with the provisions of the National Defense Education Act in 1958, the country has seen three other major legislative programs in all of which guidance and counseling not only is firmly embodied but which hold out implicit requirements for performance that now and again lead to unease. These are the Manpower Development and Training Act in 1961, the Vocational Education Act of 1963, and the staggering billion dollar Economic Opportunity Act of 1964.

The uneasy question is whether we can meet these responsibilities or whether we will be so spread that only a picture-thin veneer can be supplied. The problem is no longer one of getting a few more counselors in the program, nor how we can spread existing personnel, but how to train sufficient staff quickly and adequately enough so that the job given us can be done. We talk here not of some additional hundreds of counselors, but literally of thousands, and more probably of tens of thousands. An additional 32,000 full-time counselors are estimated to be needed between 1964 and 1967. Can this possibly be done?

The lightning has struck four times in two decades. In the 1940's and 1950's counseling was identified and liberally supported in veterans legislation. In 1954, the provisions of the Vocational Rehabilitation Act carried extensive provisions for rehabilitation counseling including the training of such personnel. In 1958, the National Defense Education Act provided budget for the enrichment of guidance services in the schools throughout the country and for the wholesale training of school counselors. Presently and inevitably the state-federal employment system must be looked to for important services on a very wide scale. There are riterated references to the need for great changes in the United States Employment Service (Subcommittee on Employment and Manpower, 1964; President's Manpower Report, 1964; AFL–CIO, 1962; President's Committee on Labor-Management, 1962), including "increased numbers of better trained and more competent employment counselors . . ." Qualifications would have to be raised as would salary levels. The burdens to be carried by the USES are enormous and all in counseling will observe with all possible interest just what does happen. No doubt there are sharp limits on what money can accomplish; the training and development of staff, however, is not one of these.

The charge given to the USES reflects the new responsibilities of all in guidance and counseling. As indicated in the new laws and official reports, there is need to provide counseling service not only to those in school, from the elementary school up, but to dropouts, young unemployed workers, those seeking training and those who do not, minority group members, displaced workers, the disabled, draft rejectees, those confronted with the apparently inevitable need to change work, and older persons. This is not a prospectus from the profession but a charter from the government. What is really startling is that the checkbook has been brought out.

Counselors are an articulate tribe and we have held out the promise of answers. Can we deliver? There is more than the discomfort of unkept promises involved here. At a number of points, policy makers seem to base their estimates of changes to be brought about—the ability to meet national needs—on availability and high quality of guidance and counseling services. If for understandable reasons we are professionally inebriated, this is or should be a sobering thought.

AND THE URGENT NEED FOR SELF EXAMINATION

We are not the neutral agents that will help smooth the way toward a new work structure, a highly trained labor force, a different society, a changed set of values and a way of life that is not the same as it has been. We are ourselves subject to these changes; we will be far from untouched.

Our own procedures in our own calling are not so immutable as to be outside investigation, and the impulse had best come from ourselves. Hull's 1928 machine or no, the computer may pattern data for us about the individual in vocational choice that just may be superior to our work. The value commitments we cherish no doubt will change with society's changing value orientation; a specific one may be the sanctity of work as such. The two-person relationship may or may not emerge as God-given; we should be ready to explore other possibilities, especially since we may have little choice about it. The neat and compartmentalized formulations we cherish about the discrete steps in vocational choice as embodied in the set definition, even if modified to include Super's points, may prove to be quite inadequate.[2] The necessary procedure, always subject to change, may provide a number of services concurrently as the client requires them. Service will not stop when a job is obtained but rather is likely to be continuous through various job changes at various times in a working life. The paths for an individual to follow, preparation, work, further training, different work, may be different one from another. At later stages, work and non-work may be seen to constitute a continuum, the various facets of which are as subject to examination and evaluation of choices for an individual as is any one part of it.

There is as much promise as threat for the future of our work. Within limits, perhaps we can affect and even make our reality. This is a superb *chance* for our work, which really is all anyone can ask.

REFERENCES

AFL-CIO Industrial Union Department. *Automation's unkept promise.* Washington, D.C.: AFL-CIO Industrial Union Department, No. 47, June 1962.

ANSHEN, M. "Managerial decisions." *Automation and technological change.* Englewood Cliffs, N.J.: Prentice-Hall, 1962.

AUMAN, F. A. "Retraining—how much of an answer to technological unemployment?" *Personnel J.,* Nov. 1962, 505–507.

BELL, D. The post-industrial society. In forum discussion on the *Impact of Tech-*

---

[2] I am indebted to Marguerite Coleman's thinking on this point in her paper given at the 43rd Annual Meeting of the Vocational Advisory Service, May 21, 1964.

nological and Social Change. June 14, 1962, Liberty Mutual Insurance Co., (Mimeo).

BRAYFIELD, A. H. "Vocational counseling today." In Williamson, E. G., ed., *Vocational counseling: a reappraisal in honor of Donald G. Paterson.* Minneapolis: University of Minnesota Press, 1961.

BROZEN, Y. *Automation, the impact of technological change.* Washington, D.C.: American Enterprise Institute for Public Policy Research, March 1963.

BRUNER, J. S. *The process of education.* Cambridge, Mass.: Harvard University Press, 1960.

CAUDILL, H. M. "The permanent poor: the lesson of eastern Kentucky." *The Atlantic, 213,* 6, 49–53.

DIEBOLD, J. "Automation: its implications for counseling." *Occupational Outlook Quarterly,* 1962, *6,* 3, 3–6.

DRUCKER, P. F. "America's next twenty years: the promise of automation." *Automation: implications for the future,* Harper's Magazine, *210* 41–47, April 1955; 39–44, May 1955.

KRANTZ, H. "A crash program to aid disadvantaged youth." *The Guidepost.* Washington, D.C.: American Personnel and Guidance Association, 1964.

Manpower Report of the President and a Report on Manpower, Requirement, Resources, Utilization and Training by the U.S. Department of Labor, March 1964, Washington, D.C. G.P.O., Superintendent of Documents.

MICHAEL, D. N. "Cybernation: the silent conquest." Santa Barbara. Fund for the Republic, 1962.

MOYNIHAN, D. P. "Morality of work and immorality of opportunity." *Vocational Guidance Quarterly,* 1964, *12,* 4, 229–236.

National Science Foundation. *Scientists, Engineers, and Technicians in the 1960's: Requirements and Supply.* Washington, D.C.: National Science Foundation, NSF 63–64.

President's Advisory Committee on Labor-Management Policy. Labor-Management Policy Committee Report on Automation. *Monthly Labor Review,* 1962, *85,* 2, 139–144.

SAMLER, J. "Where do counseling psychologists work? What do they do? What should they do?" In A. S. Thompson and D. E. Super, eds., *The professional preparation of counseling psychologists, report of the 1964 Greyston conference.* New York: Bureau of Publications, Teachers College, Columbia University, 1964.

SELIGMAN, B. B. "Man, Work, and the automated feast." *Commentary,* 1962, *34,* 9–19.

Subcommittee on Employment and Manpower, Committee on Labor and Public Welfare. *Hearings relating to the training and utilization of the manpower resources of the nation.* U.S. Senate, 88th Congress, 1st Session, G.P.O., 1963.

Subcommittee on Employment and Manpower, Committee on Labor and Public Welfare. *Report: toward full employment: proposals for a comprehensive employment and manpower policy in the U.S.* U.S. Senate, 88th Congress, 2nd Session, G.P.O., 1964.

TILGHER, A. "Work through the ages." In S. Nosow and W. H. Form, eds., *Man, work and society.* New York: Basic Books, 1962.

TYLER, L. T. "The future of vocational guidance." In E. G. Williamson, ed., *Vocational counseling: a reappraisal in honor of Donald G. Paterson,* Minnesota Studies in Student Personnel Work No. 11. Minneapolis: University of Minnesota Press, 1961.

WEINBERG, E. *The effects of technology and automation on employment of the handicapped.* Paper presented before the Mountain States Regional Meeting of the President's Committee on Employment of the Handicapped. Pueblo, Colo., June 29, 1962. U.S. Department of Labor, Bureau of Labor Statistics (Mimeo.)

WOLFBEIN, S. *"Automation and skill"* Annals of the American Academy of Political and Social Science. 1962, *340*, 53–59.

WOLFBEIN, S. *Employment and unemployment in the United States.* Chicago: Science Research Associates, 1964.

WOLFBEIN, S. "The outlook for the skilled worker in the United States: Implications for guidance and counseling." *Personnel Guid. J.*, 1961, *40*, 334–339.

WRISTON, H. M. *Perspective, in Automation and technological change.* The American Assembly, Columbia University. Englewood Cliffs, New Jersey: Prentice-Hall, 1962.

38. Automation and Counseling

Robert R. Morman

Due to rapid and marked technological advances, automation is beginning to have as great an impact in the fields of educational and vocational counseling as in business and industry. Many employees who are occupationally dislocated by these technological changes need to be apprised of the economic opportunities in automated fields of endeavor. Increasing numbers of high school and college students are evincing interest in automated fields at the various levels of formal education. However, some practicing counselors apparently still are relatively unaware of the tremendous impact of automation on counseling despite the urgent needs of present and potential clients for counsel in this field. Perhaps each counselor should query himself if he continues to program, advise, and vocationally orient clients as if automation were nonexistent; it might pay him to take inventory of his professional practices to make sure that he is equipped to acquaint counselees with the availability of necessary training opportunities to bridge the gap between unemployment and new employment.

By thinking seriously in this vein, counselors will gain greater appreciation of the fact that automation is a growing field which is extending into practically every occupational level, and consequently creating many new jobs and many related programs of instruction in various educational institutions. Undoubtedly every conscientious counselor is interested in

Robert R. Morman, "Automation and Counseling," from *Personnel and Guidance Journal*, March, 1962, pp. 594–99. Copyright © 1962 by the American Personnel and Guidance Association, Inc., Washington, D.C. Reprinted by permission.

learning of these developments, particularly in his own region, if not nationally; therefore, he will find that some knowledge of the beginning and of the history of automation will help give him an insight into its modern-day ramifications.

DEFINITION AND HISTORY

Automation, briefly defined, may be construed as any device employed to replace a portion of man's physical or motor and mental functions or both. An illustration of motor replacement would be the automatic ditch-digger replacing man's pick and shovel functions, and electronic quality control of cigarettes manufactured to specifications is an example of supplanting the inspection function of workers formerly assigned to that task. One writer termed the replacement of motor functions as the first industrial revolution and labeled the advent of "thinking devices" and "synthetic intelligences" as the second industrial revolution (Ramo, 1957). However, a more precise interpretation of automation is offered by Boelter (1957) who states, "Automation ultimately means a sequence beginning with input and proceeding to output of a product or process of desired properties to be accomplished without human direction other than to design the equipment and process, initiate and stop the sequence, and to repair and maintain the equipment." By carefully examining this definition, the reader can readily envision handling, transferring, packing, wrapping, grinding, milling, planing, weighing, measuring, enumerating, and countless other machine operations normally performed by humans.

Historically, automation probably began when primitive man first employed a lever to assist in moving a heavy object or utilized the concept of the wheel to transport heavy loads. Perhaps the most popular early example of modern-type automation is Evans' flour mill built near Philadelphia in 1784 (Shallenberger, 1957). Through the use of water power and devices like belt, bucket, and screw conveyor, grain was automatically processed into finished flour in Evans' mill without human imvolvement. Jacquard, early in the following century, is given credit as the pioneer of the "punched card principle" in the weaving of fabrics, thus bringing us a step nearer to the present-day concept of automation.

The term itself, however, is of more recent origin, being a product of the 20th century, and attributed to two individuals, Del Harder and John Diebold (Grabbe, 1957). In 1947, Del Harder of the Ford Motor Company coined the word "automation" as an abbreviation of the more unwieldy term "automatization"; then John Diebold publicized the new term extensively in his 1952 book entitled *Automation*.

Impact and Need for Automation

In view of its rapid growth, automation undoubtedly will eventually affect every occupational level in this country, whether in private enterprise or government, and the military. This prospective growth was emphasized by Ramo when he predicted that "automation will be the top industry of the future" (Ramo, 1957). To better visualize the vast potential of automation, a few examples of present-day usage are presented below, grouped so as to correspond to each of the main classifications in the *Dictionary of Occupational Titles*.

At the professional level we find automatic accounting machines, machines that translate foreign languages into English, automatic teaching machines, and machines for telemetering of intercontinental ballistic missiles. Automatic payroll computation, check-writing, inventorying, and scheduling are found at the clerical level. Processing of pre-cooked foods, food-dispensing machines, and automatic fire and lawn sprinkling systems are noted at the service level. Skilled level examples include numerical control (the use of punched cards or tapes to control complex machine-tool operations) of grinding, milling, planing, boring, shearing, and painting operations. Packaging, weighing, inspecting, and sorting exemplify the semi-skilled level. And, finally, mixing of cement, lifting, handling, loading, and transporting illustrate the unskilled level.

Quantitatively, the outlook for continued expansion of automation is given support by evidence furnished by Hugh-Jones (1956), who envisions a 25 to 30 per cent reduction in direct labor costs at the Ford Motor Company as a direct result of automation. Chrysler likewise expects to reduce its direct labor costs by one-half at a new Plymouth plant, and many other manufacturing companies look for equivalent dramatic results. In fact, economists generally agree that more than a quarter of the labor force in the United States will be affected by automation within a relatively few years, particularly in plant processing and data handling operations.

Further quantitative evidence about the effects of automation on the upgrading of the present labor force is furnished by Parker and Mayer (1956) in their comprehensive article, with figures extrapolated to 1970. This article, in essence, specifies the expected changes in the occupational distribution of jobs by making comparisons between two basic labor groups, white-collar and blue-collar. Their per cents refer to per cents of the total labor force.

Parker and Mayer predict that by 1970 there will be more white-collar workers than blue-collar workers, white-collar workers will function at the professional, managerial, technical, office, proprietorship, or sales levels, and more than half of all employed men will be liberated from manual labor. Since 1940, women have entered the labor force at a faster rate than men and have gone predominantly into white-collar jobs. As a consequence of these two trends, white-collar workers will have increased from 15 per cent in 1900 to 40 per cent by 1970. Skilled and semi-skilled workers will have expanded from 20 per cent to 40 per cent over the same time period; however, service occupations, farm, and non-farm laborers will not show any significant increase in numbers, while their corresponding proportions of the total labor force will decrease. In short, significant changes in the number and proportion of white-collar workers in the upper half of the distribution of occupations may be expected within the coming decade.

An article by former Secretary of Labor Mitchell (1958), in predicting the impact of automation on the economy, is in general agreement with the forecasts made by Parker and Mayer, but there are a few exceptions. According to Mitchell's predictions, a faster than average rate of growth is expected for service workers. The mining industry rate of growth will stabilize itself, while transportation and public utilities will expand more slowly than the other occupational fields. Proportionately more part-time employees, particularly women over 35 and young people between the ages of 14–24, will enter the job market. Mitchell's article covers the decade between 1955–1965 and emphasizes different facets of the labor force, which likely accounts for some of the discrepancies between the two forecasts.

Several concrete examples of the quantitative effects of automation in specific occupations are mentioned below to show how this has resulted in technical unemployment and occupational dislocation. Employment figures released by the American Federation of Musicians (Chase, 1958) show a steady decline by about one-third in the number of member musicians, although the total labor force has increased by more than one-third during the past 30 years. Chief reason offered for the decline is more canned music, such as records, tapes and discs.

Accounting machines like Electronic Recorded Machine Accounting (ERMA), manned by nine operators, replaced 50 bookkeepers in handling 50,000 accounts for the Bank of America. Accordingly, only one-fifth of the previous number of bookkeepers were necessary to service 500 bank branches (Pollack, 1957).

Inventory and stock control of 8,000 different goods in a large Chicago mail-order firm formerly required 60 clerks to handle the daily orders and were usually days behind in their current inventory. Now, a computer and 10 clerks perform all the necessary functions and the inventory and stock control are up to date at all times (Hugh-Jones, 1956).

The Ford Motor Company installed an automatic transfer apparatus, coupled with automatic drilling and milling machines, to produce 550 V-8 cylinder blocks in eight hours, against the 200 formerly produced by nine men in the same time, an improvement of 500 per cent (Hugh-Jones, 1956).

However, to counterbalance these grim economic predictions, a number of more hopeful eventualities are presaged to occur. Automation, through ultra-mass production and processing, is expected to create more jobs by creating expanded markets here and abroad. In particular, the need for employees in merchandising, advertising, public relations, technical representation, and sales will expand rapidly since the products of more efficient production will have to be sold. Today's luxuries will become tomorrow's necessities. New factories will create additional job opportunities for skilled operators, technicians, managers, economists, researchers, and other technically proficient personnel. Raw materials will be consumed at increasing rates, which in turn will stimulate industries producing raw materials. Since the new products must be distributed to consumers, transportation and other distribution industries will of necessity expand, resulting in further job opportunities.

When automation helps bring about the expected shorter work week, Americans will have more leisure time to devote to entertainment, sports, travel, recreation, education, literary, and other pursuits. As a result, businesses such as boat-building, small airplane and helicopter manufacture, adult education, professional sports, entertainment, and travel, which are experiencing considerable growth at the present, can be expected to expand at an even faster rate, giving a wide variety of job openings.

Counseling Implications

The advent and expansion of the field of automation has resulted in two important implications for counselors. The first implication is counseling clients regarding long-range educational and vocational plans to prepare themselves to make a living in the changed economic milieu resulting from automation. The second implication consists of advising on present and future job opportunities in the field of automation. If jobs like operations researcher, linear programmer, pendant operator, and systems engineer are mentioned by a client, the counselor will rapidly discover that standard reference sources such as the *Dictionary of Occupational Titles* (1955), *Estimates of Worker Trait Requirements for Four Thousand Jobs* (1957), or the *Minnesota Occupational Rating Scales* (Paterson, 1941) do not contain descriptions for many of these new jobs. Nor do adequate current studies exist for needed quantitative job information. Advisement or programming queries bearing on training requirements for new positions will likewise suffer from lack of recent informative material. The same problem arises in relation to workers who have been terminated because of technological changes and who have an immediate need for mustering their talents to re-enter the job market.

There are a multitude of actions available to the counselor to better inform himself in regard to the field of automation. One purpose of this article is to suggest potential sources of information on automation. Many source books and technical articles, as well as magazines and journals which cover this subject, are available in most libraries. Pertinent books and articles include Hugh-Jones (1956) *The Push Button World;* Pollack (1957) *Automation;* and Walker (1960) *Life in the Automatic Factory.* Examples of informative magazines and journals are *Business Week, Computers and Automation, Datamation, Air Force and Space Digest, Journal of Astronautics,* and *Datalink.* Of course, library catalogues, indexes and librarians can offer leads to other such source materials.

A follow-up of classified advertisements concerning new industry positions in newspapers and in professional journals such as *American Psychologist* and *Industrial Research,* by writing or telephoning to obtain further particulars, frequently results in additional usable information. Manufacturers of automatic equipment, as well as labor unions that represent their employees, will send literature on job descriptions and position requirements upon request. Examples of important sources are organizations like International Business Machines, Remington-Rand, Minnesota Mining and Manufacturing, General Electric, and American Federation of Labor.

Professional meetings and "open houses" on the subject of automation, sponsored by industrial and professional firms and associations, colleges, universities, and military organizations, offer demonstrations, lectures, discussions, and descriptive literature on the subject. Public announcements are made of industry-sponsored demonstrations and Armed Services Days; however, other types of meetings receive more limited publicity. These include management and marketing conferences, American Psychological Association meetings, research development and personnel management conferences, and human factor conclaves.

Another practical way open to counselors who wish to learn more about automation is to observe automation in action, take courses on the subject, and gain actual experience in the field. Many concerns using automated equipment welcome visitors and some even conduct guided tours. This permits counselors to observe firsthand the nature of the equipment used, conditions of work, and demands on employees, as well as offering an opportunity to discuss their jobs with the employees at work. A counselor will probably obtain maximum benefits from these visits if he plans them so that he can observe machine and data processing such as cam grinding, assembly of appliances, food processing, and payroll and insurance premium handling, so as to view various jobs at different occupational levels. Counselors who wish to obtain specific training in the field will find that adult education classes in automation, given at high schools and colleges, are being offered with increasing frequency. If none is presently given in his area, a counselor may be able to persuade his local high school or college to start such courses at the adult level. Possibly there is no better way to gain understanding and insight into automated positions and their requirements than by actual job performance. Teacher-counselors in particular have an opportunity to gain such experience during the summer months. Many companies have specific programs to cooperate with teaching institutions in this manner. Information and specific referrals can be obtained from public, private, and college placement services, as well as by contacting the companies directly.

Another possible method of gaining additional information about automation is by detailed job studies. Many possible avenues are open to the counselor who wishes to pursue this line of endeavor. As a start, he can consult audio-visual catalogues for pertinent films like McGraw-Hill's three-part series on *Automation* (Murrow, 1957). Other possible sources of such films are audio-visual equipment manufacturers and corporations like General Electric, Hughes Aircraft, and International Business Machines.

An excellent method of obtaining further information in this field is to make job analyses of several automated jobs at different occupational levels. As an aid to the beginner in job analysis, guides can be found in publications like Thorndike (1949) *Personnel Selection: Test and Measurement Techniques,* or *Estimates of Worker Trait Requirements for Four Thousand Jobs,* by the U.S. Employment Service (1957). To pursue this method further, counselors can consult books on occupational information, such as those by Baer and Roeber (1951) and Hoppick (1957), which offer descriptions and discussions on job families. The use of job families as guides in considering closely related positions to ones in which clients have training is the most feasible course in many instances as a basis for offering advisement. This is particularly true when advising job changers, terminees, and recently discharged armed services personnel who have received technical trainings. A further method of obtaining job information is by follow-up of school graduates and counselees now working in automated jobs to obtain detailed information about their new jobs.

COUNSELOR SATISFACTIONS

Although the suggestions listed above will add to the counselor's burden, he has many compensations. Automation can contribute to the solution of several perennial counseling problems and tend toward alleviation of other broad manpower issues. Even though the anticipated influx of automation is geared to the semi-skilled and skilled occupational levels, it should supply many job outlets for lesser trained persons in handling, clerical, sales, service, and distribution of goods.

Perhaps 50 per cent of high school students have poorly formulated educational and vocational plans, if any. Certain of the new areas of industrial application may strike responsive chords in those individuals and aid in stimulating more definitive thinking about their futures. Many of the new jobs should possess more appeal to them. Consequently, changes in job status hierarchies are expected.

Many studies have suggested that at least half of the high school students aspire toward professional goals but that only about a tenth of them reach this aspiration. However, automation and other concomitant economic factors are creating greater pressures for larger numbers of highly trained personnel. Civilian and military institutions have been obliged to expand their training facilities to cope with this urgency. Both industry and the military have programs of training and re-training talented individuals in their organizations. Naturally, present competency standards will still be required, but the situation will permit many more aspirants to enter professional fields. Further impetus to students at the technical, graduate, and professional training levels is obtained from expanding programs of scholarships, loans, and stipends. The National Education Defense Act is illustrative of national thinking in this regard.

Persons with physical handicaps will be able to function in many automated positions which are sedentary in nature. Button pushers, console and pendant operators, tape readers, quality controllers, inspectors, card punchers, data typists, programmers, systems analysts, designers, researchers, and other jobs of the same nature do not have high physical demands and so can probably be handled satisfactorily by properly trained personnel with physical limitations.

On a national level, automation should lead to a fuller, richer life and bring more happiness in the way of economic benefits and leisure pursuits than ever before. Improved utilization of manpower should be effected. Opportunities for persons desiring to establish their own businesses also should flourish. Many enterprising self-employment areas are open to them, particulary in fields of travel, hobby, literary, tutoring, sales, painting, programming, data processing, clothing, design, food, and "luxury" items.

Finally, there is the counselor's own feeling of satisfaction that he has counseled most capably.

Thus, there is a great deal that a counselor can do where automation is concerned. If he really desires to equip himself to perform educational and vocational counseling adequately, he really has no choice but to learn more about the field of automation. Traveznikov (1960) lends weight to this point of view when he states: "Man is headed for an automated future, no matter what tomorrow's world political organization is like." The author, however, prefers to paraphrase Pollack's (1957) expression of the future of automation in the economic picture, which is, essentially, "Automate or die."

REFERENCES

BAER, M. F., & ROEBER, E. C. *Occupational information.* Chicago: Science Research Associates, 1951.

BOELTER, L. M. K. "Introduction: reflections on automation." In Grabbe, E. M., ed., *Automation in business and industry.* New York: John Wiley & Sons, 1957.

CHASE, R. C. "Music and automation." *Voc. guid. Quart.*, 1958, 7 (2), 77–80.

Dictionary of Occupational Titles: Vol. I, *"Definitions of titles"* (2nd Ed.), March, 1949; Vol. II, *"Occupational classification and industry index"* (2nd Ed.), March, 1949; Vol. IV, *"Entry occupational classification"* (Rev. Ed.), October, 1944; *Supplement one to second edition* of Vols. I and II, March, 1955—Includes all interim releases, 2,260 new and revised definitions, and 1,322 code numbers. Washington, D.C.: U.S. Government Printing Office.

Estimates of Worker Trait Requirements for 4,000 Jobs. Washington, D.C.: U.S. Government Printing Office, 1957.

GRABBE, E. M. "The language of automation." In Grabbe, E. M., ed., *Automation in business and industry.* New York: John Wiley & Sons, 1957.

HOPPOCK, R. *Occupational information. Where to get it and how to use it in counseling and teaching.* New York: McGraw-Hill, 1957.

HUGH-JONES, E. M. A summing up. In Hugh-Jones, E. M., ed., *The push button world. Automation today.* Norman, Okla.: University of Oklahoma Press, 1956.

MITCHELL, J. P. "American labor force: prospects for the future." *Personnel guid. J.*, 1958, 35, 603–609.

MURROW, E. R., & FRIENDLY, F. W., eds. *Automation. Parts I, II, and III.* First seen on CBS television program, "See It Now." New York: McGraw-Hill, 1957.

PARKER, S. S., & MAYER, L. A. "The decade of the discretionary dollar." *Fortune*, June, 1956, 136–138.

PATERSON, D. G., et al. *The Minnesota occupational rating scales.* Chicago: Science Research Associates, 1941.

POLLACK, F. *Automation: a study of its economic and social consequences.* New York: F. A. Praeger, 1957.

RAMO, S. "Automation in business and industry." In Grabbe, E. M., ed., *Automation in business and industry.* New York: John Wiley & Sons, 1957.

SHALLENBERGER, F. S. "Economics of plant automation." In Grabbe, E. M., ed., *Automation in business and industry.* New York: John Wiley & Sons, 1957.

THORNDIKE, R. L. *Personnel selection: test and measurement techniques.* New York: John Wiley & Sons, 1949.

TRAVEZNIKOV, V. A. Automation, a Soviet view. *Air force and space digest*. Dayton, Ohio: Air Force Association, October, 1960, 67–70.

WALKER, C. R. Life in the automatic factory. In Farwell, G. F., & Peters, H. J., eds., *Guidance readings for counselors*. Chicago: Rand McNally, 1960.

SECTION NINE

The Counseling Function

Viewed as the heart or hub of guidance, counseling generates greater significance for numerous activities of the appraisal and information functions. Seen this way, counseling constitutes a necessary activity for the most effective performance of each of the other functions of guidance.

Many systematic approaches to counseling exist. Five of the most frequently mentioned groupings are: (1) trait-and-factor (Williamson); (2) psychoanalytic (Freud) and neo-Freudian (Horney, Sullivan, Adler); (3) existential or phenomenological (Rogers, May); (4) communication (Robinson); and (5) learning-theories (Wolpe, Bandura, Dollard and Miller). Other systematic approaches may represent eclectic combinations or be variants of the five broad categories listed. For example, reality therapy claims to select critical concepts from both self-theory and neobehaviorism in its process model for behavior change.

Articles selected for this section maintain a degree of parallelism between the three views of man-reactive, reactive-in-depth, and in-the-process-of-becoming (See Section Two, "Psychological Models for Guidance") and theoretical approaches to counseling. For example, in the final article Patterson makes explicit the parallel between: (1) the learning (behavioral) approaches and Allport's reactive man; (2) dynamic (psychoanalytic) approaches and Allport's reactive-in-depth man; (3) existential (humanistic or self-theory) approaches and man in the process of becoming. In this section in particular, the editors were confronted with the sharply opposing forces of an abundance of possible selections and limited space. Articles chosen were general ones that synthesize many concepts, focus on a few significant conceptual issues or summarize a body of thought.

The reader may wish first to skim Patterson's article titled "Divergences and Convergences in Counseling and Psychotherapy." The article is the summary chapter of a significant text in counseling theories, (Patterson, C. H., *Theories of counseling and psychotherapy.* New York: Harper and Row, 1966) and can serve as an excellent conceptual pattern for an extensive study of counseling theory. Patterson's central thesis is that counseling and psychotherapeutic approaches can really be dichotomized into two basic approaches: (1) man being acted upon by either internal (reactive being in depth) or external (reactive being) forces; and (2) man in the process of becoming—acting upon forces which surround him both internally and externally. Thus, without direct reference, Patterson brings the reader face to face with the critical paradox of the demonstrated ability of man to both predict and control behavior in large measure and the subjective freedom of the individual. Present day theory and research virtually demand that the honest scholar not feel free to reject glibly either the conditioning approaches of the behavior therapists or the relationship and encounter approaches of the humanistic movement. He must, instead, live with the uncomfortable paradox just delineated.

In the first selection Blocher confronts the reader with a partly historical, mostly conceptual view of dying and emerging issues. He disposes of the following illusional issues as lacking validity and relevance: (1) the directive-non-directive dichotomy; (2) "Should counselors diagnose?"; and (3) "Should counseling be personal-emotional or informational-didactic?" Blocher considers viable issues to exist in two questions: (1) "Is counseling developmental-educative and preventative in nature or is it remediating-adjustive-therapeutic?" (2) Is counseling liberating or conditioning in nature? The reader is urged to evaluate Blocher's conclusions carefully in the context of related selections in previous chapters.

Yet another problem in defining "counseling" frequently arises. How does one distinguish between "counseling" and "psychotherapy?" Traditionally, educators and administrators have tended to approach this issue emotionally, in the sense that perhaps they have avoided confronting the fact that counselors in schools or agencies often do deal with intense emotional interchanges—a province of interpersonal relationships mistakenly reserved for "psychotherapists." The three most common theoretical distinctions between counseling and psychotherapy are: (1) the counselor deals with the "normal" range of clientele, whereas psychotherapists work mostly with the "abnormal" population; (2) the counselor deals primarily with cognitive material, the psychotherapist with affect; and (3) the aim of counseling is the building up of existing strengths while that of psychotherapy is major personality reorganization.

In the second selection, however, Albert portrays the counseling-psychotherapy dichotomy as one which has limited usefulness. He points to the complexity of all therapeutic (growth producing) efforts and calls for more vigorous selection and training of counselors.

At this point, the reader may wish to turn again to Patterson for a thorough rereading of "Divergences and Convergences . . ." and begin a considered re-examination of the man-begin-acted-upon and man-acting-upon dichotomy. Additionally, Patterson's classication of counseling theories on a continuum of cognitive to affective is relevant to Albert's discussion of the distinction between counseling and psychotherapy. Finally, any student intrigued by the nature of the philosophical and scientific issues explored may wish to review the preceding chapters on philosophical, psychological and research foundations.

39.   Issues in Counseling: Elusive and Illusional

Donald H. Blocher

An examination of the questions which continue to command attention in most discussions of counseling theory, practice, and research

Donald Blocher, "Issues in Counseling: Elusive and Illusional," from *Personnel and Guidance Journal*, April, 1965, pp. 796–800. Copyright © 1965 by the American Personnel and Guidance Association, Inc., Washington, D.C. Reprinted by permission.

seems to reveal an interesting dichotomy. The first set of these questions comprises a group that are frequently discussed, often elicit considerable emotion, and are generally quite unproductive in terms of the consequences which they generate. These questions can well be called illusions in counseling. The second set of issues are frequently avoided in discussions of counseling; they are extremely difficult to frame clearly but have very important consequences. They are indeed elusive in character.

ILLUSIONS IN COUNSELING

It is perhaps easier to begin by demolishing illusions than by attempting to trap the elusive. One of the foremost illusions in counseling concerns the old question of should counseling be "directive" or "non-directive." This is one of the oldest, most decrepit, and least productive arguments in the field of counseling. Part of its feebleness is drawn from the fact that as an issue it is not even clear in meaning. Two kinds of questions are involved. The first concerns whether or not the counselor influences his client. The answer to this question is really no longer at issue. Writers as different in orientation as Williamson (1958) and Patterson (1958) agree that counselors do, should, and cannot avoid influencing clients. The relevant questions which survive around this part of the issue concern only directions and degrees of influence.

The second aspect of this sterile controversy over "directive vs. non-directive" counseling concerns the distribution of responsibility for the content of the interview or the nature of the counseling process as apart from its outcomes. Research by Robinson (1950) and others of the so-called "communications" school of counseling has indicated rather clearly that division of responsibility for the content of the counseling interview is one and only one of a number of relevant dimensions in the counseling process. This research suggests that virtually all counselors vary their behavior along this continuum from client to client or from one point to another in the counseling process. No counselors completely abdicate responsibility for the nature of the interview. For example, many so-called non-directive counselors use formal structuring techniques at the beginning of counseling which are quite "directive" in one sense. Decisions to respond to affect or content, to clarify, to accept, all require some degree of responsibility on the part of the counselor.

Again, the relevant questions which survive in this issue are merely how much and in what directions should counselor responsibility be exerted.

A second rather moribund question is whether or not counselors should diagnose. This is illusion number two. The term diagnosis has been an emotionally loaded word in the counseling vocabulary for some years. Two basic reasons seem to account for this fact. First, the term diagnosis was largely borrowed from medicine, and to many counselors it carries a strong flavor of telling clients what is wrong with them. This connotation does violence to values which many counselors hold concerning building on the assets of clients, distinguishing between counseling and psychotherapy, and so forth.

A second reason for this emotional reaction is the connection which many counselors see between diagnosis and the use of tests. Many counselors apparently feel that if they do not use tests, they also do not diagnose.

Most of the thinking surrounding both of these reactions to diagnosis is fallacious. The only philosophical assumption that really affects the question of diagnostic activity is whether or not the counselor views one of his tasks in the counseling process as that of understanding the counselee. Diagnostic activities are merely those activities which have as one of their purposes helping the counselor understand his client. Research on the nature of this kind of activity by Koester (1954), McArthur (1954), and Parker (1958) has indicated that for many counselors this activity resembles a hypothesis-testing process. The Pepinskys (1954) have called attention to the counselor as a scientist-practitioner and have described the process of observation and inference by which the counselor builds a hypothetical model through which to understand his client.

The question again is not whether or not to diagnose. All counselors who attempt to understand their clients are engaged in diagnosis. The degree to which a particular counselor is committed to differential treatment for different clients may influence the nature and extent of his diagnostic activities. The counselor with a strong client-centered approach may not vary treatment processes from one client to another to as great a degree as one who considers himself eclectic. The difference in diagnostic activity between the two refers to differential diagnosis rather than to the process of diagnosis itself, however.

Diagnosis also has nothing to do with the use of tests. Tests are merely samples of behavior from which other behavior is inferred. The moment that the counselor makes inferences about behavior from any source, he is diagnosing.

From what we know about diagnostic processes now, we must conclude that all counselors do diagnose but that diagnostic activities contribute most when they are *continuous*, *tentative*, and *testable*. Diagnosis in this sense is a continuous process that is integrated into the total counseling. It is always tentative and subject to revision as further behavior samples become available. Finally, it is testable in the sense that diagnostic constructs or hypotheses are rooted in behavior and are operationally defined so that they may be confirmed or rejected through prediction.

A third illusion revolves around the question of whether counseling is personal-emotional or informational-didactic in nature. This question is another which has generated more heat than light in recent years. When either side of this issue is explored thoroughly, it can be reduced to a set of patent absurdities.

First, examine the didactic-informational side. The logical extensions of this position are:

1. Counseling is impersonal.
2. Counseling is teaching occupational information to a class of one.
3. Only sick people have emotions.
4. The affective and intellectual functions of human beings can be separated and treated as self-contained entities.

These are obvious absurdities. A look at the opposite side of the coin, however, reveals some equally indefensible propositions.

1. Human behavior is not mediated by rational-intellectual problem-solving processes. (How did the client get to the counselor in the first place?)
2. The counseling interview is characterized by primarily verbal communication processes, but it is still an entirely emotional rather than an intellectual exchange.
3. All problems arise out of emotional conflicts rather than vice versa.
4. Personal problem-solving is not an important matter for counseling. People can solve all personal problems readily once their deep-seated emotional conflicts are removed.

These propositions seem equally absurd. If counseling is a process which helps whole human beings cope with total life situations, it seems clear that both affective and intellectual aspects of life will have to be considered.

Three illusions in counseling which have commanded research time and energy from counselors have been discussed and hopefully disposed of.

ELUSIVE ISSUES

The second set of issues which are dubbed elusive in character are naturally more difficult to discuss than those mentioned previously. These issues are important, have vital consequences, and are exceedingly difficult to resolve. The first of these is set up in terms of the following question, "Is counseling developmental-educative-preventive, or is it re-mediating-adjustive-therapeutic?"

It seems better to deal with this issue in terms of goals rather than in terms of methodologies. Efforts to distinguish between counseling and psychotherapy have dealt largely with methodologies and their applica-tions. The intensity of the process, its level of impact upon the client or patient, the setting in which it is done all have been used as distinguish-ing criteria. Writers such as Perry (1955) and Brammer and Shostrom (1968) have characterized human personality in terms of a sort of onion-skin analogy, with the counselor busy peeling away the outer layers of skin while the therapist penetrates to the inner and apparently more pungent layers of the onion core. Presumably, every counselor should stop at whatever point his eyes begin to water.

None of these kinds of distinctions seem particularly useful. Counsel-ing and psychotherapy are processes that are aimed at changing human behavior. If any real differences exist between the two processes, they must involve the kinds of outcomes which are specified for each, and possibly with the underlying assumptions which translate such outcomes into goals.

It seems to this writer that when the usual outcomes for counseling and psychotherapy are pooled and an impromptu factor analysis per-formed, two rather dominant clusters of goals appear. These can be char-acterized as (1) developmental-educative-preventive goals, and (2) remediating-adjustive-therapeutic outcomes.

It may be worthwhile examining these two clusters for a moment. One part of the first cluster deals with developmental goals. An underly-ing assumption here is that human personality grows or unfolds in terms of a largely healthy interaction between the growing organism itself and the culture or environment. From this point of view, development is seen as a reasonably ordered and patterned process of change moving in direc-tions which are typically desirable for both the individual and society. The function of counseling in such a framework is to facilitate normal development. The outcomes may be stated in terms of mastering devel-opmental tasks or moving from one stage of development to another.

The whole concept of development is closely tied to education, ob-viously. As part of this cluster, one may then include understanding of self, understanding of environment (world of work, for example), devel-opment of problem-solving skills, etc. Also associated with this cluster are preventive mental hygiene outcomes such as preventing too great frustra-tions, anxieties, or stresses; avoiding unhealthy relationships or experi-ences; etc.

The second cluster of outcomes can be described by labels such as remediative, adjustive, and therapeutic. These outcomes are generally characterized by goals that involve breaking down and replacing defenses; learning new adjustments to particular situations which may be family, institutional, or societal; and removing conflicts in personality organization. These goals cluster around concepts of removing pathological components, adjusting people to environmental demands, and restoring mental health.

When the processes which are familiarly called counseling and psychotherapy are examined in the light of these two presumed clusters of outcomes, reasons for confusion in terms become apparent. Much of what is attempted in the name of counseling has been as remediative and adjustive in purpose as anything attempted in the name of psychotherapy. Counselors have attempted to "adjust" youngsters to the demands of schools and teachers. They have attempted to remediate and remove presumed pathological elements, for example, "laziness," "negativism," "aggression," and so forth.

One important issue facing counseling is whether distinctions on the basis of the kinds of clustering that have been described will be strengthened or whether they will be further broken down and no valid differences will exist between counseling and therapy. Perhaps, of course, writers such as Rogers (1957) and Arbuckle (1961) believe this has already happened.

A second elusive issue which faces counseling today is not unrelated to the first. It can be stated in its strongest terms in this question: Is counseling liberating or conditioning in nature? Modern psychology has generally tended to look upon man, as Allport (1962) says, as a reactive being or at best a reactive being in depth. Personality or learning theories based upon such a view tend to search for a set of uniform variables to which all behavior is subject. In a sense, such a system is closed. It tends to produce models based upon homeostatic principles and to view the human being functioning in a mechanistic-deterministic environment. Changing behavior in terms of this model, whether in counseling, therapy, or whatever, involves primarily identifying and controlling these variables.

The philosophical background from which counseling and guidance has emerged is not one in which formulations of this kind are comfortable. Instead, as Beck (1963) points out, these philosophical antecedents place great emphasis upon terms like individualism, responsibility, independence, personal freedom, etc. The philosophical frame of reference and American behavioristic Zeitgeist have now collided. This collision has become disturbingly clear in the controversies between those who term themselves existential psychologists such as May (1961), Rogers (1957), Maslow (1961), and Allport (1962), and the radical behaviorists best exemplified by Skinner (1957) and represented in the guidance literature by writers such as Michael and Meyerson (1962).

Two rather distinctly alternative directions seem to open before counseling. The existentialist position seems a philosophically attractive but scientifically unclear path. The Skinnerian-behavioristic road is scientifically rigorous, but philosophically frightening. Can or should counselors specify the outcomes of counseling in rigorous behavioral terms and proceed to shape them by conditioning processes? Do they instead deal in such quasi-behavioral commodities as self-awareness, immediate experience, and self-actualization? If counseling takes the latter course, what is its eventual relationship to a behaviorist psychology? If counseling takes the path of conditioning, what becomes its commitment in a philosophical sense?

These issues are elusive but vital in terms of their consequences. Counselors above all need to spend less time and energy tilting at the illusional windmills of the past and more time in resolving the elusive but inescapable issues that will shape the future.

REFERENCES

ALLPORT, G. W. "Psychological models for guidance." *Harvard educ. Rev.,* 1962, 32 (4), 373–381.

ARBUCKLE, D. S. *Counseling: an introduction.* Boston: Allyn and Bacon, 1961.

BECK, C. *Philosophical foundations of guidance.* Englewood Cliffs, N. J.: Prentice-Hall, 1963.

BRAMMER, L., & SHOSTROM, E. *Therapeutic psychology: fundamentals of counseling and psychotherapy* (2nd. Ed.). Englewood Cliffs, N.J.: Prentice-Hall, 1968.

KOESTER, G. A. "A study of the diagnostic process." *Educ. psychol. Measmt.,* 1954, 14, 473–486.

MAY, R., ed., *Existential psychology.* New York: Random House, 1961.

McARTHUR, C. "Analyzing the clinical process." *J. counsel. Psychol.,* 1954, 1, 203–208.

MICHAEL, J., & MEYERSON, L. "A behavioral approach to counseling and guidance." *Harvard educ. Rev.,* 1962, 32, (4) 382–401.

PARKER, C. "As a clinician thinks." *J. counsel. Psychol.,* 1958, 5, (4) 253–262.

PATTERSON, C. H. "The place of values in counseling and psychotherapy." *J. counsel. Psychol.,* 1958, 5, 216–233.

PEPINSKY & PEPINSKY. *Counseling: theory and practice.* New York: Ronald Press, 1954.

PERRY, W. G. "On the relation of psychotherapy and counseling." *Annals of the New York Academy of Sciences,* 1955, 63, 396–407.

ROBINSON, F. P. *Principles and procedures in student counseling.* New York: Harper, 1950.

ROGERS, C. R. *Client-centered therapy.* Boston: Houghton-Mifflin, 1957.

SKINNER, B. F. *Verbal behavior.* New York: Appleton-Century-Crofts, 1957.

WILLIAMSON, E. G. "Value orientation in counseling." *Personnel guid. J.,* 1958, 36, 520–528.

40. If Counseling *Is* Psychotherapy—What Then?

Gerald Albert

The more the "experts" seek to define counseling and psychotherapy differentially, the more the two areas seem to blend and overlap.

Opposed to the position taken by writers like Rogers (1951), in which counseling and psychotherapy are treated as one and same thing, have been numerous statements by others like Brammer and Shostrom (1968) and Tyler (1961), who hold that in general counseling is concerned essentially with the healthy or "normal" personality and its conscious, rational aspects, and with helping individuals make life choices that are productive and with which they can live—while psychotherapy deals essentially with the abnormal personality and its unconscious, irrational aspects, and with helping individuals rectify their intrapsychic distortions.

And yet, time and time again, statements appear in the works of those who so differentiate that raise once more the question, Can this differentiation be made to stick?

Tyler, for example, asserts, "Whether the need that brings him [the counselee] to counseling grows out of his arrival at a point in his life where an important decision must be made or out of an *emotional conflict* [italics added] that is paralyzing his ability to act, the counselor will attempt to make forward movement possible." Emotional conflict is at the very heart of the psychotherapist's operational sphere. With their roots embedded in the deepest layers of personality, emotions appear in varying degrees in the conscious *and* the unconscious, the rational *and* the irrational, aspects of behavior.

Attempts to resolve this conflict have taken several forms. One writer, Evraiff (1963), simply throws up his hands and calls the whole problem "primarily one of semantics" (Evraiff, 1963, p. 8).

Another, Bordin (1955, p. 14), suggests that the difference is merely one of quantity, not quality. Blocher (1965) outlines the problem in terms of the outcomes of the two helping activities, and states: "Much of what is attempted in the name of counseling has been as remediative and adjustive in purpose as anything attempted in the name of psychotherapy."

Perhaps the problem can be brought down to a more practical level, as is done by Stewart and Warnath (1965, p. 273) when they note, "The school counselor must be an adequate diagnostician so that he can make

Gerald Albert, "If Counseling *Is* Psychotherapy—What Then?" from *Personnel and Guidance Journal*, October, 1966, pp. 124–29. Copyright © 1966 by the American Personnel and Guidance Association, Inc., Washington, D.C. Reprinted by permission.

appropriate referrals; however, the referral sources mentioned in many counseling texts do not exist in the real world of most small towns. Thus, the counselor is often faced with two alternatives: to do *something* for the disturbed student in his present environment with the resources available or to send him off to a state hospital, which may be no more than an overcrowded custodial institution." In other words, whether he is a "psychotherapist" or not, the counselor may often find himself required to deal with situations that *should* be met with psychotherapeutic skills.

Yet Stewart and Warnath hold to the traditional differentiation between the two helping professions. The bind in which they are put by this position is well illustrated by the sentence with which they conclude their discussion of this topic: "[The counselor] cannot shun his responsibility to work with all school-age young people to the limit of his capability, even when some of these young people may have serious psychological problems." *Should* he work with "serious psychological problems" if he has not been trained to do so (Stewart and Warnath, 1965)?

Wherever one attempts to draw the dividing line, one is faced finally with an inevitable reality: The school counselor's job is seen more and more as one which involves helping students with life problems. These may take the form of academic, vocational or personal-emotional difficulties. The more knowledge, understanding and experience the counselor can bring to bear on these difficulties, the better it is likely to be for the client.

Since each client is, to a greater or lesser degree, an integrated unit, all of his activities reflect and are affected by all parts of him. Excluding the unconscious, the defensively repressed, the irrational (which are part of *every* personality, however minimal or well compensated) from the remedial efforts is excluding the parts which, even in "normals," may relate most actively to the difficulties under treatment. In more severe cases, such exclusion is like treating a brain tumor with a cold compress.

Obviously, this line of thought leads inevitably to certain consequences.

THE COST OF DOING WHAT WE ARE DOING

We can go on accepting what is essentially an artificial differentiation, and train counselors as if it were valid and real. We can teach them to test and to guide, to convey information knowledgeably and well, to help students make "rational" decisions and "know" themselves—all the while pretending that ignoring the major part of their clients' personality dynamics will have no seriously crippling effect on the counseling process.

How many thousands of students may there be in need of help beyond the ability of counselors so trained to give it? We have no way of knowing. But a small illustration, of which the writer has personal knowledge, may make the point.

A capable, but traditionally trained, counselor was seen by a young male college student to get the results of certain tests. A follow-up interview was scheduled, but the counselor took ill, and the student was seen instead by another counselor, who had received training as a psychotherapist. In the course of the session, the counselor's sensitively analytic questioning brought out the fact that the student suffered from an intense homosexual problem. When asked how it was that he hadn't mentioned this in the first interview, he replied that the first counselor just didn't seem likely to understand his problem, hadn't asked any questions which could open it up, and he just couldn't get himself to bring it up for discussion on his own.

It would seem that the assumptions drilled into the first counselor (that his job is primarily to understand the problems of "normal" clients), and his inadequate training in the recognition of unconscious forces and repressed drives, had conveyed to the student an attitude which unwittingly blocked disclosure of the deeply troublesome burden he was carrying.

It is, even today, unfortunately true that most people, counselors included, have considerable apprehension about dealing with so-called "mental cases." Those who lack professional understanding of the emotionally disturbed still respond with archaic fears to their supposed dangerousness—and to the supposed dangerousness latent in the forces within their own unconscious, as well. Even in our "enlightened" time, an amazing proportion of educated people, reacting to this fear, shy away from psychotherapeutic treatment even when its need is clearly indicated.

Obviously, too, students with hidden emotional problems suffer from these problems at an infinite number of possible levels of severity, from the minuscule to the seriously disabling. A small problem can still unnecessarily hamper a youngster's development; a larger one can make him an emotional cripple. Inability to identify small-to-moderate emotional difficulties may permit them to grow into major illnesses. The counselor's responsibility is, among other things, to pick these up as early as possible—for treatment by himself or for referral elsewhere.

Supporters of the present approach to counseling usually hold that:

(a) We need more, rather than fewer, counselors. To provide the kind of advanced psychological training that would make every counselor a "psychotherapist" would reduce the supply.

To this, the answer can be made that, while it would indeed be desirable for every counselor to have the full skills of a trained therapist, all that is envisioned here is training that will enable every counselor to *know* the full range of possible emotional problems and to recognize them when they appear before him, however well hidden they may be.

(b) Problems in students can be—and are—caught and treated quite adequately under the present system. Academic performance and general behavior call attention to these problems.

The answer to this is that it simply isn't true. The therapist in private practice or at the mental hygiene center constantly sees youngsters brought in by their parents because of belated recognition of serious disturbances which never came to the awareness of school teachers or counselors.

At the college level, the writer knows of an episode in which a student took five courses, did reasonably well in all until almost the end of the semester, gave no indication of aberration to any of his professors—but was so seriously disturbed that he suddenly began threatening a former professor at a college from which he had earlier transferred, claiming the professor was secretly plotting to cause his failure at the new institution. *Many* disturbed people conceal increasingly serious aberrations for long periods of time.

How, Then, Should We Train Counselors?

It is suggested here that every counselor should be required to take courses not only in personality theory (already provided in many programs), but also in abnormal psychology (including the major approaches to psychotherapy) and in diagnostics. (This should include not only the use of tests for the determination of interests, aptitudes, values and achievement, but *also* for the identification of emotional problems.) In view of the highly significant interdisciplinary trends in psychotherapy today, it might be well to require also a course in interdisciplinary behavioral science, in which awareness at least of the effects on behavior of sociological and biological factors could be imparted to the candidates.

It is suggested, too, that increased stress be given in counseling practice to recognition of emotional difficulties as they affect the functioning of *both* so-called "normals" and "abnormals" (who are usually pretty much the same population most of the time).

It is also urged that every counselor candidate have at least an undergraduate minor in Psychology. If there is even a remote resemblance between the work of the counselor and the psychotherapist, failure to have at least this much of a background in psychology would seem highly deleterious.

With this kind of training, the counselor will be more likely to possess the skills he needs in the delicate and important functions he is called on to perform—and *less* likely to overlook well-hidden disturbances in need of early remediation. There is just no one else available to do the job that the counselor can and must do.

CHANGES THAT ARE NEEDED

The next logical step, if counseling *is* essentially a form of psychotherapy, is to be concerned about the attitudes and personality traits of the counselor. As Tyler has put it, ". . . the greatest handicaps to counseling are hostility (or in milder form indifference) and obtuseness (or a tendency to oversimplify" (Tyler, 1961, p. 248).

Whether the focus is vocational, academic, or emotional, the counselor today is dealing, in large part, with the *personality* of the client. He needs the highest measure of openness and sensitivity, as unimpaired as possible by personality problems of his own. Tyler has pointed out the desirability of personal therapy of some sort as part of every counselor's training. She notes that it can produce accepting attitudes toward other people, identify the counselor's own biases and sensitive areas, prepare him for complications that may occur in some counseling relationships, and indicate his willingness to accept his own human weaknesses just as he is willing to accept them in his clients.

While Tyler urges the usefulness of personal therapy, she questions whether it should be made a requirement for counselors, since some people can possible arrive at insight and balance in other ways.

Considering human frailty, the writer suggests that this may be too optimistic. People rarely delve into their own weaknesses and deficiencies unless forced into it. It would seem much wiser, as Tyler herself suggests is possible, to set up some form of personal therapy as part of the graduate school training program for counselors.

There is yet another reason for requiring personal therapy or counseling. Many people who become counselors have never themselves been exposed to the experience of *being* intensively counseled, as many of their own clients will be. Without this experience, how can they be expected to understand fully the reactions, the anxieties, the defensive maneuvers, the flashes of insight, that will occur in their counselees?

REQUIRE THERAPY OF COUNSELING STUDENTS

The above suggestion is an obviously controversial one. The following is probably even more so.

The private conversations of educators are constantly studded with comments about the proportion of teachers who do serious injury to young children because of their own hostilities and distortions. It may be that nothing can be done to prevent this, because of the large numbers of persons involved. There is probably a much larger proportion of such people in the general population. But can we tolerate the unchallenged appearance of such characteristics in counselors?

If the counselor does do psychotherapy, however limitedly, if his work inevitably relates to the wellsprings of emotional functioning, should anyone be allowed to practice counseling who is himself malfunctioning emotionally?

It is certainly true that the administrators of many training programs make conscientious efforts to weed out such candidates, on the basis of the personal observations of the teaching staff and the self-disclosures which do appear in counseling practice. But, considering what has been said above about the frequency of unidentified cases of emotional disturbance, and considering the powerfully self-defensive structure which all of us tend to erect to protect ourselves from unsettling self-knowledge (as well as the knowledge of others), it would be amazing if far too many unacceptable candidates do not become practicing counselors.

In view of the highly sensitive nature of the counselor's job, should not much more rigorous effort be made to keep this from happening?

It may be that more elaborate scrutiny of the candidates' activities during the course of the graduate program would make more accurate decisions possible. But this would still suffer from an element of unfairness, i.e., can we in good conscience allow a candidate to go halfway (or more) through an expensive, time-consuming program of study, and then inform him that we cannot allow him to complete it because he is psychologically unsuited for the goal he is seeking?

The alternative course of action is to require that candidates be carefully tested *before* admission to the program. There is considerable opposition to personality testing today among people who see such tests as somehow an invasion of privacy, or as insufficiently dependable to be fully trusted, and this opposition often extends to selection procedures based on tests. Yet almost every college requires a physical examination of freshman applicants, which requires that information be provided that the individual might prefer not to reveal. In fact, every time we test a student in a class, we are forcing him to tell us something about himself which he might rather we didn't know (i.e., how much he has studied, his level of ability, etc.).

Like every other test, personality tests are samples of behavior, hopefully well chosen (and validated) to reflect a whole set of behavioral responses. Counselors use tests in a great many ways. Yet counselor educators are often among those who oppose the use of tests to screen out unfit candidates from their programs, sometimes on the acknowledged grounds that the tests are imperfect, sometimes on the grounds that it would be unfair not to give the applicant a chance to rise above his weaknesses and prove his capabilities.

These are legitimate objections. No one has demonstrated that an imperfectly adjusted person necessarily makes an ineffective counselor. Nevertheless, to assume that no correlation exists between the counselor's emotional make-up and his success as a helping professional would be to vitiate almost everything we know about human behavior. Very few would contend that a seriously hostile or withdrawn counselor is unlikely to do harm to some of his clients, at least.

If the previous recommendation were followed (that all candidates undergo some form of personal therapy), much of the objection to personality tests as screening devices could be avoided. Only those candidates would be eliminated about whose personal development the most serious doubts existed. The rest would have every opportunity to achieve, through study, self-examination and personal therapy, the balance and integration considered desirable for effective professional activity in this field.

The millions of children, for whose welfare all this activity is organized, would certainly stand to gain from the resulting rise in counselor effectiveness.

Such a program would obviously take additional time and expense to complete. But in view of the sensitive position occupied by counseling personnel in the development of healthy youngsters, its importance cannot be minimized. For practical reasons, it may be that *provisional* certification (in states where such arrangements obtain) should be attainable by fulfillment of the older, less rigorous programs. In this way, the flow of needed personnel would not be curtailed. But permanent certification (or granting of the master's degree in guidance and counseling) should be awarded only to those who can really be fully trusted to help the students they counsel. And, considering the increased training of such persons, the pay scale differential between counselors and teachers, at present deplorably small, would obviously have to be considerably increased.

The result might then really be a *profession* of guidance and counseling.

CONCLUSION

If school counseling is essentially—in many functions, at least—a form of psychotherapy, we are permitting personnel with dangerously inadequate training to attempt salvage operations in water beyond their depth. Accepting the premise that the two activities are at least heavily overlapping (with "counseling" perhaps more concerned than "psycho-therapy" with the rational and conscious, while yet deeply involved, of necessity, in the realm of the *irrational* and *unconscious*), certain changes in the training programs for counselors seem logically to follow.

Counselors should be required to have taken not only the usual range of subjects called for at present, but also more advanced courses in psychological and related fields; increased stress should be given in practice to emotional functioning of clients; individuals clearly unsuited to the profession should be eliminated *in advance;* all counselor candidates should themselves experience extended counseling or therapy; pay scales should be increased to attract and reward appropriately those candidates who do qualify.

REFERENCES

BLOCHER, D. H. Issues in counseling: elusive and illusional. *Personnel and Guid. J.,* 1965, *43,* 796–800.

BORDIN, E. S. *Psychological counseling.* New York: Appleton-Century-Crofts, 1955.

BRAMMER, L., & SHOSTROM, E. *Therapeutic psychology: fundamentals of counseling and psychotherapy,* (2nd. Ed.) Englewood Cliffs, N.J.: Prentice-Hall, 1968.

EISEN, N. H. Chamberlin's method: a proposed application. *Science,* 1965, *149,* 248–249.

EVRAIFF, W. *Helping counselors grow professionally.* Englewood Cliffs, N.J.: Prentice-Hall, 1963.

ROGERS, C. R. *Client-centered therapy.* Boston: Houghton Mifflin, 1951.

STEWART, L. H., & WARNATH, C. F. *The counselor and society.* Boston: Houghton Mifflin, 1965.

TYLER, L. E. *The work of the counselor* (2nd Ed.). New York: Appleton-Century-Crofts, 1961.

41.   Divergences and Convergences in Counseling or Psychotherapy

C. H. Patterson

DIVERGENCES

PHILOSOPHY AND CONCEPTS

While there are numerous specific differences among theories of counseling or psychotherapy relating to the nature of man and the nature of emotional disturbance, these may be reduced to a single basic difference in what Allport refers to as the image of the nature of man (Allport, 1962). Allport describes three models. The first is that of man as a re-active being. Here man is viewed as a biological organism reacting to stimuli in his environment. He is determined by his experiences, by his past learning or conditioning, and by potential reconditioning. The concepts representing this point of view include reaction, reinforcement, reflex, respondent, reintegration, and reconditioning. Man as a reactive being is the image of man assumed by the behavior theorists and by counselors and psychotherapists who take a learning or behavior theory approach to counseling or psychotherapy.

Allport's second image sees man as a reactive being in depth. This is the view of depth psychology, including psychoanalysis. Rather than being conceived as a being reacting to his environment, man is seen as reacting to his innate drives, motives, and needs, and influenced by their past frustration or satisfaction. Concepts representative of this view of the nature of man include repression, regression, resistance, abreaction reaction formation, and recall and recovery of the past.

The images of the nature of man presented by the learning or behavior theory approaches and by depth psychology are similar in a basic respect. Both see man as reacting to forces or stimuli, in the one case from within, in the other from without. In the one case man is a victim of his environment; in the other, of his innate needs and drives. These two images may thus be combined to constitute a single model of man as a reactive being.

In contrast to this image is a second (Allport's third) model. Allport calls this the image of man as a being-in-the-process-of-becoming—a view of man as personal, conscious, future-oriented. Related concepts include tentativeness and commitment. This model represents the viewpoint of existentialism.

These two models appear to underly differing approaches to counseling or psychotherapy, with behavior therapy, learning theory approaches, and psychoanalysis in one group, and client-centered and existential approaches in the other.

THE COUNSELING PROCESS

The therapy process is viewed differently by the various approaches. Psychoanalysis stresses insight in relation to the past, achieved by skillful interpretation. For Kelly therapy is the process of loosening old constructs and reconditioning personal constructs. For Ellis it is a matter of convincing the client that he has been functioning irrationally and teaching him a more rational structure by which to live. The client-centered approach conceives of the counseling process as the experiencing, in a psychologically safe relationship, of feelings which have previously been too threatening for the client to experience freely and fully. Behavior therapy views counseling as the process of eliminating undesirable behavior through desensitization, extinction, and reconditioning. Existentialists see counseling as the subjective encounter of two individuals in an affective relationship.

The organization of this book is based upon a continuum in terms of the various concepts of the counseling process. The continuum varies from highly rational approaches at one end to strongly affective approaches at the other end. In the rational approach the counseling process tends to be planned, objective, and impersonal. In the affective approach it is considered as being warm, personal, and spontaneous. One approach emphasizes reason and problem-solving; the other, affect and experiencing. Although there are probably no pure forms of either approach, the above distinction appears to be one which is supported by an examination of the various points of view. In fact, it appears that there may be two divergent trends in counseling—one toward a more cognitive approach and the other toward a more affective approach, so that there may be a bimodal distribution, or a dichotomy, in the making.

Another differentiation of approaches in terms of process is the insight-action dichotomy of London (1964). He includes under the insight therapies client-centered therapy and existential analysis, as well as the various schools of psychoanalysis. Although there are differences among the insight approaches, London sees these as insignificant in comparison to their commonalities. There are two commonalities which stand out and dwarf other likenesses as well as differences: "1. The single allowable instrument of the therapy is talk, and the therapeutic sessions are deliberately conducted in such a way that, from start to finish, the patient, client, analysand, or counselee does most of the talking and most of the deciding of what will be talked about. 2. The therapist operates with a conservative bias against communicating to the patient important or detailed information about his own life, that is to say, the therapist tends to hide his personal life from the patient" (London, 1964). Techniques such as free association and permissiveness lead to exposure of the repressed or unconscious material, which is then responded to by means of reflection, empathic understanding, or interpretation by the therapist, leading to insight on the part of the client.

Action therapies, or behavior therapies, on the other hand, are not concerned with verbalizations, or talk, but with behavior, actions, or symptoms. The action therapist operates on behavior, and "he cares not a whit what the patient does or does not say about himself or even know about himself except insofar as such *behaviors* have concrete and demonstrable value for producing change." Two characteristics of action therapists, according to London, are: "1. The therapist assumes a much greater influence over the detailed conduct of the treatment sessions, and possibly over the outside life of the patient, than insight therapists would. 2. The therapist is much more responsible for the outcome of treatment, that is, for whatever changes take place in the patient, than are insight therapists" (London, 1964).

Ullmann and Krasner propose essentially the same dichotomy in their distinction between evocative or expressive therapies and behavior therapy, although they recognize that there are overlappings in techniques (Ullmann, 1965). While learning theory concepts are present in expressive therapy, in behavior therapy they are systematically applied.

In terms of the rational-affective dichotomy, both insight and action therapies may be considered as rational approaches. In insight therapy, the process or approach is rational in terms of the theory of personality and its disorders, and the techniques tend to be rational discussions of problems. In action therapy the approach is also rational in terms of its underlying theory of the causation of behavior and its theory that behavior disorders are caused by faulty learning, which must be corrected by the application of specific techniques rather than by consideration of affects or feelings in a personal relationship. Thus there would appear to be a need for another category, one that would include those approaches which minimize a rational, logical, cause-effect approach to problems and their solutions, but emphasize feelings, attitudes, and emotions and their treatment or modification by understanding, accepting, and empathizing with the client in a close personal relationship.

GOALS AND PURPOSES

If one examines the goals of different approaches, one finds an amazing range and variety. Some therapists speak of personality reorganization, others of curing a disease or illness, others of adjustment to the environment, society, or culture. Still others are concerned with the development of independence and responsibility, or with assisting the client to use his potentialities, or with helping the client to actualize himself. Yet others are concerned with helping the client feel better or with removing disturbing symptoms.

The rational therapies may emphasize the solution of problems, the making of decisions, or the learning of problem-solving behavior. The affective approaches may emphasize the development of self-esteem, congruence between the self or self-concept and the ideal self, self-acceptance, or the achievement of a sense of meaning in life.

If we use London's dichotomy, the insight therapies have as their goal self-understanding in terms of the motives, needs, and drives which have led to disturbed behavior or symptoms. Such understanding may or may not lead to or be accompanied by changed behavior. In psychoanalysis, what was id becomes ego, the unconscious or repressed becomes conscious, awareness of the historical causes of present behavior becomes insight. Action therapy has as its goal the removal of symptoms, as simply and as quickly as possible. The goal is clear, simple, and specific and does not depend upon the client's insight into or understanding of the origins of his symptoms.

To the insight therapist symptoms are literally that—indications of an underlying disturbance or problem which needs to be understood to be solved. But for the action therapist the symptom *is* the disturbance or problem, and he tries "more directly to eliminate the symptom so that the patient will feel better, and it makes no difference to him what the patient does or does not understand about anything. . . . He shapes behavior (in the lower case), not tampering with 'selves' or 'souls' or even 'personalities.' And if he can, by argument, seduction, threat, or even skillful violence (as a surgeon does), excise the symptom's painful barb, then he has done enough, but not too much" (London, 1964).

There are obviously many differences among the various approaches to counseling or psychotherapy, in methods or techniques, goals or purposes, and philosophy. Sundland and Barker studied the differences in orientation in a group of 139 psychotherapists who were members of the American Psychological Association, using a Therapist Orientation Questionnaire containing sixteen subscales (Sundland & Barker, 1962). These scales included, among others, Frequency of Activity, Type of Activity, Emotional Tenor of the Relationship, Spontaneity, Planning, Conceptualization of the Relationship, Goals of Therapy, Theory of Personal Growth, Theory of Neurosis, Theory of Motivation, and Criteria for Success. The therapists distributed themselves over the range of scores from "strongly agree" to "strongly disagree" on most of the scales. The therapists were classified into three groups—Freudians, Sullivanians, and

Rogerians—and compared on the scales. The three groups differed significantly on nine of the sixteen scales, with the Sullivanians being in the middle position in eight of these comparisons. The Freudian group, compared to the Rogerian group, believed that the therapist should be more impersonal, plan his therapy, have definite goals, inhibit his spontaneity, use interpretation, conceptualize the case, and recognize the importance of unconscious motivation. These results support those of Strupp (1955). Only one difference was found between therapists grouped by levels of experience.

A factor analysis of the sixteen scales yielded six factors. A general factor cut across most of the scales, providing a major single continuum upon which therapists vary. One end is labeled "analytic" (not simply "psychoanalytic") and the other is designated as "experiential" by Sundland and Barker. The "analytic" therapist emphasizes conceptualizing, planning therapy, unconscious processes, and restriction of spontaneity. The "experiential" therapist emphasizes nonverbal, nonrationalized experiencing; the personality of the therapist; and therapist spontaneity. More therapists tended toward the "analytic" approach than toward the "experiencing" approach.

Wallach and Strupp (1964) obtained similar results from factor analysis of the ratings of two groups of therapists on a scale of Usual Therapeutic Practices. The major factor was called the maintenance of personal distance. Four groupings of therapists—Orthodox Freudians, Psychoanalytic General, Sullivanian, and Client-centered—were compared, with the first group being highest in the personal distance factor, the second group next highest, and the remaining two about the same but lower than the other two.

McNair and Lorr (1964) studied the reported techniques of 192 male and 73 female psychotherapists (67 psychiatrists, 103 psychologists, and 95 social workers) in 44 Veterans Administration Mental Hygiene Clinics, using an instrument developed on the basis of the Sundland and Barker Therapist Orientation Scale. They hypothesized three dimensions to be measured by the AID scales: (A) psychoanalytically oriented techniques, (I) impersonal versus personal approaches to the patient, and (D) directive, active therapeutic methods. All three dimensions emerged in the factor analysis of the 49 scales included in the analysis. High scores on the A factor represent traditional psychoanalytic techniques. High scores on the I factor represent a detached, objective, impersonal approach, while low scores represent emphasis on therapist personality and the therapist-patient relationship. High scores on the D factor indicate therapist setting of goals, planning of treatment, and leading of the interview, and acceptance of social adjustment as a major goal. Low scores indicate lack of therapist direction of the interview and belief in patient determination of therapy goals. While the three factors are intercorrelated, McNair and Lorr consider them independent.

These studies support the existence of differences among therapists. The Sundland and Barker study provides evidence for the rational-affective continuum or dichotomy. The McNair and Lorr study also supports this ordering or classifying of approaches or techniques. In addition, McNair and Lorr found a factor (D) which may indicate support for London's dichotomy. Neither the Sundland and Barker nor the McNair and Lorr study would support London's classification of client-centered and existential approaches with psychoanalysis in a homogeneous insight therapy group. However, none of these studies included behavior therapists, and the results would no doubt have been different if they had. With the advent of behavior therapy, a new dimension has been added to psychotherapy and counseling, and it is the difference between this approach and all other approaches which now seems to present the major problem for the future.

It is in these approaches that the greatest differences in philosophy, methods, and goals appear. The behavior therapists are apparently interested in specific, immediate, concrete results. To obtain them the therapist takes responsibility for the process, and controls and manipulates the situation. He may disavow any ethical implications of his control by contending that he is a technician in the service of the client, who determines what the goals of the process should be.

The relationship therapist is concerned about more general, long-range goals. He gives the client the responsibility for the direction and the pace of the counseling process. While he may be very active, it is not the directive, manipulative activity of the behavior therapist, but the activity of empathizing with and understanding the client and communicating that understanding. Paradoxically, however, he may not accept the specific goals of the client, imposing his own goals of self-understanding, self-realization or self-actualization on the client. But implicit, if not explicit, in this goal is greater freedom for the client in his specific behavior. By choosing the goal of maximum future freedom for the client, a goal which is presumably that of our society, the therapist resolves the value issue of imposing his own specific goals on the client.

CONVERGENCES

With all the differences among approaches, are there no commonalities or similarities among all, or even some, of the major systems? There have been a number of attempts to discover or define common elements (Patterson, 1959). The student who has read the preceding chapters carefully will probably have noted a number of similarities among most, if not all, of the systems described.[1] The search for common elements is stimulated by the observed fact that all approaches report successes; in fact, with the exception of the claims of the behavior therapists, the rate of success claimed is approximately the same for all approaches, that is, about two thirds of those treated. It is reasoned that although the approaches may appear to be different, there must be common elements, unless there are different ways of achieving success or results. It is also possible that the same results are not achieved, but that different approaches lead to different results, that is, that the criteria for success are different among the various approaches. It is also possible, as some behaviorists point out, that the common rate of success is the result either of spontaneous recovery, with no approach being effective, or of the so-called placebo effect, which we shall consider later.

PHILOSOPHY AND CONCEPTS

It would seem to be difficult to find a common philosophy, or even a single common concept, among the points of view covered in this book. As has been indicated above, concepts relating to the nature of man and the nature of emotional disturbances vary considerably. There would seem to be little, if anything, in common between a concept of man as determined by his environment or by his internal needs and drives, on the one hand, and the concept of man as a person capable of making choices and free to do so, on the other hand; or between the concept of man as essentially an organism to be manipulated by rewards and punishments, on the one hand, and on the other, as having the potential for growth and development in the process of self-actualization.

Nevertheless, as minimal as it may appear, there is agreement in the view of man as capable of changing, or at least of being changed. He is not hopelessly predetermined, but at any stage may still be pliable. A learning theory approach actually may assume that man is infinitely susceptible to change. Skinner expresses this as follows: "It is dangerous to assert that an organism of a given species or age cannot solve a given problem. As a result of careful scheduling, pigeons, rats, and monkeys have done things in the last five years which members of their species have never done before. It is not that their forebears were incapable of such behavior; nature had simply never arranged effective sequences of schedules" (Skinner, 1958). And, regarding the possibility of molding personality, he states: "Give me the specifications, and I'll give you the man" (Skinner, 1948).

---

[1] (Editor's note) Patterson refers here to preceding Chapters in *Theories of Counseling and Psychotherapy.*

Other approaches may not be so optimistic about the changeability of personality or behavior, but clearly they assume this is possible; otherwise there would be no point to engaging in counseling or psychotherapy.

There is at least one other common element, and that is the recognition that (a) neurosis, disturbance, maladjustment, conflict, the presence of an unsolved problem, etc., is unpleasant and painful for the client and (b) such a state of affairs is undesirable and warrants attempts to change it.

A third possible common element is the recognition of the influence of the future—or of anticipations, hopes, or expectations related to the future—on present behavior. This is an element that appears to tie together approaches as different as operant conditioning and existentialism. In other words, the recognition that behavior is not entirely "caused" by the past but is also influenced by future consequences, or expectation of consequences, seems to be accepted by most points of view. Lindsley states it as follows, referring to operant conditioning: "The discovery that such [voluntary] behavior is subject to control by its consequences makes it unnecessary to explain behavior in terms of hypothetical antecedents" (Lindsley, 1963). May, presenting the existentialist position, writes that "the future, in contrast to the present or past, is the dominant mode for human beings" (May, 1958).

THE COUNSELING PROCESS

Our concern in this book is with individual counseling or psychotherapy. In this process it would appear that all approaches utilize the private interview, in which verbal interaction is the major component. The techniques of conditioning, which are a major aspect of behavior therapy, may be used outside the interview situation, of course; but the point here is that behavior therapy utilizes the interview. It is also true that the methods and techniques of other approaches may be applied in other situations than the counseling interview.

There are some behavior therapists who are interested in the application of conditioning techniques outside the interview situation. The control of the client's environment outside the interview is much more difficult than the control of the interview environment, however. It might also be maintained that the application of any of the methods or techniques of counseling or psychotherapy outside the interview situation does not constitute counseling or psychotherapy. The increasing use of the term "behavior modification" by those interested in behavior change through the use of conditioning techniques indicates their broader interests. Wolpe, however, wishes to retain the term "behavior therapy" and to consider this a method of psychotherapy.

The most widely known studies of commonalities among schools of psychotherapy in terms of process are those of Fiedler (1950, 1951). Fiedler found that therapists from different schools agreed upon the nature of the ideal therapeutic relationship, and that factor analysis yielded one common factor of "goodness" of therapeutic relationships. But how are these results to be interpreted in view of the studies referred to above, which found important differences? The answer seems to lie in the nature of the instruments used in the studies. Sundland and Barker developed their instrument by eliminating items upon which therapists agreed. Fiedler, on the other hand, appears to have assembled a group of items on which therapists agree. Sundland and Barker point out that items which they discarded because they did not result in a distribution of responses were similar to items used in Fiedler's studies. These items were concerned with empathy. There appears to be evidence, therefore, that therapists agree upon the importance of empathy and understanding, although the behavior therapists seem to deny or minimize the presence and importance of empathy. Nevertheless, it would appear that a minimum of empathic understanding is necessary for the continuation of the interaction of the counselor and the client; it is also a factor in effecting change, as will be demonstrated later. That is, it appears that a relationship characterized at least to some extent by interest, acceptance, and understanding is basic to influencing others therapeutically. Other factors may direct change along the lines the therapist desires, but it is the relationship itself that makes possible any change.

Thus, in addition to the common element of the interview, there appear to be a number of other aspects of the counseling process which most, if not all, approaches share. Among these are certain characteristics of the counselor or therapist and of the client or patient. The first characteristic of the therapist is a genuine interest in and concern for the client, a strong desire to help him, to influence or change him. Not only do counselors or therapists accept the possibility and desirability of client change, they are genuinely and strongly interested in being the agent of change in their clients. If they were not, they would not be engaged in counseling or psychotherapy.

Furthermore, all counselors or therapists expect their clients to change. This expectation may vary in its degree, in some instances approaching a highly optimistic or even enthusiastic expectation, while in others it may be minimal. But it is always present. There is always an attitude of hope and expectation of change. Again, without this expectation therapists would not continue in such work. A factor which may not be independent of or separate from those already discussed is an acceptance of or respect for the client as a person, an individual, which is present in spite of his problems and difficulties or his disagreeable characteristics. In other words, acceptance or respect is not conditioned upon the client's evidencing behavior which the counselor feels is desirable, good, healthy, etc. Acceptance does not preclude, therefore, disagreement with the attitudes, beliefs, and behavior of the client; it does not mean approval of them. It is a respect or even liking for him in spite of his unlikeable characteristics. It is the unconditional positive regard of client-centered therapy. It would appear that this must exist, at least to a minimal degree, or a counselor could not continue the relationship with a client. Counselors do not continue to work with clients when this condition does not exist; clients are therefore selected on the basis of the possibility of the existence of acceptance or respect.

Another element which appears to be common to all approaches is given various designations. In the client-centered approach it is referred to as "therapist genuineness" or "self-congruence." Others refer to it as "sincerity," "honesty," or "openness." The existentialists use the term "authenticity." Some approaches (such as that of Ellis) do not refer specifically to this characteristic, but it is apparent in their discussions, and particularly in their protocols, that this element is present.

There is a final characteristic which unites therapists of widely differing approaches. This is the fact that each therapist believes in or has confidence in the theory and method which he uses. Again, if he did not feel it was the best method or approach, he would not use it, but would adopt a different one. It might be hypothesized that success (or at least reports of success) bears a strong relationship to the degree of confidence the therapist has in his approach. The failure or inability of the therapist to commit himself to an approach apparently limits his effectiveness and makes of him a technician, or makes him technique-oriented. A common aspect of therapy thus appears to be the therapist's commitment to a particular method or approach.

Most, if not all, approaches therefore seem to include a relationship which on the part of the counselor or therapist is characterized by a belief in the possibility of client change; an expectation that the client will change; interest in and concern for the client, including a desire to help, influence, or change him; sincerity and honesty in the therapy process; and confidence in the approach used to achieve client change.

It is necessary to add one other point. This is that the crucial aspect of the therapist's impact or contribution is not his actual personality or behavior, nor even his intent in the relationship. It is the client's perception of the therapist which determines the therapist's characteristics and contribution. Thus the client's characteristics, his attitudes and set, are important aspects of the relationship.

Some common aspects of individuals who come to counselors or therapists for help are apparent. In the first place, as indicated above, they "hurt"—they are suffering or are unhappy because of conflicts, symptoms, unfulfilled desires or aspirations, feeling of failure or inadequacy, or lack of meaning in their lives. They are therefore motivated to change. Clients who are referred may not always be aware of their "hurt," or if they are, may not feel the need for help, or may not want it from a counselor or therapist. It may, of course, be maintained that everyone "hurts" in some respect and so could benefit from counseling.

Second, clients also believe that change is possible and expect to change, to be helped. Frank (1956, 1959, 1961) has emphasized the universality of this factor in clients. Cartwright and Cartwright (1958) indicate that this is a complex factor: there may be belief that improvement will occur, belief in the therapist as the major source of help, belief in the techniques or procedures as the major source of help, or belief in himself (the client) as the major source of help. These writers feel that it is only the last belief which leads to improvement in a positive linear manner. The other beliefs are probably present to some extent in all clients, however, The client must feel that the counselor is interested, concerned, and wants to help him. This belief appears to involve a complex of attitudes on the part of the client. The client must have some trust and confidence in the counselor and his methods or he would not enter counseling.

Third, the client must be active in, or participate in, the process. He is not a passive recipient, as is the physically ill patient being treated by a physician. All learning (behavior change) appears to require activity (whether motor, verbal, or intellectual) on the part of the learner. This kind of behavior in counseling or psychotherapy includes self-analysis or self-exploration. Truax and Carkhuff refer to it also as intrapersonal exploration or self-disclosure (1965). Jourard (1964) and Mowrer (1964) also speak of self-disclosure. It appears that the client as well as the counselor must be genuine, open, and honest in the therapy process.

Thus, all approaches seem to deal with clients who are in need of help, recognize this need, believe they can change, believe that the counselor can help them change, and engage in some activity in the attempt to change.

All approaches, then, appear to involve a relationship between a counselor and a client each of whom contributes to the relationship certain characteristics which lead to client change.

GOALS AND OBJECTIVES

It may be more difficult to find commonalities among goals than among concepts and techniques. However, the differences may not be as great as they at first appear. The behavior therapists, though they emphasize the removal of symptoms as an objective goal, also seem to recognize a broader goal. They apparently expect the client to feel better, to function better in life and its various aspects, to achieve at a higher level—in short, to live up to his potential. Salter (1961) for example, speaks of freeing the individual by "unbraking" him. There would seem to be at least a similarity here to the concept of self-actualization, which is accepted in one or another form, under varying names, by most other approaches. The conditioning therapists, too, appear to see increasing freedom and expressiveness as desirable results of therapy. This would seem to be similar to the spontaneity and openness to experience that Rogers describes as an objective. There also seems to be general acceptance of the desirability of responsibility and independence as outcomes of counseling or psychotherapy.

Although a concept such as self-actualization may be criticized as being subjective, vague, and abstract (Ford, 1963), it would seem to be possible to reach agreement on what it denotes in terms of actual behavior. Perhaps, with adequate definitions of terms, a statement of the goals of psychotherapy which includes the concepts mentioned above might be developed and be acceptable to various groups of counselors and therapists. Possibly such a statement would be similar to Rogers' description of the fully functioning person (Rogers, 1963).

There thus appears to be a considerable number of factors in common among the diverse approaches to counseling or psychotherapy. To some extent the various theories or points of view represent different ways of describing or explaining the same phenomena. There may be relatively little overlap in some cases—the elephant's tail is quite different from his trunk or ears, even though they are parts of the same elephant. In a sense, then, all theories are correct or have elements of truth. It is only reasonable to believe that formulations based upon the long experience and observation of competent men should have some validity and some commonality. Differences are in part related to the use of different emphases, to different perceptions of the same events, to differences in comprehensiveness of formulation. To some extent the differences may appear to be greater than they actually are. This may be due in part to the use of different terminology to refer to the same or similar concepts. A study of the various points of view reveals many concepts which are essentially the same but carry different labels. Differences may also be exaggerated by the propensity to emphasize differences rather than similarities.

The question to which we now turn is whether it is possible to develop a tentative integration of the common aspects that appear to exist, and to propose, in very general form, an approach to counseling or psychotherapy which will incorporate, or not be inconsistent with, the major theories that have been proposed.

An Attempt at Integration

Although there are many differences, there also appear to be many similarities among widely differing approaches to counseling or psychotherapy. Perhaps the greatest divergence is between the behavior therapies on the one hand and the existentialist approaches (including client-centered therapy) on the other. In spite of the similarities or agreements noted above, it appears that these two points of view are perceived by their adherents and by others as inconsistent and contradictory. The behavior therapies appear to be objective, impersonal, technique-oriented, and mechanical. The existential approaches may be seen as subjective, personal, and not concerned with technique. Is it possible to reconcile these apparently inconsistent approaches? Rogers, recognizing these divergent trends not only in psychotherapy but also in psychology, states that they "seem irreconcilable because we have not yet developed the larger frame of reference that would contain them both" (Rogers, 1961).

A possible reconciliation is suggested, deriving from a consideration of the different models of man delineated by Allport. Allport writes: "The trouble with our current theories of learning is not so much that they are wrong, but that they are partial" (Allport, 1961). It may be said, then, that the trouble with the behavior therapy or conditioning approach is not that it is wrong, but that it is incomplete as a description or theory of the nature of man and of his behavior and its modification. It is a "nothing but" approach. There can be no question about the existence of conditioning, about the fact that man is a reactive being who can be conditioned and reconditioned. But man is more than this; he is also a being in the process of becoming. He is not merely a mechanism or organism who is controlled by objective stimuli in his environment. He is also a being who lives, or exists, who thinks and feels, and who develops relationships with other beings. Man lives not by objective stimuli alone, but in the subtle and complex interrelationships he develops with others. He becomes disturbed or disordered in these relationships, and he changes and improves in them. This is a "something more" approach.

The essential nature or characteristic of counseling or psychotherapy, therefore, is that it is a relationship. It is a complex relationship, with various aspects. It is not simply a cognitive, intellectual, impersonal relationship, but an affective, experiential, highly personal relationship. It is not necessarily irrational, but it has nonrational aspects. The nature of man's ties to his fellow man is essentially affective.

Evidence seems to be accumulating that the effective element in counseling is the nature of the relationship established by the counselor. Goldstein, reviewing the literature on therapist-patient expectancies in psychotherapy, concludes: "There can no longer be any doubt as to the primary status which must be accorded the therapeutic relationship in the overall therapeutic transaction" (Goldstein, 1962). The behavior therapists appear to be unconcerned about the relationship or to minimize its importance. However, as indicated in the discussion of the approaches of Salter and Wolpe, it appears that the relationship is of greater significance in their methods than they admit. It should be apparent that the characteristics of the counselor or therapist and of the client discussed above are manifested in, or manifest themselves in, a relationship.

The counseling relationship always involves conditioning aspects. The accepting, understanding, nonthreatening atmosphere of the therapy situation offers the opportunity for the extinction of anxiety or for desensitization of threatening stimuli. In this relationship, where external threat is minimized, anxiety-arousing ideas, words, images, and feelings are free to appear. Moreover, they appear in a sequence that resembles the kind of hierarchy established by Wolpe, that is, from least anxiety-arousing to most anxiety-arousing. Thus, in any nonthreatening therapy relationship desensitization may be achieved in the same manner that it is by Wolpe. The relationship, by minimizing externally induced anxiety, makes it possible for the client to experience and bring out his internally induced anxieties or anxiety-arousing experiences at the time and the rate at which he can face and handle them in the accepting relationship.

In addition, operant conditioning serves to reinforce the production of verbalizations which the therapist believes are either therapeutic or necessary in order for therapy to occur. The therapist rewards these verbalizations by his interest and attention or by explicit praise and approval. At the beginning of therapy, negative elements may be rewarded—for example, the expression of problems, conflicts, fears, and anxieties; negative self-references; etc. As therapy progresses, the therapist may reinforce positive elements—for example, problem-solving efforts; positive thoughts, attitudes, and feelings; and positive self-references. The therapist expects progress of this kind and is sensitive to its expression in the client.

The question to be faced, to quote Jourard, is: "What conditions foster output of a kind of operant behavior in the *therapist* that we call 'patient-growth-fostering'? That is, what conditions serve to increase the rate at which the *therapist* will emit behavior which, in turn, serves as stimuli which evoke growth-conducive behavior in the *patient?*" (Jourard, 1961)

Conditioning principles have contributed to an understanding of the nature of the therapeutic process and the therapy relationship. But the conditioning which occurs is not the mechanical conditioning of a rat in a Skinner box. It is instead an aspect of the therapy relationship, and it takes place in and is influenced by the relationship. There is considerable evidence that the rate and extent of conditioning is influenced by the personality and attitudes of the experimenter and by his relationship to the subject (Ullmann & Krasner, 1965). This relationship involves characteristics of the client—his interest, motivations, thoughts, attitudes, perceptions, and expectations—as well as those of the counselor. It also is affected by the situation or setting in which the relationship occurs—what are called the demand characteristics in a research experiment. As Ullmann and Krasner note, "both the subject's and the examiner's expectancies, sets, and so forth have a major effect on the individual's response to the situation," and "the best results are obtained when the patient and the therapist form a good interpersonal relationship" (Ullmann & Krasner, 1965). The relationship, therefore, cannot be ignored, even in behavior therapy. Krasner points out that Skinner classified attention as a general reinforcer (1962). The most powerful influencers of behavior—or, in conditioning terms, reinforcers—are the respect, interest, concern, and attention of the therapist. The demonstration by research of the effects of these generalized reinforcers supports the theory of the importance of the relationship in counseling or psychotherapy.

There is a further point emphasizing the importance of the therapy relationship. Many, if not most, of the problems or difficulties of clients involve interpersonal relationships. It is being increasingly recognized that good interpersonal relationships are characterized by honesty, openness, sincerity, and spontaneity. Psychotherapy is an interpersonal relationship that has these characteristics. It is therefore a situation in which the client can learn good interpersonal relationships. In fact, thereapy would be limited if it tried to influence the client's interpersonal relationships by providing a different kind of relationship. And if it attempted to influence interpersonal relationships by avoiding the establishment of a therapeutic relationship, it would seem to be inefficient. Teaching, or conditioning, individual behavior in a mechanical manner would not appear to offer much hope of generalization to personal relationships outside of therapy.

London (1964) sees Mowrer as offering a solution to the inadequacies of insight therapy on the one hand and action therapy on the other. But Mowrer's approach, though not yet systematically developed or presented, is a relationship therapy (Mowrer, 1964). Mowrer, recognizing that personality is a product of interpersonal relationships, emphasizes the therapeutic value of openness and self-disclosure in interpersonal relationships. However, although he feels that such openness may begin in a relationship with an individual therapist, he states that it is seldom that more than one or two interviews are necessary. He feels that the client should move quickly from the group of two to the larger group of significant others in his life (to use Sullivan's phrase) or to the primary groups in his life (to use a sociological term).

There is thus no basic or necessary contradiction between behavior therapy and relationship therapy. One emphasizes the shaping or changing of specific aspects of behavior by specific rewards or reinforcers. The other emphasizes more general behavior changes (including changes of attitudes and feelings), achieved by the use of generalized reinforcers. Both utilize the principles of learning—one rather narrowly, emphasizing conditioning—the other more broadly, emphasizing what might be called a social learning approach (Murray, 1963). The behavior therapists are, as Ullmann and Krasner (1963) point out, systematic in their application of specific learning concepts. But it might also be said that many relationship therapists are also systematic in the application of generalized reinforcers. The conditioning or behavior therapy approach is supported by research evidence, including laboratory or experimental research. The relationship approach is also supported by research, including some of the research on conditioning. It is interesting and significant that both groups are coming to the same conclusions, one from laboratory work in conditioning, the other from experience and research in counseling or psychotherapy. It is important, however, that behavior therapists come to recognize the complexity of the learning process and its social or relationship aspects, and also that relationship therapists be aware of the conditioning that is an aspect of counseling or psychotherapy, too. But the total process, although it may be learning, is a complex one, involving various kinds of learning, and not simply operant or classical conditioning. It includes perceptual, cognitive, and affective elements, all of which are important in behavior and behavior change. The difficulty of providing a therapeutic relationship, with its necessary affective aspects, is greater than that of providing a laboratory conditioning relationship, or even a rational, problem-solving relationship in an interview.

There is an important implication of the complexity of the process and the importance of the therapist's interest, concern, and understanding. The process cannot be mechanized, routinized, simplified, or controlled in the sense of programming or of objective, planned manipulation of rewards in terms of expressing interest, concern, etc. This is because the therapist's behavior is only effective when it is sincere and spontaneous, not when it is a contrived technique. The therapist is most effective when he is a person—when he is, as the client-centered approach terms it, genuine in the relationship. While the behavior therapists strive for effectiveness by attempting to reduce treatment to the essentials of technique, it would appear that to be most effective the therapist must be a real, human person. The most effective influence is that of another person offering a genuine human relationship.

Jourard's comments are relevant here: "I believe we are on the brink of discovering that when an experienced therapist eschews technique, and just is *himself* in the presence of his patient, then he is in fact accomplishing the following things: 1. He is actually providing a condition which elicits real-self-being, that is, spontaneous, uncontrived self-disclosure in his patient. This is analogous with priming the pump, or showing the rat how the lever works. 2. He is providing a powerful reinforcement to real-self-being in his patient. Real-self-being begets real-self-being. 3. By *spontaneously* responding to the patient's output, the therapist not only fosters real-self-being in the patient, but he is also extinguishing many of the sickness-fostering responses emitted by the patient. 4. He is avoiding the therapy-defeating behavior of contrivance, seeming, and impersonal manipulation of himself and his patient. Rather, he is providing the patient with a role-model of honest, healthy behavior" (Jourard, 1961).

The evidence seems to point to the establishment of a particular kind of relationship as the crucial element in counseling or psychotherapy. It is a relationship characterized not so much by what techniques the therapist uses as by what he is, not so much by what he does as by the way that he does it. Rogers notes that "some of the recent studies suggest that a warmly human and genuine therapist, interested only in understanding the moment-by-moment feelings of this person who is coming into being in the relationship with him, is the most effective therapist. Certainly there is nothing to indicate that the coldly intellectual, analytical, factually minded therapist is effective" (Rogers, 1961). Much of what therapists do is superfluous or unrelated to their effectiveness; in fact, it is likely that much of their success is unrelated to what they do, or even occurs in spite of what they do, as long as they offer the relationship which it appears therapists of very differing persuasions do provide. To some extent at least, even the most extreme behaviorists provide such a relationship.

Two Questions

The conclusion that the essence of counseling or psychotherapy consists in a genuine human relationship characterized by interest, concern, empathic understanding, and genuineness on the part of the therapist leads to two questions.

1. What is there that is unique about this relationship? How does it differ from all good human relationships? If the answer is, as should be obvious, that there is nothing unique or different, then what is there that is special about the practice of counseling or psychotherapy? Fiedler

concluded from his studies that "a good therapeutic relationship is very much like any good interpersonal relationship" (Fiedler, 1950).

This view may be opposed by those who feel that it deprives counselors or therapists of unique powers, who fear that "it leaves the practitioner without a specialty" (Mowrer, 1964). But it should not be surprising that the characteristics of psychotherapy should be the characteristics of all good human relationships. Nor does it follow that if such characteristics are not limited to counseling or psychotherapy, they are not relevant or specific. The essence of emotional disturbances is disturbed human relationships. The individual has become estranged from others, has become detached from the community of men. His relationships with others have been ruptured or have been placed on an insecure, false, or untenable basis. He needs to re-establish good relationships with others.

But often he cannot do this alone, for several reasons. He may not be able to change the behavior that contributes to the poor relationships. He may not know what behaviors are involved. Others may not provide him with the opportunity to change; or even if he changes, they may not recongize, accept, or believe in the permanence of the change. Their behavior, stimulated in part at least by his own behavior, contributes to the vicious circle of poor relationships. Such a situation is not conducive to change; the individual is, or feels, threatened by others and reacts in turn by threatening them.

There is a need, then, for someone who can accept the disturbed individual, with all his disturbed, irritating, threatening behavior, and offer him a nonthreatening relationship in which he can respond in an open, nonthreatening way. Therapy offers the opportunity for learning how to relate to others in a different and more effective way. It utilizes or embodies the principles of good human relationships, which although they appear to be simple, are not widely practiced outside of therapy. If such relationships were practiced generally, there would presumably be no emotionally disturbed people, except those whose disturbances were of organic origin. Perhaps the difficulty of providing such relationships within the confines of the patterns of many human interrelationships is the basis for the practice of the therapist avoiding relationships with clients outside the therapy relationship. While there is merit in Schofield's analysis of psychotherapy as the purchase of friendship (1964), therapy is, however, more than the offering of friendship, at least in the usual sense of the word. While the viewing of psychotherapy as something dark and mysterious classifies the therapist with magicians and witch doctors, viewing it as bought friendship places him in the same category as taxi dancers, gigolos, and call girls.

2. The characteristics of counseling or psychotherapy which have been developed above have frequently been considered nonspecific ele-

ments. It is often assumed that they are not related to the specific nature of the client's disturbance, and that while they may be considered as necessary conditions of therapy, they are not sufficient. Further, such characteristics as attention, interest, concern, trust, belief, faith, and expectation are part of what is called the placebo effect in the treatment of physical diseases. While it is not usual to insist that these effects be eliminated from counseling or psychotherapy, it is generally accepted that, as nonspecific factors, they are not sufficient, and that other methods or techniques must be included to deal with the specific aspects of the disturbance. It is generally argued that any method or technique must produce greater effects than those obtained by placebo elements in order to be considered useful.

The placebo effect is a psychological effect. Where the interest or concern is with determining the physical or physiological effect of a drug or medication on a known physical disease or disturbance, it is reasonable to consider this effect as extraneous and nonspecific. Even here, however, it is of interest to recognize and study the effects of such psychological factors on physical functioning.

But the concept of the extraneousness of the placebo effect may not be applicable in counseling or psychotherapy. Here, the disorder or disturbance is psychological. Is it not logical that the specific treatment for a psychological condition should be psychological? Should it not be reasonable to suggest that the specific treatment for disturbed human relationships is the providing of a good relationship? Is the placebo effect, as Rosenthal and Frank state, "a nonspecific form of psychotherapy"? (Rosenthal, 1956)

It has long been known that any new form of treatment of emotional disturbance, from electric shock to tranquilizers, meets with great success when it is first introduced, but that its success declines with time. This is because when it is first used, it is expected to be successful—there is hope and expectation on the part of both the therapist and the patient. Patients become the object of increased interest and attention. But as time goes on, as the procedure becomes routine, as doubts or questions arise because it is not always successful, its effectiveness decreases. Its early success was the result, in whole or part, of the placebo effect. It is only reasonable, again, that in evaluating the results of an experimental treatment, this effect should be considered nonspecific. But we might also look at the apparent success of behavior therapy in the same way. How much of its success is actually the heightening of the placebo effect? Should it not be required that this effect be eliminated in order to evaluate the real effect of conditioning?

It is strange that with all the evidence of the power of the placebo effect, it has not been recognized as the most effective approach to the treatment of psychological problems. As Krasner and Ullmann put it,

"Whereas the problem had previously been conceptualized in terms of eliminating the 'placebo effects,' it would seem reasonable to maximize placebo effects in the treatment situation to increase the likelihood of client change. The evidence is growing that 'placebo effect' is a euphemism for examiner influence variables" (Krasner & Ullmann, 1965).

NECESSARY AND SUFFICIENT CONDITIONS FOR PSYCHOTHERAPY

Are there any necessary and sufficient conditions of psychotherapy, and if there are, what are they? Ellis (1959), criticizing the necessary and sufficient conditions proposed by Rogers (1957), concludes that these are no necessary conditions, but that there are a number of sufficient conditions. With the wide variety of approaches and methods in counseling or psychotherapy, all of them claiming success with some apparent justification, this would appear to be a reasonable position to take.

But if there is a common element in all methods and approaches, it would also be reasonable to conclude that this element would be the necessary and sufficient condition of psychotherapy. We have attempted to show that this common element is the relationship between the client and the therapist. The relationship is a complex one, and it is possible that we do not understand it completely and are thus not able to specify all its aspects. But at least some of its aspects are known, and they include those enumerated above. They have been demonstrated to be sufficient conditions for therapeutic personality change (Truax, 1963; Truax & Carkhuff, 1964; Truax & Carkhuff, 1965). In addition to the research on psychotherapy, there is considerable evidence of the positive influences these conditions have on behavior when they are incorporated into the programs of institutions ranging from industries to schools to mental hospitals. The effects of the use of environmental treatment in the form of the therapeutic milieu in mental hospitals seem to be evident, and they seem to proceed essentially from the change in human relationships between staff and patients. These are essentially the conditions postulated by Rogers. Whether they are necessary as well as sufficient conditions is not so easily demonstrated. If these conditions are necessary as well as sufficient, then it must be shown, not only that therapeutic personality change occurs when they are present, but that it does not occur when they are absent. It can, of course, be demonstrated that changes in behavior can be obtained when these conditions are not present, as in simple conditioning, which may not involve the presence of another person, or as in instances of coercion by the use of threat or physical force, including punishment. But it can be questioned whether such changes are therapeutic.

There is some evidence from research on psychotherapy that in the absence of these conditions in psychotherapy, positive change does not occur. Truax (Truax, 1963; Truax & Carkhuff, 1964; Truax & Carkhuff, 1965) found that while the (schizophrenic) patients of therapists evidencing high conditions of accurate empathy, unconditional positive regard, and self-congruence improved, patients of therapists evidencing low levels of these conditions showed negative personality changes. Similar results have been found with clients in college counseling centers, according to Truax. There also appears to be considerable evidence that the absence of these conditions in other situations leads to psychological disturbance. This evidence includes studies of the influence of schizophrenogenic mothers, the effects of the double bind, the effects of an institutional environment lacking in human attention on infants and children, the results of sensory isolation, and the effects of imprisonment.

There seems, then, to be evidence that the elements of the therapeutic relationship described in this chapter are common to all approaches to counseling or psychotherapy, and that where they are absent, positive change or development does not occur. There thus appears to be a basis for considering these elements the necessary and sufficient conditions for psychotherapeutic change.

REFERENCES

ALLPORT, G. W. "Psychological models for guidance." *Harvard Educ. Rev.* 1962, 32, pp. 373–381.

ALLPORT, G. W. In R. May, ed., *Existential psychology.* New York: Random House, 1961, p. 85.

CARTWRIGHT, D. S. & CARTWRIGHT, R. D. "Faith and improvement in psychotherapy." *J. of counsel. psychol.*, 1958, 5, pp. 174–177.

ELLIS, A. "Requisite conditions for basic personality change." *J. of consult. psychol.*, 1952, 23, pp. 538–540.

FIEDLER, F. "The concept of an ideal therapeutic relationship." *J. of consult. psychol.*, 1950, 14, pp. 235–245.

FIEDLER, F. "A comparison of therapeutic relationships in psychoanalytic, nondirective, and Adlerian therapy." *J. of consult. psychol.*, 1950, 14, pp. 436–445.

FIEDLER, F. "Factor analyses of psychoanalytic, nondirective, and Adlerian therapy." *J. of consult. psychol.*, 1951, 15, pp. 32–38.

FORD, D. H. & URBAN, H. B. *Systems of psychotherapy.* New York: Capricorn, 1961, p. 24.

FRANK, J. D. "The dynamics of the psychotherapeutic relationship psychiatrist," *Psychiat.*, 1959, 22, pp. 17–39.

FRANK, J. D. *Persuasion and healing.* Baltimore: Johns Hopkins Press, 1961.

GOLDSTEIN, A. P. *Therapist patient expectancies in psychotherapy.* New York: Macmillan, 1962, p. 105.

JOURARD, S. M. *The transparent self.* Princeton, N.J.: Van Nostrand, 1964.

JOURARD, S. M. "On the problem of reinforcement by the therapist of healthy behavior in the patient." In F. B. Shaw, ed., *Behavioristic approaches to counseling and psychotherapy.* Tuscalousa, Ala.: University of Alabama Press, 1961, p. 14.

KRASNER, L. "The therapist as a social reinforcement machine." In H. H. Strupp & L. Luborsky, eds., *Research in psychotherapy.* Washington, D.C.: American Psychological Association, 1962, p. 67.

KRASNER, L. & ULLMAN, L. P., eds., *Research in behavior modification.* New York: Holt, Rinehart, and Winston, 1965, p. 230.

LINDSLEY, O. "Free operant conditioning and psychotherapy." In J. Masserman and J. L. Moreno, eds., *Current psychiatric therapies.* New York: Grune & Stratton, 1963.

LONDON, P. *The Modes and morals of psychotherapy.* New York: Holt, Rinehart, and Winston, 1964.

MAY, R. "Contributions of existential psychotherapy." In R. May, E. Angel, & H. F. Ellenberger, eds., *Existence.* New York: Basic Books, 1958, p. 69.

MCNAIR, D. M. & LORR, M. "An analysis of professed psychotherapeutic techniques." *J. of consult. psychol.*, 1964, *28*, pp. 265–271.

MOWRER, O. H. *The new group therapy.* Princeton, N.J.: Van Nostrand, 1964.

MURRAY, E. J. "Learning theory and psychotherapy: biotropic versus sociotropic approaches." *J. of counsel. Psychol.*, 1963, *10*, pp. 251–255.

PATTERSON, C. H. *Counseling and psychotherapy: theory and practice.* New York: Harper & Row, 1959, chap. 12.

ROGERS, C. R. "Psychotherapy today or where do we go from here." *Amer. j. of psychother.*, 1963, *17*, pp. 5–16.

ROGERS, C. R. "The fully functioning person." *Psychotherapy: theory, research and practice*, 1963, *1*, pp. 17–26.

ROGERS, C. R. "Divergent trends." In R. May, ed., *Existential Psychology.* New York: Random House, 1961, p. 85.

ROGERS, C. R. *On becoming a person.* Boston: Houghton Mifflin, 1961, p. 269.

ROGERS, C. R. "The necessary and sufficient conditions of therapeutic personality change." *J. of consult. psychol.*, 1957, *21*, pp. 95–103.

ROSENTHAL, D. & FRANK, J. D. "Psychotherapy and the placebo effect." *Psychol. Bull.*, 1956, *53*, pp. 294–302.

SALTER, A. *Conditioned reflex therapy.* New York: Capricorn, 1961, p. 24.

SCHOFIELD, W. *Psychotherapy: The purchase of friendship.* Englewood Cliffs, New Jersey: Prentice-Hall, 1964.

SKINNER, B. F. "Reinforcement today." *Amer. Psychol.*, 1958, *14*, pp. 94–99.

SKINNER, B. F. *Walden Two*, New York: Macmillan, 1948, p. 243.

STRUPP, H. H. "An objective comparison of Rogerian and psychoanalytic techniques. *J. of consult. psychol.*, 1955, *19*, pp. 1–17.

SUNDLAND, D. M. & BARDER, E. N. "The orientations of psychotherapists." *J. of consult. psychol.*, 1962, *26*, pp. 201–212.

TRUAX, C. B. "Effective ingredients in psychotherapy: an approach to unraveling the patient-therapist interaction." *J. of counsel. psychol.*, 1963, *10*, pp. 256–264.

TRUAX, C. B. & CARKHUFF, R. P. "The old and the new: theory and research in counseling and psychotherapy." *Personnel and guid. J.*, 1964, *42*, pp. 860–866.

ULLMANN, L. P. & KRASNER, L., eds., *Case studies in behavior modification.* New York: Holt, Rinehart, and Winston, 1965.

UNGERSMA, A. J. *The search for meaning.* Philadelphia: Westminster Press, 1961, p. 55.
WALLACH, M. S. & STRUPP, H. H. "Dimensions of psychotherapist activities." *J. of consult. psychol.*, 1964, *28*, pp. 120–125.

SECTION TEN

Organizational and Administrative Functions

THE final section of this collection deals with administrative and organizational concerns and their implications for the development and performance of the guidance function. In accord with the previously stated rationale, articles were chosen to reflect conceptual elements which generally transcend a particular setting, though in this section the public school is the setting for all of the selections.

In the initial selection Kehas develops a case for functional or process organization. Thus, the responsibility for the performance of a given sphere of activities is delegated to those who possess expertise in that sphere. Authority is by knowledge rather than by sanction. The implication is that some functions such as guidance, which are developmental and pervasive through an organization, require an articulated program, preferably developed and overseen by a professional trained in that specific sphere of activities. Kehas reports the progress of such an organizational approach in the guidance Laboratory Schools at the University of Chicago. His rationale is similar to those discussed earlier: that education is not synonomous with teaching or learning, but rather is more significantly conceptualized as consisting of coequal components of instruction, administration and guidance.

Brumbaugh reports the results of social-psychologically oriented research dealing with dimensions of control, inclusion, and affection in the interpersonal relationships of school personnel. Developing the results of his and other's research toward a theory that indicates how an organization may exploit individuals, Brumbaugh sees the need for guidance personnel to become proficient in intra-organizational human relation skills, and generally in helping individuals, including other professional staff, to find acceptable ways of maximizing themselves as creative persons in an essentially organizational society.

Samler, who has had many years of experience in administering a large-scale federal government counseling service, discusses problems resulting from harmful friction between counseling personnel and administration. Samler's proposed solutions reflect a realistic and mature insight into the art and science of effective organizational development.

In a survey of typical textbooks and literature dealing with the organization and administration of guidance services in the schools Calia[1] concluded that only two main ideas, both in the need of qualification, emerge: (1) administrators should subscribe to the democratic process and (2) organizational planning must be a function of local conditions. He concludes that such a "common-sense," vague approach needs to be buttressed by sound theoretical principles and meaningful research. All the articles of this section address themselves to this call. Specifically, each of the authors exhibits concern with the development of effective and efficient means of both organizing and managing guidance function activities in order to maximize their impact on the total educational process. Further, each author maintains that professionals in guidance should draw upon the increasing body of theory and research in organizational development and administrative science as a necessary step in the improvement of practice.

[1] Calia, Vincent F. Organization theory and research: some implications for guidance programs. *Personnel and Guidance Journal.* April, 1965, p. 756.

42.   Administrative Structure and Guidance Theory

Chris D. Kehas

This article is concerned primarily with two problems: (a) the administrative structure in schools, particularly with respect to the notion of authority, and (b) the development of distinctive and powerful conceptual frameworks *of* guidance in education, i.e., theory building in guidance. It will be argued that the distribution of and the definitions of authority in schools work against the development of a distinctive guidance function, and consequently, impede the development of guidance theory and the carrying out of guidance research *in* school settings.

THE AUTHORITY DIMENSION IN SCHOOLS

Ultimate responsibility, or better, authority in school systems is associated with a superintendent; in a given school, with a principal. This is the base line, the starting point not only when one talks about school organization *per se*, but also when one goes about organizing and planning new schools. Typically, in theories or writings of educational administration, the existence of an authority dimension is simply asserted, and then defined in such phrases as "line and staff," "hierarchical arrangements," and "superior and subordinate."

Have notions of authority in schools simply been adopted from elsewhere and imposed on the school situation; have they been brought in and adapted and modified to the school situation; have they developed out of experiences and investigations *in the schools?* The last—though seemingly necessary and, to some degree, desirable—appears highly unlikely. Indeed, the movement in education to develop administrative theory *qua* administrative theory suggests that such considerations may not even be prominent.

Serious examination and study should be given to the question of authority in school systems, and primarily to the notion of the "autonomy of the principal in *his* school." Such examination and study is necessary because of the central importance of this notion in the actual administration and organization of the schools. Further, I would argue that a redistribution of authority as regards the guidance function in schools must come about—that authority for guidance in a system must reside with the

Chris D. Kehas, "Administrative Structure and Guidance Theory," from *Counselor Education and Supervision*, Spring, 1965, pp. 147–53. Copyright © 1965 by the American Personnel and Guidance Association, Inc., Washington, D.C. Reprinted by permission.

chief guidance officer of that system, and that the involvement of others with the *basic* decisions regarding guidance must be circumscribed. Simon, an influential contributor in the development of administrative theory, has stated the issue quite succinctly:

. . . A fundamental device for securing expertise in organization decisions is to locate the expert in a strategic position in the formal hierarchy of authority —that is, in a position where his decisions will be accepted as decisional premises by the other organizational members. This is a major advantage of organization by "process". . . .

. . . . .

To secure the advantages, therefore, of expertise in decision-making, it is necessary to go beyond the formal structure of authority. The "authority of ideas" must gain an importance in the organization coordinate with the "authority of sanction" . . . (1957, pp. 137–138).

This assertion obviously brings the widely-prevailing notion of the administrator as *educational* leader into serious question, suggesting, in the least, that some redefinition is necessary. The net effect of the argument here is not to ask of the administrator simply, "try to understand us better." The argument is for a functional allocation of authority in school systems, for a division of authority based on competence and expertise rather than on some unexamined notion of authority based on "ultimate responsibility." As Simon has pointed out, the principle of "unity of command" can be criticized on the ground that it does not give any reason why an individual cannot accept certain decisional premises from one superior and other non-conflicting premises from another. He suggests, as one method of resolving conflicts in authority, the possibility of a division of authority wherein "each unit in the organization is assigned some specific area over which it has exclusive authority, and that the decisional premises of any individual that fall within this area are subject to that authority" (p. 141), i.e., a functional allocation of authority. In effect, the vision is that counselors and other guidance personnel within schools would be primarily responsible and responsive to the chief guidance officer for some things, and to the principal for others. The responsibilities about the *substance* of guidance must reside with the chief guidance officer, the expert, if you will, on guidance in the situation. A major difficulty impeding this development is that guidance simply is neither seen nor experienced as a separate unit, either structurally or conceptually; it characteristically is seen as either administration or teaching, or as some combination of both.

An authority framework based simply on notions of "superordinate-subordinate" and "unity of command" is grossly inadequate for conceptualizing or even describing, let alone establishing, the working relationships among professionals. In such a framework, the subordinate is expected to act without deliberation on his own part. Such thinking may be appropriate for administrators and employees in some settings but in schools, the administrator sits with an association of professionals and his transactions with both teachers and counselors should, in the least, be collaborative. The professional must have adequate freedom to deliberate; he gains this freedom more by being responsible to one whose authority is based on ideas, i.e., on the professional knowledge, not merely on sanctions. Indeed, historically the position of the principal was based to some degree on just this authority. Such basis seems woefully inappropriate in the modern school setting.[1] For the administrator is not necessarily "more than" a teacher or a counselor, but simply "different from"; the functions are related but not necessarily in a hierarchical fashion.

Fundamentally, I view organization as the structuring of the process of administration. The purpose of structuring is to institutionalize the decision-making process. And, if authority means simply the distribution of responsibility for certain aspects of this decision-making process, it then seems logical, and valid, and desirable, to conclude that the chief guidance officer should have the responsibility for the basic guidance decisions.

My concern arises not from a concern with administration *per se*, but from a growing realization that some current administrative thinking and practice impinge severely on the purposeful development of guidance in many important ways. It has been suggested that much of our guidance activities are embedded in administrative and organizational settings that preclude the furtherance of gains, that hinder the development of guidance as a science, as a profession (Kehas, 1961). Shertzer and Stone (1963) have very cogently analyzed some of the existing administrative deterrents to such development. Peters (1963) has suggested that the Director of Guidance needs "to take visibly more active leadership in promoting guidance" and that the traditional autonomy of the principal must be qualified. However, as long as responsibility for the decisional premises regarding the substance and definition of guidance are lodged with the chief administrator—and not with a guidance administrator—I believe the *purposeful development of guidance* as a science, and as a profession, will be seriously constrained.

An attempt will be made to illustrate the notions advanced by turning to some actual explorations in the testing of these notions. The data are a school in process.

---

[1] Recent efforts by teachers in large city school systems, e.g., New York and Chicago, to gain a greater voice in the establishment of educational policies would seem to be additional evidence suggesting an examination of the notion of the administrator as chief educational officer.

Redirecting a Guidance System

A reorganization of the Laboratory Schools of the University of Chicago is being pursued with the avowed intent of reviving a sense of, and dedication to, research and experimentation in education. One aim of the reorganization is to make it possible for contributions to knowledge about guidance processes and guidance theory to develop. I will attempt to describe what sort of reorganization of the administrative structure seems necessary to move towards the fulfillment of this aim. Only a brief description of the "before" and the "after" is possible at this time, and should suffice for our purposes here.

What was the nature of the earlier system?[2] Leadership for the guidance program was lodged within an Office of Student Personnel Services, a repository of myriad functions, ranging from attendance through scheduling to academic counseling. The authority of the Director of Student Personnel Services was subordinate to that of the two Directors; moreover, in practice, he was effectively excluded from any involvement with the Primary School. His relationship to the educational processes was one primarily of *service*, his guidance functions closely akin to those of *personnel management*.

More directly, the guidance function was lodged with Grade-Level Chairmen, and was inextricably woven in with the administrative and the instructional roles. Few, if indeed any, of those charged with the guidance function viewed their guidance task as being *basically different* from either the administrative or the instructional functions. Teachers with varying degrees of training and competence in guidance—indeed, even certifiable by the State—were relieved of varying amounts of teaching responsibilities at the different levels in order to do some things that teachers would and could do if they had the time. In short, the guidance function had been defined by the administration, and was viewed primarily as a further specialization of teaching.

Such a context, it was argued, would not allow for the development of either guidance theory or research, for by definition it ruled out the development of a distinctive and unique guidance function. Now, the work of the earlier Student Personnel Services has been divided in two and made separate—(1) Administrative Services and (2) Guidance. Responsibility for the guidance function—defined as counseling, clinical, and testing activities—is resident in a Director of Guidance. The responsibilities of this Director span the Laboratory Schools, and his position

---

[2] The basic organization of the Laboratory Schools was changed in September 1963 *from* two units—Secondary and Primary Education—each headed by a Director *to* four schools—Nursery, Lower, Middle, and High—each led by a principal.

with respect to each of the Principals is being established as co-ordinate.

The posture of guidance towards students and teachers is also changing. The effect of the redefinition has been one of enlarging and expanding the notion of *basic* education within the Laboratory Schools to incorporate such dimensions of concern as personality growth, emotional development, identity formation, and establishment of self. In addition to *formally acknowledging institutional responsibilities,* the redefinition provides for new personnel—counselors—whose primary involvement resides within these areas, whose function is viewed as being *complementary* to that of teaching and just as basic, and whose primary involvement is *with students* and their concerns. In effect, the basic starting point is that there exists a set or an area of learnings which the school deals with, learnings which are *not taught,* but are learned best through involvement with a counselor. The counselors are members of the Guidance Staff, and are assigned by the Director of Guidance, in consultation with the Principals, to the separate schools. They are primarily responsible to the Director of Guidance.

The desirability of and the need for a certain amount of autonomy for a Director of Guidance in order that conceptually-oriented, professional guidance programs be developed have been recognized. That the granting of such autonomy to a Director of Guidance raises serious questions about the well-established autonomy and authority of the Principal in his school has been neither denied nor ignored. It has been confronted and, on occasion, welcomed as providing an area of study that may have ramifications in administrative theory. The impulse to eliminate the conflict has been suspended and the strain is tolerated in order that it may be examined in a way which will hopefully increase our understanding of school organization.

The kind of guidance represented here involves, then, not only more technical expertise in a function formerly performed by teachers, but the institutionalization of a *new* and distinct purpose complementary to and associated with more established concerns—and implications thereof for the organizational structure.

SOME OF THE IMPLICATIONS AND THE ISSUES

In singularly important ways, "education" is seeking to *incorporate* guidance, yet it is extremely reluctant to be changed by it; it wishes to incorporate guidance into an existing system of explicit authorities and responsibilities, of explicit foci and explicit heirarchies, i.e., into an established structure. Such attempts result in guidance being conceived of as the administrative aspects of the instructional process, or as helping to maintain the academic processes of school administration—with what I have called personnel management. However, there may well be some fundamental incompatibilities between certain conceptual structures or frameworks of guidance and the existing administrative structures or organizations of some schools. *To bring some kinds of guidance, then, into some schools may mean that some fundamental changes in definitions and in established structures are essential.*

The following knowledge seems to be emerging from our attempts to develop guidance *in* schools: Our present thinking goes somewhat like this.

In order to build a distinct and unique body of knowledge and practice in guidance, and in order for guidance to have a more purposeful development, it would seem that *movement* in the following directions must begin:

1. Towards the Schools formally acknowledging an institutional responsibility for a new function *as basic as teaching* which centers about *individual behavioral processes*, e.g., self knowledge and personal identity.

2. Towards separating out (and distinguishing professionally) the guidance portion of the total educational process.

   a. Redistributing authority in Schools such that responsibility for the guidance function resides with a chief guidance officer.

   b. Adding new personnel—counselors—whose function is viewed and established as complementary to, and as basic as that of, teaching, and whose primary involvement is with students. (Our counselors presently are involved with about 150 students. For meaningful and personal involvement to occur, this appears to be too many students for one counselor.)

To the extent that such movement occurs, the possibilities for building a distinct body of knowledge and practice, for creating a new discipline focused on helping youth develop as persons, to build a sense of self, will be maximized.

SUMMARY

What has not been argued is that simply a change in the structure or organization will in and of itself lead to a change of function. It is theoretically possible for the same function to operate within or to emerge from two differently elaborated administrative structures; and equally possible for different functional definitions of guidance to result from similarly or even identically elaborated administrative structures. Indeed, such possibilities are exciting invitations to research and investigation. Simply changing the structure is, then, insufficient. Change must occur in the functional definitions, and in the behaviorial processes of the individuals and groups concerned.

Though not directly discussed in this paper, it should be obvious that the argument does not simply revolve about authority but that considerations of the authority structure in schools are inextricably intertwined with institutional responsibilities and purposes, establishment of professional functions, and more importantly for guidance—the roles and functions of guidance personnel, conceptual frameworks for guidance theory and practice, and programs for the preparation of guidance personnel. The purpose of this paper was to define some of the problems, suggest some of the issues and identify some of the parameters, and finally, to present one attempt to test some of these notions in schools and report the findings.

REFERENCES

KEHAS, C. D. "Toward the development of theory in the administration and organization of guidance services." *Counselor Education and Supervision,* 1961, *1,* 96–101.
PETERS, H. J. "Interferences to guidance program development." *Personnel guid. J.,* 42, 1963, 119–124.
SHERTZER, B. & STONE, S. C. "Administrative deterrents to guidance program development." *Theory into practice,* 1963, 2, 24–32.
SIMON, H. A. *Administrative Behavior* (Rev. Ed.). New York: The Macmillan Co., 1957.

43.   Interpersonal Perception in the Educational Organization: Need for the Guidance Function

Robert B. Brumbaugh

Professor Jones' paper for this collection[1] has urged that "guidance must accept a strong infusion of the sociological outlook into what has

Printed by permission of the author, Dr. Robert Brumbaugh, Associate Professor of Education, Human Resources Research Institute, West Virginia University, Morgantown, West Virginia.

[1] See Section Five.

been a preponderantly psychological and psychotherapeutic outlook." The authors of a paper recently published by the *Personnel and Guidance Journal* (Willower, *et al.*, Nov., 1967) have proposed that "since students of counseling tend to be oriented primarily in psychological directions, an organizational perspective might be especially useful." There is a growing awareness among counselor educators and practitioners alike that familiarity with not only the sociological perspective, but the broad views of organization theory as well, might contribute to a better understanding of the various systems within which and on which guidance must operate.

This paper will not attempt to review the burgeoning literature of organization theory and research[2], but will focus on certain of this writer's recent empirical findings, some concepts developed from these findings, and on the resulting notes toward an organization theory of interpersonal perception. Finally, implications for guidance will be derived from the theory.

The Empirical Findings

A recent study[3] examined the perceptions of 40 public school supervising teachers and their 40 respectively assigned student teachers (each supervising teacher was assigned *one* student teacher). The student teachers were senior and postgraduate students at a mid-western university who were enrolled for practice teaching at the secondary school level.

After the supervising teachers and their respective student teachers had been in close and continuous working contact for a period of eight weeks, the Schutz FIRO-B Scale (and other instruments) were administered to the subjects. FIRO-B purports to measure the degree of expressed or wanted inclusion, control, and affection needs possessed by a subject. These three psychological need dimensions (inclusion, control, and affection), it is proposed, are most crucial in establishing interpersonal relationships (Schutz, 1958).

During administration of the test instruments, subjects were first requested to complete the FIRO-B Scale in such a manner as to truthfully reveal their own individual feelings. Following this first test administration, each subject was then administered the FIRO-B Scale again, under instructions this time to react as he imagined his respective student teacher (or supervising teacher) might have reacted to the instrument.

---

[2] See, for example, March, 1965.
[3] For more detailed descriptions of this study; see Brumbaugh *et al.*, 1966; and Brumbaugh, 1967.

Because of the transparency[4] of FIRO-B, most subjects displayed great confidence in their ability to predict the other person's reaction to the instrument.

Analysis of the FIRO-B accuracy indices of the supervising teachers as compared to those of the student teachers indicated that there were no significant differences in accuracy on the inclusion and affection dimensions. *On the control dimension,* however, *supervising teachers were significantly more likely to be accurate in their estimates of their respective student teacher's interpersonal needs* than was conversely the case.

The Concept of Control Orientation

The foregoing data indicate an apparent sensitivity on the part of the supervising teachers to the interpersonal control needs of their respective student teachers. When compared with the perceptions made by their student teachers, the supervising teachers were significantly more likely to be accurate in estimating their student teachers' needs to exercise control over others or to be controlled by others. In viewing the results of interaction with their student teachers, the supervising teachers evidently focused on their student teachers' control needs and ignored, relatively speaking, their inclusion and affection needs. Thus, the control needs of their student teachers seem to have some relevance for the supervising teacher.

It is thought that the manifested sensitivity to the control needs of their student teachers represents a control orientation toward the student teachers on the part of the supervising teachers. (Control orientation is operationally defined as the extent to which accuracy is achieved in predicting another's score on the control dimensions of the Schutz FIRO-B Scale.)

The Concepts of Superordination and Hierarchical Role Immediacy

That both superiority of organizational position and the immediacy of hierarchical role linkages must be considered in the present theoretical formulations is underscored by a number of empirical findings.

In research focusing on the mental hospital as an organization, Gilbert and Levinson found that hospital staff members whose role per-

---

[4] Transparency refers to the degree to which the particular quality or attribute being assessed by items on a paper and pencil test can be guessed or seen-through-to by the subjects taking the test.

formances involved immediate contact with and responsibility for patients were significantly more likely to endorse a custodial client-control
ideology (as contrasted with a humanistic client-control ideology) than
were staff members such as doctors who were further removed from the
patient (Gilbert and Levinson, 1957). In other research focusing on
elementary and secondary schools, Willower, Eidell, and Hoy have found
that teachers were more likely to approve the use of external control over
students than were administrators, guidance counselors, reading consultants, and others who were further removed from contact and responsibility for students (Willower *et al.*, 1967). School organizational
personnel further removed from contact and responsibility for students
were significantly more likely to approve the use of internal student
control.

While the aforementioned studies have demonstrated that superordination and hierarchical role immediacy are related to *qualitative*
differences in client- (or subordinate-) control ideology (e.g., custodial vs.
humanistic and external vs. internal), the possibility must also be considered that these two variables may be related to *quantitative* differences in control orientation toward subordinates as well.

This possibility is empirically supported, at least in part, by Kahn
and others who found that a focal person (within an organization) receives the greatest amount of pressure from his *direct* superiors. Further,
among the superior role senders in the same chain of command as the
focal person, sent pressure does not increase with status, but, on the contrary, the *immediate* supervisor sends more pressure than does the supervisor's supervisor (Kahn, *et al.*, 1964).

Notes Toward a Theory

Jones and Thibaut have proposed that we interact with others within
fairly well-defined situations and in terms of rather constraining roles.
Our main requirement, therefore, is for information *relevant* to adequate
role performance, and, fortunately for cognitive economy, we need not be
indiscriminately attentive to all the cues provided by the other actors
(Jones and Thibaut, 1958). Bruner and Tagiuri suggest that there is a
tendency for one to notice those things about another that affect the fate
of an interaction (Bruner and Tagiuri, 1954). Chowdhry and Newcomb
found that insofar as the trait to be judged is important in the interpersonal relation of judge and judged it will be more easily judged
(Chowdhry and Newcomb, 1952).

That organizational role seems to be a determinant of the perceptions of incumbents is perhaps best empirically supported by Lieberman

(1956). Kelley found that by giving his judges different role expectations (leader, follower, or unspecified) they would concern themselves with different aspects of the stimulus persons (Kelley, 1948). Katz and Kahn, in a recent treatment of open-system organizational theory, point out that research on the differential perceptions of supervisors and subordinates shows consistently that role or position in the organization is related to perceptions no less than to attitudes and values (Katz and Kahn, 1966).

As Etzioni points out, all social units have a structure and control their members, but organizations have a distinct structure and their problem of control is especially acute. The participants need to be supervised, the supervisors themselves need supervision, and so on, all the way to the top of the organization. In this sense, the organizational structure is one of control, and the hierarchy of control is the most central element of the organizational structure (Etzioni, 1965). (One of several salient attributes characterizing Weberian bureaucratic structure is that the organization of offices follows the principle of hierarchy; that is, each lower office is under the control and supervision of a higher one [Weber, 1947].)

In the present instance it is considered probable that the hierarchical nature and immediacy of the role relationship between supervising teacher and student teacher is responsible for the supervising teachers' control orientation. That the role of supervising teacher is immediately superior or superordinate to the role of student teacher is obvious and beyond debate. (It is a well-known dilemma that the public school supervising teacher is in no way empowered to delegate his legal teaching responsibility to his student teacher. The supervising teacher therefore remains immediately responsible and liable for the actions of his student-teacher charge.)

Considering the evidence cited in the preceding discussion, it is thought that a theoretical case can be built for the existence of a control orientation on behalf of every organizational superordinate in his interaction with immediate subordinates. It can be postulated that this control concern pervades each immediate superior-subordinate linkage within the structural context of the organization and results, perhaps, from the very nature of the hierarchical structure of the organization within which such interaction takes place. Quite simply put, it appears that, in order to successfully perform the superordinate role, the incumbent of such a role must view the results of interaction with immediate subordinates through a kind of cognitive reduction screen, perceptually filtering out only those particular cues which pertain to the interpersonal control needs of immediate subordinates. This interpretation receives some support from Steiner's (1955) work. Accurate cognition of the control needs of immediate subordinates (and, of course, subsequent appropriate action based on this particular information) presumably enables the superordinate to maintain his respective leader role within the organization hierarchy. He thereby remains an effective channel through which the flow of organizational authority can be transmitted.

In addition to directing some attention to the present writer's findings which suggest that supervising teachers hold a control orientation in viewing their student teachers, studies were reviewed showing that superordination and hierarchical role immediacy are related to differential client-control ideologies. A final study was cited demonstrating empirically that subordinates are subjected to most pressure by their immediate superiors in the organizational hierarchy.

In light of these findings, it is suggested that the conceptual scheme of client-control ideology might be extended to embrace the concept of control orientation within each immediate superordinate-subordinate interactional linkage throughout the entire hierarchical structure of the organization. By virtue of its higher level of abstraction, it would appear that this hypothesis possesses more explanatory power and is capable of encompassing the former findings within its broader scope of theory.

In constructing these notes toward a theory, the author's findings were used in an attempt to affect a logical rapprochement between research which indicates that those members of organizations in closest contact with and responsibility for clients are more likely to endorse a custodial client-control ideology (in contrast to a humanistic client-control ideology) than are those members of the organization further removed from client contact and responsibility and research which indicates that subordinates are subjected to most pressure by superordinates immediately above them in the organizational hierarchy.

Using his findings which point to the possibility of a control orientation being held by public school supervising teachers in their interaction with their respective student teachers, and treating the client theoretically as an integral part of the organizational hierarchy (rather than as an adjunctive entity upon which the organization operates), it has been proposed that incumbents of *all* superordinate organizational roles employ a control orientation in viewing the results of interaction between themselves and their *immediate* subordinates. It is thought that such an orientation assists the incumbent of the superordinate role to maintain his respective leader position within the organization by providing him with a frame of reference whereby he can attempt to cope with those particular interpersonal needs of his immediate subordinates which, if otherwise were unrecognized or unexploited, might threaten his leader position.

IMPLICATIONS FOR GUIDANCE

If the present theory is valid, particularly with regard to the educational organization, and interpersonal perceptions (and, possibly, relationships) of immediate superiors and subordinates at all levels are stultified or fixated on the control phases of interaction, this explicitly emphasizes the need for guidance in such organizations. (Professor Jones' paper has addressed this subject in more general terms, referring to the historical shift from *Gemeinschaft* to *Gesellschaft* social system relationships and the accompanying need for a more formalized guidance function.)

The theory points to the need for guidance to extend its "helping relationship" to members of the educational organization at *all* levels, rather than limiting its services to the student or client level as traditionally has been the practice. It points also to the need for guidance personnel to become proficient in intra-organizational sensitivity training skills, not so much to be directed at changing the dynamics of the organization (although such training can certainly be expected to have some eventual impact on these dynamics), but to enable all participants to better understand the organizational constraints which operate on their interpersonal perceptions and relationships. The counseling service can assist participants to make the necessary individual adjustments to these organizational demands.

The present theory has attempted to account for one specific way in which the organization may exploit the individual; exploit in the sense that not all the individual's interpersonal needs may be equally relevant to the accomplishment of the organization's goals. Organizations are established to attain certain specified goals and to this extent the economics associated with such goal accomplishment induce repression of the total needs of the individual. Since ours is an organizational society,[5] it may well be the major task of guidance, as a formal part of the educational organization, to help the individual to find acceptable ways of maximizing himself as a person within the calculus of the educational organization and the broader society.

REFERENCES

BLAU, PETER M. *Bureaucracy in modern society.* New York: Random House, 1956.

BRUMBAUGH, ROBERT B. *Accuracy of interpersonal perception: a function of superordinate role.* A paper presented to the American Educational Research Association, February 16, 1967 (available as an occasional paper from the Center for the Advanced Study of Educational Administration, University of Oregon).

BRUMBAUGH, ROBERT B. "Hierarchial role immediacy and superordinate control orientation." *J. of Educ. Administr.,* in press.

BRUMBAUGH, ROBERT B., HOEDT, KENNETH C., and BEISEL, WILLIAM H., Jr. "Teacher dogmatism and perceptual accuracy," *J. of Teacher Educ.,* Fall 1966, pp. 332–335.

[5] See, for example, Blau, 1956; and Presthus, 1962.

Bruner, Jerome S. and Tagiuri, Renato. "The perception of people." In Lindzey, Gardner, ed., *Handbook of social psychology*. Reading, Mass.: Addison-Wesley, 1954, p. 642.

Chowdhry, Kalma and Newcomb, T. M. "The relative abilities of leaders and non-leaders to estimate opinions of their own groups." *J. of Abnormal Social Psychol.*, XLVII, 1952.

Etzioni, Amitai. "Organizational control structure." In James G. March, ed., *Handbook of organizations*. Chicago: Rand McNally & Company, 1965, p. 650.

Gilbert, Doris C. and Levinson, Daniel J. " 'Custodialism' and 'humanism' in mental hospital structure and in staff ideology." In Greenblatt, Milton, et al., eds., *The patient and the mental hospital*. New York: Free Press of Glencoe, Inc., 1957.

Jones, Edward E. and Thibaut, John W. "Interaction goals as bases of inference in interpersonal perception." In Tagiuri, Renato and Petrullo, Luigi, eds., *Person perception and interpersonal behavior*. Stanford, Cal.: Stanford University Press, 1958, p. 152.

Kahn, Robert L. et al. *Organizational stress: studies in role conflict and ambiguity*. New York: John Wiley & Sons, 1964, p. 167.

Katz, Daniel and Kahn, Robert L. *The social psychology of organizations*. New York: John Wiley & Sons, Inc., 1966, p. 188.

Kelley, H. H. *First impressions in interpersonal relations*. Unpublished doctoral dissertation, Massachusetts Institute of Technology, 1948.

Lieberman, S. "The effects of changes in roles on the attitudes of role occupants." *Human Relations*, IX, 1956.

March, James G., ed. *Handbook of organizations*. Chicago: Rand McNally & Company, 1965.

Presthus, Robert. *The organizational society*. New York: Alfred A. Knopf, 1962.

Schultz, William C. *FIRO: A three-dimensional theory of interpersonal behavior*. New York: Holt, Rinehart & Winston, 1958.

Steiner, I. "Interpersonal behavior as influenced by accuracy of social perception." *Psychol. Rev.*, LXII, 1955, pp. 268–275.

Weber, Max in Talcott Parsons, ed.; A. M. Henderson and Talcott Parsons, trans. *The theory of social and economic organization*. New York: Oxford University Press, 1947, pp. 329–330.

Willower, Donald J., Hoy, Wayne K., and Eidell, Terry L. "The counselor and the school as a social organization." *Personnel and Guid. J.*, November 1967, pp. 228–234.

Willower, Donald J., Hoy, Wayne K., and Eidell, Terry L. *The school and pupil control ideology*. University Park, Pa.: Administrative Committee on Research, Pennsylvania State University, 1967.

44.   The Counseling Service in the Administrative Setting: Problems and Possible Solutions

Joseph Samler

The irritation of counseling personnel with administrators, and the frustration of administration with counselors is well known. There are, of course, situations where there is mutual respect for persons and roles and appreciation of the commitments of each by each. But this is not the rule, which seems to be rather that misunderstanding and suspicion are pervasive and that now and again there is open hostility. Clearly, this is a situation in which neither counselors nor administrative personnel can do their most effective work.

The problem can be generalized. In the ways in which the specialized tasks of the culture are accomplished, there are persons with specified training and particular skills engaged to do identifiable jobs of a technical nature. These persons work under others whose duties are not technical but who determine what is to be done rather than *how*, although determining where one stops and the other begins can be quite tricky. The decision-makers determine the limits of the program, budget, and interpretation and defense of policy. One group is called technical and professional—for example engineers, physicians, psychologists, social workers, counselors, teachers. The others are managers, executives, and administrators, although they too justifiably may be seen as professionals with identifiable skills and at least a claimed mystique of their own.

These are presented as if they were pure types and there are such, of course. However, there are also many technical workers who function as first-line supervisors of technical units and others who are in charge of technical programs of some size and complexity. Administrative workers also come at various levels with lesser or greater responsibility. If this is understood no one will be misled by the discussion in this paper of the two main characters in the drama as if they did only technical work or administration.

The vocational counselor enters his practice, as do other technical personnel, following a period of training. We must assume that his extensive training socializes him in the particular culture of his profession. This means only that he and others like him believe that, (1) theirs is a body of systematic knowledge that can be acquired only through extensive training, (2) only persons so trained can exercise their skills properly, (3) persons so trained have an exclusive jurisdiction, (4) major

Joseph Samler, "The Counseling Service in the Administrative Setting; Problems and Possible Solutions," from *Personnel and Guidance Journal*, March, 1966, pp. 715–22. Copyright © 1966 by the American Personnel and Guidance Association, Inc., Washington, D.C. Reprinted by permission.

commitment is to the client. The description of the professional of our time is out of the sociology of professionalization (Wilensky, 1964) and fits the counselor reasonably well. However, the literature does not reflect well enough the counselor's responsibility to the institution employing him. This responsibility is real. A similar reality is that while the preferred professional role is identified, the general public, including administrative workers, have not, or at least not yet, completely bought the picture.

With this identity, the trained counselor assumes his duties. Out of his successful socialization in the occupation, he sets a number of implicit expectations for his working situation. These start with proper physical arrangements such as the need for privacy, range through relative independence of functioning, and include firm ideas as to the nature of supervision, the need for time and money to maintain professional interests, and particular relationships to problems and clients.

These are not willful requirements nor are they idiosyncratic. Counseling literature, the burgeoning statements on professional preparation and standards, and the instructional manuals in various large programs refer to the need for privacy, staff development time, and relatively independent practice.

We have come very far in counseling in the last 20 years. It is correct to say that guidance and counseling have become public policy. Yet here and there the stream pours past sturdy rocks so that now and again there is a good deal of turbulence. The figure of speech refers to occasional administrative attitudes concerning counseling that can be skeptical or inimical. These are not pervasive attitudes but nevertheless when they occur they cause difficulty.

Such personnel seem to feel that counseling may not really be necessary and when pressed see it as a kind of coddling. Since, nevertheless, the work has to be done, they feel short cuts could be used, and the entire process rationalized. They feel that with the passage of time counselors should become sufficiently competent to do the work faster, so that production can be stepped up. They are convinced that counseling means something going on with a client; when the counselor doesn't have a person at his desk, he is goofing off.

Other attitudes are manifested by administrative personnel who are not particularly fault finders. They see counselors as special pleaders who have unbalanced views of the total problems of the organization, who always want more staff, special funds, greater status and whose interests are very narrow. They feel that counselor requirements are overstated; the job doesn't need all that fancy preparation. Even if the job is as all-fired important as counselors say, they fail to communicate this presumed importance to administrators. Counselors are unable or unwilling to abandon fancy language in favor of simple communication.

These attitudes have been collected over time and from a number of different work settings. Regarded as manifested at any one time the picture would be misleading. There is enough here, however, to warrant concern. There is reason for thinking, moreover, that our own behavior contributes to these perceptions.

When administrative personnel are good, they are very good indeed. In nearly all cases they are exceedingly bright, and gifted, therefore, in the components of brightness, in their phenomenal memories, sound evaluation, reasoning and problem-solving. To the technician-supervisor coming to them with administrative implications of work problems they can be a considerable resource in seeing clearly the alternatives offered and their implications. Decisions are available immediately and keen strategy planned for their implementation. The pressures on administrators can be enormous and time is at a great premium. It is remarkable, therefore, that the slices of time they set aside for consideration of one or another issue seem unhurried. It is impressive to note how much work they do and how seemingly easily.

But there are other aspects of the administrative personality and functioning that can be less than friendly. Perhaps this is an inevitable part of the context of the administrative line: dependence up the line, great competitive elements, understandable commitment of the executive to the organization, lack of a formulated ethic of business conduct. At least some of these characteristics need more than quick citation.

Executive and administrative positions are loci of power and as such, as Lasswell (1948) notes, attract personality types who need the exercise of power to meet their own personality needs. This in itself is not necessarily bad except when power is used for its own sake. The actual working situation, of course, is rarely so clean cut. The problem makes itself evident in the *way* in which the work is done. For example, when decisions are handed down rather than developed, the results are apparent in decreased involvement in task and personal interest and lowering of the worker's self-respect.

Perhaps many of the ills in this area stem from this source. The administrative line is a highly competitive line, so that position has to be safeguarded, skirmishes planned, advances laid out. Another issue lies in the contrast of reference points between administrative and technical personnel. For the technical worker, there are proper ways to do things in his specialty and, while very little is black and white, there are also improper ways. Of course he is supported, and perhaps this is the controlling difference, by his professional peer group which shares the same values and orientations. The ethic of administration is more difficult to discern but must relate to proper ways of dealing with people, which really is a general ethic of living and, therefore, nonspecific. All of this should be said more simply. In technical thinking it is possible to ask oneself, "What is the right thing to do?" and professional commitments will frequently enough supply at least partial answers. While rectitude, self-respect, and concern for others may act as reference points for action for administrative personnel, the situation has built-in pressures to do what in the administrator's view of the total situation is capable of achievement.

The counselor has been presented in his professional role. However, the attributes of his angelic nature need examination. Since quality of training and professional acculturation varies, counselors themselves may be unconvinced of their contribution, and the results may be self-doubt, anxiety, and professional irritability. Many ills flow from this. Defensively, there may be pomposity and upstage behavior and inability to communicate concerning the nature of counseling and what it requires if it is to function adequately. Out of fear arise shibboleths that counselors and professional personnel should not be subject to supervision. This is nonsense on the face of it. The ordinary safeguards the administrative worker hews to, coming to work on time, lunch hour limits only reasonably stretched, are seen as attacks on professional integrity. Since all jobs, including the administrator's, have their very real limits, this too is nonsense.

Last in a list that is capable of considerable expansion is the inevitable handicap of personnel down the line, including technical personnel, to understand the pressures on the person up front. The counselor may have a good appreciation of attitudes and sets with respect to his own area of work; he does not know the administrative worker's total work concerns. The administrator may be constantly chevied by his own boss, in other areas of his responsibility poor work may be turned out, other personnel may not be competent, emergencies may put a halt to all ordinary operations, or administrative detail may bog everything down. The counselor may know only that his problems are being given short shrift.

Observation suggests that there are differences in the comfort of the technical worker in different types of work settings. It is not only that a counselor working in an independent counseling service headed by a professional counselor has an easier time of it than a counselor working for instance in an industrial personnel organization and reporting to a strictly administrative type. It is rather that the technical worker in a setting where there are other professionals, even though they may belong to different disciplines, is better situated than if he works in a nontechnical setting. Thus a counselor in a school system should be better off than a counselor in a setting without other professionals, although this may seem immediately doubtful to many. There is a way to put this to the test, of course, but it is severe, and that is to change work settings and learn the hard way. There is a choice after all between being defensively patronized by school faculty and being regarded with suspicion and as a bleeding heart by real sturdy administrative types.

In the nature of things, there is potential for a good deal of frustration between administrator and technical worker. It is too facile to say that after all one of the two is in the saddle and directs which way the horse is to go. There are many ways of balking and sometimes of going in the required direction to a painful fall, perhaps for both. The policing function of the professional organizations is disregarded at some hazard; and even if the administrator regards the technician as muddle-headed, unrealistic, and an obfuscator, until he gets rid of him—sometimes in no way an easy task—or cumbersomely goes around him, he does have to suffer him. The whole situation can be very painful.

This reflection of the irritation and pain on both sides is not presented to offer self-sorrow for confirmation or to get a measure of release. It is intended as background for an examination of possible remedial measures. In some areas progress probably can be made and in one the situation seems discouraging.

Four areas should be examined. First is the nature of compromise. Second is the problem of communication. Third is the difficult area of emotional health, in which perhaps very little can be achieved. The last point relates to the need for a framework for understanding behavior.

The Nature of Compromise

Coming from the critical examination of program and research as part of his academic training, identifying with his university mentors as role models, and competent in knowledge and technique in his field, the newly trained counselor is likely to be a pretty hard pill to swallow anyway. Inevitably the technical worker hews to the standards for doing his task. Confronted with skepticism or impatience, he is as likely to get his back up as is anyone else. And yet budget limitations, competing demands from other technical groups for available funds, the reality of changed conditions, different directives, limits imposed by high authority, new interpretation of law—all of these require flexibility and the ability to adjust to change. The need for such adjustment is a reality and should be faced by counselors. This in no way is to mean that standards are sacrificed or that counselors are to hoist a flag of expediency. Probably too many of us are too readily cooperative now and just where the line is to be drawn is in part a function of common sense and wisdom, a competence that is not readily produced by didactic methods.

This may seem like a doctrine of cooperation at any price, but it is not. Actually we are all compromisers but in some situations it seems to be so natural that we don't see ourselves this way. In designing research, for example, it may be desirable to use a great many items in a questionnaire, but the hazard of reducing respondent rate compels us to keep the instrument as brief as possible. Similarly, interviews provide better data than answers on a questionnaire, but generally, except for studies with small N's, the cost is prohibitive. Examples can be multiplied many times. The basic point is that such actions do represent necessary accommodations to reality.

The populations to which service is to be extended are determined by administration, but what goes into the single service contact is in the counselor's area of competence. When he is instructed by administration to reduce the number of tests used, to be less precise and, therefore, take less time in establishing a study sample or cut down the number of interview hours, this is the time for the technical worker to take counsel with himself. The counselor's cooperation extends to number and type of program elements, not to how each single relationship is to be accomplished. While he can recommend and reason and urge for a bigger wedge of the pie, he knows that he cannot have it all; he cannot solve all the world's problems. There is a difference between being task-oriented and having service needs, and being a missionary.

In part, problems of this type are met by being filtered through various levels of supervision including the technical line. However, the characteristic of the technical worker is that even on the operating line he remains concerned with all policy that affects his work.

On Understanding Each Other

The problem of communication is central. When the shorthand of the technical language is used with laymen, that is to say administrative staff, it can lead to obscurantism and impede rather than help understanding. Similarly, when the pushes and strains of the total program of which the technical service is a part are unclear to the technical staff, there is also a lack of understanding, this time through noncommunication from administration.

As far as administration is concerned this seems to be an area in which rules of conduct even if applied mechanically can do a great deal of good. The management texts carry a good deal of wisdom. However, the question is how much of this knowledge is put to use. How regularly are staff meetings held? If such meetings are held, how are they conducted? Is there an opportunity for give and take? Are staff involved in major decisions, at least in offering advice? When final determinations are made are the reasons communicated at least in general form? Is access to administrators and supervisors relatively free or, if not, in some way regularized? These are almost the rote things. How much more could be accomplished if administration went beyond the basic steps and reached a conception of the worker as involved, task and program oriented, human and important, so that his advice and help is sought.

In another area of communication, the counselor must be held responsible for communicating concerning technical matters in English rather than psychologese. This is an essential responsibility that many have not assumed. It is very doubtful if there is any problem or technique in counseling that cannot be communicated in a relatively simple manner. This is intended to exclude no problem, including the basic nature of the counseling experience, the presumed contribution made by any one psychological test, factor analysis, or discriminant function. There are, of course, strong mysteries here, as, for instance, in the counseling relationship, how it is that one person changes perhaps remarkably as a result of spending a number of hours with another, but their intention and basic postulates can be explicated readily enough. Going upstage in professional hauteur will get for us only what it deserves, suspicion and rejection.

One positive thing we can do to help see the other point of view is to educate counselors-in-training about administration. The standard texts for guidance and pupil-personnel services include material on administration of the guidance service, but the press of problems and the pressures facing the principal of the school or the administrator of the agency and the way they have to work are missing. Could not the administrators in our own ranks be used to present material on such problems? In addition it might be useful to bring in the lay administrator who would put his urgent questions on the table and challenge the counselor-training class to convince him of their needs and priorities. The same kind of thing might be done in professional meetings or as part of in-service training. It surely should be an aspect of the internship.

On Emotional Balance

A third area of concern is in terms of mental health. Here it seems doubtful if a great deal can be done. In the final analysis the relationship between people is a function of their own security. It is now a popular slogan that personal security is at a premium in our time.

Given distortions in personality of the administrator or technical worker life can become very difficult for both. While in time, the technical worker can be moved aside, real life is never quite so simple. The general impulse is to work together as well as possible and as easily as possible. The tooth really has to pulse before strong action is taken.

Nevertheless it is not too much to say that the organization will be disaffected to the degree that any person in it suffers from personality problems. When such problems affect the person in charge the effect is greatly heightened. In a real sense, and especially over time, the administrator tends to make his organization into his own image. This may seem to be assigning too much influence to one man but research as well as observation bears it out. The organization can be highly dependent upon him, it can stifle originality or reluctantly squeeze out the semblance of creative work. At high levels such positions carry so much power that Menninger (1957) urges periodic psychiatric health checkups for such personnel.

It is not really that the personalities of staff, including technical personnel, undergo change. This is difficult to accomplish and perhaps unlikely. It is rather that those who are made uncomfortable leave when they can, others become resigned and stop caring, and still others find a self-abnegating way of maintaining favor, a way of living that may be congruent with basic personality needs. Thus the supervisor who, like God, presumably watches each sparrow fall, will drive out independent spirits and draw to him those who need to run to him with every bit of news.

This is not illness, even in a loose use of the term, but personality structure no doubt well within the normal range. There are many potential variations on the *basic* theme of the personality of the administrative head and its organizational reflections. They may include rigidity, suspiciousness, compulsivity and tight organization, great competitiveness, and in fact about all the aspects of the personality when it is engaged in its defense.

UNDERSTANDING BEHAVIOR

Not unrelated to the problem of mental health is the more intellectual area of psychological know-how. What is needed is a systematic framework for understanding the person. What is lacking, and William C. Menninger (1957) makes a point of this in talking to business executives, is acceptance of the validity of psychological data. These things can be read about, learned, studied, discussed, but to start with there has got to be a certain amount of interest, a curiosity about human beings and what has been learned about them systematically rather than through the folklore. The major areas might include for this purpose: (1) *Awareness of personality growth, development, and change.* If this is made to include unconscious motivation, the personality defenses, ways of meeting anxiety, and the normal phenomena of transference and the satisfaction of dependence needs, it may be easier to understand technical staff, since by and large they also are people. (2) *The importance of environment in personality functioning.* The central point here may very well be that, hands down, other persons are our most important environment. Also to be included, however, is the nature of the work setting and the conditions of work. This has to be considered in terms of the probable intrinsic, task-oriented work attitudes of the counselor. Finally in so brief a list the administrator should have at least (3) *a basic understanding of motivating needs and satisfactions.*

The last thing to be said is that under the benign sun of the psychological administrator, each work setting is to become a therapeutic community. This would be nice but since life is real and earnest, this is not warranted. The work has to get done and imposes requirements and standards that must be met. In its own seemingly opposite way, however, there is ample reason for thinking that in imposing structure, establishing firm standards, emotional health is in fact well served.

Clearly there are other useful areas, perhaps including the nature of language as symbolic representation as part of the problem of communication, and the psychology of roles and expectations. Maybe if this kind of training takes, the administrator may switch jobs, but this is doubtful. But perhaps we will then hear what some of us have heard in the inverted self-compliment, when the counselor or psychologist introduces his boss and says of him as the highest form of praise, "he thinks and talks like a psychologist (or counselor)."

There are in any case trends that point to greater acceptance of technical personnel. The growing acceptance of research as an operational and policy tool, the increasing use of scientific and technical staff in various policy roles, point to acknowledgment of the potential contribution of such workers.

Thus far the central elements in the counselor's identity and the administrator's work role have been identified. The generality of working well together has been noted, but major emphasis, mainly to highlight it, has been placed on the built-in factors which can lead to discord. Two specific lines of action were presented in order to increase understanding, both having particular reference to technical personnel, that is to say, to counselors. About the emotional well-being of the two chief actors it does not seem possible to be encouraging. Finally, a program of a sort was outlined for the administrator to learn about human behavior systematically.

ASPECTS OF A MODEL

Despite repeated disclaimers, there is a danger in the emphasis on the discordant elements. The hazard is that all such administrative-technical staff relationships are seen as clouded. In fact, there are very many where good, productive work has been and is being done. One will be cited not merely as a corrective, but in its own right in order to provide aspects of a model, to indicate the kind of support administration can provide. This is the program with which the present writer is asso-iated, but there is no help for it if an important point is to be made.

No pretense is made that in the Veterans Administration Vocational Rehabilitation and Education (VR&E) program things have always been rosy and that over the years the counseling staff had reserved easy chairs on cloud nine. Nor will the program's accomplishments be recounted since that story has been told elsewhere. Also left out of the outline are the detail of compromises and the clearing up of blocks in communica-tion. It is necessary to indicate finally that throughout the years, various administrative personnel, while very able, did not necessarily come to the program convinced of the staff's integrity and sanity.

A few items are selected reflecting the nature of administrative co-operation and support of counseling staff recommendations. It seems useful to note that money is always tight, the times nearly always frenetic, and the management analyst everywhere. Moreover, these roads were not built overnight. All of this should be understood.

1. When it became clear that the program was not limited in time, advanced qualification standards were established for counseling per-sonnel. They have been hewed to rigorously. In a dozen years no more than a handful of exceptions have been made and those were approved at lower grades by counseling staff and for limited functioning because no fully qualified candidates could be found.

2. Promptly with the promulgation of the new position a program of support of university training was begun with tuition and fees paid for by the agency, with time off from work on full salary. Although it has taken time and the field staff is greatly reduced, presently 85 per cent of coun-selors have been qualified as Counseling Psychologists (VR&E).

3. University-training support is continued to the doctoral level and beyond.

4. As in any centrally controlled program, policy is provided by Central Office. Thus on the books are the official strictures providing for leave for attendance at professional meetings, a specified proportion of

work time to be set aside for staff development, tight standards for professional practice including privacy for counseling, maintenance of professional libraries, and availability at each location of one-way screens and tape recorders. Approved lists of psychological consultants are available on regional office call. A panel of counseling leaders consults periodically with Central Office staff.

Sound policy is critical but promulgation and execution are different steps. The issues must be worked out again and again. But this is the shape of reality.

The essential point is that a program newly established in what basically is an administrative setting has been able with the full cooperation of administration to put up a sound framework for its functioning. Program instances of this type can be multiplied a number of times.

BEYOND PRACTICE AND OPINION

But our committed hope must be in finding out in accepted scientific ways what works, under what conditions, and why.

Following empirical studies, research hypotheses probably will flow out of formulations of role assumption, self-concept, the person's values especially in relation to work, and job satisfaction. The study population, of course, is our own group, although its likeness to psychologists and teachers as to technical and scientific personnel more generally is definitely for consideration. I suppose appropriate questions would include perceptions by technical personnel of "good" administrators and the other way around. Also it is hazardous to do more than generalize about methodology because to do so must leave out of account imaginative approaches of others. An array of many ingenious instruments is now available starting with work values inventories, Q-sort methodology, and differential press checklists, and going on from there. Criteria for identification of desirable characteristics of the two (or however many) actors and productive patterns of interaction between (and among) them might include productivity, creativity (however *that* is to be measured), quality of work (which also will take some fancy doing but is not impossible), staff and administrative morale separately and in combination, absentee rate, turnover rate, and so on.

The field is hardly virgin. Roles in work have been identified—for example, the professional and the organizational-careerist (Wilensky, 1964) and research from quite diverse sources supports these findings.

There are other dimensions to research and a leaf can be taken from the social scientists' book. Merton and Lerner (1951) note the need for systematic analysis of the process whereby certified knowledge improves policy-making. "The scientist," they note, "is called upon to contribute information useful to implement a given policy, but the policy itself is 'given,' not open to question." Specifics from our own calling come to mind. A government program is set up to train counseling personnel in two months or 10 weeks or some other short period, and counselor trainers are asked what to include in such a training period: the time limitation is taken for granted and as a matter of fact, we cooperate, as our recent history shows, and without requiring necessary safeguards, for example, in highly qualified supervision and requirements for continued training.

It may be that in addition to the steps proposed earlier that might alleviate some of the difficulty, we should look forward, as Wilensky (1964) suggests, to a mixed-type orientation resulting from interpenetration of the bureaucratic and professional cultures. Observation urges that in guidance and counseling we are talking not about interpenetration but penetration; that is, the movement is one-sided only, from the technical to the administrative, not, in the nature of things, from administrators to technicians. In one large program, numbers of counselors have moved (I hesitate to say "up") out of the technical work to administrative work including, eventually, some top-level assignments. Movement has also been to other better-paid and status-rich university jobs. It would be useful to identify the values and personality structure of counselors moving out of counseling into different areas. It has long been a plaintive cry in Division 17 that the membership is found much more in administrative than in counseling work.

Perhaps in an increasingly technical society this is an important part of an answer. Eventually, however, the technician-administrator must report to a lay administrator. This is why it is felt that answers must lie along the lines discussed at some length in this paper rather than in becoming boss.

REFERENCES

LASSWELL, H. D. *Power and personality*. New York: Norton, 1948.
MENNINGER FOUNDATION. *Toward understanding men: transcript of a seminar for industrial executives*. Topeka, Kans.: The Foundation, 1957.
MERTON, R. K., & LERNER, D. "Social scientists in the policy sciences." In D. Lerner & H. D. Lasswell, eds., *The policy sciences, recent developments in scope and method*. Stanford, Calif.: Stanford Univ. Press, 1951.
WILENSKY, H. L. "The professionalization of everyone?" *Amer. J. Sociol.*, 1964, 70, 137–158.

Name Index

SUBJECT INDEX

Adlerian theory, 142
Administration and counseling:
  implications, 485, 491–492
  empirical findings, 487–489
  problems, 494–498
  relationships, 498–502
  structure and guidance theory, 480–486
  theory, 489–491
Alienation, 242, 269 (see also Depersonalization)
American Personnel and Guidance Association (APGA), 6, 30, 46, 287, 386, 424
American Psychological Association (APA), 28, 29, 30, 31, 336, 386, 424, 458
American School Counselors Association, 46, 50, 51, 53, 54
Anthropology, cultural, 227, 234
  assumptions, 242
Anxiety, 89, 190
Appraisal function, 327 ff.
  assumptions and limitations, 353–364
  development, 329–352
  differential psychology, sources of, 329–336
  research, 361–364
  social impact, 362–374
Assessment in guidance:
  counselors' problems, 353–365
  criticism, 358
  errors, 355, 362, 364
  instruments, 358
  judgments, 357
Association for Counselor Education and Supervision (ACES), 46, 47, 52–55, 157, 160
Associationism, 177–180, 182, 183 (see also Reinforcement)
Automation (see also Labor market, Manpower, Vocational development):
  definition of, 429
  implications for counselors, 432–435
  need and impact of, 430–431

Behaviorism, 106, 168, 201, 202, 207, 209–211, 213, 232, 445, 460, 462, 467
Binet test, 12, 26, 334, 335, 338, 339 (see also Psychological tests):
  compared to Wechsler, 432
  revisions, 338–340
Biological contributions:
  genetics, 331–332

Causality, 60–61
Client-centered theory, 77–78, 144, 151 (see also in name index Rogers)
Clinical psychology defined, 27
Communication, 97–98, 106, 153, 228
  communication science, 234
  content vs. structure, 74–75
  in counseling, 250–251, 499
  empathy, 150, 152
  philosophic aspects, 69–75
  present vs. past, 72–74
  private vs. public, 70–71
Community, 38–39
  decline, 270
  Gemeinschaft, 226, 267, 268
  Gesellschaft, 226
  mobility, 38–39
  reforms, 236–237
  roles, 249
Correlations:
  correlation coefficient, 115, 121, 130, 131, 133
  factor analysis, 116
  percentiles, 131, 133, 135
  ratios (IQ), 133–134
Counseling (see also Administration, Guidance):
  and administration, 452, 496
  and automation, 429–436
  communication, private vs. public, 70
  content vs. structure, 74
  cultural influence, 41–55
  effectiveness of, 162, 224, 472–473
  functions of, 438
  goals, 81–82, 159, 161, 465
  issues, 441–446